THE TOP 500 POEMS

Other Columbia University Press Books

The Concise Columbia Book of Poetry.
William Harmon, ed. (1990)

The Columbia History of the American Novel.
Emory Elliott, ed. (1991)

Columbia Literary History of the United States.
Emory Elliott, ed. (1988)

The Columbia Granger's® Index to Poetry,
  Tenth Edition.
Edith P. Hazen, ed. (1994)

The Columbia Granger's® Dictionary of
  Poetry Quotations.
Edith P. Hazen, ed. (1992)

The Columbia Granger's® Guide to
  Poetry Anthologies.
William Katz and Linda Sternberg Katz, eds. (1990)

The Concise Columbia Encyclopedia, Second Edition.
  (1989)

The Concise Columbia Dictionary of Quotations.
Robert Andrews, ed. (1990)

The Columbia Dictionary of Modern Literary and
  Cultural Criticism.
Joseph Childers and Gary Hentzi, eds. (1995)

THE TOP 500 POEMS

EDITED

BY

WILLIAM

HARMON

A COLUMBIA ANTHOLOGY

COLUMBIA UNIVERSITY PRESS
New York

Columbia University Press wishes to express its
appreciation for assistance given by Corliss Lamont
toward the costs of publishing this book.

Columbia University Press
New York   Chichester, West Sussex
Copyright © 1992 Columbia University Press
All rights reserved

Library of Congress Cataloging-in-Publication Data
The Top 500 Poems / edited by William Harmon.
    p.   cm.
  ISBN 0-231-08028-X
  1. English poetry.   2. American poetry.
I. Harmon, William, 1938-
PR1175.C6417   1992
821.008—dc20   91-42239
                                                    CIP

Casebound editions of Columbia University Press
books are printed on permanent and durable acid-free
paper.

Printed in the United States of America

c   20   19   18   17   16   15

To
CAROLINE RUTH HARMON
for her third birthday

TABLE OF CONTENTS

Table of Contents

THE
TOP
500
POEMS

THIS IS *IT!*

I am dedicating my thoughts in this book to my three-year-old daughter Caroline, because I have had her constantly in mind (and sometimes in lap) as I wrote about the poems collected here. Already, on a daily basis, she hears poetry, and before long she will be able to read it for herself. What general book of poetry should she, or anyone, start with? Well, this collection of the 500 poems that (according to *The Columbia Granger's® Index to Poetry*) have been anthologized most often impresses me as exactly the sort of book with which I would want to welcome her to the world of poetry in English. As a poet, teacher, editor, and father, I am satisfied that these 500 poems, with a bit of commentary, will serve as a splendid way for somebody to become acquainted with the best that has been written in the shorter poetic forms for about 750 years. As I have said to myself repeatedly, this is *it!*

This is the story of poetry in English, starting in the Middle Ages in England and ending in the English-speaking world of today. It starts with poems of a simplicity of form and directness of emotion that appeal instantly to children and adults alike. But mature artistry is on display from the beginning, as is that necessary preoccupation of maturity—time. Growing children are the most vivid reminders of our own aging, and this book demonstrates, from the beginning, that English poets have been obsessed with the passage of time. Much poetry seems to be aware of its situation in time and of its relation to the metronome, the clock, and the calendar. Among the earliest poems in this book there is a sense of seasons being born:

Sumer is icumen in . . . .

When April with its sweet showers . . . .

The season or month is there to be felt; the day is there to be seized. Poetry keeps telling us what happens in time. Poems beginning

"When" are much more numerous than those beginning "Where" or "If." As the meter is running, the recurrent message tapped out by the passing of measured time is mortality. (This undercurrent may account for the melancholy and fright that turn up even in lullabies and nursery rhymes, which suggest that life is an affair of breaking boughs, falling cradles, bridges falling down, falling down, falling down.)

But generally it has occurred to me, as I thought about these 500 poems, that English-speaking people have produced one of the greatest bodies of literature the world has ever seen. The drama has been a scene of brilliance since 1590; the novel is about a century younger. In poetry, however, the English genius goes right back into the Middle Ages. Great poetry has been written in the English language for at least 600 years. Dull periods have come along from time to time, true, but in most periods since Chaucer, who died in 1400, the English language has served somebody somewhere as the instrument of breathtaking poetry: epic, dramatic, lyric, satiric, meditative, nonsensical, as well as every conceivable combination and permutation.

The greatness of English poetry in a large way reflects on the peoples who have spoken English, their culture, weather, humor, even their "character," whatever that term may suggest. They have liked songs and stories, and they have believed in talk, all the way from tavern conversation to parliamentary debate.

And they have had the English language itself. Modern English, the language in which my daughter is even now gaining fluency, incorporates Indo-European elements from northwestern and southwestern Europe—from Anglo-Saxon (Germanic) and French (Italic). Because of its history, English has become, in respect of vocabulary and syntax, practically a double language, commonly offering speakers a number of different ways of saying something. For the sake of the arts of poetry, several features of the peculiarly English language-mixture have been inexhaustibly useful. The large vocabulary furnishes a broad range of possibilities with much opportunity for nuances and ironies of meaning along with complex harmonies and textures. Some poets have favored the Germanic extreme of substantial syllables that stay close to the earth and move rather slowly, as in Hopkins's "Inversnaid":

This darksome burn, horseback brown,
His rollrock highroad roaring down,
In coop and in comb the fleece of his foam
Flutes and low to the lake falls home.

Others enjoy the interplay of Germanic and Italic colorations, as in Shakespeare's Sonnet CXVI:

Let me not to the marriage of true minds
Admit impediments . . . .

The physical condition of the language that was in place by about 1250 invited exploitation by poets of many sorts. Indo-European languages share certain basic features and change according to certain common patterns; by 1250 the general changes in English had a permanent effect on what poets could do. One tremendous change, which began many centuries ago and is still going on, has to do with the typical word-making and word-changing mechanism of a language.

Consider the Latin word *video:* it is made up from a stem (*vid-,* "see") plus a suffix (*-eo*) meaning something like "first-person singular present indicative": the English translation, "I see," must state the pronoun (1) as a separate word that (2) comes before the verb. Likewise, the *vidi* in Julius Caesar's famous claim *Veni, vidi, vici* requires two or three separate English words for an adequate translation: "I saw" or "I have seen." The drift—from single words with inflections on the right side, to collections of single words arranged on the left—has affected what we do with nouns, verbs, adjectives, and adverbs. The process had led to a language with many more monosyllables than Latin had and with many more polysyllabic words that can be stressed on the final syllables. Latin had no such words.

This is not the place to go into the details of such evolutionary developments. Indeed, there are still controversies about the whole affair. It seems, even so, that, about a thousand years ago, Indo-European languages were reaching a state in which three devices were newly available to verse-markers: (1) there were syllables that could be distinguished and measured by *quality* or accent, rather than by *quantity* or duration (as had been the uniform custom in the verse measures of Sanskrit, Greek, and Latin); (2) there were such contours of single words and of word groups—like article-plus-noun and auxiliary-plus-verb—that the accentual rhythm could be called "rising": these are chiefly the so-called *iambs* that are found in most English poems (as in the finale of Tennyson's "Ulysses": "To strive, to seek, to find, and not to yield."); (3) rhyme. Rhyme works better when the rhyming stressed syllable is not followed by unstressed material. To seize a local example, my daughter's name, "Caroline," is easier to find rhymes for than is the name of the state we live in, "North Carolina."

Now, the mood of rising that we hear in the customary rhythms of poetry coexists with the mood of falling that we find among the customary sentiments of poetry—even poetry designed for children—so that terrific torque or tension is set up in the process. There is a similar tension inherent in the double vocabulary of English, where, for example, "velocity" is a relatively abstract technical term with four little uniform syllables and "speed" is very different.

There is yet another tension available in rhyme itself, which invites us to consider words that have a common sound, yet tease us with antithetical meanings, as in the "making" and "breaking" in Dylan Thomas's "A Refusal to Mourn the Death, by Fire, of a Child in London." Rhyme, let us not forget, is much better at accenting difference and tension than is alliteration, which gives mostly the effect of sliding along the slippery slope of selfsame sounds.

Poets have been helped by the richness of the English language, but to convey their own individual visions in works of art, they have had to fashion their own individual techniques. The greatest successes are on vivid display in the pages that follow.

One can read the poets as they are arranged here, in chronological order; one can read their poems according to rank (an Appendix lists them in order of number of times they have been anthologized); or one can sample them at random. Some statistics may be interesting. Poets represented by ten or more poems are Shakespeare (29), Anonymous (21), Donne (19), Blake (18), Dickinson (14), Yeats (14), Wordsworth (13), Hopkins (12), Tennyson (11), Hardy (11), Frost (11), Keats (10). There are 160 poets here, 139 of whom are named; the 21 anonymous writers were all British. That three-quarters of the poems are British makes sense, because British poetry has been with us three times as long as American poetry in English. The breakdown by century is certainly interesting:

Century	Number of poems
XIII-XV	23
XVI	70
XVII	69
XVIII	47
XIX	169
XX	122

It is interesting to note that most seventeenth-century poems included here are from the first half of the century, while most of the eighteenth-century poems come from the last quarter of the century. Short lyrics were not much in fashion between 1660 and 1760. The nineteenth century seems to have been a golden age for poetry from first to last; I do not believe that the twentieth will ever look so good. I am not the first to remark that the very greatest writers of the twentieth century work in prose.

There is little poetry on today's radio or television, even with the advent of cable, and the newspapers report that about thirty percent of our adult population is functionally illiterate. That cannot augur anything good for poetry, but I remain hopeful, nevertheless, and I believe that this collection proves that our own generation's taste in poetry is fine indeed. I would like to thank all the poets, critics, and editors whose judgment has propelled these works into the position of the "Top 500 Poems" in English. I also have some personal thanks of my own and offer a tribute to a number of friends who put up with me even when I would say (as I heard myself say one day), "That poem that wasn't entitled 'A Farewell to Arms' maybe wasn't written by George Peele after all." Let me list their names as a way of expressing my gratitude for their forbearance and generosity: Reid Barbour, Elizabeth Core, Sally Greene, Anne Hall, Anne Harmon, Hilary Holladay, Edith Hazen, Paul Jones, Robert Kirkpatrick, Jerry Mills, John Frederick Nims, and James Raimes.

Dear Caroline: This is *it!* The Cuccu and the Tiger are waiting, and so much else. Read!

Cuckoo Song

❧❧❧

Sumer is icumen in,
  Lhudé sing cuccu;
Groweth sed and bloweth med
  And springth the wudé nu.
    Sing cuccu!
Awé bleteth after lomb,
  Lhouth after calvé cu;
Bulluc sterteth, bucké verteth;
  Murie sing cuccu.
    Cuccu, cuccu,
  Wel singés thu, cuccu,
  Ne swik thu naver nu.
Sing cuccu nu! Sing cuccu!
Sing cuccu! Sing cuccu nu!

The creature that Spenser called "The merry Cuckow, messenger of Spring" sings out his bell-like mating call at spring's threshold. The bird perches also at the threshold of anthologies: Nashe's "Spring, the Sweet Spring" (p. 120) with its vivid bird-chorus leads off Palgrave's Golden Treasury *(1861) and this admirable poem—originally scored as an extraordinary six-voice round—comes first in Quiller-Couch's* Oxford Book of English Verse *(1900). (Note that: "nu" is "now"; "lhude" is "loud"; "med" is "meadow"; "awé" is "ewe"; "verteth" is "breaks wind"; "swik" is "be silent.")*

Chaucer, who is customarily ranked as the third great-
est English poet (after Shakespeare and Milton) was a
vintner's son who gave distinguished military and civil
service to his country. He was the earliest notable poet
to be buried in the Poets' Corner of Westminster Ab-
bey.

General Prologue
to The Canterbury Tales

◆◆◆◆

When April with its sweet showers
Has pierced the drought of March to the root
And bathed every plant-vein in such liquid
As has the power to engender the flower;
When Zephyr also with its sweet breath
Has in every grove and field inspired
The tender crops, and the young sun
Has run half its course in Aries the Ram,
And small fowls make melody
That sleep all the night with open eye
(Nature pierces them so in their hearts)—
Then people long to go on pilgrimages
And palmers to seek foreign shores
To distant shrines, known in sundry lands;
And specially from every shire's end
Of England they travel to Canterbury
To seek the holy blissful martyr
That has helped them when they were sick.
It happened that one day in that season
As I lay at the Tabard Inn in Southwark
Ready to travel on my pilgrimage
To Canterbury with a most devout heart,
There came at night into that lodging-place
Twenty-nine in a group

Of sundry people, by chance fallen
Into fellowship, and they were all pilgrims
Wanting to ride toward Canterbury.
The chambers and stables were roomy,
And we were very well accommodated.
Soon, when the sun had set,
I had spoken to every one of them
So that I was immediately in their fellowship.
And we agreed to get up early
To make our way to the place I have described to you.
Nonetheless, while I have some time and room
Before passing further into this tale,
It seems reasonable to me
To tell you the condition
Of each of them, as it seemed to me,
And what they were, and of what rank,
And also in what array they were.
    I will first begin, then, with a knight. . . .

from The Canterbury Tales

Chaucer's six-hundred-year-old English is still understandable to readers without a specialized education, but my rough-and-ready translation may be helpful. The general opening to the Tales leads up to a pilgrim-by-pilgrim introduction.

Sir Patrick Spens

I. THE SAILING

The king sits in Dunfermline town
  Drinking the blude-red wine;
"O whare will I get a skeely skipper
  To sail this new ship o' mine?"

O up and spak an eldern knight,
  Sat at the king's right knee;
"Sir Patrick Spens is the best sailor
  That ever sail'd the sea."

Our king has written a braid letter,
  And seal'd it with his hand,
And sent it to Sir Patrick Spens,
  Was walking on the strand.

"To Noroway, to Noroway,
  To Noroway o'er the faem;
The king's daughter o' Noroway,
  'Tis thou must bring her hame."

The first word that Sir Patrick read
  So loud, loud laugh'd he;
The neist word that Sir Patrick read
  The tear blinded his e'e.

"O wha is this has done this deed
  And tauld the king o' me,
To send us out, at this time o' year,
  To sail upon the sea?

"Be it wind, be it weet, be it hail, be it sleet,
  Our ship must sail the faem;
The king's daughter o' Noroway,
  'Tis we must fetch her hame."

They hoysed their sails on Monenday morn
  Wi' a' the speed they may;
They hae landed in Noroway
  Upon a Wodensday.

II. THE RETURN

"Mak ready, mak ready, my merry men a'!
  Our gude ship sails the morn."
"Now ever alack, my master dear,
  I fear a deadly storm.

"I saw the new moon late yestreen
  Wi' the auld moon in her arm;
And if we gang to sea, master,
  I fear we'll come to harm."

They hadna sail'd a league, a league,
  A league but barely three,
When the lift grew dark, and the wind blew loud,
  And gurly grew the sea.

The ankers brak, and the topmast lap,
  It was sic a deadly storm:
And the waves cam owre the broken ship
  Till a' her sides were torn.

"Go fetch a web o' the silken claith,
  Another o' the twine,
And wap them into our ship's side,
  And let nae the sea come in."

They fetch'd a web o' the silken claith,
    Another o' the twine,
And they wapp'd them round that guide ship's side,
    But still the sea came in.

O laith, laith were our gude Scots lords
    To wet their cork-heel'd shoon;
But lang or a' the play was play'd
    They wat their hats aboon.

And mony was the feather bed
    That flatter'd on the faem;
And mony was the gude lord's son
    That never mair cam hame.

O lang, lang may the ladies sit,
    Wi' their fans into their hand,
Before they see Sir Patrick Spens
    Come sailing to the strand!

And lang, lang may the maidens sit
    Wi' their gowd kames in their hair,
A-waiting for their ain dear loves!
    For them they'll see nae mair.

Half-owre, half-owre to Aberdour,
    'Tis fifty fathoms deep;
And there lies gude Sir Patrick Spens,
    Wi' the Scots lords at his feet!

The poem presents its dramatically elliptical narration in the simplest ballad measure with superlative economy of design: just a few quick bold strokes and a thoroughgoing reliance on concrete detail. We are not told that the king was worried in some vague way; he is drinking and asking for help. Four brief speeches (king, knight, Sir Patrick, a nameless sailor) and then a focus on the marvelous detail of "cork heel'd shoon" (the last word in medieval chic) and floating hats. (Note that: "skeely" is "skillful"; "lift" is "sky"; "lap" is "sprang"; "laith" is "unwilling"; "aboon" is "above"; "flatter'd" is "floated," "tossing"; "kames" is "combs.")

Western Wind

>>>>>>>

Western wind, when wilt thou blow?
The small rain down can rain.
Christ, that my love were in my arms,
And I in my bed again.

In homage to this poem, which is among the very oldest in this anthology, the fine poet and editor John Frederick Nims has given the title Western Wind *to a most useful and entertaining anthology of poetry.*

Edward, Edward

"Why does your brand so drop with blood,
    Edward, Edward?
Why does your brand so drop with blood,
  And why so sad go ye, O?"
"O I have killed my hawk so good,
    Mother, mother;
O I have killed my hawk so good,
  And I have no more but he, O."

"Your hawk's blood was never so red,
    Edward, Edward;
Your hawk's blood was never so red,
  My dear son, I tell thee, O."
"O I have killed my red-roan steed,
    Mother, mother;
O I have killed my red-roan steed,
  That went so fair and free, O."

"Your steed was old, and ye have more,
    Edward, Edward;
Your steed was old, and ye have more,
  Some other dole ye dree, O."
"O I have killed my father dear,
    Mother, mother;
O I have killed my father dear,
  Alas, and woe is me, O!"

"And what penance will ye dree for that,
Edward, Edward?
What penance will ye dree for that,
My dear son, now tell me, O."
"I'll set my foot in yonder boat,
Mother, mother,
I'll set my foot in yonder boat,
And I'll fare o'er the sea, O."

"And what will ye do with your towers and your hall,
Edward, Edward?
And what will ye do with your towers and your hall,
That were so fair to see, O?"
"I'll let them stand till down they fall,
Mother, mother;
I'll let them stand till down they fall,
For here never more must I be, O."

"And what will ye leave to your bairns and your wife,
Edward, Edward?
And what will ye leave to your bairns and your wife,
When ye go o'er the sea, O?"
"The world's room: let them beg through life,
Mother, mother;
The world's room: let them beg through life,
For them never more will I see, O."

"And what will you leave to your own mother dear,
Edward, Edward?
And what will ye leave to your own mother dear,
My dear son, now tell me, O?"
"The curse of hell from me shall ye bear,
Mother, mother;
The curse of hell from me shall ye bear,
Such counsels ye gave to me, O!"

Compared with "Sir Patrick Spens," (p. 10) this ballad shows a quantum advance in sophistication and polish: the stanza is more complex, and the design is stripped to a set of quick ex post facto exchanges between a mother and a son. (Note that: "brand" is "sword"; "dree" is "suffer.")

Thomas the Rhymer

True Thomas lay oer yond grassy bank
  And he beheld a ladie gay,
A ladie that was brisk and bold,
  Come riding oer the fernie brae.

Her skirt was of the grass-green silk,
  Her mantel of the velvet fine,
At ilka tett of her horse's mane
  Hung fifty silver bells and nine.

True Thomas he took off his hat,
  And bowed him low down till his knee:
"All hail, thou mighty Queen of Heaven!
  For your peer on earth I never did see."

"O no, O no, True Thomas," she says,
  "That name does not belong to me;
I am but the queen of fair Elfland,
  And I'm come nere for to visit thee.

"But ye maun go wi me now, Thomas,
  True Thomas, ye maun go wi me,
For ye maun serve me seven years,
  Thro weel or wae as may chance to be."

She turned about her milk-white steed,
  And took True Thomas up behind,
And aye wheneer her bridle rang,
  The steed flew swifter than the wind.

For forty days and forty nights
  He wade thro red blude to the knee,
And he saw neither sun nor moon,
  But heard the roaring of the sea.

O they rade on, and further on,
   Until they came to a garden green:
"Light down, light down, ye ladie free,
   Some of that fruit let me pull to thee."

"O no, O no, True Thomas," she says,
   "That fruit maun not be touched by thee,
For a' the plagues that are in hell
   Light on the fruit of this countrie.

"But I have a loaf here in my lap,
   Likewise a bottle of claret wine,
And now ere we go farther on,
   We'll rest a while, and ye may dine."

When he had eaten and drunk his fill,
   "Lay down your head upon my knee,"
The lady sayd, "ere we climb yon hill,
   And I will show you fairlies three.

"O see not ye yon narrow road,
   So thick beset wi thorns and briers?
That is the path of righteousness,
   Tho after it but few enquires.

"And see not ye that braid braid road,
   That lies across yon lillie leven?
That is the path of wickedness,
   Tho some call it the road to heaven.

"And see not ye that bonny road,
   Which winds about the fernie brae?
That is the road to fair Elfland,
   Where you and I this night maun gae.

"But Thomas, ye maun hold your tongue,
    Whatever you may hear or see,
For gin ae word you should chance to speak,
    You will neer get back to your ain countrie,"

He has gotten a coat of the even cloth,
    And a pair of shoes of velvet green,
And till seven years were past and gone
    True Thomas on earth was never seen.

A certain Thomas of Erceldoun, who lived in the thirteenth century, was reputed to possess prophetic powers as well as talent as a poet. (Note that: "lock" is "tuft"; "fairlies" is "marvels"; "maun" is "must.")

The Wife of Usher's Well

There lived a wife at Usher's Well,
  And a wealthy wife was she;
She had three stout and stalwart sons,
  And sent them o'er the sea.

They hadna been a week from her,
  A week but barely ane,
But word came to the carlin wife
  That her three sons were gane.

They hadna been a week from her,
  A week but barely three,
Whan word came to the carlin wife
  That her sons she'd never see.

'I wish the wind may never cease,
  Nor fashes in the flood,
Till my three sons come hame to me,
  In earthly flesh and blood.'

It fell about the Martinmass,
  When nights are lang and mirk,
The carlin wife's three sons came hame,
  And their hats were o the birk.

It neither grew in syke nor ditch,
  Nor yet in ony sheugh;
But at the gates o Paradise
  That birk grew fair eneugh.

'Blow up the fire, my maidens,
  Bring water from the well;
For a' my house shall feast this night,
  Since my three sons are well.'

And she has made to them a bed,
  She's made it large and wide,
And she's taen her mantle her about,
  Sat down at the bed-side.

Up then crew the red, red cock,
  And up and crew the gray;
The eldest to the youngest said,
  ' 'Tis time we were away.'

The cock he hadna crawd but once,
  And clappd his wings at a',
When the youngest to the eldest said,
  'Brother, we must awa.'

'The cock doth craw, the day doth daw,
  The channerin worm doth chide;
Gin we be mist out o our place,
  A sair pain we maun bide.'

'Fare ye weel, my mother dear!
  Farewell to barn and byre!
And fare ye weel, the bonny lass
  That kindles my mother's fire!'

Martinmas, November 11, falls not long after All Soul's Night. The hats of birch ("birk"), as scholars have noted, would be out of season in November. (Note that: "carlin" is "old peasant"; "fashes" is "disturbances"; "sike" is "field"; "sheugh" is "furrow"; "channerin" is "fretting"; "gin" is "if"; "byre" is "stable.")

As You Came
from the Holy Land of Walsingham

As you came from the holy land
  Of Walsingham,
Met you with my true love
  By the way as you came?

How shall I know your true love
  That have met many one,
As I went to the holy land
  That have come, that have gone?

She is neither white nor brown
  But as the heavens fair,
There is none hath a form so divine
  in the earth or the air.

Such an one did I meet, good sir,
  Such an angel-like face,
Who like a queen, like a nymph, did appear
  By her gate, by her grace.

She hath left me here all alone,
  All alone as unknown,
Who sometimes did me lead with herself,
  And me loved as her own.

What's the cause that she leaves you alone
  And a new way doth take,
Who loved you once as her own
  And her joy did you make?

I have loved her all my youth,
  But now old, as you see;
Love likes not the falling fruit
  From the withered tree.

Know that love is a careless child
  And forgets promise past;
He is blind, he is deaf when he list
  And in faith never fast.

His desire is a dureless content
  And a trustless joy;
He is won with a world of despair
  And is lost with a toy.

Of womankind such indeed is the love,
  Or the word love abused,
Under which many childish desires
  And conceits are excused.

But true love is a durable fire
  In the mind ever burning;
Never sick, never old, never dead,
  From itself never turning.

If, as some scholars still believe, Sir Walter Ralegh wrote this poem, he must have done so by adapting an existing popular song; the tone and design suggest a time before the sixteenth century. Walsingham in Norfolk has long been sacred to pilgrims. Robert Lowell's "Quaker Graveyard in Nantucket" has a section called "Our Lady of Walsingham," about the shrine in Walsingham Priory.

Corpus Christi Carol

()◀▶()

Lully, lulley; lully, lulley;
The fawcon hath born my make away.

He bare hym up, he bare hym down;
He bare hym into an orchard brown.

In that orchard ther was an hall,
That was hangid with purpill and pall.

And in that hall ther was a bede;
Hit was hangid with gold so rede.

And yn that bed ther lythe a knyght,
His wowndes bledyng day and nyght.

By that bedes side ther kneleth a may,
And she wepeth both nyght and day.

And by that beddes side ther stondith a ston,
'Corpus Christi' wretyn theron.

Here, in a poem at least five hundred years old, pagan and Christian elements
are combined so economically that only the sketchiest lineaments remain. The
ever-bleeding wounds recall the Fisher King of Grail lore (see T. S. Eliot's
"Waste Land," p. 968) as well as the Body of Christ (which is what "Corpus
Christi" means). The poem, which may be a remnant or a fragment or a blend
of more than one earlier poem, has been justifiably classified as both carol and
ballad. (Note that: "make" is "mate"; "may" is "maid.")

The Three Ravens

There were three ravens sat on a tree,
Downe a downe, hay down, hay downe
There were three ravens sat on a tree,
With a downe
There were three ravens sat on a tree,
They were as black as they might be,
With a downe derrie, derrie, derrie, downe, downe.

The one of them said to his mate,
"Where shall we our breakfast take?"

"Down in yonder greene field,
There lies a knight slain under his shield.

"His hounds they lie down at his feete,
So well they can their master keepe.

"His haukes they flie so eagerly,
There's no fowle dare him come nie."

Downe there comes a fallow doe,
As great with yong as she might goe.

She lift up his bloudy hed,
And kist his wounds that were so red.

She got him up upon her backe,
And carried him to earthen lake.

She buried him before the prime,
She was dead herselfe ere even-song time.

God send every gentleman
Such haukes, such hounds, and such a leman.

Ravens and crows are everywhere in ancient and medieval literature, dark emblems of survival and disposal. In one of his late poems, W. B. Yeats said, "Another Troy must rise and set, / Another lineage feed the crow" in the same decade (the 1930s) as Eisenstein's epic film Alexander Nevsky *with its unforgettable pictures of carrion-feeders scavenging after a battle. In 1971, Ted Hughes, later to be Poet Laureate of England, published several crow poems in* Crow: From the Life and Songs of the Crow. *(Note that: "leman" is "lover.")*

Tom o' Bedlam's Song

From the hag and hungry goblin
That into rags would rend ye,
The spirit that stands by the naked man
In the Book of Moons defend ye,
That of your five sound senses
You never be forsaken,
Nor wander from yourselves with Tom
Abroad to beg your bacon,
    While I do sing, Any food, any feeding,
    Feeding, drink, or clothing;
    Come dame or maid, be not afraid,
    Poor Tom will injure nothing.

Of thirty bare years have I
Twice twenty been enraged,
And of forty been three times fifteen
In durance soundly caged
On the lordly lofts of Bedlam
With stubble soft and dainty,
Brave bracelets strong, sweet whips ding dong
With wholesome hunger plenty,
    And now I sing, etc.

With a thought I took for Maudlin
And a cruse of cockle pottage,
With a thing thus tall, sky bless you all,
I befell into this dotage.
I slept not since the Conquest,
Till then I never waked,
Till the roguish boy of love where I lay
Me found and strip't me naked.
    And now I sing, etc.

When I short have shorn my sow's face
And swigg'd my horny barrel,
In an oaken inn I pound my skin
As a suit of gilt apparel;
The moon's my constant mistress
And the lovely owl my marrow;
The flaming drake and the night crow make
Me music to my sorrow.
    While I do sing, etc.

The palsy plagues my pulses
When I prig your pigs or pullen,
Your culvers take, or matchless make
Your Chanticleer or Sullen.
When I want provant with Humphrey
I sup, and when benighted,
I repose in Paul's with waking souls
Yet never am affrighted.
    But I do sing, etc.

I know more than Apollo,
For oft when he lies sleeping
I see the stars at bloody wars
In the wounded welkin weeping;
The moon embrace her shepherd,
And the Queen of Love her warrior,
While the first doth horn the star of morn,
And the next the heavenly Farrier.
    While I do sing, etc.

The gypsies, Snap and Pedro,
Are none of Tom's comradoes,
The punk I scorn and the cutpurse sworn,
And the roaring boy's bravadoes.
The meek, the white, the gentle
Me handle, touch, and spare not;
But those that cross Tom Rynosseross
   Do what the panther dare not.
     Although I sing, etc.

With an host of furious fancies
Whereof I am commander,
With a burning spear and a horse of air,
To the wilderness I wander.
By a knight of ghosts and shadows
I summon'd am to a tourney
Ten leagues beyond the wide world's end:
Methinks it is no journey.
     Yet will I sing, etc.

The "mad song" gives a writer the chance to play with interesting irrational combinations. Thomas D'Urfey wrote one in 1688 ("I'le Sail upon the Dog-Star") that also uses "roaring boy." Tom o' Bedlam, a stock madman through the sixteenth century, is the guise that Edgar adopts in King Lear. *(Note that: "cruse" is "bowl"; "prig" is "steal"; "punk" is "whore.")*

Adam Lay I-bounden

※-※-※

Adam lay i-bounden,
  Bounden in a bond;
Four thousand winter
  Thought he not to long;
And al was for an appel,
  An appel that he took,
As clerkes finden writen
  In here book.

Ne hadde the appel take been,
  The appel take been,
Ne hadde never our Lady
  A been hevene-queen.
Blessed be the time
  That appel take was!
Therefore we moun singen
  "*Deo Gracias!*"

From data in the Old Testament, one can calculate that the Creation occurred in 4004 B.C. This little song expresses the sentiment known as the Fortunate Fall. (Note that: "Deo Gracias" is "Thanks be to God.")

Lord Randal

>>>>>>>

"O where hae ye been, Lord Randal, my son?
O where hae ye been, my handsome young man?"
"I hae been to the wild wood; mother, make my bed soon,
For I'm weary wi' hunting, and fain wald lie down."

"Where gat ye your dinner, Lord Randal, my son?
Where gat ye your dinner, my handsome young man?"
"I din'd wi' my true-love; mother, make my bed soon,
For I'm weary wi' hunting, and fain wald lie down."

"What gat ye to your dinner, Lord Randal, my son?
What gat ye to your dinner, my handsome young man?"
"I gat eels boil'd in broo; mother, make my bed soon,
For I'm weary wi' hunting, and fain wald lie down."

"What became of your bloodhounds, Lord Randal, my son?
What became of your bloodhounds, my handsome young man?"
"O they swell'd and they died; mother, make my bed soon,
For I'm weary wi' hunting, and fain wald lie down"

"O I fear ye are poison'd, Lord Randal, my son!
I fear ye are poison'd, my handsome young man!"
"O yes! I am poison'd; mother, make my bed soon,
For I'm sick at the heart, and I fain wald lie down."

As with "Edward, Edward" (p. 15), the story here is developed through a dialogue between a mother and son.

The Cherry-Tree Carol

Joseph was an old man,
  and an old man was he,
When he wedded Mary,
  in the land of Galilee.

Joseph and Mary walked
  through an orchard good,
Where was cherries and berries,
  so red as any blood.

Joseph and Mary walked
  through an orchard green,
Where was berries and cherries,
  as thick as might be seen.

O then bespoke Mary,
  so meek and so mild:
"Pluck me one cherry, Joseph,
  for I am with child."

O then bespoke Joseph,
  with words most unkind:
"Let him pluck thee a cherry
  that brought thee with child."

O then bespoke the babe,
  within his mother's womb:
"Bow down then the tallest tree,
  for my mother to have some."

Then bowed down the highest tree
   unto his mother's hand;
Then she cried, "See, Joseph,
   I have cherries at command."

O then bespake Joseph:
   "I have done Mary wrong;
But cheer up, my dearest,
   and be not cast down."

Then Mary plucked a cherry,
   as red as the blood,
Then Mary went home
   with her heavy load.

Then Mary took her babe,
   and sat him on her knee,
Saying, "My dear son, tell me
   what this world will be."

"O I shall be as dead, mother,
   as the stones in the wall;
O the stones in the streets, mother,
   shall mourn for me all.

"Upon Easter-day, mother,
   my uprising shall be;
O the sun and the moon, mother,
   shall both rise with me."

In spite of its rather rough mixture of elements from various scriptural and popular sources, this carol remains touching.

Anonymous

The Lord Is My Shepherd

◆◆◆◆◆

The Lord is my shepherd; I shall not want.
   He maketh me to lie down in green pastures: he leadeth me
      beside the still waters.
   He restoreth my soul: he leadeth me in the paths of
      righteousness for his name's sake.
   Yea, though I walk through the valley of the shadow of
      death, I will fear no evil: for thou art with me; thy rod
      and thy staff they comfort me.
   Thou preparest a table before me in the presence of mine
      enemies: thou anointest my head with oil; my cup runneth
      over.
   Surely goodness and mercy shall follow me all the days of my
      life: and I will dwell in the house of the Lord for ever.

Psalm XXIII

About half of the 150 Psalms in the Bible are attributed to David, famed as "the sweet psalmist of Israel" (Second Samuel XXIII:1). The Twenty-third is probably the best-known poem in the Old Testament and perhaps even the whole Bible. It is classified as a "song of trust," like one of the songs that David sang to pacify and heal King Saul.

I Sing of a Maiden

I sing of a maiden
  That is makèles:
King of all kings
  To her son she ches.

He came all so still
  There his mother was,
As dew in Aprìl
  That falleth on the grass.

He came all so still
  To his mother's bower,
As dew in Aprìl
  That falleth on the flower.

He came all so still
  There his mother lay,
As dew in Aprìl
  That falleth on the spray.

Mother and maiden
  Was never none but she;
Well may such a lady
  Goddès mother be.

Much pre-Reformation popular art, including songs, hymns, and prose texts, is devoted to the Blessed Virgin Mary. (Note that: "makeles" is "matchless," "mateless"; "chees" is "close"; "swich" is "such.")

A Lyke-Wake Dirge

This ae nighte, this ae nighte,
  —*Every nighte and alle,*
Fire and fleet and candle-lighte,
  And Christe receive thy saule.

When thou from hence away art past,
  —*Every nighte and alle,*
To Whinny-muir thou com'st at last;
  And Christe receive thy saule.

If ever thou gavest hosen and shoon,
  —*Every nighte and alle,*
Sit thee down and put them on;
  And Christe receive thy saule.

If hosen and shoon thou ne'er gav'st nane
  —*Every nighte and alle,*
The whinnes sall prick thee to the bare bane;
  And Christe receive thy saule.

From Whinny-muir when thou may'st pass,
  —*Every nighte and alle,*
To Brig o' Dread thou com'st at last;
  And Christe receive thy saule.

From Brig o' Dread when thou may'st pass.
  —*Every nighte and alle,*
To Purgatory fire thou com'st at last;
  And Christe receive thy saule.

If ever thou gavest meat or drink,
  —*Every nighte and alle,*
The fire sall never make thee shrink;
  And Christe receive thy saule.

If meat or drink thou ne'er gav'st nane,
  —*Every nighte and alle,*
The fire will burn thee to the bare bane;
  And Christe receive thy saule.

This ae nighte, this ae nighte,
  —*Every nighte and alle,*
Fire and fleet and candle-lighte,
  And Christe receive thy saule.

A "lyke" is a corpse, a "wake" a night watch kept over it. A "whinny-muir" is a moor with thorny shrubs. The economy of charity and punishment is not strictly Biblical, but the idea appealingly makes sense. If you never feed the hungry or clothe the naked, you are in for some answerable treatment come post-mortem time. (Note that: "bane" is "bone"; "brig" is "bridge.")

My Love in Her Attire

My love in her attire doth show her wit,
It doth so well become her:
For every season she hath dressings fit,
For winter, spring, and summer.
No beauty she doth miss,
When all her robes are on;
But Beauty's self she is,
When all her robes are gone.

This is an amorous but discreet poem of praise fit to stand alongside Herrick's "Upon Julia's Clothes" (p. 173).

The Demon Lover

"O where have you been, my long, long love,
  This long seven years and more?"
"O I'm come to seek my former vows
  Ye granted me before."

"O hold your tongue of your former vows,
  For they will breed sad strife;
O hold your tongue of your former vows
  For I am become a wife."

He turn'd him right and round about,
  And the tear blinded his ee;
"I wad never hae trodden on Irish ground,
  If it had not been for thee.

"I might have had a king's daughter,
  Far, far beyond the sea;
I might have had a king's daughter,
  Had it not been for love o' thee."

"If ye might have had a king's daughter,
  Yersell ye had to blame;
Ye might have taken the king's daughter,
  For ye kend that I was nane.

"If I was to leave my husband dear,
  And my two babes also,
O what have you to take me to,
  If with you I should go?"

"I hae seven ships upon the sea,
   The eighth brought me to land;
With four-and-twenty bold mariners,
   And music on every hand."

She has taken up her two little babes,
   Kiss'd them baith cheek and chin;
"O fair ye weel, my ain two babes,
   For I'll never see you again."

She set her foot upon the ship,
   No mariners could she behold;
But the sails were o' the taffetie,
   And the masts o' the beaten gold.

She had not sail'd a league, a league,
   A league but barely three,
When dismal grew his countenance,
   And drumlie grew his ee.

They had not sailed a league, a league,
   A league but barely three,
Until she espied his cloven foot,
   And she wept right bitterlie.

"O hold your tongue of your weeping," says he,
   "Of your weeping now let me be;
I will show you how the lilies grow
   On the banks of Italy."

"O what hills are yon, yon pleasant hills,
   That the sun shines sweetly on?"
"O yon are the hills of heaven," he said,
   "Where you will never win."

"O whaten a mountain is yon?" she said,
   "All so dreary wi' frost and snow?"
"O yon is the mountain of hell," he cried,
   "Where you and I will go."

He struck the tapmast wi' his hand,
   The foremast wi' his knee;
And he brak that gallant ship in twain,
   And sank her in the sea.

The motif of the return of the dead lover has appeared as recently as the movie Ghost *in 1990, although the film lover was human and benevolent and not at all demonic. See also the "demon lover" in Coleridge's "Kubla Khan" (p. 430). (Note that: "kend" is "knew"; "drumlic" is "gloomy.")*

Weep You No More, Sad Fountains

❖❖❖❖

Weep you no more, sad fountains;
　What need you flow so fast?
Look how the snowy mountains
　Heaven's sun doth gently waste.
　　But my sun's heavenly eyes
　　View not your weeping,
　　That now lies sleeping
　Softly, now softly lies
　　Sleeping.

Sleep is a reconciling,
　A rest that peace begets.
Doth not the sun rise smiling
　When fair at ev'n he sets?
　　Rest you then, rest, sad eyes,
　　Melt not in weeping,
　　While she lies sleeping
　Softly, now softly lies
　　Sleeping.

This verse form is a striking demonstration of the art of diminution. Thanks to the flexibility of English syntax, "A rest that peace begets" means both "rest begets peace" and "peace begets rest."

The Unquiet Grave

"The wind doth blow today, my love,
  And a few small drops of rain;
I never had but one true love,
  In cold grave she was lain.

"I'll do as much for my true love
  As any young man may;
I'll sit and mourn all at her grave
  For a twelvemonth, and a day."

The twelvemonth and a day being up,
  The dead began to speak,
"Oh who sits weeping on my grave,
  And will not let me sleep?"

" 'Tis I, my love, sits on your grave
  And will not let you sleep,
For I crave one kiss of your clay-cold lips
  And that is all I seek."

"You crave one kiss of clay-cold lips,
  But my breath smells earthy strong;
If you have one kiss of my clay-cold lips
  You time will not be long:

" 'Tis down in yonder garden green,
  Love, where we used to walk,
The finest flower that ere was seen
  Is withered to a stalk.

"The stalk is withered dry, my love,
　So will our hearts decay;
So make yourself content, my love,
　Till God calls you away."

As in many situations — including that in Romeo and Juliet *— the woman has more sense than the man; it does not matter that the man is alive and the woman is not.*

Waly, Waly

>>>>>>>

O waly, waly, up the bank,
  And waly, waly, down the brae,
And waly, waly, yon burn side,
  Where I and my love were wont to gae.

I leant my back upon an oak,
  I thought it was a trusty tree;
But first it bent, and then it broke,
  Just as my love proved false to me.

O waly, waly, love is bonny,
  A little while when it is new;
But when it's old, it waxes cold,
  And fades away like morning dew.

O wherefore should I busk my head?
  O wherefore should I comb my hair?
For my true love has me forsook,
  And says he'll never love me more.

Now Arthur's Seat shall be my bed,
  The sheets shall ne'er be filled by me:
Saint Anthony's well shall be my drink,
  Since my true love has forsaken me.

Martinmas wind, when wilt thou blow,
  And shake the green leaves off the tree?
O gentle death, when wilt thou come?
  For of my life I am weary.

'Tis not the frost, that freezes fell,
  Nor blowing snow's inclemency;
'Tis not such cold that makes me cry,
  But my love's heart grown cold to me.

When we came in by Glasgow town,
  We were a comely sight to see,
My love was clad in black velvet,
  And I myself in cramasie.

But had I wist, before I kissed,
  That love had been so ill to win,
I'd locked my heart in a case of gold,
  And pinned it with a silver pin.

And oh! if my young babe were born,
  And set upon the nurse's knee,
And I my self were dead and gone:
  For a maid again I'll never be.

The vague exclamation "Waly" (related to "wellaway" and "welladay") turns up in many versions of this ballad; some of them lack almost all specific detail (except a reference to Glasgow near the end), others are linked up with the story known as "Jamie Douglas," which concerns a domestic tragedy of the late seventeenth century. (Note that: "cramasie" is "crimson.")

JOHN SKELTON 1460?–1529

Skelton tutored Prince Henry (later Henry VIII) and
held the academic title "poet laureate" (though not the
official position, which was not instituted until later).
His poetry has considerable range, but he is remem-
bered mostly as the author of jolly doggerel and vitriolic
satire.

To Mistress Margaret Hussey

Merry Margaret,
   As midsummer flower,
Gentle as falcon
Or hawk of the tower:
With solace and gladness,
Much mirth and no madness,
All good and no badness;
     So joyously,
     So maidenly,
     So womanly
      Her demeaning
      In every thing,
      Far, far passing
      That I can indite,
      Or suffice to write
Of Merry Margaret
   As midsummer flower,
Gentle as falcon
Or hawk of the tower.
   As patient and still
And as full of good will
As fair Isaphill,
Coriander,
Sweet pomander,
Good Cassander,

Steadfast of thought,
Well made, well wrought,
Far may be sought
Ere that ye can find
So courteous, so kind
As Merry Margaret,
This midsummer flower,
Gentle as falcon
Or hawk of the tower.

from The Garlande of Laurell

Skelton had other styles, including a most dignified manner for some religious poems, but the distinctive pattern here—short lines, percussive rhythm, a piling-on of rhymes, ostensibly slipshod execution—is what has become known as Skeltonic. After five centuries, the charm, vigor, and audacity endure. (Note that: "Isaphill" is "Hypsipyle of Lemnos.")

Wyatt was born into a noble family in Kent, educated
at Cambridge, and employed as a courtier and diplomat
by Henry VIII. He was thought to have been associated
with Anne Boleyn before her marriage to the king, and
he was imprisoned briefly after her downfall. He soon
found his way back, however, into the king's favor.
Wyatt may rank as the foremost English poet in terms
of technical inventiveness, since he was the first to use
terza rima and ottava rima and was among the first to
write sonnets (all the forms mentioned here came from
Italy). In friendship and in literary relations, Wyatt is
commonly linked with the Earl of Surrey.

They Flee from Me That Sometime Did Me Seek

They flee from me that sometime did me seek
With naked foot stalking in my chamber.
I have seen them gentle, tame and meek
That now are wild and do not remember
That sometime they put themselves in danger
To take bread at my hand; and now they range
Busily seeking with a continual change.

Thanked be fortune, it hath been otherwise
Twenty times better, but once in special,
In thin array after a pleasant guise,
When her loose gown from her shoulders did fall
And she me caught in her arms long and small,
Therewithal sweetly did me kiss
And softly said, "Dear heart, how like you this?"

It was no dream: I lay broad waking.
But all is turned thorough my gentleness
Into a strange fashion of forsaking.
And I have leave to go of her goodness
And she also to use newfangleness.
But since that I so kindly am served
I fain would know what she hath deserved.

These paradoxes and complexities may foreshadow the Metaphysical poetry that was to flourish almost a hundred years later. Tottel's Miscellany *entitles this poem "The Lover Showeth How He Is Forsaken of Such as He Sometime Enjoyed" and "corrects" the seventeenth line to read "Into a bitter fashion of forsaking."*

The Lover Complaineth the Unkindness of His Love

My lute awake! perform the last
Labour that thou and I shall waste,
And end that I have now begun;
For when this song is sung and past,
My lute be still, for I have done.

As to be heard where ear is none,
As lead to grave in marble stone,
My song may pierce her heart as soon;
Should we then sigh, or sing, or moan?
No, no, my lute, for I have done.

The rocks do not so cruelly
Repulse the waves continually,
As she my suit and affection,
So that I am past remedy:
Whereby my lute and I have done.

Proud of the spoil that thou hast got
Of simple hearts thorough love's shot,
By whom, unkind, thou hast them won,
Think not he hath his bow forgot,
Although my lute and I have done.

Vengeance shall fall on thy disdain,
That makest but game on earnest pain;
Think not alone under the sun
Unquit to cause thy lovers plain,
Although my lute and I have done.

Perchance thee lie withered and old,
The winter nights that are so cold,
Plaining in vain unto the moon;
Thy wishes then dare not be told;
Care then who list, for I have done.

And then may chance thee to repent
The time that thou hast lost and spent
To cause thy lovers sigh and swoon;
Then shalt thou know beauty but lent,
And wish and want as I have done.

Now cease, my lute! this is the last
Labour that thou and I shall waste,
And ended is that we begun;
Now is this song both sung and past:
My lute, be still, for I have done.

The long title was added to this poem in Richard Tottel's Miscellany *fifteen years after Wyatt's death. The meaningful rhyme of "old," "cold," and "told," by the way, recurs in the first, fifteenth, and last stanzas of Keats's "Eve of St. Agnes" (p. 551). (Note that: "unquit" is "unrevenged"; "plain" is "complain"; "list" is "like.")*

Whoso List to Hunt

Whoso list to hunt, I know where is an hind,
But as for me, helas, I may no more.
The vain travail hath wearied me so sore,
I am of them that farthest cometh behind.
Yet may I by no means my wearied mind
Draw from the deer, but as she fleeth afore
Fainting I follow. I leave off therefore
Since in a net I seek to hold the wind.
Who list her hunt, I put him out of doubt,
As well as I may spend his time in vain.
And graven with diamonds in letters plain
There is written her fair neck round about:
"Noli me tangere for Caesar's I am,
And wild for to hold though I seem tame."

---

*Reading this brilliant but enigmatic poem, one will probably find it hard to resist
the temptation to identify the "deer" who belongs to Caesar with Anne Boleyn,
who belonged for a time to Henry VIII. This, incidentally, is the earliest sonnet
in this anthology and among the first in English. (Note that: "list" is "like";
"noli me tangere" is "I do not want you to touch me," "touch me not.")*

Ralegh was chiefly known as a military, political, and
diplomatic genius and also as a charismatic adventurer.
He wrote history and poetry of a most distinguished
order. For all his brilliance and patriotic service, how-
ever, James I still ordered Ralegh's execution, and he
was beheaded.

The Nymph's Reply to the Shepherd

If all the world and love were young,
And truth in every shepherd's tongue,
These pretty pleasures might me move
To live with thee and be thy Love.

But Time drives flocks from field to fold;
When rivers rage and rocks grow cold;
And Philomel becometh dumb;
The rest complains of cares to come.

The flowers do fade, and wanton fields
To wayward Winter reckoning yields:
A honey tongue, a heart of gall,
Is fancy's spring, but sorrow's fall.

Thy gowns, thy shoes, thy beds of roses,
Thy cap, thy kirtle, and thy posies,
Soon break, soon wither—soon forgotten,
In folly ripe, in reason rotten.

Thy belt of straw and ivy-buds,
Thy coral clasps and amber studs,—
All these in me no means can move
To come to thee and be thy Love.

But could youth last, and love still breed,
Had joys no date, nor age no need,
Then these delights my mind might move
To live with thee and be thy Love.

It is probable but not certain that Ralegh wrote this reply to Marlowe's "Passionate Shepherd to His Love" (p. 82), where there is further commentary on the responses.

The Lie

Go, Soul, the body's guest,
Upon a thankless arrant:
Fear not to touch the best;
The truth shall be thy warrant:
Go, since I needs must die,
And give the world the lie.

Say to the court, it glows
And shines like rotten wood;
Say to the church it shows
What's good, and doth no good:
If church and court reply,
Then give them both the lie.

Tell potentates, they live
Acting by others' action;
Not loved unless they give,
Not strong but by affection:
If potentates reply,
Give potentates the lie.

Tell men of high condition
That manage the estate,
Their purpose is ambition,
Their practice only hate:
And if they once reply,
Then give them all the lie.

Tell them that brave it most
They beg for more by spending,
Who, in their greatest cost,
Seek nothing but commending:
And if they make reply,
Then give them all the lie.

Tell zeal it wants devotion,
Tell love it is but lust;
Tell time it metes but motion,
Tell flesh it is but dust:
And wish them not reply,
For thou must give the lie.

Tell age it daily wasteth;
Tell honour how it alters;
Tell beauty how she blasteth;
Tell favour how it falters:
And as they shall reply,
Give every one the lie.

Tell wit how much it wrangles
In tickle points of niceness;
Tell wisdom she entangles
Herself in over-wiseness:
And when they do reply,
Straight give them both the lie.

Tell physic of her boldness;
Tell skill it is pretension;
Tell charity of coldness;
Tell law it is contention:
And as they do reply,
So give them still the lie.

Tell fortune of her blindness;
Tell nature of decay;
Tell friendship of unkindness;
Tell justice of delay:
And if they will reply,
Then give them all the lie.

Tell arts they have no soundness,
But vary by esteeming;
Tell schools they want profoundness,
And stand too much on seeming:
If arts and schools reply,
Give arts and schools the lie.

Tell faith it's fled the city;
Tell how the country erreth;
Tell manhood shakes off pity
And virtue least preferreth:
And if they do reply,
Spare not to give the lie.

So when thou hast, as I
Commanded thee, done blabbing
—Although to give the lie
Deserves no less than stabbing—
Stab at thee he that will,
No stab thy soul can kill.

Like Waller's "Go, Lovely Rose" (p. 200), "The Lie" begins as an "envoy" or "sending poem" with orders to a representative. Unlike Waller's poem, however, Ralegh's turns into a telling inventory of all that is wrong with the world—true in 1608 and still true, four centuries later.

Even Such Is Time

Even such is time that takes in trust
Our youth, our joys, our all we have,
And pays us but with age and dust,
Who in the dark and silent grave,
When we have wandered all our ways,
Shuts up the story of our days.
But from this earth, this grave, this dust,
My God shall raise me up, I trust.

---

*Just as musical themes return to their tonic or keynote, Ralegh's rhymes run
from "trust" through "dust" (twice) and back to "trust."*

The Passionate Man's Pilgrimage

Give me my scallop-shell of quiet,
My staff of faith to walk upon,
My scrip of joy, immortal diet,
My bottle of salvation,
My gown of glory, hope's true gage,
And thus I'll take my pilgrimage.

Blood must be my body's balmer,
No other balm will there be given,
Whilst my soul like a white palmer
Travels to the land of heaven,
Over the silver mountains,
Where spring the nectar fountains;
And there I'll kiss
The bowl of bliss,
And drink my eternal fill
On every milken hill.
My soul will be a-dry before,
But after it will ne'er thirst more.

And by the happy blissful way
More peaceful pilgrims I shall see,
That have shook off their gowns of clay
And go apparelled fresh like me.
I'll bring them first
To slake their thirst,
And then to taste those nectar suckets,
At the clear wells
Where sweetness dwells,
Drawn up by saints in crystal buckets.

And when our bottles and all we
Are filled with immortality,
Then the holy paths we'll travel,
Strewed with rubies thick as gravel,
Ceilings of diamonds, sapphire floors,
High walls of coral and pearl bowers.

From thence to heaven's bribeless hall
Where no corrupted voices brawl,
No conscience molten into gold,
Nor forged accusers bought and sold,
No cause deferred, nor vain-spent journey,
For there Christ is the King's Attorney,
Who pleads for all without degrees,
And he hath angels, but no fees.

When the grand twelve million jury
Of our sins with sinful fury
'Gainst our souls black verdicts give,
Christ pleads his death, and then we live.
Be thou my speaker, taintless pleader,
Unblotted lawyer, true proceeder;
Thou movest salvation even for alms,
Not with a bribed lawyer's palms.

And this is my eternal plea
To him that made heaven, earth and sea:
Seeing my flesh must die so soon,
And want a head to dine next noon,
Just at the stroke when my veins start and spread,
Set on my soul an everlasting head.
Then am I ready, like a palmer fit,
To tread those blest paths which before I writ.

Pilgrimages have fascinated English writers since the Middle Ages: Chaucer, of course, Spenser, Bunyan, T. S. Eliot (whose Four Quartets *consists of ghostly visits that have been called "totemic pilgrimages"), down to Philip Larkin, whose "Church Going" (p. 1068) represents a secular — but nonetheless passionate — pilgrimage. Ralegh's poem, which, in 1604, seemed to presage his beheading in 1618, combines a nearly Spenserian allegory of equipment and symbols with a sharp courtier's satire of earthly politics. Ralegh's authorship of this poem has recently been seriously questioned.* The New Oxford Book of Sixteenth-Century Verse *lists the poem as anonymous, maybe "written by a recusant . . . ." (Note that: "scrip" is "bag"; "gage" is "pledge"; "suckets" is "confections"; "angels" is "gold coins.")*

EDMUND SPENSER c.1552–1599

Spenser, educated at Pembroke Hall, Cambridge, earned his living in various appointive political positions. His magnum opus, *The Faerie Queene*, was begun in 1579 and never finished. In addition to its six books (and part of another), Spenser wrote a number of shorter works, including the twelve eclogues of *The Shepheardes Calender* and the 89 sonnets of *Amoretti*.

One Day I Wrote Her Name upon the Strand

>>>>>>>

One day I wrote her name upon the strand;
But came the waves, and washed it away:
Again, I wrote it with a second hand;
But came the tide, and made my pains his prey.
Vain man, said she, that dost in vain assay
A mortal thing so to immortalize;
For I myself shall like to this decay,
And eke my name be wiped out likewise.
Not so, quoth I; let baser things devise
To die in dust, but you shall live by fame:
My verse your virtues rare shall eternize,
And in the heavens write your glorious name.
    Where, whenas death shall all the world subdue,
    Our love shall live, and later life renew.

Sonnet LXXV
from Amoretti

The sonnets of Spenser's Amoretti *(1595) show the pleasures of convention — repeating sentiments and figures also used in this volume in sonnets by Sidney, Shakespeare, and others, and not so very different in the mid-twentieth-century popular song "Love Letters in the Sand" — with the complementary pleasures of invention — notable here in the engaging original rhyme scheme of the uniquely "Spenserian" sonnet (ababbcbccdcdee), a graceful compromise between the Italian and English forms.*

Prothalamion

Calm was the day, and through the trembling air
Sweet-breathing Zephyrus did softly play,
A gentle spirit, that lightly did delay
Hot Titan's beams, which then did glister fair;
When I (whom sullen care,
Through discontent of my long fruitless stay
In princes' court, and expectation vain
Of idle hopes, which still do fly away
Like empty shadows, did afflict my brain)
Walked forth to ease my pain
Along the shore of silver-streaming Thames;
Whose rutty bank, the which his river hems,
Was painted all with variable flowers,
And all the meads adorned with dainty gems
Fit to deck maidens' bowers,
And crown their paramours
Against the bridal day, which is not long:
    Sweet Thames run softly, till I end my song.

There in a meadow by the river's side
A flock of nymphs I chancèd to espy,
All lovely daughters of the flood thereby,
With goodly greenish locks all loose untied
As each had been a bride;
And each one had a little wicker basket
Made of fine twigs entrailèd curiously,
In which they gathered flowers to fill their flasket,
And, with fine fingers, cropped full feateously
The tender stalks on high.
Of every sort which in that meadow grew
They gathered some; the violet, pallid blue,
The little daisy that at evening closes,
The virgin lily and the primrose true,
With store of vermeil roses,

To deck their bridegrooms' posies
Against the bridal day, which was not long:
   Sweet Thames run softly, till I end my song.

With that I saw two swans of goodly hue
Come softly swimming down along the Lee;
Two fairer birds I yet did never see;
The snow which doth the top of Pindus strew
Did never whiter shew,
Nor Jove himself, when he a swan would be
For love of Leda, whiter did appear;
Yet Leda was, they say, as white as he,
Yet not so white as these, nor nothing near;
So purely white they were
That even the gentle stream, the which them bare,
Seemed foul to them, and bade his billows spare
To wet their silken feathers, lest they might
Soil their fair plumes with water not so fair,
And mar their beauties bright,
That shone as heaven's light,
Against their bridal day, which was not long:
   Sweet Thames run softly, till I end my song.

Eftsoons the nymphs, which now had flowers their fill,
Ran all in haste to see that silver brood
As they came floating on the crystal flood;
Whom when they saw, they stood amazèd still
Their wondering eyes to fill;
Them seemed they never saw a sight so fair,
Of fowls so lovely that they sure did deem
Them heavenly born, or to be that same pair
Which through the sky draw Venus' silver team;
For sure they did not seem
To be begot of any earthly seed,
But rather angels, or of angels' breed;
Yet were they bred of summer's-heat, they say,
In sweetest season, when each flower and weed
The earth did fresh array;

So fresh they seemed as day,
Even as their bridal day, which was not long:
   Sweet Thames run softly, till I end my song.

Then forth they all out of their baskets drew
Great store of flowers, the honour of the field,
That to the sense did fragrant odours yield,
All which upon those goodly birds they threw,
And all the waves did strew,
That like old Peneus' waters they did seem
When down along by pleasant Tempe's shore,
Scattered with flowers, through Thessaly they stream,
That they appear, through lilies' plenteous store,
Like a bride's chamber-floor.
Two of those nymphs meanwhile two garlands bound
Of freshest flowers which in that mead they found,
The which presenting all in trim array,
Their snowy foreheads therewithal they crowned,
Whilst one did sing this lay
Prepared against that day,
Against their bridal day, which was not long:
   Sweet Thames run softly, till I end my song.

"Ye gentle birds! the world's fair ornament,
And heaven's glory, whom this happy hour
Doth lead unto your lovers' blissful bower,
Joy may you have, and gentle heart's content
Of your love's couplement;
And let fair Venus, that is queen of love,
With her heart-quelling son upon you smile,
Whose smile, they say, hath virtue to remove
All love's dislike, and friendship's faulty guile
For ever to assoil.
Let endless peace your steadfast hearts accord,
And blessed plenty wait upon your board,
And let your bed with pleasures chaste abound,
That fruitful issue may to you afford,
Which may your foes confound,

[67]

And make your joys redound
Upon your bridal day, which is not long:
 Sweet Thames run softly, till I end my song."

So ended she; and all the rest around
To her redoubled that her undersong,
Which said their bridal day should not be long:
And gentle Echo from the neighbour ground
Their accents did resound.
So forth those joyous birds did pass along,
Adown the Lee that to them murmured low,
As he would speak but that he lacked a tongue,
Yet did by signs his glad affection show,
Making his stream run slow.
And all the fowl which in his flood did dwell
Gan flock about these twain, that did excel
The rest, so far as Cynthia doth shend
The lesser stars. So they, enrangèd well,
Did on those two attend,
And their best service lend
Against their wedding day, which was not long:
 Sweet Thames run softly, till I end my song.

At length they all to merry London came,
To merry London, my most kindly nurse,
That to me gave this life's first native source,
Though from another place I take my name,
An house of ancient fame:
There when they came whereas those bricky towers
The which on Thames' broad aged back do ride,
Where now the studious lawyers have their bowers,
There whilom wont the Templar knights to bide,
Till they decayed through pride:
Next whereunto there stands a stately place,
Where oft I gainèd gifts and goodly grace
Of that great lord, which therein wont to dwell,
Whose want too well now feels my friendless case;
But ah! here fits not well

Old woes, but joys to tell
Against the bridal day, which is not long:
  Sweet Thames run softly, till I end my song.

Yet therein now doth lodge a noble peer,
Great England's glory and the world's wide wonder,
Whose dreadful name late through all Spain did thunder,
And Hercules' two pillars standing near
Did make to quake and fear:
Fair branch of honour, flower of chivalry!
That fillest England with thy triumphs' fame,
Joy have thou of thy noble victory,
And endless happiness of thine own name
That promiseth the same;
That through thy prowess and victorious arms
Thy country may be freed from foreign harms,
And great Eliza's glorious name may ring
Through all the world, filled with thy wide alarms,
Which some brave Muse may sing
To ages following,
Upon the bridal day, which is not long:
  Sweet Thames run softly, till I end my song.

From those high towers this noble lord issuing,
Like radiant Hesper when his golden hair
In the ocean billows he hath bathèd fair,
Descended to the river's open viewing,
With a great train ensuing.
Above the rest were goodly to be seen
Two gentle knights of lovely face and feature,
Beseeming well the bower of any queen,
With gifts of wit and ornaments of nature
Fit for so goodly stature,
That like the twins of Jove they seemed in sight
Which deck the baldric of the heavens bright;
They two, forth pacing to the river's side,
Received those two fair brides, their love's delight,
Which, at the appointed tide,

Each one did make his bride
Against their bridal day, which is not long:
    Sweet Thames run softly, till I end my song.

Spenser published his "Epithalamion" in 1595 in honor of his own wedding. The next year, he coined "Prothalamion" as a name for a "Spousall Verse" or a betrothal poem celebrating a ceremony technically somewhat in advance of the nuptials proper. It was a double wedding involving the two eldest daughters of the Earl of Worcester and their fiancés. The river-refrain returns in T. S. Eliot's "Waste Land" (p. 968). (Note that: "entraylèd" is "interlaced"; "flasket" is "basket"; "breede" is "race"; "whylome" is "formerly"; "tyde" is "time.")

SIR PHILIP SIDNEY 1554–1586

Sidney's charismatic presence pervades the literature of England at the end of the sixteenth century and the beginning of the seventeenth; and even this book honors not only Sidney's poetry but also his birthplace (in Jonson's "To Penshurst") and his sister (in Browne's "On the Countess Dowager of Pembroke"). Although his life was short and busy, Sidney wrote a prose romance, an important critical treatise, and many poems, all in his spare time, as it were. He died in battle in the Netherlands and was buried in St. Paul's Cathedral.

With How Sad Steps, O Moon, Thou Climb'st the Skies!

With how sad steps, O moon, thou climb'st the skies,
How silently, and with how wan a face.
What, may it be that even in heavenly place
That busy archer his sharp arrows tries?
Sure, if that long-with-love-acquainted eyes
Can judge of love, thou feel'st a lover's case;
I read it in thy looks; thy languished grace
To me, that feel the like, thy state descries.
Then, even of fellowship, O moon, tell me,
Is constant love deemed there but want of wit?
Are beauties there as proud as here they be?
Do they above love to be loved, and yet
Those lovers scorn whom that love doth possess?
Do they call virtue there ungratefulness?

Sonnet XXXI
from Astrophil and Stella

One can be so troubled by love that the woes are projected onto everything around, even celestial objects. The moon's pallor and mutability make it an apt correlative for any number of emotional states. Loony tunes are nothing new and will never go out of style. About four centuries after Sidney, Philip Larkin wrote a moon poem called "Sad Steps."

Leave Me, O Love,
Which Reachest But to Dust

Leave me, O Love, which reachest but to dust,
　And thou, my mind, aspire to higher things!
Grow rich in that which never taketh rust:
　Whatever fades but fading pleasure brings.
Draw in thy beams, and humble all thy might
　To that sweet yoke where lasting freedoms be,
Which breaks the clouds and opens forth the light,
　That doth both shine and give us sight to see.
O take fast hold; let that light be thy guide
　In this small course which birth draws out to death;
And think how evil becometh him to slide,
　Who seeketh heaven, and comes of heavenly breath.
　　Then farewell, world; thy uttermost I see;
　　Eternal Love, maintain thy life in me.

Some earlier editors placed this poem as Sonnet CX in the sonnet sequence
Astrophil and Stella, *but now there is general agreement that it belongs at the*
end of the volume called Certain Sonnets.

My True Love Hath My Heart

My true love hath my heart, and I have his,
   By just exchange, one for the other given.
I hold his dear, and mine he cannot miss,
   There never was a better bargain driven.
His heart in me keeps me and him in one,
   My heart in him his thoughts and senses guides;
He loves my heart, for once it was his own,
   I cherish his, because in me it bides.
His heart his wound receivèd from my sight,
   My heart was wounded with his wounded heart;
For as from me on him his hurt did light,
   So still methought in me his hurt did smart.
     Both equal hurt, in this change sought our bliss:
     My true love hath my heart and I have his.

from Arcadia

The tricky story-within-a-story in Book III of Arcadia *is too complicated to be summarized; suffice it to say that a young woman sings this lovely song to a young man.*

Loving in Truth,
and Fain in Verse My Love to Show

()◀━()

Loving in truth, and fain in verse my love to show,
That she, dear she, might take some pleasure of my pain,
Pleasure might cause her read, reading might make her know,
Knowledge might pity win, and pity grace obtain,
I sought fit words to paint the blackest face of woe:
Studying inventions fine, her wits to entertain,
Oft turning others' leaves, to see if thence would flow
Some fresh and fruitful showers upon my sunburn'd brain.
But words came halting forth, wanting Invention's stay;
Invention, Nature's child, fled stepdame Study's blows;
And others' feet still seemed but strangers in my way.
Thus, great with child to speak, and helpless in my throes,
Biting my truant pen, beating myself for spite:
"Fool," said my Muse to me, "look in thy heart and write!"

Sonnet I
from Astrophil and Stella

This first sonnet in the Astrophil and Stella *cycle may seem to advise one to indulge in unfettered creative writing, but the poem itself is a marvel of artifice and craft. It is a very rare sort of sonnet, rhyming* abababababcdcdee *and using hexameters—lines with six iambic feet—rather than the usual pentameters. (Note that: "trewand" is "truant.")*

Come Sleep! O Sleep, the Certain Knot of Peace

Come, Sleep, O Sleep, the certain knot of peace,
  The baiting-place of wit, the balm of woe,
The poor man's wealth, the prisoner's release,
  The indifferent judge between the high and low;
With shield of proof shield me from out the press
  Of those fierce darts Despair at me doth throw:
O make in me those civil wars to cease;
  I will good tribute pay, if thou do so.
Take thou of me smooth pillows, sweetest bed,
  A chamber deaf to noise and blind to light,
A rosy garland and a weary head;
  And if these things, as being thine by right,
    Move not thy heavy grace, thou shalt in me,
    Livelier than elsewhere, Stella's image see.

Sonnet XXXIX
from Astrophil and Stella

An exercise in finding clever ways to praise and court sleep, this poem is also an expression of the power of love. (Note that: "baiting" is "resting.")

GEORGE PEELE c.1558–c.1597

Peele seems to have been one of those engaging hell-raisers that distinguish certain expansive ages of literature. He was himself a performer as well as a playwright and lyric poet. He also specialized in that type of poem known as "gratulatory."

His Golden Locks Time Hath to Silver Turned

◆◇◆◇◆

His golden locks time hath to silver turned;
  O time too swift, O swiftness never ceasing!
His youth 'gainst time and age hath ever spurned,
  But spurned in vain; youth waneth by increasing.
Beauty, strength, youth are flowers but fading seen;
Duty, faith, love are roots, and ever green.

His helmet now shall make a hive for bees,
  And, lovers' sonnets turned to holy psalms,
A man-at-arms must now serve on his knees,
  And feed on prayers, which are age his alms:
But though from court to cottage he depart,
His saint is sure of his unspotted heart.

And when he saddest sits in homely cell,
  He'll teach his swains this carol for a song—
"Blest be the hearts that wish my sovereign well,
  Curst be the souls that think her any wrong."
Goddess, allow this agèd man his right,
To be your beadsman now that was your knight.

from Polyhymnia

This poem, which was first printed as part of Peele's "Polyhymnia," was long thought to be Peele's work, written for the ceremony in 1590 when the Queen's Champion, Sir Henry Lee, aged sixty, gave up his position. It has recently been persuasively argued, however, that the poem is not by Peele but by Lee himself. The poem has also been titled "A Farewell to Arms," by which name it was presumably known to Ernest Hemingway in the 1920s.

Whenas the Rye Reach to the Chin

When as the rye reach to the chin,
And chopcherry, chopcherry ripe within,
Strawberries swimming in the cream,
And school-boys playing in the stream;
   Then O, then O, then O my true love said,
    Till that time come again,
  She could not live a maid.

from The Old Wives' Tale

This song seems to be an amiable riddle, along the lines of "blue moon" and "month of Sundays."

ROBERT SOUTHWELL c.1561–1595

Canonized in 1970, Southwell is the only saint among the poets in this book. He was educated by Jesuits on the continent and took holy orders. Back in England, he was arrested on his way to celebrate Mass. He was imprisoned and brutally tortured before being executed. Most of his poems were written during his three-year imprisonment.

The Burning Babe

As I in hoary winter's night stood shivering in the snow,
Surprised I was with sudden heat which made my heart to glow;
And lifting up a fearful eye to view what fire was near,
A pretty Babe all burning bright did in the air appear;
Who, scorched with excessive heat, such floods of tears did shed,
As though his floods should quench his flames which with his
    tears were fed.
"Alas!" quoth he, "but newly born in fiery heats I fry,
Yet none approach to warm their hearts or feel my fire but I.
My faultless breast the furnace is, the fuel wounding thorns;
Love is the fire, and sighs the smoke, the ashes shame and
    scorns;
The fuel justice layeth on, and mercy blows the coals;
The metal in this furnace wrought are men's defiled souls;
For which, as now on fire I am to work them to their good,
So will I melt into a bath to wash them in my blood."
With this he vanished out of sight and swiftly shrunk away,
And straight I called unto mind that it was Christmas Day.

In the limited scope of sixteen lines, Southwell combines many traditions and conventions: the seven-stress line of folk ballads, the alliteration of Old English, the sustained allegory of Medieval theology, the piercing vision of mysticism, and the heritage of solstitial observances, including Christmas.

SAMUEL DANIEL 1562–1619

Daniel wrote tragedies and masques as well as the son-
net sequence *Delia,* which is the source of his poem in
this anthology. He also engaged in literary controversy,
answering Thomas Campion's *Observations in the Art of
English Poesie* with his robust *A Defence of Ryme.*

Care-Charmer Sleep,
Son of the Sable Night

•◦•

Care-charmer Sleep, son of the sable Night,
  Brother to Death, in silent darkness born,
Relieve my languish, and restore the light;
  With dark forgetting of my cares return.
And let the day be time enough to mourn
  The shipwreck of my ill-adventured youth;
Let waking eyes suffice to wail their scorn
  Without the torment of the night's untruth.
Cease, dreams, th' images of day-desires,
  To model forth the passions of the morrow;
Never let rising sun approve you liars,
  To add more grief to aggravate my sorrow.
    Still let me sleep, embracing clouds in vain,
    And never wake to feel the day's disdain.

from Delia

---

*Without claiming for Daniel the last word in Freudian sophistication, we may
still admire the way he could recognize that dreams deal with "our day-desires,"
often in ways that disturb our needed repose.*

MICHAEL DRAYTON 1563–1631

Drayton, who, like Shakespeare, came from Warwick-
shire, was a Jack of all poetic genres, excelling in the
sonnet and also in historical and topographical poems;
moreover, he collaborated on various dramatic works.
He was among the earliest of the professional men of
letters and is buried, fittingly, in Westminster Abbey.

Since There's No Help,
Come Let Us Kiss and Part

Since there's no help, come let us kiss and part;
Nay, I have done, you get no more of me,
And I am glad, yea, glad with all my heart
That thus so cleanly I myself can free;
Shake hands for ever, cancel all our vows,
And when we meet at any time again,
Be it not seen in either of our brows
That we one jot of former love retain.
Now at the last gasp of Love's latest breath,
When, his pulse failing, Passion speechless lies,
When Faith is kneeling by his bed of death,
And Innocence is closing up his eyes,
   Now if thou wouldst, when all have given him over,
   From death to life thou mightst him yet recover.

Sonnet LXI
from Idea

---

*It is thought that Anne Goodere, daughter of Drayton's patron, was the inspi-
ration for his* Idea *or* Ideas Mirrour *(1594). Drayton's language is plainer
than Shakespeare's, and the introductory sonnet of* Idea *sounds quite modern:
"My verse is the true image of my mind." The first three lines of this sonnet
consist exclusively of ordinary monosyllables.*

Marlowe was born at Canterbury, educated at Cambridge, and murdered at Deptford, presumably in a quarrel over the bill at a tavern. In the swift blaze of his career, Marlowe produced a half-dozen tragedies as well as translations from Ovid. In an age of matchless greatness in literature, only Shakespeare was greater than Marlowe.

The Passionate Shepherd to His Love

Come live with me and be my love,
And we will all the pleasures prove
That valleys, groves, hills, and fields,
Woods, or steepy mountain yields.

And we will sit upon the rocks,
Seeing the shepherds feed their flocks
By shallow rivers, to whose falls
Melodious birds sing madrigals.

And I will make thee beds of roses
And a thousand fragrant posies;
A cap of flowers and a kirtle
Embroidered all with leaves of myrtle;

A gown made of the finest wool
Which from our pretty lambs we pull;
Fair linèd slippers for the cold,
With buckles of the purest gold;

A belt of straw and ivy buds,
With coral clasps and amber studs.
And if these pleasures may thee move,
Come live with me and be my Love.

The shepherds' swains shall dance and sing
For thy delight each May morning.
If these delights thy mind may move,
Then live with me and be my Love.

This gentle pseudo-pastoral was first published in 1599, some years after Marlowe's death, in a collection called The Passionate Pilgrim. *The next year,* England's Helicon *included this poem along with a reply that may be by Sir Walter Ralegh (see "The Nymph's Reply to the Shepherd," p. 55). In 1633 John Donne's "Bait" began, "Come live with me and be my love, / And we will some new pleasures prove . . . ."*

In spite of his eminence as the greatest English poet and one of the greatest poets ever in the world, we know little about Shakespeare's life. His father was a prominent citizen of Stratford-upon-Avon. When Shakespeare was eighteen he married a somewhat older woman, Anne Hathaway, who gave birth to a daughter six months after the wedding. During the 1590s Shakespeare worked in the London theater as actor and playwright. Early in his career, he wrote some long poems, and it is probable that the sonnets that make up more than half of his poems in this book were written during the 1590s. His three dozen plays, for which he is most famous, are grouped as histories or chronicle plays, comedies, romances, and tragedies.

That Time of Year
Thou Mayst in Me Behold

That time of year thou mayst in me behold
When yellow leaves, or none, or few, do hang
Upon those boughs which shake against the cold,
Bare ruin'd choirs where late the sweet birds sang.
In me thou see'st the twilight of such day
As after sunset fadeth in the west,
Which by and by black night doth take away,
Death's second self, that seals up all in rest.
In me thou see'st the glowing of such fire,
That on the ashes of his youth doth lie,
As the death-bed whereon it must expire,
Consum'd with that which it was nourish'd by.
   This thou perceiv'st, which makes thy love more strong,
   To love that well which thou must leave ere long.

Sonnet LXXIII

It is as though the measured pace of poetry implicitly says, "The clock is ticking, the meter is running." Music and poetry are themselves reminders of time, and time's passing leads finally to a state of inexorable mortality, ever clearer as one ages. But, as Wallace Stevens was to say in "Sunday Morning" (p. 920) dozens of decades later, "Death is the mother of beauty": the meter-matrix of mortality gives birth to much great poetry.

Shall I Compare Thee to a Summer's Day?

()◀▬▶()

Shall I compare thee to a summer's day?
Thou art more lovely and more temperate:
Rough winds do shake the darling buds of May,
And summer's lease hath all too short a date;
Sometime too hot the eye of heaven shines,
And often is his gold complexion dimm'd;
And every fair from fair sometime declines,
By chance or nature's changing course untrimm'd:
But thy eternal summer shall not fade
Nor lose possession of that fair thou ow'st;
Nor shall Death brag thou wand'rest in his shade,
When in eternal lines to time thou grow'st;
   So long as men can breathe or eyes can see,
   So long lives this, and this gives life to thee.

Sonnet XVIII

Elizabethan sonneteers inherited a packet of conventions from Italian precursors, most notably Francesco Petrarch. "Petrarchan" designates the rhetoric of love poems involving fanciful comparisons and fantastic exaggeration. But this sonnet, like Sonnet CXXX, "My mistress' eyes are nothing like the sun," on p. 97, could be called anti-Petrarchan, since it begins by denying comparisons. The final claim—that the very verse we are reading is what confers eternal life—is a convention derived from Horace's Odes. (Note that: "ow'st" is "ownest.")

Let Me Not
to the Marriage of True Minds

Let me not to the marriage of true minds
Admit impediments. Love is not love
Which alters when it alteration finds,
Or bends with the remover to remove.
O, no! it is an ever-fixèd mark
That looks on tempests and is never shaken;
It is the star to every wand'ring bark,
Whose worth's unknown, although his height be taken.
Love's not Time's fool, though rosy lips and cheeks
Within his bending sickle's compass come;
Love alters not with his brief hours and weeks,
But bears it out even to the edge of doom.
    If this be error and upon me proved,
    I never writ, nor no man ever loved.

Sonnet CXVI

Shakespeare's Julius Caesar claims to be as "constant as the northern star"—that is, the Pole Star that seems not to move while all other stars revolve around it and which can still be used in informal navigation. Ink has been spilt over the reading of line 8, which probably refers to the star (whose elevation or celestial altitude can be known by instruments) but may refer to the bark (ship).

Fear No More the Heat o' the Sun

❖·❖·❖·❖

Fear no more the heat o' the sun
　　Nor the furious winter's rages;
Thou thy worldly task hast done,
　　Home art gone, and ta'en thy wages:
Golden lads and girls all must,
As chimney-sweepers, come to dust.

Fear no more the frown o' the great,
　　Thou art past the tyrant's stroke;
Care no more to clothe and eat;
　　To thee the reed is as the oak:
The scepter, learning, physic, must
All follow this, and come to dust.

Fear no more the lightning flash,
　　Nor the all-dreaded thunder stone;
Fear not slander, censure rash;
　　Thou hast finished joy and moan:
All lovers young, all lovers must
Consign to thee, and come to dust.

No exorciser harm thee!
Nor no witchcraft charm thee!
Ghost unlaid forbear thee!
Nothing ill come near thee!
Quiet consummation have;
And renownèd be thy grave!

from Cymbeline

In the fourth act of Cymbeline, *the princes Guiderius and Arviragus "say" this
funeral song over the supposedly dead body of the supposed boy Fidele — really the
living body of the woman Imogen. (Shakespeare's theater, which had no ac-
tresses, specialized in plots involving change or confusion of sex; there were, in
addition, many make-believe deaths.)*

When Icicles Hang by the Wall

When icicles hang by the wall,
  And Dick the shepherd blows his nail
And Tom bears logs into the hall,
  And milk comes frozen home in pail,
When blood is nipp'd and ways be foul,
Then nightly sings the staring owl,
To-whit!
To-who! — a merry note,
While greasy Joan doth keel the pot.

When all aloud the wind doth blow,
  And coughing drowns the parson's saw,
And birds sit brooding in the snow,
  And Marian's nose looks red and raw,
When roasted crabs hiss in the bowl,
Then nightly sings the staring owl,
To-whit!
To-who! — a merry note,
While greasy Joan doth keel the pot.

from Love's Labour's Lost

Two songs are sung at the end of Love's Labour's Lost, *one associated with "Ver, the Spring" and the cuckoo ("When daisies pied and violets blue") and this complementary companion piece, associated with "Hiems, Winter" and the owl. Marian, or at least her nose "red and raw," is immortal, and forever will "greasy Joan" be at her pot. (Note that: "keel" is "stir"; "crabs" is "crab apples.")*

Full Fathom Five Thy Father Lies

>>>>>>>

Full fathom five thy father lies;
   Of his bones are coral made;
Those are pearls that were his eyes:
   Nothing of him that doth fade
But doth suffer a sea-change
Into something rich and strange.
Sea-nymphs hourly ring his knell:
Ding-dong.
Hark! now I hear them,—ding-dong, bell.

from The Tempest

In The Tempest, *the spirit Ariel sings this little song to Ferdinand, who believes that his father has been drowned in a shipwreck. Ferdinand is mistaken, as Ariel knows, so that the potential cruelty in the message is softened somewhat.*

When to the Sessions
of Sweet Silent Thought

When to the sessions of sweet silent thought
I summon up remembrance of things past,
I sigh the lack of many a thing I sought,
And with old woes new wail my dear time's waste.
Then can I drown an eye, unus'd to flow,
For precious friends hid in death's dateless night,
And weep afresh love's long since cancell'd woe,
And moan th' expense of many a vanish'd sight.
Then can I grieve at grievances foregone,
And heavily from woe to woe tell o'er
The sad account of fore-bemoaned moan,
Which I new pay as if not paid before.
But if the while I think on thee, dear friend,
All losses are restor'd and sorrows end.

Sonnet XXX

Here we see an exoskeleton as distinct as a grasshopper's: "When . . . Then . . . Then . . . But . . . ." The vocabulary owes much to the no-nonsense realms of law and commerce. This sonnet is a complaint, a favorite type of writing with English poets from Chaucer to the present. Here, as in celebrated soliloquies in Macbeth *and* Hamlet, *Shakespeare seems to relish the chance to inventory the woes of the world. This poem, by the way, is the source of the title of the English translation of Marcel Proust's* À la recherche du temps perdu. *(Note that: "tell" is "count.")*

Oh Mistress Mine

Oh mistress mine! where are you roaming?
Oh! stay and hear; your true love's coming,
   That can sing both high and low.
Trip no further, pretty sweeting;
Journeys end in lovers meeting,
   Every wise man's son doth know.

What is love? 'tis not hereafter;
Present mirth hath present laughter;
   What's to come is still unsure:
In delay there lies no plenty;
Then come kiss me, sweet and twenty,
   Youth's a stuff will not endure.

from Twelfth Night

This song from Twelfth Night, *sung by the clown Feste, is like sea-foam. It oscillates cheerfully between nonsense and platitude, finally sounding the familiar refrain of* carpe diem *— "seize the day."*

The Expense of Spirit
in a Waste of Shame

The expense of spirit in a waste of shame
Is lust in action; and, till action, lust
Is perjured, murderous, bloody, full of blame,
Savage, extreme, rude, cruel, not to trust;
Enjoyed no sooner but despisèd straight;
Past reason hunted, and no sooner had,
Past reason hated as a swallowed bait
On purpose laid to make the taker mad;
Mad in pursuit, and in possession so;
Had, having, and in quest to have, extreme;
A bliss in proof, and proved, a very woe,
Before, a joy proposed; behind, a dream.
   All this the world well knows, yet none knows well
   To shun the heaven that leads men to this hell.

Sonnet CXXIX

The antiquity of these stoic sentiments is also attested by Ben Jonson's hard-hitting translation of a fragment by Petronius, a member of Nero's entourage: "Doing a filthy pleasure is, and short; / And done we straight repent us of the sport . . . ."

When, in Disgrace
with Fortune and Men's Eyes

When, in disgrace with fortune and men's eyes,
I all alone beweep my outcast state,
And trouble deaf heaven with my bootless cries,
And look upon myself, and curse my fate,
Wishing me like to one more rich in hope,
Featured like him, like him with friends possessed,
Desiring this man's art, and that man's scope,
With what I most enjoy contented least;
Yet in these thoughts myself almost despising,
Haply I think on thee, and then my state,
Like to the lark at break of day arising
From sullen earth, sings hymns at heaven's gate;
   For thy sweet love remembered such wealth brings
   That then I scorn to change my state with kings.

Sonnet XXIX

T. S. Eliot appropriated a phrase from this sonnet for "Ash-Wednesday," in which Shakespeare's line becomes "Desiring this man's gift and that man's scope." The "Yet" at the head of line 9 marks the "turn" (volta) that distinguishes the architecture of the classic sonnet.

When Daisies Pied

()◄━━►()

When daisies pied and violets blue,
  And lady-smocks all silver-white,
And cuckoo-buds of yellow hue
  Do paint the meadows with delight,
The cuckoo then, on every tree,
Mocks married men, for thus sings he,
    "Cuckoo;
      Cuckoo, cuckoo": Oh word of fear,
      Unpleasing to a married ear!

When shepherds pipe on oaten straws,
  And merry larks are plouwmen's clocks,
When turtles tread, and rooks, and daws,
  And maidens bleach their summer smocks,
The cuckoo then, on every tree,
Mocks married men, for thus sings he,
    "Cuckoo;
      Cuckoo, cuckoo": Oh word of fear,
      Unpleasing to a married ear!

from Love's Labour's Lost

These lines, along with their companion piece "When Icicles Hang by the Wall" (p. 89), come at the end of Love's Labour's Lost. *The pun on "cuckoo" and "cuckold" is a reminder that the words are related, supposedly because of the behavior of the female bird.*

It Was a Lover and His Lass

It was a lover and his lass,
    With a hey, and a ho, and a hey nonino,
That o'er the green corn field did pass
    In springtime, the only pretty ring time,
When birds do sing, hey ding a ding, ding:
Sweet lovers love the spring.

Between the acres of the rye,
    With a hey, and a ho, and a hey nonino,
These pretty country folks would lie,
    In springtime, etc.

This carol they began that hour,
    With a hey, and a ho, and a hey nonino,
How that a life was but a flower
    In springtime, etc.

And therefore take the present time,
    With a hey, and a ho, and a hey nonino;
For love is crownèd with the prime
    In springtime, etc.

from As You Like It

Two pages sing this song to Touchstone and Audrey in the last act of As You
Like It. *Touchstone comments afterwards, "Truly, young gentlemen, though
there was no great matter in the ditty, yet the note was very untuneable" (with
"ditty," related to "diction," meaning the words).*

My Mistress' Eyes
Are Nothing like the Sun

◆◆◆◆

My mistress' eyes are nothing like the sun;
Coral is far more red than her lips' red;
If snow be white, why then her breasts are dun;
If hairs be wires, black wires grow on her head.
I have seen roses damasked, red and white,
But no such roses see I in her cheeks,
And in some perfumes there is more delight
Than in the breath that from my mistress reeks.
I love to hear her speak, yet well I know
That music hath a far more pleasing sound;
I grant I never saw a goddess go:
My mistress when she walks treads on the ground.
   And yet by heaven I think my love as rare
   As any she belied with false compare.

Sonnet CXXX

In somewhat the same key as Sonnet XVIII ("Shall I compare thee to a summer's day?" on p. 86), this poem amounts to a denial of a set of conventional metaphors. The exaggerated figures of praise for a beloved woman come from many sources, to be sure, but the sonnets of Petrarch are the chief source for Renaissance poets.

Poor Soul,
the Center of My Sinful Earth

Poor soul, the center of my sinful earth,
My sinful earth, these rebel powers that thee array,
Why dost thou pine within and suffer dearth,
Painting thy outward walls so costly gay?
Why so large cost, having so short a lease,
Dost thou upon thy fading mansion spend?
Shall worms, inheritors of this excess,
Eat up thy charge? Is this thy body's end?
Then, soul, live thou upon thy servant's loss,
And let that pine to aggravate thy store.
Buy terms divine in selling hours of dross,
Within be fed, without be rich no more.
  So shalt thou feed on Death, that feeds on men,
  And Death once dead, there's no more dying then.

Sonnet CXLVI

The theme of the "death of death" returns in John Donne's Holy Sonnet X ("Death, be not proud," p. 125) and, in varied form, in Dylan Thomas's "Refusal to Mourn the Death, by Fire, of a Child in London" (p. 1054).

Hark! Hark! the Lark

>>>>>>>

Hark! hark! the lark at heaven's gate sings,
 And Phoebus 'gins arise,
His steeds to water at those springs
 On chaliced flowers that lies;
And winking Mary-buds begin
 To ope their golden eyes:
With every thing that pretty is,
 My lady sweet, arise!
 Arise, arise!

from Cymbeline

In need of a wooing song, the lewd Cloten commands his musicians: "First, a very excellent good-conceited thing; after, a wonderful sweet air with admirable rich words to it . . . ."

Take, O Take Those Lips Away

Take, O take, those lips away,
   That so sweetly were forsworn;
And those eyes, the break of day,
   Lights that do mislead the morn:
But my kisses bring again
     Bring again:
Seals of love but sealed in vain,
    —Sealed in vain!

from Measure for Measure

This song is sung by Mariana and a boy in "the moated grange" (see Tennyson's "Mariana," p. 654).

Farewell!
Thou Art Too Dear for My Possessing

Farewell! thou art too dear for my possessing,
And like enough thou know'st thy estimate:
The charter of thy worth gives thee releasing;
My bonds in thee are all determinate.
For how do I hold thee but by thy granting?
And for that riches where is my deserving?
The cause of this fair gift in me is wanting,
And so my patent back again is swerving.
Thyself thou gav'st, thy own worth then not knowing,
Or me, to whom thou gav'st it, else mistaking;
So thy great gift, upon misprision growing,
Comes home again, on better judgement making.
Thou have I had thee, as a dream doth flatter,
In sleep a king, but, waking, no such matter.

Sonnet LXXXVII

From the beginning, this sonnet vacillates between two realms, the erotic and the commercial, a traffic facilitated in part by the multiple meanings of "dear" and "possessing."

Where the Bee Sucks, There Suck I

Where the bee sucks, there suck I;
In a cowslip's bell I lie;
There I couch when owls do cry.
On the bat's back I do fly
After summer merrily.
Merrily, merrily shall I live now
Under the blossom that hangs on the bough.

from The Tempest

The "airy spirit" Ariel sings this happy song, looking forward to being freed from service to Prospero.

When That I Was
and a Little Tiny Boy

>∾∾∾∾<

When that I was and a little tiny boy,
  With hey, ho, the wind and the rain,
A foolish thing was but a toy,
  For the rain it raineth every day.

But when I came to man's estate
  With hey, ho, the wind and the rain,
'Gainst knaves and thieves men shut their gate,
  For the rain it raineth every day.

But when I came, alas! to wive,
  With hey, ho, the wind and the rain,
By swaggering could I never thrive,
  For the rain it raineth every day.

But when I came unto my beds,
  With hey, ho, the wind and the rain,
With toss-pots still had drunken heads,
  For the rain it raineth every day.

A great while ago the world begun,
  With hey, ho, the wind and the rain,
But that's all one, our play is done,
  And we'll strive to please you every day.

from Twelfth Night

The clown Feste sings these verses at the end of Twelfth Night. *The serious possibilities lurking in the design and the refrain are explored by Thomas Hardy in "During Wind and Rain" (p. 784) and by Robert Frost in "The Wind and the Rain." Twelfth Night falls in early January.*

Full Many a Glorious Morning Have I Seen

Full many a glorious morning have I seen
Flatter the mountain-tops with sovereign eye,
Kissing with golden face the meadows green,
Gilding pale streams with heavenly alchemy;
Anon permit the basest clouds to ride
With ugly rack on his celestial face,
And from the forlorn world his visage hide,
Stealing unseen to west with this disgrace:
Even so my son one early morn did shine
With all-triumphant splendour on my brow;
But, out, alack! he was but one hour mine,
The region cloud hath mask'd him from me now.
    Yet him for this my love no whit disdaineth;
    Suns of the world may stain when heaven's sun staineth.

Sonnet XXXIII

Renaissance poets were in love with concentric patterns whereby a human life is likened to the progress of a day or a year. In this sonnet, the comparison is buttressed by a pun on "eye" and "I" and, perhaps, on "sun" and "son."

No Longer Mourn For Me When I Am Dead

No longer mourn for me when I am dead
Than you shall hear the surly sullen bell
Give warning to the world that I am fled
From this vile world, with vilest worms to dwell:
Nay, if you read this line, remember not
The hand that writ it; for I love you so,
That I in your sweet thoughts would be forgot,
If thinking on me then should make you woe.
O, if, I say, you look upon this verse
When I perhaps compounded am with clay,
Do not so much as my poor name rehearse,
But let your love even with my life decay;
   Lest the wise world should look into your moan,
   And mock you with me after I am gone.

Sonnet LXXI

It is fitting that a poem about life and death should follow an elementary design of simple sounds: "No . . . Nay . . . Oh . . . Lest . . . ."

Tired with All These, for Restful Death I Cry

❖❖❖❖

Tired with all these, for restful death I cry,
As, to behold desert a beggar born,
And needy nothing trimm'd in jollity,
And purest faith unhappily forsworn,
And gilded honour shamefully misplac'd,
And maiden virtue rudely strumpeted,
And right perfection wrongfully disgrac'd,
And strength by limping sway disabled,
And art made tongue-tied by authority,
And folly, doctor-like, controlling skill,
And simple truth miscall'd simplicity,
And captive good attending captain ill:
　　Tir'd with all these, from these would I be gone,
　　Save that, to die, I leave my love alone.

Sonnet LXVI

The meaning and technique are both remarkable here: the poem is a bill of complaints (a familiar device in Shakespeare's tragedies as well), and ten of the fourteen lines begin with the same word.

Like as the Waves
Make towards the Pebbled Shore

‹‹‹-‹‹‹-‹‹‹

Like as the waves make towards the pebbled shore,
So do our minutes hasten to their end;
Each changing place with that which goes before,
In sequent toil all forwards do contend.
Nativity, once in the main of light,
Crawls to maturity, where with being crowned,
Crooked eclipses 'gainst his glory fight,
And Time that gave doth now his gift confound.
Time doth transfix the flourish set on youth
And delves the parallels in beauty's brow,
Feeds on the rarities of nature's truth,
And nothing stands but for his scythe to mow:
   And yet to times in hope my verse shall stand,
   Praising thy worth, despite his cruel hand.

Sonnet LX

Like Sonnet LXV ("Since Brass, nor Stone, nor Earth, nor Boundless Sea," on p. 110), this poem makes a conventional claim for the ability of poems of praise to endure and to preserve love.

When Daffodils Begin to Peer

>>>>>>>

When daffodils begin to peer,
    With heigh! the doxy, over the dale,
Why, then comes in the sweet o' the year;
    For the red blood reigns in the winter's pale.

The white sheet bleaching on the hedge,
    With heigh! the sweet birds, O, how they sing!
Doth set my pugging tooth on edge,
    For a quart of ale is a dish for a king.

The lark, that tirra-lirra chants,
    With heigh! with heigh! the thrush and the jay,
Are summer songs for me and my aunts,
    While we lie tumbling in the hay.

                              from The Winter's Tale

Autolycus the rogue sings this lusty number: both "doxy" and "aunts" refer to prostitution.

How like a Winter
Hath My Absence Been

How like a winter hath my absence been
From thee, the pleasure of the fleeting year!
What freezings have I felt, what dark days seen!
What old December's bareness everywhere!
And yet this time removed was summer's time.
The teeming autumn, big with rich increase,
Bearing the wanton burthen of the prime,
Like widowed wombs after their lords' decease;
Yet this abundant issue seemed to me
But hope of orphans and unfathered fruit;
For summer and his pleasures wait on thee,
And, thou away, the very birds are mute;
   Or, if they sing, 'tis with so dull a cheer
   That leaves look pale, dreading the winter's near.

Sonnet XCVII

The "wanton burden" evidently means the fruit or harvest of wantonness. (Note that: "prime" is "the spring"; "cheer" is "disposition.")

Since Brass, nor Stone, nor Earth, nor Boundless Sea

Since brass, nor stone, nor earth, nor boundless sea,
But sad mortality o'ersways their power,
How with this rage shall beauty hold a plea,
Whose action is no stronger than a flower?
O how shall summer's honey breath hold out
Against the wrackful siege of batt'ring days,
When rocks impregnable are not so stout,
Nor gates of steel so strong but time decays?
O fearful meditation, where alack,
Shall Time's best jewel from Time's chest lie hid?
Or what strong hand can hold his swift foot back,
Or who his spoil of beauty can forbid?
   O none, unless this miracle have might,
   That in black ink my love may still shine bright.

Sonnet LXV

Brass, made of copper and zinc, has long been a symbol of durability; it has also come to mean money, shamelessness, and audacity. Here and elsewhere (as in Sonnet LV: "Not marble, nor the gilded monuments / Of princes, shall outlive this powerful rhyme"), Shakespeare enters the formulaic boastful claim about the ability of his art to preserve his love.

Come Away, Come Away, Death

Come away, come away, death,
  And in sad cypress let me be laid.
Fly away, fly away, breath;
  I am slain by a fair cruel maid.
My shroud of white, stuck all with yew,
    O! prepare it.
My part of death, no one so true
    Did share it.

Not a flower, not a flower sweet,
  On my black coffin let there be strown;
Not a friend, not a friend greet
  My poor corpse, where my bones shall be thrown.
A thousand thousand sighs to save,
    Lay me, O! where
Sad true lover never find my grave,
    To weep there.

from Twelfth Night

Twelfth Night *begins with the Duke's "If music be the food of love, play on . . . ." He asks the clown to sing again "the song we had last night" and calls it "old and plain." He also says it is "silly sooth," meaning "simple truth."*

Come unto These Yellow Sands

Come unto these yellow sands,
   And then take hands:
Court'sied when you have, and kissed,
   The wild waves whist, —
Foot it featly here and there;
And, sweet sprites, the burden bear.
     Hark, hark!
       Bow, wow,
    The watch-dogs bark:
       Bow, wow.
    Hark, hark! I hear
The strain of strutting chanticleer
Cry, Cock-a-diddle-dow!

from The Tempest

---

*After hearing this song sung by an invisible Ariel, Ferdinand muses in words
later echoed in T. S. Eliot's "Waste Land" (p. 968):*

Sitting on a bank,
Weeping again the King my father's wrack,
This music crept by me upon the waters . . . .

Tell Me Where Is Fancy Bred

()◀━▶()

Tell me, where is fancy bred,
Or in the heart, or in the head?
How begot, how nourished?
  Reply, reply.
It is engend'red in the eyes,
With gazing fed; and fancy dies
In the cradle where it lies.
  Let us all ring fancy's knell.
  I'll begin it—Ding, dong, bell.

All: Ding, dong, bell.

from The Merchant of Venice

The stage direction in The Merchant of Venice *reads, "A song the whilst Bassanio comments on the caskets to himself." As elsewhere in Shakespeare, "fancy" here means "love" or perhaps "fond infatuation."*

THOMAS CAMPION 1567–1620

Campion was a trained physician, a musician competent
enough to compose music for his own poems, a bold
and expressive poet in English and Latin, and a vigor-
ous controversialist in some of the ongoing literary wars
of his time. Among the poets in this anthology, he
stands virtually alone in his ability to write a memorable
lyric not based on recurring syllabic accent.

My Sweetest Lesbia

My sweetest Lesbia, let us live and love,
And though the sager sort our deeds reprove,
Let us not weigh them. Heaven's great lamps do dive
Into their west, and straight again revive,
But soon as once set is our little light,
Then must we sleep one ever-during night.

If all would lead their lives in love like me,
Then bloody swords and armor should not be;
No drum nor trumpet peaceful sleeps should move,
Unless alarm came from the camp of love.
But fools do live, and waste their little light,
And seek with pain their ever-during night.

When timely death my life and fortune ends,
Let not my hearse be vexed with mourning friends,
But let all lovers, rich in triumph, come
And with sweet pastimes grace my happy tomb;
And, Lesbia, close up thou my little light,
And crown with love my ever-during night.

---

*Here Campion is imitating, and in part translating, an early poem of Catullus
to his "Lesbia" (whose real name was Clodia). The poem has been translated
into English by many others, including Richard Crashaw in the seventeenth
century and John Frederick Nims in the twentieth.*

Rose-cheeked Laura

◈◈◈◈

Rose-cheeked Laura, come,
Sing thou smoothly with thy beauty's
Silent music, either other
　Sweetly gracing.

Lovely forms do flow
From concent divinely framèd;
Heav'n is music, and thy beauty's
　Birth is heavenly.

These dull notes we sing
Discords need for helps to grace them;
Only beauty purely loving
　Knows no discord,

But still moves delight,
Like clear springs renewed by flowing,
Ever perfect, ever in them-
　selves eternal.

This lyric is one of the most successful of the many Elizabethan experiments in basing versification on principles drawn from classical antiquity. It contains no rhyme, the rhythm is based on quantity (length of syllable) as well as quality (accent), lines are made up of different kinds of foot, and a word may be broken at the end of a line—a very rare occurrence in serious poetry. (Note that: "concent" is "harmonious music-making.")

There Is a Garden in Her Face

There is a garden in her face,
　Where roses and white lilies grow;
A heavenly paradise is that place,
　Wherein all pleasant fruits do flow.
There cherries grow which none may buy,
　Till "Cherry-ripe" themselves do cry.

Those cherries fairly do enclose
　Of orient pearl a double row,
Which when her lovely laughter shows,
　They look like rosebuds filled with snow.
Yet them nor peer nor prince can buy,
　Till "Cherry-ripe" themselves do cry.

Her eyes like angels watch them still;
　Her brows like bended bows do stand,
Threatening with piercing frowns to kill
　All that attempt with eye or hand
Those sacred cherries to come nigh,
　Till "Cherry-ripe" themselves do cry.

Campion plays with many conventions, including the music and lore of street-vendors' cries (which can still be heard) and the farfetched comparisons of erotic verse from Italy and France (which also can still be heard). In chapter 24 of Tess of the d'Urbervilles, *Thomas Hardy describes Angel Clare's reaction to Tess's beautiful face by saying, "He had never before seen a woman's lips and teeth which forced upon his mind with such persistent iteration the old Elizabethan simile of roses filled with snow"; and the line "Late roses filled with early snow" returns in T. S. Eliot's "East Coker"* (Four Quartets).

Thrice Toss These Oaken Ashes in the Air

>>>>>>>

Thrice toss these oaken ashes in the air;
Thrice sit thou mute in this enchanted chair;
Then thrice three times tie up this true love's knot,
And murmur soft: "She will, or she will not."

Go burn these poisonous weeds in yon blue fire,
These screech-owl's feathers and this prickling briar,
This cypress gathered at a dead man's grave,
That all thy fears and cares an end may have.

Then come, you fairies, dance with me a round;
Melt her hard heart with your melodious sound.
In vain are all the charms I can devise;
She hath an art to break them with her eyes.

Poets are fond of lists, catalogues, and superstitions, especially those involving numbers. This may be all in fun, but it makes a convincing love poem as well as a valuable collection of data for folklorists.

The life of the anti-Puritan satirist Thomas Nashe looks like a perfect example of Thomas Hobbes's formulation of human life in a state of nature: solitary, nasty, brutish, poor, and short. Nashe has, nevertheless, an appealing charm and impressive inventiveness, and he managed, in a short and vexed life, to distinguish himself in comic drama, satire, and prose fiction, writing one of the very earliest adventure novels, *The Unfortunate Traveler; or, The Life of Jack Wilton.*

Adieu, Farewell, Earth's Bliss

Adieu, farewell earth's bliss;
This world uncertain is;
Fond are life's lustful joys;
Death proves them all but toys;
None from his darts can fly;
I am sick, I must die.
   Lord, have mercy on us!

Rich men, trust not in wealth,
Gold cannot buy you health;
Physic himself must fade.
All things to end are made,
The plague full swift goes by;
I am sick, I must die.
   Lord, have mercy on us!

Beauty is but a flower
Which wrinkles will devour;
Brightness falls from the air;
Queens have died young and fair;
Dust hath closed Helen's eye.
I am sick, I must die.
   Lord, have mercy on us!

Strength stoops unto the grave,
Worms feed on Hector brave;
Swords may not fight with fate,
Earth still holds ope her gate.
"Come, come" the bells do cry.
I am sick, I must die.
   Lord, have mercy on us.

Wit with his wantonness
Tasteth death's bitterness;
Hell's executioner
Hath no ears for to hear
What vain art can reply.
I am sick, I must die.
   Lord, have mercy on us.

Haste, therefore, each degree,
To welcome destiny;
Heaven is our heritage,
Earth but a player's stage;
Mount we unto the sky.
I am sick, I must die.
   Lord, have mercy on us.

              from Summer's Last Will and Testament

Nashe's comedy Summer's Last Will and Testament *contains two songs that have outlasted their original setting: "Spring, the Sweet Spring" (p. 120) and this litany. A formal church litany involves clergy and congregation alternating supplications and responses. We can hear Nashe, notoriously witty, wanton, bitter, and artful, in the castigation of "vain art" and in the plangent couplet about "Wit with his wantonness." (Note that: "fond" is "foolish"; "toys" is "trifles.")*

Spring, the Sweet Spring

Spring, the sweet spring, is the year's pleasant king;
Then blooms each thing, then maids dance in a ring,
Cold doth not sting, the pretty birds do sing,
  "Cuckoo, jug-jug, pu-we, to-witta-woo!"

The palm and may make country houses gay,
Lambs frisk and play, the shepherds pipe all day,
And we hear aye birds tune this merry lay,
  "Cuckoo, jug-jug, pu-we, to-witta-woo."

The fields breathe sweet, the daisies kiss our feet,
Young lovers meet, old wives a-sunning sit,
In every street these tunes our ears do greet,
  "Cuckoo, jug-jug, pu-we, to-witta-woo!"
  Spring, the sweet spring!

               from Summer's Last Will and Testament

Although leading off Palgrave's Golden Treasury *(1861) certainly added to this song's fame, it is meritorious in its own right. Most of Great Britain is hundreds of miles farther north than most of the United States, so that—the Gulf Stream notwithstanding—winter is usually cold, dark, and damp, and spring is always welcome. (Note that, "cuckoo . . .," is "the conventional cry of cuckoo, nightingale, lapwing, and owl.")*

Tichborne came from a prominent Catholic family and took part in the Babington conspiracy to assassinate Queen Elizabeth. With others in the group, he was arrested, tried, and gruesomely executed. His age at the time of his death is not certainly known, but it is probable that he was no more than eighteen.

Tichborne's Elegy

Elegy Written with His Own Hand in the Tower before His Execution

My prime of youth is but a frost of cares,
   My feast of joy is but a dish of pain,
My crop of corn is but a field of tares,
   And all my good is but vain hope of gain:
The day is past, and yet I saw no sun,
And now I live, and now my life is done.

My tale was heard, and yet it was not told,
   My fruit is fall'n, and yet my leaves are green,
My youth is spent, and yet I am not old,
   I saw the world, and yet I was not seen:
My thread is cut, and yet it is not spun,
And now I live, and now my life is done.

I sought my death, and found it in my womb,
   I looked for life, and saw it was a shade,
I trod the earth, and knew it was my tomb,
   And now I die, and now I was but made:
My glass is full, and now my glass is run,
And now I live, and now my life is done.

Tichborne was hanged and quartered on September 20, 1586. He was in the spring of life, and he died just before the autumnal equinox—as is reflected in the "prime" and "frost" of the opening of his elegy, supposedly written on the eve of execution. Hilary Holladay has noticed that the poem contains eighteen lines, one for each year of the poet's life. Of the 180 words in the poem, 179 are outright monosyllables, and even the lone exception ("fallen") is sounded and counted as a monosyllable ("fall'n").

SIR HENRY WOTTON 1568–1639

Wotton served as secretary to the Earl of Essex and later, between 1604 and 1624, was involved in various diplomatic and intelligence-gathering positions. His literary writings were not published until twelve years after his death.

On His Mistress, the Queen of Bohemia

⟫⟫⟫⟫⟪

You meaner beauties of the night
    That poorly satisfy our eyes
More by your number than your light,
    You common people of the skies,
    What are you when the moon doth rise?

You wandering chanters of the wood
    That warble forth Dame Nature's lays,
Thinking your passions understood
    By weaker accents, what's your praise
    When Philomel her voice doth raise?

You violets that first appear,
    By your pure purple mantles known,
Like the proud virgins of the year,
    As if the spring were all your own,
    What are you when the rose is blown?

So, when my mistress shall be seen
    In form and beauty of her mind,
By virtue first, then choice, a queen,
    Oh tell if she were not designed
    The eclipse and glory of her kind?

Elizabeth of Bohemia, daughter of James I of England, was Wotton's employer—and that is what "Mistress" here means. In 1620 Wotton was a diplomat temporarily in her service. The success of his poem owes something to a balancing act: the diplomat indulges in exaggerated praise but tempers that extremism by using rhetorical questions that have a subtler effect than outright declarations. (A slightly later poem addressed to Elizabeth of Bohemia and attributed to "G. H." may be by George Herbert.)

JOHN DONNE 1572-1631

Donne was a Roman Catholic but later, while studying
law, joined the Church of England. He was a traveler,
diplomat, and courtier. Rather late in life, he became a
preacher and was soon famous for his sermons; he was
made Dean of St. Paul's in 1621. As the poems in this
anthology demonstrate, Donne could write, with equal
facility and depth, passionate poems of secular love and
passionate poems of sacred love, both sorts informed by
large-minded wit.

Death, Be Not Proud

Death, be not proud, though some have callèd thee
Mighty and dreadful, for thou art not so;
For those whom thou think'st thou dost overthrow,
Die not, poor Death, nor yet canst thou kill me.
From rest and sleep, which but thy pictures be,
Much pleasure; then from thee much more must flow,
And soonest our best men with thee do go,
Rest of their bones, and soul's delivery.
Thou'rt slave to fate, chance, kings, and desperate men,
And dost with poison, war, and sickness dwell;
And poppy or charms can make us sleep as well
And better than thy stroke; why swell'st thou then?
One short sleep past, we wake eternally,
And death shall be no more: Death, thou shalt die.

Holy Sonnet X

*Three of Donne's Holy Sonnets are included in this anthology: this one, the
seventh (p. 128), and the fourteenth (pp. 126). They are much alike, especially
in their common reliance on imperatives, dramatic paradoxes, and subtle-seeming
ratiocination.*

Batter My Heart, Three-Personed God

Batter my heart, three-personed God; for, you
As yet but knock, breathe, shine, and seek to mend;
That I may rise, and stand, o'erthrow me, and bend
Your force, to break, blow, burn, and make me new.
I, like an usurped town, to another due,
Labour to admit you, but oh, to no end,
Reason your viceroy in me, me should defend,
But is captived, and proves weak or untrue,
Yet dearly I love you, and would be loved fain,
But am bethrothed unto your enemy,
Divorce me, untie, or break that knot again,
Take me to you, imprison me, for I
Except you enthrall me, never shall be free,
Nor ever chaste, except you ravish me.

Holy Sonnet XIV

Before Donne, the sonnet was a relatively unholy secular love lyric that could become intensely erotic and also lightheartedly satirical. And it could exploit love's capacity for exaggeration and paradox. Donne's Holy Sonnets lift the level of love from secular to sacred but keep the dramatic emphasis on paradox.

The Good Morrow

❖❖❖❖

I wonder by my troth, what thou, and I
    Did, till we loved? were we not weaned till then,
But sucked on country pleasures, childishly?
    Or snorted we in the seven sleepers' den?
'Twas so; but this, all pleasures fancies be.
If ever any beauty I did see,
Which I desired, and got, 'twas but a dream of thee.

And now good-morrow to our waking souls,
    Which watch not one another out of fear;
For love, all love of other sights controls,
    And makes one little room, an every where.
Let sea-discoverers to new worlds have gone,
Let maps to other, worlds on worlds have shown,
Let us possess one world, each hath one, and is one.

My face in thine eye, thine in mine appears,
    And true plain hearts do in the faces rest,
Where can we find two better hemispheres
    Without sharp North, without declining West?
Whatever dies, was not mixed equally;
If our two loves be one, or, thou and I
Love so alike, that none do slacken, none can die.

John Dryden and Samuel Johnson doubted the wisdom of using intellectual arguments in love poetry. In our time, on the other hand, T. S. Eliot has praised Donne for preserving a unity of sensibility missing in Dryden, who so sharply separated mind from heart. For Donne, mind and heart were one, and love could employ the idiom of physics, and vice versa.

At the Round Earth's Imagined Corners

At the round earth's imagined corners, blow
Your trumpets, angels, and arise, arise
From death, you numberless infinities
Of souls, and to your scattered bodies go,
All whom the flood did, and fire shall o'erthrow,
All whom war, dearth, age, agues, tyrannies,
Despair, law, chance, hath slain, and you whose eyes,
Shall behold God, and never taste death's woe.
But let them sleep, Lord, and me mourn a space,
For, if above all these, my sins abound,
'Tis late to ask abundance of thy grace,
When we are there; here on this lowly ground,
Teach me how to repent; for that's as good
As if thou hadst sealed my pardon, with thy blood.

Holy Sonnet VII

We can glimpse here something of Donne's fondness for paradox and education: this poet knows that the earth is round, with "corners" that are merely imaginary; he also knows that angels are not bound by literal laws of physics. Angels, like the vernacular today, still observe "the four corners of the world."

Go and Catch a Falling Star

>>>>>>>

Go and catch a falling star,
  Get with child a mandrake root,
Tell me where all past years are,
  Or who cleft the Devil's foot,
Teach me to hear mermaids singing,
  Or to keep off envy's stinging,
    And find
    What wind
Serves to advance an honest mind.

If thou be'st borne to strange sights,
  Things invisible to see,
Ride ten thousand days and nights,
  Till age snow white hairs on thee.
Thou, when thou return'st, wilt tell me
  All strange wonders that befell thee,
    And swear
    Nowhere
Lives a woman true, and fair.

If thou find'st one, let me know,
  Such a pilgrimage were sweet;
Yet do not, I would not go,
  Though at next door we might meet;
Though she were true, when you met her,
  And last, till you write your letter,
    Yet she
    Will be
False, ere I come, to two, or three.

Like many of the Holy Sonnets, this poem begins with a robust series of imperatives. The impossible things are more or less conventional, but the terms are joined by certain dark underlying similarities (the devil is a sort of falling star, the mandrake root is supposedly anthropomorphic); conceivably, the prevalence of dishonesty and inconstancy is a result of the Fall.

The Sun Rising

Busy old fool, unruly sun,
  Why dost thou thus,
Through windows, and through curtains call on us?
Must to thy motions lovers' seasons run?
    Saucy pedantic wretch, go chide
    Late school-boys, and sour prentices,
  Go tell court-huntsmen that the King will ride,
  Call country ants to harvest offices;
Love, all alike, no season knows, nor clime,
Nor hours, days, months, which are the rags of time.

    Thy beams, so reverend, and strong
    Why shouldst thou think?
I could eclipse and cloud them with a wink,
But that I would not lose her sight so long:
    If her eyes have not blinded thine,
    Look, and tomorrow late, tell me,
  Whether both th' Indias of spice and mine
  Be where thou left'st them, or lie here with me.
Ask for those kings whom thou saw'st yesterday,
And thou shalt hear, All here in one bed lay.

    She's all states, and all princes, I,
    Nothing else is.
Princes do but play us; compared to this,
All honor's mimic; all wealth alchemy.
    Thou sun art half as happy as we,
    In that the world's contracted thus;
  Thine age asks ease, and since thy duties be
  To warm the world, that's done in warming us.
Shine here to us, and thou art everywhere;
This bed thy center is, these walls, thy sphere.

The playful overstatement here about the sun's mistaken self-image "so reverend and strong" resembles the much more serious statement in Holy Sonnet X (p. 125) about death's mistaken self-image as "Mighty and dreadful." Donne delights in deflation of the overrated, so that the genuinely worthy—in this case, sexual love—can be suitably praised.

A Valediction: Forbidding Mourning

◆◆◆◆◆

As virtuous men pass mildly away,
    And whisper to their souls to go,
Whilst some of their sad friends do say,
    The breath goes now, and some say, no:

So let us melt, and make no noise,
    No tear-floods, nor sigh-tempests move,
'Twere profanation of our joys
    To tell the laity our love.

Moving of the earth brings harms and fears,
    Men reckon what it did and meant,
But trepidation of the spheres,
    Though greater far, is innocent.

Dull sublunary lovers' love,
    Whose soul is sense, cannot admit
Absence, because it doth remove
    Those things which elemented it.

But we by a love so much refined
    That our selves know not what it is,
Interassurèd of the mind,
    Care less eyes, lips, and hands to miss.

Our two souls therefore, which are one,
    Though I must go, endure not yet
A breach, but an expansion,
    Like gold to airy thinness beat.

If they be two, they are two so
   As stiff twin compasses are two,
Thy soul, the fixed foot, makes no show
   To move, but doth if th' other do.

And though it in the center sit,
   Yet when the other far doth roam,
It leans, and hearkens after it,
   And grows erect as that comes home.

Such wilt thou be to me, who must
   Like th' other foot, obliquely run;
The firmness makes my circle just,
   And makes me end where I begun.

Here, in one of Donne's many poems of parting and farewell ("valediction"), we see what is probably the most celebrated of the so-called Metaphysical conceits: conceptualizations that range far afield for metaphoric likenesses. With remarkable wit and virtuosity, Donne succeeds in likening lovers to a metal drafting instrument.

A Hymn to God the Father

Wilt Thou forgive that sin where I begun,
 Which was my sin, though it were done before?
Wilt Thou forgive that sin through which I run,
 And do run still, though still I do deplore?
  When Thou hast done, Thou hast not done,
   For I have more.

Wilt Thou forgive that sin which I have won
 Others to sin and made my sin their door?
Wilt Thou forgive that sin which I did shun
 A year, or two, but wallowed in a score?
  When Thou hast done, Thou hast not done,
   For I have more.

I have a sin of fear, that when I have spun
 My last thread, I shall perish on the shore;
Swear by thyself that at my death Thy Son
 Shall shine as He shines now, and heretofore;
  And having done that, Thou hast done,
   I fear no more.

Seeing God as the Father prompts Donne to join "Son" and "Sun." The poet's own name enters into the punning, since "thou hast done" sound like "thou hast Donne."

The Ecstasy

Where, like a pillow on a bed,
　A pregnant bank swelled up, to rest
The violet's reclining head,
　Sat we two, one another's best.
Our hands were firmly cemented
　With a fast balm, which thence did spring,
Our eye-beams twisted, and did thread
　Our eyes, upon one double string;
So t'intergraft our hands, as yet
　Was all the means to make us one,
And pictures in our eyes to get
　Was all our propagation.
As 'twixt two equal armies, fate
　Suspends uncertain victory,
Our souls (which to advance their state
　Were gone out) hung 'twixt her, and me.
And whilst our souls negotiate there,
　We like sepulchral statues lay;
All day, the same our postures were,
　And we said nothing, all the day.
If any, so by love refined,
　That he soul's language understood,
And by good love were grown all mind,
　Within convenient distance stood,
He (though he knew not which soul spake,
　Because both meant, both spake the same)
Might thence a new concoction take,
　And part far purer than he came.
"This ecstasy doth unperplex"
　(We said) "and tell us what we love;
We see by this, it was not sex;
　We see, we saw not what did move:
But as all several souls contain
　Mixture of things, they know not what,

Love, these mixed souls doth mix again,
   And makes both one, each this and that.
A single violet transplant,
   The strength, the color, and the size,
(All which before was poor, and scant)
   Redoubles still, and multiplies.
When love, with one another so
   Interinanimates two souls,
That abler soul, which thence doth flow,
   Defects of loneliness controls.
We then, who are this new soul, know
   Of what we are composed, and made,
For, the atomies of which we grow,
   Are souls, whom no change can invade.
But oh alas, so long, so far
   Our bodies why do we forbear?
They are ours, though they are not we; we are
   The intelligences, they the sphere.
We owe them thanks, because they thus,
   Did us, to us, at first convey,
Yielded their forces, sense, to us,
   Nor are dross to us, but allay.
On man heaven's influence works not so,
   But that it first imprints the air,
So soul into the soul may flow,
   Though it to body first repair.
As our blood labors to beget
   Spirits, as like souls as it can,
Because such fingers need to knit
   That subtle knot, which makes us man:
So must pure lovers' souls descend
   To affections, and to faculties,
Which sense may reach and apprehend,
   Else a great prince in prison lies.
To our bodies turn we then, that so
   Weak men on love revealed may look;
Love's mysteries in souls do grow,
   But yet the body is his book.

And if some lover, such as we,
  Have heard this dialogue of one,
Let him still mark us, he shall see
  Small change, when we're to bodies gone."

As Donne would have known, "ecstasy" comes from Greek ekstasis, *the opposite of* stasis. *The various meanings of* ekstasis *include "distraction" and "trance," along with the idea of being moved in space (as the lovers' souls "were gone out" in the fourth stanza of Donne's poem). See also the ecstatic moments in Hopkins's "Windhover" (p. 790) and Hardy's "Darkling Thrush" (p. 770). Martin Heidegger said, "Time is ecstasy." (Note that: "atomies" is "indivisible units.")*

The Canonization

For God's sake hold your tongue, and let me love,
   Or chide my palsy, or my gout,
   My five grey hairs, or ruined fortune flout;
With wealth your state, your mind with arts improve,
     Take you a course, get you a place,
     Observe his Honor, or his Grace;
Or the king's real, or his stamped face
   Contemplate; what you will, approve,
   So you will let me love.

Alas, alas, who's injured by my love?
   What merchant's ships have my sighs drowned?
   Who says my tears have overflowed his ground?
When did my colds a forward spring remove?
     When did the heats which my veins fill
     Add one more to the plaguy bill?
Soldiers find wars, and lawyers find out still
   Litigious men, which quarrels move,
   Though she and I do love.

Call us what you will, we are made such by love;
   Call her one, me another fly,
   We're tapers too, and at our own cost die,
And we in us find the eagle and the dove
     The phœnix riddle hath more wit
     By us; we two being one are it.
So to one neutral thing both sexes fit,
   We die and rise the same, and prove
   Mysterious by this love.

We can die by it, if not live by love,
   And if unfit for tomb or hearse
   Our legend be, it will be fit for verse;
And if no piece of chronicle we prove,
     We'll build in sonnets pretty rooms;
     As well a well-wrought urn becomes
The greatest ashes, as half-acre tombs,
   And by these hymns all shall approve
   Us canonized for love:

And thus invoke us, "You, whom reverend love
   Made one another's hermitage;
   You, to whom love was peace, that now is rage;
Who did the whole world's soul contract, and drove
     Into the glasses of your eyes
     (So made such mirrors, and such spies,
That they did all to you epitomize);
   Countries, towns, courts beg from above
   A pattern of your love."

With many erotic puns (especially the equation of death and orgasm) and much sexual lore, Donne here presents a tissue of exaggerations that confirm the strength of his love. We remember that "stanza" in Italian means "room" and that Cleanth Brooks's distinguished study of paradox in poetry is called The Well-Wrought Urn.

The Flea

Mark but this flea, and mark in this,
How little that which thou deniest me is;
Me it sucked first, and now sucks thee,
And in this flea our two bloods mingled be;
Thou know'st that this cannot be said
A sin, or shame, or loss of maidenhead,
   Yet this enjoys before it woo,
    And pampered swells with one blood made of two,
    And this, alas, is more than we would do.

Oh stay, three lives in one flea spare,
Where we almost, nay more than married are.
This flea is you and I, and this
Our marriage bed and marriage temple is;
Though parents grudge, and you, we are met,
And cloistered in these living walls of jet.
   Though use make you apt to kill me
   Let not to that, self-murder added be,
   And sacrilege, three sins in killing three.

Cruel and sudden, hast thou since
Purpled thy nail in blood of innocence?
Wherein could this flea guilty be,
Except in that drop which it sucked from thee?
Yet thou triumph'st, and say'st that thou
Find'st not thy self nor me the weaker now;
   'Tis true; then learn how false fears be:
   Just so much honor, when thou yield'st to me,
   Will waste, as this flea's death took life from thee.

There just has to be an element of aimless showing off in "The Flea," as though Donne had been challenged to make something out of nearly nothing. Since it is inconceivable that any coy mistress could be swayed by an argument so silly, one may conclude that the poet is merely demonstrating the strength of his passion, devotion, and ingenuity. (Note that: "use" is "habit.")

Hymn to God My God, in My Sickness

Since I am coming to that holy room
  Where, with thy choir of saints for evermore,
I shall be made thy music; as I come
   I tune the instrument here at the door,
   And what I must do then, think now before.

Whilst my physicians by their love are grown
  Cosmographers, and I their map, who lie
Flat on this bed, that by them may be shown
   That this is my southwest discovery
   Per fretum febris, by these straits to die,

I joy, that in these traits, I see my West,
  For, though their currents yield return to none,
What shall my West hurt me? As West and East
   In all flat maps (and I am one) are one,
   So death doth touch the resurrection.

Is the Pacific Sea my home? Or are
  The Eastern riches? Is Jerusalem?
Anyan, and Magellan, and Gibraltar,
   All straits, and none but straits, are ways to them,
   Whether where Japhet dwelt, or Cham, or Shem.

We think that Paradise and Calvary,
  Christ's cross and Adam's tree, stood in one place;
Look, Lord and find both Adams met in me;
   As the first Adam's sweat surrounds my face,
   May the last Adam's blood my soul embrace.

So, in his purple wrapped, receive me, Lord;
  By these his thorns give me his other crown;
And, as to others' souls I preached thy word,
  Be this my text, my sermon to mine own:
  Therefore that he may raise the Lord throws down.

The great circumnavigators of the sixteenth century, whose adventures continued into Donne's day, established the virtual unity of West and East, a seeming paradox with religious implications for the believer who sees Christ's death on Good Friday "touching" the Resurrection on Easter Sunday (see also Donne's "Good Friday, 1613. Riding Westward," p. 153). According to medieval lore, the "tree" of Adam's fall and the "tree" of the Crucifixion stood in the same place; and Creation, Fall, and Crucifixion all took place in April. (Note that: "per fretum febris" is "through the strait of fever.")

Sweetest Love, I Do Not Go

Sweetest love, I do not go
  For weariness of thee,
Nor in hope the world can show
  A fitter love for me;
    But since that I
Must die at last, 'tis best
To use myself in jest
    Thus by feigned deaths to die.

Yesternight the sun went hence,
  And yet is here today;
He hath no desire nor sense,
  Nor half so short a way.
    Then fear not me,
But believe that I shall make
Speedier journeys, since I take
  More wings and spurs than he.

O how feeble is man's power,
  That, if good fortune fall,
Cannot add another hour
  Nor a lost hour recall!
    But come bad chance,
And we join to it our strength,
And we teach it art and length,
  Itself o'er us to advance.

When thou sigh'st thou sigh'st not wind,
　But sigh'st my soul away;
When thou weep'st, unkindly kind,
　My life's blood doth decay.
　　It cannot be
That thou lov'st me as thou say'st,
If in thine my life thou waste:
　That art the best of me.

Let not thy divining heart
　Forethink me any ill;
Destiny may take thy part,
　And may thy fears fulfil.
　　But think that we
Are but turned aside to sleep:
They who one another keep
　Alive, ne'er parted be.

This song is one of Donne's many valedictions: formal farewells or poems of parting. At the end of the poem, Donne indulges in a delicate trick of verbal magic to argue that the lovers are never parted.

A Nocturnal upon St. Lucy's Day, Being the Shortest Day

>>>>>>>

'Tis the year's midnight, and it is the day's,
Lucy's, who scarce seven hours herself unmasks;
  The sun is spent, and now his flasks
  Send forth light squibs, no constant rays;
    The world's whole sap is sunk;
The general balm the hydroptic earth hath drunk,
Whither, as to the bed's-feet, life is shrunk,
Dead and interred; yet all these seem to laugh,
Compared with me, who am their epitaph.

Study me then, you who shall lovers be
At the next world, that is, at the next spring:
  For I am every dead thing,
  In whom love wrought new alchemy.
    For his art did express
A quintessence even from nothingness,
From dull privations, and lean emptiness:
He ruined me, and I am re-begot
Of absence, darkness, death: things which are not.

All others, from all things, draw all that's good,
Life, soul, form, spirit, whence they being have;
  I, by Love's limbeck, am the grave
  Of all, that's nothing. Oft a flood
    Have we two wept, and so
Drowned the whole world, us two; oft did we grow
To be two Chaoses, when we did show
Care to aught else; and often absences
Withdrew our souls, and made us carcasses.

But I am by her death (which word wrongs her)
Of the first nothing the elixir grown;
   Were I a man, that I were one
   I needs must know; I should prefer,
     If I were any beast,
Some ends, some means; yea plants, yea stones detest,
And love; all, all some properties invest;
If I an ordinary nothing were,
As shadow, a light and body must be here.

But I am none; nor will my sun renew.
You lovers, for whose sake the lesser sun
   At this time to the Goat is run
   To fetch new lust, and give it you,
     Enjoy your summer all;
Since she enjoys her long night's festival,
Let me prepare towards her, and let me call
This hour her Vigil, and her Eve, since this
Both the year's, and the day's deep midnight is.

St. Lucy's Day is December 13, and in Donne's time the winter solstice was observed on December 12. Although the solstice is the shortest day (that is, having the least daylight), it is the moment of the sun's rebirth, and the daylight hours will increase for six months until the summer solstice. It was once noted that "solar heroes," or divinities, are born in December, under the sign of Capricorn. (Note that: "hydroptic" is "dropsical," "insatiably thirsty"; "limbeck" is "alembic"; "goat" is "Capricorn.")

The Funeral

Whoever comes to shroud me, do not harm
　　　　Nor question much
That subtle wreath of hair which crowns my arm;
The mystery, the sign you must not touch,
　　　　For 'tis my outward Soul,
Viceroy to that, which then to heaven being gone,
　　　　Will leave this to control,
And keep these limbs, her Provinces, from dissolution.

For if the sinewy thread my brain lets fall
　　　　Through every part
Can tie those parts, and make me one of all;
These hairs which upward grew, and strength and art
　　　　Have from a better brain,
Can better do it; except she meant that I
　　　　By this should know my pain,
As prisoners then are manacled, when they're condemned to die.

Whate'er she meant by it, bury it with me,
　　　　For since I am
Love's martyr, it might breed idolatry,
If into others' hands these Relics came;
　　　　As 'twas humility
To afford to it all that a Soul can do,
　　　　So, 'tis some bravery,
That since you would save none of me, I bury some of you.

Both "The Funeral" and "The Relic" (p. 151) concern a wreath or bracelet of the lover's hair to be worn by the speaker in the grave.

The Apparition

When by thy scorn, O murderess, I am dead,
And that thou think'st thee free
From all solicitation from me,
Then shall my ghost come to thy bed,
And thee, feigned vestal, in worse arms shall see;
Then thy sick taper will begin to wink,
And he, whose thou art then, being tired before,
Will, if thou stir, or pinch to wake him, think
  Thou call'st for more,
And in false sleep will from thee shrink,
And then, poor aspen wretch, neglected thou
Bathed in a cold quicksilver sweat wilt lie
  A verier ghost than I;
What I will say, I will not tell thee now,
Lest that preserve thee; and since my love is spent,
I had rather thou shouldst painfully repent,
Than by my threatenings rest still innocent.

Donne would have been aware that the Latin apparitio *means not only "appearance" but also "attendance" and "service"; the meaning of "ghost" is newer. Quicksilver (mercury), an apt figure to describe postcoital sweat, also calls up uses in alchemy (to refine precious metal from ore) and medicine (to treat syphilis).*

The Relic

When my grave is broke up again
Some second guest to entertain,
(For graves have learned that woman-head
To be to more than one a bed)
    And he that digs it, spies
A bracelet of bright hair about the bone,
    Will he not let us alone,
And think that there a loving couple lies,
Who thought that this device might be some way
To make their souls, at the last busy day,
Meet at this grave, and make a little stay?

If this fall in a time, or land,
Where mis-devotion doth command,
Then, he that digs us up will bring
Us to the Bishop and the King,
    To make us relics; then
Thou shalt be a Mary Magdalen, and I
    A something else thereby;
All women shall adore us, and some men;
And since at such time, miracles are sought,
I would have that age by this paper taught
What miracles we harmless lovers wrought.

First, we loved well and faithfully,
Yet knew not what we loved, nor why,
Difference of sex no more we knew,
Than our guardian angels do;
    Coming and going, we
Perchance might kiss, but not between those meals;
    Our hands ne'er touched the seals,
Which nature, injured by late law, sets free;
These miracles we did; but now alas,
All measure, and all language, I should pass,
Should I tell what a miracle she was.

Shakespeare presumably put a curse on those who would disturb his bones (as Yorick's are disturbed in Hamlet*). Donne seems to accept the situation, since the reuse of graves was a common practice. The line "A bracelet of bright hair about the bone" still has plenary power to shock and move.*

Good Friday, 1613. Riding Westward

Let man's soul be a sphere, and then in this
The intelligence that moves, devotion is;
And as the other spheres, by being grown
Subject to foreign motions, lose their own,
And being by others hurried every day
Scarce in a year their natural form obey,
Pleasure or business, so, our souls admit
For their first mover, and are whirled by it.
Hence is't that I am carried towards the west
This day, when my soul's form bends toward the east.
There I should see a sun, by rising set,
And by that setting, endless day beget;
But that Christ on this cross did rise and fall,
Sin had eternally benighted all.
Yet dare I almost be glad I do not see
That spectacle of too much weight for me.
Who sees God's face, that is self life, must die;
What a death were it then to see God die!
It made his own lieutenant, Nature, shrink;
It made his footstool crack, and the sun wink.
Could I behold those hands which span the poles
And tune all spheres at once; pierced with those holes?
Could I behold that endless height, which is
Zenith to us and to our antipodes,
Humbled below us? or that blood which is
The seat of all our souls, if not of his,
Make dirt of dust, or that flesh which was worn
By God for his apparel, ragged and torn?
If on these things I durst not look, durst I
Upon his miserable mother cast mine eye,
Who was God's partner here, and furnished thus
Half of that sacrifice which ransomed us?
Though these things, as I ride, be from mine eye,

They are present yet unto my memory,
For that looks towards them; and thou look'st towards me,
O Savior, as thou hang'st upon the tree;
I turn my back to thee but to receive
Corrections, till thy mercies bid thee leave.
Oh, think me worth thine anger, punish me,
Burn off my rusts, and my deformity;
Restore thine image, so much, by thy grace,
That thou mayst know me, and I'll turn my face.

One major axis of this turning poem is that from East to West, with a reminder, on a Good Friday, that the words "east" and "Easter" (and eos, Greek for "dawn") are related. Although "sun" and "son" are not etymologically related, they are joined by a common pun, especially when the Son of God rises at sunrise on Easter Sunday.

The Anniversary

()◀▶()

All kings, and all their favorites,
All glory of honors, beauties, wits.
The sun itself, which makes times, as they pass,
Is elder by a year, now, than it was
When thou and I first one another saw:
All other things, to their destruction draw,
Only our love hath no decay;
This, no tomorrow hath, nor yesterday;
Running, it never runs from us away,
But truly keeps his first, last, everlasting day.

Two graves must hide thine and my corse,
If one might, death were no divorce;
Alas, as well as other princes, we
(Who prince enough in one another be)
Must leave at last in death, these eyes, and ears,
Oft fed with true oaths, and with sweet salt tears;
But souls where nothing dwells but love
(All other thoughts being inmates) then shall prove
This, or a love increasèd there above,
When bodies to their graves, souls from their graves remove.

And then we shall be thoroughly blest,
But we no more, than all the rest;
Here upon earth, we are kings, and none but we
Can be such kings, nor of such subjects be;
Who is so safe as we? where none can do
Treason to us, except one of us two.
True and false fears let us refrain,
Let us love nobly, and live, and add again
Years and years unto years, till we attain
To write threescore: this is the second of our reign.

It is typical of some lovers to act as their own fanatic accountants who know the day—or in some cases the hour or even the very minute—when they met or fell in love or became engaged. Donne's cleverness plays with the notion of time standing still and love persisting even as time runs on.

BEN JONSON 1572–1637

Ben Jonson is the earliest English writer who is routinely called by a nickname, a familiarity that seems justified by Jonson's vigor, charm, and good humor. He was a successful playwright, producing tragedies as well as comedies; a translator, conversationalist, and critic of great learning and distinction; and, above all, a lyric poet whose grace and energy are the equal of his best classical precursors.

Drink to Me Only with Thine Eyes

Drink to me only with thine eyes,
   And I will pledge with mine;
Or leave a kiss but in the cup,
   And I'll not look for wine.
The thirst that from the soul doth rise
   Doth ask a drink divine;
But might I of Jove's nectar sup,
   I would not change for thine.
I sent thee late a rosy wreath,
   Not so much honoring thee
As giving it a hope that there
   It could not withered be.
But thou thereon didst only breathe,
   And sent'st it back to me;
Since when it grows, and smells, I swear,
   Not of itself, but thee.

It is unlikely that many among the general reading public will know poems in this collection as true lyrics, songs meant to be sung. But this gem of Jonson's, his Song: To Celia, is still, after almost four hundred years, one of the loveliest and most popular of songs in English.

On My First Son

Farewell, thou child of my right hand, and joy;
  My sin was too much hope of thee, loved boy.
Seven years thou wert lent to me, and I thee pay,
  Exacted by thy fate, on the just day.
Oh, could I lose all father now! For why
  Will man lament the state he should envy?
To have so soon 'scaped world's and flesh's rage,
  And, if no other misery, yet age?
Rest in soft peace, and, asked, say here doth lie
  Ben Jonson his best piece of poetry;
For whose sake, henceforth, all his vows be such,
  As what he loves may never like too much.

Jonson's son, who died on his seventh birthday, was a junior. As Jonson knew, "Benjamin" means "son of the right hand" or "favorite." He also knew that "poem" means "thing made" or "product," so that one may speak of one's poetry as children and of one's children as poetry.

Hymn to Diana

Queen and huntress, chaste and fair,
Now the sun is laid to sleep,
Seated in thy silver chair,
State in wonted manner keep:
    Hesperus entreats thy light,
    Goddess excellently bright.

Earth, let not thy envious shade
Dare itself to interpose;
Cynthia's shining orb was made
Heaven to clear when day did close:
    Bless us then with wishèd sight,
    Goddess excellently bright.

Lay thy bow of pearl apart,
And thy crystal-shining quiver;
Give unto the flying hart
Space to breathe, how short soever:
    Thou that mak'st a day of night,
    Goddess excellently bright.

from Cynthia's Revels

Like "Slow, Slow, Fresh Fount" (p. 164), this is a song from Cynthia's Revels. Hesperus sings the hymn to Cynthia (or Diana), virgin goddess of the moon and the hunt.

Still to Be Neat

>>>>>>>

Still to be neat, still to be dressed,
As you were going to a feast;
Still to be powdered, still perfumed:
Lady, it is to be presumed,
Though art's hid causes are not found,
All is not sweet, all is not sound.

Give me a look, give me a face,
That makes simplicity a grace;
Robes loosely flowing, hair as free:
Such sweet neglect more taketh me
Than all the adulteries of art;
They strike mine eyes, but not my heart.

from The Silent Woman

Robert Herrick, who called Jonson "Saint Ben," helped himself to parts of this marvelous song from one of Jonson's plays. The "sweet" and "neglect" are used also in Herrick's "Delight in Disorder" (p. 174), and "taketh" (was ever a mot more juste?) *also graces Herrick's "Upon Julia's Clothes" (p. 173).*

The Triumph of Charis

See the Chariot at hand here of Love,
  Wherein my Lady rideth!
Each that draws is a swan or a dove,
  And well the car Love guideth
As she goes, all hearts do duty
      Unto her beauty;
And enamour'd do wish, so they might
      But enjoy such a sight,
That they still were to run by her side,
Thorough swords, thorough seas, whither she would ride.

Do but look on her eyes, they do light
  All that Love's world compriseth!
Do but look on her hair, it is bright
  As Love's star when it riseth!
Do but mark, her forehead's smoother
      Than words that soothe her;
And from her arch'd brows such a grace
      Sheds itself through the face,
As alone there triumphs to the life
All the gain, all the good, of the elements' strife.

Have you seen but a bright lily grow
  Before rude hands have touch'd it?
Have you mark'd but the fall of the snow
  Before the soil hath smutch'd it?
Have you felt the wool of the beaver,
      Or swan's down ever?
Or have smelt of the bud of the brier,
      Or the nard in the fire?
Or have tasted the bag of the bee?
O so white, O so soft, O so sweet is she!

from A Celebration of Charis in Ten Lyric Pieces

The phrase "or swan's down ever" occurs also at the end of Ezra Pound's Pisan Cantos. *This "triumph" is the fourth part of Jonson's "Celebration of Charis in Ten Lyric Pieces." No person has been identified as the original of "Charis," whose name means "grace." (Note that: "whether" is "whithersoever"; "nard" is "spikenard," an aromatic plant.)*

Epitaph on S. P.

◆◆◆◆◆

Weep with me, all you that read
   This little story;
And know, for whom a tear you shed
   Death's self is sorry.
'Twas a child that so did thrive
   In grace and feature,
As Heaven and Nature seemed to strive
   Which owned the creature.
Years he numbered scarce thirteen
   When Fates turned cruel,
Yet three filled Zodiacs had he been
   The Stages' jewel;
And did act (what now we moan)
   Old men so duly,
As sooth the Parcae thought him one,
   He played so truly.
So, by error, to his fate
   They all consented;
But, viewing him since, alas, too late!
   They have repented;
And have sought, to give new birth,
   In baths to steep him;
But, being so much too good for earth,
   Heaven vows to keep him.

The boy-actor Salomon Pavy acted in some of the plays that Jonson wrote for the Children of Queen Elizabeth's Chapel. (Note that: "Parcae" is "the Fates.")

Slow, Slow, Fresh Fount,
Keep Time with My Salt Tears

Slow, slow, fresh fount, keep time with my salt tears;
  Yet slower yet, oh faintly gentle springs:
List to the heavy part the music bears,
  "Woe weeps out her division when she sings."
Droop herbs and flowers;
Fall grief in showers;
"Our beauties are not ours":
    Oh, I could still,
Like melting snow upon some craggy hill,
  Drop, drop, drop, drop,
Since nature's pride is, now, a withered daffodil.

from Cynthia's Revels

In Cynthia's Revels, *the nymph Echo sings this pretty echoic song for Narcissus, metamorphosed into a flower related to the daffodil. (Note that: "division" is "subdividing one long note into several shorter ones.")*

Come, My Celia, Let Us Prove

Come, my Celia, let us prove
While we may the sports of love;
Time will not be ours forever,
He at length our good will sever.
Spend not then his gifts in vain.
Suns that set may rise again,
But if once we lost this light,
'Tis with us perpetual night.
Why should we defer our joys?
Fame and rumor are but toys.
Cannot we delude the eyes
Of a few poor household spies?
Or his easier ears beguile,
So removèd by our wile?
'Tis no sin love's fruit to steal,
But the sweet theft to reveal:
To be taken, to be seen,
These have crimes accounted been.

from Volpone

Volpone includes this song in his assault on the virtuous wife Celia, to whose husband, Corvino, the "easier ears" in line 13 belong. The model for the beginning of the poem seems to be much the same lines from Catullus as inspired Campion's "My Sweetest Lesbia" (p. 114).

To Penshurst

Thou art not, Penshurst, built to envious show,
Of touch or marble; nor canst boast a row
Of polished pillars, or a roof of gold;
Thou hast no lantern whereof tales are told,
Or stair, or courts; but stand'st an ancient pile,
And, these grudged at, art reverenced the while.
Thou joy'st in better marks, of soil, of air,
Of wood, of water; therein thou art fair.
Thou hast thy walks for health, as well as sport;
Thy mount, to which the dryads do resort,
Where Pan and Bacchus their high feasts have made,
Beneath the broad beech and the chestnut shade,
That taller tree, which of a nut was set
At his great birth where all the Muses met.
There in the writhèd bark are cut the names
Of many a sylvan, taken with his flames;
And thence the ruddy satyrs oft provoke
The lighter fauns to reach thy Lady's Oak.
Thy copse too, named of Gamage, thou hast there,
That never fails to serve thee seasoned deer
When thou wouldst feast, or exercise, thy friends.
The lower land, that to the river bends,
Thy sheep, thy bullocks, kine, and calves do feed;
The middle grounds thy mares and horses breed.
Each bank doth yield thee conies; and the tops,
Fertile of wood, Ashore and Sidney's copse,
To crown thy open table, doth provide
The purpled pheasant with the speckled side;
The painted partridge lies in every field,
And for thy mess is willing to be killed.
And if the high-swollen Medway fail thy dish,
Thou hast thy ponds that pay thee tribute fish,
Fat agèd carps that run into thy net,
And pikes, now weary their own kind to eat,

As loath the second draught or cast to stay,
Officiously at first themselves betray;
Bright eels that emulate them, and leap on land
Before the fisher, or into his hand.
Then hath thy orchard fruit, thy garden flowers,
Fresh as the air, and new as are the hours.
The early cherry, with the later plum,
Fig, grape, and quince, each in his time doth come:
The blushing apricot and woolly peach
Hang on thy walls, that every child may reach.
And though thy walls be on the country stone,
They're reared with no man's ruin, no man's groan;
There's none that dwell about them wish them down,
But all come in, the farmer and the clown,
And no one empty-handed, to salute
Thy lord and lady, though they have no suit.
Some bring a capon, some a rural cake,
Some nuts, some apples; some that think they make
The better cheeses bring 'em, or else send
By their ripe daughters, whom they would commend
This way to husbands, and whose baskets bear
An emblem of themselves in plum or pear.
But what can this (more than express their love)
Add to thy free provisions, far above
The need of such? whose liberal board doth flow
With all that hospitality doth know;
Where comes no guest but is allowed to eat,
Without his fear, and of thy lord's own meat;
Where the same beer and bread, and selfsame wine,
That is his lordship's shall be also mine.
And I not fain to sit (as some this day
At great men's tables), and yet dine away.
Here no man tells my cups; nor, standing by,
A waiter doth my gluttony envỳ,
But gives me what I call, and lets me eat;
He knows below he shall find plenty of meat.
Thy tables hoard not up for the next day;
Nor, when I take my lodging, need I pray

For fire, or lights, or livery; all is there,
As if thou then wert mine, or I reigned here:
There's nothing I can wish, for which I stay.
That found King James when, hunting late this way
With his brave son, the prince, they saw thy fires
Shine bright on every hearth, as the desires
Of thy Penates had been set on flame
To entertain them; or the country came
With all their zeal to warm their welcome here.
What (great I will not say, but) sudden cheer
Didst thou then make 'em! and what praise was heaped
On thy good lady then! who therein reaped
The just reward of her high housewifery;
To have her linen, plate, and all things nigh,
When she was far; and not a room but dressed
As if it had expected such a guest!
These, Penshurst, are thy praise, and yet not all.
Thy lady's noble, fruitful, chaste withal.
His children thy great lord may call his own,
A fortune in this age but rarely known.
They are, and have been, taught religion; thence
Their gentler spirits have sucked innocence.
Each morn and even they are taught to pray,
With the whole household, and may, every day,
Read in their virtuous parents' noble parts
The mysteries of manners, arms, and arts.
Now, Penshurst, they that will proportion thee
With other edifices, when they see
Those proud, ambitious heaps, and nothing else,
May say, their lords have built, but thy lord dwells.

So-called topographical poetry, of which "To Penshurst" is one of the greatest examples in English, has persisted since the seventeenth century, exercising a poet's skills in architecture, history, rhetoric, and the arts of verse-writing. Penshurst, in Kent, enjoyed the superlative distinction of being the seat of the Sidneys, one of the most illustrious families of Elizabethan and Jacobean England. (Note that: "touch" is "touchstone," a fine marble; "lantherne" is a glassed-in room like a greenhouse on top of a house; "clowne" is "rural peasant," "rustic"; "penates" is "household gods"; "proportion" is "compare.")

JOHN WEBSTER c.1578–c.1632

In the manner of the Elizabethan theater, John Webster freely collaborated—with William Rowley, Thomas Dekker, Thomas Heywood, John Marston, and Cyril Tourneur—but his most famous tragedies were his alone: *The White Devil* and *The Duchess of Malfi*. Of the poets in this book, Webster was the only one who was also a coachmaker.

Call for the Robin Redbreast and the Wren

Call for the Robin Redbreast and the Wren,
Since o'er shady groves they hover,
And with leaves and flowers do cover
The friendless bodies of unburied men.
Call unto his funeral Dole
The Ante, the field-mouse, and the mole
To rear him hillocks, that shall keep him warm,
And (when gay tombs are robb'd) sustain no harm,
But keep the wolf far thence, that's foe to men,
For with his nails he'll dig them up agen.

from The White Devil

"Webster was much possessed by death," according to T. S. Eliot's "Whispers of Immortality". This end of Cornelia's song or dirge from Webster's White Devil *also appears, varied slightly, in Eliot's "Waste Land" (p. 968).*

Browne's narrative and lyric poems have been impor-
tant models for many writers, including Milton and
Keats.

On the Countess Dowager of Pembroke

Underneath this sable hearse
Lies the subject of all verse:
Sidney's sister, Pembroke's mother:
Death, ere thou has slain another,
Fair and learned and good as she,
Time shall throw a dart at thee.

Marble piles let no man raise
To her name: for after days
Some kind woman born as she,
Reading this, like Niobe,
Shall turn marble, and become
Both her mourner and her tomb.

Mary Herbert, Countess of Pembroke (1561–1621), was the younger sister of Sir Philip Sidney. She was also one of the most accomplished people in an age of prodigious accomplishment. A poet and translator herself, she befriended and helped many writers, including Samuel Daniel and Ben Jonson.

Superficially, Herrick was a good deal like his contemporary George Herbert: a poet and clergyman educated at Cambridge. But, markedly unlike the pious and saintly Herbert, Herrick was a much better secular poet than a sacred one. In his marvelously constructed lyrics there is an appreciation of nature and the physical—including the body, with and without clothes.

To the Virgins, to Make Much of Time

Gather ye rose-buds while ye may,
   Old Time is still a-flying;
And this same flower that smiles today,
   Tomorrow will be dying.

The glorious lamp of heaven, the sun,
   The higher he's a-getting,
The sooner will his race be run,
   And nearer he's to setting.

That age is best which is the first,
   When youth and blood are warmer;
But being spent, the worse, and worst
   Times, still succeed the former.

Then be not coy, but use your time,
   And while ye may, go marry;
For having lost but once your prime,
   You may for ever tarry.

This gem of a poem is a good deal like Andrew Marvell's carpe diem *poem "To His Coy Mistress" (p. 229). Unlike Marvell's clever pseudo-syllogism, however, Herrick's little song simply asserts some pretty hackneyed propositions, including a variant of "time flies," followed by the imperatives "be not coy," "use your time," and "go marry."*

Upon Julia's Clothes

Whenas in silks my Julia goes,
Then, then, methinks, how sweetly flows
That liquefaction of her clothes.

Next, when I cast mine eyes and see
That brave vibration each way free,
O how that glittering taketh me!

The highlights of the poem are the surprisingly technical "liquefaction" and the brilliant stroke (abetted by alliteration) of "brave vibration" ("brave" as in "brave new world," meaning "splendid").

Delight in Disorder

A sweet disorder in the dress
Kindles in clothes a wantonness.
A lawn about the shoulders thrown
Into a fine distractión;
An erring lace, which here and there
Enthralls the crimson stomacher;
A cuff neglectful, and thereby
Ribbons to flow confusèdly;
A winning wave, deserving note,
In the tempestuous petticoat;
A careless shoestring, in whose tie
I see a wild civility;
Do more bewitch me than when art
Is too precise in every part.

Herrick cleverly says that poetry, a model of order, could be used to praise erotic disorder. In saluting disorder (praise echoed in our time by Roland Barthes), Herrick practices what he preaches by exhibiting modest disorder in rhetoric, logic, grammar, and versification.

To Daffodils

◆◆◆◆◆

Fair daffodils, we weep to see
  You haste away so soon:
As yet the early-rising sun
  Has not attained his noon.
      Stay, stay,
    Until the hasting day
       Has run
    But to the evensong;
And, having prayed together, we
    Will go with you along.

We have short time to stay, as you,
  We have as short a spring;
As quick a growth to meet decay,
  As you, or anything.
      We die,
    As your hours do, and dry
       Away,
    Like to the summer's rain;
Or as the pearls of morning's dew
    Ne'er to be found again.

It makes sense that a poem about the brevity of life, whether floral or human, should be in short lines made up mostly of notably short words—molecular syllables like "see," "so," "day," "do," "die."

The Argument of His Book

I sing of brooks, of blossoms, birds and bowers,
Of April, May, of June and Jùly-flowers;
I sing of May-poles, hock-carts, wassails, wakes,
Of bridegrooms, brides and of their bridal cakes;
I write of youth, of love, and have access
By these to sing of cleanly wantonness;
I sing of dews, of rains, and piece by piece
Of balm, of oil, of spice and ambergris;
I sing of times trans-shifting, and I write
How roses first came red and lilies white;
I write of groves, of twilights, and I sing
The Court of Mab, and of the Fairy King;
I write of hell; I sing (and ever shall)
Of heaven, and hope to have it after all.

"Argument" here means the subject matter. Herrick speaks truly: he wrote several hundred poems on a great variety of subjects and kept his head and heart through it all.

Corinna's Going a-Maying

Get up, get up for shame! The blooming morn
Upon her wings presents the god unshorn.
  See how Aurora throws her fair,
  Fresh-quilted colors through the air.
  Get up, sweet slug-a-bed, and see
  The dew bespangling herb and tree!
Each flower has wept and bowed toward the east
Above an hour since, yet you not dressed;
  Nay! not so much as out of bed?
  When all the birds have matins said
  And sung their thankful hymns, 'tis sin,
  Nay, profanation, to keep in,
Whenas a thousand virgins on this day
Spring, sooner than the lark, to fetch in May.

Rise and put on your foliage, and be seen
To come forth, like the springtime, fresh and green,
  And sweet as Flora. Take no care
  For jewels for your gown or hair.
  Fear not; the leaves will strew
  Gems in abundance upon you.
Besides, the childhood of the day has kept,
Against you come, some orient pearls unwept.
  Come, and receive them while the light
  Hangs on the dew-locks of the night;
  And Titan on the eastern hill
  Retires himself, or else stands still
Till you come forth. Wash, dress, be brief in praying;
Few beads are best when once we go a-Maying.

Come, my Corinna, come; and, coming, mark
How each field turns a street, each street a park,
  Made green and trimmed with trees; see how
  Devotion gives each house a bough
  Or branch: each porch, each door, ere this,
  An ark, a tabernacle is,
Made up of white-thorn neatly interwove,
As if here were those cooler shades of love.
  Can such delights be in the street
  And open fields, and we not see't?
  Come, we'll abroad; and let's obey
  The proclamation made for May,
And sin no more, as we have done, by staying;
But, my Corinna, come, let's go a-Maying.

There's not a budding boy or girl this day
But is got up and gone to bring in May.
  A deal of youth, ere this, is come
  Back, and with white-thorn laden home.
  Some have dispatched their cakes and cream,
  Before that we have left to dream;
And some have wept, and wooed, and plighted troth,
And chose their priest, ere we can cast off sloth.
  Many a green-gown has been given,
  Many a kiss, both odd and even,
  Many a glance, too, has been sent
  From out the eye, love's firmament;
Many a jest told of the keys betraying
This night, and locks picked; yet we're not a-Maying!

Come, let us go, while we are in our prime,
And take the harmless folly of the time!
   We shall grow old apace, and die
   Before we know our liberty.
   Our life is short, and our days run
   As fast away as does the sun.
And, as a vapor or a drop of rain,
Once lost, can ne'er be found again,
   So when or you or I are made
   A fable, song, or fleeting shade,
   All love, all liking, all delight
   Lies drowned with us in endless night.
Then, while time serves and we are but decaying,
Come, my Corinna, come, let's go a-Maying.

Here is a carpe diem *poem urging the almost literal seizure of the day (see Herrick's "To the Virgins, to Make Much of Time," p. 172). Since "Corinna" could be a diminutive of "Cora," another name for Persephone, the poem gains a dimension from classical myth that adds complexity and profundity, although the mischievous Herrick is not above mildly lewd jests about keys and locks. Some of the arguments, and even some of the language, come out of the mouths of "the ungodly" in the Old Testament.*

The Night-Piece to Julia

Her eyes the glow-worm lend thee,
The shooting stars attend thee;
   And the elves also,
   Whose little eyes glow
Like the sparks of fire, befriend thee.

No will-o'-th'-wisp mislight thee,
Nor snake or slow-worm bite thee;
   But on, on thy way,
   Not making a stay,
Since ghost there's none to affright thee.

Let not the dark thee cumber;
What though the moon does slumber?
   The stars of the night
   Will lend thee their light
Like tapers clear without number.

Then, Julia, let me woo thee,
Thus, thus to come unto me;
   And when I shall meet
   Thy silv'ry feet
My soul I'll pour into thee.

Even in parts of the world with advanced civilization, enchanting rural lore persists, four hundred years after Herrick's birth. Glow-worms and shooting stars have a special place in literature, from Shakespeare's Midsummer-Night's Dream *and Marvell's "Mower to the Glow-Worms" (p. 244) to Robert Frost's "Fireflies in the Garden." (Note that: "slow-worm" is "small lizard" or (the earlier and more probable meaning) "an adder.")*

Grace for a Child

Here a little child I stand,
Heaving up my either hand;
Cold as Paddocks though they be,
Here I lift them up to Thee,
For a Benizon to fall
On our meat, and on us all. *Amen.*

The seven other poems by Herrick in this anthology come from a book called Hesperides; *this child's prayer is from Herrick's more pious collection,* Noble Numbers. *(Note that: "Paddocks" are "toads" or "frogs"; a "Benizon" is a "blessing.")*

HENRY KING, BISHOP OF CHICHESTER 1592–1669

King, who was friendly with John Donne and Isaak
Walton, in time became Bishop of Chichester.

Exequy on His Wife

❖·❖·❖·❖

Accept, thou shrine of my dead Saint!
Instead of dirges this complaint;
And for sweet flowers to crown thy hearse,
Receive a strew of weeping verse
From thy griev'd friend, whom thou might'st see
Quite melted into tears for thee.
  Dear loss! since thy untimely fate
My task hath been to meditate
On thee, on thee: thou art the book,
The library whereon I look
Though almost blind. For thee (lov'd clay!)
I languish out, not live the day,
Using no other exercise
But what I practise with mine eyes.
By which wet glasses I find out
How lazily time creeps about
To one that mourns: this, only this
My exercise and bus'ness is:
So I compute the weary hours
With sighs dissolved into showers.
  Nor wonder if my time go thus
Backward and most preposterous;
Thou hast benighted me. Thy set
This eve of blackness did beget,
Who wast my day, (though overcast
Before thou had'st thy noon-tide passed)
And I remember must in tears,

Thou scarce had'st seen so many years
As day tells hours. By thy clear sun
My love and fortune first did run;
But thou wilt never more appear
Folded within my hemisphere:
Since both thy light and motion
Like a fled star is fall'n and gone;
And twixt me and my soul's dear wish
The earth now interposed is,
With such a strange eclipse doth make
As ne'er was read in almanake.

   I could allow thee for a time
To darken me annd my sad clime,
Were it a month, a year, or ten,
I would thy exile live till then;
And all that space my mirth adjourn
So thou wouldst promise to return;
And putting off thy ashy shroud
At length disperse this sorrow's cloud.

   But woe is me! the longest date
Too narrow is to calculate
These empty hopes. Never shall I
Be so much blest, as to descry
A glimpse of thee, till that day come
Which shall the earth to cinders doom,
And a fierce fever must calcine
The body of this world, like thine
(My Little World!). That fit of fire
Once off, our bodies shall aspire
To our souls' bliss: then we shall rise,
And view ourselves with clearer eyes
In that calm region, where no night
Can hide us from each other's sight.

   Meantime, thou hast her earth: much good
May my harm do thee. Since it stood
With Heaven's will I might not call
Her longer mine, I give thee all
My short-liv'd right and interest

In her, whom living I lov'd best:
With a most free and bounteous grief,
I give thee what I could not keep.
Be kind to her, and prithee look
Thou write into thy Doomsday book
Each parcel of this rarity
Which in thy casket shrin'd doth lie:
See that thou make thy reck'ning straight,
And yield her back again by weight;
For thou must audit on thy trust
Each grain and atom of this dust:
As thou wilt answer Him, that lent,
Not gave thee, my dear monument.

   So close the ground, and 'bout her shade
Black curtains draw, my bride is laid.

   Sleep on (my love!) in thy cold bed
Never to be disquieted,
My last good night! Thou wilt not wake
Till I thy fate shall overtake:
Till age, or grief, or sickness must
Marry my body to that dust
It so much loves; and fill the room
My heart keeps empty in thy tomb.
Star for me there; I will not fail
To meet thee in that hollow vale.
And think not much of my delay;
I am already on the way,
And follow thee with all the speed
Desire can make, or sorrows breed.
Each minute is a short degree
And ev'ry hour a step towards thee.
At night when I betake to rest,
Next morn I rise nearer my west
Of life, almost by eight hours' sail,
Than when sleep breath'd his drowsy gale.

   Thus from the sun my bottom steers,
And my days' compass downward bears.
Nor labour I to stem the tide,

Through which to thee I swiftly glide.
    'Tis true; with shame and grief I yield,
Thou, like the van, first took'st the field,
And gotten hast the victory
In thus adventuring to die
Before me; whose more years might crave
A just precedence in the grave.
But hark! My pulse, like a soft drum
Beats my approach, tells thee I come;
And slow howe'er my marches be,
I shall at last sit down by thee.
    The thought of this bids me go on,
And wait my dissolution
With hope and comfort. Dear! (forgive
The crime) I am content to live
Divided, with but half a heart,
Till we shall meet and never part.

In lines admired by Edgar Allan Poe and T. S. Eliot, Henry King memorialized his dead wife. As was typical at the time, King used some of the witty devices of the Metaphysicals (such as employing technical terms from geometry: sixty minutes of arc equal one degree). But King's most durable achievement is the registration of passionate love and profound theology. (Note that: "straw" is "scattering"; "calcine" is "burn to dust"; "bottom" is "sea-going craft.")

After a time as an apprentice courtier, Herbert took
orders in his early thirties and spent the remaining few
years of his life as a most devout clergyman and a re-
ligious poet of great intellect and passion. Herbert's po-
etry, mostly contained in *The Temple; or, Sacred Poems
and Private Ejaculations,* was not published until after his
death.

Love Bade Me Welcome

Love bade me welcome; yet my soul drew back,
  Guilty of dust and sin.
But quick-eyed Love, observing me grow slack
  From my first entrance in,
Drew nearer to me, sweetly questioning
  If I lacked any thing.

"A guest," I answered, "worthy to be here";
  Love said, "You shall be he."
"I the unkind, ungrateful? Ah my dear,
  I cannot look on Thee."
Love took my hand, and smiling did reply,
  "Who made the eyes but I?"

"Truth Lord, but I have marred them: let my shame
  Go where it doth deserve."
"And know you not," says Love, "who bore the blame?"
  "My dear, then I will serve."
"You must sit down," says Love, "and taste My meat."
  So I did sit and eat.

Like "The Collar" (p. 188), this "Love" (one of three poems Herbert wrote with that title) is a brightly colored, highly dramatized account of a conflict between a person and a principle—a man and a god. The Love here seems to be a pagan Eros, but this Lord merges with the Christian God: the God who is Love. Something of medieval "light" philosophy may persist in the notion that Love made eyes in the first place. (Louis L. Martz points out a question from Psalm XCIV: "He that formed the eye, shall he not see?")

The Collar

≫≫≫≫≫

I struck the board, and cried, No more.
    I will abroad.
  What? shall I ever sigh and pine?
My lines and life are free; free as the road,
  Loose as the wind, as large as store.
    Shall I be still in suit?
  Have I no harvest but a thorn
  To let me blood, and not restore
  What I have lost with cordial fruit?
    Sure there was wine
Before my sighs did dry it: there was corn
    Before my tears did drown it.
  Is the year only lost to me?
    Have I no bays to crown it?
No flowers, no garlands gay? all blasted?
    All wasted?
  Not so, my heart: but there is fruit,
    And thou hast hands.
  Recover all thy sigh-blown age
On double pleasures: leave thy cold dispute
Of what is fit, and not. Forsake thy cage,
    Thy rope of sands,
Which petty thoughts have made, and made to thee
  Good cable, to enforce and draw,
    And be thy law,
  While thou didst wink and wouldst not see.
    Away, Take Heed,
    I will abroad,
Call in thy death's head there: tie up thy fears.
    He that forbears
  To suit and serve his need,
    Deserves his load.

But as I raved and grew more fierce and wild
    At every word,
Me thought I heard one calling, *Child!*
    And I replied, *My Lord.*

Herbert puns on "collar/choler." The "board" struck in the first line is a table—a usage surviving today only in such locutions as "bed and board"; in this poem it refers not only to the table for meals but also to that used for Holy Communion.

Virtue

Sweet day, so cool, so calm, so bright,
The bridal of the earth and sky:
The dew shall weep thy fall tonight;
    For thou must die.

Sweet, rose, whose hue angry and brave
Bids the rash gazer wipe his eye:
Thy root is ever in its grave,
    And thou must die.

Sweet spring, full of sweet days and roses,
A box where sweets compacted lie;
My music shows ye have your closes,
    And all must die.

Only a sweet and virtuous soul,
Like seasoned timber, never gives;
But though the whole world turn to coal,
    Then chiefly lives.

As Louis L. Martz observes, "Virtue" is constructed according to a process of deepening the meaning of "sweet," from the simple sensual pleasure (in Herbert's day as much a matter of smell as of taste) to a moral asset of the soul.

The Pulley

When God at first made man,
Having a glass of blessings standing by,
"Let us," said He, "pour on him all we can:
Let the world's riches, which dispersed lie,
　　Contract into a span."

So Strength first made a way;
Then Beauty flowed, then Wisdom, Honor, Pleasure:
When almost all was out, God made a stay,
Perceiving that alone of all His treasure
　　Rest in the bottom lay.

"For if I should," said He,
"Bestow this jewel also on My creature,
He would adore My gifts instead of Me,
And rest in Nature, not the God of Nature:
　　So both should losers be.

"Yet let him keep the rest,
But keep them with repining restlessness:
Let him be rich and weary, that at least,
If goodness lead him not, yet weariness
　　May toss him to My breast."

Although related to any number of fanciful Creation myths, including the Hebrew and the Greek, Herbert's "Pulley" is a charmingly original explanation of why we are so restless. Restively, the poet puns on various senses of "rest" as verb and noun.

Redemption

Having been tenant long to a rich lord,
   Not thriving, I resolvèd to be bold,
   And make a suit unto him, to afford
A new small-rented lease, and cancel the old.
In heaven at his manor I him sought:
   They told me there, that he was lately gone
   About some land, which he had dearly bought
Long since on earth, to take possession.
I straight returned, and knowing his great birth,
   Sought him accordingly in great resorts,
   In cities, theaters, gardens, parks, and courts.
At length I heard a ragged noise and mirth
   Of thieves and murderers: there I him espied,
   Who straight, "Your suit is granted," said, and died.

Of the eight Herbert poems here, only two are sonnets—this and "Prayer the Church's Banquet" (p. 195). This poem uses the sonnet form for a parable that combines homely domestic details, theological concepts, and the melodramatic structure that Herbert and many other preachers like.

Easter Wings

Lord, who createdst man in wealth and store,
Though foolishly he lost the same,
Decaying more and more
Till he became
Most poor:
With Thee
O let me rise
As larks, harmoniously,
And sing this day Thy victories:
Then shall the fall further the flight in me.

My tender age in sorrow did begin:
And still with sicknesses and shame
Thou did'st so punish sin,
That I became
Most thin.
With thee
Let me combine
And feel thy victory:
For, if I imp my wing on thine,
Affliction shall advance the flight in me.

Herbert composed a few poems that belong to the tradition of the carmen fig-
uratum *or figure poem — that is, one whose shape on the page suggests its subject
or theme. There are some ancient Greek examples, and Richard Willes published
several (in Latin) in 1573. Among the moderns, the most notable practitioners
of shaped poetry in English have been E. E. Cummings, Dylan Thomas, and
John Hollander. Herbert makes a stanza that suggests the shape of wings and
also the form of his argument; the stanza grows poorest and thinnest with the
words "Most poor" and "Most thin." (Note that: "imp" is "graft.")*

[193]

Jordan

Who says that fictions only and false hair
Become a verse? Is there in truth no beauty?
Is all good structure in a winding stair?
May no lines pass, except they do their duty
   Not to a true, but painted chair?

Is it no verse, except enchanted groves
And sudden arbours shadow coarse-spun lines?
Must purling streams refresh a lover's loves?
Must all be veiled, while he that reads, divines,
   Catching the sense at two removes?

Shepherds are honest people; let them sing:
Riddle who list, for me, and pull for prime:
I envy no man's nightingale or spring;
Nor let them punish me with loss of rhyme,
   Who plainly say, *My God, My King.*

Herbert wrote two poems entitled "Jordan" having to do with poetry itself, as though to let the baptismal River Jordan replace the Pierian Spring of the secular Muses of classical antiquity. Such artful rejection of artfulness—the crafty denial of craft—is among the oldest of rhetorical gimmicks. (Note that: "pull for prime" is to try to draw a lucky card in the game called primero.)

Prayer the Church's Banquet

Prayer, the Church's banquet; Angels' age,
God's breath in man returning to his birth,
The soul in paraphrase, heart in pilgrimage,
The Christian plummet, sounding heaven and earth;
Engine against th' Almighty, sinner's tower,
Reversed thunder, Christ-side-piercing spear,
The six-days' world-transposing in an hour,
A kind of tune, which all things hear and fear;
Softness, and peace, and joy, and love, and bliss,
Exalted Manna, gladness of the best;
Heaven in ordinary, man well dressed,
The milky way, the bird of Paradise,
   Church-bells beyond the stars heard, the souls blood,
   The land of spices; something understood.

In one of his richest and boldest poems, Herbert uses the sonnet form (fairly rare for him) to provide a catalogue of subjects with no verb or predicate of any kind. More than any other poem in this anthology, this one is a pure list, like a paradigmatic outline for a sermon or lecture.

Carew, a lawyer's son, was educated in the law at Oxford and the Middle Temple. He is included among the Courtly poets who specialized in lighthearted lyrics in praise of love.

Ask Me No More Where Jove Bestows

Ask me no more where Jove bestows,
When June is past, the fading rose;
For in your beauty's orient deep
These flowers, as in their causes, sleep.

Ask me no more whither do stray
The golden atoms of the day;
For in pure love heaven did prepare
Those powders to enrich your hair.

Ask me no more whither doth haste
The nightingale when May is past,
For in your sweet dividing throat
She winters, and keeps warm her note.

Ask me no more where those stars light
That downwards fall in dead of night,
For in your eyes they sit, and there
Fixed become, as in their sphere.

Ask me no more if east or west
The phoenix builds her spicy nest,
For unto you at last she flies
And in your fragrant bosom dies.

The "causes" here come from Aristotle, for whom anything results from the operation of four causes (final, formal, material, efficient). Things inhere in their causes; so roses may be said to "sleep" in theirs. "Dividing" is a technical term in music; in Carew's day an atom ("uncuttable") was an indivisible particle.

To My Inconstant Mistress

When thou, poor Excommunicate
   From all the joys of Love, shalt see
The full reward and glorious fate
   Which my strong faith shall purchase me,
   Then curse thine own inconstancy!

A fairer hand than thine shall cure
   That heart which thy false oaths did wound;
And to my soul a soul more pure
   Than thine shall by Love's hand be bound,
   And both with equal glory crown'd.

Then shalt thou weep, entreat, complain
   To Love, as I did once to thee;
When all thy tears shall be as vain
   As mine were then: for thou shalt be
   Damn'd for thy false apostasy.

Carew adds technical terms from Christian theology to themes dating back to Catullus and Propertius.

SIR WILLIAM DAVENANT 1606–1668

Davenant (also called D'Avenant) was said to be Shakespeare's godson, and rumors persisted that he was Shakespeare's natural son as well. He was a busy and varied man of letters, producing comedies, tragedies, and the heroic poem *Gondibert,* which is still readable. He was made poet laureate and knighted by Charles I. A loyal Cavalier, he was imprisoned in the Tower in the early 1650s, saved supposedly by Milton. Davenant returned the favor during the Restoration, when Milton was jailed.

The Lark Now Leaves His Watery Nest

≫≫≫≫≫

The lark now leaves his watery nest,
  And climbing, shakes his dewy wings;
He takes this window for the east,
  And to implore your light, he sings,
Awake, awake, the morn will never rise,
Till she can dress her beauty at your eyes.

The merchant bows unto the seaman's star,
  The ploughman from the sun his season takes;
But still the lover wonders what they are,
  Who look for day before his mistress wakes.
Awake, awake, break through your veils of lawn,
Then draw your curtains, and begin the dawn.

This aubade *(morning song) is reminiscent of Shakespeare's "Hark! Hark! the* Lark" *(p. 99). The phrase "watery nest" is also found in Shakespeare's "Rape of Lucrece".*

A complex man surviving in most complex times, Waller was a politician in the good and bad senses. He was a lawyer and, at sixteen, a member of Parliament, seeming to support the Parliamentarians but really a Royalist who, when exposed in 1643, displayed treachery, cowardice, and faithlessness. No matter: his lovely poetry shines with a clear light and true voice, and all the double-crossing and crookedness evaporate.

Go, Lovely Rose

Go, lovely rose,
Tell her that wastes her time and me
That now she knows,
When I resemble her to thee,
How sweet and fair she seems to be.

Tell her that's young
And shuns to have her graces spied,
That, hadst thou sprung
In deserts where no men abide,
Thou must have uncommended died.

Small is the worth
Of beauty from the light retired:
Bid her come forth,
Suffer herself to be desired,
And not blush so to be admired.

Then die, that she
The common fate of all things rare
    May read in thee,
How small a part of time they share
    That are so wondrous sweet and fair.

This is an "envoy," a sending poem acting as a go-between for a poet who for some reason cannot address his or her love directly. Waller's contemporary Henry Lawes set "Go, Lovely Rose" to music.

On a Girdle

That which her slender waist confined,
Shall now my joyful temples bind;
No monarch but would give his crown,
His arms might do what this has done.

It was my heaven's extremest sphere,
The pale which held that lovely deer;
My joy, my grief, my hope, my love,
Did all within this circle move!

A narrow compass! and yet there
Dwelt all that's good, and all that's fair!
Give me but what this riband bound,
Take all the rest the sun goes round!

Here "girdle" means a belt or sash and not the modern elasticized foundation garment.

JOHN MILTON 1608–1674

Milton, who is customarily ranked as the second-greatest poet in English (after Shakespeare), was born in London and educated at Cambridge. Thereafter he spent several years in retirement, preparing himself for great things. For about the middle twenty years of his life, he took on some unpoetic chores as Latin Secretary to Cromwell's Council of State. His sight was failing during his State service, and by 1652 he was totally blind. His greatest work, *Paradise Lost*, was published in 1667, *Paradise Regained* and *Samson Agonistes* four years later.

Lycidas

Yet once more, O ye laurels, and once more,
Ye myrtles brown, with ivy never-sere,
I come to pluck your berries harsh and crude,
And with forc'd fingers rude
Shatter your leaves before the mellowing year.
Bitter constraint and sad occasion dear
Compels me to disturb your season due:
For Lycidas is dead, dead ere his prime
Young Lycidas, and hath not left his peer.
Who would not sing for Lycidas? he well knew
Himself to sing, and build the lofty rhyme.
He must not float upon his watery bier
Unwept, and welter to the parching wind
Without the meed of some melodious tear.
    Begin then, Sisters of the sacred well
That from beneath the seat of Jove doth spring;
Begin, and somewhat loudly sweep the string:
Hence with denial vain, and coy excuse.
So may some gentle Muse
With lucky words favor my destin'd urn,
And as he passes, turn

And bid fair peace be to my sable shroud.
For we were nurs'd upon the self-same hill,
Fed the same flock, by fountain, shade and rill.

   Together both, ere the high lawns appear'd
Under the glimmering eyelids of the morn,
We drove afield, and both together heard
What time the gray-fly winds her sultry horn,
Battening our flocks with the fresh dews of night,
Oft till the ev'n-star bright
Toward heav'n's descent had slop'd his burnish'd wheel.
Meanwhile the rural ditties were not mute
Temper'd to the'oaten flute:
Rough Satyrs danc'd, and Fauns with cloven heel
From the glad sound would not be absent long,
And old Dametas lov'd to hear our song.

   But O the heavy change, now thou art gone,
Now thou art gone, and never must return!
Thee shepherd, thee the woods and desert caves
With wild thyme and the gadding vine o'ergrown
And all their echoes mourn.
The willows and the hazel copses green
Shall now no more be seen
Fanning their joyous leaves to thy soft lays.
As killing as the canker to the rose,
Or taint-worm to the weanling herds that graze,
Or frost to flowers that their gay wardrobe wear
When first the whitethorn blows,
Such, Lycidas, thy loss to shepherd's ear.

   Where were ye Nymphs when the remorseless deep
Clos'd o'er the head of your lov'd Lycidas?
For neither were ye playing on the steep,
Where your old bards the famous Druids lie,
Nor on the shaggy top of Mona high,
Nor yet where Deva spreads her wizard stream.
Ay me, I fondly dream!
Had ye been there . . . for what could that have done?
What could the Muse herself that Orpheus bore,
The Muse herself, for her enchanting son?

Whom universal nature did lament,
When by the rout that made the hideous roar
His gory visage down the stream was sent,
Down the swift Hebrus to the Lesbian shore.
    Alas! What boots it with uncessant care
To tend the homely slighted shepherd's trade,
And strictly meditate the thankless Muse?
Were it not better done as others use,
To sport with Amaryllis in the shade,
Hid in the tangles of Neaera's hair?
Fame is the spur that the clear spirit doth raise
(That last infirmity of noble mind)
To scorn delights and live laborious days;
But the fair guerdon when we hope to find,
And think to burst out into sudden blaze,
Comes the blind Fury with th'abhorred shears
And slits the thin-spun life. "But not the praise,"
Phoebus repli'd, and touch'd my trembling ears.
"Fame is no plant that grows on mortal soil,
Nor in the glistering foil
Set off to th'world, nor in broad rumor lies;
But lives, and spreads aloft by those pure eyes
And perfect witness of all-judging Jove:
As he pronounces lastly on each deed,
Of so much fame in Heav'n expect thy meed."
    O fountain Arethuse, and thou honor'd flood,
Smooth-sliding Mincius, crown'd with vocal reeds,
That strain I heard was of a higher mood.
But now my oat proceeds,
And listens to the herald of the sea
That came in Neptune's plea.
He ask'd the waves, and ask'd the felon winds,
"What hard mishap hath doom'd this gentle swain?"
And question'd every gust of rugged wings
That blows from off each beaked promontory.
They knew not of his story,
And sage Hippotades their answer brings
That not a blast was from his dungeon stray'd;

The air was calm, and on the level brine
Sleek Panope with all her sisters play'd.
It was that fatal and perfidious bark,
Built in th'eclipse, and rigg'd with curses dark,
That sunk so low that sacred head of thine.
   Next Camus (reverend sire) went footing slow,
His mantle hairy and his bonnet sedge
Inwrought with figures dim, and on the edge
Like to that sanguine flower inscrib'd with woe.
"Ah! Who hath reft" (quoth he) "my dearest pledge?"
Last came, and last did go,
The pilot of the Galilean lake.
Two massy keys he bore of metals twain
(The golden opes, the iron shuts amain).
He shook his mitr'd locks, and stern bespake:
"How well could I have spar'd for thee, young swain,
Enough of such as for their bellies' sake
Creep and intrude and climb into the fold?
Of other care they little reckoning make
Than how to scramble at the shearers' feast
And shove away the worthy bidden guest.
Blind mouths! that scarce themselves know how to hold
A sheephook, or have learn'd ought else the least
That to the faithful herdman's art belongs!
What recks it them? What need they? They are sped.
And when they list their lean and flashy songs
Grate on their scrannel pipes of wretched straw,
The hungry sheep look up, and are not fed,
But that two-handed engine at the door
Stands ready to smites once, and smites no more."
Besides what the grim wolf with privy paw
Daily devours apace, and little said.
But that two-handed engine at the door
Stands ready to smite once, and smites no more."
   Return, Alpheus, the dread voice is pass'd
That shrunk thy streams; return, Sicilian Muse,
And call the vales and bid them hither cast
Their bells and flowerets of a thousand hues.

Ye valleys low, where the mild whispers use
Of shades and wanton winds and gushing brooks,
On whose fresh lap the swart star sparely looks,
Throw hither all your quaint enamel'd eyes
That on the green turf suck the honey'd showers,
And purple all the ground with vernal flowers.
Bring the rathe primrose that forsaken dies,
The tufted crow-toe and pale jessamine,
The white pink, and the pansy freak'd with jet,
The glowing violet,
The musk-rose and the well-attir'd woodbine,
With cowslips wan that hang the pensive head,
And every flower that sad embroidery wears;
Bid amaranthus all his beauty shed,
And daffodillies fill their cups with tears
To strew the laureate hearse where Lycid lies.
For so, to interpose a little ease,
Let our frail thoughts dally with false surmise;
Ay me! whilst thee the shores and sounding seas
Wash far away, where e'er thy bones are hurl'd,
Whether beyond the stormy Hebrides,
Where thou perhaps under the whelming tide
Visit'st the bottom of the monstrous world,
Or whether thou, to our moist vows deni'd,
Sleep'st by the fable of Bellerus old,
Where the great vision of the guarded Mount
Looks toward Namancos and Bayona's hold.
Look homeward Angel now, and melt with ruth,
And O ye dolphins, waft the hapless youth.
　　Weep no more, woeful shepherds, weep no more;
For Lycidas your sorrow is not dead,
Sunk though he be beneath the watery floor:
So sinks the daystar in the ocean bed,
And yet anon repairs his drooping head
And tricks his beams and with new-spangl'd ore
Flames in the forehead of the morning sky;
So Lycidas sunk low, but mounted high
Through the dear might of him that walk'd the waves,

Where other groves and other streams along
With nectar pure his oozy locks he laves
And hears the unexpressive nuptial song
In the bless'd kingdoms meek of joy and love.
There entertain him all the saints above
In solemn troops and sweet societies,
That sing, and singing in their glory move,
And wipe the tears for ever from his eyes.
Now, Lycidas, the shepherds weep no more.
Henceforth thou art the genius of the shore
In thy large recompense, and shalt be good
To all that wander in that perilous flood.

   Thus sang the uncouth swain to th'oaks and rills,
While the still morn went out with sandals gray;
He touch'd the tender stops of various quills,
With eager thought warbling his Doric lay.
And now the sun had stretch'd out all the hills,
And now was dropp'd into the western bay;
At last he rose, and twitch'd his mantle blue,
Tomorrow to fresh woods and pastures new.

"Pastor" originally meant "shepherd," and the fiction of such pastoral elegies as "Lycidas" is that the dead subject—usually a poet—is a shepherd lamented by others. Samuel Johnson, doubting Milton's sincerity, said, "Where there is leisure for fiction there is little grief." But the poem is still read and loved. (Note that: "scrannel" is "flimsy"; "unexpressive" is "ineffable.")

On His Deceased Wife

Methought I saw my late espoused saint
Brought to me like Alcestis from the grave,
Whom Jove's great son to her glad husband gave,
Rescued from Death by force, though pale and faint.
Mine, as whom washed from spot of childbed taint
Purification in the Old Law did save,
And such as yet once more I trust to have
Full sight of her in heaven without restraint,
Came vested all in white, pure as her mind.
Her face was veiled; yet to my fancied sight
Love, sweetness, goodness, in her person shined
So clear as in no face with more delight.
But, O! as to embrace me she inclined,
I waked, she fled, and day brought back my night.

Milton wrote nothing more personal or more touching. This account of a blind widower's dream may be about Milton's first wife, Mary, who died just after giving birth in 1652, or his second wife, Katherine, who died a few months after giving birth in 1658. Most scholars favor the choice of Katherine, since Milton never set eyes on her.

On His Blindness

()◀▬▶()

When I consider how my light is spent,
Ere half my days, in this dark world and wide,
And that one talent which is death to hide
Lodged with me useless, though my soul more bent
To serve therewith my Maker, and present
My true account, lest he returning chide,
"Doth God exact day labor, light denied?"
I fondly ask; by Patience, to prevent
That murmur, soon replies: "God doth not need
Either man's work or his own gifts; who best
Bear his mild yoke, they serve him best. His state
Is kingly: thousands at his bidding speed
And post o'er land and ocean without rest.
They also serve who only stand and wait."

By 1652 Milton was completely blind. He was aware of connections with other blind men, preeminently Homer and Samson. (The last word of Samson Agonistes *is "spent.") (Note that: "fondly" is "foolishly.")*

On the Late Massacre in Piedmont

Avenge, O Lord, thy slaughtered saints, whose bones
Lie scattered on the Alpine mountains cold;
Even them who kept thy truth so pure of old
When all our fathers worshipped stocks and stones,
Forget not: in thy book record their groans
Who were thy sheep and in their ancient fold
Slain by the bloody Piemontese, that rolled
Mother with infant down the rocks. Their moans
The vales redoubled to the hills, and they
To heaven. Their martyred blood and ashes sow
O'er all the Italian fields where still doth sway
The triple tyrant; that from these may grow
A hundredfold, who, having learnt thy way,
Early may fly the Babylonian woe.

The Waldenses or Waldensians, a dissenting sect founded by Peter Waldo in the twelfth century, continue to live in the French and Italian Alps. In the sixteenth century they accepted the Protestant doctrine of the Reformation. The massacre took place on April 24, 1655. (Note that: "stocks" is "idols"; "triple tyrant" is the Pope.)

L'Allegro

Hence loathèd Melancholy
  Of Cerberus and blackest Midnight born,
In Stygian cave forlorn
  'Mongst horrid shapes, and shrieks, and sights unholy,
Find out some uncouth cell,
  Where brooding Darkness spreads his jealous wings,
And the night-raven sings;
  There under ebon shades and low-browed rocks,
As ragged as thy locks,
  In dark Cimmerian desert ever dwell.
But come thou Goddess fair and free,
In Heaven ycleaped Euphrosyne,
And by men, heart-easing Mirth,
Whom lovely Venus at a birth
With two sister Graces more
To ivy-crownèd Bacchus bore;
Or whether (as some sager sing)
The frolic wind that breathes the spring,
Zephyr with Aurora playing,
As he met her once a-Maying,
There on beds of violets blue,
And fresh-blown roses washed in dew,
Filled her with thee, a daughter fair,
So buxom, blithe, and debonair.
Haste thee Nymph, and bring with thee
Jest and youthful jollity,
Quips and cranks, and wanton wiles,
Nods, and becks, and wreathèd smiles,
Such as hang on Hebe's cheek,
And love to live in dimple sleek;
Sport that wrinkled Care derides,
And Laughter holding both his sides.
Come, and trip it as ye go
On the light fantastic toe,

And in thy right hand lead with thee,
The mountain nymph, sweet Liberty;
And if I give thee honor due,
Mirth, admit me of thy crew
To live with her, and live with thee,
In unreprovèd pleasures free:
To hear the lark begin his flight,
And singing startle the dull night,
From his watchtower in the skies,
Till the dappled dawn doth rise;
Then to come in spite of sorrow,
And at my window bid good morrow,
Through the sweetbrier, or the vine,
Or the twisted eglantine;
While the cock with lively din,
Scatters the rear of darkness thin,
And to the stack or the barn door,
Stoutly struts his dames before;
Oft listening how the hounds and horn
Cheerly rouse the slumbering morn,
From the side of some hoar hill,
Through the high wood echoing shrill.
Some time walking not unseen
By hedgerow elms, on hillocks green,
Right against the eastern gate,
Where the great sun begins his state,
Robed in flames and amber light,
The clouds in thousand liveries dight;
While the ploughman near at hand
Whistles o'er the furrowed land,
And the milkmaid singeth blithe,
And the mower whets his scythe,
And every shepherd tells his tale
Under the hawthorn in the dale.
Straight mine eye hath caught new pleasures
Whilst the lantskip round it measures:
Russet lawns and fallows gray,
Where the nibbling flocks do stray,

Mountains on whose barren breast
The laboring clouds do often rest,
Meadows trim with daisies pied,
Shallow brooks and rivers wide.
Towers and battlements it sees
Bosomed high in tufted trees,
Where perhaps some beauty lies,
The cynosure of neighboring eyes.
Hard by, a cottage chimney smokes,
From betwixt two agèd oaks,
Where Corydon and Thyrsis met,
Are at their savory dinner set
Of herbs and other country messes,
Which the neat-handed Phyllis dresses;
And then in haste her bower she leaves,
With Thestylis to bind the sheaves;
Or if the earlier season lead,
To the tanned haycock in the mead.
Sometimes with secure delight
The upland hamlets will invite,
When the merry bells ring round,
And the jocund rebecks sound
To many a youth and many a maid,
Dancing in the chequered shade;
And young and old come forth to play
On a sunshine holiday,
Till the livelong daylight fail;
Then to the spicy nut-brown ale,
With stories told of many a feat,
How fairy Mab the junkets eat;
She was pinched and pulled, she said,
And he, by friar's lanthorn led,
Tells how the drudging goblin sweat,
To earn his cream-bowl duly set,
When in one night, ere glimpse of morn,
His shadowy flail hath threshed the corn
That ten day-laborers could not end;
Then lies him down the lubber fend,

And stretched out all the chimney's length,
Basks at the fire his hairy strength;
And crop-full out of doors he flings,
Ere the first cock his matin rings.
Thus done the tales, to bed they creep,
By whispering winds soon lulled asleep.
Towered cities please us then,
And the busy hum of men,
Where throngs of knights and barons bold
In weeds of peace high triumphs hold,
With store of ladies, whose bright eyes
Rain influence, and judge the prize
Of wit or arms, while both contend
To win her grace whom all commend.
There let Hymen oft appear
In saffron robe, with taper clear,
And pomp, and feast, and revelry,
With masque and antique pageantry:
Such sights as youthful poets dream
On summer eves by haunted stream.
Then to the well-trod stage anon,
If Jonson's learnèd sock be on,
Or sweetest Shakespeare, Fancy's child,
Warble his native wood-notes wild;
And ever against eating cares,
Lap me in soft Lydian airs,
Married to immortal verse,
Such as the meeting soul may pierce
In notes with many a winding bout
Of linkèd sweetness long drawn out,
With wanton heed and giddy cunning,
The melting voice through mazes running,
Untwisting all the chains that tie
The hidden soul of harmony;
That Orpheus' self may heave his head
From golden slumber on a bed
Of heaped Elysian flowers, and hear
Such strains as would have won the ear

Of Pluto, to have quite set free
His half-regained Eurydice.
These delights if thou canst give,
Mirth, with thee I mean to live.

Milton, like Browning, delighted in complementary companion poems, a classification that suits Paradise Lost *and* Paradise Regained *as well as the pair of set pieces* "L'Allegro" *("The Mirthful Man") and* "Il Penseroso" *("The Thoughtful Man"). (Note that: "buxom" is "jolly"; "dight" is "decked," "dressed"; "secure" is "carefree"; "friar's lantern" is "will-o'-the-wisp"; "lubber" is "crude"; "weeds" is "clothing.")*

Il Penseroso

Hence vain deluding Joys,
  The brood of Folly without father bred,
How little you bestead,
  Or fill the fixèd mind with all your toys;
Dwell in some idle brain,
  And fancies fond with gaudy shapes possess,
As thick and numberless
  As the gay motes that people the sunbeams,
Or likest hovering dreams,
  The fickle pensioners of Morpheus' train.
But hail thou Goddess, sage and holy,
Hail divinest Melancholy,
Whose saintly visage is too bright
To hit the sense of human sight,
And therefore to our weaker view
O'erlaid with black, staid Wisdom's hue;
Black, but such as in esteem
Prince Memnon's sister might beseem,
Or that starred Ethiop queen that strove
To set her beauty's praise above
The sea nymphs, and their powers offended;
Yet thou art higher far descended:
Thee bright-haired Vesta long of yore
To solitary Saturn bore;
His daughter she (in Saturn's reign
Such mixture was not held a stain).
Oft in glimmering bowers and glades
He met her, and in secret shades
Of woody Ida's inmost grove,
Whilst yet there was no fear of Jove.
Come pensive Nun, devout and pure,
Sober, steadfast, and demure,
All in a robe of darkest grain,
Flowing with majestic train,

And sable stole of cypress lawn,
Over thy decent shoulders drawn.
Come, but keep thy wonted state,
With even step and musing gait,
And looks commercing with the skies,
Thy rapt soul sitting in thine eyes;
There held in holy passion still,
Forget thyself to marble, till
With a sad leaden downward cast,
Thou fix them on the earth as fast.
And join with thee calm Peace and Quiet,
Spare Fast, that oft with gods doth diet,
And hears the Muses in a ring
Aye round above Jove's altar sing.
and add to these retired Leisure,
That in trim gardens takes his pleasure;
But first and chiefest, with thee bring
Him that yon soars on golden wing,
Guiding the fiery-wheelèd throne,
The Cherub Contemplation;
And the mute Silence hist along,
'Less Philomel will deign a song,
In her sweetest, saddest plight,
Smoothing the rugged brow of Night,
While Cynthia checks her dragon yoke,
Gently o'er th' accustomed oak;
Sweet bird that shunn'st the noise of folly,
Most musical, most melancholy!
Thee, chauntress, oft the woods among,
I woo to hear thy evensong;
And missing thee, I walk unseen
On the dry smooth-shaven green,
To behold the wandering moon,
Riding near her highest noon,
Like one that had been led astray
Through the heavens' wide pathless way;
And oft, as if her head she bowed,
Stooping through a fleecy cloud.

Oft on a plat of rising ground
I hear the far-off curfew sound,
Over some wide-watered shore,
Swinging slow with sullen roar;
Or if the air will not permit,
Some still, removèd place will fit,
Where glowing embers through the room
Teach light to counterfeit a gloom,
Far from all resort of mirth,
Save the cricket on the hearth,
Or the bellman's drowsy charm,
To bless the doors from nightly harm.
Or let my lamp at midnight hour
Be seen in some high lonely tower,
Where I may oft outwatch the Bear,
With thrice-great Hermes, or unsphere
The spirit of Plato to unfold
What worlds or what vast regions hold
Th' immortal mind that hath forsook
Her mansion in this fleshly nook;
And of those daemons that are found
In fire, air, flood, or under ground,
Whose power hath a true consent
With planet or with element.
Sometime let gorgeous Tragedy
In sceptered pall come sweeping by,
Presenting Thebes, or Pelops' line,
Or the tale of Troy divine,
Or what (though rare) of later age
Ennobled hath the buskined stage.
But, O sad Virgin, that thy power
Might raise Musaeus from his bower,
Or bid the soul of Orpheus sing
Such notes as, warbled to the string,
Drew iron tears down Pluto's cheek,
And made Hell grant what love did seek;
Or call up him that left half told
The story of Cambuscan bold,

Of Camball, and of Algarsife,
And who had Canace to wife,
That owned the virtuous ring and glass,
And of the wondrous horse of brass,
On which the Tartar king did ride;
And if aught else great bards beside
In sage and solemn tunes have sung,
Of tourneys and of trophies hung,
Of forests and enchantments drear,
Where more is meant than meets the ear.
Thus Night oft see me in thy pale career,
Till civil-suited Morn appear,
Not tricked and frounced as she was wont
With the Attic boy to hunt,
But kerchiefed in a comely cloud,
While rocking winds are piping loud,
Or ushered with a shower still,
When the gust hath blown his fill,
Ending on the rustling leaves,
With minute-drops from off the eaves.
And when the sun begins to fling
His flaring beams, me Goddess bring
To archèd walks of twilight groves,
And shadows brown that Sylvan loves,
Of pine or monumental oak,
Where the rude axe with heavèd stroke
Was never heard the nymphs to daunt,
Or fright them from their hallowed haunt.
There in close covert by some brook,
Where no profaner eye may look,
Hide me from Day's garish eye,
While the bee with honied thigh,
That at her flowery work doth sing,
And the waters murmuring,
With such consort as they keep,
Entice the dewy-feathered Sleep;
And let some strange mysterious dream
Wave at his wings in airy stream

Of lively portraiture displayed,
Softly on my eyelids laid.
And as I wake, sweet music breathe
Above, about, or underneath,
Sent by some spirit to mortals good,
Or th' unseen Genius of the wood.
But let my due feet never fail
To walk the studious cloister's pale,
And love the high embowèd roof,
With antic pillars massy proof,
And storied windows richly dight,
Casting a dim, religious light.
There let the pealing organ blow
To the full-voiced choir below,
In service high and anthems clear,
As may with sweetness, through mine ear,
Dissolve me into ecstasies,
And bring all Heaven before mine eyes.
And may at last my weary age
Find out the peaceful hermitage,
The hairy gown and mossy cell,
Where I may sit and rightly spell
Of every star that heaven doth show,
And every herb that sips the dew;
Till old experience do attain
To something like prophetic strain.
These pleasures Melancholy give,
And I with thee will choose to live.

It seems significant that "Il Penseroso," though beginning and ending with the same words as "L'Allegro," should be longer by two dozen lines. Readers of long poems seem to prefer the dark to the light, putting Paradise Lost *and Dante's* Inferno *ahead of* Paradise Regained *and the* Paradiso; *but, among short poems, "L'Allegro" is somewhat more popular than "Il Penseroso." (Note that: "bestead" is "profit"; "hit" is "affect"; "hist" is "summon"; "plat" is "plot"; "virtuous" is "powerful"; "frounced" is "curled"; "dight" is "decked," "dressed"; "spell" is "speculate.")*

Sir John Suckling 1609–1642

The son of a knight who had served as Secretary of
State and Comptroller of the Household under James I,
Suckling was born in Middlesex and educated at Cam-
bridge. He was a loyal supporter of Charles I; he fled
to the Continent early in the Civil War and died in
Paris, purportedly a suicide. John Aubrey credits
Suckling with the invention of cribbage.

Why So Pale and Wan, Fond Lover?

>>>>>>>

Why so pale and wan, fond lover?
   Prithee, why so pale?
Will, when looking well can't move her,
   Looking ill prevail?
   Prithee, why so pale?

Why so dull and mute, young sinner?
   Prithee, why so mute?
Will, when speaking well can't win her,
   Saying nothing do't?
   Prithee, why so mute?

Quit, quit, for shame; this will not move,
   This cannot take her.
If of herself she will not love,
   Nothing can make her:
   The devil take her!

from Aglaura

---

*This easy song has a good deal of prosodic sophistication as well as rhetorical
drama: in one dimension, the speaker works against the lover (who may be
himself); in another, the speaker and lover work together against the woman.
And the percussively reiterated questions work against the final imperative,
"Quit, quit."*

ANNE BRADSTREET c.1612–1672

Anne Bradstreet was the daughter of one governor of the Massachusetts Bay Colony (Thomas Dudley) and the wife of another (Simon Bradstreet). She came to America at age eighteen, raised eight children, and lived to see her work published in 1650 as *The Tenth Muse Lately Sprung Up in America.*

To My Dear and Loving Husband

If ever two were one, then surely we.
If ever man were loved by wife, then thee;
If ever wife was happy in a man,
Compare with me, ye women, if you can.
I prize thy love more then whole mines of gold,
Or all the riches that the East doth hold.
My love is such that rivers cannot quench,
Nor aught but love from thee, give recompense.
Thy love is such I can no way repay,
The heavens reward thee manifold, I pray.
Then while we live, in love let's so persever
That when we live no more, we may live ever.

Anne Bradstreet considered her poems her "offspring" (see Jonson's "On My First Son," p. 158). Three centuries after the first publication of her poems, John Berryman produced Homage to Mistress Bradstreet.

Lovelace was gifted, handsome, amiable, and wealthy, but he lost everything in supporting the Royalist cause. His most durable poems reflect the circumstances of his turbulent life: he really was in prison (in 1642, for supporting the King), and he really did go to the wars, fighting and being wounded.

To Lucasta, Going to the Wars

Tell me not, Sweet, I am unkind
   That from the nunnery
Of thy chaste breast and quiet mind,
   To war and arms I fly.

True, a new mistress now I chase,
   The first foe in the field;
And with a stronger faith embrace
   A sword, a horse, a shield.

Yet this inconstancy is such
   As you too shall adore;
I could not love thee, Dear, so much,
   Loved I not Honour more.

The real name of Lovelace's fiancée was Lucy Sacheverell. He did, in fact, love honor more than Lucy-Lucasta, and he did, in fact, go to war. When, by an error, his death was reported to her, she married somebody else. The quaint argument may seem silly today when ideals of chivalry and honor have just about perished.

To Althea, from Prison

When Love with unconfinèd wings
  Hovers within my gates,
And my divine Althea brings
  To whisper at the grates;
When I lie tangled in her hair
  And fetter'd to her eye,
The birds that wanton in the air
  Know no such liberty.

When flowing cups run swiftly round
  With no allaying Thames,
Our careless heads with roses bound,
  Our hearts with loyal flames;
When thirsty grief in wine we steep,
  When healths and draughts go free —
Fishes that tipple in the deep
  Know no such liberty.

When, like committed linnets, I
  With shriller throat shall sing
The sweetness, mercy, majesty,
  And glories of my King;
When I shall voice aloud how good
  He is, how great should be,
Enlargèd winds, that curl the flood,
  Know no such liberty.

Stone walls do not a prison make,
  Nor iron bars a cage;
Minds innocent and quiet take
  That for an hermitage;
If I have freedom in my love
  And in my soul am free,
Angels alone, that soar above,
  Enjoy such liberty.

Lovelace wrote this song while incarcerated for his Royalist views in 1642. Lovelace can coin memorable paradoxical phrases—e.g., "Stone walls do not a prison make"—but there is nothing farfetched about the sentiment. His eloquence is matched only by his sincerity.

The Grasshopper

O thou that swing'st upon the waving hair
  Of some well-filled oaten beard,
Drunk every night with a delicious tear
  Dropp'd thee from heav'n where now th' art rear'd;

The joys of earth and air are thine entire,
  That with thy feet and wings dost hop and fly;
And when thy poppy works, thou dost retire
  To thy carv'd acorn-bed to lie.

Up with the day, the sun thou welcomest then,
  Sport'st in the gilt plats of his beams,
And all these merry days mak'st merry men,
  Thyself, and melancholy streams.

But ah the sickle! golden ears are cropp'd,
  Ceres and Bacchus bid good night;
Sharp frosty fingers all your flow'rs have topp'd,
  And what scythes spar'd, winds shave off quite.

Poor verdant fool, and now green ice! thy joys,
  Large and as lasting as thy perch of grass,
Bid us lay in 'gainst winter rain, and poise
  Their floods with an o'erflowing glass.

Thou best of men and friends! we will create
  A genuine summer in each other's breast;
And spite of this cold time and frozen fate,
  Thaw us a warm seat to our rest.

Our sacred hearths shall burn eternally
   As vestal flames; the North-wind, he
Shall strike his frost-stretch'd wings, dissolve, and fly
   This Ætna in epitome.

Dropping December shall come weeping in,
   Bewail th' usurping of his reign;
But when in showers of old Greek we begin,
   Shall cry he hath his crown again.

Night as clear Hesper shall our tapers whip
   From the light casements where we play,
And the dark hag from her black mantle strip,
   And stick there everlasting day.

Thus richer than untempted kings are we,
   That asking nothing, nothing need:
Though lord of all what seas embrace, yet he
   That wants himself is poor indeed.

The cautionary fable invoked here reaches from Aesop in the 6th century, B.C., to the episode of the Ondt and the Gracehoper in James Joyce's Finnegans Wake *(1939). Since Lovelace was loyal to the Crown, the grasshopper may stand for the Cavaliers in "this cold time" after the establishment of the Commonwealth in 1649. (Note that: "gilt-plats" is "gold-colored meadows"; "poise" is "counterbalance"; "strike" is "fold.")*

ANDREW MARVELL 1621–1678

Marvell was born in Yorkshire and educated at Cambridge. Like Edmund Waller, he was a Member of Parliament, and in a busy career he served both the court of Charles II and the Cromwellians. Marvell assisted Milton for a time in the Latin Secretaryship to the Council of State. Marvell was a celebrated controversialist and satirist as well as a splendid lyric poet.

To His Coy Mistress

Had we but world enough and time,
This coyness, Lady, were no crime.
We would sit down and think which way
To walk, and pass our long love's day.
Thou by the Indian Ganges' side
Shouldst rubies find; I by the tide
Of Humber would complain. I would
Love you ten years before the Flood,
And you should, if you please, refuse
Till the Conversion of the Jews.
My vegetable love should grow
Vaster than empires, and more slow.
An hundred years should go to praise
Thine eyes, and on thy forehead gaze,
Two hundred to adore each breast,
But thirty thousand to the rest.
An age at least to every part,
And the last age should show your heart.
For, Lady, you deserve this state,
Nor would I love at lower rate.
     But at my back I always hear
Time's winged chariot hurrying near,
And yonder all before us lie
Deserts of vast eternity.

Thy beauty shall no more be found,
Nor in thy marble vault shall sound
My echoing song; then worms shall try
That long preserved virginity,
And your quaint honor turn to dust,
And into ashes all my lust.
The grave's a fine and private place,
But none, I think, do there embrace.
   Now therefore, while the youthful hue
Sits on thy skin like morning glew,
And while thy willing soul transpires
At every pore with instant fires,
Now let us sport us while we may;
And now, like amorous birds of prey,
Rather at once our time devour
Than languish in his slow-chapped power.
Let us roll all our strength and all
Our sweetness up into one ball
And tear our pleasures with rough strife
Thorough the iron gates of life.
Thus, though we cannot make our sun
Stand still, yet we will make him run.

---

*T. S. Eliot noticed that this great poem of seduction has a lucidly logical struc-
ture: (1) If we had time, you could hold out; (2) We don't have time; (3) "Now
therefore . . . ." Like Herrick's "To the Virgins, to Make Much of Time" (p.
172), this poem belongs to the category of* carpe diem: *seize the day. The poem
also partakes of that special kind of erotic encomium called a* blason, *usually
a top-to-toe inventory of physical attractions (but see also Hopkins's "Habit of
Perfection," p. 800).*

The Garden

How vainly men themselves amaze
To win the palm, the oak, or bays,
And their incessant labors see
Crown'd from some single herb or tree,
Whose short and narrow-vergèd shade
Does prudently their toils upbraid;
While all flowers and all trees do close
To weave the garlands of repose!

Fair Quiet, have I found thee here,
And Innocence, thy sister dear?
Mistaken long, I sought you then
In busy companies of men:
Your sacred plants, if here below,
Only among the plants will grow:
Society is all but rude
To this delicious solitude.

No white nor red was ever seen
So amorous as this lovely green.
Fond lovers, cruel as their flame,
Cut in these trees their mistress' name:
Little, alas! they know or heed
How far these beauties hers exceed!
Fair trees, wheresoe'er your barks I wound,
No name shall but your own be found.

When we have run our passion's heat,
Love hither makes his best retreat:
The gods, that mortal beauty chase,
Still in a tree did end their race;
Apollo hunted Daphne so
Only that she might laurel grow;
And Pan did after Syrinx speed
Not as a nymph, but for a reed.

What wondrous life in this I lead!
Ripe apples drop about my head;
The luscious clusters of the vine
Upon my mouth do crush their wine;
The nectarine and curious peach
Into my hands themselves do reach;
Stumbling on melons, as I pass,
Ensnared with flowers, I fall on grass.

Meanwhile the mind from pleasure less
Withdraws into its happiness;
The mind, that ocean where each kind
Does straight its own resemblance find;
Yet it creates, transcending these,
Far other worlds, and other seas;
Annihilating all that's made
To a green thought in a green shade,

Here at the fountain's sliding foot,
Or at some fruit-tree's mossy root,
Casting the body's vest aside,
My soul into the boughs does glide;
There, like a bird, it sits and sings,
Then whets and combs its silver wings,
And, till prepared for longer flight,
Waves in its plumes the various light.

Such was that happy Garden-state
While man there walked without a mate:
After a place so pure and sweet,
What other help could yet be meet!
But 'twas beyond a mortal's share
To wander solitary there:
Two paradises 'twere in one,
To live in Paradise alone.

How well the skillful gard'ner drew
Of flowers and herbs, this dial new!
Where, from above, the milder sun
Does through a fragrant zodiac run:
And, as it works, th' industrious bee
Computes its time as well as we.
How could such sweet and wholesome hours
Be reckon'd but with herbs and flowers!

In ridiculing the use of certain trees for emblematic purposes (palms for athletes, bays for poetry) and highlighting the cruelty of carving in the bark of trees, Marvell offers a revisionist reading of ancient myths, suggesting that metamorphoses, such as those of Daphne and Syrinx, were by design, and that Adam's loss of paradise dated from the introduction of Eve.

The Definition of Love

My love is of a birth as rare
As 'tis for object strange and high;
It was begotten by despair
Upon impossibility.

Magnanimous despair alone
Could show me so divine a thing,
Where feeble hope could ne'er have flown,
But vainly flapped its tinsel wing.

And yet I quickly might arrive
Where my extended soul is fixed,
But fate does iron wedges drive,
And always crowds itself betwixt.

For fate with jealous eye does see
Two perfect loves, nor lets them close;
Their union would her ruin be,
And her tyrannic power depose.

And therefore her decrees of steel
Us as the distant poles have placed,
Though love's whole world on us doth wheel,
Not by themselves to be embraced;

Unless the giddy heaven fall,
And earth some new convulsion tear,
And, us to join, the world should all
Be cramped into a planisphere.

As lines, so loves, oblique may well
Themselves in every angle greet;
But ours so truly parallel,
Though infinite, can never meet.

Therefore the love which us doth bind,
But fate so enviously debars,
Is the conjunction of the mind,
And opposition of the stars.

As scholars have noted, the defining at work here is not only the familiar affair of telling what something is, but it is also the setting of a limit or boundary. This love, offspring of Despair and Impossibility, is utterly thwarted. (Note that: "close" is "unite"; "planisphere" is a flat two-dimensional representation of three-dimensional reality.)

Bermudas

Where the remote Bermudas ride,
In the Ocean's bosom unespied,
From a small boat, that rowed along,
The listening winds received this song:

"What should we do but sing His praise,
That led us through the watery maze,
Unto an isle so long unknown,
And yet far kinder than our own?
Where He the huge sea-monsters wracks
That lift the deep upon their backs,
He lands us on a grassy stage,
Safe from the storms' and prelates' rage:
He gave us this eternal Spring
Which here enamels everything,
And sends the fowls to us in care
On daily visits through the air:
He hangs in shades the orange bright,
Like golden lamps in a green night,
And does in the pomegranates close
Jewels more rich than Ormus shows;
He makes the figs our mouths to meet,
And throws the melons at our feet;
But apples plants of such a price
No tree could ever bear them twice.
With cedars, chosen by His hand
From Lebanon, He stores the land,
And makes the hollow seas, that roar,
Proclaim the ambergris on shore.
He cast (of which we rather boast)
The Gospel's pearl upon our coast;
And in these rocks for us did frame
A temple where to sound His name.

Oh! let our voice His praise exalt,
Till it arrive at Heaven's vault,
Which, thence (perhaps) rebounding, may
Echo beyond the Mexique bay."

Thus sung they, in the English boat,
A holy and a cheerful note;
And all the way, to guide their chime,
With falling oars they kept the time.

Juan de Bermúdez discovered the island group that bears his name early in the sixteenth century. Reports of the fine vegetation and weather formed part of the inspiration of Shakespeare's Tempest. *Some Puritans known to Marvell sought refuge there. Marvell travelled all over Europe, including Denmark and Russia, but never visited the islands. (Note that: "apples" is "pineapples.")*

An Horatian Ode
upon Cromwell's Return from Ireland

>>>>>>>

The forward Youth that would appear
Must now forsake his Muses dear,
   Nor in the Shadows sing
   His Numbers languishing.
'Tis time to leave the Books in dust,
And oyl th' unused Armours rust:
   Removing from the Wall
   The Corslet of the Hall.
So restless Cromwel could not cease
In the inglorious Arts of Peace,
   But through adventrous War
   Urged his active Star:
And, like the three-fork'd Lightning, first
Breaking the Clouds where it was nurst,
   Did thorough his own Side
   His fiery way divide.
For 'tis all one to Courage high
The Emulous or Enemy;
   And with such to inclose
   Is more then to oppose.
Then burning through the Air he went,
And Pallaces and Temples rent:
   And Caesars head at last
   Did through his Laurels blast.
'Tis Madness to resist or blame
The force of angry Heavens flame;
   And, if we would speak true,
   Much to the Man is due:
Who, from his private Gardens, where
He liv'd reserved and austere,
   As if his highest plot
   To plant the Bergamot,

Could by industrious Valour climbe
To ruine the great Work of Time,
  And cast the Kingdoms old
  Into another Mold.
Though Justice against Fate complain,
And plead the antient Rights in vain:
  But those do hold or break
  As Men are strong or weak.
Nature that hateth emptiness,
Allows of penetration less:
  And therefore must make room
  Where greater Spirits come.
What Field of all the Civil Wars
Where his were not the deepest Scars?
  And Hampton shows what part
  He had of wiser Art:
Where, twining subtile fears with hope,
He wove a Net of such a scope,
  That Charles himself might chase
  To Caresbrooks narrow case:
That thence the *Royal Actor* born
The Tragick Scaffold might adorn,
  While round the armed Bands
  Did clap their bloody hands.
He nothing common did, or mean,
Upon the memorable Scene:
  But with his keener Eye
  The Axes edge did try:
Nor call'd the Gods with vulgar spight
To vindicate his helpless Right,
  But bow'd his comely Head
  Down, as upon a Bed.
This was that memorable Hour
Which first assur'd the forced Pow'r.
  So when they did design
  The Capitols first Line,
A bleeding Head where they begun,
Did fright the Architects to run;

And yet in that the State
Foresaw its happy Fate.
And now the Irish are asham'd
To see themselves in one Year tam'd:
So much one Man can do,
That does both act and know.
They can affirm his Praises best,
And have, though overcome, confest
How good he is, how just,
And fit for highest Trust:
Nor yet grown stiffer with Command,
But still in the Republick's hand:
How fit he is to sway
That can so well obey.
He to the Commons Feet presents
A Kingdome, for his first years rents:
And, what he may, forbears
His Fame to make it theirs:
And has his Sword and Spoyls ungirt,
To lay them at the Publick's skirt.
So when the Falcon high
Falls heavy from the Sky,
She, having kill'd, no more does search,
But on the next green Bow to pearch;
Where, when he first does lure,
The Falckner has her sure.
What may not then our Isle presume
While Victory his Crest does plume;
What may not others fear,
If thus he crown each Year!
A Caesar he ere long to Gaul,
To Italy an Hannibal,
And to all States not free
Shall Clymacterick be.
The Pict no shelter now shall find
Within his party-colour'd Mind;
But from this Valour sad
Shrink underneath the Plad:

Happy if in the tufted brake
The English Hunter him mistake,
   Nor lay his Hounds in near
   The Caledonian Deer.
But thou the Wars and Fortunes Son
March indefatigably on,
   And for the last effect
   Still keep thy Sword erect:
Besides the force it has to fright
The Spirits of the shady Night;
   The same Arts that did gain
   A Pow'r must it maintain.

Frank Kermode and Keith Walker have said of Marvell's state of mind in the spring of 1650, when Oliver Cromwell came back from his expedition to Ireland, "The reason why there is so much uncertainty about his position is that . . . he expressed himself not in prose but in poetry, with a higher degree of obliquity and a concern for more than topical significance. 'An Horatian Ode on Cromwell's Return from Ireland' is a manifestly great poem, yet it is also baffling to anybody who wants simply to know where the poet stood with Cromwell in 1650." (Note that: "bergamot" is a pear-shaped citrus fruit; "climacteric" is "crucial time.")

The Picture of Little T. C. in a Prospect of Flowers

See with what simplicity
This nymph begins her golden days!
   In the green grass she loves to lie,
And there with her fair aspect tames
The wilder flowers, and gives them names;
   But only with the roses plays,
      And them does tell
What colour best becomes them, and what smell.

Who can foretell for what high cause
This darling of the gods was born?
   Yet this is she whose chaster laws
The wanton Love shall one day fear,
And, under her command severe,
   See his bow broke and ensigns torn.
      Happy who can
Appease this virtuous enemy of man!

O then let me in time compound
And parley with those conquering eyes,
   Ere they have tried their force to wound;
Ere with their glancing wheels they drive
In triumph over hearts that strive,
   And them that yield but more despise:
      Let me be laid,
Where I may see thy glories from some shade.

Meantime, whilst every verdant thing
Itself does at thy beauty charm,
   Reform the errors of the Spring;
Make that the tulips may have share
Of sweetness, seeing they are fair,
   And roses of their thorns disarm;
      But most procure
That violets may a longer age endure.

But O, young beauty of the woods,
Whom Nature courts with fruits and flowers,
   Gather the flowers, but spare the buds;
Lest Flora, angry at thy crime
To kill her infants in their prime,
   Do quickly make the example yours;
      And ere we see,
Nip in the blossom all our hopes and thee.

The title initials are thought to belong to a child named Theophila Cornewall. Her first name, which means "Beloved of God," may be referred to in line 10 ("darling of the gods"). Marvell's curious title has caught the fancy of modern poets: consider Charles Tomlinson's "Picture of J. T. in a Prospect of Stone" and John Ashbery's "Picture of Little J. A. in a Prospect of Flowers."

The Mower to the Glow-Worms

Ye living lamps, by whose dear light
The nightingale does sit so late
And studying all the summer night,
Her matchless songs does meditate;

Ye country comets, that portend
No war, nor prince's funeral,
Shining unto no higher end
Than to presage the grasses' fall;

Ye glow-worms, whose officious flame
To wandering mowers shows the way,
That in the night have lost their aim,
And after foolish fires do stray;

Your courteous lights in vain you waste,
Since Juliana here is come,
For she my mind hath so displaced
That I shall never find my home.

At various stages of their lives, members of the well-named Lampyridae family are called glow-worms, fireflies, lightning bugs, and lightning beetles. Poets from all over the world have loved them for centuries. They are magnets for all sorts of lore and literature. Marvell gets a good deal of charm and information into a short, modest poem. (Note that: "foolish fires"—ignes fatui in Latin—is the spooky light from burning marsh-gas, also called "will-o'-the-wisp" and "jack-o'-lantern"; "officious" is "obliging.")

A Dialogue between the Soul and Body

SOUL:
   O who shall from this dungeon raise
A soul enslaved so many ways?
With bolts of bones, that fettered stands
In feet; and manacled in hands:
Here blinded with an eye; and there
Deaf with the drumming of an ear;
A soul hung up, as 'twere, in chains
Of nerves, and arteries, and veins;
Tortured, besides each other part,
In a vain head and double heart.

BODY:
   O who shall me deliver whole
From bonds of this tyrannic soul?
Which, stretched upright, impales me so
That mine own precipice I go;
And warms and moves this needless frame
(A fever could but do the same);
And, wanting where its spite to try,
Has made me live to let me die;
A body that could never rest,
Since this ill spirit it possessed.

SOUL:

        What magic could me thus confine
Within another's grief to pine?
Where whatsoever it complain,
I feel, that cannot feel, the pain.
And all my care itself employs
That to preserve, which me destroys;
Constrained not only to endure
Diseases, but, what's worse, the cure;
And ready oft the port to gain,
Am shipwrecked into health again.

BODY:

        But physic yet could never reach
The maladies thou me dost teach:
Whom first the cramp of hope does tear;
And then the palsy shakes of fear;
The pestilence of love does heat;
Or hatred's hidden ulcer eat;
Joy's cheerful madness does perplex,
Or sorrow's other madness vex;
Which knowledge forces me to know,
And memory will not forgo.
What but a soul could have the wit
To build me up for sin so fit?
So architects do square and hew
Green trees that in the forest grew.

There is bibliographical evidence that much of Marvell's poem has been lost. The loss is all the more regrettable in view of Marvell's genius in giving both contestants such interesting and original arguments. (Note that: "needless" is "not in need"; "physic" is "medicine.")

Since Henry Vaughan and his twin brother Thomas were born in a part of Wales once inhabited by a tribe called the Silures, Vaughan styled himself a "Silurist." He studied both law and medicine, and his poems are saturated with religious feeling. Vaughan was extraordinarily devoted to the memory of George Herbert and modelled his own writings on those in Herbert's *The Temple*. Vaughan's passionate feelings affected Wordsworth very strongly, a century after Vaughan's death.

The Retreat

Happy those early days! when I
Shined in my angel-infancy.
Before I understood this place
Appointed for my second race,
Or taught my soul to fancy ought
But a white, celestial thought,
When yet I had not walked above
A mile or two, from my first love,
And looking back (at that short space)
Could see a glimpse of his bright face;
When on some *gilded cloud* or *flower*
My gazing soul would dwell an hour,
And in those weaker glories spy
Some shadows of eternity;
Before I taught my tongue to wound
My conscience with a sinful sound,
Or had the black art to dispense
A sev'ral sin to ev'ry sense,
But felt through all this fleshly dress
Bright *shoots* of everlastingness.
　O, how I long to travel back
And tread again that ancient track!

That I might once more reach that plain,
Where first I left my glorious train;
From whence th' inlightened spirit sees
That shady city of palm trees;
But (ah!) my soul with too much stay
Is drunk, and staggers in the way.
Some men a forward motion love,
But I by backward steps would move,
And when this dust falls to the urn
In that state I came, return.

"Retreat" means both a movement backward and a place of shelter. Vaughan plays also on the "re-" prefix that means both "back" and "again" in the title and the last word. This poem is a precursor of Wordsworth's "Intimations" ode (p. 400).

The World

I saw Eternity the other night,
Like a great ring of pure and endless light,
  All calm, as it was bright;
And round beneath it, time in hours, days, years,
  Driven by the spheres
Like a vast shadow moved; in which the world
  And all her train were hurled:
The doting lover in his quaintest strain
  Did there complain;
Near him, his lute, his fancy, and his flights,
  Wit's sour delights,
With gloves and knots, the silly snares of pleasure,
  Yet his dear treasure,
All scattered lay, while he his eyes did pour
  Upon a flower.

The darksome statesman, hung with weights and woe,
Like a thick midnight-fog, moved there so slow,
  He did not stay, nor go;
Condemning thoughts, like sad eclipses, scowl
  Upon his soul,
And clouds of crying witnesses without
  Pursued him with one shout;
Yet digged the mole, and lest his ways be found
  Worked underground,
Where he did clutch his prey, but One did see
  That policy;
Churches and altars fed him; perjuries
  Were gnats and flies;
It rained about him blood and tears, but he
  Drank them as free.

The fearful miser on a heap of rust
Sat pining all his life there, did scarce trust
   His own hands with the dust,
Yet would not place one piece above, but lives
   In fear of thieves.
Thousands there were as frantic as himself,
   And hugged each one his pelf:
The downright epicure placed heav'n in sense,
   And scorned pretense;
While others, slipped into a wide excess,
   Said little less;
The weaker sort slight trivial wares enslave,
   Who think them brave;
And poor, despised Truth sat counting by
   Their victory.

Yet some, who all this while did weep and sing,
And sing and weep, soared up into the ring;
   But most would use no wing.
O fools, said I, thus to prefer dark night
   Before true light!
To live in grots and caves, and hate the day
   Because it shows the way;
The way which from this dead and dark abode
   Leads up to God;
A way where you might tread the sun, and be
   More bright than he!
But as I did their madness so discuss,
   One whispered thus:
This ring the Bridegroom did for none provide
   But for His bride.

Even after 350 years, Vaughan's genius retains its peculiar power to astonish. The grandeur of "I saw Eternity" is balanced by the colloquial humility of "the other night." Throughout, the poem—a detailed gloss on First John II:16–17— keeps both the grand vision and the common touch; each element validates the other. (Note that: "brave" is "flashy.")

They Are All Gone
into the World of Light

They are all gone into the world of light!
  And I alone sit ling'ring here;
There very memory is fair and bright,
    And my sad thoughts doth clear.

It glows and glitters in my cloudy breast,
  Like stars upon some gloomy grove,
Or those faint beams in which this hill is dressed,
    After the sun's remove.

I see them walking in an air of glory,
  Whose light doth trample on my days:
My days, which are at best but dull and hoary,
    Mere glimmering and decays.

O holy Hope! and high Humility,
  High as the heavens above!
These are your walks, and you have showed them me,
    To kindle my cold love.

Dear, beauteous Death! the jewel of the just,
  Shining nowhere, but in the dark;
What mysteries do lie beyond thy dust,
    Could man outlook that mark!

He that hath found some fledged bird's nest, may know
  At first sight if the bird be flown;
But what fair well or grove he sings in now,
    That is to him unknown.

And yet, as angels in some brighter dreams
   Call to the soul when man doth sleep,
So some strange thoughts transcend our wonted themes,
    And into glory peep.

If a star were confin'd into a tomb,
   Her captive flames must needs burn there;
But when the hand that locked her up, gives room,
    She'll shine through all the sphere.

O Father of eternal life, and all
   Created glories under Thee!
Resume Thy spirit from this world of thrall
    Into true liberty.

Either disperse these mists, which blot and fill
   My perspective, still, as they pass:
Or else remove me hence unto that hill
    Where I shall need no glass.

Most of Vaughan's material here is biblical, but the imagery of the last stanza relies on the technology of the mid-seventeenth century. "Perspective" means "telescope"; the "glass" at the end is primarily a telescope but also secondarily alludes to the metal mirror in First Corinthians XIII in the Bible (about seeing "through a glass darkly").

Peace

❖❖❖❖

My soul, there is a country
    Far beyond the stars,
Where stands a winged sentry
    All skillful in the wars.
There, above noise and danger,
    Sweet Peace sits crowned with smiles,
And One born in a manger
    Commands the beauteous files.
He is thy gracious friend,
    And (Oh, my Soul awake!)
Did in pure love descend
    To die here for thy sake.
If thou canst get but thither,
    There grows the flower of peace,
The rose that cannot wither,
    Thy fortress and thy ease;
Leave then thy foolish ranges;
    For none can thee secure
But One who never changes,
    Thy God, thy life, thy cure.

As is typical of Vaughan's best poems, "Peace" combines a cosmic vision with ordinary diction, as in the most memorable passage "If thou canst get but thither . . . ." (we still say "get" in this sense).

The Night

Through that pure Virgin-shrine,
That sacred veil drawn o'er thy glorious noon
That men might look and live as glow-worms shine,
    And face the moon,
  Wise Nicodemus saw such light
  As made him know his God by night.

    Most blest believer he!
Who in that land of darkness and blind eyes
Thy long-expected healing wings could see,
    When thou didst rise,
  And what can never more be done
  Did at midnight speak with the Sun!

    O who will tell me where
He found thee at that dead and silent hour!
What hallowed solitary ground did bear
    So rare a flower,
  Within whose sacred leaves did lie
  The fullness of the Deity.

    No mercy-seat of gold,
No dead and dusty *Cherub*, nor carv'd stone,
But his own living works did my Lord hold
    And lodge alone;
  Where *trees* and *herbs* did watch and peep
  And wonder, while the *Jews* did sleep.

    Dear night! this worlds defeat;
The stop to busie fools; cares check and curb;
The day of Spirits; my souls calm retreat
    Which none disturb!
  Christs progress, and his prayer time;
  The hours to which high Heaven doth chime.

Gods silent, searching flight:
When my Lords head is fill'd with dew, and all
His locks are wet with the clear drops of night;
        His still, soft call;
    His knocking time; The souls dumb watch,
    When Spirits their fair kinred catch.

    Were all my loud, evil days
Calm and unhaunted as is thy dark Tent,
Whose peace but by some *Angels* wing or voice
        Is seldom rent;
    Then I in Heaven all the long year
    Would keep, and never wander here.

    But living where the Sun
Doth all things wake, and where all mix and tyre
Themselves and others, I consent and run
        To ev'ry myre,
    And by this worlds ill-guiding light,
    Erre more then I can do by night.

    There is in God (some say)
A deep, but dazling darkness; As men here
Say it is late and dusky, because they
        See not all clear;
    O for that night! where I in him
    Might live invisible and dim.

The reference to John III:2 in the Bible concerns Nicodemus, who "came to Jesus by night, and said unto him, Rabbi, we know that thou art a teacher come from God: for no man can do these miracles that thou doest, except God be with him." T. S. Eliot's "Mr. Eliot's Sunday Morning Service" quotes the final words of Vaughan's poem. (Note that: "kinred" is "kindred.")

During the quarter-century between Milton's death in 1674 and his own death in 1700, Dryden was the most considerable and accomplished poet in England. A product of Westminster and Cambridge, he was brilliant as a dramatist, a critic, a translator, and a satirist. Now and then he looked back to the work of Chaucer, Shakespeare, and Jonson, occasionally attempting modernized adaptations of earlier work, but he also looked ahead—so much so that he is often regarded as an eighteenth-century poet, even though he died in the seventeenth century.

To the Memory of Mr. Oldham

›››››››

Farewell, too little and too lately known,
Whom I began to think and call my own;
For sure our souls were near allied, and thine
Cast in the same poetic mold with mine.
One common note on either lyre did strike,
And knaves and fools we both abhorred alike.
To the same goal did both our studies drive:
The last set out the soonest did arrive.
Thus Nissus fell upon the slippery place,
While his young friend performed and won the race.
O early ripe! to thy abundant store
What could advancing age have added more?
It might (what Nature never gives the young)
Have taught the numbers of thy native tongue.
But satire needs not those, and wit will shine
Through the harsh cadence of a rugged line.
A noble error, and but seldom made,
When poets are by too much force betrayed.
Thy gen'rous fruits, though gathered ere their prime,
Still showed a quickness; and maturing time
But mellows what we write to the dull sweets of rhyme.

Once more, hail, and farewell! farewell, thou young
But ah! too short, Marcellus of our tongue!
Thy brows with ivy and with laurels bound;
But fate and gloomy night encompass thee around.

John Oldham (1653–1683) died young after publishing Satire against Virtue
(1679) and Satires upon the Jesuits *(1681). (Note that: "Nisus" is a youth
who fell into a pool of blood; "Marcellus" is the illustrious nephew of Augustus
who died at age twenty. Both Nisus and Marcellus are in Virgil's* Aeneid.*)*

Mac Flecknoe

All human things are subject to decay,
And, when Fate summons, monarchs must obey:
This Flecknoe found, who, like Augustus, young
Was called to empire and had governed long;
In prose and verse was owned, without dispute
Through all the realms of Nonsense, absolute.
This agèd prince, now flourishing in peace
And blessed with issue of a large increase,
Worn out with business, did at length debate
To settle the succession of the state;
And pondering which of all his sons was fit
To reign, and wage immortal war with wit,
Cried: " 'Tis resolved; for nature pleads that he
Should only rule who most resembles me:
Sh——— alone my perfect image bears,
Mature in dullness from his tender years.
Sh——— alone, of all my sons, is he
Who stands confirmed in full stupidity.
The rest to some faint meaning make pretense,
But Sh——— never deviates into sense.
Some beams of wit on other souls may fall,
Strike through and make a lucid inverval,
But Sh———'s genuine night admits no ray,
His rising fogs prevail upon the day;
Besides his goodly fabric fills the eye,
And seems designed for thoughtless majesty:
Thoughtless as monarch oaks that shade the plain
And, spread in solemn state, supinely reign.
Heywood and Shirley were but types of thee,
Thou last great prophet of tautology.
Even I, a dunce of more renown than they,
Was sent before but to prepare thy way;
And coarsely clad in Norwich drugget came
To teach the nations in thy greater name.

My warbling lute, the lute I whilom strung
When to King John of Portugal I sung,
Was but the prelude to that glorious day,
When thou on silver Thames didst cut thy way
With well-timed oars before the royal barge,
Swelled with the pride of thy celestial charge;
And big with hymn, commander of an host,
The like was ne'er in *Epsom* blankets tossed.
Methinks I see the new Arion sail,
The lute still trembling underneath thy nail;
At thy well-sharpened thumb from shore to shore
The treble squeaks for fear, the basses roar;
Echoes from Pissing-Alley Sh — — — call,
And Sh — — — they resound from A — — — Hall.
About thy boat the little fishes throng
As at the morning toast that floats along.
Sometimes as prince of thy harmonious band
Thou wield'st thy papers in thy threshing hand.
St. André's feet ne'er kept more equal time,
Not even the feet of thy own *Psyche's* rhyme,
Though they in number as in sense excel;
So just, so like tautology they fell,
That, pale with envy, Singleton forswore   }
The lute and sword which he in triumph bore   }
And vowed he ne'er would act Villerius more."   }
Here stopped the good old sire, and wept for joy
In silent raptures of the hopeful boy.
All arguments, but most his plays, persuade
That for anointed dullness he was made.

   Close to the walls which fair Augusta bind
(The fair Augusta much to fears inclined),
An ancient fabric, raised t' inform the sight,
There stood of yore and Barbican it hight.
A watchtower once; but now, so Fate ordains,
Of all the pile an empty name remains.
From its old ruins brothel-houses rise,
Scenes of lewd loves and of polluted joys.
Where their vast courts the mother-strumpets keep,

And, undisturbed by watch, in silence sleep.
Near these a Nursery erects its head,
Where queens are formed and future heroes bred;
Where unfledged actors learn to laugh and cry, ⎫
Where infant punks their tender voices try, ⎬
And little Maximins the gods defy. ⎭
Great Fletcher never treads in buskins here,
Nor greater Jonson dares in socks appear;
But gentle Simkin just reception finds
Amidst this monument of vanished minds;
Pure clinches the suburbian muse affords,
And Panton waging harmless war with words.
Here Flecknoe, as a place to fame well known,
Ambitiously designed his Sh — — —'s throne.
For ancient Dekker prophesied long since ⎫
That in this pile should reign a mighty prince, ⎬
Born for a scourge of wit and flail of sense; ⎭
To whom true dullness should some *Psyches* owe,
But worlds of *Misers* from his pen should flow;
Humorists and *Hypocrites* it should produce,
Whole Raymond families and tribes of Bruce.
    Now Empress Fame had published the renown
Of Sh — — —'s coronation through the town.
Roused by report of Fame, the nations meet
From near Bunhill and distant Watling Street.
No Persian carpets spread th' imperial way,
But scattered limbs of mangled poets lay;
From dusty shops neglected authors come,
Martyrs of pies and relics of the bum.
Much Heywood, Shirley, Ogleby there lay,
But loads of Sh — — — almost choked the way.
Bilked stationers for yeomen stood prepared,
And H — — — was Captain of the Guard.
The hoary Prince in majesty appeared,
High on a throne of his own labors reared.
At his right hand our young Ascanius sate,
Rome's other hope and pillar of the state.
His brows thick fogs, instead of glories, grace,

And lambent dullness played around his face.
As Hannibal did to the altars come,
Sworn by his sire a mortal foe to Rome;
So Sh———— swore, nor should his vow be vain,
That he till death true dullness would maintain,
And in his father's right and realm's defense
Ne'er to have peace with wit nor truce with sense.
The King himself the sacred unction made,
As king by office, and as priest by trade:
In his sinister hand instead of ball
He placed a mighty mug of potent ale;
Love's Kingdom to his right he did convey,
At once his scepter and his rule of sway,
Whose righteous lore the Prince had practiced young,
And from whose loins recorded *Psyche* sprung.
His temples last with poppies were o'erspread,
That nodding seemed to consecrate his head.
Just at that point of time, if fame not lie,
On his left hand twelve reverend owls did fly:
So Romulus, 'tis sung, by Tiber's brook
Presage of sway from twice six vultures took.
Th' admiring throng loud acclamations make,
And omens of his future empire take.
The sire then shook the honors of his head,
And from his brows damps of oblivion shed
Full on the filial dullness:long he stood
Repelling from his breast the raging god; }
At length burst out in this prophetic mood:
"Heavens bless my son, from Ireland let him reign
To far Barbadoes on the western main;
Of his dominion may no end be known,
And greater than his father's be his throne.
Beyond *Love's Kingdom* let him stretch his pen."
He paused, and all the people cried, "Amen."
"Then thus," continued he, "my son, advance
Still in new impudence, new ignorance.
Success let others teach, learn thou from me
Pangs without birth and fruitless industry.

Let *Virtuosos* in five years be writ,
Yet not one thought accuse thy toil of wit.
Let gentle George in triumph tread the stage,
Make Dorimant betray, and Loveit rage;
Let Cully, Cockwood, Fopling, charm the pit,
And in their folly show the writer's wit.
Yet still thy fools shall stand in thy defense,
And justify their author's want of sense.
Let 'em be all by thy own model made
Of dullness, and desire no foreign aid,
That they to future ages may be known
Not copies drawn but issue of thy own.
Nay, let thy men of wit, too, be the same,
All full of thee and differing but in name;
But let no alien S—dl—y interpose
To lard with wit thy hungry *Epsom* prose.
And when false flowers of rhetoric thou wouldst cull,
Trust nature, do not labor to be dull;
But write thy best, and top; and in each line
Sir Formal's oratory will be thine.
Sir Formal, though unsought, attends thy quill
And does thy northern dedications fill.
Nor let false friends seduce thy mind to fame
By arrogating Jonson's hostile name.
Let Father Flecknoe fire thy mind with praise,
And Uncle Ogleby thy envy raise.
Thou art my blood, where Jonson has no part;
What share have we in nature or in art?
Where did his wit on learning fix a brand
And rail at arts he did not understand?
Where made he love in Prince Nicander's vein,
Or swept the dust in *Psyche's* humble strain?
Where sold he bargains, whip-stitch, kiss my arse,
Promised a play and dwindled to a farce?
When did his muse from Fletcher scenes purloin,
As thou whole Etherege dost transfuse to thine?
But so transfused as oil on waters flow,
His always floats above, thine sinks below.

This is thy province, this thy wondrous way,
New humors to invent for each new play;
This is that boasted bias of thy mind
By which one way, to dullness, 'tis inclined,
Which makes thy writings lean on one side still,
And in all changes that way bends thy will.
Nor let thy mountain belly make pretense
Of likeness; thine's a tympany of sense.
A tun of man in thy large bulk is writ,
But sure thou 'rt but a kilderkin of wit.
Like mine thy gentle numbers feebly creep,
Thy tragic muse gives smiles, thy comic sleep.
With whate'er gall thou sett'st thyself to write,
Thy inoffensive satires never bite.
In thy felonious heart though venom lies,
It does but touch thy Irish pen, and dies.
Thy genius calls thee not to purchase fame
In keen iambics but mild anagram;
Leave writing plays, and choose for thy command
Some peaceful province in acrostic land.
There thou may'st wings display and altars raise,
And torture one poor word ten thousand ways.
Or, if thou wouldst thy different talents suit,
Set thy own songs and sing them to thy lute."
He said, but his last words were scarcely heard, ⎫
For Bruce and Longville had a trap prepared, ⎬
And down they sent the yet declaiming bard. ⎭
Sinking, he left his drugget robe behind,
Borne upwards by a subterranean wind.
The mantle fell to the young prophet's part,
With double portion of his father's art.

Dryden insults Thomas Shadwell (1642?–1692) by making him out to be the son ("Mac") of Richard Flecknoe (who died about 1678), a Roman Catholic priest and minor poet whose only positive fame comes from his having written one of the first English operas. (He is nastily caricatured in Andrew Marvell's "Flecknoe, an English Priest at Rome.") For reasons unknown, Dryden constructs an elaborate mock-epic to ridicule not only Shadwell's work but his person as well (he was fat and addicted to opium). The contagious style of "Mac Flecknoe" occupied the center of English satiric verse from Dryden's heyday in the 1670s right through Byron's 150 years further on. (Note that: "fabric" is "building"; "clinches" is "puns"; "stationers" is "printers and publishers"; "sinister" is "left"—the literal meaning; "kilderkin" is "small cask.")

A Song for St. Cecilia's Day, 1687

I

From harmony, from heavenly harmony
  This universal frame began:
  When Nature underneath a heap
    Of jarring atoms lay,
  And could not heave her head,
The tuneful voice was heard from high:
  "Arise, ye more than dead."
Then cold, and hot, and moist, and dry,
In order to their stations leap,
  And Music's power obey.
From harmony, from heavenly harmony
  This universal frame began:
  From harmony to harmony
Through all the compass of the notes it ran,
The diapason closing full in man.

II

What passion cannot Music raise and quell!
  When Jubal struck the corded shell,
  His listening brethren stood around,
  And, wondering, on their faces fell
  To worship that celestial sound.
Less than a god they thought there could not dwell
  Within the hollow of that shell
  That spoke so sweetly and so well.
What passion cannot Music raise and quell!

III

The trumpet's loud clangor
　　Excites us to arms,
With shrill notes of anger,
　　And mortal alarms.
The double double double beat
　　Of the thundering drum
Cries: "Hark! the foes come;
Charge, charge, 'tis too late to retreat."

IV

The soft complaining flute
In dying notes discovers
The woes of hopeless lovers,
Whose dirge is whispered by the warbling lute.

V

Sharp violins proclaim
Their jealous pangs, and desperation,
Fury, frantic indignation,
Depth of pains, and height of passion,
　　For the fair, disdainful dame.

VI

But O! what art can teach,
What human voice can reach,
The sacred organ's praise?
Notes inspiring holy love,
Notes that wing their heavenly ways
To mend the choirs above.

VII

Orpheus could lead the savage race;
And trees unrooted left their place,
  Sequacious of the lyre;
But bright Cecilia raised the wonder higher:
When to her organ vocal breath was given,
An angel heard, and straight appeared,
  Mistaking earth for heaven.

GRAND CHORUS

As from the power of sacred lays
  The spheres began to move,
And sung the great Creator's praise
  To all the blest above;
So, when the last and dreadful hour
This crumbling pageant shall devour,
The trumpet shall be heard on high,
The dead shall live, the living die,
And Music shall untune the sky.

For several years at the end of the seventeenth century, a London music society sponsored a celebration on November 22, the day of St. Cecilia, patron saint of music and, according to legend, inventor of the organ. Dryden's song was the official ode for the observance in 1687; "Alexander's Feast" (p. 268) performed the same honor in 1697.

Alexander's Feast;
or, The Power of Music

I

'Twas at the royal feast, for Persia won
    By Philip's warlike son:
    Aloft in awful state
    The god-like hero sate
    On his imperial throne:
    His valiant peers were placed around;
Their brows with roses and with myrtles bound.
    (So should desert in arms be crowned:)
The lovely Thaïs by his side,
Sat like a blooming Eastern bride
In flower of youth and beauty's pride.
    Happy, happy, happy pair!
    None but the Brave
    None but the Brave
    None but the Brave deserves the Fair.

CHORUS

Happy, happy, happy pair!
None but the Brave
None but the Brave
None but the Brave deserves the Fair.

II

Timotheus placed on high
    Amid the tuneful choir,
     With flying fingers touched the lyre:
The trembling notes ascend the sky,
And heavenly joys inspire.
The song began from Jove;
Who left his blissful seats above,
(Such is the power of mighty Love.)
A dragon's fiery form belied the god:
Sublime on radiant spires he rode,
    When he to fair Olympia pressed,
    And while he sought her snowy breast:
Then, round her slender waist he curled,
And stamped an image of himself, a sovereign of the world.
The listening crowd admire the lofty sound,
"A present Deity," they shout around:
"A present Deity," the vaulted roofs rebound.
     With ravished ears
     The Monarch hears,
     Assumes the god,
     Affects to nod,
    And seems to shake the spheres.

CHORUS

With ravished ears
The Monarch hears,
Assumes the god,
Affects to nod,
And seems to shake the spheres.

III

The praise of Bacchus then the sweet musician sung,
    Of Bacchus ever fair and ever young;
        The jolly god in triumph comes;
        Sound the trumpets, beat the drums:
            Flushed with a purple grace
            He shows his honest face;
Now give the hautboys breath: he comes, he comes!
      "Bacchus, ever fair and young,
        Drinking joys did first ordain;
    Bacchus' blessings are a treasure;
    Drinking is the soldier's pleasure;
        Rich the treasure,
        Sweet the pleasure;
    Sweet is pleasure after pain."

CHORUS

Bacchus' blessings are a treasure;
Drinking is the soldier's pleasure;
    Rich the treasure,
    Sweet the pleasure;
Sweet is pleasure after pain.

IV

Soothed with the sound the King grew vain,
    Fought all his battles o'er again;
And thrice he routed all his foes, and thrice he slew the slain.
      The master saw the madness rise,
      His glowing cheeks, his ardent eyes;
      And while he heaven and earth defied,
      Changed his hand, and checked his pride.
        He chose a mournful Muse
        Soft pity to infuse:
      He sung Darius great and good,
        By too severe a fate,
    Fallen, fallen, fallen, fallen,
      Fallen from his high estate
And weltering in his blood;
      Deserted at his utmost need
      By those his former bounty fed;
      On the bare earth exposed he lies,
      With not a friend to close his eyes.

With downcast looks the joyless victor sate,
    Revolving in his altered soul
      The various turns of chance below;
    And, now and then, a sigh he stole,
    And tears began to flow.

CHORUS

Revolving in his altered soul
    The various turns of chance below;
And, now and then, a sigh he stole,
    And tears began to flow.

V

The mighty master smiled to see
That love was in the next degree:
'Twas but a kindred sound to move,
For pity melts the mind to love.
    Softly sweet, in Lydian measures
    Soon he soothed his soul to pleasures.
    "War," he sung, "is toil and trouble;
    Honour but an empty bubble.
      Never ending, still beginning,
    Fighting still, and still destroying;
      If the world be worth thy winning,
    Think, O think it worth enjoying.
      Lovely Thaïs sits beside thee,
      Take the good the Gods provide thee."

The many rend the skies with loud applause;
So Love was crowned, but Music won the cause.
    The Prince, unable to conceal his pain,
      Gazed on the Fair
      Who caused his care,
    And sighed and looked, sighed and looked,
Sighed and looked, and sighed again:
At length, with love and wine at once oppressed,
The vanquished victor sunk upon her breast.

CHORUS

The Prince, unable to conceal his pain,
    Gazed on the Fair
    Who caused his care,
    And sighed and looked, sighed and looked,
Sighed and looked, and sighed again:
At length, with love and wine at once oppressed,
The vanquished victor sunk upon her breast.

VI

Now strike the golden lyre again,
A louder yet, and yet a louder strain.
Break his bands of sleep asunder,
And rouse him, like a rattling peal of thunder.
        Hark, hark, the horrid sound
            Has raised up his head,
            As awaked from the dead,
        And amazed he stares around.
"Revenge, revenge!" Timotheus cries,
        "See the Furies arise!
        See the snakes that they rear,
        How they hiss in their hair,
    And the sparkles that flash from their eyes!
        Behold a ghastly band,
        Each a torch in his hand!
Those are Grecian ghosts that in battle were slain,
And unburied remain
Inglorious on the plain.
                Give the vengeance due
                To the valiant crew.
Behold how they toss their torches on high,
        How they point to the Persian abodes,
And glittering temples of their hostile gods!"
The Princes applaud with a furious joy,
And the King seized a flambeau, with zeal to destroy;
            Thaïs led the way
            To light him to his prey,
And, like another Helen, fired another Troy.

CHORUS
And the King seized a flambeau, with zeal to destroy;
            Thaïs led the way
            To light him to his prey,
And, like another Helen, fired another Troy.

VII

Thus, long ago,
Ere heaving bellows learned to blow,
While organs yet were mute;
Timotheus, to his breathing flute
And sounding lyre,
Could swell the soul to rage, or kindle soft desire.
At last divine Cecilia came,
Inventress of the vocal frame;
The sweet Enthusiast, from her sacred store,
Enlarged the former narrow bounds,
And added length to solemn sounds,
With Nature's mother wit, and arts unknown before.
Let old Timotheus yield the prize,
Or both divide the crown;
He raised a mortal to the skies,
She drew an angel down.

GRAND CHORUS

At last divine Cecilia came,
Inventress of the vocal frame;
The sweet Enthusiast, from her sacred store,
Enlarged the former narrow bounds,
And added length to solemn sounds,
With Nature's mother wit, and arts unknown before.
Let old Timotheus yield the prize,
Or both divide the crown;
He raised a mortal to the skies,
She drew an angel down.

The title feast was held in Persepolis to celebrate Alexander's victory over the Persians. Some power—Dryden nominates the musician Timotheus—moved Alexander to burn Persepolis in retaliation for the Persians' burning of Athens. The notion of "another Troy," by the way, recurs in much of William Butler Yeats's poetry and verbatim in his "Two Songs from a Play." See the commentary on Dryden's "Song for St. Cecilia's Day," p. 265. (Note that: "admire" is "wonder at"; "hautboys" is "oboes"; "flambeau" is "torch.")

EDWARD TAYLOR c.1645–1729

Taylor, born in England, came to Massachusetts in 1668, studied at Harvard, and served as pastor and physician in the town of Westfield for more than fifty years. None of his poetry was published until 1939, more than two centuries after his death.

Huswifery

Make me, O Lord, Thy spining wheel complete.
  Thy Holy Word my distaff make for me.
Make mine affections Thy swift flyers neat
  And make my soul Thy holy spool to be.
  My conversation make to be Thy reel
  And reel the yarn thereon spun of Thy wheel.

Make me Thy loom then, knit therein this twine:
  And make Thy Holy Spirit, Lord, wind quills:
Then weave the web Thyself. The yarn is fine.
  Thine ordinances make my fulling mills.
  Then dye the same in heavenly colors choice,
  All pinked with varnished flowers of paradise.

Then clothe therewith mine understanding, will,
  Affections, judgment, conscience, memory,
My words, and actions, that their shine may fill
  My ways with glory and Thee glorify.
  Then mine apparel shall display before Ye
  That I am clothed in holy robes for glory.

Taylor's devotional poems, among the earliest to be written in America, owe some of their imagery and feeling to such English exemplars as Donne and Herbert. The itemized domestic allegory of "Huswifery"—related to textile jobs like spinning, weaving, dyeing, and sewing—was a staple feature of sermons and didactic verse.

JONATHAN SWIFT 1667–1745

Gulliver's Travels has conferred absolute immortality on
Swift; on account of it and it alone he belongs with the
greatest of writers. Historically, however, he is impor-
tant for contributions to political thought, particularly
on the treatment of Ireland. He was born and educated
in Dublin and from 1713 served as Dean of St.
Patrick's there. He is not known to have married, but
he maintained close relationships with Esther Johnson
("Stella") and Esther Vanhomrigh ("Vanessa").

A Description of the Morning

Now hardly here and there an hackney coach
Appearing, showed the ruddy morn's approach.
Now Betty from her master's bed had flown,
And softly stole to discompose her own;
The slipshod 'prentice from his master's door
Had pared the dirt, and sprinkled round the floor.
Now Moll had whirled her mop with dextrous airs,
Prepared to scrub the entry and the stairs.
The youth with broomy stumps began to trace
The kennel's edge, where wheels had worn the place.
The small-coal man was heard with cadence deep,
Till drowned in shriller notes of chimney sweep:
Duns at his lordship's gate began to meet;
And brickdust Moll had screamed through half the street.
The turnkey now his flock returning sees,
Duly let out a-nights to steal for fees:
The watchful bailiffs take their silent stands,
And schoolboys lag with satchels in their hands.

This vision of a modern urban morning—first published in The Tatler *in
1709—should be compared with Blake's "London" (p. 361), written almost a
century later. (Note that: "kennel" is "gutter," "sewer"; "duns" is "bill collec-
tors.")*

Pope was the greatest English poet for a third of the
eighteenth century: from about 1711, when he wrote
his "Essay on Criticism," until his death thirty-three
years later. He was most successful as a translator of
Homer, but his reputation rests largely on his genius as
a satirist, especially in the mock-epic mode displayed in
"The Rape of the Lock" and *The Dunciad*. As the "Epis-
tle to Dr. Arbuthnot" demonstrates, Pope was among
the finest epistolary poets in English.

Know Then Thyself

Know then thyself, presume not God to scan,
The proper study of mankind is Man.
Placed on this isthmus of a middle state,
A being darkly wise and rudely great:
With too much knowledge for the Sceptic side,
With too much weakness for the Stoic's pride,
He hangs between; in doubt to act or rest,
In doubt to deem himself a God or Beast,
In doubt his mind or body to prefer;
Born but to die, and reasoning but to err;
Alike in ignorance, his reason such
Whether he thinks too little or too much:
Chaos of thought and passion, all confused;
Still by himself abused, or disabused;
Created half to rise and half to fall;
Great lord of all things,yet a prey to all;
Sole judge of truth, in endless error hurled;
The glory, jest, and riddle of the world!
  Go, wondrous creature! mount where science guides:
Go, measure earth, weigh air, and state the tides:
Instruct the planets in what orbs to run,
Correct old time and regulate the Sun;
Go, soar with Plato to th' empyreal sphere,

To the first good, first perfect, and first fair;
Or tread the mazy round his follow'rs trod
And quitting sense call imitating God—
As Eastern priests in giddy circles run,
And turn their heads to imitate the Sun.
Go, teach Eternal Wisdom how to rule:
Then drop into thyself, and be a fool!
　　Superior beings, when of late they saw
A mortal man unfold all nature's law,
Admired such wisdom in an earthly shape,
And showed a NEWTON as we show an ape.
　　Could he, whose rules the rapid comet bind,
Describe or fix one movement of his mind?
Who saw its fires here rise and there descend,
Explain his own beginning or his end?
Alas, what wonder: man's superior part
Unchecked may rise, and climb from art to art,
But when his own great work is but begun,
What reason weaves by passion is undone.

from An Essay on Man

These eighteen lines open the second epistle (of four) in "An Essay on Man," described in Pope's Argument as being "Of the Nature and State of Man, with respect to Himself, as an Individual."

Epistle to Dr. Arbuthnot

P. Shut, shut the door, good John! (fatigued, I said),
Tie up the knocker, say I'm sick, I'm dead.
The Dog Star rages! nay 'tis past a doubt
All Bedlam, or Parnassus, is let out:
Fire in each eye, and papers in each hand,
They rave, recite, and madden round the land.

What walls can guard me, or what shades can hide?
They pierce my thickets, through my grot they glide,
By land, by water, they renew the charge,
They stop the chariot, and they board the barge.
No place is sacred, not the church is free;
Even Sunday shines no Sabbath day to me:
Then from the Mint walks forth the man of rhyme,
Happy to catch me just at dinner time.

Is there a parson, much bemused in beer,
A maudlin poetess, a rhyming peer,
A clerk foredoomed his father's soul to cross,
Who pens a stanza when he should engross?
Is there who, locked from ink and paper, scrawls
With desperate charcoal round his darkened walls?
All fly to Twit'nam, and in humble strain
Apply to me to keep them mad or vain.
Arthur, whose giddy son neglects the laws,
Imputes to me and my damned works the cause:
Poor Cornus sees his frantic wife elope,
And curses wit, and poetry, and Pope.

Friend to my life (which did not you prolong,
The world had wanted many an idle song)
What drop or nostrum can this plague remove?
Or which must end me, a fool's wrath or love?
A dire dilemma! either way I'm sped,
If foes, they write, if friends, they read me dead.
Seized and tied down to judge, how wretched I!
Who can't be silent, and who will not lie.

To laugh were want of goodness and of grace,
And to be grave exceeds all power of face.
I sit with sad civility, I read
With honest anguish and an aching head,
And drop at last, but in unwilling ears,
This saving counsel, "Keep your piece nine years."
   "Nine years!" cries he, who high in Drury Lane,
Lulled by soft zephyrs through the broken pane,
Rhymes ere he wakes, and prints before term ends
Obliged by hunger and request of friends:
"The piece, you think, is incorrect? why, take it,
I'm all submission, what you'd have it, make it."
   Three things another's modest wishes bound,
My friendship, and a prologue, and ten pound.
   Pitholeon sends to me: "You know his Grace,
I want a patron; ask him for a place."
Pitholeon libeled me—"but here's a letter
Informs you, sir, 'twas when he knew no better.
Dare you refuse him? Curll invites to dine,
He'll write a *Journal,* or he'll turn Divine."
Bless me! a packet—" 'Tis a stranger sues,
A virgin tragedy, an orphan Muse."
If I dislike it, "Furies, death, and rage!"
If I approve, "Commend it to the stage."
There (thank my stars) my whole commission ends,
The players and I are, luckily, no friends.
Fired that the house reject him," " 'Sdeath, I'll print it,
And shame the fools—Your interest, sir, with Lintot!"
Lintot, dull rogue, will think your price too much.
"Not, sir, if you revise it, and retouch."
All my demurs but double his attacks;
At last he whispers, "Do; and we go snacks."
Glad of a quarrel, straight I clap the door,
"Sir, let me see your works and you no more."
   'Tis sung, when Midas' ears began to spring
(Midas, a sacred person and a king),
His very minister who spied them first,
(Some say his queen) was forced to speak, or burst.

And is not mine, my friend a sorer case,
When every coxcomb perks them in my face?
   A. Good friend, forbear! you deal in dangerous things.
I'd never name queens, ministers, or kings;
Keep close to ears, and those let asses prick;
'Tis nothing — — —P. Nothing? if they bite and kick?
Out with it, *Dunciad!* Let the secret pass,
That secret to each fool, that he's an ass:
The truth once told (and wherefore should we lie?)
The queen of Midas slept, and so may I.
   You think this cruel? take it for a rule,
No creature smarts so little as a fool.
Let peals of laughter, Codrus! round thee break,
Thou unconcerned canst hear the mighty crack.
Pit, box, and gallery in convulsions hurled,
Thou stand'st unshook amidst a bursting world.
Who shames a scribbler? break one cobweb through,
He spins the slight, self-pleasing thread anew:
Destroy his fib or sophistry, in vain;
The creature's at his dirty work again,
Throned in the center of his thin designs,
Proud of a vast extent of flimsy lines.
Whom have I hurt? has poet yet or peer
Lost the arched eyebrow or Parnassian sneer?
And has not Colley still his lord and whore?
His butchers Henley? his freemasons Moore?
Does not one table Bavius still admit?
Still to one bishop Philips seem a wit?
Still Sappho — — —A. Hold! for God's sake—you'll offend.
No names—be calm—learn prudence of a friend.
I too could write, and I am twice as tall;
But foes like these! — — —P. One flatterer's worse than all.
Of all mad creatures, if the learn'd are right,
It is the slaver kills, and not the bite.
A fool quite angry is quite innocent:
Alas! 'Tis ten times worse when they repent.
   One dedicates in high heroic prose,
And ridicules beyond a hundred foes;

One from all Grub Street will my fame defend,
And, more abusive, calls himself my friend.
This prints my letters, that expects a bribe,
And others roar aloud, "Subscribe, subscribe!"
    There are, who to my person pay their court:
I cough like Horace, and, though lean, am short;
Ammon's great son one shoulder had too high,
Such Ovid's nose, and "Sir! you have an eye—"
Go on, obliging creatures, make me see
All that disgraced my betters met in me.
Say for my comfort, languishing in bed,
"Just so immortal Maro held his head":
And when I die, be sure you let me know
Great Homer died three thousand years ago.
    Why did I write? what sin to me unknown
Dipped me in ink, my parents', or my own?
As yet a child, not yet a fool to fame,
I lisped in numbers, for the numbers came.
I left no calling for this idle trade,
No duty broke, no father disobeyed.
The Muse but served to ease some friend, not wife,
To help me through this long disease, my life,
To second, Arbuthnot! thy art and care,
And teach the being you preserved, to bear.
    A. But why then publish? P. Granville the polite,
And knowing Walsh, would tell me I could write;
Well-natured Garth inflamed with early praise,
And Congreve loved, and Swift endured my lays;
The courtly Talbot, Somers, Sheffield, read;
Even mitered Rochester would nod the head,
And St. John's self (great Dryden's friends before)
With open arms received one poet more.
Happy my studies, when by these approved!
Happier their author, when by these beloved!
From these the world will judge of men and books,
Not from the Burnets. Oldmixons, and Cookes.
    Soft were my numbers; who could take offense
While pure description held the place of sense?

Like gentle Fanny's was my flowery theme,
A painted mistress, or a purling stream.
Yet then did Gildon draw his venal quill;
I wished the man a dinner, a sat still.
Yet then did Dennis rave in furious fret;
I never answered, I was not in debt.
If I want provoked, or madness made them print,
I waged no war with Bedlam or the Mint.
  Did some more sober critic come abroad?
If wrong, I smiled; if right, I kissed the rod.
Pains, reading, study are their just pretense,
And all they want is spirit, taste, and sense.
Commas and points they set exactly right,
And 'twere a sin to rob them of their mite.
Yet ne'er one sprig of laurel graced these ribalds,
From slashing Bentley down to piddling Tibbalds.
Each wight who reads not, and but scans and spells,
Each word-catcher that lives on syllables,
Even such small critics some regard may claim,
Preserved in Milton's or in Shakespeare's name.
Pretty! in amber to observe the forms
Of hairs, or straws, or dirt, or grubs, or worms!
The things, we know, are neither rich nor rare,
But wonder how the devil they got there.
  Were others angry? I excused them too;
Well might they rage; I gave them but their due.
A man's true merit 'tis not hard to find;
But each man's secret standard in his mind,
That casting weight pride adds to emptiness,
This, who can gratify? for who can guess?
The bard whom pilfered pastorals renown,
Who turns a Persian tale for half a crown,
Just writes to make his barrenness appear,
And strains from hard-bound brains eight lines a year:
He, who still wanting, though he lives on theft,
Steals much, spends little, yet has nothing left;
And he who now to sense, now nonsense leaning,
Means not, but blunders round about a meaning:

And he whose fustian's so sublimely bad,
It is not poetry, but prose run mad:
All these, my modest satire bade translate,
And owned that nine such poets made a Tate.
How did they fume, and stamp, and roar, and chafe!
And swear, not Addison himself was safe.
  Peace to all such! but were there one whose fires
True Genius kindles, and fair Fame inspires;
Blessed with each talent and each art to please,
And born to write, converse, and live with ease:
Should such a man, too fond to rule alone,
Bear, like the Turk, no brother near the throne;
View him with scornful, yet with jealous eyes,
And hate for arts that caused himself to rise;
Damn with faint praise, assent with civil leer,
And without sneering, teach the rest to sneer;
Willing to wound, and yet afraid to strike,
Just hint a fault, and hesitate dislike;
Alike reserved to blame or to commend,
A timorous foe, and a suspicious friend;
Dreading even fools; by flatterers besieged,
And so obliging that he ne'er obliged;
Like Cato, give his little senate laws,
And sit attentive to his own applause;
While wits and Templars every sentence raise,
And wonder with a foolish face of praise—
Who but must laugh, if such a man there be?
Who would not weep, if Atticus were he?
  What though my name stood rubric on the walls
Or plastered posts, with claps, in capitals?
Or smoking forth, a hundred hawkers' load,
On wings of winds came flying all abroad?
I sought no homage from the race that write;
I kept, like Asian monarchs, from their sight:
Poems I heeded (now berhymed so long)
No more than thou, great George! a birthday song.
I ne'er with wits or witlings passed my days
To spread about the itch of verse and praise;

Nor like a puppy daggled through the town
To fetch and carry sing-song up and down;
Nor at rehearsals sweat, and mouthed, and cried,
With handkerchief and orange at my side;
But sick of fops, and poetry, and prate,
To Bufo left the whole Castalian state.
   Proud as Apollo on his forkéd hill,
Sat full-blown Bufo, puffed by every quill;
Fed with soft dedication all day long,
Horace and he went hand in hand in song.
His library (where busts of poets dead
And a true Pindar stood without a head)
Received of wits an undistinguished race,
Who first his judgment asked, and then a place:
Much they extolled his pictures, much his seat,
And flattered every day, and some days eat:
Till grown more frugal in his riper days,
He paid some bards with port, and some with praise;
To some a dry rehearsal was assigned,
And others (harder still) he paid in kind.
Dryden alone (what wonder?) came not nigh;
Dryden alone escaped this judging eye:
But still the great have kindness in reserve;
He helped to bury whom he helped to starve.
   May some choice patron bless each gray goose quill!
May every Bavius have his Bufo still!
So when a statesman wants a day's defense,
Or Envy holds a whole week's war with Sense,
Or simple Pride for flattery makes demands,
May dunce by dunce he whistled off my hands!
Blessed be the great! for those they take away,
And those they left me—for they left me Gay;
Left me to see neglected genius bloom,
Neglected die, and tell it on his tomb;
Of all thy blameless life the sole return
My verse, and Queensberry weeping o'er thy urn!
Oh, let me live my own, and die so too!
("To live and die is all I have to do")

Maintain a poet's dignity and ease,
And see what friends, and read what books I please;
Above a patron, though I condescend
Sometimes to call a minister my friend.
I was not born for courts or great affairs;
I pay my debts, believe, and say my prayers,
Can sleep without a poem in my head,
Nor know if Dennis be alive or dead.

Why am I asked what next shall see the light?
Heavens! was I born for nothing but to write?
Has life no joys for me? or (to be grave)
Have I no friend to serve, no soul to save?
"I found him close with Swift"—"Indeed? no doubt"
Cries prating Balbus, "something will come out."
'Tis all in vain, deny it as I will.
"No, such a genius never can lie still,"
And then for mine obligingly mistakes
The first lampoon Sir Will or Bubo makes.
Poor guiltless I! and can I choose but smile,
When every coxcomb knows me by my style?

Cursed be the verse, how well soe'er it flow,
That tends to make one worthy man my foe,
Give Virtue scandal, Innocence a fear,
Or from the soft-eyed virgin steal a tear!
But he who hurts a harmless neighbor's peace.
Insults fallen worth, or Beauty in distress,
Who loves a lie, lame Slander helps about,
Who writes a libel, or who copies out:
That fop whose pride affects a patron's name,
Yet absent, wounds an author's honest fame;
Who can your merit selfishly approve,
And show the sense of it without the love;
Who has the vanity to call your friend,
Yet wants the honour, injured, to defend;
Who tells whate'er you think, whate'er you say,
And, if he lie not, must at least betray:
Who to the *Dean*, and *silver bell* can swear,
And sees at *Cannons* what was never there;

Who reads, but with a lust to misapply,
Make satire a lampoon, and fiction, lie.
A lash like mine no honest man shall dread,
But all such babbling blockheads in his stead.
   Let *Sporus* tremble—"What? that thing of silk,
Sporus, that mere white curd of ass's milk?
Satire or sense, alas! can Sporus feel?
Who breaks a butterfly upon a wheel?"
Yet let me flap this bug with gilded wings,
This painted child of dirt that stinks and stings;
Whose buzz the witty and the fair annoys,
Yet wit ne'er tastes, and beauty ne'er enjoys:
So well-bred spaniels civilly delight
In mumbling of the game they dare not bite.
Eternal smiles his emptiness betray,
As shallow streams run dimpling all the way.
Whether in florid impotence he speaks,
And, as the prompter breathes, the puppet squeaks;
Or at the ear of Eve, familiar toad,
Half froth, half venom, spits himself abroad,
In puns, or politics, or tales, or lies,
Or spite, or smut, or rhymes, or blasphemies.
His wit all seesaw, between *that* and *this*,
Now high, now low, now master up, now miss,
And he himself one vile antithesis.
Amphibious thing! that acting either part,
The trifling head, or the corrupted heart,
Fop at the toilet, flatterer at the board,
Now trips a Lady, and now struts a Lord.
Eve's tempter thus the Rabbins have exprest,
A cherub's face, a reptile all the rest;
Beauty that shocks you, parts that none will trust,
Wit that can creep, and pride that licks the dust.
   Not Fortune's worshipper, nor fashion's fool,
Not lucre's madman, nor ambition's tool,
Not proud, nor servile; be one poet's praise,
That, if he pleased, he pleased by manly ways:
That flattery, even to kings, he held a shame,

And thought a lie in verse or prose the same.
That not in fancy's maze he wandered long,
But stooped to truth and moralized his song:
That not for fame, but virtue's better end,
He stood the furious foe, the timid friend,
The damning critic, half-approving wit,
The coxcomb hit, or fearing to be hit;
Laughed at the loss of friends he never had,
The dull, the proud, the wicked, and the mad;
The distant threats of vengeance on his head,
The blow unfelt, the tear he never shed;
The tale revived, the lie so oft o'erthrown,
The imputed trash, and dulness not his own;
The morals blackened when the writings 'scape,
The libeled person, and the pictured shape;
Abuse, on all he loved, or loved him, spread,
A friend in exile, or a father, dead;
The whisper, that to greatness still too near,
Perhaps, yet vibrates on his SOVEREIGN'S ear—
Welcome for thee, fair Virtue! all the past:
For thee, fair Virtue! welcome even the *last!*
  "But why insult the poor, affront the great?"
A knave's a knave, to me, in every state:
Alike my scorn, if he succeed or fail,
Sporus at court, or Japhet in a jail,
A hireling scribbler, or a hireling peer,
Knight of the post corrupt, or of the shire;
If on a pillory, or near a throne,
He gain his Prince's ear, or lose his own.
Yet soft by nature, more a dupe than wit,
Sappho can tell you how this man was bit:
This dreaded satirist Dennis will confess
Foe to his pride, but friend to his distress,
So humble, he has knocked at Tibbald's door,
Has drunk with Cibber, nay, has rhymed for Moore.
Full ten years slandered, did he once reply?
Three thousand suns went down on Welsted's lie.
To please a mistress one aspersed his life;

He lashed him not, but let her be his wife:
Let Budgell charge low Grubstreet on his quill,
And write whate'er he pleased, except his will;
Let the two Curlls of town and court, abuse
His father, mother, body, soul, and Muse.
Yet why? that father held it for a rule,
It was a sin to call our neighbor fool;
That harmless mother thought no wife a whore:
Hear this, and spare his family, James Moore!
Unspotted names, and memorable long,
If there be force in virtue, or in song.
  Of gentle blood (part shed in honor's cause,
While yet in Britain honor had applause)
Each parent sprung— — —A. What fortune,
    pray? — — —P. Their own,
And better got than Bestia's from the throne.
Born to no pride, inheriting no strife,
Nor marrying discord in a noble wife,
Stranger to civil and religious rage,
The good man walked innoxious through his age.
No courts he saw, no suits would ever try,
Nor dared an oath, nor hazarded a lie.
Unlearn'd, he knew no schoolman's subtle art,
No language but the language of the heart.
By nature honest, by experience wise,
Healthy by temperature, and by exercise;
His life, though long, to sickness passed unknown,
His death was instant, and without a groan.
Oh, grant me thus to live, and thus to die!
Who sprung from kings shall know less joy than I.
  O friend! may each domestic bliss be thine!
Be no unpleasing melancholy mine:
Me, let the tender office long engage,
To rock the cradle of reposing Age,
With lenient arts extend a mother's breath,
Make Languor smile, and smooth the bed of Death,
Explore the thought explain the asking eye,
And keep a while one parent from the sky!

On cares like these if length of days attend,
May heaven, to bless those days, preserve my friend,
Preserve him social, cheerful, and serene,
And just as rich as when he served a Queen!
    A. Whether that blessing be denied or given,
Thus far was right—the rest belongs to Heaven.

In a mode and style much indebted to Horace, Pope's epistle to his distinguished friend and physician is a dialogue inside a letter. The imagined responses of Arbuthnot identify him as the addressee and the interlocutor who boosts the movement of the satire, so that some editors label speeches in the poem "P." and "A." The dialogue of the epistle, is as much of a confessional autobiography as Pope cared to commit to paper. (Note that: "sped" is "ruined"; "snacks" is "shares"; "Templars" is "law students"; "rubric" is "in red"; "claps" is "posters"; "bit" is "deceived.")

An Essay on Criticism

❦❦❦

PART 1

'Tis hard to say, if greater want of skill
Appear in writing or in judging ill;
But of the two less dangerous is the offense
To tire our patience than mislead our sense.
Some few in that, but numbers err in this,
Ten censure wrong for one who writes amiss;
A fool might once himself alone expose,
Now one in verse makes many more in prose.
    'Tis with our judgments as our watches, none
Go just alike, yet each believes his own.
In poets as true genius is but rare,
True taste as seldom is the critic's share;
Both must alike from Heaven derive their light,
These born to judge, as well as those to write.
Let such teach others who themselves excel,
And censure freely who have written well.
Authors are partial to their wit, 'tis true,
But are not critics to their judgment too?
    Yet if we look more closely, we shall find
Most have the seeds of judgment in their mind:
Nature affords at least a glimmering light;
The lines, though touched but faintly, are drawn right.
But as the slightest sketch, if justly traced, ⎫
Is by ill coloring but the more disgraced, ⎬
So by false learning is good sense defaced: ⎭
Some are bewildered in the maze of schools,
And some made coxcombs Nature meant but fools.
In search of wit these lose their common sense,
And then turn critics in their own defense:
Each burns alike, who can, or cannot write,
Or with a rival's or an eunuch's spite.
All fools have still an itching to deride,

And fain would be upon the laughing side.
If Maevius scribble in Apollo's spite,
There are who judge still worse than he can write.
   Some have at first for wits, then poets passed,
Turned critics next, and proved plain fools at last.
Some neither can for wits nor critics pass,
As heavy mules are neither horse nor ass.
Those half-learn'd witlings, numerous in our isle,
As half-formed insects on the banks of Nile;
Unfinished things, one knows not what to call,
Their generation's so equivocal:
To tell them would a hundred tongues require,
Or one vain wit's, that might a hundred tire.
   But you who seek to give and merit fame,
And justly bear a critic's noble name,
Be sure yourself and your own reach to know,
How far your genius, taste, and learning go;
Launch not beyond your depth, but be discreet,
And mark that point where sense and dullness meet.
   Nature to all things fixed the limits fit,
And wisely curbed proud man's pretending wit.
As on the land while here the ocean gains,
In other parts it leaves wide sandy plains;
Thus in the soul while memory prevails,
The solid power of understanding fails;
Where beams of warm imagination play,
The memory's soft figures melt away.
One science only will one genius fit,
So vast is art, so narrow human wit.
Not only bounded to peculiar arts,
But oft in those confined to single parts.
Like kings we lose the conquests gained before,
By vain ambition still to make them more;
Each might his several province well command,
Would all but stoop to what they understand.
   First follow Nature, and your judgment frame
By her just standard, which is still the same;
Unerring Nature, still divinely bright,

One clear, unchanged, and universal light,
Life, force, and beauty must to all impart,
At once the source, and end, and test of art.
Art from that fund each just supply provides,
Works without show, and without pomp presides.
In some fair body thus the informing soul
With spirits feeds, with vigor fills the whole,
Each motion guides, and every nerve sustains;
Itself unseen, but in the effects remains.
Some, to whom Heaven in wit has been profuse,
Want as much more to turn it to its use;
For wit and judgment often are at strife,
Though meant each other's aid, like man and wife.
'Tis more to guide than spur the Muse's steed,
Restrain his fury than provoke his speed;
The wingèd courser, like a generous horse,
Shows most true mettle when you check his course.
    Those rules of old discovered, not devised,
Are Nature still, but Nature methodized;
Nature, like liberty, is but restrained
By the same laws which first herself ordained.
    Hear how learn'd Greece her useful rules indites,
When to repress and when indulge our flights:
High on Parnassus' top her sons she showed,
And pointed out those arduous paths they trod;
Held from afar, aloft, the immortal prize,
And urged the rest by equal steps to rise.
Just precepts thus from great examples given,
She drew from them what they derived from Heaven.
The generous critic fanned the poet's fire,
And taught the world with reason to admire.
Then criticism the Muse's handmaid proved,
To dress her charms, and make her more beloved:
But following wits from that intention strayed,
Who could not win the mistress, wooed the maid;
Against the poets their own arms they turned,
Sure to hate most the men from whom they learned.
So modern 'pothecaries, taught the art

By doctor's bills to play the doctor's part,
Bold in the practice of mistaken rules,
Prescribe, apply, and call their masters fools.
Some on the leaves of ancient authors prey,
Nor time nor moths e'er spoiled so much as they.
Some dryly plain, without invention's aid,
Write dull receipts how poems may be made.
These leave the sense their learning to display,
And those explain the meaning quite away.

   You then whose judgment the right course would steer,
Know well each ancient's proper character;
His fable, subject, scope in every page;
Religion, country, genius of his age:
Without all these at once before your eyes,
Cavil you may, but never criticize.
Be Homer's works your study and delight,
Read them by day, and meditate by night;
Thence form your judgment, thence your maxims bring,
And trace the Muses upward to their spring.
Still with itself compared, his text peruse;
And let your comment be the Mantuan Muse.

   When first young Maro in his boundless mind
A work to outlast immortal Rome designed,
Perhaps he seemed above the critic's law,
And but from Nature's fountains scorned to draw;
But when to examine every part he came,
Nature and Homer were, he found, the same.
Convinced, amazed, he checks the bold design, ⎫
And rules as strict his labored work confine ⎬
As if the Stagirite o'erlooked each line. ⎭
Learn hence for ancient rules a just esteem;
To copy Nature is to copy them.

   Some beauties yet no precepts can declare,
For there's a happiness as well as care.
Music resembles poetry, in each ⎫
Are nameless graces which no methods teach, ⎬
And which a master hand alone can reach. ⎭
If, where the rules not far enough extend

(Since rules were made but to promote their end)
Some lucky license answers to the full
The intent proposed, that license is a rule.
Thus Pegasus, a nearer way to take,
May boldly deviate from the common track.
From vulgar bounds with brave disorder part,
And snatch a grace beyond the reach of art,
Which without passing through the judgment, gains
The heart, and all its end at once attains.
In prospects thus, some objects please our eyes, ⎫
Which out of Nature's common order rise,   ⎬
The shapeless rock, or hanging precipice.   ⎭
Great wits sometimes may gloriously offend,
And rise to faults true critics dare not mend;
But though the ancients thus their rules invade
(As kings dispense with laws themselves have made)
Moderns, beware! or if you must offend
Against the precept, ne'er transgress its end;
Let it be seldom, and compelled by need;
And have at least their precedent to plead.
The critic else proceeds without remorse,
Seizes your fame, and puts his laws in force.
　　I know there are, to whose presumptuous thoughts
Those freer beauties, even in them, seem faults.
Some figures monstrous and misshaped appear,
Considered singly, or beheld too near,
Which, but proportioned to their light or place,
Due distance reconciles to form and grace.
A prudent chief not always must display
His powers in equal ranks and fair array,
But with the occasion and the place comply,
Conceal his force, nay seem sometimes to fly.
Those oft are stratagems which errors seem,
Nor is it Homer nods, but we that dream.
　　Still green with bays each ancient altar stands
Above the reach of sacrilegious hands,
Secure from flames, from envy's fiercer rage,
Destructive war, and all-involving age.

See, from each clime the learn'd their incense bring!
Here in all tongues consenting paeans ring!
In praise so just let every voice be joined,
And fill the general chorus of mankind.
Hail, bards triumphant! born in happier days,
Immortal heirs of universal praise!
Whose honors with increase of ages grow,
As streams roll down, enlarging as they flow;
Nations unborn your mighty names shall sound,
And worlds applaud that must not yet be found!
Oh, may some spark of your celestial fire,
The last, the meanest of your sons inspire
(That on weak wings, from far, pursues your flights,
Glows while he reads, but trembles as he writes)
To teach vain wits a science little known,
To admire superior sense, and doubt their own!

PART 2

Of all the causes which conspire to blind
Man's erring judgment, and misguide the mind,
What the weak head with strongest bias rules,
Is pride, the never-failing vice of fools.
Whatever Nature has in worth denied,
She gives in large recruits of needful pride;
For as in bodies, thus in souls, we find
What wants in blood and spirits swelled with wind:
Pride, where wit fails, steps in to our defense,
And fills up all the mighty void of sense.
If once right reason drives that cloud away,
Truth breaks upon us with resistless day.
Trust not yourself: but your defects to know,
Make use of every friend—and every foe.
   A little learning is a dangerous thing;
Drink deep, or taste not the Pierian spring.
There shallow draughts intoxicate the brain,
And drinking largely sobers us again.
Fired at first sight with what the Muse imparts,
In fearless youth we tempt the heights of arts,

While from the bounded level of our mind
Short views we take, nor see the lengths behind;
But more advanced, behold with strange surprise
New distant scenes of endless science rise!
So pleased at first the towering Alps we try,
Mount o'er the vales, and seem to tread the sky,
The eternal snows appear already past,
And the first clouds and mountains seem the last;
But, those attained, we tremble to survey
The growing labors of the lengthened way,
The increasing prospect tires our wandering eyes,
Hills peep o'er hills, and Alps on Alps arise!
   A perfect judge will read each work of wit
With the same spirit that its author writ:
Survey the whole, nor seek slight faults to find
Where Nature moves, and rapture warms the mind;
Nor lose, for that malignant dull delight,
The generous pleasure to be charmed with wit.
But in such lays as neither ebb nor flow,
Correctly cold, and regularly low,
That, shunning faults, one quiet tenor keep,
We cannot blame indeed—but we may sleep.
In wit, as nature, what affects our hearts
Is not the exactness of peculiar parts;
'Tis not a lip, or eye, we beauty call,
But the joint force and full result of all.
Thus when we view some well-proportioned dome
(The world's just wonder, and even thine, O Rome!),
No single parts unequally surprise,
All comes united to the admiring eyes:
No monstrous height, or breadth, or length appear;
The whole at once is bold and regular.
   Whoever thinks a faultless piece to see,
Thinks what ne'er was, nor is, nor e'er shall be.
In every work regard the writer's end,
Since none can compass more than they intend;
And if the means be just, the conduct true,
Applause, in spite of trivial faults, is due.

As men of breeding, sometimes men of wit,
To avoid great errors must the less commit,
Neglect the rules each verbal critic lays,
For not to know some trifles is a praise.
Most critics, fond of some subservient art,
Still make the whole depend upon a part:
They talk of principles, but notions prize,
And all to one loved folly sacrifice.
    Once on a time La Mancha's knight, they say,
A certain bard encountering on the way,
Discoursed in terms as just, with looks as sage,
As e'er could Dennis, of the Grecian stage;
Concluding all were desperate sots and fools
Who durst depart from Aristotle's rules.
Our author, happy in a judge so nice,
Produced his play, and begged the knight's advice;
Made him observe the subject and the plot,
The manners, passions, unities; what not?
All which exact to rule were brought about,
Were but a combat in the lists left out.
"What! leave the combat out?" exclaims the knight.
"Yes, or we must renounce the Stagirite."
"Not so, by Heaven!" he answers in a rage,
"Knights, squires, and steeds must enter on the stage."
"So vast a throng the stage can ne'er contain."
"Then build a new, or act it in a plain."
    Thus critics of less judgment than caprice,
Curious, not knowing, not exact, but nice,
Form short ideas, and offend in arts
(As most in manners), by a love to parts.
    Some to conceit alone their taste confine,
And glittering thoughts struck out at every line;
Pleased with a work where nothing's just or fit,
One glaring chaos and wild heap of wit.
Poets, like painters, thus unskilled to trace
The naked nature and the living grace,
With gold and jewels cover every part,
And hide with ornaments their want of art.

True wit is Nature to advantage dressed,
What oft was thought, but ne'er so well expressed;
Something whose truth convinced at sight we find,
That gives us back the image of our mind.
As shades more sweetly recommend the light,
So modest plainness sets off sprightly wit;
For works may have more wit than does them good,
As bodies perish through excess of blood.
   Others for language all their care express,
And value books, as women men, for dress.
Their praise is still—the style is excellent;
The sense they humbly take upon contènt.
Words are like leaves; and where they most abound,
Much fruit of sense beneath is rarely found.
False eloquence, like the prismatic glass,
Its gaudy colors spreads on every place;
The face of Nature we no more survey,
All glares alike, without distinction gay.
But true expression, like the unchanging sun, ⎫
Clears and improves whate'er it shines upon;   ⎬
It gilds all objects, but it alters none.   ⎭
Expression is the dress of thought, and still
Appears more decent as more suitable.
A vile conceit in pompous words expressed
Is like a clown in regal purple dressed:
For different styles with different subjects sort,
As several garbs with country, town, and court.
Some by old words to fame have made pretense,
Ancients in phrase, mere moderns in their sense.
Such labored nothings, in so strange a style,
Amaze the unlearn'd, and make the learned smile;
Unlucky as Fungoso in the play,   ⎫
These sparks with awkward vanity display ⎬
What the fine gentleman wore yesterday; ⎭
And but so mimic ancient wits at best,
As apes our grandsires in their doublets dressed.
In words as fashions the same rule will hold,
Alike fantastic if too new or old:

Be not the first by whom the new are tried,
Nor yet the last to lay the old aside.
  But most by numbers judge a poet's song,
And smooth or rough with them is right or wrong.
In the bright Muse though thousand charms conspire,
Her voice is all these tuneful fools admire,
Who haunt Parnassus but to please their ear, ⎫
Not mend their minds; as some to church repair, ⎬
Not for the doctrine, but the music there. ⎭
These equal syllables alone require,
Though oft the ear the open vowels tire,
While expletives their feeble aid do join,
And ten low words oft creep in one dull line:
While they ring round the same unvaried chimes,
With sure returns of still expected rhymes;
Where'er you find "the cooling western breeze,"
In the next line, it "whispers through the trees";
If crystal streams "with pleasing murmurs creep,"
The reader's threatened (not in vain) with "sleep";
Then, at the last and only couplet fraught
With some unmeaning thing they call a thought,
A needless Alexandrine ends the song
That, like a wounded snake, drags its slow length along.
Leave such to tune their own dull rhymes, and know
What's roundly smooth or languishingly slow;
And praise the easy vigor of a line
Where Denham's strength and Waller's sweetness join.
True ease in writing comes from art, not chance,
As those move easiest who have learned to dance.
'Tis not enough no harshness gives offense,
The sound must seem an echo to the sense.
Soft is the strain when Zephyr gently blows,
And the smooth stream in smoother numbers flows;
But when loud surges lash the sounding shore,
The hoarse, rough verse should like the torrent roar.
When Ajax strives some rock's vast weight to throw,
The line too labors, and the words move slow;
Not so when swift Camilla scours the plain,

Flies o'er the unbending corn, and skims along the main.
Hear how Timotheus' varied lays surprise,
And bid alternate passions fall and rise!
While at each change the son of Libyan Jove
Now burns with glory, and then melts with love;
Now his fierce eyes with sparkling fury glow,
Now sighs steal out, and tears begin to flow:
Persians and Greeks like turns of nature found
And the world's victor stood subdued by sound!
The power of music all our hearts allow,
And what Timotheus was is Dryden now.

Avoid extremes; and shun the fault of such
Who still are pleased too little or too much.
At every trifle scorn to take offense:
That always shows great pride, or little sense.
Those heads, as stomachs, are not sure the best,
Which nauseate all, and nothing can digest.
Yet let not each gay turn thy rapture move;
For fools admire, but men of sense approve:
As things seem large which we through mists descry,
Dullness is ever apt to magnify.

Some foreign writers, some our own despise;
The ancients only, or the moderns prize.
Thus wit, like faith, by each man is applied
To one small sect, and all are damned beside.
Meanly they seek the blessing to confine,
And force that sun but on a part to shine,
Which not alone the southern wit sublimes,
But ripens spirits in cold northern climes;
Which from the first has shone on ages past,
Enlights the present, and shall warm the last;
Though each may feel increases and decays,
And see now clearer and now darker days.
Regard not then if wit be old or new,
But blame the false and value still the true.

Some ne'er advance a judgment of their own,
But catch the spreading notion of the town;
They reason and conclude by precedent,

And own stale nonsense which they ne'er invent.
Some judge of authors' names, not works, and then
Nor praise nor blame the writings, but the men.
Of all this servile herd the worst is he
That in proud dullness joins with quality,
A constant critic at the great man's board,
To fetch and carry nonsense for my lord.
What woeful stuff this madrigal would be
In some starved hackney sonneteer or me!
But let a lord once own the happy lines,
How the wit brightens! how the style refines!
Before his sacred name flies every fault,
And each exalted stanza teems with thought!
   The vulgar thus through imitation err;
As oft the learn'd by being singular;
So much they scorn the crowd, that if the throng
By chance go right, they purposely go wrong.
So schismatics the plain believers quit,
And are but damned for having too much wit.
Some praise at morning what they blame at night,
But always think the last opinion right.
A Muse by these is like a mistress used,
This hour she's idolized, the next abused;
While their weak heads like towns unfortified,
'Twixt sense and nonsense daily change their side.
Ask them the cause; they're wiser still, they say;
And still tomorrow's wiser than today.
We think our fathers fools, so wise we grow;
Our wiser sons, no doubt, will think us so.
Once school divines this zealous isle o'erspread;
Who knew most sentences was deepest read.
Faith, Gospel, all seemed made to be disputed,
And none had sense enough to be confuted.
Scotists and Thomists now in peace remain
Amidst their kindred cobwebs in Duck Lane.
If faith itself has different dresses worn,
What wonder modes in wit should take their turn?
Oft, leaving what is natural and fit,

The current folly proves the ready wit;
And authors think their reputation safe,
Which lives as long as fools are pleased to laugh.
    Some valuing those of their own side or mind,
Still make themselves the measure of mankind:
Fondly we think we honor merit then,
When we but praise ourselves in other men.
Parties in wit attend on those of state,
And public faction doubles private hate.
Pride, Malice, Folly against Dryden rose,
In various shapes of parsons, critics, beaux;
But sense survived, when merry jests were past;
For rising merit will buoy up at last.
Might he return and bless once more our eyes,
New Blackmores and new Milbourns must arise.
Nay, should great Homer lift his awful head,
Zoilus again would start up from the dead.
Envy will merit, as its shade, pursue,
But like a shadow, proves the substance true;
For envied wit, like Sol eclipsed, makes known
The opposing body's grossness, not its own.
When first that sun too powerful beams displays,
It draws up vapors which obscure its rays;
But even those clouds at last adorn its way,
Reflect new glories, and augment the day.
    Be thou the first true merit to befriend;
His praise is lost who stays till all commend.
Short is the date, alas! of modern rhymes,
And 'tis but just to let them live betimes.
No longer now that golden age appears,
When patriarch wits survived a thousand years:
Now length of fame (our second life) is lost,
And bare threescore is all even that can boast;
Our sons their fathers' failing language see,
And such as Chaucer is shall Dryden be.
So when the faithful pencil has designed
Some bright idea of the master's mind,
Where a new world leaps out at his command,

And ready Nature waits upon his hand;
When the ripe colors soften and unite,
And sweetly melt into just shade and light;
When mellowing years their full perfection give,
And each bold figure just begins to live,
The treacherous colors the fair art betray,
And all the bright creation fades away!
　　Unhappy wit, like most mistaken things,
Atones not for that envy which it brings.
In youth alone its empty praise we boast,
But soon the short-lived vanity is lost;
Like some fair flower the early spring supplies,
That gaily blooms, but even in blooming dies,
What is this wit, which must our cares employ?
The owner's wife, that other men enjoy;
Then most our trouble still when most admired,
And still the more we give, the more required;
Whose fame with pains we guard, but lose with ease,
Sure some to vex, but never all to please;
'Tis what the vicious fear, the virtuous shun,
By fools 'tis hated, and by knaves undone!
　　If wit so much from ignorance undergo,
Ah, let not learning too commence its foe!
Of old those met rewards who could excel,
And such were praised who but endeavored well;
Though triumphs were to generals only due,
Crowns were reserved to grace the soldiers too.
Now they who reach Parnassus' lofty crown
Employ their pains to spurn some others down;
And while self-love each jealous writer rules,
Contending wits become the sport of fools;
But still the worst with most regret commend,
For each ill author is as bad a friend.
To what base ends, and by what abject ways,
Are mortals urged through sacred lust of praise!
Ah, ne'er so dire a thirst of glory boast,
Nor in the critic let the man be lost!

Good nature and good sense must ever join;
To err is human, to forgive divine.
  But if in noble minds some dregs remain
Nor yet purged off, of spleen and sour disdain,
Discharge that rage on more provoking crimes,
Nor fear a dearth in these flagitious times.
No pardon vile obscenity should find,
Though wit and art conspire to move your mind;
But dullness with obscenity must prove
As shameful sure as impotence in love.
In the fat age of pleasure, wealth, and ease
Sprung the rank weed, and thrived with large increase:
When love was all an easy monarch's care,
Seldom at council, never in a war;
Jilts ruled the state, and statesmen farces writ;
Nay, wits had pensions, and young lords had wit;
The fair sat panting at a courtier's play,
And not a mask went unimproved away;
The modest fan was lifted up no more,
And virgins smiled at what they blushed before.
The following license of a foreign reign
Did all the dregs of bold Socinus drain;
Then unbelieving priests reformed the nation,
And taught more pleasant methods of salvation;
Where Heaven's free subjects might their rights dispute,
Lest God himself should seem too absolute;
Pulpits their sacred satire learned to spare,
And Vice admired to find a flatterer there!
Encouraged thus, wit's Titans braved the skies,
And the press groaned with licensed blasphemies.
These monsters, critics! with your darts engage,
Here point your thunder, and exhaust your rage!
Yet shun their fault, who, scandalously nice,
Will needs mistake an author into vice;
All seems infected that the infected spy,
As all looks yellow to the jaundiced eye.

PART 3

Learn then what morals critics ought to show,
For 'tis but half a judge's task, to know.
'Tis not enough, taste, judgment, learning, join;
In all you speak, let truth and candor shine:
That not alone what to your sense is due
All may allow; but seek your friendship too.

Be silent always when you doubt your sense;
And speak, though sure, with seeming diffidence:
Some positive, persisting fops we know,
Who, if once wrong, will needs be always so;
But you, with pleasure own your errors past,
And make each day a critic on the last.

'Tis not enough, your counsel still be true;
Blunt truths more mischief than nice falsehoods do;
Men must be taught as if you taught them not,
And things unknown proposed as things forgot.
Without good breeding, truth is disapproved;
That only makes superior sense beloved.

Be niggards of advice on no pretense;
For the worst avarice is that of sense.
With mean complacence ne'er betray your trust,
Nor be so civil as to prove unjust.
Fear not the anger of the wise to raise;
Those best can bear reproof, who merit praise.

'Twere well might critics still this freedom take;
But Appius reddens at each word you speak,
And stares, tremendous! with a threatening eye,
Like some fierce tyrant in old tapestry.
Fear most to tax an honorable fool,
Whose right it is, uncensured to be dull;
Such, without wit, are poets when they please,
As without learning they can take degrees.
Leave dangerous truths to unsuccessful satyrs,
And flattery to fulsome dedicators,
Whom, when they praise, the world believes no more,
Than when they promise to give scribbling o'er.

'Tis best sometimes your censure to restrain,
And charitably let the dull be vain:
Your silence there is better than your spite,
For who can rail so long as they can write?
Still humming on, their drowsy course they keep,
And lashed so long, like tops, are lashed asleep.
False steps but help them to renew the race,
As, after stumbling, jades will mend their pace.
What crowds of these, impenitently bold,
In sounds and jingling syllables grown old,
Still run on poets, in a raging vein,
Even to the dregs and squeezings of the brain,
Strain out the last dull droppings of their sense,
And rhyme with all the rage of impotence.
  Such shameless bards we have, and yet 'tis true,
There are as mad, abandoned critics too.
The bookful blockhead, ignorantly read,
With loads of learned lumber in his head.
With his own tongue still edifies his ears,
And always listening to himself appears.
All books he reads, and all he reads assails,
From Dryden's *Fables* down to Durfey's *Tales*.
With him, most authors steal their works, or buy;
Garth did not write his own *Dispensary*.
Name a new play, and he's the poet's friend,
Nay showed his faults—but when would poets mend?
No place so sacred from such fops is barred,
Nor is Paul's church more safe than Paul's churchyard:
Nay, fly to altars; *there* they'll talk you dead:
For fools rush in where angels fear to tread.
Distrustful sense with modest caution speaks,　⎱
It still looks home, and short excursions makes;　⎰
But rattling nonsense in full volleys breaks,
And never shocked, and never turned aside,
Bursts out, resistless, with a thundering tide.
  But where's the man, who counsel can bestow,
Still pleased to teach, and yet not proud to know?
Unbiased, or by favor, or by spite:

[307]

Not dully prepossessed, nor blindly right;
Though learned, well-bred; and though well-bred, sincere;
Modestly bold, and humanly severe:
Who to a friend his faults can freely show,
And gladly praise the merit of a foe?
Blessed with a taste exact, yet unconfined;
A knowledge both of books and humankind;
Gen'rous converse; a soul exempt from pride;
And love to praise, with reason on his side?
  Such once were critics; such the happy few,
Athens and Rome in better ages knew.
The mighty Stagirite first left the shore,
Spread all his sails, and durst the deeps explore;
He steered securely, and discovered far,
Led by the light of the Mæonian star.
Poets, a race long unconfined, and free,
Still fond and proud of savage liberty,
Received his laws; and stood convinced 'twas fit,
Who conquered nature, should preside o'er wit.
  Horace still charms with graceful negligence,
And without method talks us into sense;
Will, like a friend, familiarly convey
The truest notions in the easiest way.
He, who supreme in judgment, as in wit,
Might boldly censure, as he boldly writ,
Yet judged with coolness, though he sung with fire;
His precepts teach but what his works inspire.
Our critics take a contrary extreme,
They judge with fury, but they write with fle'me.
Nor suffers Horace more in wrong translations
By wits, than critics in as wrong quotations.
  See Dionysius Homer's thoughts refine,
And call new beauties forth from every line!
  Fancy and art in gay Petronius please,
The scholar's learning, with the courtier's ease.
  In grave Quintilian's copious work, we find
The justest rules, and clearest method joined:
Thus useful arms in magazines we place,

All ranged in order, and disposed with grace,
But less to please the eye, than arm the hand,
Still fit for use, and ready at command.
  Thee, bold Longinus! all the nine inspire,
And bless their critic with a poet's fire.
An ardent judge, who, zealous in his trust,
With warmth gives sentence, yet is always just;
Whose own example strengthens all his laws,
And is himself that great sublime he draws.
  Thus long succeeding critics justly reigned,
License repressed, and useful laws ordained.
Learning and Rome alike in empire grew;
And arts still followed where her eagles flew;
From the same foes, at last, both felt their doom,
And the same age saw learning fall, and Rome.
With tyranny, then superstition joined,
As that the body, this enslaved the mind;
Much was believed, but little understood,
And to be dull was construed to be good;
A second deluge learning thus o'errun,
And the monks finished what the Goths begun.
  At length Erasmus, that great, injured name
(The glory of the priesthood, and the shame!),
Stemmed the wild torrent of a barb'rous age,
And drove those holy Vandals off the stage.
  But see! each Muse, in Leo's golden days,
Starts from her trance, and trims her withered bays!
Rome's ancient Genius, o'er its ruins spread,
Shakes off the dust, and rears his reverend head.
Then sculpture and her sister-arts revive;
Stones leaped to form, and rocks began to live;
With sweeter notes each rising temple rung;
A Raphael painted, and a Vida sung.
Immortal Vida: on whose honored brow
The poet's bays and critic's ivy grow:
Cremona now shall ever boast thy name,
As next in place to Mantua, next in fame!

But soon by impious arms from Latium chased,
Their ancient bounds the banished Muses passed;
Thence arts o'er all the northern world advance,
But critic-learning flourished most in France:
The rules a nation, born to serve, obeys;
And Boileau still in right of Horace sways.
But we, brave Britons, foreign laws despised,
And kept unconquered—and uncivilized;
Fierce for the liberties of wit, and bold,
We still defied the Romans, as of old.
Yet some there were, among the sounder few
Of those who less presumed, and better knew,
Who durst assert the juster ancient cause,
And here restored wit's fundamental laws.
Such was the Muse, whose rules and practice tell,
"Nature's chief masterpiece is writing well."
Such was Roscommon, not more learned than good,
With manners gen'rous as his noble blood;
To him the wit of Greece and Rome was known,
And every author's merit, but his own.
Such late was Walsh—the Muse's judge and friend,
Who justly knew to blame or to commend;
To failings mild, but zealous for desert;
The clearest head, and the sincerest heart.
This humble praise, lamented shade! receive,
This praise at least a grateful Muse may give:
The Muse, whose early voice you taught to sing,
Prescribed her heights, and pruned her tender wing,
(Her guide now lost) no more attempts to rise,
But in low numbers short excursions tries:
Content, if hence the unlearned their wants may view,
The learned reflect on what before they knew:
Careless of censure, nor too fond of fame;
Still pleased to praise, yet not afraid to blame;
Averse alike to flatter, or offend;
Not free from faults, nor yet too vain to mend.

Pope produced his effervescent essay at about the age of twenty. The period around 1710 was probably the last time anybody writing literary criticism in Europe could in effect limit his inquiry to poetry. Pope's main exemplars are Horace and Boileau, to whom he acknowledges his debt. A verse essay on verse labors under the double burden of needing to succeed as precept and as example. (Note that: "to tell them" is "to tally them"; "science" is "branch of knowledge"; "doctors' bills" is "prescriptions"; "receipts" is "recipes"; "tempt" is "attempt"; "clown" is "hick"; "flagitious" is "scandalously evil"; "lumber" is "trash"; "fle'me" is "phlegm"; "low numbers" is "humble poems.")

We think so much of Samuel Johnson, the imposing "Doctor Johnson," that we call his day the Age of Johnson, reflecting chiefly his stature both as a great lexicographer and prose-writer and as the subject of what is indisputably the most wonderful literary biography in the language. We are likely to forget the Samuel Johnson who was also among the finest poets of his age. Although he died more than 200 years ago, his example remains brightly in view when we think about the history of periodical writing, biography, dictionaries, the profession of the writer, and the place of the "man of letters."

A Short Song of Congratulation

»»»»»

Long-expected one and twenty
  Ling'ring year at last is flown,
Pomp and pleasure, pride and plenty,
  Great Sir John, are all your own.

Loosened from the minor's tether;
  Free to mortgage or to sell,
Wild as wind, and light as feather
  Bid the slaves of thrift farewell.

Call the Bettys, Kates, and Jennys
  Every name that laughs at care,
Lavish of your grandsire's guineas,
  Show the spirit of an heir.

All that prey on vice and folly
  Joy to see their quarry fly:
Here the gamester light and jolly,
  There the lender grave and sly.

Wealth, Sir John, was made to wander,
   Let it wander as it will;
See the jockey, see the pander,
   Bid them come, and take their fill.

When the bonny blade carouses,
   Pockets full, and spirits high,
What are acres? What are houses?
   Only dirt, or wet or dry.

If the guardian or the mother
   Tell the woes of willful waste,
Scorn their counsel and their pother,
   You can hang or drown at last.

Johnson included this marvel of irony in a letter to Hester Thrale, saying, "You have heard in the papers how Sir J. Lade is come to age, I have enclosed a short song of congratulation, which you must not show to any body . . . ." Sir John was a notorious hell-raiser. He happened to be Mrs. Thrale's nephew, and he came to no good.

On the Death of Mr. Robert Levet, a Practiser in Physic

Condemned to Hope's delusive mine,
  As on we toil from day to day,
By sudden blasts or slow decline
  Our social comforts drop away.

Well tried through many a varying year,
  See Levet to the grave descend;
Officious, innocent, sincere,
  Of every friendless name the friend.

Yet still he fills affection's eye,
  Obscurely wise and coarsely kind;
Nor, lettered Arrogance, deny
  Thy praise to merit unrefined.

When fainting nature called for aid,
  And hovering death prepared the blow,
His vigorous remedy displayed
  The power of art without the show.

In Misery's darkest cavern known,
  His useful care was ever nigh,
Where hopeless Anguish poured his groan,
  And lonely Want retired to die.

No summons mocked by chill delay,
  No petty gain disdained by pride;
The modest wants of every day
  The toil of every day supplied.

His virtues walked their narrow round,
  Nor made a pause, nor left a void;
And sure the Eternal Master found
  The single talent well employed.

The busy day, the peaceful night,
  Unfelt, uncounted, glided by;
His frame was firm—his powers were bright,
  Though now his eightieth year was nigh.

Then with no fiery throbbing pain,
  No cold gradations of decay,
Death broke at once the vital chain,
  And freed his soul the nearest way.

By as much as Sir John Lade (in "A Short Song of Congratulation," p. 312) falls short of decency, Robert Levet—sometimes styled "Doctor" although he was not licensed—exceeded normal expectations. Although ungainly and grotesque, Levet had a good heart and knew enough about medicine to be of help to those in need. He lived for many years in Johnson's house. (Note that: "officious" is "kind," "performing good works.")

The Vanity of Human Wishes: The Tenth Satire of Juvenal Imitated

Let Observation with extensive View,
Survey Mankind, from *China to Peru;*
Remark each anxious Toil, each eager Strife,
And watch the busy Scenes of crouded Life;
Then say how Hope and Fear, Desire and Hate,
O'erspread with Snares the clouded Maze of Fate,
Where wav'ring Man, betray'd by vent'rous Pride,
To tread the dreary Paths without a Guide;
As treach'rous Phantoms in the Mist delude,
Shuns fancied Ills, or chases airy Good.
How rarely Reason guides the stubborn Choice,
Rules the bold Hand, or prompts the suppliant Voice,
How Nations sink, by darling Schemes oppress'd,
When Vengeance listens to the Fool's Request.
Fate wings with ev'ry Wish th' afflictive Dart,
Each Gift of Nature, and each Grace of Art,
With fatal Heat impetuous Courage glows,
With fatal Sweetness Elocution flows,
Impeachment stops the Speaker's pow'rful Breath,
And restless Fire precipitates on Death.

But scarce observ'd the Knowing and the Bold,
Fall in the gen'ral Massacre of Gold;
Wide-wasting Pest! that rages unconfin'd,
And crouds with Crimes the Records of Mankind,
For Gold his Sword the Hireling Ruffian draws,
For Gold the hireling Judge distorts the Laws;
Wealth heap'd on Wealth, nor Truth nor Safety buys,
The Dangers gather as the Treasures rise.

Let Hist'ry tell where rival Kings command,
And dubious Title shakes the madded Land,
When Statutes glean the Refuse of the Sword,
How much more safe the Vassal than the Lord,

Low sculks the Hind beneath the Rage of Pow'r,
And leaves the wealthy Traytor in the *Tow'r,*
Untouch'd his Cottage, and his Slumbers sound,
Tho' Confiscation's Vulturs hover round.

The needy Traveller, serene and gay,
Walks the wild Heath, and sings his Toil away.
Dos Envy seize thee? crush th' upbraiding Joy,
Increase his Riches and his Peace destroy,
Now Fears in dire Vicissitude invade,
The rustling Brake alarms, and quiv'ring Shade,
Nor Light nor Darkness bring his Pain Relief,
One shews the Plunder, and one hides the Thief.

Yet still one gen'ral Cry the Skies assails,
And Gain and Grandeur load the tainted Gales;
Few know the toiling Statesman's Fear or Care,
Th' insidious Rival and the gaping Heir.

Once more, *Democritus,* arise on Earth,
With chearful Wisdom and instructive Mirth,
See motly Life in modern Trappings dress'd,
And feed with varied Fools th' eternal Jest:
Thou who couldst laugh where Want enchain'd Caprice
Toil crush'd Conceit, and Man was of a Piece;
Where Wealth unlov'd without a Mourner dy'd;
And scarce a Sycophant was fed by Pride;
Where ne'er was known the Form of mock Debate,
Or seen a new-made Mayor's unwieldly State;
Where Change of Fav'rites made no Change of Laws,
And Senates heard before they judg'd a Cause;
How wouldst thou shake at *Britain's* modish Tribe,
Dart the quick Taunt, and edge the piercing Gibe?
Attentive Truth and Nature to descry,
And pierce each Scene with Philosophic Eye.
To thee were solemn Toys or empty Shew,
The Robes of Pleasure and the Veils of Woe:
All aid the Farce, and all thy Mirth maintain,
Whose Joys are causeless, or whose Griefs are vain.

Such was the Scorn that fill'd the Sage's Mind,
Renew'd at ev'ry Glance on Humankind;

How just that Scorn ere yet thy Voice declare,
Search every State, and canvass ev'ry Pray'r.
   Unnumber'd Suppliants croud Preferment's Gate,
Athirst for Wealth, and burning to be great;
Delusive Fortune hears th' incessant Call,
They mount, they shine, evaporate, and fall.
On ev'ry Stage the Foes of Peace attend,
Hate dogs their Flight, and Insult mocks their End.
Love ends with Hope, the sinking Statesman's Door
Pours in the Morning Worshiper no more;
For growing Names the weekly Scribbler lies,
To growing Wealth the Dedicator flies,
From every Room descends the painted Face,
That hung the bright *Palladium* of the Place,
And smoak'd in Kitchens, or in Auctions sold,
To better Features yields the Frame of Gold;
For now no more we trace in ev'ry Line
Heroic Worth, Benevolence Divine:
The Form distorted justifies the Fall,
And Detestation rids th' indignant Wall.
   But will not *Britain* hear the last Appeal,
Sign her Foes Doom, or guard her Fav'rites Zeal;
Through Freedom's Sons no more Remonstrance rings,
Degrading Nobles and controuling Kings;
Our supple Tribes repress their Patriot Throats,
And ask no Questions but the Price of Votes;
With Weekly Libels and Septennial Ale,
Their Wish is full to riot and to rail.
   In full-blown Dignity, see *Wolsey* stand,
Law in his Voice, and Fortune in his Hand:
To him the Church, the Realm, their Pow'rs consign,
Thro' him the Rays of regal Bounty shine,
Turn'd by his Nod the Stream of Honour flows,
His Smile alone Security bestows:
Still to new Heights his restless Wishes tow'r,
Claim leads to Claim, and Pow'r advances Pow'r;
Till Conquest unresisted ceas'd to please,
And Rights submitted, left him none to seize.

At length his Sov'reign frowns—the Train of State
Mark the keen Glance, and watch the Sign to hate;
Where-e'er he turns he meets a Stranger's Eye,
His Suppliants scorn him, and his Followers fly;
Now drops at once the Pride of aweful State,
The golden Canopy, the glitt'ring Plate,
The regal Palace, the luxurious Board,
The liv'ried Army, and the menial Lord.
With Age, with Cares, with Maladies oppress'd,
He seeks the Refuge of Monastic Rest.
Grief aids Disease, remember'd Folly stings,
And his last Sighs reproach the Faith of Kings.

Speak thou, whose Thoughts at humble Peace repine,
Shall *Wolsey's* Wealth, with *Wolsey's* End be thine?
Or liv'st thou now, with safer Pride content,
The wisest Justice on the Banks of *Trent?*
For why did *Wolsey* near the Steeps of Fate,
On weak Foundations raise th' enormous Weight?
Why but to sink beneath Misfortune's Blow,
With louder Ruin to the Gulphs below?

What gave great *Villiers* to th' Assassin's Knife,
And fix'd Disease on *Harley's* closing Life?
What murder'd *Wentworth*, and what exil'd *Hyde*,
By Kings protected, and to Kings ally'd?
What but their Wish indulg'd in Courts to shine,
And Pow'r too great to keep or to resign?

When first the College Rolls receive his Name,
The young Enthusiast quits his Ease for Fame;
Through all his Veins the Fever of Renown
Burns from the strong Contagion of the Gown;
O'er *Bodley's* Dome his future Labours spread,
And *Bacon's* Mansion trembles o'er his Head.
Are these thy Views? proceed, illustrious Youth,
And Virtue guard thee to the Throne of Truth!
Yet should thy Soul indulge the gen'rous Heat,
Till captive Science yields her last Retreat;
Should Reason guide thee with her brightest Ray,
And pour on misty Doubt resistless Day;

Should no false Kindness lure to loose Delight,
Nor Praise relax, nor Difficulty fright;
Should tempting Novelty thy Cell refrain,
And Sloth effuse her opiate Fumes in vain;
Should Beauty blunt on Fops her fatal Dart,
Nor claim the Triumph of a letter'd Heart;
Should no Disease thy torpid Veins invade,
Nor Melancholy's Phantoms haunt thy Shade;
Yet hope not Life from Grief or Danger free,
Nor think the Doom of Man revers'd for thee:
Deign on the passing World to turn thine Eyes,
And pause awhile from Letters, to be wise;
These mark what Ills the Scholar's Life assail,
Toil, Envy, Want, the Patron, and the Jail.
See Nations slowly wise, and meanly just,
To buried Merit raise the tardy Bust.
If Dreams yet flatter, once again attend,
Hear *Lydiat's* life, and *Galileo's* end.

   Nor deem, when Learning her last Prize bestows
The glitt'ring Eminence exempt from Foes;
See when the Vulgar 'scape, despis'd or aw'd,
Rebellion's vengeful Talons seize on *Laud*.
From meaner Minds, tho' smaller Fines content
The plunder'd Palace or sequester'd Rent;
Mark'd out by dangerous Parts he meets the Shock,
And fatal Learning leads him to the Block:
Around his Tomb let Art and Genius weep,
But hear his Death, ye Blockheads, hear and sleep.

   The festal Blazes, the triumphal Show,
The ravish'd Standard, and the captive Foe,
The Senate's Thanks, the Gazette's pompous Tale,
With Force resistless o'er the Brave prevail.
Such Bribes the rapid *Greek* o'er *Asia* whirl'd,
For such the steady *Romans* shook the World;
For such in distant Lands the *Britons* shine,
And stain with Blood the *Danube* or the *Rhine*;
This Pow'r has Praise, that Virtue scarce can warm,
Till Fame supplies the universal Charm.

Yet Reason frowns on War's unequal Game,
Where wasted Nations raise a single Name,
And mortgag'd States their Grandsires Wreaths regret,
From Age to Age in everlasting Debt;
Wreaths which at last the dear-bought Right convey
To rust on Medals, or on Stones decay.
   On what Foundation stands the Warrior's Pride,
How just his Hopes let *Swedish Charles* decide;
A Frame of Adamant, a Soul of Fire,
No Dangers fright him, and no Labours tire;
O'er Love, o'er Fear extends his wide Domain,
Unconquer'd Lord of Pleasure and of Pain;
No Joys to him pacific Scepters yield,
War sounds the Trump, he rushes to the Field;
Behold surrounding Kings their Pow'rs combine,
And One capitulate, and One resign;
Peace courts his Hand, but spreads her Charms in vain;
"Think Nothing gain'd," he cries, "till nought remain,
On *Moscow's* Walls till *Gothic* Standards fly,
And All be mine beneath the Polar Sky."
The March begins in Military State,
And Nations on his Eye suspended wait;
Stern Famine guards the solitary Coast,
And Winter barricades the Realms of Frost;
He comes, nor Want nor Cold his Course delay;—
Hide, blushing Glory, hide *Pultowa's* Day:
The vanquish'd Hero leaves his broken Bands,
And shews his Miseries in distant Lands;
Condemn'd a needy Supplicant to wait,
While Ladies interpose, and Slaves debate.
But did not Chance at length her Error mend?
Did no subverted Empire mark his End?
Did rival Monarchs give the fatal Wound?
Or hostile Millions press him to the Ground?
His Fall was destin'd to a barren Strand,
A petty Fortress, and a dubious Hand;
He left the Name, at which the World grew pale,
To point a Moral, or adorn a Tale.

All Times their Scenes of pompous Woes afford,
From *Persia's* Tyrant to *Bavaria's* Lord.
In gay Hostility, and barb'rous Pride,
With half Mankind embattled at his Side,
Great *Xerxes* comes to seize the certain Prey,
And starves exhausted Regions in his Way;
Attendant Flatt'ry counts his Myriads o'er,
Till counted Myriads sooth his Pride no more;
Fresh Praise is try'd till Madness fires his Mind,
The Waves he lashes, and enchains the Wind;
New Pow'rs are claim'd, new Pow'rs are still bestow'd,
Till rude Resistance lops the spreading God;
The daring *Greeks* deride the Martial Shew,
And heap their Vallies with the gaudy Foe;
Th' insulted Sea with humbler Thoughts he gains,
A single Skiff to speed his Flight remains;
Th' incumber'd Oar scarce leaves the dreaded Coast
Through purple Billows and a floating Host.
    The bold *Bavarian*, in a luckless Hour,
Tries the dread Summits of *Cesarean* Pow'r,
With unexpected Legions bursts away,
And sees defenceless Realms receive his Sway;
Short Sway! fair *Austria* spreads her mournful Charms,
The Queen, the Beauty, sets the World in Arms;
From Hill to Hill the Beacons rousing Blaze
Spreads wide the Hope of Plunder and of Praise;
The fierce *Croatian*, and the wild *Hussar*,
With all the Sons of Ravage croud the War;
The baffled Prince in Honour's flatt'ring Bloom
Of hasty Greatness finds the fatal Doom,
His foes Derision, and his Subjects Blame,
And steals to Death from Anguish and from Shame.
    Enlarge my Life with Multitude of Days,
In Health, in Sickness, thus the Suppliant prays;
Hides from himself his State, and shuns to know,
That Life protracted is protracted Woe.
Time hovers o'er, impatient to destroy,
And shuts up all the Passages of Joy:

In vain their Gifts the bounteous Seasons pour,
The Fruit Autumnal, and the Vernal Flow'r,
With listless Eyes the Dotard views the Store,
He views, and wonders that they please no more;
Now pall the tastless Meats, and joyless Wines,
And Luxury with Sighs her Slave resigns.
Approach, ye Minstrels, try the soothing Strain,
Diffuse the tuneful Lenitives of Pain:
No Sounds alas would touch th' impervious Ear,
Though dancing Mountains witness'd *Orpheus* near;
Nor Lute nor Lyre his feeble Pow'rs attend,
Nor sweeter Musick of a virtuous Friend,
But everlasting Dictates croud his Tongue,
Perversely grave, or positively wrong.
The still returning Tale, and ling'ring Jest,
Perplex the fawning Niece and pamper'd Guest,
While growing Hopes scarce awe the gath'ring Sneer,
And scarce a Legacy can bribe to hear;
The watchful Guests still hint the last Offence,
The Daughter's Petulance, the Son's Expence,
Improve his heady Rage with treach'rous Skill,
And mould his Passions till they make his Will.

   Unnumber'd Maladies his Joints invade,
Lay Siege to Life and press the dire Blockade;
But unextinguish'd Av'rice still remains,
And dreaded Losses aggravate his Pains;
He turns, with anxious Heart and cripled Hands,
His Bonds of Debt, and Mortgages of Lands;
Or views his Coffers with suspicious Eyes,
Unlocks his Gold, and counts it till he dies.

   But grant, the Virtues of a temp'rate Prime
Bless with an Age exempt from Scorn or Crime;
An Age that melts with unperceiv'd Decay,
And glides in modest Innocence away;
Whose peaceful Day Benevolence endears,
Whose Night congratulating Conscience cheers;
The gen'ral Fav'rite as the gen'ral Friend:
Such Age there is, and who shall wish its End?

Yet ev'n on this her Load Misfortune flings,
To press the weary Minutes flagging Wings:
New Sorrow rises as the Day returns,
A Sister sickens, or a Daughter mourns.
Now Kindred Merit fills the sable Bier,
Now lacerated Friendship claims a Tear.
Year chases Year, Decay pursues Decay,
Still drops some Joy from with'ring Life away;
New Forms arise, and diff'rent Views engage,
Superfluous lags the Vet'ran on the Stage,
Till pitying Nature signs the last Release,
And bids afflicted Worth retire to Peace.

But few there are whom Hours like these await,
Who set unclouded in the Gulphs of Fate.
From *Lydia's* Monarch should the Search descend,
By *Solon* caution'd to regard his End,
In Life's last Scene what Prodigies surprise,
Fears of the Brave, and Follies of the Wise?
From *Marlb'rough's* Eyes the Streams of Dotage flow,
And *Swift* expires a Driv'ler and a Show.

The teeming Mother, anxious for her Race,
Begs for each Birth the Fortune of a Face:
Yet *Vane* could tell what Ills from Beauty spring;
And *Sedley* curs'd the Form that pleas'd a King.
Ye Nymphs of rosy Lips and radiant Eyes,
Whom Pleasure keeps too busy to be wise,
Whom Joys with soft Varieties invite,
By Day the Frolick, and the Dance by Night,
Who frown with Vanity, who smile with Art,
And ask the latest Fashion of the Heart,
What Care, what Rules your heedless Charms shall save,
Each Nymph your Rival, and each Youth your Slave?
Against your Fame with Fondness Hate combines,
The Rival batters, and the Lover mines.
With distant Voice neglected Virtue calls,
Less heard and less, the faint Remonstrance falls;
Tir'd with Contempt, she quits the slipp'ry Reign,
And Pride and Prudence take her Seat in vain.

In croud at once, where none the Pass defend,
The harmless Freedom, and the private Friend.
The Guardians yield, by Force superior ply'd;
To Int'rest, Prudence; and to Flatt'ry, Pride.
Here Beauty falls betray'd, despis'd, distress'd,
And hissing Infamy proclaims the rest.
    Where then shall Hope and Fear their Objects find?
Must dull Suspence corrupt the stagnant Mind?
Must helpless Man, in Ignorance sedate,
Roll darkling down the Torrent of his Fate?
Must no Dislike alarm, no Wishes rise,
Nor Cries invoke the Mercies of the Skies?
Enquirer, cease, Petitions yet remain,
Which Heav'n may hear, nor deem Religion vain.
Still raise for Good the supplicating Voice,
But leave to Heav'n the Measure and the Choice.
Safe in his Pow'r, whose Eyes discern afar
The secret Ambush of a specious Pray'r.
Implore his Aid, in his Decisions rest,
Secure whate'er he gives, he gives the best.
Yet when the Sense of sacred Presence fires,
And Strong Devotion to the Skies aspires,
Pour forth thy Fervours for a healthful Mind,
Obedient Passions, and a Will resign'd;
For Love, which scarce collective Man can fill;
For Patience sov'reign o'er transmuted Ill;
For Faith, that panting for a happier Seat,
Counts Death kind Nature's Signal of Retreat:
These Goods for Man the Laws of Heav'n ordain,
These Goods he grants, who grants the Pow'r to gain;
With these celestial Wisdom calms the Mind,
And makes the Happiness she does not find.

So powerfully does Johnson adapt Juvenal's dignified satirical manner that the poem can reach back to such familiar examples from classical antiquity as Xerxes and Alexander, can graciously include a touching sketch of the senile Swift (who had died in 1745, just four years before Johnson's poem was written), and can reach forward to our own time. Johnson's "remembered folly stings" is very probably one ancestor of Eliot's "fools' approval stings" in "Little Gidding" (p. 987). (Note that: "lenitives" are substances that lighten pain.)

THOMAS GRAY 1716-1771

Gray was born in London and educated at Eton and Cambridge. Although he held a law degree, he devoted his life to the study of language and literature. Toward the end of his life he was made Professor of Modern History at Cambridge. Gray could be regarded as a bridge, or at least a bridge-builder, between the neo-classical values of the Augustan Age and the romantic values of the later eighteenth century, and also between the interest of scholarly learning and the fascination of great popularity.

Elegy Written in a Country Churchyard

The curfew tolls the knell of parting day,
The lowing herd wind slowly o'er the lea,
The plowman homeward plods his weary way,
And leaves the world to darkness and to me.

Now fades the glimmering landscape on the sight,
And all the air a solemn stillness holds,
Save where the beetle wheels his droning flight,
And drowsy tinklings lull the distant folds;

Save that from yonder ivy-mantled tower
The moping owl does to the moon complain
Of such as, wand'ring near her secret bower,
Molest her ancient solitary reign.

Beneath those rugged elms, that yew tree's shade,
Where heaves the turf in many a mold'ring heap,
Each in his narrow cell for ever laid,
The rude forefathers of the hamlet sleep.

The breezy call of incense-breathing morn,
The swallow twitt'ring from the straw-built shed,
The cock's shrill clarion, or the echoing horn,
No more shall rouse them from their lowly bed.

For them no more the blazing hearth shall burn,
Or busy houswife ply her evening care;
No children run to lisp their sire's return,
Or climb his knees the envied kiss to share.

Oft did the harvest to their sickle yield,
Their furrow oft the stubborn glebe has broke;
How jocund did they drive their team afield!
How bowed the woods beneath their sturdy stroke!

Let not Ambition mock their useful toil,
Their homely joys, and destiny obscure;
Nor Grandeur hear with a disdainful smile
The short and simple annals of the poor.

The boast of heraldry, the pomp of pow'r,
And all that beauty, all that wealth e'er gave,
Awaits alike th' inevitable hour.
The paths of glory lead but to the grave.

Nor you, ye Proud, impute to these the fault,
If Mem'ry o'er their tomb no trophies raise,
Where through the long-drawn aisle and fretted vault
The pealing anthem swells the note of praise.

Can storied urn or animated bust
Back to its mansion call the fleeting breath?
Can Honor's voice provoke the silent dust,
Or Flatt'ry soothe the dull cold ear of Death?

Perhaps in this neglected spot is laid
Some heart once pregnant with celestial fire;
Hands that the rod of empire might have swayed,
Or waked to ecstasy the living lyre.

But Knowledge to their eyes her ample page
Rich with the spoils of time did ne'er unroll;
Chill Penury repressed their noble rage,
And froze the genial current of the soul.

Full many a gem of purest ray serene,
The dark unfathomed caves of ocean bear:
Full many a flower is born to blush unseen,
And waste its sweetness on the desert air.

Some village Hampden, that with dauntless breast
The little tyrant of his fields withstood;
Some mute inglorious Milton here may rest,
Some Cromwell, guiltless of his country's blood.

Th' applause of list'ning senates to command,
The threats of pain and ruin to despise,
To scatter plenty o'er a smiling land,
And read their hist'ry in a nation's eyes.

Their lot forbade; nor circumscribed alone
Their glowing virtues, but their crimes confined;
Forbade to wade through slaughter to a throne,
And shut the gates of mercy on mankind.

The struggling pangs of conscious truth to hide,
To quench the blushes of ingenuous shame,
Or heap the shrine of Luxury and Pride
With incense kindled at the Muse's flame.

Far from the madding crowd's ignoble strife,
Their sober wishes never learned to stray;
Along the cool sequestered vale of life
They kept the noiseless tenor of their way.

Yet ev'n these bones from insult to protect
Some frail memorial still erected nigh,
With uncouth rhymes and shapeless sculpture decked,
Implores the passing tribute of a sigh.

Their name, their years, spelt by th' unlettered Muse,
The place of fame and elegy supply:
And many a holy text around she strews,
That teach the rustic moralist to die.

For who to dumb Forgetfulness a prey,
This pleasing anxious being e'er resigned,
Left the warm precincts of the cheerful day,
Nor cast one longing ling'ring look behind?

On some fond breast the parting soul relies,
Some pious drops the closing eye requires;
Ev'n from the tomb the voice of Nature cries,
Ev'n in our ashes live their wonted fires.

For thee, who mindful of th' unhonor'd dead
Dost in these lines their artless tale relate;
If chance, by lonely contemplation led,
Some kindred spirit shall inquire thy fate,

Haply some hoary-headed swain may say,
"Oft have we seen him at the peep of dawn
Brushing with hasty steps the dews away
To meet the sun upon the upland lawn.

"There at the foot of yonder nodding beech
That wreathes its old fantastic roots so high,
His listless length at noontide would he stretch,
And pore upon the brook that babbles by.

"Hard by yon wood, now smiling as in scorn,
Mutt'ring his wayward fancies he would rove,
Now drooping, woeful wan, like one forlorn,
Or crazed with care, or crossed in hopeless love.

"One morn I missed him, on the customed hill,
Along the heath and near his fav'rite tree;
Another came; nor yet beside the rill,
Nor up the lawn, nor at the wood was he;

"The next with dirges due in sad array
Slow through the churchway path we saw him borne.
Approach and read (for thou can'st read) the lay,
Graved on the stone beneath yon aged thorn."

The Epitaph

Here rests his head upon the lap of Earth
A youth to Fortune and to Fame unknown.
Fair Science frowned not on his humble birth,
And Melancholy marked him for her own.

Large was his bounty, and his soul sincere,
Heav'n did a recompence as largely send:
He gave to Mis'ry all he had, a tear,
He gained from Heav'n ('twas all he wished) a friend.

No farther seek his merits to disclose,
Or draw his frailties from their dread abode,
(There they alike in trembling hope repose),
The bosom of his Father and his God.

Gray's lines reach us through phrases that are virtually proverbial ("purest ray serene"), through such titles as Hardy's Far from the Madding Crowd *and* Humphrey Cobb's Paths of Glory, *and through overt echoes and allusions in poems by T. S. Eliot, John Crowe Ransom, Hart Crane, Philip Larkin, and George Starbuck. The meditation set in a sacred place continues through Wordsworth's "Tintern Abbey" (p. 407), Hardy's "Darkling Thrush" (p. 770), Eliot's "Little Gidding" (p. 987), and Larkin's "Church Going" (p. 1068). (Note that: "rude" is "uneducated"; "glebe" is "ground"; "provoke" is "call forth" (literally); "madding" is "milling.")*

Ode on the Death of a Favorite Cat, Drowned in a Tub of Gold Fishes

Twas on a lofty vase's side,
Where China's gayest art had dyed
    The azure flowers that blow;
Demurest of the tabby kind,
The pensive Selima reclined,
    Gazed on the lake below.

Her conscious tail her joy declared;
The fair round face, the snowy beard,
    The velvet of her paws,
Her coat, that with the tortoise vies,
Her ears of jet, and emerald eyes,
    She saw; and purr'd applause.

Still had she gazed; but 'midst the tide
Two angel forms were seen to glide,
    The Genii of the stream:
Their scaly armor's Tyrian hue
Thro' richest purple to the view
    Betray'd a golden gleam.

The hapless Nymph with wonder saw:
A whisker first and then a claw,
    With many an ardent wish,
She stretch'd in vain to reach the prize.
What female heart can gold despise?
What Cat's averse to fish?

Presumptuous Maid! with looks intent
Again she stretch'd, again she bent,
  Nor knew the gulf between.
(Malignant Fate sat by, and smil'd)
The slipp'ry verge her feet beguil'd,
  She tumbled headlong in.

Eight times emerging from the flood
She mew'd to ev'ry watry God,
  Some speedy aid to send.
No Dolphin came, no Nereid stirr'd:
Nor cruel *Tom*, nor *Susan* heard.
  A Fav'rite has no friend!

From hence, ye Beauties, undeceiv'd,
Know, one false step is ne'er retriev'd,
  And be with caution bold.
Not all that tempts your wand'ring eyes
And heedless hearts, is lawful prize;
  Nor all, that glisters, gold.

Gray's "Elegy" (p. 327) is somber and earnest; this "Ode" is flippant and airy. It belongs among the animal fables whose pedigree goes back to Aesop and comes forward to the bestiary maintained in today's cartoons. The favorite cat belonged to the estimable Horace Walpole. (Note that: "blow" is "bloom.")

WILLIAM COLLINS 1721–1759

Collins was a gifted and learned poet, but he had to
work during unfavorable times and amid uncongenial
surroundings. He was subject to melancholia and died
insane.

Ode to Evening

()◀━━▶()

If aught of Oaten Stop, or Pastoral Song
May hope, chaste Eve, to soothe thy modest ear,
    Like thy own solemn springs,
    Thy springs and dying gales,
O nymph reserved, while now the bright-haired sun
Sits in yon western tent, whose cloudy skirts,
    With brede ethereal wove,
    O'erhang his wavy bed;
Now air is hushed, save where the weak-ey'd bat
With short shrill shriek flits by on leathern wing,
    Or where the beetle winds
    His small but sullen horn,
As oft he rises midst the twilight path,
Against the pilgrim borne in heedless hum:
    Now teach me, Maid composed,
    To breathe some softened strain,
Whose numbers stealing through thy darkening vale
May not unseemly with its stillness suit;
    As musing slow, I hail
    Thy genial loved return!
For when thy folding star arising shows
His paly circlet, at his warning lamp
    The fragrant Hours, and elves
    Who slept in flowers the day,

And many a nymph who wreathes her brows with sedge,
And sheds the freshening dew, and, lovelier still,
   The Pensive Pleasures sweet,
   Prepare thy shadowy car.
Then lead, calm votaress, where some sheety lake
Cheers the lone heath, or some time-hallowed pile,
   Or upland fallows grey,
   Reflect its last cool gleam.
But when chill blustering winds or driving rain
Forbid my willing feet, be mine the hut
   That from the mountain's side
   Views wilds and swelling floods,
And hamlets brown, and dim-discovered spires,
And hears their simple bell, and marks o'er all
   Thy dewy fingers draw
   The gradual dusky veil.
While Spring shall pour his showers, as oft he wont,
And bathe thy breathing tresses, meekest Eve!
   While Summer loves to sport
   Beneath thy lingering light;
While sallow Autumn fills thy lap with leaves,
Or Winter, yelling through the troublous air,
   Affrights thy shrinking train,
   And rudely rends they robes;
So long, sure-found beneath the sylvan shed,
Shall Fancy, Friendship, Science, rose-lipped Health,
   Thy gentlest influence own,
   And hymn thy favourite name!

Collins modelled his ode on some of Horace's. Marvell's "Horatian Ode upon Cromwell's Return from Ireland" (p. 238) also uses an English adaptation of Horace's so-called Alcaic stanza, two longer lines followed by two shorter ones. Unlike Marvell, however, Collins courageously imitated his Roman exemplar in writing an unrhymed *lyric (the earliest in this anthology) and producing thereby a bewitchingly peculiar music. (Note that: "brede" is "embroidery"; "folding-star" is "evening star.")*

How Sleep the Brave

How sleep the brave who sink to rest
By all their country's wishes blest!
When Spring, with dewy fingers cold,
Returns to deck their hallowed mold,
She there shall dress a sweeter sod
Than Fancy's feet have ever trod.

By fairy hands their knell is rung,
By forms unseen their dirge is sung;
There Honor comes, a pilgrim gray,
To bless the turf that wraps their clay,
And Freedom shall awhile repair,
To dwell a weeping hermit there!

In 1745 and early 1746 the British army suffered defeat in one battle in Belgium and two in Scotland. This is Collins's "Ode Written in the Beginning of the Year 1746."

OLIVER GOLDSMITH c.1730–1774

Goldsmith was educated at Trinity College, Dublin, but failed to be ordained, even though his father was a clergyman. He received some medical training and worked for a time as a physician. He became a successful professional writer, distinguishing himself as a journalist, historian, biographer, and all-round literary author, producing not only the poems in this anthology but popular plays (such as *She Stoops to Conquer*) and *The Vicar of Wakefield*, one of the most beloved novels in English.

When Lovely Woman Stoops to Folly

When lovely woman stoops to folly,
   And finds too late that men betray,
What charm can soothe her melancholy,
   What art can wash her guilt away?

The only art her guilt to cover,
   To hide her shame from every eye,
To give repentance to her lover,
   And wring his bosom—is to die.

from The Vicar of Wakefield

This song from Goldsmith's novel The Vicar of Wakefield *also contributes a few lines to T. S. Eliot's "Waste Land" (p. 968).*

An Elegy on the Death of a Mad Dog

Good people all, of every sort,
　Give ear unto my song;
And if you find it wond'rous short,
　It cannot hold you long.

In Islington there was a man,
　Of whom the world might say,
That still a godly race he ran,
　Whene'er he went to pray.

A kind and gentle heart he had,
　To comfort friends and foes;
The naked every day he clad,
　When he put on his clothes.

And in that town a dog was found,
　As many dogs there be,
Both mongrel, puppy, whelp, and hound,
　And curs of low degree.

This dog and man at first were friends;
　But when a pique began,
The dog, to gain some private ends,
　Went mad and bit the man.

Around from all the neighboring streets
　The wond'ring neighbors ran,
And swore the dog had lost its wits,
　To bite so good a man.

The wound it seem'd both sore and sad
   To every Christian eye;
And while they swore the dog was mad,
   They swore the man would die.

But soon a wonder came to light,
   That showed the rogues they lied:
The man recover'd of the bite,
   The dog it was that died.

from The Vicar of Wakefield

Like "When Lovely Woman Stoops to Folly" (p. 338), this variant on the folk-irony of The Biter Bit is a number from The Vicar of Wakefield, *performed as incidental (and parodic) entertainment by a member of the vicar's family. Sir Walter Scott, a generation younger than Goldsmith, could produce comparably durable verses in respectable prose works. Charles Kingsley, in a smaller way, could do something of the sort a hundred years later. Peacock, Waugh, and DeVries, among the comedians, could handle parodies from time to time. By now, the art has all but died; among contemporary novelists, just about the only practitioner writing passable song-lyrics is Thomas Pynchon.*

The Deserted Village

>>>>>>>

SWEET AUBURN! loveliest village of the plain,
Where health and plenty cheered the laboring swain,
Where smiling spring its earliest visit paid,
And parting summer's lingering blooms delayed.
Dear lovely bowers of innocence and ease,
Seats of my youth, when every sport could please,
How often have I loitered o'er thy green,
Where humble happiness endeared each scene!
How often have I paused on every charm,
The sheltered cot, the cultivated farm,
The never-failing brook, the busy mill.
The decent church that topped the neighboring hill,
The hawthorn-bush, with seats beneath the shade,
For talking age and whispering lovers made!

How often have I blessed the coming day,
When toil remitting lent its turn to play,
And all the village train, from labor free,
Led up their sports beneath the spreading tree,
While many a pastime circled in the shade,
The young contending as the old surveyed;
And many a gambol frolicked o'er the ground,
And sleights of art and feats of strength went round;
And still, as each repeated pleasure tired,
Succeeding sports the mirthful band inspired;
The dancing pair that simply sought renown,
By holding out, to tire each other down;
The swain mistrustless of his smutted face,
While secret laughter tittered round the place;

The bashful virgin's sidelong looks of love,
The matron's glance that would those looks reprove, —
These were thy charms, sweet village! sports like these,
With sweet succession, taught e'en toil to please;
These round thy bowers their cheerful influence shed,
These were thy charms, —but all these charms are fled!

Sweet smiling village, loveliest of the lawn,
Thy sports are fled, and all thy charms withdrawn;
Amidst thy bowers the tyrant's hand is seen,
And desolation saddens all thy green;
One only master grasps the whole domain,
And half a tillage stints thy smiling plain;
No more thy glassy brook reflects the day,
But, choked with sedges, works its weedy way;
Along thy glades, a solitary guest,
The hollow-sounding bittern guards its nest;
Amidst thy desert walks the lapwing flies,
And tires their echoes with unvaried cries.
Sunk are thy bowers in shapeless ruin all,
And the long grass o'ertops the mouldering wall,
And, trembling, shrinking from the spoiler's hand,
Far, far away thy children leave the land.

Ill fares the land, to hastening ills a prey,
Where wealth accumulates and men decay:
Princes and lords may flourish, or may fade;
A breath can make them, as a breath has made;
But a bold peasantry, their country's pride,
When once destroyed, can never be supplied.

A time there was, ere England's griefs began,
When every rood of ground maintained its man;
For him light Labor spread her wholesome store,
Just gave what life required, but gave no more;
His best companions, innocence and health;
And his best riches, ignorance of wealth.

But times are altered; trade's unfeeling train
Usurp the land and dispossess the swain;
Along the lawn, where scattered hamlets rose,
Unwieldy wealth and cumbrous pomp repose,
And every want to luxury allied,
And every pang that folly pays to pride.
Those gentle hours that plenty bade to bloom,
Those calm desires that asked but little room,
Those healthful sports that graced the peaceful scene,
Lived in each look, and brightened all the green, —
These, far departing, seek a kinder shore,
And rural mirth and manners are no more.

Sweet Auburn! parent of the blissful hour,
Thy glades forlorn confess the tyrant's power.
Here, as I take my solitary rounds,
Amidst thy tangling walks and ruined grounds,
And, many a year elapsed, return to view
Where once the cottage stood, the hawthorn grew,
Remembrance wakes, with all her busy train,
Swells at my breast, and turns the past to pain.

In all my wanderings round this world of care,
In all my griefs — and God has given my share —
I still had hopes my latest hours to crown,
Amidst these humble bowers to lay me down;
To husband out life's taper at the close,
And keep the flame from wasting by repose;
I still had hopes — for pride attends us still —
Amidst the swains to show my book-learned skill,
Around my fire an evening group to draw,
And tell of all I felt and all I saw;
And, as a hare, whom hounds and horns pursue,
Pants to the place from whence at first she flew,
I still had hopes, my long vexations past,
Here to return, — and die at home at last.

O blest retirement! friend to life's decline,
Retreats from care, that never must be mine,
How blest is he who crowns in shades like these
A youth of labor with an age of ease;
Who quits a world where strong temptations try,
And, since 't is hard to combat, learns to fly!
For him no wretches, born to work and weep,
Explore the mine, or tempt the dangerous deep;
No surly porter stands in guilty state,
To spurn imploring famine from the gate:
But on he moves to meet his latter end,
Angels around befriending virtue's friend;
Sinks to the grave with unperceived decay,
While resignation gently slopes the way;
And, all his prospects brightening to the last,
His heaven commences ere the world be past.

Sweet was the sound, when oft, at evening's close,
Up yonder hill the village murmur rose;
There, as I passed with careless steps and slow,
The mingling notes came softened from below;
The swain responsive as the milkmaid sung,
The sober herd that lowed to meet their young;
The noisy geese that gabbled o'er the pool,
The playful children just let loose from school;
The watch-dog's voice that bayed the whispering wind,
And the loud laugh that spoke the vacant mind, —
These all in sweet confusion sought the shade,
And filled each pause the nightingale had made.
But now the sounds of population fail,
No cheerful murmurs fluctuate in the gale,
No busy steps the grass-grown foot-way tread,
But all the bloomy flush of life is fled.
All but yon widowed, solitary thing,
That feebly bends beside the plashy spring;
She, wretched matron, forced in age, for bread,
To strip the brook with mantling cresses spread,

To pick her wintry fagot from the thorn,
To seek her nightly shed, and weep till morn;
She only left of all the harmless train,
The sad historian of the pensive plain.

Near yonder copse, where once the garden smiled,
And still where many a garden-flower grows wild;
There, where a few torn shrubs the place disclose,
The village preacher's modest mansion rose.
A man he was to all the country dear,
And passing rich with forty pounds a year;
Remote from towns he ran his godly race,
Nor e'er had changed, nor wished to change, his place;
Unskilful he to fawn, or seek for power,
By doctrines fashioned to the varying hour;
Far other aims his heart had learned to prize,
More bent to raise the wretched than to rise.
His house was known to all the vagrant train.
He chid their wanderings, but relieved their pain;
The long-remembered beggar was his guest,
Whose beard descending swept his aged breast.
The ruined spendthrift, now no longer proud,
Claimed kindred there, and had his claims allowed;
The broken soldier, kindly bade to stay,
Sate by his fire, and talked the night away;
Wept o'er his wounds, or tales of sorrow done,
Shouldered his crutch, and showed how fields were won.
Pleased with his guests, the good man learned to glow,
And quite forgot their vices in their woe;
Careless their merits or their faults to scan,
His pity gave ere charity began.

Thus to relieve the wretched was his pride,
And e'en his failings leaned to Virtue's side;
But in his duty prompt at every call,
He watched and wept, he prayed and felt for all;

And, as a bird each fond endearment tries,
To tempt its new-fledged offspring to the skies,
He tried each art, reproved each dull delay,
Allured to brighter worlds, and led the way.

Beside the bed where parting life was laid,
And sorrow, guilt, and pain by turns dismayed,
The reverend champion stood. At his control,
Despair and anguish fled the struggling soul;
Comfort came down the trembling wretch to raise,
And his last faltering accents whispered praise.

At church, with meek and unaffected grace,
His looks adorned the venerable place;
Truth from his lips prevailed with double sway,
And fools, who came to scoff, remained to pray.
The service past, around the pious man,
With steady zeal, each honest rustic ran;
E'en children followed with endearing wile,
And plucked his gown, to share the good man's smile.
His ready smile a parent's warmth expressed,
Their welfare pleased him, and their cares distressed;
To them his heart, his love, his griefs were given,
But all his serious thoughts had rest in heaven.
As some tall cliff, that lifts its awful form,
Swells from the vale, and midway leaves the storm,
Though round its breast the rolling clouds are spread,
Eternal sunshine settles on its head.

Beside yon straggling fence that skirts the way,
With blossomed furze unprofitably gay,
There, in his noisy mansion, skilled to rule,
The village master taught his little school;
A man severe he was, and stern to view,
I knew him well, and every truant knew;
Well had the boding tremblers learned to trace
The day's disasters in his morning face;

Full well they laughed with counterfeited glee
At all his jokes, for many a joke had he;
Full well the busy whisper circling round
Conveyed the dismal tidings when he frowned;
Yet he was kind, or, if severe in aught,
The love he bore to learning was in fault.
The village all declared how much he knew,
'T was certain he could write, and cipher too;
Lands he could measure, times and tides presage,
And e'en the story ran that he could gauge;
In arguing too, the parson owned his skill,
For, e'en though vanquished, he could argue still,
While words of learnèd length and thundering sound
Amazed the gazing rustics ranged around;
And still they gazed, and still the wonder grew
That one small head could carry all he knew.

But past is all his fame. The very spot
Where many a time he triumphed is forgot. —
Near yonder thorn, that lifts its head on high,
Where once the sign-post caught the passing eye,
Low lies that house where nut-brown draughts inspired,
Where graybeard mirth and smiling toil retired,
Where village statesmen talked with looks profound,
And news much older than their ale went round.
Imagination fondly stoops to trace
The parlor splendors of that festive place, —
The whitewashed wall; the nicely sanded floor;
The varnished clock that ticked behind the door;
The chest, contrived a double debt to pay,
A bed by night, a chest of drawers by day;
The pictures placed for ornament and use;
The twelve good rules; the royal game of goose;
The hearth, except when winter chilled the day,
With aspen boughs and flowers and fennel gay;
While broken teacups, wisely kept for show,
Ranged o'er the chimney, glistened in a row.

Vain, transitory splendor! could not all
Reprieve the tottering mansion from its fall?
Obscure it sinks, nor shall it more impart
An hour's importance to the poor man's heart;
Thither no more the peasant shall repair
To sweet oblivion of his daily care;
No more the farmer's news, the barber's tale,
No more the woodman's ballad shall prevail;
No more the smith his dusky brow shall clear,
Relax his ponderous strength, and lean to hear;
The host himself no longer shall be found
Careful to see the mantling bliss go round;
Nor the coy maid, half willing to be prest,
Shall kiss the cup to pass it to the rest.

Yes! let the rich deride, the proud disdain,
These simple blessings of the lowly train;
To me more dear, congenial to my heart,
One native charm, than all the gloss of art.
Spontaneous joys, where nature has its play,
The soul adopts, and owns their first-born sway;
Lightly they frolic o'er the vacant mind,
Unenvied, unmolested, unconfined:
But the long pomp, the midnight masquerade,
With all the freaks of wanton wealth arrayed, —
In these, ere triflers half their wish obtain,
The toiling pleasure sickens into pain;
And, e'en while fashion's brightest arts decoy,
The heart, distrusting, asks if this be joy.

Ye friends to truth, ye statesmen, who survey
The rich man's joys increase, the poor's decay,
'T is yours to judge, how wide the limits stand
Between a splendid and a happy land.

Proud swells the tide with loads of freighted ore,
And shouting Folly hails them from her shore;
Hoards e'en beyond the miser's wish abound,
And rich men flock from all the world around.
Yet count our gains. This wealth is but a name
That leaves our useful products still the same.
Not so the loss. The man of wealth and pride
Takes up a space that many poor supplied;
Space for his lake, his park's extended bounds,
Space for his horses, equipage, and hounds:
The robe that wraps his limbs in silken sloth
Has robbed the neighboring fields of half their growth;
His seat, where solitary sports are seen,
Indignant spurns the cottage from the green;
Around the world each needful product flies,
For all the luxuries the world supplies:
While thus the land, adorned for pleasure all,
In barren splendor feebly waits the fall.

As some fair female unadorned and plain,
Secure to please while youth confirms her reign,
Slights every borrowed charm that dress supplies,
Nor shares with art the triumph of her eyes,
But when those charms are past, —for charms are frail, —
When time advances, and when lovers fail,
She then shines forth, solicitous to bless,
In all the glaring impotence of dress;
Thus fares the land by luxury betrayed,
In nature's simplest charms at first arrayed,
But verging to decline, its splendors rise,
Its vistas strike, its palaces surprise;
While, scourged by famine from the smiling land,
The mournful peasant leads his humble band;
And while he sinks, without one arm to save,
The country blooms, —a garden and a grave.

Where then, ah! where shall poverty reside,
To 'scape the pressure of contiguous pride?
If to some common's fenceless limits strayed
He drives his flock to pick the scanty blade,
Those fenceless fields the sons of wealth divide,
And e'en the bare-worn common is denied.
If to the city sped;—what waits him there?
To see profusion that he must not share;
To see ten thousand baneful arts combined
To pamper luxury and thin mankind;
To see each joy the sons of pleasure know
Extorted from his fellow-creature's woe.
Here while the courtier glitters in brocade,
There the pale artist plies the sickly trade;
Here while the proud their long-drawn pomps display,
There the black gibbet glooms beside the way.
The dome where Pleasure holds here midnight reign,
Here, richly decked, admits the gorgeous train:
Tumultuous grandeur crowds the blazing square,
The rattling chariots clash, the torches glare.
Sure scenes like these no troubles e'er annoy!
Sure these denote one universal joy!
Are these thy serious thoughts?—Ah, turn thine eyes
Where the poor houseless shivering female lies.
She once, perhaps, in village plenty blest,
Has wept at tales of innocence distrest;
Her modest looks the cottage might adorn,
Sweet as the primrose peeps beneath the thorn;
Now lost to all: her friends, her virtue fled,
Near her betrayer's door she lays her head,
And, pinched with cold, and shrinking from the shower,
With heavy heart deplores that luckless hour,
When idly first, ambitious of the town,
She left her wheel and robes of country brown.

Do thine, sweet Auburn, thine, the loveliest train,
Do thy fair tribes participate her pain?
E'en now, perhaps, by cold and hunger led,
At proud men's doors they ask a little bread!

Ah, no! To distant climes, a dreary scene,
Where half the convex world intrudes between,
Through torrid tracks with fainting steps they go,
Where wild Altama murmurs to their woe.
Far different there from all that charmed before,
The various terrors of that horrid shore, —
Those blazing suns that dart a downward ray,
And fiercely shed intolerable day;
Those matted woods where birds forget to sing,
But silent bats in drowsy clusters cling;
Those poisonous fields with rank luxuriance crowned,
Where the dark scorpion gathers death around;
Where at each step the stranger fears to wake
The rattling terrors of the vengeful snake;
Where crouching tigers wait their hapless prey,
And savage men more murderous still than they;
While oft in whirls the mad tornado flies,
Mingling the ravaged landscape with the skies.
Far different these from every former scene,
The cooling brook, the grassy vested green,
The breezy covert of the warbling grove,
That only sheltered thefts of harmless love.

Good Heaven! what sorrows gloomed that parting day
That called them from their native walks away;
When the poor exiles, every pleasure past,
Hung round the bowers, and fondly looked their last,
And took a long farewell, and wished in vain
For seats like these beyond the western main;
And shuddering still to face the distant deep,
Returned and wept, and still returned to weep.
The good old sire the first prepared to go
To new-found worlds, and wept for others' woe;
But for himself in conscious virtue brave,
He only wished for worlds beyond the grave.
His lovely daughter, lovelier in her tears,
The fond companion of his helpless years,

Silent went next, neglectful of her charms,
And left a lover's for her father's arms.
With louder plaints the mother spoke her woes,
And blessed the cot where every pleasure rose;
And kissed her thoughtless babes with many a tear,
And clasped them close, in sorrow doubly dear;
Whilst her fond husband strove to lend relief
In all the silent manliness of grief.

O luxury! thou curst by Heaven's decree,
How ill exchanged are things like these for thee!
How do thy potions, with insidious joy,
Diffuse their pleasures only to destroy!
Kingdoms by thee, to sickly greatness grown,
Boast of a florid vigor not their own.
At every draught more large and large they grow,
A bloated mass of rank, unwieldy woe;
Till, sapped their strength, and every part unsound,
Down, down they sink, and spread a ruin round.

Even now the devastation is begun,
And half the business of destruction done;
Even now, methinks, as pondering here I stand,
I see the rural virtues leave the land.
Down where yon anchoring vessel spreads the sail
That idly waiting flaps with every gale,
Downward they move, a melancholy band,
Pass from the shore, and darken all the strand.
Contended toil, and hospitable care,
And kind connubial tenderness, are there;
And piety with wishes placed above,
And steady loyalty, and faithful love.
And thou, sweet Poetry, thou loveliest maid,
Still first to fly where sensual joys invade;
Unfit, in these degenerate times of shame,
To catch the heart, or strike for honest fame;
Dear charming nymph, neglected and decried,
My shame in crowds, my solitary pride;

Thou source of all my bliss and all my woe,
That found'st me poor at first, and keep'st me so;
Thou guide, by which the nobler arts excel,
Thou nurse of every virtue, fare thee well!
Farewell; and O, where'er thy voice be tried,
On Torno's cliffs, or Pambamarca's side,
Whether where equinoctial fervors glow,
Or winter wraps the polar world in snow,
Still let thy voice, prevailing over time,
Redress the rigors of the inclement clime;
Aid slighted truth with thy persuasive strain;
Teach erring man to spurn the rage of gain;
Teach him, that states of native strength possest,
Though very poor, may still be very blest;
That trade's proud empire hastes to swift decay,
As ocean sweeps the labored mole away;
While self-dependent power can time defy,
As rocks resist the billows and the sky.

One line from "The Deserted Village"—"And still they gazed, and still the wonder grew"—seems to be one model of a line in T. S. Eliot's "Waste Land": "And still she cried, and still the world pursues" (see p. 968). The general melancholy of wasted lands and deserted villages touches both British and American poetry from the eighteenth century onward (see Robert Frost's "Directive," p. 908). (Note that: "vacant" is "idle," "vacationing"; "guage" is "estimate the capacity"; "labored mole" is "breakwater constructed with much labor.")

Cowper could produce effective satires and engaging historical pieces and he was a fine letter-writer, but for the purposes of this anthology he was most successful as an author of hymns. Cowper (sounded "Cooper," by the way) seems to have been a sweet-tempered man but was tormented by depression and mania most of his adult life.

Light Shining out of Darkness

God moves in a mysterious way,
   His wonders to perform;
He plants his footsteps in the sea,
   And rides upon the storm.

Deep in unfathomable mines
   Of never-failing skill,
He treasures up his bright designs,
   And works his sovereign will.

Ye fearful saints fresh courage take,
   The clouds ye so much dread
Are big with mercy, and shall break
   In blessings on your head.

Judge not the Lord by feeble sense,
   But trust him for his grace;
Behind a frowning providence,
   He hides a smiling face.

His purposes will ripen fast,
   Unfolding ev'ry hour;
The bud may have a bitter taste,
   But sweet will be the flow'r.

Blind unbelief is sure to err,
And scan his work in vain;
God is his own interpreter,
And he will make it plain.

With Isaac Watts, Charles Wesley, A. M. Toplady, and many others, the eighteenth century was one of the greatest ages of Protestant hymn-writing. Cowper wrote the famous Olney Hymns *with John Newton, curate of Olney. Newton is best remembered today for "Amazing Grace."*

The Poplar Field

The poplars are felled, farewell to the shade
And the whispering sound of the cool colonnade,
The winds play no longer, and sing in the leaves,
Nor Ouse on his bosom their image receives.

Twelve years have elapsed since I last took a view
Of my favourite field and the bank where they grew,
And now in the grass behold they are laid,
And the tree is my seat that once lent me a shade.

The blackbird has fled to another retreat
Where the hazels afford him a screen from the heat,
And the scene where his melody charmed me before,
Resounds with his sweet-flowing ditty no more.

My fugitive years are all hasting away,
And I must ere long lie as lowly as they,
With a turf on my breast, and a stone at my head,
Ere another such grove shall arise in its stead.

'Tis a sight to engage me, if any thing can,
To muse on the perishing pleasures of man;
Though his life be a dream, his enjoyments, I see,
Have a being less durable even than he.

---

*A century after Cowper's poem, Gerard Manley Hopkins wrote one much like it
on the same subject: "Binsey Poplars."*

PHILIP FRENEAU 1752–1832

Freneau came along just in time to take part in literary activities related to the American Revolution, and he lived long enough to keep up the production of patriotic and satirical verses through the War of 1812. Early in the life of the Republic he was an adherent of Thomas Jefferson and such an enemy of Alexander Hamilton that George Washington complained about "that rascal Freneau."

The Indian Burying Ground

In spite of all the learned have said,
　I still my old opinion keep;
The posture, that we give the dead,
　Points out the soul's eternal sleep.

Not so the ancients of these lands—
　The Indian, when from life released,
Again is seated with his friends,
　And shares again the joyous feast.

His imaged birds, and painted bowl,
　And venison, for a journey dressed,
Bespeak the nature of the soul,
　Activity, that knows no rest.

His bow, for action ready bent,
　And arrows, with a head of stone,
Can only mean that life is spent,
　And not the old ideas gone.

Thou, stranger, that shalt come this way,
　No fraud upon the dead commit—
Observe the swelling turf, and say
　They do not lie, but here they sit.

Here still a lofty rock remains,
    On which the curious eye may trace
(Now wasted, half, by wearing rains)
    The fancies of a ruder race.

Here still an aged elm aspires,
    Beneath whose far-projecting shade
(And which the shepherd still admires)
    The children of the forest played!

There oft a restless Indian queen
    (Pale Shebah, with her braided hair)
And many a barbarous form is seen
    To chide the man that lingers there.

By midnight moons, o'er moistening dews;
    In habit for the chase arrayed,
The hunter still the deer pursues,
    The hunter and the deer, a shade!

And long shall timorous fancy see
    The painted chief, and pointed spear,
And Reason's self shall bow the knee
    To shadows and delusions here.

Freneau seems to be deliberately echoing the form and content of Gray's "Elegy Written in a Country Churchyard" (p. 327) with these alternately rhyming quatrains (although Freneau's meter is a foot shorter than Gray's heroic pentameter). But these "rude forefathers" are not laid out as though asleep; these members of a "ruder race" are buried in a sitting position.

WILLIAM BLAKE 1757–1827

Blake was a splendid graphic artist as well as a literary genius. After an early period of relatively unsophisticated lyrics, he produced visionary poems of remarkable scope and originality. His influence has increased steadily since his death, and among his literary descendants can be counted D. G. Rossetti, W. B. Yeats, and Allen Ginsberg.

The Tyger

Tyger, Tyger, burning bright
In the forests of the night;
What immortal hand or eye,
Could frame thy fearful symmetry?

In what distant deeps or skies
Burnt the fire of thine eyes!
On what wings dare he aspire?
What the hand, dare seize the fire?

And what shoulder, & what art,
Could twist the sinews of thy heart?
And when thy heart began to beat,
What dread hand? & what dread feet?

What the hammer? what the chain?
In what furnace was thy brain?
What the anvil? what dread grasp
Dare its deadly terrors clasp?

When the stars threw down their spears
And water'd heaven with their tears:
Did he smile his work to see?
Did he who made the Lamb make thee?

Tiger, Tiger, burning bright,
In the forests of the night:
What immortal hand or eye,
Dare frame thy fearful symmetry?

from Songs of Experience

"The Tiger," from the celebrated Songs of Experience *(1794), is, indeed, a song of experience, vividly and memorably. Its powerful rhythm seems pounded out on an instrument of percussion, something that beats like a heart or a hammer, both of which are named in the poem. The mighty beast is the whole world of experience outside ourselves, a world of igneous creation and destruction. Faced with such terrifying beauty, the poet can only ask; the poem is nothing but one wondering question after another.*

London

I wander thro' each charter'd street,
Near where the charter'd Thames does flow.
And mark in every face I meet
Marks of weakness, marks of woe.

In every cry of every Man,
In every Infants cry of fear,
In every voice: in every ban,
The mind-forg'd manacles I hear,

How the Chimney-sweepers cry
Every blackning Church appalls,
And the hapless Soldiers sigh
Runs in blood down Palace walls,

But most thro' midnight streets I hear
How the youthful Harlots curse
Blasts the new-born Infants tear
And blights with plagues the Marriage hearse.

from Songs of Experience

"The Tiger" (p. 359) contains no "I" and no statements; "London" centers on an "I" and is nothing but statements in a strikingly original idiom that foreshadows surrealist combinations of sensory images.

And Did Those Feet in Ancient Time

And did those feet in ancient time
Walk upon England's mountains green?
And was the holy Lamb of God
On England's pleasant pastures seen?

And did the Countenance Divine
Shine forth upon our clouded hills?
And was Jerusalem builded here,
Among these dark Satanic Mills?

Bring me my Bow of burning gold:
Bring me my Arrows of desire:
Bring me my Spear: O clouds unfold!
Bring me my Chariot of fire!

I will not cease from Mental Fight,
Nor shall my Sword sleep in my hand,
Till we have built Jerusalem
In England's green & pleasant Land.

from Milton

Blake's words (some of which furnished the movie title Chariots of Fire) *are very likely the most inspiriting ever written by an Englishman for Englishmen. A tradition of rugged struggle extends from Milton and Bunyan in the seventeenth century, through Blake and Wordsworth in the eighteenth and nineteenth, down to our own time in writers as diverse as W. B. Yeats and Joyce Cary.*

Piping down the Valleys Wild

◆◇◆◇◆

Piping down the valleys wild
Piping songs of pleasant glee
On a cloud I saw a child,
And he laughing said to me,

"Pipe a song about a Lamb";
So I piped with merry chear.
"Piper pipe that song again" —
So I piped, he wept to hear.

"Drop thy pipe thy happy pipe
Sing thy songs of happy chear";
So I sung the same again
While he wept with joy to hear.

"Piper sit thee down and write
In a book that all may read" —
So he vanish'd from my sight.
And I pluck'd a hollow reed,

And I made a rural pen,
And I stain'd the water clear,
And I wrote my happy songs
Every child may joy to hear.

from Songs of Experience

Blake introduces his Songs of Innocence *with a song of innocence of sorts —
innocence without idiocy, innocence with sophistication. There is weeping with
laughter (as fits babies and adults alike), and there must be misgiving in
recognizing that the passage from piping and singing to writing is a downward
motion that involves a stain on clarity.*

The Sick Rose

O Rose, thou art sick.
The invisible worm
That flies in the night
In the howling storm

Has found out thy bed
Of crimson joy,
And his dark secret love
Does thy life destroy.

from Songs of Experience

The conjunction of "joy" and "destroy" echoes Book IX of Paradise Lost, *in which another flying enemy invades a paradise. Milton's epic is mostly unrhymed, but "destroy" and "joy" end consecutive lines in one of Satan's soliloquies.*

The Lamb

Little Lamb, who made thee?
Dost thou know who made thee?
Gave thee life, and bid thee feed
By the stream and o'er the mead;
Gave thee clothing of delight,
Softest clothing, woolly, bright;
Gave thee such a tender voice,
Making all the vales rejoice?
Little Lamb, who made thee?
Dost thou know who made thee?

Little Lamb, I'll tell thee,
Little Lamb, I'll tell thee:
He is called by thy name,
For he calls himself a Lamb,
He is meek, and he is mild;
He became a little child.
I a child, and thou a lamb,
We are called by his name.
Little Lamb, God bless thee!
Little Lamb, God bless thee!

from Songs of Experience

Blake so designed Songs of Experience *that many of the poems therein work as companion pieces to some in* Songs of Innocence, *in some cases even sharing the same title. "The Lamb" is the emblem of innocence, corresponding to "The Tiger" (p. 359) as the emblem of experience.*

Ah! Sun-Flower

Ah Sun-flower! weary of time,
Who countest the steps of the Sun,
Seeking after that sweet golden clime
Where the traveller's journey is done;

Where the Youth pined away with desire,
And the pale Virgin shrouded in snow,
Arise from their graves and aspire,
Where my Sun-flower wishes to go.

from Songs of Experience

It is characteristic of the Songs of Experience *to saturate a natural creature with human emotions and to translate all such creatures into symbols of human desire.*

Hear the Voice of the Bard

Hear the voice of the Bard!
Who Present, Past and Future, sees
Whose ears have heard
The Holy Word,
That walk'd among the ancient trees.

Calling the lapsed Soul
And weeping in the evening dew;
That might controll
The starry pole;
And fallen, fallen light renew!

O Earth, O Earth, return!
Arise from out the dewy grass;
Night is worn,
And the morn
Rises from the slumberous mass.

Turn away no more:
Why wilt thou turn away
The starry floor
The wat'ry shore
Is giv'n thee till the break of day.

from Songs of Experience

Blake, recalling the ancient attribution of vatic powers and public duties to the bard—a specialized term retaining a Celtic dignity well into the nineteenth century, thanks to Thomas Gray's "The Bard" (1757)—placed this invocation at the beginning of Songs of Experience.

Auguries of Innocence

To see a World in a Grain of Sand
And a Heaven in a Wild Flower,
Hold Infinity in the palm of your hand
And Eternity in an hour.

A Robin Redbreast in a Cage
Puts all Heaven in a Rage.
A dove house fill'd with doves and Pigeons
Shudders Hell thro' all its regions.
A dog starv'd at his Master's Gate
Predicts the ruin of the State.
A Horse misus'd upon the Road
Calls to Heaven for Human blood.
Each outcry of the hunted Hare
A fibre from the Brain does tear.
A Skylark wounded in the wing,
A Cherubim does cease to sing.
The Game Cock clip'd and arm'd for fight
Does the Rising Sun affright.
Every Wolf's and Lion's howl
Raises from Hell a Human Soul.
The wild deer, wand'ring here and there,
Keeps the Human Soul from Care.
The Lamb Misus'd breeds Public strife
And yet forgives the Butcher's Knife.
The Bat that flits at close of Eve
Has left the Brain that won't Believe.
The Owl that calls upon the Night
Speaks the Unbeliever's fright.
He who shall hurt the little Wren
Shall never be belov'd by Men.
He who the Ox to wrath has mov'd
Shall never be by Woman lov'd.

The wanton Boy that kills the Fly
Shall feel the Spider's enmity.
He who torments the Chafer's sprite
Weaves a Bower in endless Night.
The Catterpiller on the Leaf
Repeats to thee thy Mother's grief.
Kill not the Moth nor Butterfly,
For the Last Judgement draweth nigh.
He who shall train the Horse to War
Shall never pass the Polar Bar.
The Beggar's Dog and Widow's Cat,
Feed them and thou wilt grow fat.
The Gnat that sings his Summer's song
Poison gets from Slander's tongue.
The poison of the Snake and Newt
Is the sweat of Envy's Foot.
The Poison of the Honey Bee
Is the Artist's Jealousy.
The Prince's Robes and Beggar's Rags
Are Toadstools on the Miser's Bags.
A truth that's told with bad intent
Beats all the Lies you can invent.
It is right it should be so;
Man was made for Joy and Woe;
And when this we rightly know
Thro' the World we safely go.
Joy and Woe are woven fine,
A Clothing for the Soul divine;
Under every grief and pine
Runs a joy with silken twine.
The Babe is more than swaddling Bands;
Throughout all these Human Lands
Tools were made, and Born were hands,
Every Farmer Understands.
Every Tear from Every Eye
Becomes a Babe in Eternity;
This is caught by Females bright
And return'd to its own delight.

The Bleat, the Bark, Bellow and Roar
Are Waves that Beat on Heaven's Shore.
The Babe that weeps the Rod beneath
Writes Revenge in realms of death.
The Beggar's Rags, fluttering in Air,
Does to Rags the Heavens tear.
The Soldier, arm'd with Sword and Gun,
Palsied strikes the Summer's Sun.
The poor Man's Farthing is worth more
Than all the Gold on Afric's Shore.
One Mite wrung from the Labrer's hands
Shall buy and sell the Miser's Lands:
Or, if protected from on high,
Does that whole Nation sell and buy.
He who mocks the Infant's Faith
Shall be mock'd in Age and Death.
He who shall teach the Child to Doubt
The rotting Grave shall ne'er get out.
He who respects the Infant's faith
Triumphs over Hell and Death.
The Child's Toys and the Old Man's Reasons
Are the Fruits of the Two seasons.
The Questioner, who sits so sly,
Shall never know how to Reply.
He who replies to words of Doubt
Doth put the Light of Knowledge out.
The Strongest Poison ever known
Came from Caesar's Laurel Crown.
Nought can deform the Human Race
Like to the Armour's iron brace.
When Gold and Gems adorn the Plow
To peaceful Arts shall Envy Bow.
A Riddle or the Cricket's Cry
Is to Doubt a fit Reply.
The Emmet's Inch and Eagle's Mile
Make Lame Philosophy to smile.
He who Doubts from what he sees
Will ne'er Believe, do what you Please.

If the Sun and Moon should doubt,
They'd immediately Go out.
To be in a Passion you Good may do,
But no Good if a Passion is in you.
The Whore and Gambler, by the State
Licenc'd, build that Nation's Fate.
The Harlot's cry from Street to Street
Shall weave Old England's winding Sheet.
The Winner's Shout, the Loser's Curse,
Dance before dead England's Hearse.
Every Night and every Morn
Some to Misery are Born.
Every Morn and every Night
Some are Born to sweet delight.
Some are Born to sweet delight,
Some are Born to Endless Night.
We are led to Believe a Lie
When we see not Thro' the Eye
Which was Born in a Night to perish in a Night
When the Soul Slept in Beams of Light.
God Appears and God is Light
To those poor Souls who dwell in Night,
But does a Human Form Display
To those who Dwell in Realms of day.

These miscellaneous sayings, from a notebook kept in 1803, were not published until 1863, many years after Blake's death. More than any of his Romantic contemporaries or successors, Blake kept up the Augustan habit of registering moral truths in epigrams, rather like Alexander Pope and Benjamin Franklin.

How Sweet I Roam'd from Field to Field

How sweet I roam'd from field to field
And tasted all the summer's pride,
Till I the Prince of Love beheld
Who in the sunny beams did glide!

He show'd me lilies for my hair,
And blushing roses for my brow;
He led me through his gardens fair,
Where all his golden pleasures grow.

With sweet May dews my wings were wet,
And Phoebus fir'd my vocal rage;
He caught me in his silken net,
And shut me in his golden cage.

He loves to sit and hear me sing,
Then, laughing, sports and plays with me;
Then stretches out my golden wing,
And mocks my loss of liberty.

Blake's Poetical Sketches *(1783) consists of poems written from Blake's adolescence, in some cases as early as 1769. Of Blake's poems in this anthology, this song is the earliest.*

The Little Black Boy

My mother bore me in the southern wild,
And I am black, but O! my soul is white;
White as an angel is the English child,
But I am black as if bereav'd of light.

My mother taught me underneath a tree,
And sitting down before the heat of day,
She took me on her lap and kissèd me,
And pointing to the east, began to say:

"Look on the rising sun: there God does live,
And gives his light, and gives his heat away;
And flowers and trees and beasts and men receive
Comfort in morning, joy in the noon day.

"And we are put on earth a little space,
That we may learn to bear the beams of love,
And these black bodies and this sun-burnt face
Is but a cloud, and like a shady grove.

"For when our souls have learn'd the heat to bear,
The cloud will vanish; we shall hear his voice,
Saying, 'Come out from the grove, my love & care,
And round my golden tent like lambs rejoice.' "

Thus did my mother say, and kissèd me;
And thus I say to little English boy:
When I from black and he from white cloud free,
And round the tent of God like lambs we joy,

I'll shade him from the heat till he can bear
To lean in joy upon our father's knee;
And then I'll stand and stroke his silver hair,
And be like him, and he will then love me.

from Songs of Experience

"The Little Black Boy" is in the same heroic quatrain as Gray's "Elegy" (p. 327). Although not a stanza much used by Blake, it serves here to ennoble its subject.

A Poison Tree

I was angry with my friend:
I told my wrath, my wrath did end.
I was angry with my foe:
I told it not, my wrath did grow.

And I water'd it in fears,
Night and morning with my tears;
And I sunnèd it with smiles,
And with soft deceitful wiles.

And it grew both day and night,
Till it bore an apple bright;
And my foe beheld it shine,
And he knew that it was mine,

And into my garden stole
When the night had veil'd the pole;
In the morning glad I see
My foe outstretch'd beneath the tree.

from Songs of Experience

Blake retells the legend of the deadly apple in terms that will reappear in Eliot's "Gerontion" (p. 984): "These tears are shaken from the wrath-bearing tree."

The Chimney Sweeper

·◇·◇·◇·◇·

When my mother died I was very young,
And my father sold me while yet my tongue
Could scarcely cry *'weep' 'weep' 'weep' 'weep'*!
So your chimneys I sweep, & in soot I sleep.

There's little Tom Dacre, who cried when his head,
That curled like a lamb's back, was shaved; so I said,
"Hush Tom never mind it, for when your head's bare,
You know that the soot cannot spoil your white hair."

And so he was quiet, & that very night,
As Tom was asleeping he had such a sight—
That thousands of sweepers Dick, Joe, Ned & Jack,
Were all of them locked up in coffins of black;

And by came an Angel who had a bright key,
And he opened the coffins & set them all free;
Then down a green plain leaping, laughing they run,
And wash in a river and shine in the sun.

Then naked & white, all their bags left behind,
They rise upon clouds, and sport in the wind.
And the angel told Tom, if he'd be a good boy,
He'd have God for his father & never want joy.

And so Tom awoke, and we rose in the dark,
And got with our bags & our brushes to work.
Though the morning was cold, Tom was happy & warm;
So if all do their duty, they need not fear harm.

from Songs of Innocence

Blake wrote two poems called "The Chimney Sweeper": this one in Songs of Innocence *and another in* Songs of Experience. *This poem is longer than its companion piece and perhaps more naive. Chimney sweepers' work was dirty and dangerous; since the spaces were small and confined, younger children were in demand.*

To the Evening Star

Thou Fair-haired Angel of the Evening,
Now, whilst the sun rests on the mountains, light
Thy bright torch of love; thy radiant crown
Put on, and smile upon our evening bed!
Smile on our loves; and while thou drawest the
Blue curtains of the sky, scatter thy silver dew
On every flower that shuts its sweet eyes

In timely sleep. Let thy West Wind sleep on
The lake; speak silence with thy glimmering eyes,
And wash the dusk with silver. Soon, full soon,
Dost thou withdraw; then the wolf rages wide,
And the lion glares through the dun forest:
The fleeces of the flocks are covered with
Thy sacred dew: protect them with thine influence.

The evening star is the planet Venus, named for the Roman goddess of love. Although this is an early poem of Blake's, it is technically very mature and advanced: a sonnet by virtue of its fourteen lines but with no rhyme or regular rhythm. Lines ending "the" and "with" are common nowadays but were nearly unprecedented in 1783. Blake's decision to avoid rhyme in an evening poem may owe something to Collins's unrhymed "Ode to Evening" (p. 335).

The Garden of Love

>>>>>>>

I went to the Garden of Love,
And saw what I never had seen:
A Chapel was built in the midst,
Where I used to play on the green.

And the gates of this Chapel were shut,
And "Thou shalt not" writ over the door;
So I turn'd to the Garden of Love
That so many sweet flowers bore;

And I saw it was filled with graves,
And tomb-stones where flowers should be;
And Priests in black gowns were walking their rounds,
And binding with briars my joys and desires.

from Songs of Experience

This song of experience recounts the familiar dilemma: our biological nature is thwarted by much of our civil law and established religion. The strain between the antithetical parts of human life gives torque to Blake's work in all media.

The Clod and the Pebble

"Love seeketh not Itself to please,
Nor for itself hath any care,
But for another gives its ease,
And builds a Heaven in Hell's despair."

So sang a little Clod of Clay
Trodden with the cattle's feet,
But a Pebble of the brook
Warbled out these metres meet:

"Love seeketh only Self to please,
To bind another to Its delight,
Joys in another's loss of ease,
And builds a Hell in Heaven's despite."

from Songs of Experience

Blake could invent an original fable as engaging as any in folklore but without an overload of obvious allegory. Wisdom literature commonly proffers contradictory advice (as in Proverbs XXVI: "Answer not a fool according to his folly" and "Answer a fool according to his folly").

Holy Thursday

'Twas on a Holy Thursday, their innocent faces clean,
The children walking two & two, in red & blue & green,
Grey-headed beadles walked before with wands as white as
    snow,
Till into the high dome of Paul's they like Thames' waters flow.

O what a multitude they seemed, these flowers of London town!
Seated in companies they sit with radiance all their own.
The hum of multitudes was there, but multitudes of lambs,
Thousands of little boys & girls raising their innocent hands.

Now like a mighty wind they raise to Heaven the voice of song,
Or like harmonious thunderings the seats of Heaven among.
Beneath them sit the aged men, wise guardians of the poor;
Then cherish pity, lest you drive an angel from your door.

from Songs of Innocence

Blake wrote two poems entitled "Holy Thursday," in Songs of Innocence *and in* Songs of Experience. *The more popular is this one from* Songs of Innocence. *Holy Thursday (Ascension Day) was celebrated in London by having poor children from charity schools march to St. Paul's Cathedral for a special service.*

Mock On, Mock On, Voltaire, Rousseau

Mock on, mock on, Voltaire, Rousseau;
Mock on, mock on, 'Tis all in vain.
You throw the sand against the wind,
And the wind blows it back again.

And every sand becomes a Gem
Reflected in the beams divine;
Blown back, they blind the mocking Eye,
But still in Israel's paths they shine.

The Atoms of Democritus
And Newton's Particles of light
Are sands upon the Red sea shore,
Where Israel's tents do shine so bright.

Democritus and Newton probably do not deserve to be grouped with mockers like Voltaire and Rousseau, but it is not Blake's business to be fair or exact. Scientists and philosophical skeptics are drawn into an irresistible vortex where they receive the same scorn as that heaped on Israel's enemies in the Old Testament.

ROBERT BURNS 1759–1796

Burns is honored as the national poet of Scotland. He was genuinely convivial and modest in company but also intelligent enough to master his craft—chiefly as a writer or re-writer of songs—and to understand the eighteenth-century fashion for the primitive and the rustic. His engaging face can still be seen on cigar boxes and shortbread tins.

A Red, Red Rose

〰〰〰

O my Luve's like a red, red rose,
   That's newly sprung in June:
O my Luve's like the melodie
   That's sweetly played in tune!

As fair art thou, my bonnie lass,
   So deep in luve am I;
And I will luve thee still, my dear,
   Till a' the seas gang dry.

Till a' the seas gang dry, my dear,
   And the rocks melt wi' the sun;
I will luve thee still, my dear,
   While the sands o' life shall run.

And fare thee weel, my only Luve,
   And fare thee weel a while!
And I will come again, my Luve,
   Though it were ten thousand mile.

This, Burns's most famous poem, is among the purest expressions of love in any literature.

To a Mouse on Turning Her Up in Her Nest with the Plough, November, 1785

Wee, sleekit, cow'rin', tim'rous beastie,
O, what a panic's in thy breastie!
Thou need na start awa sae hasty,
  Wi' bickering brattle!
I wad be laith to rin an' chase thee,
  Wi' murd'ring pattle!

I'm truly sorry Man's dominion
Has broken Nature's social union,
An' justifies that ill opinion
  Which makes thee startle,
At me, thy poor, earth-born companion,
  An' fellow-mortal!

I doubt na, whiles, but thou may thieve;
What then? poor beastie, thou maun live!
A daimen icker in a thrave
  'S a sma' request:
I'll get a blessin wi' the lave,
  An' never miss 't!

Thy wee-bit housie, too, in ruin!
It's silly wa's the win's are strewin!
An' naething, now, to big a new ane,
  O' foggage green!
An' bleak December's winds ensuin,
  Baith snell an' keen!

Thou saw the fields laid bare an' waste,
An' weary Winter comin fast,
An' cozie here, beneath the blast,
   Thou thought to dwell,
Till crash! the cruel coulter past
   Out thro' thy cell.

That wee-bit heap o' leaves an' stibble,
Has cost thee monie a weary nibble!
Now thou's turn'd out, for a' thy trouble,
   But house or hald,
To thole the winter's sleety dribble,
   An' cranreuch cauld!

But Mousie, thou are no thy lane,
In proving foresight may be vain:
The best laid schemes o' mice an' men,
   Gang aft a-gley,
An' lea'e us nought but grief an' pain,
   For promis'd joy!

Still, thou art blest, compar'd wi' me!
The present only toucheth thee:
But Och! I backward cast my e'e,
   On prospects drear!
An' forward, tho' I canna see,
   I guess an' fear!

It was like Burns to find the deepest meaning in the humblest creatures, such as lice or mice. His description of the mouse is like Uncle Toby's treatment of the fly in Sterne's Tristram Shandy.

John Anderson, My Jo

John Anderson my jo, John,
  When we were first acquent;
Your locks were like the raven,
  Your bony brow was brent;
But now your brow is beld, John,
  Your locks are like the snaw;
But blessings on your frosty pow,
  John Anderson my Jo.

John Anderson my jo, John,
  We clamb the hill the gither;
And mony a canty day, John,
  We've had wi' ane anither:
Now we maun totter down, John,
  And hand in hand we'll go;
And sleep the gither at the foot,
  John Anderson my Jo.

This is one of the many poems that Burns produced by rewriting an anonymous work from folklore.

The Banks o' Doon

❖·❖·❖·❖

Ye flowery banks o' bonnie Doon,
　How can ye blume sae fair!
How can ye chant, ye little birds,
　And I sae fu' o' care!

Thou'll break my heart, thou bonnie bird
　That sings upon the bough;
Thou minds me o' the happy days
　When my fause Luve was true.

Thou'll break my heart, thou bonnie bird
　That sings beside thy mate;
For sae I sat, and sae I sang,
　And wist na o' my fate.

Aft hae I roved by bonnie Doon
　To see the woodbine twine,
And ilka bird sang o' its love;
　And sae did I o' mine.

Wi' lightsome heart I pu'd a rose,
　Frae aff its thorny tree;
And my fause luver staw the rose,
　But left the thorn wi' me.

The Doon is a river in Burns's native Ayrshire in the western Lowlands. When Gerard Manley Hopkins decided to write about a stream in Scotland, in "Inversnaid" (p. 799), he modelled some of his diction on Burns's (including the word burn, *which means "brook.")*

For A' That and A' That

Is there for honest poverty
That hings his head, and a' that?
The coward slave, we pass him by;
We dare be poor for a' that!
For a' that, and a' that,
Our toils obscure, and a' that;
The rank is but the guinea's stamp—
The man's the gowd for a' that!

What tho' on hamely fare we dine,
Wear hodden gray, and a' that?
Gie fools their silks, and knaves their wine—
A man's a man for a' that!
For a' that, and a' that,
Their tinsel show, and a' that;
The honest man, though e'er sae poor,
Is king o' men, for a' that!

Ye see yon birkie, ca'd a lord,
Wha struts, an' stares, an' a' that—
Tho' hundreds worship at his word,
He's but a coof for a' that;
For a' that, and a' that,
His riband, star, and a' that;
The man of independent mind,
He looks an' laughs at a' that.

A prince can mak a belted knight,
A marquis, duke, and a' that;
But an honest man's aboon his might—
Gude faith, he mauna fa' that!
For a' that, and a' that,
Their dignities, an' a' that;
The pith o' sense, and pride o' worth,
Are higher rank than a' that.

Then let us pray that come it may,—
As come it will for a' that,—
That sense and worth, o'er a' the earth,
May bear the gree, an' a' that.
For a' that, and a' that,
It's comin' yet, for a' that—
That man to man, the warld o'er,
Shall brithers be for a' that.

Intellectual poets of the seventeenth century delighted in paradox; some of their eighteenth-century successors delighted in less complicated affirmations of equality and identity. We now glibly repeat such verdicts as Burns's "A man's a man for a' that," but the sentiment was far from cant or cliché two centuries ago.

Holy Willie's Prayer

>>>>>>>

O Thou that in the heavens does dwell!
Wha, as it pleases best Thysel,
Sends ane to heaven and ten to hell,
   A' for Thy glory!
And no for ony gude or ill
   They've done before Thee!

I bless and praise Thy matchless might,
When thousands Thou has left in night,
That I am here before Thy sight,
   For gifts and grace,
A burning and a shining light
   To a' this place.

What was I, or my generation,
That I should get such exaltation?
I, wha deserved most just damnation
   For broken laws,
Sax thousand years ere my creation,
   Thro' Adam's cause!

When from my mother's womb I fell,
Thou might hae plunged me deep in hell,
To gnash my gooms, and weep, and wail,
   In burning lakes,
Where damned devils roar and yell,
   Chained to their stakes.

Yet I am here, a chosen sample,
To shew Thy grace is great and ample;
I'm here, a pillar o' Thy temple,
   Strong as a rock,
A guide, a buckler, and example,
   To a' Thy flock.

O Lord, Thou kens what zeal I bear,
When drinkers drink, and swearers swear,
And singin' here, and dancin' there,
   Wi' great an' sma';
For I am keepet by Thy fear,
   Free frae them a'.

But yet, O Lord, confess I must,
At times I'm fashed wi' fleshly lust;
And sometimes too, in warldly trust,
   Vile Self gets in;
But Thou remembers we are dust,
   Defiled wi' sin.

O Lord! yestreen, Thou kens—wi' Meg—
Thy pardon I sincerely beg!
O may't ne'er be a living plague,
   To my dishonor!
And I'll ne'er lift a lawless leg
   Again upon her.

Besides, I farther maun allow,
Wi' Leezie's lass, three times—I trow—
But Lord, that Friday I was fou
   When I cam near her;
Or else, Thou kens, Thy servant true
   Wad never steer her.

Maybe Thou lets this fleshy thorn
Buffet Thy servant e'en and morn,
Lest he o'er proud and high should turn,
   That he's sae gifted;
If sae, Thy hand maun e'en be borne
   Until Thou lift it.

Lord, bless Thy Chosen in this place,
For here Thou has a chosen race:
But God, confound their stubborn face,
   And blast their name,
Wha bring Thy rulers to disgrace
   And public shame.

Lord mind Gaun Hamilton's deserts!
He drinks, and swears, and plays at cartes,
Yet has sae mony taking arts
   Wi' Great and Sma',
Frae God's ain priest the people's hearts
   He steals awa.

And when we chastened him therefore,
Thou kens how he bred sic a splore,
And set the warld in a roar
   O' laughing at us—
Curse Thou his basket and his store,
   Kail and potatoes.

Lord, hear my earnest cry and prayer
Against that Presbytry of Ayr!
Thy strong right hand, Lord, make it bare
   Upon their heads!
Lord visit them, and dinna spare,
   For their misdeeds!

O Lord, my God, that glib-tongued Aiken!
My very heart and flesh are quaking
To think how I sat, sweating, shaking,
    And pissed wi' dread,
While he wi' hingin lip and sneaking
    Held up his head!

Lord, in Thy day o' vengeance try him!
Lord, visit them that did employ him!
And pass not in Thy mercy by them,
    Nor hear their prayer;
But for Thy people's sake destroy them,
    And dinna spare!

But Lord, remember me and mine
Wi' mercies temporal and divine!
That I for grace and gear may shine,
    Excelled by nane!
And a' the glory shall be Thine!
    AMEN! AMEN!

"Holy Willie" was William Fisher, a Kirk (Scottish church) Elder who, according to Burns, "was much and justly famed for that polemical chattering which ends in tippling orthodoxy, and for that spiritualized bawdry which refines to liquorish devotion." The hypocrite's prayer is offered up after he has been bested in a church court by Gavin Hamilton and Robert Aiken.

In his long and eventful life, Wordsworth had more to do with the nature of English poetry than any other poet of the past two centuries. Educated at Cambridge, he spent time in France at the height of the Revolution. Legacies and sinecures enabled Wordsworth and his sister Dorothy to live simply, without needing to earn a living. They occupied dwellings in Dorset, then in Somerset, near Coleridge, then at Grasmere in the Lake Country, and finally—in 1813, after he had married Mary Hutchinson—at Rydal Mount. An on-again-off-again friendship with Coleridge was clearly the most important association of Wordsworth's literary life. The two collaborated on the volume called *Lyrical Ballads, with a Few Other Poems,* containing Coleridge's "The Rime of the Ancient Mariner" and a number of Wordsworth's poems, including the meditative masterpiece "Tintern Abbey." Wordsworth was much honored in his later years and from 1843 until his death was Poet Laureate.

The World Is Too Much with Us

The world is too much with us; late and soon,
Getting and spending, we lay waste our powers:
Little we see in Nature that is ours;
We have given our hearts away, a sordid boon!
This Sea that bares her bosom to the moon;
The winds that will be howling at all hours,
And are up-gathered now like sleeping flowers;
For this, for everything, we are out of tune;

It moves us not. — Great God! I'd rather be
A Pagan suckled in a creed outworn;
So might I, standing on this pleasant lea,
Have glimpses that would make me less forlorn;
Have sight of Proteus rising from the sea;
Or hear old Triton blow his wreathèd horn.

The form of this sonnet refers back to sixteenth- and seventeenth-century precursors. Some of the details refer back as well: the description of Proteus (the Old Man of the Sea) recalls Milton's description of the same figure; that of the sea-god Triton recalls Spenser's.

I Wandered Lonely as a Cloud

I wandered lonely as a cloud
That floats on high o'er vales and hills,
When all at once I saw a crowd,
A host, of golden daffodils;
Beside the lake, beneath the trees,
Fluttering and dancing in the breeze.

Continuous as the stars that shine
And twinkle on the milky way,
They stretched in never-ending line
Along the margin of a bay:
Ten thousand saw I at a glance,
Tossing their heads in sprightly dance.

The waves beside them danced; but they
Out-did the sparkling waves in glee:
A poet could not but be gay,
In such a jocund company:
I gazed—and gazed—but little thought
What wealth the show to me had brought:

For oft, when on my couch I lie
In vacant or in pensive mood,
They flash upon that inward eye
Which is the bliss of solitude;
And then my heart with pleasure fills,
And dances with the daffodils.

A doctrine of simple-hearted harmony with rural nature was a foundation-stone of Romanticism, and Wordsworth was the most eloquent exponent of that belief. One could conceivably force complications into such poetry, because it is profound, but the essential feeling is as simple as it is familiar.

Composed upon Westminster Bridge, September 3, 1802

Earth has not anything to show more fair;
Dull would he be of soul who could pass by
A sight so touching in its majesty:
This City now doth, like a garment, wear
The beauty of the morning; silent, bare,
Ships, towers, domes, theaters, and temples lie
Open unto the fields, and to the sky;
All bright and glittering in the smokeless air.
Never did sun more beautifully steep
In his first splendor, valley, rock, or hill;
Ne'er saw I, never felt, a calm so deep!
The river glideth at his own sweet will:
Dear God! the very houses seem asleep;
And all that mighty heart is lying still!

According to Wordsworth's sister, the actual experience occurred on July 31, 1802. The "City" of London is the financial district, a square mile that includes London Bridge and is distinguished by fine commercial and religious buildings. It is much the same neighborhood as that in T. S. Eliot's "Waste Land" (p. 968).

The Solitary Reaper

Behold her, single in the field,
Yon solitary Highland Lass!
Reaping and singing by herself;
Stop here, or gently pass!
Alone she cuts and binds the grain,
And sings a melancholy strain;
O listen! for the Vale profound
Is overflowing with the sound.

No Nightingale did ever chaunt
More welcome notes to weary bands
Of travelers in some shady haunt,
Among Arabian sands:
A voice so thrilling ne'er was heard
In spring-time from the Cuckoo-bird,
Breaking the silence of the seas
Among the farthest Hebrides.

Will no one tell me what she sings? —
Perhaps the plaintive numbers flow
For old, unhappy, far-off things,
And battles long ago:
Or is it some more humble lay,
Familiar matter of today?
Some natural sorrow, loss, or pain,
That has been, and may be again?

Whate'er the theme, the Maiden sang
As if her song could have no ending;
I saw her singing at her work,
And o'er the sickle bending: —
I listened, motionless and still;
And, as I mounted up the hill,
The music in my heart I bore,
Long after it was heard no more.

Although deriving most of his material from his own experience, Wordsworth acknowledged that this vision of a lone working-woman singing in Gaelic came from Thomas Wilkinson's Tour of Scotland. The poet asks, "Will no one tell me what she sings?" because he cannot understand her language.

Ode: Intimations of Immortality from Recollections of Early Childhood

I

There was a time when meadow, grove and stream,
The earth and every common sight,
　　To me did seem
　Apparelled in celestial light,
The glory and the freshness of a dream.
It is not now as it hath been of yore;—
　Turn wheresoe'er I may,
　　By night or day,
The things which I have seen I now can see no more.

II

　The Rainbow comes and goes,
　And lovely is the Rose,
　The Moon doth with delight
Look round her when the heavens are bare,
　Waters on a starry night
　Are beautiful and fair;
The sunshine is a glorious birth;
But yet I know, where'er I go,
That there hath past away a glory from the earth.

III

Now, while the birds thus sing a joyous song,
　And while the young lambs bound
　　As to the tabor's sound,
To me alone there came a thought of grief:
A timely utterance gave that thought relief,
　　And I again am strong:

The cataracts blow their trumpets from the steep;
No more shall grief of mine the season wrong;
I hear the Echoes through the mountains throng,
The Winds come to me from the fields of sleep,
  And all the earth is gay
    Land and sea
  Give themselves up to jollity,
    And with the heart of May
  Doth every Beast keep holiday; —
    Thou child of Joy,
Shout round me, let me hear thy shouts, thou happy
  Shepherd-boy!

IV

Ye blessèd Creatures, I have heard the call
  Ye to each other make; I see
The heavens laugh with you in your jubilee;
  My heart is at your festival,
    My head hath its coronal,
The fulness of your bliss, I feel—I feel it all.
  Oh evil day! if I were sullen
  While Earth herself is adorning,
    This sweet May-morning,
  And the Children are culling
    On every side,
  In a thousand valleys far and wide,
  Fresh flowers; while the sun shines warm,
And the Babe leaps up on his Mother's arm: —
  I hear, I hear, with joy I hear!
  —But there's a Tree, of many, one,
A single Field which I have looked upon,
Both of them speak of something that is gone:
  The Pansy at my feet
  Doth the same tale repeat:
Whither is fled the visionary gleam?
Where is it now, the glory and the dream?

V

Our birth is but a sleep and a forgetting:
The Soul that rises with us, our life's Star,
   Hath had elsewhere its setting,
    And cometh from afar:
   Not in entire forgetfulness,
   And not in utter nakedness,
But trailing clouds of glory do we come
   From God, who is our home:
Heaven lies about us in our infancy!
Shades of the prison-house begin to close
   Upon the growing Boy,
But He beholds the light, and whence it flows,
   He sees it in his joy;
The Youth, who daily farther from the east
   Must travel, still is Nature's Priest,
   And by the vision splendid
   Is on his way attended;
At length the Man perceives it die away,
And fade into the light of common day.

VI

Earth fills her lap with pleasures of her own;
Yearnings she hath in her own natural kind,
And even with something of a Mother's mind,
   And no unworthy aim
   The homely Nurse doth all she can
To make her Foster-child, her Inmate Man,
   Forget the glories he hath known,
And that imperial palace whence he came.

VII

Behold the Child among his new-born blisses,
A six years' Darling of a pigmy size!
See where 'mid work of his own hand he lies.
Fretted by sallies of his mother's kisses,
With light upon him from his father's eyes!
See, at his feet, some little plan or chart,

Some fragment from his dream of human life,
Shaped by himself with newly-learned art;
   A wedding or a festival,
   A mourning or a funeral;
     And this hath now his heart,
     And unto this he frames his song:
       Then will he fit his tongue
To dialogues of business, love, or strife;
   But it will not be long
   Ere this be thrown aside,
   And with new joy and pride
The little Actor cons another part;
Filling from time to time his "humorous stage"
With all the Persons, down to palsied Age,
That Life brings with her in her equipage;
   As if his whole vocation
   Were endless imitation.

VIII

Thou whose exterior semblance doth belie
   Thy Soul's immensity;
Thou best Philosopher, who yet dost keep
Thy heritage, thou Eye among the blind,
That, deaf and silent, read'st the eternal deep,
Haunted for ever by the eternal mind,—
   Mighty Prophet! Seer blest!
   On whom those truths do rest,
Which we are toiling all our lives to find,
In darkness lost, the darkness of the grave;
Thou, over whom thy Immortality
Broods like the Day, a Master o'er a Slave,
A Presence which is not to be put by;
Thou little Child, yet glorious in the might
Of heaven-born freedom on thy being's height,
Why with such earnest pains dost thou provoke
The years to bring the inevitable yoke,
Thus blindly with thy blessedness at strife?
Full soon thy Soul shall have her earthly freight,

[403]

And custom lie upon thee with a weight,
Heavy as frost, and deep almost as life!

IX

O joy! that in our embers
Is something that doth live,
That nature yet remembers
What was so fugitive!
The thought of our past years in me doth breed
Perpetual benediction; not indeed
For that which is most worthy to be blest;
Delight and liberty, the simple creed
Of Childhood, whether busy or at rest,
With new-fledged hope still fluttering in his breast:—
Not for these I raise
The song of thanks and praise;
But for those obstinate questionings
Of sense and outward things,
Fallings from us, vanishings;
Blank misgivings of a Creature
Moving about in worlds not realized,
High instincts before which our mortal Nature
Did tremble like a guilty Thing surprised:
But for those first affections,
Those shadowy recollections,
Which, be they what they may,
Are yet the fountain-light of all our day,
Are yet a master-light of all our seeing;
Uphold us, cherish, and have power to make
Our noisy years seem moments in the being
Of the eternal Silence: truths that wake,
To perish never:
Which neither listlessness, nor mad endeavour,
Nor Man nor Boy,
Nor all that is at enmity with joy,
Can utterly abolish or destroy!
Hence in a season of calm weather
Though inland far we be,

Our Souls have sight of that immortal sea
   Which brought us hither,
  Can in a moment travel thither,
And see the Children sport upon the shore,
And hear the mighty waters rolling evermore.

X

Then sing, ye Birds, sing, sing a joyous song!
   And let the young Lambs bound
   As to the tabor's sound!
We in thought will join your throng,
   Ye that pipe and ye that play,
   Ye that through your hearts today
   Feel the gladness of the May!
What though the radiance which was once so bright
Be now for ever taken from my sight,
  Though nothing can bring back the hour
Of splendour in the grass, of glory in the flower;
   We will grieve not, rather find
   Strength in what remains behind;
   In the primal sympathy
   Which having been must ever be;
   In the soothing thoughts that spring
   Out of human suffering;
   In the faith that looks through death,
In years that bring the philosophic mind.

XI

And O, ye Fountains, Meadows, Hills, and Groves,
Forbode not any severing of our loves!
Yet in my heart of hearts I feel your might
I only have relinquished one delight
To live beneath your more habitual sway.
I love the Brooks which down their channels fret,
Even more than when I tripped lightly as they;
The innocent brightness of a new-born Day
   Is lovely yet;
The Clouds that gather round the setting sun

[405]

Do take a sober colouring from an eye
That hath kept watch o'er man's mortality;
Another race hath been, and other palms are won.
Thanks to the human heart by which we live,
Thanks to its tenderness, its joys, and fears,
To me the meanest flower that blows can give
Thoughts that do often lie too deep for tears.

According to Wordsworth's own testimony, he wrote the last seven stanzas of this poem two years after the first four. The poem looks back to Vaughan's "Retreat" (p. 247) and has more intimate connections with Coleridge's "Dejection: An Ode" (p. 458). The concentration on childhood and the suggestion of "a prior state of existence" also relate the poem to Yeats's "Among School Children" (p. 860).

Lines Composed a Few Miles above Tintern Abbey

Five years have passed; five summers, with the length
Of five long winters! and again I hear
These waters, rolling from their mountain-springs
With a sweet inland murmur.—Once again
Do I behold these steep and lofty cliffs,
Which on a wild secluded scene impress
Thoughts of more deep seclusion; and connect
The landscape with the quiet of the sky.
The day is come when I again repose
Here, under this dark sycamore, and view
These plots of cottage-ground, these orchard-tufts,
Which, at this season, with their unripe fruits,
Are clad in one green hue, and lose themselves
Mid groves and copses. Once again I see
These hedge-rows, hardly hedge-rows, little lines
Of sportive wood run wild; these pastoral farms
Green to the very door; and wreathes of smoke
Sent up, in silence, from among the trees,
With some uncertain notice, as might seem,
Of vagrant dwellers in the houseless woods,
Or of some hermit's cave, where by his fire
The hermit sits alone.

                    Those beauteous forms,
Through a long absence, have not been to me
As is a landscape to a blind man's eye:
But oft, in lonely rooms, and mid the din
Of towns and cities, I have owed to them,
In hours of weariness, sensations sweet,
Felt in the blood, and felt along the heart,
And passing even into my purer mind

With tranquil restoration: — feelings too
Of unremembered pleasure; such, perhaps,
As have no slight or trivial influence
On that best portion of a good man's life;
His little, nameless, unremembered acts
Of kindness and of love. Nor less, I trust,
To them I may have owed another gift,
Of aspect more sublime; that blessed mood,
In which the burthen of the mystery,
In which the heavy and the weary weight
Of all this unintelligible world
Is lightened: — that serene and blessed mood,
In which the affections gently lead us on,
Until, the breath of this corporeal frame,
And even the motion of our human blood
Almost suspended, we are laid asleep
In body, and become a living soul:
While with an eye made quiet by the power
Of harmony, and the deep power of joy,
We see into the life of things.
                                    If this
Be but a vain belief, yet, oh! how oft,
In darkness, and amid the many shapes
Of joyless day-light; when the fretful stir
Unprofitable, and the fever of the world,
Have hung upon the beatings of my heart,
How oft, in spirit, have I turned to thee
O sylvan Wye! Thou wanderer through the woods,
How often has my spirit turned to thee!

And now, with gleams of half-extinguished thought,
With many recognitions dim and faint,
And somewhat of a sad perplexity,
The picture of the mind revives again:
While here I stand, not only with the sense
Of present pleasure, but with pleasing thoughts
That in this moment there is life and food
For future years. And so I dare to hope

Though changed, no doubt, from what I was, when first
I came among these hills; when like a roe
I bounded o'er the mountains, by the sides
Of the deep rivers, and the lonely streams,
Wherever nature led; more like a man
Flying from something that he dreads, than one
Who sought the thing he loved. For nature then
(The coarser pleasures of my boyish days,
And their glad animal movements all gone by,)
To me was all in all.—I cannot paint
What then I was. The sounding cataract
Haunted me like a passion: the tall rock,
The mountain, and the deep and gloomy wood,
Their colours and their forms, were then to me
An appetite: a feeling and a love,
That had no need of a remoter charm,
By thought supplied, or any interest
Unborrowed from the eye.— That time is past,
And all its aching joys are now no more,
And all its dizzy raptures. Not for this
Faint I, nor mourn nor murmur: other gifts
Have followed, for such loss, I would believe,
Abundant recompence. For I have learned
To look on nature, not as in the hour
Of thoughtless youth, but hearing oftentimes
The still, sad music of humanity,
Not harsh nor grating, though of ample power
To chasten and subdue. And I have felt
A presence that disturbs me with the joy
Of elevated thoughts; a sense sublime
Of something far more deeply interfused,
Whose dwelling is the light of setting suns,
And the round ocean, and the living air,
And the blue sky, and in the mind of man,
A motion and a spirit, that impels
All thinking things, all objects of all thought,
And rolls through all things. Therefore am I still
A lover of the meadows and the woods,

And mountains; and of all that we behold
From this green earth; of all the mighty world
Of eye and ear, both what they half-create,
And what perceive; well pleased to recognize
In nature and the language of the sense,
The anchor of my purest thoughts, the nurse,
The guide, the guardian of my heart, and soul
Of all my moral being.
     Nor, perchance,
If I were not thus taught, should I the more
Suffer my genial spirits to decay:
For thou art with me, here, upon the banks
Of this fair river; thou, my dearest friend,
My dear, dear friend, and in thy voice I catch
The language of my former heart, and read
My former pleasures in the shooting lights
Of thy wild eyes. Oh! yet a little while
May I behold in thee what I was once,
My dear, dear sister! And this prayer I make,
Knowing that Nature never did betray
The heart that loved her, 'tis her privilege,
Through all the years of this our life, to lead
From joy to joy: for she can so inform
The mind that is within us, so impress
With quietness and beauty, and so feed
With lofty thoughts, that neither evil tongues,
Rash judgments, nor the sneers of selfish men,
Nor greetings where no kindness is, nor all
The dreary intercourse of daily life,
Shall e'er prevail against us, or disturb
Our cheerful faith that all which we behold
Is full of blessings. Therefore let the moon
Shine on thee in thy solitary walk;
And let the misty mountain winds be free
To blow against thee: and in after years,
When these wild ecstasies shall be matured
Into a sober pleasure, when thy mind

Shall be a mansion for all lovely forms,
Thy memory be as a dwelling-place
For all sweet sounds and harmonies; Oh! then,
If solitude, or fear, or pain, or grief,
Should be thy portion, with what healing thoughts
Of tender joy wilt thou remember me,
And these my exhortations! Nor, perchance,
If I should be, where I no more can hear
Thy voice, nor catch from thy wild eyes these gleams
Of past existence, wilt thou then forget
That on the banks of this delightful stream
We stood together; and that I, so long
A worshipper of Nature, hither came,
Unwearied in that service: rather say
With warmer love, oh! with far deeper zeal
Of holier love. Nor wilt thou then forget,
That after many wanderings, many years
Of absence, these steep woods and lofty cliffs,
And this green pastoral landscape, were to me
More dear, both for themselves, and for thy sake.

In a poem that is essentially an ode in all but name, Wordsworth expresses the profound meanings of a pilgrimage or return to a special sacred place—a theme that animates much poetry in English, from Chaucer's Canterbury Tales *(p. 8) through Gray's "Elegy Written in a Country Churchyard" (p. 328) to such distinguished modern work as Eliot's "Little Gidding" (p. 987) and Larkin's "Church Going" (p. 1068).*

Lucy

Comprising:
She Dwelt among the Untrodden Ways,
I Traveled among Unknown Men,
Strange Fits of Passion Have I Known,
Three Years She Grew in Sun and Shower
A Slumber Did My Spirit Seal

◆◆◆◆

(I)

She dwelt among the untrodden ways
　　Beside the springs of Dove,
A Maid whom there were none to praise
　　And very few to love:

A violet by a mossy stone
　　Half hidden from the eye!
Fair as a star, when only one
　　Is shining in the sky.

She lived unknown, and few could know
　　When Lucy ceased to be;
But she is in her grave, and oh,
　　The difference to me!

(II)

I traveled among unknown men,
　　In lands beyond the sea;
Nor, England! did I know till then
　　What love I bore to thee.

'Tis past, that melancholy dream!
　　Nor will I quit thy shore
A second time; for still I seem
　　To love thee more and more.

Among thy mountains did I feel
   The joy of my desire;
And she I cherished turned her wheel
   Beside an English fire.

Thy mornings showed, thy nights concealed,
   The bowers where Lucy played;
And time too is the last green field
   That Lucy's eyes surveyed.

(III)

Strange fits of passion have I known:
And I will dare to tell,
But in the Lover's ear alone,
What once to me befell.

When she I loved looked every day
Fresh as a rose in June,
I to her cottage bent my way,
Beneath an evening-moon.

Upon the moon I fixed my eye,
All over the wide lea;
With quickening pace my horse drew nigh
Those paths so dear to me.

And now we reached the orchard-plot;
And, as we climbed the hill,
The sinking moon to Lucy's cot
Came near, and nearer still.

In one of those sweet dreams I slept,
Kind Nature's gentlest boon!
And all the while my eyes I kept
On the descending moon.

My horse moved on; hoof after hoof
He raised, and never stopped:
When down behind the cottage roof,
At once, the bright moon dropped.

What fond and wayward thoughts will slide
Into a Lover's head!
"O mercy!" to myself I cried,
"If Lucy should be dead!"

(IV)

Three years she grew in sun and shower;
Then Nature said, "A lovelier flower
    On earth was never sown;
This child I to myself will take;
She shall be mine, and I will make
    A lady of my own.

"Myself will to my darling be
Both law and impulse: and with me
    The girl, in rock and plain,
In earth and heaven, in glade and bower,
Shall feel an overseeing power
    To kindle or restrain.

"She shall be sportive as the fawn
That wild with glee across the lawn
    Or up the mountain springs;
And hers shall be the breathing balm,
And hers the silence and the calm
    Of mute insensate things.

"The floating clouds their state shall lend
To her; for her the willow bend;
    Nor shall she fail to see
Even in the motions of the storm
Grace that shall mould the maiden's form
    By silent sympathy.

"The stars of midnight shall be dear
To her; and she shall lean her ear
   In many a secret place
Where rivulets dance their wayward round,
And beauty born of murmuring sound
   Shall pass into her face.

"And vital feelings of delight
Shall rear her form to stately height,
   Her virgin bosom swell;
Such thoughts to Lucy I will give
While she and I together live
   Here in this happy dell."

Thus Nature spake—The work was done—
How soon my Lucy's race was run!
   She died, and left to me
This heath, this calm and quiet scene;
The memory of what has been,
   And never more will be.

(V)

A slumber did my spirit seal;
   I had no human fears:
She seemed a thing that could not feel
   The touch of earthly years.

No motion has she now, no force;
   She neither hears nor sees;
Rolled round in earth's diurnal course,
   With rocks, and stones, and trees.

These five lyrics, along with a sixth called "Lucy Gray," are customarily grouped as "the Lucy poems." Although "I Traveled among Unknown Men" was slightly later than the others, Wordsworth said that it belonged after "She Dwelt among the Untrodden Ways." No actual persons or occasions mentioned in the poem have been identified with any certainty.

It Is a Beauteous Evening

It is a beauteous evening, calm and free,
The holy time is quiet as a Nun
Breathless with adoration; the broad sun
Is sinking down in its tranquillity;
The gentleness of heaven broods o'er the Sea:
Listen! the mighty Being is awake,
And doth with his eternal motion make
A sound like thunder—everlastingly.
Dear Child! dear Girl! that walkest with me here,
If thou appear untouched by solemn thought,
Thy nature is not therefore less divine:
Thou liest in Abraham's bosom all the year;
And worshipp'st at the Temple's inner shrine,
God being with thee when we know it not.

The "dear Girl" in this sonnet is thought to be Wordsworth's natural daughter Caroline, who was about ten years old when the poem was written in the late summer of 1802.

London, 1802

Milton! thou should'st be living at this hour:
England hath need of thee; she is a fen
Of stagnant waters; altar, sword, and pen,
Fireside, the heroic wealth of hall and bower
Have forfeited their ancient English dower
Of inward happiness. We are selfish men;
Oh raise us up, return to us again
And give us manners, virtue, freedom, power.
Thy soul was like a star, and dwelt apart;
Thou hadst a voice whose sound was like the sea:
Pure as the naked heavens, majestic, free,
So didst thou travel on life's common way,
In cheerful godliness; and yet thy heart
The lowliest duties on herself did lay.

After Milton, the sonnet form went into a 130-year hibernation, stirring now and then in Gray or Bowles but not fully reawakening until Wordsworth. Inspired by reading Milton's polemical prose, he addressed this ringing appeal to his mighty precursor as sonnet-writer and as moral exemplar.

My Heart Leaps Up

My heart leaps up when I behold
   A rainbow in the sky:
So was it when my life began;
So is it now I am a man;
So be it when I shall grow old,
   Or let me die!
The Child is father of the Man;
And I could wish my days to be
Bound each to each by natural piety.

The last three lines of this prismatic poem reappear as the epigraph of Words-
worth's "Ode: Intimations of Immortality from Recollections of Early Childhood"
(p. 400).

Surprised by Joy

Surprised by joy—impatient as the wind
   I turned to share the transport—Oh! with whom
   But thee, deep buried in the silent tomb,
That spot which no vicissitude can find?
Love, faithful love, recalled thee to my mind—
   But how could I forget thee? Through what power,
   Even for the least division of an hour,
Have I been so beguiled as to be blind
To my most grievous loss!—That thought's return
   Was the worst pang that sorrow ever bore,
Save one, one only, when I stood forlorn,
   Knowing my heart's best treasure was no more;
That neither present time, nor years unborn
   Could to my sight that heavenly face restore.

Wordsworth said that this tender poem was suggested by memories of his daughter Catherine, who died in 1812 at the age of four.

She Was a Phantom of Delight

She was a phantom of delight
When first she gleamed upon my sight;
A lovely apparition, sent
To be a moment's ornament;
Her eyes as stars of twilight fair;
Like twilight's, too, her dusky hair;
But all things else about her drawn
From May-time and the cheerful dawn;
A dancing shape, an image gay,
To haunt, to startle and waylay.

I saw her upon nearer view,
A Spirit, yet a Woman too!
Her household motions light and free,
And steps of virgin liberty;
A countenance in which did meet
Sweet records, promises as sweet;
A creature not too bright or good
For human nature's daily food;
For transient sorrows, simple wiles,
Praise, blame, love, kisses, tears, and smiles.

And now I see with eye serene
The very pulse of the machine;
A being breathing thoughtful breath,
A traveller between life and death;
The reason firm, the temperate will,
Endurance, foresight, strength, and skill;
A perfect Woman, nobly planned,
To warn, to comfort, and command;
And yet a Spirit still, and bright
With something of angelic light.

Wordsworth wrote this poem about his wife.

Resolution and Independence

THERE was a roaring in the wind all night;
The rain came heavily and fell in floods;
But now the sun is rising calm and bright;
The birds are singing in the distant woods;
Over his own sweet voice the stock-dove broods;
The jay makes answer as the magpie chatters;
And all the air is filled with pleasant noise of waters.

All things that love the sun are out of doors;
The sky rejoices in the morning's birth;
The grass is bright with rain-drops; — on the moors
The hare is running races in her mirth;
And with her feet she from the plashy earth
Raises a mist; that, glittering in the sun,
Runs with her all the way, wherever she doth run.

I was a Traveler then upon the moor;
I saw the hare that raced about with joy;
I heard the woods and distant waters roar;
Or heard them not, as happy as a boy:
The pleasant season did my heart employ:
My old remembrances went from me wholly;
And all the ways of men, so vain and melancholy.

But, as it sometimes chanceth, from the might
Of joy in minds that can no further go,
As high as we have mounted in delight
In our dejection do we sink as low;
To me that morning did it happen so;
And fears and fancies thick upon me came;
Dim sadness — and blind thoughts, I knew not, nor could name.

I heard the sky-lark warbling in the sky;
And I bethought me of the playful hare:
Even such a happy Child of earth am I;
Even as these blissful creatures do I fare;
Far from the world I walk, and from all care;
But there may come another day to me —
Solitude, pain of heart, distress, and poverty.

My whole life I have lived in pleasant thought,
As if life's business were a summer mood;
As if all needful things would come unsought
To genial faith, still rich in genial good;
But how can he expect that others should
Build for him, sow for him, and at his call
Love him, who for himself will take no heed at all?

I thought of Chatterton, the marvellous Boy,
The sleepless Soul that perished in his pride;
Of Him who walked in glory and in joy
Following his plough, along the mountain-side:
By our own spirits are we deified:
We Poets in our youth begin in gladness;
But thereof come in the end despondency and madness.

Now, whether it were by peculiar grace,
A leading from above, a something given,
Yet it befell that, in this lonely place,
When I with these untoward thoughts had striven,
Beside a pool bare to the eye of heaven
I saw a Man before me unawares:
The oldest man he seemed that ever wore grey hairs.

As a huge stone is sometimes seen to lie
Couched on the bald top of an eminence;
Wonder to all who do the same espy,
By what means it could thither come, and whence;
So that it seems a thing endued with sense:
Like a sea-beast crawled forth, that on a shelf
Of rock or sand reposeth, there to sun itself;

Such seemed this Man, not all alive nor dead,
Nor all asleep—in his extreme old age:
His body was bent double, feet and head
Coming together in life's pilgrimage;
As if some dire constraint of pain, or rage
Of sickness felt by him in times long past,
A more than human weight upon his frame had cast.

Himself he propped, limbs, body, and pale face,
Upon a long grey staff of shaven wood:
And, still as I drew near with gentle pace,
Upon the margin of that moorish flood
Motionless as a cloud the old Man stood,
That heareth not the loud winds when they call;
And moveth all together, if it move at all.

At length, himself unsettling, he the pond
Stirred with his staff, and fixedly did look
Upon the muddy water, which he conned,
As if he had been reading in a book:
And now a stranger's privilege I took;
And, drawing to his side, to him did say,
"This morning gives us promise of a glorious day."

A gentle answer did the old Man make,
In courteous speech which forth he slowly drew:
And him with further words I thus bespake,
"What occupation do you there pursue?
This is a lonesome place for one like you."
Ere he replied, a flash of mild surprise
Broke from the sable orbs of his yet-vivid eyes.

His words came feebly, from a feeble chest,
But each in solemn order followed each,
With something of a lofty utterance drest —
Choice word and measured phrase, above the reach
Of ordinary men; a stately speech;
Such as grave Livers do in Scotland use,
Religious men, who give to God and man their dues.

He told, that to these waters he had come
To gather leeches, being old and poor:
Employment hazardous and wearisome!
And he had many hardships to endure:
From pond to pond he roamed, from moor to moor;
Housing, with God's good help, by choice or chance;
And in this way he gained an honest maintenance.

The old Man still stood talking by my side;
But now his voice to me was like a stream
Scarce heard; nor word from word could I divide;
And the whole body of the Man did seem
Like one whom I had met with in a dream;
Or like a man from some far region sent,
To give me human strength, by apt admonishment.

My former thoughts returned: the fear that kills;
And hope that is unwilling to be fed;
Cold, pain, and labour, and all fleshly ills;
And mighty Poets in their misery dead.
— Perplexed, and longing to be comforted,
My question eagerly did I renew,
"How is it that you live, and what is it you do?"

He with a smile did then his words repeat;
And said that, gathering leeches, far and wide
He travelled; stirring thus about his feet
The waters of the pools where they abide.
"Once I could meet with them on every side;
But they have dwindled long by slow decay;
Yet still I persevere, and find them where I may."

While he was talking thus, the lonely place,
The old Man's shape, and speech — all troubled me:
In my mind's eye I seemed to see him pace
About the weary moors continually,
Wandering about alone and silently.
While I these thoughts within myself pursued,
He, having made a pause, the same discourse renewed.

And soon with this he other matter blended,
Cheerfully uttered, with demeanour kind,
But stately in the main; and when he ended,
I could have laughed myself to scorn to find
In that decrepit Man so firm a mind.
"God," said I, "be my help and stay secure;
I'll think of the Leech-gatherer on the lonely moor!"

For a poem about the humblest of humankind — an infirm old man with one of the worst jobs anybody has ever had — Wordsworth deliberately chose a stanza called Rhyme Royal, which had been associated with kings. Wordsworth's poem is travestied in "I'll Tell Thee Everything I Can" by "Lewis Carroll" (p. 755).

SIR WALTER SCOTT 1771–1832

Beginning in 1797 and continuing for thirty-five years, Scott published at least one book a year, and sometimes two: poetry, historical fiction, collections of folklore, and editions and biographies of earlier writers. Although the direct influence of his verse has diminished somewhat since the nineteenth century, his importance is still strongly felt in opera, historical fiction, and antiquarian studies. It is also worth noting that the modern sense of "glamour" comes from Scott.

Proud Maisie

Proud Maisie is in the wood,
　　Walking so early;
Sweet Robin sits on the bush,
　　Singing so rarely.

"Tell me, thou bonny bird,
　　When shall I marry me?"
"When six braw gentlemen
　　Kirkward shall carry ye."

"Who makes the bridal bed,
　　Birdie, say truly?"
"The grey-headed sexton
　　That delves the grave duly.

"The glowworm o'er grave and stone
　　Shall light thee steady.
The owl from the steeplesing,
　　'Welcome, proud lady.' "

from The Heart of Midlothian

Scott seems to have been the last writer who produced still-readable novels containing poems that qualify for an anthology based on popularity. "Proud Maisie," from chapter 40 of The Heart of Midlothian, *is the last song sung by Madge Wildfire.*

Breathes There the Man
with Soul So Dead

Breathes there the man with soul so dead,
   Who never to himself hath said,
   This is my own, my native land!
Whose heart hath ne'er within him burn'd,
As home his footsteps he hath turn'd
   From wandering on a foreign strand!
If such there breathe, go, mark him well;
For him no Minstrel raptures swell;
High though his titles, proud his name,
Boundless his wealth as wish can claim;
Despite those titles, power, and pelf,
The wretch, concentred all in self,
Living, shall forfeit fair renown,
And, doubly dying, shall go down
To the vile dust, from whence he sprung,
Unwept, unhonour'd, and unsung.

                  from The Lay of the Last Minstrel

These lines open canto 6 of "The Lay of the Last Minstrel." Today, two centuries later, Scotland ("Caledonia") still inspires patriotic fervor. Any number of immensely popular romances amply demonstrate that the land continues to impress us as wild, rugged, and exciting. The turning point of Edward Everett Hale's "Man without a Country," by the way, comes when the hero, Philip Nolan, reads these lines by Scott.

Lochinvar

❖❖❖❖

Oh, young Lochinvar is come out of the West, —
Through all the wide Border his steed was the best,
And, save his good broadsword, he weapon had none, —
He rode all unarmed, and he rode all alone.
So faithful in love, and so dauntless in war,
There never was knight like the young Lochinvar.

He stayed not for brake, and he stopped not for stone,
He swam the Eske river where ford there was none,
But, ere he alighted at Netherby gate,
The bride had consented, the gallant came late;
For a laggard in love, and a dastard in war,
Was to wed the fair Ellen of brave Lochinvar.

So boldly he entered the Netherby hall,
Among bridesmen, and kinsmen, and brothers, and all.
Then spoke the bride's father, his hand on his sword,
(For the poor craven bridegroom said never a word),
"Oh, come ye in peace here, or come ye in war,
Or to dance at our bridal, young Lord Lochinvar?"

"I long wooed your daughter, my suit you denied; —
Love swells like the Solway, but ebbs like its tide; —
And now am I come, with this lost love of mine,
To lead but one measure, drink one cup of wine.
There are maidens in Scotland more lovely by far,
That would gladly be bride to the young Lochinvar."

The bride kissed the goblet, the knight took it up,
He quaffed off the wine, and he threw down the cup.
She looked down to blush, and she looked up to sigh,
With a smile on her lips,and a tear in her eye.
He took her soft hand ere her mother could bar:
"Now tread we a measure," said young Lochinvar.

So stately his form, and so lovely her face,
That never a hall such a galliard did grace;
While her mother did fret, and her father did fume,
And the bridegroom stood dangling his bonnet and plume,
And the bridemaidens whispered, " 'Twere better by far
To have matched our fair cousin with young Lochinvar."

One touch to her hand, and one word in her ear,
When they reached the hall-door, and the charger stood near;
So light to the croupe the fair lady he swung,
So light to the saddle before her he sprung!
"She is won! we are gone! over bank, bush, and scaur;
They'll have fleet steeds that follow," quoth young Lochinvar.

There was mounting 'mong Græmes of the Netherby clan;
Forsters, Fenwicks, and Musgraves, they rode and they ran;
There was racing and chasing on Cannobie Lee,
But the lost bride of Netherby ne'er did they see.
So daring in love, and so dauntless in war,
Have ye e'er heard of gallant like young Lochinvar?

from Marmion

---

*In the chivalric tale "Marmion," Lady Heron sings "Lochinvar," which Scott
based on a folk ballad.*

Paradoxically, the most philosophical of philosophical critics, fit for the company of Plato and Bacon, is also the least philosophical of poets, fit for the company of the anonymous authors of "Sir Patrick Spens" and other ballads. The son of a vicar, Coleridge received a spotty but stimulating education and led a particularly vexed life, which included a dependency on opium. He was, however, most fortunate in his associations; he was close to Charles Lamb, William Wordsworth, and Robert Southey, and he was supported for several years by the philanthropy of Josiah and Thomas Wedgwood, still famous for their china.

Kubla Khan

In Xanadu did Kubla Khan
A stately pleasure-dome decree:
Where Alph, the sacred river, ran
Through caverns measureless to man
  Down to a sunless sea.
So twice five miles of fertile ground
With walls and towers were girdled round;
And here were gardens bright with sinuous rills,
Where blossomed many an incense-bearing tree;
And here were forests ancient as the hills,
Enfolding sunny spots of greenery.

But oh! that deep romantic chasm which slanted
Down the green hill athwart a cedarn cover!
A savage place! as holy and enchanted
As e'er beneath a waning moon was haunted
By woman wailing for her demon-lover!
And from this chasm, with ceaseless turmoil seething,
As if this earth in fast thick pants were breathing,
A mighty fountain momently was forced:
Amid whose swift half-intermitted burst
Huge fragments vaulted like rebounding hail,
Or chaffy grain beneath the thresher's flail:
And 'mid these dancing rocks at once and ever
It flung up momently the sacred river.
Five miles meandering with a mazy motion
Through wood and dale the sacred river ran,
Then reached the caverns measureless to man,
And sank in tumult to a lifeless ocean:
And 'mid this tumult Kubla heard from far
Ancestral voices prophesying war!

    The shadow of the dome of pleasure
    Floated midway on the waves;
    Where was heard the mingled measure
    From the fountain and the caves.
It was a miracle of rare device,
A sunny pleasure-dome with caves of ice!

A damsel with a dulcimer
In a vision once I saw:
It was an Abyssinian maid,
And on her dulcimer she played,
Singing of Mount Abora.
Could I revive within me
Her symphony and song,
To such a deep delight 'twould win me,
That with music loud and long,
I would build that dome in air,
That sunny dome! those caves of ice!
And all who heard should see them there,
And all should cry, Beware! Beware!
His flashing eyes, his floating hair!
Weave a circle round him thrice,
And close your eyes with holy dread,
For he on honey-dew hath fed,
And drunk the milk of Paradise.

We meet in Coleridge a genius-level mentality (here, in 1797, about twenty-five years of age), with his deep desires given special form and color by fabulously comprehensive reading and profound thinking. The desires take the form of a Paradise, which literally means "a walled enclosure." Then, reading about another walled enclosure devoted to pleasure and lulled by both opium and the charms of repeated sounds in exotic words, the genius falls asleep and dreams this poem.

The Rime of the Ancient Mariner

IN SEVEN PARTS

*Facile credo, plures esse Naturas invisibles
quam visibiles in rerum universitate. Sed ho-
rum [sic] omnium familiam quis nobis enar-
rabit? et gradus et cognationes et discrimina et
singulorum munera? Quid agunt? quae loca
habitant? Harum rerum notitiam semper am-
bivit ingenium humanum, nunquam attigit.
Juvat, inverea, non diffiteor, quandoque, in
animo, in tabulâ, majoris et melioris mundi
imaginem contemplari: ne mens assuefacta
hodiernae vitae minutiis se contrahat nimis, et
tota subsidat in pusillas cogitationes. Sed ver-
itati interea invigilandum est, modusque ser-
vandus, ut certa ab incertis, diem a nocte,
distinguamus.* —T. BURNET

PART I

*An ancient Mariner meeteth
three Gallants bidden to a
Wedding feast, and detaineth
one.*

It is an ancient Mariner
And he stoppeth one of three.
—"By thy long gray beard and glittering
     eye,
Now wherefore stopp'st thou me?

The Bridegroom's doors are opened wide,
And I am next of kin;
The guests are met, the feast is set:
May'st hear the merry din."

He holds him with his skinny hand,
"There was a ship," quoth he.
"Hold off! unhand me, graybeard loon!"
Eftsoons his hand dropped he.

*The Wedding Guest is
spellbound by the eye of the
old seafaring man, and
constrained to hear his tale.*

He holds him with his glittering eye—
The Wedding Guest stood still,
And listens like a three years' child:
The Mariner hath his will.

The Wedding Guest sat on a stone:
He cannot choose but hear;
And thus spake on that ancient man,
The bright-eyed Mariner.

"The ship was cheered, the harbor cleared,
Merrily did we drop
Below the kirk, below the hill,
Below the lighthouse top.

The Mariner tells how the ship sailed southward with a good wind and fair weather, till it reached the line.

The Sun came up upon the left,
Out of the sea came he!
And he shone bright, and on the right
Went down into the sea.

Higher and higher every day,
Till over the mast at noon—"
The Wedding Guest here beat his breast,
For he heard the loud bassoon.

The Wedding Guest heareth the bridal music; but the Mariner continueth his tale.

The bride hath placed into the hall,
Red as a rose is she;
Nodding their heads before her goes
The merry minstrelsy.

The Wedding Guest he beat his breast,
Yet he cannot choose but hear;
And thus spake on that ancient man,
The bright-eyed Mariner.

The ship driven by a storm toward the South Pole.

"And now the STORM-BLAST came and he
Was tyrannous and strong;
He struck with his o'ertaking wings,
And chased us south along.

With sloping masts and dipping prow,
As who pursued with yell and blow
Still treads the shadow of his foe,
And forward bends his head,
The ship drove fast, loud roared the blast,
And southward aye we fled.

And now there came both mist and snow,
And it grew wondrous cold:
And ice, mast-high, came floating by,
As green as emerald.

The land of ice, and of fearful sounds where no living thing was to be seen.

And through the drifts the snowy clifts
Did send a dismal sheen:
Nor shapes of men nor beasts we ken—
The ice was all between.

The ice was here, the ice was there,
The ice was all around:
It cracked and growled, and roared and
    howled,
Like noises in a swound!

Till a great sea bird, called the Albatross, came through the snowfog, and was received with great joy and hospitality.

At length did cross an Albatross,
Thorough the fog it came;
As if it had been a Christian soul,
We hailed it in God's name.

It ate the food it ne'er had eat,
And round and round it flew.
The ice did split with a thunder-fit;
The helmsman steered us through!

And lo! the Albatross proveth a
bird of good omen, and
followeth the ship as it
returned northward through fog
and floating ice.

And a good south wind sprung up behind;
The Albatross did follow,
And every day, for food or play,
Came to the mariners' hollo!

In mist or cloud, on mast or shroud,
It perched for vespers nine;
Whiles all the night, through fog-smoke
   white,
Glimmered the white Moon-shine."

The ancient Mariner
inhospitably killeth the pious
bird of good omen.

"God save thee, ancient Mariner!
From the fiends, that plague thee thus! —
Why look'st thou so?"—With my crossbow
I shot the ALBATROSS.

PART II

The Sun now rose upon the right:
Out of the sea came he,
Still hid in mist, and on the left
Went down into the sea.

And the good south wind still blew behind,
But no sweet bird did follow,
Nor any day for food or play
Came to the mariners' hollo!

His shipmates cry out against
the ancient Mariner, for killing
the bird of good luck.

And I had done a hellish thing,
And it would work 'em woe:
For all averred, I had killed the bird
That made the breeze to blow.
Ah wretch! said they, the bird to slay,
That made the breeze to blow!

But when the fog cleared off, they justify the same, and thus make themselves accomplices in the crime.

Nor dim nor red, like God's own head,
The glorious Sun uprist:
Then all averred, I had killed the bird
That brought the fog and mist.
'Twas right, said they, such birds to slay,
That bring the fog and mist.

The fair breeze continues; the ship enters the Pacific Ocean, and sails northward, even till it reaches the Line.

The fair breeze blew, the white foam flew,
The furrow followed free;
We were the first that ever burst
Into that silent sea.

The ship hath been suddenly becalmed.

Down dropped the breeze, the sails
    dropped down,
'Twas sad as sad could be;
And we did speak only to break
The silence of the sea!

All in a hot and copper sky,
The bloody Sun, at noon,
Right up above the mist did stand,
No bigger than the Moon.

Day after day, day after day,
We stuck, nor breath nor motion;
As idle as a painted ship
Upon a painted ocean.

And the Albatross begins to be avenged.

Water, water, everywhere,
And all the boards did shrink;
Water, water, everywhere,
Nor any drop to drink.

The very deep did rot: O Christ!
That ever this should be!
Yea, slimy things did crawl with legs
Upon the slimy sea.

About, about, in reel and rout
The death-fires danced at night;
The water, like a witch's oils,
Burnt green, and blue and white.

And some in dreams assuréd were
Of the Spirit that plagued us so;
Nine fathom deep he had followed us
From the land of mist and snow.

*A Spirit had followed them;
one of the invisible inhabitants
of this planet, neither departed
souls nor angels; concerning
whom the learned Jew,
Josephus, and the Platonic
Constantinopolitan, Michael
Psellus, may be consulted.
They are very numerous, and
there is no climate or element
without one or more.*

And every tongue, through utter drought,
Was withered at the root;
We could not speak, no more than if
We had been choked with soot.

*The shipmates, in their sore
distress, would fain throw the
whole guilt on the ancient
Mariner: in sign whereof they
hang the dead sea bird round
his neck.*

Ah! well-a-day! what evil looks
Had I from old and young!
Instead of the cross, the Albatross
About my neck was hung.

PART III

There passed a weary time. Each throat
Was parched, and glazed each eye.
A weary time! a weary time!
How glazed each weary eye,
When looking westward, I beheld
A something in the sky.

At first it seemed a little speck,
And then it seemed a mist;
It moved and moved, and took at last
A certain shape, I wist.

A speck, a mist, a shape, I wist!
And still it neared and neared:
As if it dodged a water sprite,
It plunged and tacked and veered.

With throats unslaked, with black lips
    baked,
We could nor laugh nor wail;
Through utter drought all dumb we stood!
I bit my arm, I sucked the blood,
And cried, a sail! a sail!

With throats unslaked, with black lips
    baked,
Agape they heard me call:
Gramercy! they for joy did grin,
And all at once their breath drew in,
As they were drinking all.

And horror follows. For can it
be a ship that comes onward
without wind or tide?

See! see! (I cried) she tacks no more!
Hither to work us weal;
Without a breeze, without a tide,
She steadies with upright keel!

The western wave was all aflame.
The day was well nigh done!
Almost upon the western wave
Rested the broad bright Sun;
When that strange shape drove suddenly
Betwixt us and the Sun.

It seemeth him but the skeleton
of a ship.

And straight the Sun was flecked with bars,
(Heaven's Mother send us grace!)
As if through a dungeon grate he peered
With broad and burning face.

And its ribs are seen as bars
on the face of the setting Sun.

Alas! (thought I, and my heart beat loud)
How fast she nears and nears!
Are those *her* sails that glance in the Sun,
Like restless gossameres?

The Specter-Woman and her
Deathmate, and no other on
board the skeleton ship.

Are those *her* ribs through which the Sun
Did peer, as through a grate?
And is that Woman all her crew?
Is that a DEATH? and are there two?
Is DEATH that woman's mate?

Like vessel, like crew!

Her lips were red, *her* looks were free,
Her locks were yellow as gold:
Her skin was as white as leprosy,
The Nightmare LIFE-IN-DEATH was she,
Who thicks man's blood with cold.

Death and Life-in-Death have diced for the ship's crew, and she (the latter) winneth the ancient Mariner.

The naked hulk alongside came,
And the twain were casting dice;
"The game is done! I've won! I've won!"
Quoth she, and whistles thrice.

No twilight within the courts of the Sun.

The Sun's rim dips; the stars rush out:
At one stride comes the dark;
With far-heard whisper, o'er the sea,
Off shot the specter-bark.

At the rising of the Moon,

We listened and looked sideways up!
Fear at my heart, as at a cup,
My lifeblood seemed to sip!
The stars were dim, and thick the night,
The steersman's face by his lamp gleamed
    white;
From the sails the dew did drip—
Till clomb above the eastern bar
The hornéd Moon, with one bright star
Within the nether tip.

One after another,

One after one, by the star-dogged Moon,
Too quick for groan or sigh,
Each turned his face with ghastly pang,
And cursed me with his eye.

His shipmates drop down dead.

Four times fifty living men,
(And I heard nor sigh nor groan)
With heavy thump, a lifeless lump,
They dropped down one by one.

But Life-in-Death begins her
work on the ancient Mariner.

The souls did from their bodies fly—
They fled to bliss or woe!
And every soul, it passed me by,
Like the whizz of my cross-bow!

PART IV

The Wedding Guest feareth
that a Spirit is talking to him.

"I fear thee, ancient Mariner!
I fear thy skinny hand!
And thou art long, and lank, and brown,
As is the ribbed sea-sand.

I fear thee and thy glittering eye,
And thy skinny hand, so brown."—
Fear not, fear not, thou Wedding Guest!
This body dropped not down.

But the ancient Mariner
assureth him of his bodily life,
and proceedeth to relate his
horrible penance.

Alone, alone, all, all alone,
Alone on a wide wide sea!
And never a saint took pity on
My soul in agony.

He despiseth the creatures of
the calm,

The many men, so beautiful!
And they all dead did lie:
And a thousand thousand slimy things
Lived on; and so did I.

And envieth that they should
live, and so many lie dead.

I looked upon the rotting sea,
And drew my eyes away;
I looked upon the rotting deck,
And there the dead men lay.

I looked to heaven, and tried to pray;
But or ever a prayer had gushed,
A wicked whisper came, and made
My heart as dry as dust.

I closed my lids, and kept them close,
And the balls like pulses beat,
For the sky and the sea, and the sea and
    the sky
Lay like a load on my weary eye,
And the dead were at my feet.

But the curse liveth for him in the eye of the dead men.

The cold sweat melted from their limbs,
Nor rot nor reek did they:
The look with which they looked on me
Had never passed away.

An orphan's curse would drag to hell
A spirit from on high;
But oh! more horrible than that
Is the curse in a dead man's eye!
Seven days, seven nights, I saw that curse,
And yet I could not die.

The moving Moon went up the sky,
And nowhere did abide;
Softly she was going up,
And a star or two beside—

In his loneliness and fixedness he yearneth towards the journeying Moon, and the stars that still sojourn, yet still move onward; and everywhere the blue sky belongs to them, and is their appointed rest, and their native country and their own natural homes, which they enter unannounced, as lords that are certainly expected and yet there is a silent joy at their arrival.

Her beams bemocked the sultry main,
Like April hoar-frost spread;
But where the ship's huge shadow lay,
The charmèd water burnt alway
A still and awful red.

By the light of the Moon he beholdeth God's creatures of the great calm.

Beyond the shadow of the ship,
I watched the water snakes:
They moved in tracks of shining white,
And when they reared, the elfish light
Fell off in hoary flakes.

Within the shadow of the ship
I watched their rich attire:
Blue, glossy green, and velvet black,
They coiled and swam; and every track
Was a flash of golden fire.

Their beauty and their happiness.

He blesseth them in his heart.

O happy living things! no tongue
Their beauty might declare:
A spring of love gushed from my heart,
And I blessed them unaware:
Sure my kind saint took pity on me,
And I blessed them unaware.

The spell begins to break.

The self-same moment I could pray;
And from my neck so free
The Albatross fell off, and sank
Like lead into the sea.

PART V

Oh sleep! it is a gentle thing,
Beloved from pole to pole!
To Mary Queen the praise be given!
She sent the gentle sleep from Heaven,
That slid into my soul.

Be grace of the holy Mother, the ancient Mariner is refreshed with rain.

The silly buckets on the deck,
That had so long remained,
I dreamt that they were filled with dew;
And when I awoke, it rained.

My lips were wet, my throat was cold,
My garments all were dank;
Sure I had drunken in my dreams,
And still my body drank.

I moved, and could not feel my limbs;
I was so light—almost
I thought that I had died in sleep,
And was a blessèd ghost.

He heareth sounds and seeth strange sights and commotions in the sky and the element.

And soon I heard a roaring wind:
It did not come anear;
But with its sound it shook the sails,
That were so thin and sere.

The upper air burst into life!
And a hundred fire-flags sheen,
To and fro they were hurried about!
And to and fro, and in and out,
The wan stars danced between.

And the coming wind did roar more loud,
And the sails did sigh like sedge;
And the rain poured down from one black
    cloud;
The Moon was at its edge.

The thick black cloud was cleft, and still
The Moon was at its side:
Like waters shot from some high crag,
The lightning fell with never a jag,
A river steep and wide.

The bodies of the ship's crew are inspirited, and the ship moves on;

The loud wind never reached the ship,
Yet now the ship moved on!
Beneath the lightning and the Moon
The dead men gave a groan.

They groaned, they stirred, they all uprose,
Nor spake, nor moved their eyes;
It had been strange, even in a dream,
To have seen those dead men rise.

The helmsman steered, the ship moved on;
Yet never a breeze up-blew;
The mariners all 'gan work the ropes,
Where they were wont to do;
They raised their limbs like lifeless tools—
We were a ghastly crew.

The body of my brother's son
Stood by me, knee to knee:
The body and I pulled at one rope,
But he said nought to me.

But not by the souls of the men, nor by demons of earth or middle air, but by a blessèd troop of angelic spirits, sent down by the invocation of the guardian saint.

"I fear thee, ancient Mariner!"
Be calm, thou Wedding Guest!
'Twas not those souls that fled in pain,
Which to their corses came again,
But a troop of spirits blest:

For when it dawned—they dropped their
   arms,
And clustered round the mast;
Sweet sounds rose slowly through their
mouths,
And from their bodies passed.

Around, around, flew each sweet sound,
Then darted to the Sun;
Slowly the sounds came back again,
Now mixed, now one by one.

Sometimes a-dropping from the sky
I heard the sky-lark sing;
Sometimes all little birds that are,
How they seemed to fill the sea and air
With their sweet jargoning!

And now 'twas like all instruments,
Now like a lonely flute;
And now it is an angel's song,
That makes the heavens be mute.

It ceased; yet still the sails made on
A pleasant noise till noon,
A noise like of a hidden brook
In the leafy month of June,
That to the sleeping woods all night
Singeth a quiet tune.

Till noon we quietly sailed on,
Yet never a breeze did breathe:
Slowly and smoothly went the ship,
Moved onward from beneath.

The lonesome Spirit from the South Pole carries on the ship as far as the Line, in obedience to the angelic troop, but still requireth vengeance.

Under the keel nine fathom deep,
From the land of mist and snow,
The spirit slid: and it was he
That made the ship to go.
The sails at noon left off their tune,
And the ship stood still also.

The Sun, right up above the mast,
Had fixed her to the ocean:
But in a minute she 'gan stir,
With a short uneasy motion—
Backwards and forwards half her length
With a short uneasy motion.

Then like a pawing horse let go,
She made a sudden bound:
It flung the blood into my head,
And I fell down in a swound.

*The Polar Spirit's fellow
demons, the invisible
inhabitants of the element,
take part in his wrong; and
two of them relate, one to
the other, that penance long
and heavy for the ancient
Mariner hath been accorded
to the Polar Spirit, who
returneth southward.*

How long in that same fit I lay,
I have not to declare;
But ere my living life returned,
I heard and in my soul discerned
Two voices in the air.

"Is it he?" quoth one, "Is this the man?
By him who died on cross,
With his cruel bow he laid full low
The harmless Albatross.

The spirit who bideth by himself
In the land of mist and snow,
He loved the bird that loved the man
Who shot him with his bow."

The other was a softer voice,
As soft as honey-dew:
Quoth he, "The man hath penance done,
And penance more will do."

PART VI

FIRST VOICE:

"But tell me, tell me! speak again,
Thy soft response renewing—
What makes that ship drive on so fast?
What is the ocean doing?"

SECOND VOICE:

"Still as a slave before his lord,
The ocean hath no blast;
His great bright eye most silently
Up to the Moon is cast—

If he may know which way to go;
For she guides him smooth or grim.
See, brother, see! how graciously
She looketh down on him."

The Mariner hath been cast into a trance; for the angelic power causeth the vessel to drive northward faster than human life could endure.

FIRST VOICE:

"But why drives on that ship so fast,
Without or wave or wind?"

SECOND VOICE:

"The air is cut away before,
And closes from behind.

Fly, brother, fly! more high, more high!
Or we shall be belated:
For slow and slow that ship will go,
When the Mariner's trance is abated."

The supernatural motion is retarded; the Mariner awakes, and his penance begins anew.

I woke, and we were sailing on
As in a gentle weather:
'Twas night, calm night, the moon was high;
The dead men stood together.

All stood together on the deck,
For a charnel-dungeon fitter:
All fixed on me their stony eyes,
That in the Moon did glitter.

The pang, the curse, with which they died,
Had never passed away:
I could not draw my eyes from theirs,
Nor turn them up to pray.

The curse is finally expiated.   And now this spell was snapped: once more
I viewed the ocean green,
And looked far forth, yet little saw
Of what had else been seen—

Like one, that on a lonesome road
Doth walk in fear and dread,
And having once turned round walks on,
And turns no more his head;
Because he knows, a frightful fiend
Doth close behind him tread.

But soon there breathed a wind on me,
Nor sound nor motion made:
Its path was not upon the sea,
In ripple or in shade.

It raised my hair, it fanned my cheek
Like a meadow-gale of spring—
It mingled strangely with my fears,
Yet it felt like a welcoming.

Swiftly, swiftly flew the ship,
Yet she sailed softly too:
Sweetly, sweetly blew the breeze—
On me alone it blew.

*And the ancient Mariner
beholdeth his native country.*

Oh! dream of joy! is this indeed
The lighthouse top I see?
Is this the hill? is this the kirk?
Is this mine own countree?

We drifted o'er the harbor-bar,
And I with sobs did pray—
O let me be awake, my God!
Or let me sleep alway.

The harbor-bay was clear as glass,
So smoothly it was strewn!
And on the bay the moonlight lay,
And the shadow of the Moon.

The rock shone bright, the kirk no less,
That stands above the rock:
The moonlight steeped in silentness
The steady weathercock.

*The angelic spirits leave the
dead bodies,*

And the bay was white with silent light,
Till rising from the same,
Full many shapes, that shadows were,
In crimson colors came.

*And appear in their own forms
of light.*

A little distance from the prow
Those crimson shadows were:
I turned my eyes upon the deck—
Oh, Christ! what saw I there!

Each corse lay flat, lifeless and flat,
And, by the holy rood!
A man all light, a seraph-man,
On every corse there stood.

This seraph-band, each waved his hand:
It was a heavenly sight!
They stood as signals to the land,
Each one a lovely light;

This seraph-band, each waved his hand,
No voice did they impart—
No voice; but oh! the silence sank
Like music on my heart.

But soon I heard the dash of oars,
I heard the Pilot's cheer;
My head was turned perforce away
And I saw a boat appear.

The Pilot and the Pilot's boy,
I heard them coming fast:
Dear Lord in Heaven! it was a joy
The dead men could not blast.

I saw a third—I heard his voice:
It is the Hermit good!
He singeth loud his godly hymns
That he makes in the wood.
He'll shrieve my soul, he'll wash away
The Albatross's blood.

PART VII

The Hermit of the Wood

This Hermit good lives in that wood
Which slopes down to the sea.
How loudly his sweet voice he rears!
He loves to talk with mariners
That come from a far countree.

He kneels at morn, and noon, and eve—
He hath a cushion plump:
It is the moss that wholly hides
The rotted old oak stump.

The skiff-boat neared: I heard them talk,
"Why, this is strange, I trow!
Where are those lights so many and fair,
That signal made but now?"

*Approacheth the ship with
wonder.*

"Strange, by my faith!" the Hermit said—
"And they answered not our cheer!
The planks looked warped! and see those
    sails,
How thin they are and sere!
I never saw aught like to them,
Unless perchance it were

Brown skeletons of leaves that lag
My forest-brook along;
When the ivy tod is heavy with snow,
And the owlet whoops to the wolf below,
That eats the she-wolf's young."

"Dear Lord! it hath a fiendish look,"
The Pilot made reply,
"I am a-feared"—"Push on, push on!"
Said the Hermit cheerily.

The boat came closer to the ship,
But I nor spake nor stirred;
The boat came close beneath the ship,
And straight a sound was heard.

The ship suddenly sinketh.

Under the water it rumbled on,
Still louder and more dread:
It reached the ship, it split the bay;
The ship went down like lead.

*The ancient Mariner is saved
in the Pilot's boat.*

Stunned by that loud and dreadful sound,
Which sky and ocean smote,
Like one that hath been seven days drowned
My body lay afloat;
But swift as dreams, myself I found
Within the Pilot's boat.

Upon the whirl, where sank the ship,
The boat spun round and round;
And all was still, save that the hill
Was telling of the sound.

I moved my lips—the Pilot shrieked
And fell down in a fit;
The holy Hermit raised his eyes,
And prayed where he did sit.

I took the oars: the Pilot's boy,
Who now doth crazy go,
Laughed loud and long, and all the while
His eyes went to and fro.
"Ha! ha!" quoth he, "full plain I see,
The Devil knows how to row."

And now, all in my own countree,
I stood on the firm land!
The Hermit stepped forth from the boat,
And scarcely he could stand.

The ancient Mariner earnestly entreateth the Hermit to shrieve him; and the penance of life falls on him.

"O shrieve me, shrieve me, holy man!"
The Hermit crossed his brow.
"Say quick," quoth he, "I bid thee say—
What manner of man art thou?"

Forthwith this frame of mine was
          wrenched
With a woeful agony,
Which forced me to begin my tale;
And then it left me free.

And ever and anon throughout his future life an agony constraineth him to travel from land to land;

Since then, at an uncertain hour,
That agony returns:
And till my ghastly tale is told,
This heart within me burns.

I pass, like night, from land to land;
I have strange power of speech;
That moment that his face I see,
I know the man that must hear me:
To him my tale I teach.

What loud uproar bursts from the door!
The wedding guests are there:
But in the garden-bower the bride
And bridemaids singing are:
And hark the little vesper bell,
Which biddeth me to prayer!

O Wedding Guest! this soul hath been
Alone on a wide sea:
So lonely 'twas, that God himself
Scarce seeméd there to be.

O sweeter than the marriage feast,
'Tis sweeter far to me,
To walk together to the kirk
With a goodly company!

To walk together to the kirk,
And all together pray,
While each to his great Father bends,
Old men, and babes, and loving friends
And youths and maidens gay!

And to teach, by his own example, love and reverence to all things that God made and loveth.

Farewell, farewell! but this I tell
To thee, thou Wedding Guest!
He prayeth well, who loveth well
Both man and bird and beast.

He prayeth best, who loveth best
All things both great and small;
For the dear God who loveth us,
He made and loveth all.

The Mariner, whose eye is bright,
Whose beard with age is hoar,
Is gone: and now the Wedding Guest
Turned from the bridegroom's door.

He went like one that hath been stunned,
And is of sense forlorn:
A sadder and a wiser man,
He rose the morrow morn.

"The Rime of the Ancient Mariner" is at once a fascinating adventure story and a parabolical analysis of ethics; a long poem and an economical narrative; a sober tragedy but also, being told by the mariner to a wedding guest, a jubilant epithalamium; a recalling and recounting of immemorial hauntings and myth-makings and a present-tense realization of absolute immediacy, beginning "It is . . . ." (Note that, in Part VII: "tod" is "clump.")

Dejection: An Ode

Late, late yestreen I saw the new Moon
With the old Moon in her arms;
And I fear, I fear, my master, dear!
We shall have a deadly storm.
Ballad of Sir Patrick Spens

Well! If the Bard was weather-wise, who made
  The grand old ballad of Sir Patrick Spence,
  This night, so tranquil now, will not go hence
Unroused by winds, that ply a busier trade
Than those which mould you cloud in lazy flakes,
Or the dull sobbing draft, that moans and rakes
Upon the strings of this Æolian lute,
    Which better far were mute.
  For lo! the New-moon winter-bright!
  And overspread with phantom light,
  (With swimming phantom light o'erspread
  But rimmed and circled by a silver thread)
I see the old Moon in her lap, foretelling
  The coming-on of rain and squally blast.
And oh! that even now the gust were swelling,
  And the slant night-shower driving loud and fast!
Those sounds which oft have raised me, whilst they awed,
    And sent my soul abroad,
Might now perhaps their wonted impulse give,
Might startle this dull pain, and makie it move and live!

A grief without a pant, void, dark, and drear,
  A stifled, drowsy, unimpassioned grief,
  Which finds no natural outlet, no relief,
    In word, or sigh, or tear —
O Lady! in this wan and heartless mood,
To other thoughts by yonder throstle wooed,

All this long eve, so balmy and serene,
Have I been gazing on the western sky,
  And its peculiar tint of yellow green:
And still I gaze—and with how blank an eye!
And those thin clouds above, in flakes and bars,
That give away their motion to the stars;
Those stars, that glide behind them or between,
Now sparkling, now bedimmed, but always seen:
Yon crescent Moon, as fixed as if it grew
In its own cloudless, starless lake of blue;
I see them all so excellently fair,
I see, not feel, how beautiful they are!

  My genial spirits fail;
  And what can these avail
To lift the smothering weight from off my breast?
  It were a vain endeavour,
  Though I should gaze for ever
On that green light that lingers in the west:
I may not hope from outward forms to win
The passion and the life, whose fountains are within.

O Lady! we receive but what we give,
And in our life alone does Nature live:
Ours is her wedding garment, ours her shroud!
  And would we aught behold, of higher worth,
Than that inanimate cold world allowed
To the poor loveless ever-anxious crowd,
  Ah! from the soul itself must issue forth
A light, a glory, fair luminous cloud
  Enveloping the Earth—
And from the soul itself must there be sent
  A sweet and potent voice, of its own birth,
Of all sweet sounds the life and element!

O pure of heart! thou need'st not ask of me
What this strong music in the soul may be!
What, and wherein it doth exist,
This light, this glory, this fair luminous mist,
This beautiful and beauty-making power.
   Joy, virtuous Lady! Joy that ne'er was given,
Save to the pure, and in their purest hour,
Life, and Life's effluence, cloud at once and shower,
Joy, Lady! is the spirit and the power,
Which wedding Nature to us gives in dower
   A new Earth and new Heaven,
Undreamt of by the sensual and the proud—
Joy is the sweet voice, Joy the luminous cloud—
     We in ourselves rejoice!
And thence flows all that charms or ear or sight,
   All melodies the echoes of that voice,
All colours a suffusion from that light.

There was a time when, though my path was rough,
   This joy within me dallied with distress,
And all misfortunes were but as the stuff
   Whence Fancy made me dreams of happiness:
For hope grew round me, like the twining vine,
And fruits, and foliage, not my own, seemed mine.
But now afflictions bow me down to earth:
Nor care I that they rob me of my mirth;
    But oh! each visitation
Suspends what nature gave me any my birth,
   My shaping spirit of Imagination.
For not to think of what I needs must feel,
   But to be still and patient, all I can;
And haply by abstruse research to steal
   From my own nature all the natural man—
   This was my sole resource, my only plan:
Till that which suits a part infects the whole,
And now is almost grown the habit of my soul.

Hence, viper thoughts, that coil around my mind,
     Reality's dark dream!
I turn from you, and listen to the wind,
     Which long has raved unnoticed. What a scream
Of agony by torture lengthened out
That lute sent forth! Thou Wind, that rav'st without,
     Bare crag, or mountain-tairn, or blasted tree,
Or pine-grove whither woodman never clomb,
Or lonely house, long held the witches' home,
     Methinks were fitter instruments for thee,
Mad Lutanist! who in this month of showers,
Of dark-brown gardens, and of peeping flowers,
Mak'st Devils' yule, with worse than wintry song,
The blossoms, buds, and timorous leaves among.
     Thou Actor, perfect in all tragic sounds!
Thou mighty Poet, e'en to frenzy bold!
          What tell'st thou now about?
          'Tis of the rushing of an host in rout,
     With groans, of trampled men, with smarting wounds—
At once they groan with pain, and shudder with the cold!
But hush! there is a pause of deepest silence!
     And all that noise, as of a rushing crowd,
With groans, and tremulous shudderings—all is over—
It tells another tale, with sounds less deep and loud!
          A tale of less affright,
          And tempered with delight,
As Otway's self had framed the tender lay,—
          'Tis of a little child
          Upon a lonesome wild,
Not far from home, but she hath lost her way:
And now moans low in bitter grief and fear,
And now screams loud, and hopes to make her mother hear.

'Tis midnight, but small thoughts have I of sleep:
Full seldom may my friend such vigils keep!
Visit her, gentle Sleep! with wings of healing,
   And may this storm be but a mountain-birth,
May all the stars hang bright above her dwelling,
   Silent as though they watched the sleeping Earth!
     With light heart may she rise,
     Gay fancy, cheerful eyes,
   Joy lift her spirit, joy attune her voice;
To her may all things live, from the pole to pole,
Their life the eddying of her living soul!
   O simple spirit, guided from above,
Dear Lady! friend devoutest of my choice,
Thus may'st thou ever, evermore rejoice.

On an April night in 1802, after hearing his friend Wordsworth recite the early part of his "Ode: Intimations of Immortality from Recollections of Early Childhood" (p. 400), Coleridge wrote a long verse-letter to Sara Hutchinson, sister of Wordsworth's fiancée. Coleridge was married, but in love with Sara. This ode is the result of a severe revision of that letter.

Frost at Midnight

The Frost performs its secret ministry,
Unhelped by any wind. The owlet's cry
Came loud—and hark, again! loud as before.
The inmates of my cottage, all at rest,
Have left me to that solitude, which suits
Abstruser musings: save that at my side
My cradled infant slumbers peacefully.
'Tis calm indeed! so calm, that it disturbs
And vexes meditation, with its strange
And extreme silentness. Sea, hill, and wood,
This populous village! Sea, and hill, and wood,
With all the numberless goings-on of life,
Inaudible as dreams! the thin blue flame
Lies on my low-burnt fire, and quivers not;
Only that film, which fluttered on the grate,
Still flutters there, the sole unquiet thing.
Methinks its motion in this hush of nature
Gives it dim sympathies with me who live,
Making it a companionable form,
Whose puny flaps and freaks the idling Spirit
By its own moods interprets, everywhere
Echo or mirror seeking of itself,
And makes a toy of Thought.

       But O! how oft,
How oft, at school, with most believing mind,
Presageful, have I gazed upon the bars,
To watch that fluttering *stranger*! and as oft
With unclosed lids, already had I dreamt
Of my sweet birthplace, and the old church tower,
Whose bells, the poor man's only music, rang
From morn to evening, all the hot fair-day,
So sweetly, that they stirred and haunted me
With a wild pleasure, falling on mine ear

Most like articulate sounds of things to come!
So gazed I, till the soothing things, I dreamt,
Lulled me to sleep, and sleep prolonged by dreams!
And so I brooded all the following morn,
Awed by the stern preceptor's face, mine eye
Fixed with mock study on my swimming book:
Save if the door half-opened, and I snatched
A hasty glance, and still my heart leaped up,
For still I hoped to see the *stranger's* face,
Townsman, or aunt, or sister more beloved,
My playmate when we both were clothed alike!

Dear Babe, that sleepest cradled by my side,
Whose gentle breathings, heard in this deep calm,
Fill up the interspersèd vacancies
And momentary pauses of the thought!
My babe so beautiful! it thrills my heart
With tender gladness, thus to look at thee,
And think that thou shalt learn far other lore,
And in far other scenes! For I was reared
In the great city, pent 'mid cloisters dim,
And saw nought lovely but the sky and stars.
But *thou*, my babe! shalt wander like a breeze
By lakes and sandy shores, beneath the crags
Of ancient mountain, and beneath the clouds,
Which image in their bulk both lakes and shores
And mountain crags: so shalt thou see and hear
The lovely shapes and sounds intelligible
Of that eternal language, which thy God
Utters, who from eternity doth teach
Himself in all, and all things in himself.
Great universal Teacher! he shall mold
Thy spirit, and by giving make it ask.

Therefore all seasons shall be sweet to thee,
Whether the summer clothe the general earth
With greenness, or the redbreast sit and sing
Betwixt the tufts of snow on the bare branch
Of mossy apple tree, while the nigh thatch
Smokes in the sun-thaw; whether the eave-drops fall
Heard only in the trances of the blast,
Or if the secret ministry of frost
Shall hang them up in silent icicles,
Quietly shining to the quiet Moon.

The Coleridges were living in a cottage at Nether Stowey in Somersetshire, not very far from Coleridge's "sweet birthplace" in Devonshire. The "cradled infant" in this poem is Hartley Coleridge, who was born in 1796. (He is also mentioned in Coleridge's "Nightingale.")

Southey was extraordinarily productive and versatile, turning out many volumes of poetry, history, and biography. He and Samuel Taylor Coleridge were married to sisters and were friends for decades. From 1813 until his death thirty years later, Southey served as Poet Laureate. Byron made Southey one of his favorite targets for satire and outright abuse, much of which now seems exaggerated and undeserved.

The Battle of Blenheim

It was a summer evening,
　Old Kaspar's work was done;
And he before his cottage door
　Was sitting in the sun,
And by him sported on the green
His little grandchild Wilhelmine.

She saw her brother Peterkin
　Roll something large and round,
That he beside the rivulet,
　In playing there, had found;
He came to ask what he had found,
That was so large, and smooth, and round.

Old Kaspar took it from the boy,
　Who stood expectant by;
And then the old man shook his head,
　And with a natural sigh,
'Tis some poor fellow's skull, said he,
Who fell in the great victory.

I find them in the garden, for
    There's many here about,
And often when I go to plough
    The ploughshare turns them out;
For many thousand men, said he,
Were slain in the great victory.

Now tell us what 'twas all about,
    Young Peterkin he cries,
And little Wilhelmine looks up
    With wonder-waiting eyes;
Now tell us all about the war,
And what they kill'd each other for.

It was the English, Kaspar cried,
    That put the French to rout;
But what they kill'd each other for,
    I could not well make out.
But everybody said, quoth he,
That 'twas a famous victory.

My father lived at Blenheim then,
    Yon little stream hard by;
They burnt his dwelling to the ground,
    And he was forced to fly:
So with his wife and child he fled,
Nor had he where to rest his head.

With fire and sword the country round
    Was wasted far and wide,
And many a childing mother then,
    And new-born infant, died.
But things like that, you know, must be
At every famous victory.

They say it was a shocking sight,
 After the field was won,
For many thousand bodies here
 Lay rotting in the sun;
But things like that, you know, must be
After a famous victory.

Great praise the Duke of Marlbro' won,
 And our good Prince Eugene. —
Why, 'twas a very wicked thing!
 Said little Wilhelmine. —
Nay—nay—my little girl, quoth he,
It was a famous victory.

And everybody praised the Duke
 Who such a fight did win. —
But what good came of it at last?
 Quoth little Peterkin. —
Why that I cannot tell, said he,
But 'twas a famous victory.

The Duke of Marlborough and Prince Eugene of Austria commanded a combined force that defeated the French at Blenheim (Bavaria) in 1704. Southey's poem suggests the unwitting wisdom of innocent children compared with the thoughtlessness of an adult—a contrast sharpened by the increasingly ironic ring of the repeated "victory."

In a long and varied career, Landor wrote much epic and dramatic poetry as well as several ingenious "imaginary conversations" of literary and political personages. The general reader, however, and the majority of anthologies that serve the general reader, will remember Landor exclusively as the author of lapidary lyrics that possess a quality of irreducible perfection.

Rose Aylmer

Ah what avails the sceptered race,
  Ah what the form divine!
What every virtue, every grace!
  Rose Aylmer, all were thine.
Rose Aylmer, whom these wakeful eyes
  May weep, but never see,
A night of memories and of sighs
  I consecrate to thee.

There really was a Rose Aylmer. The daughter of Baron Aylmer, she died in 1800.

Dirce

Stand close around, ye Stygian set,
  With Dirce in one boat convey'd,
Or Charon, seeing, may forget
  That he is old, and she a shade.

from Pericles and Aspasia

The last three words vividly show the strength of alliteration combined with ellipsis ("is" being omitted).

I Strove with None

I strove with none, for none was worth my strife:
Nature I loved, and next to Nature, Art:
I warmed both hands before the fire of Life;
It sinks; and I am ready to depart.

from The Last Fruit off an Old Tree

These lines are a heroic quatrain in more than one sense. Such pure stoicism is rare in English. One of Robert Frost's later poems, "Lucretius Versus the Lake Poets," continues the discussion.

Past Ruined Ilion Helen Lives

❖◦❖◦❖◦❖

Past ruined Ilion Helen lives,
    Alcestis rises from the shades;
Verse calls them forth; 'tis verse that gives
    Immortal youth to mortal maids.

Soon shall Oblivion's deepening veil
    Hide all the peopled hills you see,
The gay, the proud, while lovers hail
    These many summers you and me.

Innumerable verses from three millennia call Helen forth, and even Alcestis endures in Milton's "On His Deceased Wife" (p. 209) and, wholly transformed, in T. S. Eliot's Cocktail Party.

THOMAS CAMPBELL 1777–1844

Although Campbell, the son of a Scottish merchant, was a prominent reformer and one of the founders of London University, his reputation today is based solely on a number of war-songs.

Hohenlinden

On Linden, when the sun was low,
All bloodless lay the untrodden snow,
And dark as winter was the flow
   Of Iser, rolling rapidly.

But Linden saw another sight
When the drum beat at dead of night,
Commanding fires of death to light
   The darkness of her scenery.

By torch and trumpet fast arrayed,
Each horseman drew his battle blade,
And furious every charger neighed
   To join the dreadful revelry.

Then shook the hills with thunder riven,
Then rushed the steed to battle driven,
And louder than the bolts of heaven
   Far flashed the red artillery.

But redder yet that light shall glow
On Linden's hills of stainèd snow,
And bloodier yet the torrent flow
   Of Iser, rolling rapidly.

'Tis morn, but scarce yon level sun
Can pierce the war-clouds, rolling dun,
Where furious Frank and fiery Hun
　Shout in their sulphurous canopy.

The combat deepens. On, ye brave,
Who rush to glory, or the grave!
Wave, Munich! all thy banners wave,
　And charge with all thy chivalry!

Few, few shall part where many meet!
The snow shall be their winding-sheet,
And every turf beneath their feet
　Shall be a soldier's sepulchre.

The "furious Frank" beat the "fiery Hun"; that is, the French defeated the Austrians at Hohenlinden, Bavaria, in December of 1800. Winter battles were rare.

CLEMENT CLARKE MOORE 1779–1863

Moore, a professor of religion, published his one celebrated poem in the *Troy Sentinel* (in Troy, New York) in time for Christmas 1823.

A Visit from St. Nicholas

>>>>>>>

'Twas the night before Christmas, when all through the house
Not a creature was stirring, not even a mouse.
The stockings were hung by the chimney with care,
In hopes that St. Nicholas soon would be there;
The children were nestled all snug in their beds,
While visions of sugarplums danced in their heads;
And mamma in her 'kerchief, and I in my cap,
Had just settled our brains for a long winter's nap,
When out on the lawn there arose such a clatter,
I sprang from the bed to see what was the matter.
Away to the window I flew like a flash,
Tore open the shutters and threw up the sash.
The moon on the breast of the new-fallen snow
Gave the luster of mid-day to objects below,
When, what to my wondering eyes should appear,
But a miniature sleigh, and eight tiny reindeer,
With a little old driver, so lively and quick,
I knew in a moment it must be St. Nick.
More rapid than eagles his coursers they came,
And he whistled, and shouted, and called them by name:
"Now, *Dasher!* now, *Dancer!* now, *Prancer* and *Vixen!*
On, *Comet!* on, *Cupid!* on, *Donder* and *Blitzen!*
To the top of the porch! to the top of the wall!
Now dash away! dash away! dash away all!"
As dry leaves that before the wild hurricane fly,
When they meet with an obstacle, mount to the sky,
So up to the house-top the coursers they flew,
With the sleigh full of toys, and St. Nicholas too.

And then, in a twinkling, I heard on the roof
The prancing and pawing of each little hoof.
As I drew in my head, and was turning around,
Down the chimney St. Nicholas came with a bound.
He was dressed all in fur, from his head to his foot,
And his clothes were all tarnished with ashes and soot;
A bundle of toys he had flung on his back,
And he looked like a peddler just opening his pack.
His eyes—how they twinkled! his dimples how merry!
His cheeks were like roses, his nose like a cherry!
His droll little mouth was drawn up like a bow,
And the beard of his chin was as white as the snow;
The stump of a pipe he held tight in his teeth,
And the smoke it encircled his head like a wreath;
He had a broad face and a little round belly,
That shook, when he laughed, like a bowlful of jelly.
He was chubby and plump, a right jolly old elf,
And I laughed when I saw him, in spite of myself;
A wink of his eye and a twist of his head,
Soon gave me to know I had nothing to dread.
He spoke not a word, but went straight to his work,
And filled all the stockings; then turned with a jerk,
And laying his finger aside of his nose
And giving a nod, up the chimney he rose.
He sprang to his sleigh, to his team gave a whistle,
And away they all flew like the down of a thistle,
But I heard him exclaim, ere he drove out of sight,
" *Happy Christmas to all, and to all a good-night.*"

This Santa, small and dressed in fur, may not quite match the icon of today, but Moore contributed as much to his development as any other creator. Christmas seems everlasting, but most of our modern practices come from the nineteenth century, especially from such writers as Moore and Dickens.

LEIGH HUNT 1784–1859

Hunt was eventually to publish an *Autobiography* and *Table Talk*. He was always an able versifier, but he will be most fondly remembered as a supporter of writers (including Keats and Byron) and as an editor of several periodicals, including the *Examiner*, the *Reflector*, and the *Indicator*.

Jenny Kissed Me

Jenny kissed me when we met,
    Jumping from the chair she sat in.
Time, you thief, who love to get
    Sweets into your list, put that in.
Say I'm weary, say I'm sad;
    Say that health and wealth have missed me;
Say I'm growing old, but add—
    Jenny kissed me!

Hunt, the story goes, was kissed by Jane Welsh Carlyle when he delivered the news that a piece written by her husband Thomas had been accepted by the publisher. Technically, the poem is a rondeau only by the most relaxed definition—but Hunt seems to have been a relaxed and sympathetic person.

Abou Ben Adhem

Abou Ben Adhem (may his tribe increase!)
Awoke one night from a deep dream of peace,
And saw, within the moonlight in his room,
Making it rich, and like a lily in bloom,
An Angel writing in a book of gold:

Exceeding peace had made Ben Adhem bold,
And to the Presence in the room he said,
"What writest thou?" The Vision raised its head,
And with a look made of all sweet accord
Answered, "The names of those who love the Lord."

"And is mine one?" said Abou. "Nay, not so,"
Replied the Angel. Abou spoke more low,
But cheerly still; and said, "I pray thee, then,
Write me as one that loves his fellow-men."

The Angel wrote, and vanished. The next night
It came again with a great wakening light,
And showed the names whom love of God had blessed,
And, lo! Ben Adhem's name led all the rest!

This rather Dickensian story has enjoyed immense popularity since its first appearance in an anthology in 1838. Like Shelley, Byron, Poe, and many others, Hunt took advantage of a general taste for matters vaguely Asian.

GEORGE GORDON NOEL BYRON, 6TH BARON BYRON 1788–1824

Byron is uniquely distinguished for his personality and life as much as for his poetry. He is, indeed, widely regarded as a very great poet and especially as a wit and satirist. Byron was not only a genius but also a millionaire, a hero, a nobleman, a sinner, and a beauty. Born into a tormented and tempestuous family, he succeeded to the family title when he was ten; his schooling was at Harrow and Cambridge. By 1812 he was one of the most famous poets in England. He married most unhappily in 1815 and in the next year—hounded by accusations of insanity and incest—exiled himself permanently. Byronism is still with us, as is the Byronic hero: dark, moody, aloof, misanthropic, courageous, brilliant, audacious, tortured.

So We'll Go No More a-Roving

So, we'll go no more a-roving
  So late into the night,
Though the heart be still as loving,
  And the moon be still as bright.

For the sword outwears its sheath,
  And the soul outwears the breast,
And the heart must pause to breathe,
  And love itself have rest.

Though the night was made for loving,
  And the day returns too soon,
Yet we'll go no more a-roving
  By the light of the moon.

In his earlier poetry, Byron, who was partly Scottish, followed the lead of such other Scots as Robert Burns and Sir Walter Scott in reviving old ballads and composing new ones—or, as here, of grafting new material onto old. Regretful decrepitude may seem a fatuous pose in a writer not yet thirty, but Byron had scarcely seven more years to live when he wrote this.

She Walks in Beauty

〰〰〰〰

I

She walks in Beauty, like the night
    Of cloudless climes and starry skies;
And all that's best of dark and bright
    Meet in her aspect and her eyes:
Thus mellowed to that tender light
    Which Heaven to gaudy day denies.

II

One shade the more, one ray the less,
    Had half impaired the nameless grace
Which waves in every raven tress,
    Or softly lightens o'er her face;
Where thoughts serenely sweet express,
    How pure, how dear their dwelling-place.

III

And on that cheek, and o'er that brow,
    So soft, so calm, yet eloquent,
The smiles that win, the tints that glow,
    But tell of days in goodness spent,
A mind at peace with all below,
    A heart whose love is innocent!

This lyric, like "The Destruction of Sennacherib" (p. 482), was written for the volume called Hebrew Melodies *(1815) with traditional music adapted by Isaac Nathan. Most things about Byron are fabulously romantic, including the story that he met a lovely cousin by marriage at a ball and wrote "She Walks in Beauty" the next morning.*

The Destruction of Sennacherib

The Assyrian came down like the wolf on the fold,
And his cohorts were gleaming in purple and gold,
And the sheen of their spears was like stars on the sea,
When the blue wave rolls nightly on deep Galilee.

Like the leaves of the forest when summer is green,
That host with their banners at sunset were seen:
Like the leaves of the forest when autumn hath blown,
That host on the morrow lay wither'd and strown.

For the Angel of Death spread his wings on the blast,
And breathed in the face of the foe as he pass'd
And the eyes of the sleepers wax'd deadly and chill,
And their hearts but once heaved, and forever grew still!

And there lay the steed with his nostril all wide,
But through it there roll'd not the breath of his pride;
And the foam of his gasping lay white on the turf,
And cold as the spray of the rock-beating surf.

And there lay the rider distorted and pale,
With the dew on his brow, and the rust on his mail:
And the tents were all silent, the banners alone,
The lances unlifted, the trumpet unblown.

And the widows of Ashur are loud in their wail,
And the idols are broke in the temple of Baal;
And the might of the Gentile, unsmote by the sword,
Hath melted like snow in the glance of the Lord!

The durability of this poem is shown by the opening of the Prologue of Tom Clancy's Sum of All Fears *(1991): " 'Like a wolf on the fold.' In recounting the Syrian attack on the Israeli-held Golan Heights at 1400 hours, local time, on Saturday, October 6, 1973, most commentators automatically recalled Lord Byron's famous line."*

When We Two Parted

When we two parted
  In silence and tears,
Half broken-hearted
  To sever for years,
Pale grew thy cheek and cold,
  Colder thy kiss;
Truly that hour foretold
  Sorrow to this.

The dew of the morning
  Sunk chill on my brow—
It felt like the warning
  Of what I feel now.
Thy vows are all broken,
  And light is thy fame;
I hear thy name spoken,
  And share in its shame.

They name thee before me,
  A knell to mine ear;
A shudder comes o'er me—
  Why wert thou so dear?
They know not I knew thee,
  Who knew thee too well:—
Long, long shall I rue thee,
  Too deeply to tell.

In secret we met—
　In silence I grieve,
That thy heart could forget,
　Thy spirit deceive.
If I should meet thee
　After long years,
How should I greet thee?
　With silence and tears.

Byron was twenty when he wrote these haunting lines. The emotion is definite and powerful even though the dramatis personae *are no more than pronouns.*

The Ocean

❖❖❖❖

There is a pleasure in the pathless woods,
There is a rapture on the lonely shore,
There is society where none intrudes
By the deep sea, and music in its roar:
I love not man the less, but nature more,
From these our interviews, in which I steal
From all I may be, or have been before,
To mingle with the universe, and feel
What I can ne'er express, yet cannot all conceal.

Roll on, thou deep and dark blue Ocean,—roll!
Ten thousand fleets sweep over thee in vain;
Man marks the earth with ruin,—his control
Stops with the shore;—upon the watery plain
The wrecks are all thy deed, nor doth remain
A shadow of man's ravage, save his own,
When, for a moment, like a drop of rain,
He sinks into thy depths with bubbling groan,
Without a grave, unknelled, uncoffined, and unknown.

His steps are not upon thy paths,—thy fields
Are not a spoil for him,—thou dost arise
And shake him from thee; the vile strength he wields
For earth's destruction thou dost all despise,
Spurning him from thy bosom to the skies,
And send'st him, shivering in thy playful spray
And howling, to his gods, where haply lies
His petty hope in some near port or bay,
And dashest him again to earth:—there let him lay.

The armaments which thunderstrike the walls
Of rock-built cities, bidding nations quake
And monarchs tremble in their capitals,
The oak leviathans, whose huge ribs make
Their clay creator the vain title take
Of lord of thee and arbiter of war, —
These are thy toys, and, as the snowy flake,
They melt into thy yeast of waves, which mar
Alike the Armada's pride or spoils of Trafalgar.

Thy shores are empires, changed in all save thee;
Assyria, Greece, Rome, Carthage, what are they?
Thy waters wasted them while they were free,
And many a tyrant since; their shores obey
The stranger, slave, or savage; their decay
Has dried up realms to deserts: not so thou;
Unchangeable save to thy wild waves' play,
Time writes no wrinkles on thine azure brow;
Such as creation's dawn beheld, thou rollest now.

Thou glorious mirror, where the Almighty's form
Glasses itself in tempests; in all time,
Calm or convulsed, — in breeze, or gale, or storm,
Icing the pole, or in the torrid clime
Dark-heaving; boundless, endless, and sublime,
The image of Eternity, — the throne
Of the Invisible! even from out thy slime
The monsters of the deep are made; each zone
Obeys thee; thou goest forth, dread, fathomless, alone.

And I have loved thee, Ocean! and my joy
Of youthful sports was on thy breast to be
Borne, like thy bubbles, onward; from a boy
I wantoned with thy breakers,—they to me
Were a delight; and if the freshening sea
Made them a terror, 't was a pleasing fear;
For I was as it were a child of thee,
And trusted to thy billows far and near,
And laid my land upon thy mane,—as I do here.

from Childe Harold's Pilgrimage

Henry James drolly ridiculed the Romantics who "besought the deep blue sea to roll." It may be absurd to encourage natural forces to keep up what they cannot help doing ("Shine on, harvest moon"), but we do it, perhaps as a way of fixing our place and role in the world.

There Was a Sound of Revelry by Night

There was a sound of revelry by night,
And Belgium's capital had gathered then
Her beauty and her chivalry, and bright
The lamps shone o'er fair women and brave men;
A thousand hearts beat happily; and when
Music arose with its voluptuous swell,
Soft eyes looked love to eyes which spake again,
And all went merry as a marriage-bell;
But hush! hark! a deep sound strikes like a rising knell!

Did ye not hear it? — No; 'twas but the wind,
Or the car rattling o'er the stony street;
On with the dance! let joy be unconfined;
No sleep till morn, when Youth and Pleasure meet
To chase the glowing Hours with flying feet.
But hark! that heavy sound breaks in once more,
As if the clouds its echo would repeat;
And nearer, clearer, deadlier than before!
Arm! arm! it is — it is — the cannon's opening roar!

Within a windowed niche of that high hall
Sate Brunswick's fated chieftain; he did hear
That sound, the first amidst the festival,
And caught its tone with Death's prophetic ear;
And when they smiled because he deemed it near,
His heart more truly knew that peal too well
Which stretched his father on a bloody bier,
And roused the vengeance blood alone could quell:
He rushed into the field, and, foremost fighting, fell.

Ah! then and there was hurrying to and fro,
And gathering tears, and tremblings of distress,
And cheeks all pale, which but an hour ago
Blushed at the praise of their own loveliness;
And there were sudden partings, such as press
The life from out young hearts, and choking sighs
Which ne'er might be repeated: who would guess
If evermore should meet those mutual eyes,
Since upon night so sweet such awful morn could rise!

And there was mounting in hot haste: the steed,
The mustering squadron, and the clattering car,
Went pouring forward with impetuous speed,
And swiftly forming in the ranks of war;
And the deep thunder peal on peal afar;
And near, the beat of the alarming drum
Roused up the soldier ere the morning star;
While thronged the citizens with terror dumb,
Or whispering with white lips,—"The foe! they come! they come!"

And wild and high the "Cameron's gathering" rose,
The war-note of Lochiel, which Albyn's hills
Have heard,—and heard, too, have her Saxon foes;
How in the noon of night that pibroch thrills
Savage and shrill! But with the breath which fills
Their mountain pipe, so fill the mountaineers
With the fierce native daring which instils
The stirring memory of a thousand years,
And Evan's, Donald's fame rings in each clansman's ears!

And Ardennes waves above them her green leaves,
Dewy with nature's tear-drops, as they pass,
Grieving, if aught inanimate e'er grieves,
Over the unreturning brave,—alas!
Ere evening to be trodden like the grass
Which now beneath them, but above shall grow
In its next verdure, when this fiery mass
Of living valor, rolling on the foe,
And burning with high hope, shall moulder cold and low.

Last noon beheld them full of lusty life,
Last eve in Beauty's circle proudly gay,
The midnight brought the signal-sound of strife,
The morn the marshalling in arms—the day
Battle's magnificently stern array!
The thunder-clouds close o'er it, which when rent
The earth is covered thick with other clay,
Which her own clay shall cover, heaped and pent,
Rider and horse,—friend, foe,—in one red burial blent!

Their praise is hymned by loftier harps than mine;
Yet one I would select from that proud throng,
Partly because they blend me with his line,
And partly that I did his sire some wrong,
And partly that bright names will hallow song!
And his was of the bravest, and when showered
The death-bolts deadliest the thinned files along,
Even where the thickest of war's tempest lowered,
They reached no nobler breast than thine, young, gallant Howard!

There have been tears and breaking hearts for thee,
And mine were nothing, had I such to give;
But when I stood beneath the fresh green tree,
Which living waves where thou didst cease to live,
And saw around me the wide field revive
With fruits and fertile promise, and the Spring
Come forth her work of gladness to contrive,
With all her reckless birds upon the wing,
I turned from all she brought to those she could not bring.

I turned to thee, to thousands, of whom each
And one as all a ghastly gap did make
In his own kind and kindred, whom to teach
Forgetfulness were mercy for their sake;
The Archangel's trump, not glory's, must awake
Those whom they thirst for; though the sound of Fame
May for a moment soothe, it cannot slake
The fever of vain longing, and the name
So honored, but assumes a stronger, bitterer claim.

They mourn, but smile at length; and, smiling, mourn;
The tree will wither long before it fall;
The hull drives on, though mast and sail be torn;
The roof-tree sinks, but moulders on the hall
In massy hoariness; the ruined wall
Stands when its wind-worn battlements are gone;
The bars survive the captive they inthrall;
The day drags through though storms keep out the sun;
And thus the heart will break, yet brokenly live on:

Even as a broken mirror, which the glass
In every fragment multiplies; and makes
A thousand images of one that was,
The same, and still the more, the more it breaks;
And thus the heart will do which not forsakes,
Living in shattered guise, and still, and cold,
And bloodless, with its sleepless sorrow aches,
Yet withers on till all without is old,
Showing no visible sign, for such things are untold.

from Childe Harold's Pilgrimage

Byron shares with Thackeray the honor of superlatively realizing all the brilliance and irony of the Duchess of Richmond's ball on the eve of the Battle of Waterloo in June 1815—probably the single most important event in nineteenth-century Europe.

CHARLES WOLFE 1791–1823

Charles Wolfe, then a student at Trinity College, Dublin, read Southey's prose account (published in 1817) of the death and burial of Sir John Moore, which had taken place in early 1809. Wolfe's poem on the subject is his only work to achieve any fame, but it was immensely celebrated—and debated and even parodied—all through the nineteenth century.

The Burial of Sir John Moore
after Corunna

Not a drum was heard, not a funeral note,
As his corse to the rampart we hurried;
Not a soldier discharged his farewell shot
O'er the grave where our hero we buried.

We buried him darkly at dead of night,
The sods with our bayonets burning,
By the struggling moonbeam's misty light
And the lanthorn dimly burning.

No useless coffin enclosed his breast,
Not in sheet or in shroud we wound him;
But he lay like a warrior taking his rest
With his martial cloak around him.

Few and short were the prayers we said,
And we spoke not a word of sorrow;
But we steadfastly gazed on the face of the dead,
And we bitterly thought of the morrow.

We thought, as we hollow'd his narrow bed
And smooth'd down his lonely pillow,
That the foe and the stranger would tread o'er his head,
And we far away on the billow!

Lightly they'll talk of the spirit that's gone,
And o'er his cold ashes upbraid him—
But little he'll reck, if they let him sleep on
In the grave where a Briton has laid him.

But half of our heavy task was done
When the clock struck the hour for retiring;
And we heard the distant and random gun
That the foe was sullenly firing.

Slowly and sadly we laid him down,
From the field of his fame fresh and gory;
We carved not a line, and we raised not a stone,
But we left him alone with his glory.

A small English force, retreating before a French army ten times as great, was leaving from the port of La Caruña in northwest Spain; Lieutenant General Sir John Moore was killed during the embarkation and had to be buried in haste in an unmarked grave. A temporary monument was erected by England's Spanish allies, with a permanent tomb overlooking the Atlantic erected later.

Shelley was born into a substantial Sussex family and educated at Eton and Oxford, being expelled from the latter because of an atheistic pamphlet. His life was complex and turbulent, with an early marriage to Harriet Westbrook, whom he subsequently abandoned for Mary Godwin, the daughter of William Godwin and his first wife, Mary Wollstonecraft. After Harriet's suicide in 1816, Shelley and Mary were married. Shelley was a distinguished translator as well as a great lyric and dramatic poet. He drowned when his yacht *Ariel* foundered in a storm off the Italian coast. His body, washed ashore after a week, was cremated in the presence of Byron and Leigh Hunt.

Ozymandias

I met a traveler from an antique land
Who said: Two vast and trunkless legs of stone
Stand in the desert. Near them, on the sand,
Half sunk, a shattered visage lies, whose frown,
And wrinkled lip, and sneer of cold command,
Tell that its sculptor well those passions read
Which yet survive, stamped on these lifeless things,
The hand that mocked them and the heart that fed;
And on the pedestal these words appear:
"My name is Ozymandias, king of kings:
Look on my works, ye Mighty, and despair!"
Nothing beside remains. Round the decay
Of that colossal wreck, boundless and bare
The lone and level sands stretch far away.

The joke seems to be on Ozymandias, of whose boasting nothing remains but some fragments in a legend, with an easy moral: take care how you brag. But maybe the joke is on somebody besides the king. For one thing, he, Ramses II of Egypt, may still endure as a mummy. And, even if the monumental statue is broken and the inscription sounds fatuous, what remains of anybody else of that age?

Ode to the West Wind

◆◆◆◆◆

I

O wild West Wind, thou breath of Autumn's being,
Thou, from whose unseen presence the leaves dead
Are driven, like ghosts from an enchanter fleeing,

Yellow, and black, and pale, and hectic red,
Pestilence-stricken multitudes: O Thou,
Who chariotest to their dark wintry bed

The winged seeds, where they lie cold and low,
Each like a corpse within its grave, until
Thine azure sister of the Spring shall blow

Her clarion o'er the dreaming earth, and fill
(Driving sweet buds like flocks to feed in air)
With living hues and odors plain and hill:

Wild Spirit, which art moving everywhere;
Destroyer and Preserver; hear, O hear!

II

Thou on whose stream, mid the steep sky's commotion,
Loose clouds like earth's decaying leaves are shed,
Shook from the tangled boughs of Heaven and Ocean,

Angels of rain and lightning: there are spread
On the blue surface of thine aëry surge,
Like the bright hair uplifted from the head

Of some fierce Mænad, even from the dim verge
Of the horizon to the zenith's height,
The locks of the approaching storm. Thou dirge

Of the dying year, to which this closing night
Will be the dome of a vast sepulcher,
Vaulted with all thy congregated might

Of vapors, from whose solid atmosphere
Black rain, and fire, and hail will burst: O hear!

III

Thou who didst waken from his summer dreams
The blue Mediterranean, where he lay,
Lulled by the coil of his chrystalline streams,

Beside a pumice isle in Baiæ's bay,
And saw in sleep old palaces and towers
Quivering within the wave's intenser day,

All overgrown with azure moss and flowers
So sweet, the sense faints picturing them! Thou
For whose path the Atlantic's level powers

Cleave themselves into chasms, while far below
The sea-blooms and the oozy woods which wear
The sapless foliage of the ocean, know

Thy voice, and suddenly grow gray with fear,
And tremble and despoil themselves: O hear!

IV

If I were a dead leaf thou mightest bear;
If I were a swift cloud to fly with thee;
A wave to pant beneath thy power, and share

The impulse of thy strength, only less free
Than thou, O Uncontrollable! If even
I were as in my boyhood, and could be

[498]

The comrade of thy wanderings over Heaven,
As then, when to outstrip thy skiey speed
Scarce seemed a vision; I would ne'er have striven

As thus with thee in prayer in my sore need.
Oh, lift me as a wave, a leaf, a cloud!
I fall upon the thorns of life! I bleed!

A heavy weight of hours has chained and bowed
One too like thee: tameless, and swift, and proud.

V

Make me thy lyre, even as the forest is:
What if my leaves are falling like its own!
The tumult of thy mighty harmonies

Will take from both a deep, autumnal tone,
Sweet though in sadness. Be thou, Spirit fierce,
My spirit! Be thou me, impetuous one!

Drive my dead thoughts over the universe
Like withered leaves to quicken a new birth!
And, by the incantation of this verse,

Scatter, as from an unextinguished hearth
Ashes and sparks, my words among mankind!
Be through my lips to unawakened earth

The trumpet of a prophecy! O Wind,
If Winter comes, can Spring be far behind?

---

*Shelley wrote this ode in Italy, one autumn two or three years before his death.
The poem soars on the loftiness of elementary ideas: elements, seasons, points of
the compass. Normally these are differential and separate us from nature and
from one another. But here, in a complex and passionate synthesis, Shelley
connects the death of leaves in autumn to the birth of seeds to come in the spring.*

To a Skylark

Hail to thee, blithe spirit!
  Bird thou never wert,
That from heaven, or near it,
  Pourest thy full heart
In profuse strains of unpremeditated art.

Higher still and higher,
  From the earth thou springest
Like a cloud of fire;
  The blue deep thou wingest,
And singing still dost soar, and soaring ever singest.

In the golden lightning
  Of the sunken sun,
O'er which clouds are bright'ning,
  Thou dost float and run,
Like an unbodied joy whose race is just begun.

The pale purple even
  Melts around thy flight;
Like a star of heaven
  In the broad daylight
Thou art unseen, but yet I hear thy shrill delight.

Keen as are the arrows
  Of that silver sphere,
Whose intense lamp narrows
  In the white dawn clear,
Until we hardly see, we feel that it is there.

All the earth and air
   With thy voice is loud,
As, when night is bare,
   From one lonely cloud
The moon rains out her beams, and heaven is overflowed.

What thou art we know not;
   What is most like thee?
From rainbow clouds there flow not
   Drops so bright to see,
As from thy presence showers a rain of melody.

Like a poet hidden
   In the light of thought,
Singing hymns unbidden,
   Till the world is wrought
To sympathy with hopes and fears it heeded not:

Like a high-born maiden
   In a palace tower,
Soothing her love-laden
   Soul in secret hour
With music sweet as love, which overflows her bower:

Like a glow-worm golden
   In a dell of dew,
Scattering unbeholden
   Its aerial hue
Among the flowers and grass, which screen it from the view:

Like a rose embowered
   In its own green leaves,
By warm winds deflowered,
   Till the scent it gives
Makes faint with too much sweet those heavy-winged thieves:

Sound of vernal showers
   On the twinkling grass,
Rain-awakened flowers,
   All that ever was,
Joyous, and clear, and fresh, thy music doth surpass.

Teach us, sprite or bird,
   What sweet thoughts are thine:
I have never heard
   Praise of love or wine
That panted forth a flood of rapture so divine.

Chorus hymeneal,
   Or triumphal chaunt,
Matched with thine would be all
   But an empty vaunt—
A thing wherein we feel there is some hidden want.

What objects are the fountains
   Of thy happy strain?
What fields, or waves, or mountains?
What shapes of sky or plain?
What love of thine own kind? what ignorance of pain?

With thy clear keen joyance,
   Languor cannot be:
Shadow of annoyance
   Never came near thee:
Thou lovest, but never knew love's sad satiety.

Waking as asleep,
   Thou of death must deem
Things more true and deep
   Than we mortals dream,
Or how could thy notes flow in such a crystal stream?

We look before and after,
    And pine for what is not:
Our sincerest laughter
    With some pain is fraught;
Our sweetest songs are those that tell of saddest thought.

Yet if we could scorn
    Hate, and pride, and fear;
If we were things born
    Not to shed a tear,
I know not how thy joy we ever should come near.

Better than all measures
    Of delightful sound,
Better than all treasures
    That in books are found,
Thy skill to poet were, thou scorner of the ground!

Teach me half the gladness
    That thy brain must know,
Such harmonious madness
    From my lips would flow,
The world should listen then, as I am listening now.

Shelley wrote "To a Skylark" in 1820 while living at Leghorn, Italy. Sixty-seven years later, visiting the place, Thomas Hardy wrote "Shelley's Skylark":

> *Somewhere afield here something lies*
> *In Earth's oblivious eyeless trust*
> *That moved a poet to prophecies . . .*

Music, When Soft Voices Die

Music, when soft voices die,
Vibrates in the memory;
Odours, when sweet violets sicken,
Live within the sense they quicken.

Rose leaves, when the rose is dead,
Are heaped for the beloved's bed;
And so thy thoughts, when thou art gone,
Love itself shall slumber on.

This poem, found in a notebook, was published after Shelley's death by his widow. Since the poem is probably unfinished, some of the obscurities may never be understood. The "beloved" seems to be the dead rose; "thy thoughts" seems to mean "my thoughts of thee."

To Night

I

Swiftly walk o'er the western wave,
  Spirit of Night!
Out of the misty eastern cave,
Where, all the long and lone daylight,
Thou wovest dreams of joy and fear,
Which make thee terrible and dear, —
  Swift by thy flight!

II

Wrap thy form in a mantle gray,
  Star-inwrought!
Blind with thine hair the eyes of Day;
Kiss her until she be wearied out,
Then wander o'er city, and sea, and land,
Touching all with thine opiate wand —
  Come, long-sought!

III

When I arose and saw the dawn,
  I sighed for thee;
When light rode high, and the dew was gone,
And noon lay heavy on flower and tree,
And the weary Day turned to his rest,
Lingering like an unloved guest,
  I sighed for thee.

IV

Thy brother Death came, and cried,
　Wouldst thou me?
Thy sweet child Sleep, the filmy-eyed,
Murmured like a noontide bee,
Shall I nestle near thy side?
Wouldst thou me? — And I replied,
　No, not thee!

V

Death will come when thou art dead,
　Soon, too soon —
Sleep will come when thou art fled;
Of neither would I ask the boon
I ask of thee, beloved Night —
Swift be thine approaching flight,
　Come soon, soon!

"To Night" was written in the year before Shelley's death and first published in Posthumous Poems *in 1824. The metaphors are magically protean: Day is female in the second stanza, male in the third.*

England in 1819

An old, mad, blind, despised, and dying king,
Princes, the dregs of their dull race, who flow
Through public scorn,—mud from a muddy spring,—
Rulers who neither see, nor feel, nor know,
But leech-like to their fainting country cling,
Till they drop, blind in blood, without a blow,—
A people starved and stabbed in the untilled field,—
An army, which liberticide and prey
Makes as a two-edged sword to all who wield,—
Golden and sanguine laws which tempt and slay;
Religion Christless, Godless—a book sealed;
A Senate,—Time's worst statute unrepealed,—
Are graves, from which a glorious Phantom may
Burst, to illumine our tempestuous day.

This grammatically remarkable sonnet—twelve lines of subject before a two-line predicate—should be compared with Wordsworth's "London, 1802" (p. 417).

To____

❖❖*❖*❖*

One word is too often profaned
 For me to profane it,
One feeling too falsely disdained
 For thee to disdain it;
One hope is too like despair
 For prudence to smother,
And pity from thee more dear
 Than that from another.

I can give not what men call love,
 But wilt thou accept not
The worship the heart lifts above
 And the Heavens reject not,—
The desire of the moth for the star,
 Of the night for the morrow,
The devotion to something afar
 From the sphere of our sorrow?

These lines, though included in Palgrave's Golden Treasury *(1861) and Quiller-Couch's* Oxford Book of English Verse *(1900), seem to have fallen somewhat out of favor, perhaps because of obscurity and awkwardness. But those very qualities can also create a beautiful and lifelike indefiniteness.*

Adonais

I

I weep for Adonais—he is dead!
  Oh weep for Adonais, though our tears
Thaw not the frost which binds so dear a head!
    And thou, sad Hour selected from all years
    To mourn our loss, rouse thy obscure compeers,
And teach them thine own sorrow! Say: "With me
    Died Adonais! Till the future dares
Forget the past, his fate and fame shall be
An echo and a light unto eternity."

II

Where wert thou, mighty Mother, when he lay,
  When thy son lay, pierced by the shaft which flies
In darkness? Where was lorn Urania
    When Adonais died? With veilèd eyes,
    Mid listening Echoes, in her paradise
She sate, while one, with soft enamoured breath.
    Rekindled all the fading melodies
With which, like flowers that mock the corse beneath,
He had adorned and hid the coming bulk of Death.

III

Oh weep for Adonais—he is dead!—
  Wake, melancholy Mother, wake and weep!—
Yet wherefore? Quench within their burning bed
    Thy fiery tears, and let thy loud heart keep,
    Like his, a mute and uncomplaining sleep;
For he is gone where all things wise and fair
    Descend. Oh dream not that the amorous deep
Will yet restore him to the vital air;
Death feeds on his mute voice, and laughs at our despair.

IV

Most musical of mourners, weep again!
   Lament anew, Urania!—He died
Who was the sire of an immortal strain,
    Blind, old, and lonely, when his country's pride
    The priest, the slave, and the liberticide,
Trampled and mocked with many a loathèd rite
    Of lust and blood. He went unterrified
Into the gulf of death; but his clear sprite
Yet reigns o'er earth, the third among the Sons of Light.

V

Most musical of mourners, weep anew!
   Not all to that bright station dared to climb:
And happier they their happiness who knew,
    Whose tapers yet burn through that night of time
    In which suns perished. Others more sublime,
Struck by the envious wrath of man or god,
    Have sunk, extinct in their refulgent prime;
And some yet live, treading the thorny road
Which leads, through toil and hate, to Fame's serene abode.

VI

But now thy youngest, dearest one has perished,
   The nursling of thy widowhood, who grew,
Like a pale flower by some sad maiden cherished,
    And fed with true-love tears instead of dew.
    Most musical of mourners, weep anew!
Thy extreme hope, the loveliest and the last,
    The bloom whose petals, nipped before they blew,
Died on the promise of the fruit, is waste;
The broken lily lies—the storm is overpast.

VII

To that high Capital where kingly Death
    Keeps his pale court in beauty and decay
He came; and bought, with price of purest breath,
    A grave among the eternal.—Come away!
    Haste, while the vault of blue Italian day
Is yet his fitting charnel-roof, while still
    He lies as if in dewy sleepy he lay.
Awake him not! surely he takes his fill
Of deep and liquid rest, forgetful of all ill.

VIII

He will awake no more, oh never more!
    Within the twilight chamber spreads apace
The shadow of white Death, and at the door
    Invisible Corruption waits to trace
    His extreme way to her dim dwelling-place;
The eternal Hunger sits, but pity and awe
    Soothe her pale rage, nor dares she to deface
So fair a prey, till darkness and the law
Of change shall o'er his sleep the mortal curtain draw.

IX

Oh weep for Adonais!—The quick Dreams,
    The passion-wingèd ministers of thought,
Who were his flocks, whom near the living streams
    Of his young spirit he fed, and whom he taught
    The love which was its music, wander not—
Wander no more from kindling brain to brain,
    But droop there whence they sprung; and mourn
        their lot
Round the cold heart where, after their sweet pain,
They ne'er will gather strength or find a home again.

X

And one with trembling hands clasps his cold head,
  And fans him with her moonlight wings, and cries,
"Our love, our hope, our sorrow, is not dead!
  See, on the silken fringe of his faint eyes,
  Like dew upon a sleeping flower, there lies
A tear some dream has loosened from his brain."
  Lost angel of a ruined paradise!
She knew not 'twas her own,—as with no stain
She faded, like a cloud which had outwept its rain.

XI

One from a lucid urn of starry dew
  Washed her light limbs, as if embalming them;
Another clipped her profuse locks, and threw
  The wreath upon him, like an anadem
  Which frozen tears instead of pearls begem;
Another in her wilful grief would break
  Her bow and wingèd reeds, as if to stem
A greater loss with one which was more weak,—
And dull the bardèd fire against his frozen cheek.

XII

Another Splendour on his mouth alit,
  That mouth whence it was wont to draw the breath
Which gave it strength to pierce the guarded wit,
  And pass into the panting heart beneath
  With lightning and with music: the damp death
Quenched its caress upon his icy lips,
  And, as a dying meteor stains a wreath
Of moonlight vapour which the cold night clips,
It flushed through his pale limbs, and passed to its eclipse.

XIII

And others came. Desires and Adorations;
　　Wingèd Persuasions, and veiled Destinies;
Splendours, and Glooms, and glimmering Incarnations
　　Of Hopes and Fears, and twilight Fantasies;
　　And Sorrow, with her family of Sighs;
And Pleasure, blind with tears, led by the gleam
　　Of her own dying smile instead of eyes, —
　　Came in slow pomp; — the moving pomp might seem
Like pageantry of mist on an autumnal stream.

XIV

All he had loved, and moulded into thought
　　From shape and hue and odour and sweet sound,
Lamented Adonais. Morning sought
　　Her eastern watch-tower, and her hair unbound,
　　Wet with the tears which should adorn the ground,
Dimmed the aërial eyes that kindle day;
　　Afar the melancholy Thunder moaned,
　　Pale Ocean in unquiet slumber lay,
And the wild Winds flew round, sobbing in their dismay.

XV

Lost Echo sits amid the voiceless mountains,
　　And feeds her grief with his rememberd lay;
And will no more reply to winds or fountains,
　　Or amorous birds perched on the young green spray,
　　Or herdsman's horn, or bell at closing day;
Since she can mimic not his lips, more dear
　　Than those for whose disdain she pined away
　　Into a shadow of all sounds: — a drear
Murmur, between their songs, is all the woodmen hear.

XVI

Grief made the young Spring wild, and she threw down
   Her kindling buds, as if she Autumn were,
Or they dead leaves; since her delight is flown,
    For whom should she have waked the sullen Year?
    To Phoebus was not Hyacinth so dear,
Not to himself Narcissus, as to both
    Thou, Adonais: wan they stand and sere
Amid the faint companions of their youth,
With dew all turned to tears,—odour, to sighing ruth.

XVII

Thy spirit's sister, the lorn nightingale,
   Mourns not her mate with such melodious pain;
Not so the eagle, who like thee could scale
    Heaven, and could nourish in the sun's domain
    Her mighty youth with morning, doth complain,
Soaring and screaming round her empty nest,
    As Albion wails for thee: the curse of Cain
Light on his head who pierced thy innocent breast,
And scared the angel soul that was its earthly guest!

XVIII

Ah woe is me! Winter is come and gone,
   But grief returns with the revolving year.
The airs and streams renew their joyous tone;
    The ants, the bees, the swallows, re-appear;
    Fresh leaves and flowers deck the dead Seasons' bier;
The amorous birds now pair in every brake,
    And build their mossy homes in field and brere;
And the green lizard and the golden snake,
Like unimprisoned flames, out of their trance awake.

XIX

Through wood and stream and field and hill and ocean,
   A quickening life from the Earth's heart has burst,
   As it has ever done, with change and motion,
   From the great morning of the world when first
   God dawned on chaos. In its stream immersed,
The lamps of heaven flash with a softer light;
   All baser things pant with life's sacred thirst,
Diffuse themselves, and spend in love's delight
The beauty and the joy of their renewèd might.

XX

The leprous corpse, touched by this spirit tender,
   Exhales itself in flowers of gentle breath;
Like incarnations of the stars, when splendour
   Is changed to fragrance, they illumine death,
   And mock the merry worm that wakes beneath.
Nought we know dies: shall that alone which knows
   Be as a sword consumed before the sheath
By sightless lightning? The intense atom glows
A moment, then is quenched in a most cold repose.

XXI

Alas, that all we loved of him should be,
   But for our grief, as if it had not been,
And grief itself be mortal! Woe is me!
   Whence are we, and why are we? of what scene
   The actors and spectators? Great and mean
Meet massed in death, who lends what life must borrow.
   As long as skies are blue and fields are green,
Evening must usher night, night urge the morrow,
Month follow month with woe, and year wake year to sorrow.

XXII

He will awake no more, oh never more!
    "Wake thou," cried Misery, "childless Mother! Rise
Out of thy sleep, and slake in thy heart's core
    A wound more fierce than his, with tears and sighs."
    And all the Dreams that watched Urania's eyes,
And all the Echoes whom their Sister's song
    Had held in holy silence, cried "Arise";
Swift as a thought by the snake Memory stung,
From her ambrosial rest the fading Splendour sprung.

XXIII

She rose like an autumnal Night that springs
    Out of the east, and follows wild and drear
The golden Day, which, on eternal wings,
    Even as a ghost abandoning a bier,
    Had left the Earth a corpse. Sorrow and fear
So struck, so roused, so rapt, Urania;
    So saddened round her like an atmosphere
Of stormy mist; so swept her on her way,
Even to the mournful place where Adonais lay.

XXIV

Out of her secret paradise she sped,
    Through camps and cities rough with stone and steel
And human hearts, which, to her aery tread
    Yielding not, wounded the invisible
    Palms of her tender feet where'er they fell.
And barbèd tongues, and thoughts more sharp than they,
    Rent the soft form they never could repel,
Whose sacred blood, like the young tears of May,
Paved with eternal flowers that undeserving way.

XXV

In the death-chamber for a moment Death,
  Shamed by the presence of that living Might,
Blushed to annihilation, and the breath
    Revisited those lips, and life's pale light
    Flashed through those limbs so late her dear delight.
"Leave me not wild and drear and comfortless,
    As silent lightning leaves the starless night!
Leave me not!" cried Urania. Her distress
Roused Death: Death rose and smiled, and met her vain
  caress.

XXVI

"Stay yet awhile! speak to me once again!
  Kiss me, so long but as a kiss may live!
And in my heartless breast and burning brain
    That word, that kiss, shall all thoughts else survive,
    With food of saddest memory kept alive,
Now thou art dead, as if it were a part
    Of thee, my Adonais! I would give
All that I am, to be as thou now art: —
But I am chained to Time, and cannot thence depart.

XXVII

"O gentle child, beautiful as thou wert,
  Why didst thou leave the trodden paths of men
Too soon, and with weak hands though mighty heart
    Dare the unpastured dragon in his den?
    Defenceless as thou wert, oh where was then
Wisdom the mirrored shield, or Scorn the spear?
    Or, hadst thou waited the full cycle when
Thy spirit should have filled its crescent sphere,
The monsters of life's waste had fled from thee like deer.

XXVIII

"The herded wolves bold only to pursue,
    The obscene ravens clamorous o'er the dead,
The vultures to the conqueror's banner true,
    Who feed where Desolation first has fed,
    And whose wings rain contagion,—how they fled,
When, like Apollo from his golden bow,
    The Pythian of the age one arrow sped,
And smiled!—The spoilers tempt no second blow,
They fawn on the proud feet that spurn them lying low.

XXIX

"The sun comes forth, and many reptiles spawn;
    He sets, and each ephemeral insect then
Is gathered into death without a dawn,
    And the immortal stars awake again.
    So is it in the world of living men:
A godlike mind soars forth, in its delight
    Making earth bare and veiling heaven; and, when
It sinks, the swarms that dimmed or shared its light
Leave to its kindred lamps the spirit's awful night."

XXX

Thus ceased she: and the Mountain Shepherds came,
    Their garlands sere, their magic mantles rent.
The Pilgrim of Eternity, whose fame
    Over his living head like heaven is bent,
    An early but enduring monument,
Came, veiling all the lightnings of his song
    In sorrow. From her wilds Ierne sent
The sweetest lyrist of her saddest wrong,
And love taught grief to fall like music from his tongue.

XXXI

Midst others of less note came one frail form,
  A phantom among men, companionless
As the last cloud of an expiring storm,
  Whose thunder is its knell. He, as I guess,
  Had gazed on Nature's naked loveliness
Actaeon-like; and now he fled astray
  With feeble steps o'er the world's wilderness,
And his own thoughts along that rugged way
Pursued like raging hounds their father and their prey.

XXXII

A pard-like Spirit beautiful and swift—
  A love in desolation masked—a power
Girt round with weakness; it can scarce uplift
  The weight of the superincumbent hour.
  It is a dying lamp, a falling shower,
A breaking billow;—even whilst we speak
  Is it not broken? On the withering flower
The killing sun smiles brightly: on a cheek
The life can burn in blood even while the heart may break.

XXXIII

His head was bound with pansies overblown,
  And faded violets, white and pied and blue;
And a light spear topped with a cypress-cone,
  Round whose rude shaft dark ivy-tresses grew
  Yet dripping with the forest's noonday dew,
Vibrated, as the ever-beating heart
  Shook the weak hand that grasped it. Of that crew
He came the last, neglected and apart;
A herd-abandoned deer struck by the hunter's dart.

XXXIV

All stood aloof, and at his partial moan
   Smiled through their tears. Well knew that gentle band
Who in another's fate now wept his own.
   As in the accents of an unknown land
   He sang new sorrow, sad Urania scanned
The Stranger's mien, and murmured "Who art thou?"
   He answered not, but with a sudden hand
Made bare his branded and ensanguined brow,
Which was like Cain's or Christ's—oh that it should be so!

XXXV

What softer voice is hushed over the dead?
   Athwart what brow is that dark mantle thrown?
What form leans sadly o'er the white death-bed,
   In mockery of monumental stone,
   The heavy heart heaving without a moan?
If it be he who, gentlest of the wise,
   Taught, soothed, loved, honoured, the departed one,
Let me not vex with inharmonious sighs
The silence of that heart's accepted sacrifice.

XXXVI

Our Adonais has drunk poison—oh
   What deaf and viperous murderer could crown
Life's early cup with such a draught of woe?
   The nameless worm would now itself disown;
   It felt, yet could escape, the magic tone
Whose prelude held all envy, hate, and wrong,
   But what was howling in one breast alone,
Silent with expectation of the song
Whose master's hand is cold, whose silver lyre unstrung.

XXXVII

Live thou, whose infamy is not thy fame!
  Live! fear no heavier chastisement from me,
Thou noteless blot on a remembered name!
  But be thyself, and know thyself to be!
  And ever at thy season be thou free
To spill the venom which thy fangs o'erflow:
  Remorse and self-contempt shall cling to thee,
Hot shame shall burn upon thy secret brow,
And like a beaten hound tremble thou shalt—as now.

XXXVIII

Nor let us weep that our delight is fled
  Far from these carrion-kites that scream below.
He wakes or sleeps with the enduring dead;
  Thou canst not soar where he is sitting now.
  Dust to the dust: but the pure spirit shall flow
Back to the burning fountain whence he came,
  A portion of the Eternal, which must glow
Through time and change, unquenchably the same,
Whilst thy cold embers choke the sordid hearth of shame.

XXXIX

Peace, peace! he is not dead, he doth not sleep!
  He hath awakened from the dream of life.
'Tis we who, lost in stormy visions, keep
  With phantoms an unprofitable strife,
  And in mad trance strike with our spirit's knife
Invulnerable nothings. We decay
  Like corpses in a charnel; fear and grief
Convulse us and consume us day by day,
And cold hopes swarm like worms within our living clay.

XL

He has outsoared the shadow of our night.
Envy and calumny and hate and pain,
And that unrest which men miscall delight,
Can touch him not and torture not again.
From the contagion of the world's slow stain
He is secure; and now can never mourn
A heart grown cold, a head grown grey in vain —
Nor, when the spirit's self has ceased to burn,
With sparkless ashes load an unlamented urn.

XLI

He live, he wakes — 'tis Death is dead, not he;
Mourn not for Adonais. — Thou young Dawn,
Turn all thy dew to splendour, for from thee
The spirit thou lamentest is not gone!
Ye caverns and ye forests, cease to moan!
Cease, ye faint flowers and fountains! and, thou Air,
Which like a mourning-veil thy scarf hadst thrown
O'er the abandoned Earth, now leave it bare
Even to the joyous stars which smile on its despair!

XLII

He is made one with Nature. There is heard
His voice in all her music, from the moan
Of thunder to the song of night's sweet bird.
He is a presence to be felt and known
In darkness and in light, from herb and stone, —
Spreading itself where'er that Power may move
Which has withdrawn his being to its own,
Which wields the world with never-wearied love,
Sustains it from beneath, and kindles it above.

XLIII

He is a portion of the loveliness
   Which once he made more lovely. He doth bear
His part, while the One Spirit's plastic stress
   Sweeps through the dull dense world; compelling there
   All new successions to the forms they wear;
Torturing the unwilling dross, that checks its flight,
   To its own likeness, as each mass may bear;
And bursting in its beauty and its might
From trees and beasts and men into the heaven's light.

XLIV

The splendours of the firmament of time
   May be eclipsed, but are extinguished not;
Like stars to their appointed height they climb,
   And death is a low mist which cannot blot
   The brightness it may veil. When lofty thought
Lifts a young heart above its mortal lair
   And love and life contend in it for what
Shall be its earthly doom, the dead live there,
And move like winds of light on dark and stormy air.

XLV

The inheritors of unfulfilled renown
   Rose from their thrones, built beyond mortal thought
Far in the unapparent. Chatterton
   Rose pale, his solemn agony had not
   Yet faded from him: Sidney, as he fought,
And as he fell, and as he lived and loved,
   Sublimely mild, a spirit without spot,
Arose; And Lucan, by his death approved; —
Oblivion as they rose shrank like a thing reproved.

XLVI

And many more, whose names on earth are dark,
But whose transmitted effluence cannot die
So long as fire outlives the parent spark,
Rose, robed in dazzling immortality.
"Thou art become as one of us," they cry;
"It was for thee yon kingless sphere has long
Swung blind in unascended majesty,
Silent alone amid an heaven of song.
Assume thy wingèd throne, thou Vesper of our throng!"

XLVII

Who mourns for Adonais? Oh come forth,
Fond wretch, and know thyself and him aright.
Clasp with thy panting soul the pendulous earth;
As from a centre, dart thy spirit's light
Beyond all worlds, until its spacious might
Satiate the void circumference: then shrink
Even to a point within our day and night;
And keep thy heart light, lest it make thee sink,
When hope has kindled hope, and lured thee to the brink.

XLVIII

Or go to Rome, which is the sepulchre,
Oh not of him, but of our joy. 'Tis nought
That ages, empires, and religions, there
Lie buried in the ravage they have wrought;
For such as he can lend—they borrow not
Glory from those who made the world their prey;
And he is gathered to the kings of thought
Who waged contention with their time's decay,
And of the past are all that cannot pass away.

XLIX

Go thou to Rome,—at once the paradise,
    The grave, the city, and the wilderness;
And where its wrecks like shattered mountains rise,
    And flowering weeds and fragrant copses dress
    The bones of Desolation's nakedness,
Pass, till the Spirit of the spot shall lead
    Thy footsteps to a slope of green access,
Where, like an infant's smile, over the dead
A light of laughing flowers along the grass is spread.

L

And grey walls moulder round, on which dull Time
    Feeds, like slow fire upon a hoary brand;
And one keen pyramid with wedge sublime,
    Pavilioning the dust of him who planned
    This refuge for his memory, doth stand
Like flame transformed to marble; and beneath
    A field is spread, on which a newer band
Have pitched in heaven's smile their camp of death,
Welcoming him we lose with scarce-extinguished breath.

LI

Here pause. These graves are all too young as yet
    To have outgrown the sorrow which consigned
Its charge to each; and, if the seal is set
    Here on one fountain of a mourning mind,
    Break it not thou! too surely shalt thou find
Thine own well full, if thou returnest home,
    Of tears and gall. From the world's bitter wind
Seek shelter in the shadow of the tomb.
What Adonais is why fear we to become?

LII

The One remains, the many change and pass;
   Heaven's light for ever shines, earth's shadows fly;
Life, like a dome of many-coloured glass,
   Stains the white radiance of eternity,
   Until Death tramples it of fragments. — Die,
If thou wouldst be with that which thou dost seek!
   Follow where all is fled! — Rome's azure sky,
Flowers, ruins, statues, music, words, are weak
The glory they transfuse with fitting truth to speak.

LIII

Why linger, why turn back, why shrink, my heart?
   Thy hopes are gone before: from all things here
They have departed; thou shouldst now depart.
   A light is past from the revolving year,
   And man and woman; and what still is dear
Attracts to crush, repels to make thee wither.
   The soft sky smiles, the low mind whispers near:
'Tis Adonais calls! Oh hasten thither!
No more let life divide what death can join together.

LIV

That light whose smile kindles the universe,
   That beauty in which all things work and move,
That benediction which the eclipsing curse
   Of birth can quench not, that sustaining Love
   Which, through the web of being blindly wove
By man and beast and earth and air and sea,
   Burns bright or dim, as each are mirrors of
The fire for which all thirst, now beams on me,
Consuming the last clouds of cold mortality.

LV

The breath whose might I have invoked in song
　Descends on me; my spirit's bark is driven
Far from the shore, far from the trembling throng
　Whose sails were never to the tempest given.
　The massy earth and spherèd skies are riven!
I am borne darkly, fearfully afar!
　Whilst, burning through the inmost veil of heaven,
The soul of Adonais, like a star,
Beacons from the abode where the Eternal are.

Just as Auden was to write a Yeatsian poem on Yeats's death (p. 1028), Shelley wrote a Keatsian poem on Keats's. The Spenserian stanza in "Adonais" is the measure used in Keats's "Eve of St. Agnes" (p. 551). Such a pastoral elegy, inherited from the Greeks, has long been used by one poet who laments the passing of another, as is the case with Milton's "Lycidas" (p. 203). "Adonais" stands alone, however, since both Shelley and Keats are poets of the very first rank.

JOHN CLARE 1793–1864

Despite a life marked by poverty, misery, insanity, and confinement to asylums, Clare managed to be one of the most productive poets in English; his complete works are still not available 130 years after his death. Praised at one time as a rustic primitive on the model of Burns, he was later honored as a sainted madman on the model of Smart, Collins, and Cowper. In time, he may receive recognition as a very good poet, sometimes even a great one.

I Am

>>>>>>>

I am: yet what I am none cares or knows:
  My friends forsake me like a memory lost,
I am the self-consumer of my woes—
  They rise and vanish in oblivious host,
Like shadows in love's frenzied stifled throes—
And yet I am, and live—like vapors tossed

Into the nothingness of scorn and noise,
  Into the living sea of waking dreams,
Where there is neither sense of life or joys,
  But the vast shipwreck of my life's esteems;
Even the dearest, that I love the best,
And strange—nay, rather stranger than the rest.

I long for scenes where man has never trod,
  A place where woman never smiled or wept—
There to abide with my Creator, God,
  And sleep as I in childhood sweetly slept,
Untroubling and untroubled where I lie,
The grass below—above the vaulted sky.

You would have to have a very hard heart indeed not to feel pity for Clare and to hear the utter truth, sincerity, and pathos of "I Am," written (along with hundreds of other poems) while he was confined in the General Lunatic Asylum in Northampton, where he spent about the last third of his life.

Bryant established himself as a poet in his teens and was generally regarded as the leading American poet from about 1825 until his death more than fifty years later. He was trained as a lawyer and employed as a journalist. Originally a Democrat, he later became one of the founders of the Republican Party.

To a Waterfowl

Whither, 'midst falling dew,
While glow the heavens with the last steps of day,
Far, through their rosy depths, dost thou pursue
    Thy solitary way?

Vainly the fowler's eye
Might mark thy distant flight to do thee wrong,
As, darkly painted on the crimson sky,
    Thy figure floats along.

Seek'st thou the plashy brink
Of weedy lake, or marge of river wide,
Or where the rocking billows rise and sink
    On the chafed ocean side?

There is a Power whose care
Teaches thy way along that pathless coast, —
The desert and illimitable air, —
    Lone wandering, but not lost.

All day thy wings have fanned,
At that far height, the cold, thin atmosphere,
Yet stoop not, weary, to the welcome land,
　　Though the dark night is near.

And soon that toil shall end;
Soon shalt thou find a summer home, and rest,
And scream among thy fellows; reeds shall bend,
　　Soon, o'er thy sheltered nest.

Thou'rt gone, the abyss of heaven
Hath swallowed up thy form; yet, on my heart
Deeply hath sunk the lesson thou hast given,
　　And shall not soon depart.

He who, from zone to zone,
Guides through the boundless sky thy certain flight,
In the long way that I must tread alone,
　　Will lead my steps aright.

Some modern readers resent having a poem spell out its moral and theological "lesson" so baldly, but a work with so much accuracy of observation and grace of form has earned the right to a bit of sententiousness. Matthew Arnold called this "the most perfect brief poem in the language."

Thanatopsis

To him who in the love of Nature holds
Communion with her visible forms, she speaks
A various language; for his gayer hours
She has a voice of gladness, and a smile
And eloquence of beauty, and she glides
Into his darker musings, with a mild
And gentle sympathy, that steals away
Their sharpness, ere he is aware. When thoughts
Of the last bitter hour come like a blight
Over thy spirit, and sad images
Of the stern agony, and shroud, and pall,
And breathless darkness, and the narrow house
Make thee to shudder, and grow sick at heart;—
Go forth under the open sky, and list
To Nature's teachings, while from all around—
Earth and her waters, and the depths of air,—
Comes a still voice—Yet a few days, and thee
The all-beholding sun shall see no more
In all his course; nor yet in the cold ground,
Where thy pale form was laid, with many tears,
Nor in the embrace of ocean shall exist
Thy image. Earth, that nourished thee, shall claim
Thy growth, to be resolv'd to earth again;
And, lost each human trace, surrend'ring up
Thine individual being, shalt thou go
To mix forever with the elements,
To be a brother to th' insensible rock
And to the sluggish clod, which the rude swain
Turns with his share, and treads upon. The oak
Shall send his roots abroad, and pierce thy mould.
Yet not to thy eternal resting place
Shalt thou retire alone—nor couldst thou wish
Couch more magnificent. Thou shalt lie down
With patriarchs of the infant world—with kings

The powerful of the earth—the wise, the good,
Fair forms, and hoary seers of ages past,
All in one mighty sepulchre.—The hills
Rock-ribb'd and ancient as the sun,—the vales
Stretching in pensive quietness between;
The venerable woods—rivers that move
In majesty, and the complaining brooks
That make the meadows green; and pour'd round all,
Old ocean's grey and melancholy waste,—
Are but the solemn decorations all
Of the great tomb of man. The golden sun,
The planets, all the infinite host of heaven,
Are shining on the sad abodes of death,
Through the still lapse of ages. All that tread
The globe are but a handful to the tribes
That slumber in its bosom.—Take the wings
Of morning—and the Barcan desert pierce,
Or lose thyself in the continuous woods
Where rolls the Oregan, and hears no sound,
Save his own dashings—yet—the dead are there,
And millions in those solitudes, since first
The flight of years began, have laid them down
In their last sleep—the dead reign there alone.—
So shalt thou rest—and what if thou shalt fall
Unnoticed by the living—and no friend
Take note of thy departure? All that breathe
Will share thy destiny. The gay will laugh
When thou art gone, the solemn brood of care
Plod on, and each one as before will chase
His favourite phantom; yet all these shall leave
Their mirth and their employments, and shall come,
And make their bed with thee. As the long train
Of ages glide away, the sons of men,
The youth in life's green spring, and he who goes
In the full strength of years, matron, and maid,
The bow'd with age, the infant in the smiles
And beauty of its innocent age cut off,—
Shall one by one be gathered to they side,

By those, who in their turn shall follow them.
So live, that when thy summons comes to join
The innumerable caravan, that moves
To the pale realms of shade, where each shall take
His chamber in the silent halls of death,
Thou go not, like the quarry-slave at night,
Scourged to his dungeon, but sustain'd and sooth'd
By an unfaltering trust, approach thy grave,
Like one who wraps the drapery of his couch
About him, and lies down to pleasant dreams.

Bryant began his sophisticated "view of death" as a teenager. The first version was shorter than this final version by about thirty lines but still displayed a mature stoicism and discipline. "Thanatopsis" has long been a favorite moral poem for Americans.

JOHN KEATS 1795–1821

No poet in this anthology produced more great poetry at an earlier age than John Keats. Both his parents died while he was very young. Keats was apprenticed to a surgeon, moved to London in 1815, and was qualified as a "dresser" and subsequently as a surgeon, in accordance with the medical regulations of the day. Keats's earliest poems were written under the influence of Edmund Spenser, and all of Keats's work shows something of a Spenserian blend of sensuousness and intellectual depth. Keats was never a formal critic of the sort who writes essays, reviews, and dissertations, but, in his marvelous letters, he displays one of the finest critical intelligences in English literature.

To Autumn

I

Season of mists and mellow fruitfulness,
   Close bosom-friend of the maturing sun;
Conspiring with him how to load and bless
   With fruit the vines that round the thatch-eves run;
To bend with apples the mossed cottage-trees,
   And fill all fruit with ripeness to the core;
     To swell the gourd, and plump the hazel shells
   With a sweet kernel; to set budding more,
And still more, later flowers for the bees,
Until they think warm days will never cease,
     For summer has o'er-brimmed their clammy cells.

II

Who hath not seen thee oft amid thy store?
  Sometimes whoever seeks abroad may find
Thee sitting careless on a granary floor,
  Thy hair soft-lifted by the winnowing wind;
Or on a half-reaped furrow sound asleep,
  Drowsed with the fume of poppies, while thy hook
    Spares the next swath and all its twinèd flowers:
And sometimes like a gleaner thou dost keep
  Steady thy laden head across a brook;
  Or by a cider-press, with patient look,
    Thou watchest the last oozings hours by hours.

III

Where are the songs of Spring? Ay, where are they?
  Think not of them, thou hast thy music too,—
While barrèd clouds bloom the soft-dying day,
  And touch the stubble-plains with rosy hue;
Then in a wailful choir the small gnats mourn
  Among the river swallows, borne aloft
    Or sinking as the light wind lives or dies;
And full-grown lambs loud bleat from hilly bourn;
  Hedge-crickets sing; and now with treble soft
  The red-breast whistles from a garden-croft;
    And gathering swallows twitter in the skies.

Most of Keats's six great odes were written in May 1819; true to its subject, however, this, the last, was written just a day or two before the autumnal equinox of 1819. Keats makes autumn "the human season," not much like the super-human creativity of spring or the otherworldly extremism of summer and winter. The poet here exploits to the full his matchless genius for sensual realization — how things look and sound and also how they smell, taste, and feel. (Note that: "bourn" is "region"; "croft" is "small enclosed field.")

La Belle Dame sans Merci

O what can ail thee, Knight at arms,
  Alone and palely loitering?
The sedge has withered from the Lake
  And no birds sing!

O what can ail thee, Knight at arms,
  So haggard and so woe begone?
The Squirrel's granary is full
  And the harvest's done.

I see a lily on thy brow
  With anguish moist and fever dew,
And on thy cheeks a fading rose
  Fast withereth too —

I met a Lady in the Meads,
  Full beautiful, a faery's child
Her hair was long, her foot was light
  And her eyes were wild —

I made a Garland for her head,
  And bracelets too, and fragrant Zone
She look'd at me as she did love
  And made sweet moan —

I set her on my pacing steed
  And nothing else saw all day long
For sidelong would she bend and sing
  A faery's song —

She found me roots of relish sweet
And honey wild and manna dew
And sure in language strange she said
I love thee true —

She took me to her elfin grot
And there she wept, and sigh'd full sore,
And there I shut her wild wild eyes
With kisses four.

And there she lulled me asleep
And there I dream'd — Ah woe betide!
The latest dream I ever dreamt
On the cold hill side.

I saw pale Kings, and Princes too
Pale warriors, death pale were they all;
They cried, La belle dame sans merci
Hath thee in thrall.

I saw their starv'd lips in the gloom
With horrid warning gaped wide,
And I awoke, and found me here
On the cold hill's side.

And this is why I sojourn here
Alone and palely loitering;
Though the sedge is withered from the Lake,
And no birds sing —

La Belle Dame sans Merci
(Revised Version)

Ah, what can ail thee, wretched wight,
 Alone and palely loitering;
The sedge has wither'd from the lake,
 And no birds sing.

Ah, what can ail thee, wretched wight,
 So haggard and so woe-begone?
The squirrel's granary is full,
 And the harvest's done.

I see a lilly on thy brow,
 With anguish moist and fever dew;
And on thy cheek a fading rose
 Fast withereth too.

I met a Lady in the meads
 Full beautiful, a fairy's child;
Her hair was long, her foot was light,
 And her eyes were wild.

I set her on my pacing steed,
 And nothing else saw all day long;
For sideways would she lean, and sing
 A faery's song.

I made a garland for her head,
 And bracelets too, and fragrant zone;
She look'd at me as she did love,
 And made sweet moan.

She found me roots of relish sweet,
　　And honey wild, and manna dew,
And sure in language strange she said,
　　I love thee true.

She took me to her elfin grot,
　　And there she gaz'd and sighed deep,
And there I shut her wild sad eyes—
　　So kiss'd to sleep.

And there we slumber'd on the moss,
　　And there I dream'd, ah woe betide
The latest dream I ever dream'd
　　On the cold hill side.

I saw pale kings, and princes too,
　　Pale warriors, death-pale were they all;
Who cry'd—"La belle Dame sans mercy
　　Hath thee in thrall!"

I saw their starv'd lips in the gloom
　　With horrid warning gaped wide,
And I awoke, and found me here
　　On the cold hill side.

And this is why I sojourn here
　　Alone and palely loitering,
Though the sedge is wither'd from the lake,
　　And no birds sing.

Keats's "Eve of St. Agnes" (p. 551) includes "an ancient ditty . . . In Provence called 'La belle dame sans merci.' " There is a medieval song with that title (which means "The Lovely Lady without Pity") by Alain Chartier. Like many of his Romantic contemporaries, Keats adapted the ballad stanza and also followed the ballad convention of casting the entire poem in the form of questions and answers. Keats wrote two versions of this strangely powerful story. Since they are short, and since critics disagree about which is better, both are given here.

On First Looking into Chapman's Homer

Much have I traveled in the realms of gold,
   And many goodly states and kingdoms seen;
   Round many western islands have I been
Which bards in fealty to Apollo hold.
Oft of one wide expanse had I been told
   That deep-browed Homer ruled as his demesne,
   Yet did I never breathe its pure serene
Till I heard Chapman speak out loud and bold.
Then felt I like some watcher of the skies
   When a new planet swims into his ken;
Or like stout Cortez when with eagle eyes
   He stared at the Pacific— and all his men
Looked at each other with a wild surmise—
   Silent, upon a peak in Darien.

Keats made two very apt choices of metaphors for his exciting and inspiring glimpse of Homer, whose Greek he could not read, through the translations of George Chapman. Keats erred in giving Cortez credit for what Balboa had done, but it was still brilliant of the poet to connect the Renaissance explorers with later discoverers.

Ode to a Nightingale

I

My heart aches, and a drowsy numbness pains
   My sense, as though of hemlock I had drunk,
Or emptied some dull opiate to the drains
   One minute past, and Lethe-wards had sunk.
'Tis not through envy of thy happy lot,
   But being too happy in thine happiness, —
      That thou, light-wingèd Dryad of the trees,
         In some melodious plot
   Of beechen green, and shadows numberless,
   Singest of summer in full-throated ease.

II

O for a draught of vintage! that hath been
   Cool'd a long age in the deep-delvèd earth,
Tasting of Flora and the country green,
   Dance, and Provençal song, and sunburnt mirth!
O for a beaker full of the warm South,
   Full of the true, the blushful Hippocrene,
      With beaded bubbles winking at the brim,
         And purple-stainèd mouth;
   That I might drink, and leave the world unseen,
   And with thee fade away into the forest dim:

III

Fade far away, dissolve, and quite forget
    What thou among the leaves hast never known,
The weariness, the fever, and the fret
    Here, where men sit and hear each other groan;
Where palsy shakes a few, sad, last gray hairs,
    Where youth grows pale, and specter-thin, and dies;
        Where but to think is to be full of sorrow
            And leaden-eyed despairs,
    Where Beauty cannot keep her lustrous eyes,
        Or new Love pine at them beyond to-morrow.

IV

Away! away! for I will fly to thee,
    Not charioted by Bacchus and his pards,
But on the viewless wings of Poesy,
    Though the dull brain perplexes and retards:
Already with thee! tender is the night,
    And haply the Queen-Moon is on her throne,
        Clustered around by all her starry Fays;
            But here there is no light,
    Save what from heaven is with the breezes blown
        Through verdurous glooms and winding mossy ways.

V

I cannot see what flowers are at my feet,
    Nor what soft incense hangs upon the boughs,
But, in embalmèd darkness, guess each sweet
    Wherewith the seasonable month endows
The grass, the thicket, and the fruit-tree wild;
    White hawthorn, and the pastoral eglantine;
        Fast fading violets cover'd up in leaves;
            And mid-May's eldest child,
    The coming musk-rose, full of dewy wine,
        The murmurous haunt of flies on summer eves.

VI

Darkling I listen; and for many a time
  I have been half in love with easeful Death,
Call'd him soft names in many a musèd rhyme,
  To take into the air my quiet breath;
Now more than ever seems it rich to die,
  To cease upon the midnight with no pain,
    While thou art pouring forth thy soul abroad
      In such an ecstasy!
  Still wouldst thou sing, and I have ears in vain—
  To thy high requiem become a sod.

VII

Thou wast not born for death, immortal Bird!
  No hungry generations tread thee down;
The voice I hear this passing night was heard
  In ancient days by emperor and clown:
Perhaps the self-same song that found a path
  Through the sad heart of Ruth, when, sick for home,
    She stood in tears amid the alien corn;
      The same that oft-times hath
  Charm'd magic casements, opening on the foam
  Of perilous seas, in faery lands forlorn.

VIII

Forlorn! the very word is like a bell
  To toll me back from thee to my sole self!
Adieu! the fancy cannot cheat so well
  As she is fam'd to do, deceiving elf.
Adieu! adieu! thy plaintive anthem fades
  Past the near meadows, over the still stream,
    Up the hill-side; and now 'tis buried deep
      In the next valley-glades:
  Was it a vision, or a waking dream?
    Fled is that music:—Do I wake or sleep?

Keats's "Ode on a Grecian Urn" (p. 546) is virtually selfless, hinting only at a vague plural first-person pronoun toward the end. This beautiful ode, on the other hand, smacks more of the Romantic concentration on the singular self, with "My" at the beginning and "I" near the end.

Ode on a Grecian Urn

❖❖❖❖

Thou still unravished bride of quietness,
   Thou foster-child of silence and slow time,
Sylvan historian, who canst thus express
   A flowery tale more sweetly than our rhyme:
What leaf-fringed legend haunts about thy shape
   Of deities or mortals, or of both,
      In Tempe or the dales of Arcady?
   What men or gods are these? What maidens loth?
What mad pursuit? What struggle to escape?
      What pipes and timbrels? What wild ecstasy?

Heard melodies are sweet, but those unheard
   Are sweeter; therefore, ye soft pipes, play on;
Not to the sensual ear, but, more endeared,
   Pipe to the spirit ditties of no tone:
Fair youth, beneath the trees, thou canst not leave
   Thy song, nor ever can those trees be bare;
      Bold Lover, never, never canst thou kiss,
Though winning near the goal—yet, do not grieve;
   She cannot fade, though thou hast not thy bliss,
   For ever wilt thou love, and she be fair!

Ah, happy, happy boughs! that cannot shed
   Your leaves, nor ever bid the Spring adieu;
And, happy melodist, unwearièd,
   For ever piping songs for ever new;
More happy love! more happy, happy love!
   For ever warm and still to be enjoyed,
      For ever panting, and for ever young;
All breathing human passion far above,
   That leaves a heart high-sorrowful and cloyed,
      A burning forehead, and a parching tongue.

Who are these coming to the sacrifice?
    To what green altar, O mysterious priest,
Lead'st thou that heifer lowing at the skies,
    And all her silken flanks with garlands drest?
What little town by river or sea shore,
    Or mountain-built with peaceful citadel,
        Is emptied of this folk, this pious morn?
And, little town, thy streets for evermore
    Will silent be; and not a soul to tell
        Why thou art desolate, can e'er return.

O Attic shape! Fair attitude! with brede
    Of marble men and maidens overwrought,
With forest branches and the trodden weed;
    Thou, silent form, dost tease us out of thought
As doth Eternity: Cold Pastoral!
    When old age shall this generation waste,
        Thou shalt remain, in midst of other woe
    Than ours, a friend to man, to whom thou say'st,
Beauty is truth, truth beauty,—that is all
        Ye know on earth, and all ye need to know.

Compared with his Romantic "Ode to a Nightingale" (p. 542), this ode seems closer to the Classical spirit. Its subject is an artifact from classical antiquity, and the handling of the subject has an impersonal quality, reflected in the structural poise of the poem. Because of some confusing punctuation, it is unclear whether the urn says all of the last two lines or just "Beauty is truth, truth beauty."

When I Have Fears

When I have fears that I may cease to be
  Before my pen has gleaned my teeming brain,
Before high-piled books, in charactery,
  Hold like rich garners the full ripened grain;
When I behold, upon the night's starred face,
  Huge cloudy symbols of a high romance,
And think that I may never live to trace
  Their shadows, with the magic hand of chance;
And when I feel, fair creature of an hour,
  That I shall never look upon thee more,
Never have relish in the faery power
  Of unreflecting love; — then on the shore
Of the wide world I stand alone, and think
Till love and fame to nothingness do sink.

Keats parallels the typical Shakespeare sonnet in rhyme scheme, in the tightly efficient "When . . . then . . ." architecture, and even in particulars of wording ("wide world" echoes Shakespeare's ". . . the prophetic soul of the wide world . . ." in Sonnet CVII). One of the last books by the modern American poet John Berryman is called Love and Fame *(1970).*

Ode on Melancholy

>>>>>>>

I

No, no, go not to Lethe, neither twist
  Wolf's-bane, tight-rooted, for its poisonous wine;
Nor suffer thy pale forehead to be kiss'd
  By nightshade, ruby grape of Proserpine;
Make not your rosary of yew-berries,
  Nor let the beetle, nor the death-moth be
    Your mournful Psyche, nor the downy owl
A partner in your sorrow's mysteries;
  For shade to shade will come too drowsily,
    And drown the wakeful anguish of the soul.

II

But when the melancholy fit shall fall
  Sudden from heaven like a weeping cloud,
That fosters the droop-headed flowers all,
  And hides the green hill in an April shroud;
Then glut thy sorrow on a morning rose,
  Or on the rainbow of the salt sand-wave,
    Or on the wealth of globed peonies;
Or if thy mistress some rich anger shows,
  Emprison her soft hand, and let her rave,
    And feed deep, deep upon her peerless eyes.

III

She dwells with Beauty—Beauty that must die;
  And Joy, whose hand is ever at his lips
Bidding adieu; and aching Pleasure nigh,
  Turning to poison while the bee-mouth sips:
Ay, in the very temple of Delight
  Veil'd Melancholy has her sovran shrine,
    Though seen of none save him whose strenuous tongue
  Can burst Joy's grape against his palate fine;
His soul shall taste the sadness of her might,
  And be among her cloudy trophies hung.

Although we may have outgrown the primitive pathology that regards melancholia as the result of too much black bile, we still recognize the condition as a true affliction of the spirit. Keats sounds quite modern in his rejection of the usual dark emblems, emphasizing instead that the better images for melancholy are those of beauty, joy, and life itself, since we know they must perish. Keats, somewhat like Blake, devised an original mythology with melancholy's shrine right in the temple of delight.

The Eve of St. Agnes

I

St. Agnes' Eve—Ah, bitter chill it was!
The owl, for all his feathers, was a-cold;
The hare limped trembling through the frozen grass,
And silent was the flock in woolly fold:
Numb were the Beadsman's fingers, while he told
His rosary, and while his frosted breath,
Like pious incense from a censer old,
Seemed taking flight for heaven, without a death,
Past the sweet Virgin's picture, while his prayer he saith.

II

His prayer he saith, this patient, holy man;
Then takes his lamp, and riseth from his knees,
And back returneth, meager, barefoot, wan,
Along the chapel aisle by slow degrees:
The sculptured dead, on each side, seem to freeze,
Emprisoned in black, purgatorial rails:
Knights, ladies, praying in dumb orat'ries,
He passeth by; and his weak spirit fails
To think how they may ache in icy hoods and mails.

III

Northward he turneth through a little door,
And scarce three steps, ere Music's golden tongue
Flattered to tears this aged man and poor;
But no—already had his deathbell rung:
The joys of all his life were said and sung:
His was harsh penance on St. Angnes' Eve:
Another way he went, and soon among
Rough ashes sat he for his soul's reprieve,
And all night kept awake, for sinners' sake to grieve.

IV

That ancient Beadsman heard the prelude soft;
And so it chanced, for many a door was wide,
From hurry to and fro. Soon, up aloft,
The silver, snarling trumpets' 'gan to chide:
The level chambers, ready with their pride,
Were glowing to receive a thousand guests:
The carvèd angels, ever eager-eyed,
Stared, where upon their heads the cornice rests,
With hair blown back, and wings put cross-wise on their
    breasts.

V

At length burst in the argent revelry,
With plume, tiara, and all rich array,
Numerous as shadows haunting faerily
The brain, new-stuffed, in youth, with triumphs gay
Of old romance. These let us wish away,
And turn, sole-thoughted, to one Lady there,
Whose heart had brooded, all that wintry day,
On love, and winged St. Agnes' saintly care,
As she had heard old dames full many times declare.

VI

They told her how, upon St. Agnes' Eve,
Young virgins might have visions of delight,
And soft adorings from their loves receive
Upon the honeyed middle of the night,
If ceremonies due they did aright;
As, supperless to bed they must retire,
And couch supine their beauties, lily-white,
Nor look behind, nor sideways, but require
Of Heaven with upward eyes for all that they desire.

VII

Full of this whim was thoughtful Madeline:
The music, yearning like a God in pain,
She scarcely heard: her maiden eyes divine,
Fixed on the floor, saw many a sweeping train
Pass by—she heeded not at all: in vain
Came many a tiptoe, amorous cavalier,
And back retired; not cooled by high disdain,
But she saw not: her heart was otherwhere:
She sighed for Agnes' dreams, the sweetest of the year.

VIII

She danced along with vague, regardless eyes,
Anxious her lips, her breathing quick and short:
The hallowed hour was near at hand: she sighs
Amid the timbrels, and the thronged resort
Of whisperers in anger, or in sport;
'Mid looks of love, defiance, hate, and scorn,
Hoodwinked with faery fancy; all amort,
Save to St. Agnes and her lambs unshorn,
And all the bliss to be before tomorrow morn.

IX

So, purposing each moment to retire,
She lingered still. Meantime, across the moors,
Had come young Porphyro, with heart on fire
For Madeline. Beside the portal doors,
Buttressed from moonlight, stands he, and implores
All saints to give him sight of Madeline,
But for one moment in the tedious hours,
That he might gaze and worship all unseen;
Perchance speak, kneel, touch, kiss—in sooth such things have
    been.

X

He ventures in: let no buzzed whisper tell:
All eyes be muffled, or a hundred swords
Will storm his heart, Love's feverous citadel:
For him, those chambers held barbarian hordes,
Hyena foemen, and hot-blooded lords,
Whose very dogs would execrations howl
Against his lineage: not one breast affords
Him any mercy, in that mansion foul,
Save one old beldame, weak in body and in soul.

XI

Ah, happy chance! the aged creature came,
Shuffling along with ivory-headed wand,
To where he stood, hid from the torch's flame,
Behind a broad hall-pillar, far beyond
The sound of merriment and chorus bland:
He startled her; but soon she knew his face,
And grasped his fingers in her palsied hand,
Saying, "Mercy, Porphyro! hie thee from this place;
They are all here tonight, the whole blood-thirsty race!

XII

"Get hence! get hence! there's dwarfish Hildebrand;
He had a fever late, and in the fit
He curséd thee and thine, both house and land:
Then there's that old Lord Maurice, not a whit
More tame for his gray hairs—Alas me! flit!
Flit like a ghost away."—"Ah, Gossip dear,
We're safe enough; here in this arm-chair sit,
And tell me how"—"Good Saints! not here, not here;
Follow me, child, or else these stones will be thy bier."

XIII

He followed through a lowly archèd way,
Brushing the cobwebs with his lofty plume,
And as she muttered "Well-a—well-a-day!"
He found him in a little moonlight room,
Pale, latticed, chill, and silent as a tomb.
"Now tell me where is Madeline," said he,
"O tell me, Angela, by the holy loom
Which none but secret sisterhood may see,
When they St. Agnes' wool are waving piously."

XIV

"St. Agnes! Ah! it is St. Agnes' Eve—
Yet men will murder upon holy days:
Thou must hold water in a witch's sieve,
And be liege-lord of all the Elves and Fays,
To venture so: it fills me with amaze
To see thee, Porphyro!—St. Agnes' Eve!
God's help! my lady fair the conjuror plays
This very night: good angels her deceive!
But let me laugh awhile, I've mickle time to grieve."

XV

Feebly she laugheth in the languid moon,
While Porphyro upon her face doth look,
Like puzzled urchin on an aged crone
Who keepeth closed a wonderous riddle-book,
As spectacled she sits in chimney nook.
But soon his eyes grew brilliant, when she told
His lady's purpose; and he scarce could brook
Tears, at the thought of those enchantments cold,
And Madeline asleep in lap of legends old.

XVI

Sudden a thought came like a full-blown rose,
Flushing his brow, and in his painèd heart
Made purple riot: then doth he propose
A stratagem, that makes the beldame start:
"A cruel man and impious thou art:
Sweet lady, let her pray, and sleep, and dream
Alone with her good angels, far apart
From wicked men like thee. Go, go! — I deem
Thou canst not surely be the same that thou didst seem."

XVII

"I will not harm her, by all saints I swear,"
Quoth Porphyro: "O may I ne'er find grace
When my weak voice shall whisper its last prayer,
If one of her soft ringlets I displace,
Or look with ruffian passion in her face:
Good Angela, believe me by these tears;
Or I will, even in a moment's space,
Awake, with horrid shout, my foemen's ears,
And beard them, though they be more fanged than wolves and
  bears."

XVIII

"Ah! why wilt thou affright a feeble soul?
A poor, weak, palsy-stricken, churchyard thing,
Whose passing-bell may ere the midnight toll;
Whose prayers for thee, each morn and evening,
Were never missed." — Thus plaining, doth she bring
A gentler speech from burning Porphyro;
So woeful, and of such deep sorrowing,
That Angela gives promise she will do
Whatever he shall wish, betide her weal or woe.

XIX

Which was, to lead him, in close secrecy,
Even to Madeline's chamber, and there hide
Him in a closet, of such privacy
That he might see her beauty unespied,
And win perhaps that night a peerless bride,
While legioned faeries paced the coverlet,
And pale enchantment held her sleepy-eyed.
Never on such a night have lovers met,
Since Merlin paid his Demon all the monstrous debt.

XX

"It shall be as thou wishest," said the Dame:
"All cates and dainties shall be storèd there
Quickly on this feast-night: by the tambour frame
Her own lute thou wilt see: no time to spare,
For I am slow and feeble, and scarce dare
On such a catering trust my dizzy head.
Wait here, my child, with patience; kneel in prayer
The while: Ah! thou must needs the lady wed,
Or may I never leave my grave among the dead."

XXI

So saying, she hobbled off with busy fear.
The lover's endless minutes slowly passed;
The dame returned, and whispered in his ear
To follow her; with agéd eyes aghast
From fright of dim espial. Safe at last,
Through many a dusky gallery, they gain
The maiden's chamber, silken, hushed, and chaste;
Where Porphyro took covert, pleased amain.
His poor guide hurried back with agues in her brain.

XXII

Her faltering hand upon the balustrade,
Old Angela was feeling for the stair,
When Madeline, St. Agnes' charmèd maid,
Rose, like a missioned spirit, unaware:
With silver taper's light, and pious care,
She turned, and down the agéd gossip led
To a safe level matting. Now prepare,
Young Porphyro, for gazing on that bed;
She comes, she comes again, like ring dove frayed and fled.

XXIII

Out went the taper as she hurried in;
Its little smoke, in pallid moonshine, died:
She closed the door, she panted, all akin
To spirits of the air, and visions wide:
No uttered syllable, or, woe betide!
But to her heart, her heart was voluble,
Paining with eloquence her balmy side;
As though a tongueless nightingale should swell
Her throat in vain, and die, heart-stifled, in her dell.

XXIV

A casement high and triple-arched there was,
All garlanded with carven imag'ries
Of fruits, and flowers, and bunches of knot-grass,
And diamonded with panes of quaint device,
Innumerable of stains and splendid dyes,
As are the tiger-moth's deep-damasked wings;
And in the midst, 'mong thousand heraldries,
And twilight saints, and dim emblazonings,
A shielded scutcheon blushed with blood of queens and kings.

XXV

Full on this casement shone the wintry moon,
And threw warm gules on Madeline's fair breast,
As down she knelt for heaven's grace and boon;
Rose-bloom fell on her hands, together pressed,
And on her silver cross soft amethyst,
And on her hair a glory, like a saint:
She seemed a splendid angel, newly dressed,
Save wings, for heaven — Porphyro grew faint:
She knelt, so pure a thing, so free from mortal taint.

XXVI

Anon his heart revives: her vespers done,
Of all its wreathèd pearls her hair she frees;
Unclasps her warmèd jewels one by one;
Loosens her fragrant bodice; by degrees
Her rich attire creeps rustling to her knees:
Half-hidden, like a mermaid in sea-weed,
Pensive awhile she dreams awake, and sees,
In fancy, fair St. Agnes in her bed,
But dares not look behind, or all the charm is fled.

XXVII

Soon, trembling in her soft and chilly nest,
In sort of wakeful swoon, perplexed she lay,
Until the poppied warmth of sleep oppressed
Her soothèd limbs, and soul fatigued away;
Flown, like a thought, until the morrow-day;
Blissfully havened both from joy and pain;
Clasped like a missal where swart Paynims pray;
Blinded alike from sunshine and from rain,
As though a rose should shut, and be a bud again.

XXVIII

Stol'n to this paradise, and so entranced,
Porphyro gazed upon her empty dress,
And listened to her breathing, if it chanced
To wake into a slumberous tenderness;
Which when he heard, that minute did he bless,
And breathed himself: then from the closet crept,
Noiseless as fear in a wide wilderness,
And over the hushed carpet, silent, stepped,
And 'tween the curtains peeped, where, lo!—how fast she slept.

XXIX

Then by the bedside, where the faded moon
Made a dim, silver twilight, soft he set
A table, and, half anguished, threw thereon
A cloth of woven crimson, gold, and jet—
O for some drowsy Morphean amulet!
The boisterous, midnight, festive clarion,
The kettledrum, and far-heard clarinet,
Affray his ears, though but in dying tone—
The hall door shuts again, and all the noise is gone.

XXX

And still she slept an azure-lidded sleep,
In blanchèd linen, smooth, and lavendered,
While he from forth the closet brought a heap
Of candied apple, quince, and plum, and gourd;
With jellies soother than the creamy curd,
And lucent syrups, tinct with cinnamon;
Manna and dates, in argosy transferred
From Fez; and spicéd dainties, every one,
From silken Samarcand to cedared Lebanon.

XXXI

These delicates he heaped with glowing hand
On golden dishes and in baskets bright
Of wreathéd silver: sumptuous they stand
In the retired quiet of the night,
Filling the chilly room with perfume light.
"And now, my love, my seraph fair, awake!
Thou art my heaven, and I thine eremite:
Open thine eyes, for meek St. Agnes' sake,
Or I shall drowse beside thee, so my soul doth ache."

XXXII

Thus whispering, his warm, unnervèd arm
Sank in her pillow. Shaded was her dream
By the dusk curtains:—'twas a midnight charm
Impossible to melt as iced stream:
The lustrous salvers in the moonlight gleam;
Broad golden fringe upon the carpet lies:
It seemed he never, never could redeem
From such a steadfast spell his lady's eyes;
So mused awhile, entoiled in woofèd fantasies.

XXXIII

Awakening up, he took her hollow lute—
Tumultuous—and, in chords that tenderest be,
He played an ancient ditty, long since mute,
In Provence called, "La belle dame sans merci":
Close to her ear touching the melody—
Wherewith disturbed, she uttered a soft moan:
He ceased—she panted quick—and suddenly
Her blue affrayèd eyes wide open shone:
Upon his knees he sank, pale as smooth-sculptured stone.

XXXIV

Her eyes were open, but she still beheld,
Now wide awake, the vision of her sleep:
There was a painful change, that nigh expelled
The blisses of her dream so pure and deep,

At which fair Madeline began to weep,
And moan forth witless words with many a sigh;
While still her gaze on Porphyro would keep;
Who knelt, with joinèd hands and piteous eye,
Fearing to move or speak, she looked so dreamingly.

XXXV

"Ah, Porphyro!" said she, "but even now
Thy voice was at sweet tremble in mine ear,
Made tunable with every sweetest vow;
And those sad eyes were spiritual and clear:
How changed thou art! how pallid, chill, and drear!
Give me that voice again, my Porphyro,
Those looks immortal, those complainings dear!
Oh leave me not in this eternal woe,
For if thou diest, my Love, I know not where to go."

XXXVI

Beyond a mortal man impassioned far
At these voluptuous accents, he arose,
Ethereal, flushed, and like a throbbing star
Seen 'mid the sapphire heaven's deep repose
Into her dream he melted, as the rose
Blendeth its odor with the violet —
Solution sweet: meantime the frost-wind blows
Like Love's alarum pattering the sharp sleet
Against the windowpanes; St. Agnes' moon hath set.

XXXVII

'Tis dark: quick pattereth the flaw-blown sleet:
"This is no dream, my bride, my Madeline!"
'Tis dark: the icèd gusts still rave and beat:
"No dream, alas! alas! and woe is mine!
Porphyro will leave me here to fade and pine, —
Cruel! what traitor could thee hither bring?
I curse not, for my heart is lost in thine,
Though thou forsakest a deceivèd thing; —
A dove forlorn and lost with sick unpruned wing."

XXXVIII

"My Madeline! sweet dreamer! lovely bride!
Say, may I be for aye thy vassal blest?
Thy beauty's shield, heart-shaped and vermeil dyed?
Ah, silver shrine, here will I take my rest
After so many hours of toil and quest,
A famished pilgrim—saved by miracle.
Though I have found, I will not rob thy nest
Saving of thy sweet self; if thou think'st well
To trust, fair Madeline, to no rude infidel.

XXXIX

"Hark! 'tis an elfin-storm from faery land,
Of haggard seeming, but a boon indeed:
Arise—arise! the morning is at hand;—
The bloated wassaillers will never heed;—
Let us away, my love, with happy speed;
There are no ears to hear, or eyes to see,—
Drowned all in Rhenish and the sleepy mead:
Awake! arise! my love, and fearless be,
For o'er the southern moors I have a home for thee."

XL

She hurried at his words, beset with fears,
For there were sleeping dragons all around,
At glaring watch, perhaps, with ready spears—
Down the wide stairs a darkling way they found.—
In all the house was heard no human sound.
A chain-drooped lamp was flickering by each door;
The arras, rich with horseman, hawk, and hound,
Fluttered in the besieging wind's uproar;
And the long carpets rose along the gusty floor.

XLI

They glide, like phantoms, into the wide hall;
Like phantoms, to the iron porch, they glide;
Where lay the Porter, in uneasy sprawl,
With a huge empty flagon by his side:
The wakeful bloodhound rose, and shook his hide,
But his sagacious eye an inmate owns:
By one, and one, the bolts full easy slide:—
The chains lie silent on the footworn stones;—
The key turns, and the door upon its hinges groans.

XLII

And they are gone: ay, ages long ago
These lovers fled away into the storm.
That night the Baron dreamt of many a woe,
And all his warrior-guests, with shade and form
Of witch, and demon, and large coffin-worm,
Were long be-nightmared. Angela the old
Died palsy-twitched, with meager face deform;
The Beadsman, after thousand ave's told,
For aye unsought for slept among his ashes cold.

Keats's first poem was an "Imitation of Spenser" in the complex nine-line Spenserian stanza that, after 200 years of disuse, found favor with Byron (see "The Ocean," p. 486, and "There Was a Sound of Revelry by Night," p. 489) and Shelley (see "Adonais," p. 509). The romantic story is based on the legend that, on St. Agnes' Eve (January 20), a maiden can obtain a vision of her husband-to-be by performing certain rituals. The legend and the winter setting gave Keats a chance to experiment with many kinds of sensuous poetry, both in verbal devices and in sound effects. The thirtieth stanza is justly celebrated for its unusual gustatory and tactile appeals. There is also a measure of verbal humor, as in the line "Out went the taper as she hurried in."

Bright Star

Bright star, would I were steadfast as thou art—
Not in lone splendor hung aloft the night,
And watching, with eternal lids apart,
Like nature's patient sleepless Eremite,
The moving waters at their priestlike task
Of pure ablution round earth's human shores,
Or gazing on the new soft fallen mask
Of snow upon the mountains and the moors:
No—yet still steadfast, still unchangeable,
Pillowed upon my fair love's ripening breast
To feel for ever its soft fall and swell,
Awake for ever in a sweet unrest;
Still, still to hear her tender-taken breath,
And so live ever—or else swoon to death.

Keats began this sonnet in 1819 and later, not long before his death, copied a version in a volume of Shakespeare's poems. The "fair love" is Fanny Brawne.

Ode to Psyche

✕✕✕✕✕

O Goddess! hear these tuneless numbers, wrung
  By sweet enforcement and remembrance dear,
And pardon that thy secrets should be sung
  Even into thine own soft-conchèd ear:
Surely I dreamed today, or did I see
  The wingèd Psyche with awakened eyes?
I wandered in a forest thoughtlessly,
  And, on the sudden, fainting with surprise,
Saw two fair creatures, couchèd side by side
    In deepest grass, beneath the whispering roof
    Of leaves and trembled blossoms, where there ran
      A brooklet, scarce espied:
'Mid hushed, cool-rooted flowers fragrant-eyed,
  Blue, silver-white, and budded Tyrian.
They lay calm-breathing on the bedded grass;
    Their arms embracèd, and their pinions too;
    Their lips touched not, but had not bade adieu,
As if disjoinèd by soft-handed slumber,
And ready still past kisses to outnumber
    At tender eye-dawn of aurorean love:
      The wingèd boy I knew
    But who wast thou, O happy, happy dove?
      His Psyche true!

O latest-born and loveliest vision far
  Of all Olympus' faded hierarchy!
Fairer than Phoebe's sapphire-regioned star,
  Or Vesper, amorous glow-worm of the sky;
Fairer than these, though temple thou hast none,
    Nor altar heaped with flowers;
Nor Virgin choir to make delicious moan
    Upon the midnight hours;
No voice, no lute, no pipe, no incense sweet
  From chain-swung censer teeming;
No shrine, no grove, no oracle, no heat
  Of pale-mouthed prophet dreaming.

O brightest! though too late for antique vows,
  Too, too late for the fond believing lyre,
When holy were the haunted forest boughs,
  Holy the air, the water, and the fire;
Yet even in these days so far retired
    From happy pieties, thy lucent fans,
    Fluttering among the faint Olympians,
I see, and sing, by my own eyes inspired.
So let me be thy choir, and make a moan
    Upon the midnight hours;
Thy voice, thy lute, thy pipe, thy incense sweet
  From swinged censer teeming:
Thy shrine, thy grove, thy oracle, thy heat
  Of pale-mouthed prophet dreaming.

Yes, I will be thy priest, and build a fane
   In some untrodden region of my mind,
Where branchèd thoughts, new grown with pleasant pain
   Instead of pines shall murmur in the wind:
Far, far around shall those dark-clustered trees
   Fledge the wild-ridgèd mountains steep by steep;
And there by zephyrs, streams, and birds, and bees,
   The moss-lain Dryads shall be lulled to sleep;
And in the midst of this wide quietness
A rosy sanctuary will I dress
With the wreathed trellis of a working brain,
   With buds, and bells, and stars without a name,
With all the gardener Fancy e'er could feign,
   Who, breeding flowers, will never breed the same;
And there shall be for thee all soft delight
    That shadowy thought can win,
A bright torch, and a casement ope at night,
    To let the warm Love in!

Keats wrote five great odes in April and May 1819. Of this one, the first to be finished, he wrote in a letter to his sister and brother: "The following Poem—the last I have written is the first and the only one with which I have taken even moderate pains . . . . You must recollect that Psyche was not embodied as a goddess before the time of Apuleius the Platonist who lived after the Augustan age, and consequently the Goddess was never worshipped or sacrificed to with any of the ancient fervour . . . ."

Like Edgar Allan Poe and others of their generation,
Hood was a magazine writer; he also served as editor of
a succession of periodicals, including one called *Hood's
Magazine*. He is known for humorous verse and satire.
His son, who is called "Tom" Hood, carried on the
tradition with undiminished vigor.

I Remember, I Remember

I remember, I remember,
The house where I was born,
The little window where the sun
Came peeping in at morn;
He never came a wink too soon,
Nor brought too long a day,
But now, I often wish the night
Had borne my breath away!

I remember, I remember,
The roses, red and white,
The violets, and the lily-cups,
Those flowers made of light!
The lilacs where the robin built,
And where my brother set
The laburnum on his birthday, —
The tree is living yet!

I remember, I remember,
Where I was used to swing,
And thought the air must rush as fresh
To swallows on the wing;
My spirit flew in feathers then,
That is so heavy now,
And summer pools could hardly cool
The fever on my brow!

I remember, I remember
The fir trees dark and high;
I used to think their slender tops
Were close against the sky;
It was a childish ignorance,
But now 'tis little joy
To know I'm farther off from Heaven
Than when I was a boy.

After the unrelenting thunderstorms of the early-nineteenth-century Romantics, the more temperate weather of such minor Victorians as Hood can come as a pleasant relief.

It was only after his suicide that Beddoes's best-remembered work, the play called *Death's Jest-Book, or The Fool's Tragedy*, appeared. It was Elizabethan in style, including such incidental lyrics as "Old Adam, the Carrion Crow."

Old Adam, the Carrion Crow

()◄═══► ()

Old Adam, the carrion crow,
  The old crow of Cairo;
He sat in the shower, and let it flow
Under his tail and over his crest;
    And through every feather
    Leaked the wet weather;
And the bough swung under his nest;
For his beak it was heavy with marrow.
  Is that the wind dying? O no;
  It's only two devils, that blow
  Through a murderer's bones, to and fro,
    In the ghosts' moonshine.

Ho! Eve, my grey carrion wife,
   When we have supped on king's marrow,
Where shall we drink and make merry our life?
   Our nest it is queen Cleopatra's skull,
      'Tis cloven and cracked,
      And battered and hacked,
But with tears of blue eyes it is full:
Let us drink then, my raven of Cairo.
   Is that the wind dying? O no;
   It's only two devils, that blow
Through a murderer's bones, to and fro,
   In the ghosts' moonshine.

from Death's Jest Book

Ezra Pound called Beddoes "Prince of morticians." In this lyric, the theme (seen earlier in "The Three Ravens," p. 26) is varied with an idiom that one must call macabre *(a term it is hard to avoid when one is talking about Beddoes). The repeated "Is that the wind dying?" is echoed in the second part of T. S. Eliot's "Waste Land" (p. 968).*

Emerson spent most of his long life in Massachusetts, where he was born. He was a schoolmaster and Unitarian pastor but from about the age of thirty earned his living as an essayist and lecturer. Although his poetry is respected, his fame rests much more on his peculiarly American labors as a thinker. It is to his credit that he was among the first to recognize the genius of Whitman.

Concord Hymn

Sung at the Completion of the Battle Monument, July 4, 1837

By the rude bridge that arched the flood,
  Their flag to April's breeze unfurled,
Here once the embattled farmers stood
  And fired the shot heard round the world.

The foe long since in silence slept;
  Alike the conqueror silent sleeps;
And Time the ruined bridge has swept
  Down the dark stream which seaward creeps.

On this green bank, by this soft stream,
  We set to-day a votive stone;
That memory may their deed redeem,
  When, like our sires, our sons are gone.

Spirit, that made those heroes dare
  To die, and leave their children free,
Bid Time and Nature gently spare
  The shaft we raise to them and thee.

This hymn, not at all typical of Emerson's work in prose or verse, seems to survive in spite of itself, an occasional poem that has so outlived its occasion that many readers will not know which Concord is involved, or why. Even more will not be able to remember any of the stanzas beyond the first, on which rests all of the poem's fame.

The Snow-Storm

◆◇◆◇

Announced by all the trumpets of the sky,
Arrives the snow, and, driving o'er the fields,
Seems nowhere to alight: the whited air
Hides hills and woods, the river, and the heaven,
And veils the farm-house at the garden's end.
The sled and traveller stopped, the courier's feet
Delayed, all friends shut out, the housemates sit
Around the radiant fireplace, enclosed
In a tumultuous privacy of storm.

Come see the north wind's masonry.
Out of an unseen quarry evermore
Furnished with tile, the fierce artificer
Curves his white bastions with projected roof
Round every windward stake, or tree, or door.
Speeding, the myriad-handed, his wild work
So fanciful, so savage, nought cares he
For number or proportion. Mockingly,
On coop or kennel he hangs Parian wreaths;
A swan-like form invests the hidden thorn;
Fills up the farmer's lane from wall to wall,
Maugre the farmer's sighs; and at the gate
A tapering turret overtops the work.
And when his hours are numbered, and the world
Is all his own, retiring, as he were not,
Leaves, when the sun appears, astonished Art
To mimic in slow structures, stone by stone,
Built in an age, the mad wind's night-work,
The frolic architecture of the snow.

Emerson was steeped in humanity and humaneness, but in this poem, once he removed our species from the scene, he can appreciate that, in a few winter hours, nature can project both superhuman grandeur and uncanny frivolity.

The Rhodora

On Being Asked, Whence is The Flower?

In May, when sea-winds pierced our solitudes,
I found the fresh Rhodora in the woods,
Spreading its leafless blooms in a damp nook,
To please the desert and the sluggish brook.
The purple petals, fallen in the pool,
Made the black water with their beauty gay;
Here might the red-bird come his plumes to cool,
And court the flower that cheapens his array.
Rhodora! if the sages ask thee why
This charm is wasted on the earth and sky,
Tell them, dear, that if eyes were made for seeing,
Then Beauty is its own excuse for being:
Why thou wert there, O rival of the rose!
I never thought to ask, I never knew:
But, in my simple ignorance, suppose
The self-same Power that brought me there brought you.

Gray's "Elegy Written in a Country Churchyard" (p. 327) seems to accept the fact that "Full many a flower is born to blush unseen, / And waste its sweetness on the desert air." The sentiment that "Beauty is its own excuse for being" was comforting enough to serve as a motto of the Art-for-Art's-Sake movement late in the nineteenth century—to say nothing of the emblematic Ars Gratia Artis *of such an un-Emersonian institution as the leonine Metro-Goldwyn-Mayer Studios.*

Brahma

If the red slayer think he slays,
    Or if the slain think he is slain,
They know not well the subtle ways
    I keep, and pass, and turn again.

Far or forgot to me is near;
    Shadow and sunlight are the same;
The vanish'd gods to me appear;
    And one to me are shame and fame.

They reckon ill who leave me out;
    When me they fly, I am the wings;
I am the doubter and the doubt,
    And I the hymn the Brahmin sings.

The strong gods pine for my abode,
    And pine in vain the sacred Seven;
But thou, meek lover of the good!
    Find me, and turn thy back on heaven.

These mystical paradoxes represent Emerson's version of certain principles of Hinduism, in which Brahma is the supreme divinity. Emerson's immediate source was the Vishnu Purana, *but much the same doctrine can be found in the* Bhagavad-Gita *(and also in "The Dry Salvages" in T. S. Eliot's* Four Quartets*).*

Fable

The mountain and the squirrel
Had a quarrel,
And the former called the latter " Little Prig";
Bun replied,
"You are doubtless very big;
But all sorts of things and weather
Must be taken in together,
To make up a year
And a sphere.
And I think it no disgrace
To occupy my place.
If I'm not so large as you,
You are not so small as I,
And not half so spry.
I'll not deny you make
A very pretty squirrel track;
Talents differ; all is well and wisely put;
If I cannot carry forests on my back,
Neither can you crack a nut."

It takes a very special kind of imagination to conceive of a mountain that calls a squirrel "Little Prig," but Emerson possessed just such imagination and magnanimity.

Days

Daughters of Time, the hypocritic Days,
Muffled and dumb like barefoot dervishes,
And marching single in an endless file,
Bring diadems and fagots in their hands.
To each they offer gifts after his will,
Bread, kingdoms, stars, and sky that holds them all.
I, in my pleached garden, watched the pomp,
Forgot my morning wishes, hastily
Took a few herbs and apples, and the Day
Turned and departed silent. I, too late,
Under her solemn fillet saw the scorn.

Emerson proudly cultivated the American style of talking about dervishes, diadems, and apples in the same breath.

ELIZABETH BARRETT BROWNING 1806–1861

When she was about thirty-two years old, Elizabeth Barrett Browning was seriously ill and remained an invalid for some years. In spite of the overprotection of a forbidding father, she became secretly engaged to Robert Browning and married him in 1846, when she was forty. They are the only married couple among the many poets in this anthology.

How Do I Love Thee? Let Me Count the Ways

How do I love thee? Let me count the ways.
I love thee to the depth and breadth and height
My soul can reach, when feeling out of sight
For the ends of Being and ideal Grace.
I love thee to the level of every day's
Most quiet need; by sun and candle-light.
I love thee freely, as men strive for Right;
I love thee purely, as they turn from Praise.
I love thee with the passion put to use
In my old griefs, and with my childhood's faith.
I love thee with a love I seemed to lose
With my lost saints, — I love thee with the breath,
Smiles, tears, of all my life! — and, if God choose,
I shall but love thee better after death.

Sonnet XLII
from Sonnets from the Portuguese

At first, Elizabeth Barrett Browning called her love poems "Sonnets Translated from the Bosnian," changing the title later to Sonnets from the Portuguese, *as though to camouflage intensely personal poems as translations. It is possible that Robert Browning, knowing her earlier poem "Catarina to Camoëns" about famous Portuguese literary lovers, called her "the Portuguese."*

HENRY WADSWORTH LONGFELLOW 1807–1882

Longfellow was a great teacher in two senses: he was an innovator in the teaching of modern languages at Harvard, and he graciously submitted his art to what he perceived to be the duty of poetry—to deliver academic and moral lessons. He was probably the greatest and most effective didactic poet ever to write in the United States; people who know almost no other poems will know "Listen, my children, and you shall hear. . . ." Longfellow is also notable as an innovator in developing a long unrhymed measure that was *not* blank verse; he wrote two fine long poems in unrhymed dactylic hexameter (*Evangeline* and *The Courtship of Miles Standish*) and an unforgettable epic in unrhymed trochaic tetrameter (*The Song of Hiawatha*).

My Lost Youth

Often I think of the beautiful town
　　That is seated by the sea;
Often in thought go up and down
The pleasant streets of that dear old town,
　　And my youth comes back to me.
　　　And a verse of a Lapland song
　　　Is haunting my memory still:
"A boy's will is the wind's will,
And the thoughts of youth are long, long thoughts."

I can see the shadowy lines of its trees,
  And catch, in sudden gleams,
The sheen of the far-surrounding seas,
And islands that were the Hesperides
  Of all my boyish dreams.
    And the burden of that old song,
    It murmurs and whispers still:
  "A boy's will is the wind's will,
And the thoughts of youth are long, long thoughts."

I remember the black wharves and the slips,
  And the sea-tides tossing free;
And Spanish sailors with bearded lips,
And the beauty and mystery of the ships,
  And the magic of the sea.
    And the voice of that wayward song
    Is singing and saying still:
  "A boy's will is the wind's will,
And the thoughts of youth are long, long thoughts."

I remember the bulwarks by the shore,
  And the fort upon the hill;
The sun-rise gun, with its hollow roar,
The drum-beat repeated o'er and o'er,
  And the bugle wild and shrill.
    And the music of that old song
    Throbs in my memory still:
  "A boy's will is the wind's will,
And the thoughts of youth are long, long thoughts."

I remember the sea-fight far away,
How it thundered o'er the tide!
And the dead captains, as they lay
In their graves, o'erlooking the tranquil bay,
Where they in battle died.
And the sound of that mournful song
Goes through me with a thrill:
"A boy's will is the wind's will,
And the thoughts of youth are long, long thoughts."

I can see the breezy dome of groves,
The shadows of Deering's Woods;
And the friendships old and the early loves
Come back with a Sabbath sound, as of doves
In quiet neighborhoods.
And the verse of that sweet old song,
It flutters and murmurs still:
"A boy's will is the wind's will,
And the thoughts of youth are long, long thoughts."

I remember the gleams and glooms that dart
Across the schoolboy's brain;
The song and the silence in the heart,
That in part are prophecies, and in part
Are longings wild and vain.
And the voice of that fitful song
Sings on, and is never still:
"A boy's will is the wind's will,
And the thoughts of youth are long, long thoughts."

There are things of which I may not speak;
 There are dreams that cannot die;
There are thoughts that make the strong heart weak,
And bring a pallor into the cheek,
 And a mist before the eye.
  And the words of that fatal song
  Come over me like a chill:
 "A boy's will is the wind's will,
And the thoughts of youth are long, long thoughts."

Strange to me now are the forms I meet
 When I visit the dear old town;
But the native air is pure and sweet,
And the trees that o'ershadow each well-known street,
 As they balance up and down,
  Are singing the beautiful song,
  Are sighing and whispering still:
 "A boy's will is the wind's will,
And the thoughts of youth are long, long thoughts."

And Deering's Woods are fresh and fair,
 And with joy that is almost pain
My heart goes back to wander there,
And among the dreams of the days that were,
 I find my lost youth again.
  And the strange and beautiful song,
  The groves are repeating it still:
 "A boy's will is the wind's will,
And the thoughts of youth are long, long thoughts."

Longfellow's language still lives in the title of Robert Frost's first book, A Boy's Will *(1913); and "The Pasture," which opens Frost's volume, follows the unusual abbc rhyme scheme of Longfellow's refrain.*

Paul Revere's Ride

Listen, my children, and you shall hear
Of the midnight ride of Paul Revere,
On the eighteenth of April, in Seventy-five;
Hardly a man is now alive
Who remembers that famous day and year.

He said to his friend, "If the British march
By land or sea from the town tonight,
Hang a lantern aloft in the belfry arch
Of the North Church tower as a signal light,—
One, if by land, and two, if by sea;
And I on the opposite shore will be,
Ready to ride and spread the alarm
Through every Middlesex village and farm,
For the country folk to be up and to arm."

Then he said, "Good night!" and with muffled oar
Silently rowed to the Charlestown shore,
Just as the moon rose over the bay,
Where swinging wide at her moorings lay
The *Somerset*, British man-of-war;
A phantom ship, with each mast and spar
Across the moon like a prison bar,
And a huge black hulk, that was magnified
By its own reflection in the tide.

Meanwhile, his friend through alley and street
Wanders and watches, with eager ears,
Till in the silence around him he hears
The muster of men at the barrack door,
The sound of arms, and the tramp of feet,
And the measured tread of the grenadiers,
Marching down to their boats on the shore.

Then he climbed the tower of the Old North Church,
By the wooden stairs, with stealthy tread,
To the belfry-chamber overhead,
And startled the pigeons from their perch
On the sombre rafters, that round him made
Masses and moving shapes of shade, —
By the trembling ladder, steep and tall,
To the highest window in the wall,
Where he paused to listen and look down
A moment on the roofs of the town
And the moonlight flowing over all.

Beneath, in the churchyard, lay the dead,
In their night-encampment on the hill,
Wrapped in silence so deep and still
That he could hear, like a sentinel's tread,
The watchful night-wind, as it went
Creeping along from tent to tent,
And seeming to whisper, "All is well!"
A moment only he feels the spell
Of the place and the hour, and the secret dread
Of the lonely belfry and the dead;
For suddenly all his thoughts are bent
On a shadowy something far away,
Where the river widens to meet the bay, —
A line of black that bends and floats
On the rising tide, like a bridge of boats.

Meanwhile, impatient to mount and ride,
Booted and spurred, with a heavy stride
On the opposite shore walked Paul Revere.
Now he patted his horse's side,
Now gazed at the landscape far and near,
Then, impetuous, stamped the earth,
And turned and tightened his saddle girth;
But mostly he watched with eager search
The belfry's tower of the Old North Church,
As it rose above the graves on the hill,

Lonely and spectral and sombre and still.
And lo! as he looks, on the belfry height
A glimmer, and then a gleam of light!
He springs to the saddle, the bridle he turns,
But lingers and gazes, till full on his sight
A second lamp in the belfry burns!

A hurry of hoofs in a village street,
A shape in the moonlight, a bulk in the dark,
And beneath, from the pebbles, in passing, a spark
Struck out by a steed flying fearless and fleet;
That was all! And yet, through the gloom and the light,
The fate of a nation was riding that night;
And the spark struck out by that steed, in his flight,
Kindled the land into flame with its heat.
He has left the village and mounted the steep,
And beneath him, tranquil and broad and deep,
Is the Mystic, meeting the ocean tides;
And under the alders that skirt its edge,
Now soft on the sand, now loud on the ledge,
Is heard the tramp of his steed as he rides.

It was twelve by the village clock,
When he crossed the bridge into Medford town.
He heard the crowing of the cock,
And the barking of the farmer's dog,
And he felt the damp of the river fog,
That rises after the sun goes down.

It was one by the village clock,
When he galloped into Lexington.
He saw the gilded weathercock
Swim in the moonlight as he passed,
And the meeting-house windows, blank and bare,
Gaze at him with a spectral glare,
As if they already stood aghast
At the bloody work they would look upon.

It was two by the village clock,
When he came to the bridge in Concord town.
He heard the bleating of the flock,
And the twitter of birds among the trees,
And felt the breath of the morning breeze
Blowing over the meadows brown.
And one was safe and asleep in his bed
Who at the bridge would be first to fall,
Who that day would be lying dead,
Pierced by a British musket-ball.

You know the rest. In books you have read,
How the British Regulars fired and fled, —
How the farmers gave them ball for ball,
From behind each fence and farmyard wall,
Chasing the redcoats down the lane,
Then crossing the fields to emerge again
Under the trees at the turn of the road,
And only pausing to fire and load.
So through the night rode Paul Revere;
And so through the night went his cry of alarm
To every Middlesex village and farm, —
A cry of defiance, and not of fear,
A voice in the darkness, a knock at the door,
And a word that shall echo for evermore!
For, borne on the night-wind of the Past,
Through all our history, to the last,
In the hour of darkness and peril and need,
The people will waken and listen to hear
The hurrying hoof-beats of that steed,
And the midnight message of Paul Revere.

from Tales of a Wayside Inn

Even now, more than a century after Longfellow's death, much of what many Americans think they know about certain episodes and personages of their own country's history—Miles Standish, the Acadians in Canada and Louisiana, Paul Revere, Native American lore and language—comes from Longfellow's memorable verses. Revere's ride took place on the night before the battle commemorated in Emerson's "Concord Hymn" (p. 573).

Chaucer

An old man in a lodge within a park;
The chamber walls depicted all around
With portraitures of huntsman, hawk, and hound,
And the hurt deer. He listeneth to the lark,
Whose song comes with the sunshine through the dark
Of painted glass in leaden lattice bound;
He listeneth and he laugheth at the sound,
Then writeth in a book like any clerk.
He is the poet of the dawn, who wrote
The Canterbury Tales and his old age
Made beautiful with song; and as I read
I hear the crowing cock, I hear the note
Of lark and linnet, and from every page
Rise odors of ploughed field or flowery mead.

Longfellow wrote rather educational sonnets on a number of great English poets, but they are much better poems than "educational" may suggest. Longfellow was one of the greatest American sonnet-writers of the nineteenth century.

Whittier was an ardent Quaker and Abolitionist. His first master and exemplar was Burns, whose manner he imitated. Later he wrote vigorous political poetry of a propagandistic sort. From the end of the Civil War until his death, Whittier concentrated on the rural scene. He wrote the words of the familiar hymn "Dear Lord and Father of Mankind."

Barbara Frietchie

Up from the meadows rich with corn,
Clear in the cool September morn,

The clustered spires of Frederick stand
Green-walled by the hills of Maryland.

Round about them orchards sweep,
Apple and peach tree fruited deep,

Fair as the garden of the Lord
To the eyes of the famished rebel horde,

On that pleasant morn of the early fall
When Lee marched over the mountain-wall;

Over the mountains winding down,
Horse and foot, into Frederick town.

Forty flags with their silver stars,
Forty flags with their crimson bars,

Flapped in the morning wind: the sun
Of noon looked down, and saw not one.

Up rose old Barbara Frietchie then,
Bowed with her fourscore years and ten;

Bravest of all in Frederick town,
She took up the flag the men hauled down;

In her attic window the staff she set,
To show that one heart was loyal yet.

Up the street came the rebel tread,
Stonewall Jackson riding ahead.

Under his slouched hat left and right
He glanced; the old flag met his sight.

"Halt!"—the dust-brown ranks stood fast.
"Fire!"—out blazed the rifle-blast.

It shivered the window, pane and sash;
It rent the banner with seam and gash.

Quick, as it fell, from the broken staff
Dame Barbara snatched the silken scarf.

She leaned far out on the window-sill,
And shook it forth with a royal will.

"Shoot, if you must, this old gray head,
But spare your country's flag," she said.

A shade of sadness, a blush of shame,
Over the face of the leader came;

The nobler nature within him stirred
To life at that woman's deed and word;

"Who touches a hair of yon gray head
Dies like a dog! March on!" he said

All day long through Frederick street
Sounded the tread of marching feet:

All day long that free flag tossed
Over the heads of the rebel host.

Ever its torn folds rose and fell
On the loyal winds that loved it well;

And through the hill-gaps sunset light
Shone over it with a warm good-night.

Barbara Frietchie's work is o'er,
And the Rebel rides on his raids no more.

Honor to her! and let a tear
Fall, for her sake, on Stonewall's bier.

Over Barbara Frietchie's grave,
Flag of Freedom and Union, wave!

Peace and order and beauty draw
Round thy symbol of light and law;

And ever the stars above look down
On thy stars below in Frederick town!

---

*By the time Whittier's poem was published in 1864, General Jackson was dead.
He was shot by his own men by mistake on May 3, 1863, and died a week later.
At thirty-nine, he was less than half Barbara Frietchie's age when she died, aged
ninety.*

Snow-Bound; A Winter Idyl

>>>>>>>

The sun that brief December day
Rose cheerless over hills of gray,
And, darkly circled, gave at noon
A sadder light than waning moon.
Slow tracing down the thickening sky
Its mute and ominous prophecy,
A portent seeming less than threat,
It sank from sight before it set.
A chill no coat, however stout,
Of homespun stuff could quite shut out,
A hard, dull bitterness of cold,
That checked, mid-vein, the circling race
Of life-blood in the sharpened face,
The coming of the snow-storm told.
The wind blew east; we heard the roar
Of Ocean on his wintry shore,
And felt the strong pulse throbbing there
Beat with low rhythm our inland air.

Meanwhile we did our nightly chores, —
Brought in the wood from out of doors,
Littered the stalls, and from the mows
Raked down the herd's-grass for the cows:
Heard the horse whinnying for his corn;
And, sharply clashing horn on horn,
Impatient down the stanchion rows
The cattle shake their walnut bows;
While, peering from his early perch
Upon the scaffold's pole of birch,
The cock his crested helmet bent
And down his querulous challenge sent.

Unwarmed by any sunset light
The gray day darkened into night,
A night made hoary with the swarm
And whirl-dance of the blinding storm,
As zigzag, wavering to and fro,
Crossed and recrossed the wingëd snow:
And ere the early bedtime came
The white drift piled the window-frame,
And through the glass the clothes-line posts
Looked in like tall and sheeted ghosts.

So all night long the storm roared on:
The morning broke without a sun;
In tiny spherule traced with lines
Of Nature's geometric signs,
In starry flake, and pellicle,
All day the hoary meteor fell;
And, when the second morning shone,
We looked upon a world unknown,
On nothing we could call our own.
Around the glistening wonder bent
The blue walls of the firmament,
No cloud above, no earth below, —
A universe of sky and snow!
The old familiar sights of ours
Took marvellous shapes; strange domes and towers
Rose up where sty or corn-crib stood,
Or garden-wall, or belt of wood;
A smooth white mound the brush-pile showed,
A fenceless drift what once was road;
The bridle-post an old man sat
With loose-flung coat and high cocked hat;
The well-curb had a Chinese roof;
And even the long sweep, high aloof,
In its slant splendor, seemed to tell
Of Pisa's leaning miracle.

A prompt, decisive man, no breath
Our father wasted: "Boys, a path!"
Well pleased, (for when did farmer boy
Count such a summons less than joy?)
Our buskins on our feet we drew;
With mittened hands, and caps drawn low,
To guard our necks and ears from snow,
We cut the solid whiteness through.
And, where the drift was deepest, made
A tunnel walled and overlaid
With dazzling crystal: we had read
Of rare Aladdin's wondrous cave,
And to our own his name we gave,
With many a wish the luck were ours
To test his lamp's supernal powers.
We reached the barn with merry din,
And roused the prisoned brutes within:
The old horse thrust his long head out,
And grave with wonder gazed about;
The cock his lusty greeting said,
And forth his speckled harem led;
The oxen lashed their tails, and hooked,
And mild reproach of hunger looked;
The hornëd patriarch of the sheep,
Like Egypt's Amun roused from sleep,
Shook his sage head with gesture mute,
And emphasized with stamp of foot.

All day the gusty north-wind bore
The loosening drift its breath before;
Low circling round its southern zone,
The sun through dazzling snow-mist shone.
No church-bell lent its Christian tone
To the savage air, no social smoke
Curled over woods of snow-hung oak.
A solitude made more intense
By dreary-voicëd elements,
The shrieking of the mindless wind,

The moaning tree-boughs swaying blind,
And on the glass the unmeaning beat
Of ghostly finger-tips of sleet.
Beyond the circle of our hearth
No welcome sound of toil or mirth
Unbound the spell, and testified
Of human life and thought outside.
We minded that the sharpest ear
The buried brooklet could not hear,
The music of whose liquid lip
Had been to us companionship,
And, in our lonely life, had grown
To have an almost human tone.

As night drew on, and, from the crest
Of wooded knolls that ridged the west,
The sun, a snow-blown traveller, sank
From sight beneath the smothering bank,
We piled, with care, our nightly stack
Of wood against the chimney-back, —
The oaken log, green, huge, and thick,
And on its top the stout back-stick;
The knotty forestick laid apart,
And filled between with curious art
The ragged brush; then, hovering near,
We watched the first red blaze appear,
Heard the sharp crackle, caught the gleam
On whitewashed wall and sagging beam,
Until the old, rude-furnished room
Burst, flower-like, into rosy bloom;
While radiant with a mimic flame
Outside the sparkling drift became,
And through the bare-boughed lilac-tree
Our own warm hearth seemed blazing free.
The crane and pendent trammels showed,
The Turks' heads on the andirons glowed;
While childish fancy, prompt to tell
The meaning of the miracle,

Whispered the old rhyme: *"Under the tree,*
When fire outdoors burns merrily,
There the witches are making tea."

The moon above the eastern wood
Shone at its full; the hill-range stood
Transfigured in the silver flood,
Its blown snows flashing cold and keen,
Dead white, save where some sharp ravine
Took shadow, or the sombre green
Of hemlocks turned to pitchy black
Against the whiteness at their back.
For such a world and such a night
Most fitting that unwarming light,
Which only seemed where'er it fell
To make the coldness visible.

Shut in from all the world without,
We sat the clean-winged hearth about,
Content to let the north-wind roar
In baffled rage at pane and door,
While the red logs before us beat
The frost-line back with tropic heat;
And ever, when a louder blast
Shook beam and rafter as it passed,
The merrier up its roaring draught
The great throat of the chimney laughed;
The house-dog on his paws outspread
Laid to the fire his drowsy head,
The cat's dark silhouette on the wall
A couchant tiger's seemed to fall;
And, for the winter fireside meet,
Between the andirons' straddling feet,
The mug of cider simmered slow,
The apples sputtered in a row,
And, close at hand, the basket stood
With nuts from brown October's wood.

What matter how the night behaved?
What matter how the north-wind raved?
Blow high, blow low, not all its snow
Could quench our hearth-fire's ruddy glow.
O Time and Change! — with hair as gray
As was my sire's that winter day,
How strange it seems, with so much gone
Of life and love, to still live on!
Ah, brother! only I and thou
Are left of all that circle now, —
The dear home faces whereupon
That fitful firelight paled and shone.
Henceforward, listen as we will,
The voices of that hearth are still;
Look where we may, the wide earth o'er,
Those lighted faces smile no more.
We tread the paths their feet have worn,
　　We sit beneath their orchard trees,
　　We hear, like them, the hum of bees
And rustle of the bladed corn;
We turn the pages that they read,
　　Their written words we linger o'er,
But in the sun they cast no shade,
No voice is heard, no sign is made,
　　No step is on the conscious floor!
Yet Love will dream, and Faith will trust,
(Since He who knows our need is just,)
That somehow, somewhere, meet we must.
Alas for him who never sees
The stars shine through his cypress-trees!
Who, hopeless, lays his dead away,
Nor looks to see the breaking day
Across the mournful marbles play!
Who hath not learned, in hours of faith,
　　The truth to flesh and sense unknown,
That Life is ever lord of Death,
　　And Love can never lose its own!

We sped the time with stories old,
Wrought puzzles out, and riddles told,
Or stammered from our school-book lore
"The Chief of Gambia's golden shore."
How often since, when all the land
Was clay in Slavery's shaping hand,
As if a far-blown trumpet stirred
The languorous sin-sick air, I heard:
"Does not the voice of reason cry,
  Claim the first right which Nature gave,
From the red scourge of bondage fly,
  Nor deign to live a burdened slave!"
Our father rode again his ride
On Memphremagog's wooded side;
Sat down again to moose and samp
In trapper's hut and Indian camp;
Lived o'er the old idyllic ease
Beneath St. Francois' hemlock-trees;
Again for him the moonlight shone
On Norman cap and bodiced zone;
Again he heard the violin play
Which led the village dance away.
And mingled in its merry whirl
The grandam and the laughing girl.
Or, nearer home, our steps he led
Where Salisbury's level marshes spread
  Mile-wide as flies the laden bee;
Where merry mowers, hale and strong,
Swept, scythe on scythe, their swaths along
  The low green prairies of the sea.
We share the fishing off Boar's Head,
  And round the rocky Isles of Shoals
  The hake-broil on the drift-wood coals;
The chowder on the sand-beach made,
Dipped by the hungry, steaming hot,
With spoons of clam-shell from the pot.
We heard the tales of witchcraft old,
And dream and sign and marvel told

To sleepy listeners as they lay
Stretched idly on the salted hay,
Adrift along the winding shores,
When favoring breezes deigned to blow
The square sail of the gundelow
And idle lay the useless oars.

Our mother, while she turned her wheel
Or run the new-knit stocking-heel,
Told how the Indian hordes came down
At midnight on Cocheco town,
And how her own great-uncle bore
His cruel scalp-mark to fourscore.
Recalling, in her fitting phrase,
  So rich and picturesque and free,
  (The common unrhymed poetry
Of simple life and country ways,)
The story of her early days, —
She made us welcome to her home;
Old hearths grew wide to give us room;
We stole with her a frightened look
At the gray wizard's conjuring-book,
The fame whereof went far and wide
Through all the simple country side;
We heard the hawks at twilight play,
The boat-horn on Piscataqua,
The loon's weird laughter far away;
We fished her little trout-brook, knew
What flowers in wood and meadow grew,
What sunny hillsides autumn-brown
She climbed to shake the ripe nuts down,
Saw where in sheltered cove and bay
The ducks' black squadron anchored lay,
And heard the wild-geese calling loud
Beneath the gray November cloud.

Then, haply, with a look more grave,
And soberer tone, some tale she gave
From painful Sewel's ancient tome,
Beloved in every Quaker home,
Of faith fire-winged by martyrdom,
Or Chalkley's Journal, old and quaint, —
Gentlest of skippers, rare sea-saint! —
Who, when the dreary calms prevailed,
And water-butt and bread-cask failed,
And cruel, hungry eyes pursued
His portly presence mad for food,
With dark hints muttered under breath
Of casting lots for life or death,
Offered, if Heaven withheld supplies,
To be himself the sacrifice.
Then, suddenly, as if to save
The good man from his living grave,
A ripple on the water grew,
A school of porpoise flashed in view.
"Take, eat," he said, "and be content;
These fishes in my stead are sent
By Him who gave the tangled ram
To spare the child of Abraham."

Our uncle, innocent of books,
Was rich in lore of fields and brooks,
The ancient teachers never dumb
Of Nature's unhoused lyceum.
In moons and tides and weather wise,
He read the clouds as prophecies,
And foul or fair could well divine,
By many an occult hint and sign,
Holding the cunning-warded keys
To all the woodcraft mysteries;
Himself to Nature's heart so near
That all her voices in his ear
Of beast or bird had meanings clear,
Like Apollonius of old,

Who knew the tales the sparrows told,
Or Hermes who interpreted
What the sage cranes of Nilus said;
A simple, guileless, childlike man,
Content to live where life began;
Strong only on his native grounds,
The little world of sights and sounds
Whose girdle was the parish bounds,
Whereof his fondly partial pride
The common features magnified,
As Surrey hills to mountains grew
In White of Selborne's loving view, —
He told how teal and loon he shot,
And how the eagle's egg he got,
The feats on pond and river done,
The prodigies of rod and gun;
Till, warming with the tales he told,
Forgotten was the outside cold,
The bitter wind unheeded blew,
From ripening corn the pigeons flew,
The partridge drummed i' the wood, the mink
Went fishing down the river-brink.
In fields with bean or clover gay,
The woodchuck, like a hermit gray,
    Peered from the doorway of his cell:
The muskrat plied the mason's trade,
And tier by tier his mud-walls laid;
And from the shagbark overhead
    The grizzled squirrel dropped his shell.
Next, the dear aunt, whose smile of cheer
And voice in dreams I see and hear, —
The sweetest woman ever Fate
Perverse denied a household mate,

Who, lonely, homeless, not the less
Found peace in love's unselfishness,
And welcome wheresoe'er she went,
A calm and gracious element,
Whose presence seemed the sweet income
And womanly atmosphere of home, —
Called up her girlhood memories,
The huskings and the apple-bees,
The sleigh-rides and the summer sails.
Weaving through all the poor details
And homespun warp of circumstance
A golden woof-thread of romance.
For well she kept her genial mood
And simple faith of maidenhood;
Before her still a cloud-land lay,
The mirage loomed across her way;
The morning dew, that dries so soon
With others, glistened at her noon;
Through years of toil and soil and care,
From glossy tress to thin gray hair,
All unprofaned she held apart
The virgin fancies of the heart.
Be shame to him of woman born
Who hath for such but thought of scorn.

There, too, our elder sister plied
Her evening task the stand beside;
A full, rich nature, free to trust,
Truthful and almost sternly just,
Impulsive, earnest, prompt to act,
And make her generous thought a fact,
Keeping with many a light disguise
The secret of self-sacrifice.
O heart sore-tried! thou hast the best

That Heaven itself could give thee, — rest,
Rest from all bitter thoughts and things!
　How many a poor one's blessing went
　With thee beneath the low green tent
Whose curtain never outward swings!

As one who held herself a part
Of all she saw, and let her heart
　Against the household bosom lean,
Upon the motley-braided mat
Our youngest and our dearest sat,
Lifting her large, sweet, asking eyes,
　Now bathed in the unfading green
And holy peace of Paradise.
Oh, looking from some heavenly hill,
　Or from the shade of saintly palms,
　Or silver reach of river calms,
Do those large eyes behold me still?
With me one little year ago: —
The chill weight of the winter snow
　For months upon her grave has lain;
And now, when summer south-winds blow
　And brier and harebell bloom again,
I tread the pleasant paths we trod,
I see the violet-sprinkled sod
Whereon she leaned, too frail and weak
The hillside flowers she loved to seek,
Yet following me where'er I went
With dark eyes full of love's content.
The birds are glad; the brier-rose fills
The air with sweetness; all the hills
Stretch green to June's unclouded sky;
But still I wait with ear and eye
For something gone which should be nigh,
A loss in all familiar things,
In flower that blooms, and bird that sings.
And yet, dear heart! remembering thee,
　Am I not richer than of old?

Safe in thy immortality,
  What change can reach the wealth I hold?
  What chance can mar the pearl and gold
Thy love hath left in trust with me?
And while in life's late afternoon,
  Where cool and long the shadows grow,
I walk to meet the night that soon
  Shall shape and shadow overflow,
I cannot feel that thou art far,
Since near at need the angels are;
And when the sunset gates unbar,
  Shall I not see thee waiting stand,
And, white against the evening star,
  The welcome of thy beckoning hand?

Brisk wielder of the birch and rule,
The master of the district school
Held at the fire his favored place,
Its warm glow lit a laughing face
Fresh-hued and fair, where scarce appeared
The uncertain prophecy of beard.
He teased the mitten-blinded cat,
Played cross-pins on my uncle's hat,
Sang songs, and told us what befalls
In classic Dartmouth's college halls.
Born the wild Northern hills among,
From whence his yeoman father wrung
By patient toil subsistence scant,
Not competence and yet not want,
He early gained the power to pay
His cheerful, self-reliant way;
Could doff at ease his scholar's gown
To peddle wares from town to town;
Or through the long vacation's reach
In lonely lowland districts teach,
Where all the droll experience found
At stranger hearths in boarding round,
The moonlit skater's keen delight,

The sleigh-drive through the frosty night,
The rustic-party, with its rough
Accompaniment of blind-man's-buff,
And whirling-plate, and forfeits paid,
His winter task a pastime made.
Happy the snow-locked homes wherein
He tuned his merry violin,
Or played the athlete in the barn,
Or held the good dame's winding-yarn,
Or mirth-provoking versions told
Of classic legends rare and old,
Wherein the scenes of Greece and Rome
Had all the commonplace of home,
And little seemed at best the odds
'Twixt Yankee pedlers and old gods;
Where Pindus-born Arachthus took
The guise of any grist-mill brook,
And dread Olympus at his will
Became a huckleberry hill.

A careless boy that night he seemed;
   But at his desk he had the look
And air of one who wisely schemed,
   And hostage from the future took
   In trained thought and lore of book.
Large-brained, clear-eyed, of such as he
Shall Freedom's young apostles be,
Who, following in War's bloody trail,
Shall every lingering wrong assail;
All chains from limb and spirit strike,
Uplift the black and white alike;
Scatter before their swift advance
The darkness and the ignorance,
The pride, the lust, the squalid sloth,
Which nurtured Treason's monstrous growth,
Made murder pastime, and the hell
Of prison-torture possible;
The cruel lie of caste refute,

Old forms remould, and substitute
For Slavery's lash the freeman's will,
For blind routine, wise-handed skill;
A school-house plant on every hill,
Stretching in radiate nerve-lines thence
The quick wires of intelligence;
Till North and South together brought
Shall own the same electric thought,
In peace a common flag salute,
And, side by side in labor's free
And unresentful rivalry,
Harvest the fields wherein they fought.

Another guest that winter night
Flashed back from lustrous eyes the light.
Unmarked by time, and yet not young,
The honeyed music of her tongue
And words of meekness scarcely told
A nature passionate and bold,
Strong, self-concentred, spurning guide,
Its milder features dwarfed beside
Her unbent will's majestic pride.
She sat among us, at the best,
A not unfeared, half-welcome guest,
Rebuking with her cultured phrase
Our homeliness of words and ways.
A certain pard-like, treacherous grace
Swayed the lithe limbs and drooped the lash,
Lent the white teeth their dazzling flash;
And under low brows, black with night,
Rayed out at times a dangerous light;
The sharp heat-lightnings of her face
Presaging ill to him whom Fate
Condemned to share her love or hate.
A woman tropical, intense
In thought and act, in soul and sense,
She blended in a like degree
The vixen and the devotee,

Revealing with each freak or feint
  The temper of Petruchio's Kate,
The raptures of Siena's saint.
Her tapering hand and rounded wrist
Had facile power to form a fist;
The warm, dark languish of her eyes
Was never safe from wrath's surprise.
Brows saintly calm and lips devout
Knew every change of scowl and pout;
And the sweet voice had notes more high
And shrill for social battle-cry.

Since then what old cathedral town
Has missed her pilgrim staff and gown,
What convent-gate has held its lock
Against the challenge of her knock!
Through Smyrna's plague-hushed thoroughfares,
Up sea-set Malta's rocky stairs,
Gray olive slopes of hills that hem
  Thy tombs and shrines, Jerusalem,
Or startling on her desert throne
The crazy Queen of Lebanon
With claims fantastic as her own,
Her tireless feet have held their way;
And still, unrestful, bowed, and gray,
She watches under Eastern skies,
  With hope each day renewed and fresh,
  The Lord's quick coming in the flesh,
Whereof she dreams and prophesies!

Where'er her troubled path may be,
  The Lord's sweet pity with her go!
The outward wayward life we see,
  The hidden springs we may not know.
Nor is it given us to discern
  What threads the fatal sisters spun,
  Through what ancestral years has run
The sorrow with the woman born,

[608]

What forged her cruel chain of moods,
What set her feet in solitudes,
 And held the love within her mute,
What mingled madness in the blood,
 A life-long discord and annoy,
 Water of tears with oil of joy,
And hid within the folded bud
 Perversities of flower and fruit.
It is not ours to separate
 The tangled skein of will and fate,
To show what metes and bounds should stand
Upon the soul's debatable land,
And between choice and Providence
Divide the circle of events;
But He who knows our frame is just,
Merciful and compassionate,
And full of sweet assurances
And hope for all the language is,
That He remembereth we are dust!

At last the great logs, crumbling low,
Sent out a dull and duller glow,
The bull's-eye watch that hung in view,
Ticking its weary circuit through,
Pointed with mutely warning sign
Its black hand to the hour of nine.
That sign the pleasant circle broke:
My uncle ceased his pipe to smoke,
Knocked from its bowl the refuse gray,
And laid it tenderly away;
Then roused himself to safely cover
The dull red brands with ashes over.
And while, with care, our mother laid
The work aside, her steps she stayed
One moment, seeking to express
Her grateful sense of happiness
For food and shelter, warmth and health,
And love's contentment more than wealth,

With simple wishes (not the weak,
Vain prayers which no fulfilment seek,
But such as warm the generous heart,
O'er-prompt to do with Heaven its part)
That none might lack, that bitter night,
For bread and clothing, warmth and light.

Within our beds awhile we heard
The wind that round the gables roared,
With now and then a ruder shock,
Which made our very bedsteads rock.
We heard the loosened clapboards tost,
The board-nails snapping in the frost;
And on us, through the unplastered wall,
Felt the light sifted snow-flakes fall.
But sleep stole on, as sleep will do
When hearts are light and life is new;
Faint and more faint the murmurs grew,
Till in the summer-land of dreams
They softened to the sound of streams,
Low stir of leaves, and dip of oars,
And lapsing waves on quiet shores.

Next morn we wakened with the shout
Of merry voices high and clear;
And saw the teamsters drawing near
To break the drifted highways out.
Down the long hillside treading slow
We saw the half-buried oxen go,
Shaking the snow from heads uptost,
Their straining nostrils white with frost.
Before our door the straggling train
Drew up, an added team to gain.
The elders threshed their hands a-cold,
    Passed, with the cider-mug, their jokes
    From lip to lip; the younger folks
Down the loose snow-banks, wrestling, rolled,
Then toiled again the cavalcade

O'er windy hill, through clogged ravine,
  And woodland paths that wound between
Low drooping pine-boughs winter-weighed.
From every barn a team afoot,
At every house a new recruit,
Where, drawn by Nature's subtlest law,
Haply the watchful young men saw
Sweet doorway pictures of the curls
And curious eyes of merry girls,
Lifting their hands in mock defence
Again the snow-ball's compliments,
And reading in each missive tost
The charm with Eden never lost.

We heard once more the sleigh-bells' sound;
  And, following where the teamsters led,
The wise old Doctor went his round,
Just pausing at our door to say,
In the brief autocratic way
Of one who, prompt at Duty's call,
Was free to urge her claim on all,
  That some poor neighbor sick abed
At night our mother's aid would need.
For, one in generous thought and deed,
  What mattered in the sufferer's sight
  The Quaker matron's inward light,
The Doctor's mail of Calvin's creed?
All hearts confess the saints elect
  Who, twain in faith, in love agree,
And melt not in an acid sect
  The Christian pearl of charity!

So days went on: a week had passed
Since the great world was heard from last.
The Almanac we studied o'er,
Read and reread our little store
Of books and pamphlets, scarce a score;
One harmless novel, mostly hid

From younger eyes, a book forbid,
And poetry, (or good or bad,
A single book was all we had,)
Where Ellwood's meek, drab-skirted Muse,
 A stranger to the heathen Nine,
 Sang, with a somewhat nasal whine,
The wars of David and the Jews.
At last the floundering carrier bore
The village paper to our door.
Lo! broadening outward as we read,
To warmer zones the horizon spread
In panoramic length unrolled
We saw the marvels that it told.
Before us passed the painted Creeks,
 And daft McGregor on his raids
 In Costa Rica's everglades.
And up Taygetos winding slow
Rode Ypsilanti's Mainote Greeks,
A Turk's head at each saddle-bow!
Welcome to us its week-old news,
Its corner for the rustic Muse,
 Its monthly gauge of snow and rain,
Its record, mingling in a breath
The wedding bell and dirge of death:
Jest, anecdote, and love-lorn tale,
The latest culprit sent to jail;
Its hue and cry of stolen and lost,
Its vendue sales and goods at cost,
 And traffic calling loud for gain.
We felt the stir of hall and street,
The pulse of life that round us beat;
The chill embargo of the snow
Was melted in the genial glow;
Wide swung again our ice-locked door,
And all the world was ours once more!

Clasp, Angel of the backward look
 And folded wings of ashen gray

And voice of echoes far away,
The brazen covers of thy book;
The weird palimpsest old and vast,
Wherein thou hid'st the spectral past;
Where, closely mingling, pale and glow
The characters of joy and woe;
The monographs of outlived years,
Or smile-illumed or dim with tears,
    Green hills of life that slope to death,
And haunts of home, whose vistaed trees
Shade off to mournful cypresses
    With the white amaranths underneath
Even while I look, I can but heed
    The restless sands' incessant fall,
Importunate hours that hours succeed,
Each clamorous with its own sharp need,
    And duty keeping pace with all.
Shut down and clasp the heavy lids;
I hear again the voice that bids
The dreamer leave his dream midway
For larger hopes and graver fears;
Life greatens in these later years,
The century's aloe flowers to-day!

Yet, haply, in some lull of life,
Some Truce of God, which breaks its strife,
The worldling's eyes shall gather dew,
    Dreaming in throngful city ways
Of winter joys his boyhood knew;
And dear and early friends— the few
Who yet remain—shall pause to view
    These Flemish pictures of old days;
Sit with me by the homestead hearth,
And stretch the hands of memory forth
    To warm them at the wood-fire's blaze!
And thanks untraced to lips unknown
Shall greet me like the odors blown
From unseen meadows newly mown,

Or lilies floating in some pond,
Wood-fringed, the wayside gaze beyond;
The traveller owns the grateful sense
Of sweetness near, he knows not whence,
And, pausing, takes with forehead bare
The benediction of the air.

Writing toward the end of the American Civil War in 1864–1865, Whittier looked back forty-five years to an episode from his childhood. The group at the Whittier homestead included the poet's parents, his brother and two sisters, an uncle and an aunt (both unmarried), a schoolmaster lodging with them, and an eccentric woman named Harriet Livermore, who, as even the tolerant Quaker Whittier had to concede, was "fantastic and mentally strained."

Holmes was a Harvard medical doctor who practiced privately for many years; he also taught anatomy and physiology at Harvard and spent six years as dean of the university's medical school. In a long and productive literary life he produced criticism, fiction, conversation, and much occasional verse. It was also Holmes who named *The Atlantic Monthly*.

The Deacon's Masterpiece;
or, The Wonderful "One-Hoss Shay"
A Logical Story

Have you heard of the wonderful one-hoss shay,
That was built in such a logical way
It ran a hundred years to a day,
And then, of a sudden, it—ah, but stay,
I'll tell you what happened without delay,
Scaring the parson into fits,
Frightening people out of their wits, —
Have you heard of that, I say?

SEVENTEEN HUNDRED AND FIFTY-FIVE.
Georgius Secundus was then alive, —
Snuffy old drone from the German hive.
That was the year when Lisbon-town
Saw the earth open and gulp her down,
And Braddock's army was done so brown,
Left without a scalp to its crown.
It was on the terrible, Earthquake-day
That the Deacon finished the one-hoss shay.

Now in building of chaises, I tell you what,
There is always *somewhere* a weakest spot, —
In hub, tire, felloe, in spring or thill,
In panel, or crossbar, or floor, or sill,
In screw, bolt, thoroughbrace, —lurking still,
Find it somewhere you must and will, —
Above or below, or within or without, —
And that's the reason, beyond a doubt,
A chaise *breaks down*, but doesn't *wear out*.

But the Deacon swore (as Deacons do,
With an "I dew vum," or an "I tell *yeou*")
He would build one shay to beat the taown
'N the keounty 'n' all the kentry raoun':
It should be so built that it *couldn'* break daown:
"Fur," said the Deacon, " 't's mighty plain
Thut the weakes' places mus' stan' the strain;
'N' the way t' fix it, uz I maintain, is only jest
T' make that place uz strong uz the rest."

So the Deacon inquired of the village folk
Where he could find the strongest oak,
That couldn't be split nor bent nor broke, —
That was for spokes and floor and sills;
He sent for lancewood to make the thills;
The crossbars were ash, from the straightest trees;
The panels of whitewood, that cuts like cheese,
But lasts like iron for things like these;
The hubs of logs from the "Settler's ellum," —
Last of its timber, —they couldn't sell 'em,
Never an axe had seen their chips,
And the wedges flew from between their lips,
Their blunt ends frizzled like celery-tips;

Step and prop-iron, bolt and screw,
Spring, tire, axle, and linchpin too,
Steel of the finest, bright and blue;
Thoroughbrace bison-skin, thick and wide;
Boot, top, dasher, from tough old hide
Found in the pit when the tanner died.
That was the way he "put her through."
"There!" said the Deacon, "naow she'll dew!"

Do! I tell you, I rather guess
She was a wonder, and nothing less!
Colts grew horses, beards turned gray,
Deacon and deaconess dropped away,
Children and grandchildren—where were they?
But there stood the stout old one-hoss shay
As fresh as on Lisbon-earthquake-day!

EIGHTEEN HUNDRED;—it came and found
The Deacon's masterpiece strong and sound.
Eighteen hundred increased by ten;—
"Hahnsum kerridge" they called it then.
Eighteen hundred and twenty came;—
Running as usual; much, the same.
Thirty and forty at last arrive,
And then come fifty, and FIFTY-FIVE.
Little of all we value here
Wakes on the morn of its hundredth year
Without both feeling and looking queer.
In fact, there's nothing that keeps its youth,
So far as I know, but a tree and truth.
(This is a moral that runs at large;
Take it.—You're welcome.—No extra charge.)

First of November, — the Earthquake-day. —
There are traces of age in the one-hoss shay,
A general flavor of mild decay,
But nothing local as one may say.
There couldn't be, — for the Deacon's art
Had made it so like in every part
That there wasn't a chance for one to start,
For the wheels were just as strong as the thills,
And the floor was just as strong as the sills,
And the panels just as strong as the floor,
And the whipple-tree neither less nor more,
And the back-crossbar as strong as the fore,
And spring and axle and hub *encore.*
And yet, *as a whole,* it is past a doubt
In another hour it will be *worn out!*

First of November, 'Fifty-five!
This morning the parson takes a drive.
Now, small boys, get out of the way!
Here comes the wonderful one-hoss shay,
Drawn by a rat-tailed, ewe-necked bay.
"Huddup!" said the parson. Off went they.
The parson was working his Sunday's text, —
Had got to *fifthly,* and stopped perplexed
At what the — Moses — was coming next.
All at once the horse stood still,
Close by the meet'n'-house on the hill.
— First a shiver, and then a thrill,
Then something decidedly like a spill, —
And the parson was sitting upon a rock,
At half-past nine by the meet'n'-house clock, —
Just the hour of the Earthquake shock!

—What do you think the parson found,
When he got up and stared around?
The poor old chaise in a heap or mound,
As if it had been to the mill and ground!
You see, of course, if you're not a dunce,
How it went to pieces all at once, —
All at once, and nothing first, —
Just as bubbles do when they burst.

End of the wonderful one-hoss shay.
Logic is logic. That's all I say.

from The Autocrat of the Breakfast Table

In more ways than one—in tone, rhythm, attention to detail—Holmes here sounds as though he is anticipating Dr. Seuss (Theodore Seuss Geisel), who was almost a hundred years younger. Few consumers nowadays even bother to scoff at "dynamic obsolescence" whereby products are deliberately designed to fall apart, sometimes before they are paid for.

The Chambered Nautilus

This is the ship of pearl, which, poets feign,
   Sails the unshadowed main, —
   The venturous bark that flings
On the sweet summer wind its purpled wings
In gulfs enchanted, where the Siren sings,
   And coral reefs lie bare,
Where the cold sea-maids rise to sun their streaming hair.

Its webs of living gauze no more unfurl!
   Wrecked is the ship of pearl!
   And every chambered cell,
Where its dim dreaming life was wont to dwell,
As the frail tenant shaped his growing shell,
   Before thee lies revealed, —
Its irised ceiling rent, its sunless crypt unsealed!

Year after year beheld the silent toil
   That spread his lustrous coil;
   Still, as the spiral grew,
He left the past year's dwelling for the new,
Stole with soft step its shining archway through,
   Built up its idle door,
Stretched in his last-found home, and knew the old no more.

Thanks for the heavenly message brought by thee,
   Child of the wandering sea,
   Cast from her lap, forlorn!
From thy dead lips a clearer note is born
Than ever Triton blew from wreathèd horn!
   While on mine ear it rings,
Through the deep caves of thought I hear a voice that sings: —

Build thee more stately mansions, O my soul,
  As the swift seasons roll!
  Leave thy low-vaulted past!
Let each new temple, nobler than the last,
Shut thee from heaven with a dome more vast,
  Till thou at length art free,
Leaving thine outgrown shell by life's unresting sea!

from The Autocrat of The Breakfast Table

In the first decade of the nineteenth century, an ambitious (although flawed) program of universal free public education was started all across the English-speaking world. By 1830, a new literate audience was demanding not only something to read but also guidance in the intellectual and ethical value of the reading matter. Holmes—along with Bryant, Whittier, Longfellow, and Lowell—came along just in time to answer both needs. They were fine poets, but—much to the disgust of their even finer contemporary, Edgar Allan Poe—they felt pressured to announce their moral lessons overtly. These "schoolroom poets" were finally rejected so robustly by generations of resentful readers that few advocates survive who can see the wonderful aesthetic qualities in many of their poems.

Old Ironsides

Ay, tear her tattered ensign down!
Long has it waved on high,
And many an eye has danced to see
That banner in the sky;
Beneath it rung the battle shout,
And burst the cannon's roar; —
The meteor of the ocean air
Shall sweep the clouds no more!

Her deck, once red with heroes' blood,
Where knelt the vanquished foe,
When winds were hurrying o'er the flood,
And waves were white below,
No more shall feel the victor's tread,
Or know the conquered knee; —
The harpies of the shore shall pluck
The eagle of the sea!

O, better that her shattered hulk
Should sink beneath the wave;
Her thunders shook the mighty deep,
And there should be her grave;
Nail to the mast her holy flag,
Set every threadbare sail,
And give her to the god of storms,
The lightning and the gale!

At twenty-one, Holmes wrote this rhetorical exercise in response to an announcement that the frigate Constitution, *famous for exploits in the War of 1812, was to be scrapped. The ploy worked, the ship was spared and can still be seen in Boston, 160 years after Holmes's verse.*

EDGAR ALLAN POE 1809–1849

Although he was born in Boston, Poe, having been or-
phaned at an early age, was raised in Virginia. In a
pitifully short career as a literary editor and journalist,
he made himself famous as a fabulous inventor—a true
American Daedalus—so that it can be persuasively ar-
gued that Poe, just about singlehandedly, invented the
short story, science fiction, detective fiction, the sym-
bolist poem, and the New Criticism. Poe remains the
American writer with just about the greatest influence:
he understood humankind's deepest fears and desires.
His shadow stretches over many literary provinces,
from Jules Verne to Oscar Wilde to Vladimir Nabokov
to the novels of Thomas Pynchon and the films of Stan-
ley Kubrick.

To Helen

Helen, thy beauty is to me
   Like those Nicéan barks of yore,
That gently, o'er a perfumed sea,
   The weary, way-worn wanderer bore
   To his own native shore.

On desperate seas long wont to roam,
   Thy hyacinth hair, thy classic face,
Thy Naiad airs have brought me home
   To the glory that was Greece,
And the grandeur that was Rome.

Lo! in yon brilliant window-niche
   How statue-like I see thee stand,
The agate lamp within thy hand!
Ah, Psyche, from the regions which
   Are Holy-Land!

Seemingly a conglomeration of imperfections, Poe's "To Helen" somehow, un-accountably, creates a living and durable work of art that for 150 years has been the greatest American lyric poem. In meter and rhyme, the stanzas don't match; "long wont" is a ludicrous dangling modifier; some of the rhymes are of types that Poe castigated in others ("face" and "Greece" rhyme too little, "roam" and "Rome" too much). Poe suggested that the subject was a young woman named Jane Stith Stanard, who died when Poe was fifteen. The classical trappings are both allusive and elusive, as though the poet preferred suggestion to assertion. Nobody has explained "Nicéan"; "Naiad" and "Psyche" remain indeterminate. The poem is, nevertheless, a gem. First drafted when the poet was fourteen, "To Helen" probably had a younger author than any other poem in this book.

The Raven

Once upon a midnight dreary, while I pondered, weak and
    weary,
Over many a quaint and curious volume of forgotten lore,
While I nodded, nearly napping, suddenly there came a
    tapping,
As of some one gently rapping, rapping at my chamber door.
" 'Tis some visitor," I muttered, "tapping at my chamber
    door—
        Only this, and nothing more."

Ah, distinctly I remember it was in the bleak December,
And each separate dying ember wrought its ghost upon the
    floor.
Eagerly I wished the morrow;— vainly I had sought to
    borrow
From my books surcease of sorrow— sorrow for the lost
    Lenore—
For the rare and radiant maiden whom the angels name
    Lenore—
        Nameless here for evermore.

And the silken sad uncertain rustling of each purple curtain
Thrilled me—filled me with fantastic terrors never felt before;
So that now, to still the beating of my heart, I stood
    repeating
" 'Tis some visitor entreating entrance at my chamber
    door;—
Some late visitor entreating at my chamber door
        This it is, and nothing more."

Presently my soul grew stronger; hesitating then no longer,
"Sir," said I, "or Madam, truly your forgiveness I implore;
But the fact is I was napping, and so gently you came
      rapping,
And so faintly you come tapping, tapping at my chamber
      door,
That I scarce was sure I heard you"—here I opened wide the
      door;—
            Darkness there, and nothing more.

Deep into that darkness peering, long I stood there
      wondering, fearing,
Doubting, dreaming dreams no mortal ever dared to dream
      before;
But the silence was unbroken, and the darkness gave no
      token,
And the only word there spoken was the whispered word,
      "Lenore!"
This I whispered, and an echo murmured back the word,
      "Lenore!"—
            Merely this, and nothing more.

Back into the chamber turning, all my soul within me
      burning,
Soon I heard again a tapping somewhat louder than before.
"Surely," said I, "surely that is something at my window
      lattice;
Let me see, then, what thereat is, and this mystery explore—
Let my heart be still a moment and this mystery explore;—
            'Tis the wind and nothing more!"

Open here I flung the shutter, when, with many a flirt and
    flutter,
In there stepped a stately raven of the saintly days of yore;
Not the least obeisance made he; not an instant stopped or
    stayed he;
But, with mien of lord or lady, perched above my chamber
    door—
Perched upon a bust of Pallas just above my chamber door—
        Perched, and sat, and nothing more.

Then this ebony bird beguiling my sad fancy into smiling,
By the grave and stern decorum of the countenance it wore,
"Though thy crest be shorn and shaven, thou," I said, "art
    sure no craven,
Ghastly grim and ancient raven wandering from the Nightly
    shore—
Tell me what thy lordly name is on the Night's Plutonian
    shore!"
        Quoth the raven, "Nevermore."

Much I marvelled this ungainly fowl to hear discourse so
    plainly,
Though its answer little meaning—little relevancy bore,
For we cannot help agreeing that no living human being
Ever yet was blessed with seeing bird above his chamber
    door—
Bird or beast upon the sculptured bust above his chamber
    door,
        With such name as "Nevermore."

But the raven, sitting lonely on the placid bust, spoke only
That one word, as if his soul in that one word he did outpour.
Nothing farther then he uttered—not a feather then he
    fluttered—
Till I scarcely more than muttered "Other friends have flown
    before—
On the morrow *he* will leave me, as my hopes have flown
    before."

Then the bird said "Nevermore."

Startled at the stillness broken by reply so aptly spoken,
"Doubtless," said I, "what it utters is its only stock and store
Caught from some unhappy master whom unmerciful Disaster
Followed fast and followed faster till his songs one burden
    bore—
Till the dirges of his Hope that melancholy burden bore
        Of 'Never—nevermore.' "

But the raven still beguiling all my sad soul into smiling,
Straight I wheeled a cushioned seat in front of bird and bust
    and door;
Then, upon the velvet sinking, I betook myself to linking
Fancy unto fancy, thinking what his ominous bird of yore—
What this grim, ungainly, ghastly, gaunt, and ominous bird of
    yore
        Meant in croaking "Nevermore."

This I sat engaged in guessing, but no syllable expressing
To the fowl whose fiery eyes now burned into my bosom's
    core;
This and more I sat divining, with my head at ease reclining
On the cushion's velvet lining that the lamplight gloated o'er,
But whose velvet violet lining with the lamplight gloating o'er,
        She shall press, ah, nevermore!

Then, methought, the air grew denser, perfumed from an
    unseen censer
Swung by angels whose faint foot-falls tinkled on the tufted
    floor.
"Wretch," I cried, "thy God hath lent thee—by these angels
    he hath sent thee
Respite—respite and nepenthe from thy memories of Lenore!
Quaff, oh quaff this kind nepenthe and forget this lost
    Lenore!"
        Quoth the raven, "Nevermore."

"Prophet!" said I, "thing of evil!—prophet still, if bird or
  devil!—
Whether Tempter sent, or whether tempest tossed thee here
  ashore,
Desolate, yet all undaunted, on this desert land enchanted—
On this home by Horror haunted—tell me truly, I implore—
Is there—*is* there balm in Gilead?—tell me—tell me, I
  implore!"
          Quoth the raven, "Nevermore."

"Prophet!" said I, "thing of evil—prophet still, if bird or devil!
By that Heaven that bends above us—by that God we both
  adore—
Tell this soul with sorrow laden if, within the distant Aidenn,
It shall clasp a sainted maiden whom the angels name
  Lenore—
Clasp a rare and radiant maiden whom the angels name
  Lenore."
          Quoth the raven, "Nevermore."

"Be that word our sign of parting, bird or fiend!" I shrieked,
  upstarting—
"Get thee back into the tempest and the Night's Plutonian
  shore!
Leave no black plume as a token of that lie thy soul hath
  spoken!
Leave my loneliness unbroken!—quit the bust above my door!
Take thy beak from out my heart, and take thy form from off
  my door!"
          Quoth the raven, "Nevermore."

And the raven, never flitting, still is sitting, still is sitting
On the pallid bust of Pallas just above my chamber door;
And his eyes have all the seeming of a demon's that is
   dreaming,
And the lamp-light o'er him streaming throws his shadow on
   the floor;
And my soul from out that shadow that lies floating on the
   floor
      Shall be lifted— nevermore!

No poem in this book has stimulated more poetic responses, direct or indirect, than "The Raven." From Mallarmé's Igitur *and D. G. Rossetti's "Blessed Damozel" in the nineteenth century—and possibly as early as canto 13 of Longfellow's "Song of Hiawatha" just after Poe's death—artists have repeated or countered the terms of Poe's powerful vision. (See Stevens's "Thirteen Ways of Looking at a Blackbird," p. 932, and William Carlos Williams's "Red Wheelbarrow," p. 935. Farther afield, see T. S. Eliot's "Burnt Norton" and Robert Frost's "Dust of Snow.")*

Annabel Lee

It was many and many a year ago,
    In a kingdom by the sea,
That a maiden there lived whom you may know
    By the name of Annabel Lee;
And this maiden she lived with no other thought
    Than to love and be loved by me.

She was a child and *I* was a child,
    In this kingdom by the sea,
But we loved with a love that was more than love—
    I and my Annabel Lee—
With a love that the wingèd seraphs of Heaven
    Coveted her and me.

And this was the reason that, long ago,
    In this kingdom by the sea,
A wind blew out of a cloud by night
    Chilling my Annabel Lee;
So that her high-born kinsmen came
    And bore her away from me,
To shut her up in a sepulchre
    In this kingdom by the sea.

The angels, not half so happy in Heaven,
    Went envying her and me:—
Yes! that was the reason (as all men know,
    In this kingdom by the sea)
That the wind came out of the cloud chilling
    And killing my Annabel Lee.

But our love it was stronger by far than the love
   Of those who were older than we—
   Of many far wiser than we—
And neither the angels in Heaven above
   Nor the demons down under the sea
Can ever dissever my soul from the soul
   Of the beautiful Annabel Lee:—

For the moon never beams without bringing me dreams
   Of the beautiful Annabel Lee;
And the stars never rise but I feel the bright eyes
   Of the beautiful Annabel Lee:
And so all the night-tide, I lie down by the side
Of my darling, my darling, my life and my bride
   In her sepulchre there by the sea—
   In her tomb by the side of the sea.

Although it uses a relatively primitive ballad technique, "Annabel Lee" was one of Poe's last poems, and its power has lasted right into the modern age, all the way from the mid-century pop tune "Too Young" (a hit record for Nat "King" Cole) to, a few years later, Vladimir Nabokov's Lolita.

The City in the Sea

Lo! Death has reared himself a throne
In a strange city lying alone
Far down within the dim West,
Where the good and the bad and the worst and the best
Have gone to their eternal rest.
There shrines and palaces and towers
(Time-eaten towers that tremble not!)
Resemble nothing that is ours.
Around, by lifting winds forgot,
Resignedly beneath the sky
The melancholy waters lie.

No rays from the holy heaven come down
On the long night-time of that town;
But light from out the lurid sea
Streams up the turrets silently—
Gleams up the pinnacles far and free
Up domes—up spires—up kingly halls—
Up fanes—up Babylon-like walls—
Up shadowy long-forgotten bowers
Of sculptured ivy and stone flowers—
Up many and many a marvellous shrine
Whose wreathéd friezes intertwine
The viol, the violet, and the vine.

Resignedly beneath the sky
The melancholy waters lie.
So blend the turrets and shadows there
That all seem pendulous in air,
While from a proud tower in the town
Death looks gigantically down.

There open fanes and gaping graves
Yawn level with the luminous waves;
But not the riches there that lie
In each idol's diamond eye—
Not the gaily-jewelled dead
Tempt the waters from their bed;
For no ripples curl, alas!
Along that wilderness of glass—
No swellings tell that winds may be
Upon some far-off happier sea—
No heavings hint that winds have been
On seas less hideously serene.

But lo, a stir is in the air!
The wave—there is a movement there!
As if the towers had thrust aside,
In slightly sinking, the dull tide—
As if their tops had feebly given
A void within the filmy Heaven.
The waves have now a redder glow—
The hours are breathing faint and low—
And when, amid no earthly moans,
Down, down that town shall settle hence,
Hell, rising from a thousand thrones,
Shall do it reverence.

Poe's imaginings, however exotic and elaborate, are firmly based in a sober recognition of realistic fears and desires (many more fears than desires). Besides, Poe's stories unfold with telling execution and masterful technique. Later poets may reject Poe's vulgarity, but almost nobody denies his tremendous influence and importance. Matter from "The City in the Sea" returns in works by T. S. Eliot: "wilderness of glass" comes back as "wilderness of mirrors" in "Gerontion" (p. 984); the upside-down city reappears in the fifth part of "The Waste Land" (p. 968).

The Bells

≫≫≫≫≫≫

I

Hear the sledges with the bells—
Silver bells!
What a world of merriment their melody foretells!
How they tinkle, tinkle, tinkle,
In the icy air of night!
While the stars that oversprinkle
All the heavens, seem to twinkle
With a crystalline delight;
Keeping time, time, time,
In a sort of Runic rhyme,
To the tintinnabulation that so musically wells
From the bells, bells, bells, bells,
Bells, bells, bells,—
From the jingling and the tinkling of the bells.

II

Hear the mellow wedding bells—
Golden bells!
What a world of happiness their harmony foretells!
Through the balmy air of night
How they ring out their delight!—
From the molten-golden notes,
And all in tune,
What a liquid ditty floats
To the turtle-dove that listens, while she gloats
On the moon!
Oh, from out the sounding cells,

What a gush of euphony voluminously wells!
How it swells!
How it dwells
On the Future!—how it tells
Of the rapture that impels
To the swinging and the ringing
Of the bells, bells, bells,—
Of the bells, bells, bells, bells,
Bells, bells, bells,
To the rhyming and the chiming of the bells!

III

Hear the loud alarum bells—
Brazen bells!
What a tale of terror, now, their turbulency tells!
In the startled ear of night
How they scream out their affright!
Too much horrified to speak,
They can only shriek, shriek,
Out of tune,
In a clamorous appealing to the mercy of the fire,
In a mad expostulation with the deaf and frantic fire,
Leaping higher, higher, higher,
With a desperate desire,
And a resolute endeavor
Now—now to sit, or never,
By the side of the pale-faced moon.
Oh, the bells, bells, bells!
What a tale their terror tells
Of Despair!
How they clang, and clash, and roar!
What a horror they outpour

On the bosom of the palpitating air!
 Yet the ear, it fully knows,
  By the twanging
  And the clanging,
 How the danger ebbs and flows;
Yet the ear distinctly tells,
  In the jangling
  And the wrangling,
 How the danger sinks and swells,
By the sinking or the swelling in the anger of the bells —
 Of the bells, —
 Of the bells, bells, bells, bells,
  Bells, bells, bells —
In the clamor and the clangor of the bells!

IV

 Hear the tolling of the bells —
  Iron bells!
What a world of solemn thought their monody compels!
 In the silence of the night,
 How we shiver with affright
At the melancholy menace of their tone!
  For every sound that floats
  From the rust within their throats
   Is a groan.
  And the people — ah, the people —
  They that dwell up in the steeple,
   All alone,
 And who tolling, tolling, tolling,
  In that muffled monotone,
 Feel a glory in so rolling
  On the human heart a stone —

They are neither man nor woman —
They are neither brute nor human —
    They are Ghouls: —
  And their king it is who tolls: —
  And he rolls, rolls, rolls,
      Rolls
    A paean from the bells!
  And his merry bosom swells
    With the paean of the bells!
  And he dances, and he yells;
Keeping time, time, time,
In a sort of Runic rhyme,
    To the paean of the bells —
      Of the bells: —
Keeping time, time, time,
In a sort of Runic rhyme,
    To the throbbing of the bells —
    Of the bells, bells, bells —
    To the sobbing of the bells,
  Keeping time, time, time,
    As he knells, knells, knells,
  In a happy Runic rhyme,
    To the rolling of the bells —
    Of the bells, bells, bells: —
    To the tolling of the bells,
  Of the bells, bells, bells, bells,
    Bells, bells, bells —
To the moaning and the groaning of the bells.

What a tour de force! Poe's most entertaining poem is a curriculum driven by the powers of sound, all organized according to foursomes: metals, ages and Ages, seasons, and appropriate emotional registers, with verbal and acoustic coefficients.

The Haunted Palace

In the greenest of our valleys,
  By good angels tenanted,
Once a fair and stately palace
  (Radiant palace) reared its head.
In the monarch Thought's dominion
  It stood there!
Never seraph spread a pinion
  Over fabric half so fair.

Banners yellow, glorious, golden,
  On its roof did float and flow
(This, all this, was in the olden
  Time long ago);
And every gentle air that dallied
  In that sweet day,
Along the ramparts plumed and pallid,
  A wingèd odor went away.

Wanderers in that happy valley
  Through two luminous windows, saw
Spirits moving musically
  To a lute's well-tuned law;
Round about a throne where, sitting
  (Porphyrogene!)
In state his glory well befitting,
  The ruler of the realm was seen.

And all with pearl and ruby glowing
　　Was the fair palace door,
Through which came flowing, flowing, flowing,
　　And sparkling evermore,
A troop of echoes, whose sweet duty
　　Was but to sing,
In voices of surpassing beauty,
　　The wit and wisdom of their king.

But evil things, in robes of sorrow,
　　Assailed the monarch's high estate
(Ah! let us mourn, for never morrow
　　Shall dawn upon him, desolate);
And round about his home the glory
　　That blushed and bloomed
Is but a dim-remembered story
　　Of the old time entombed.

And travellers, now, within that valley,
　　Through the red-litten windows see
Vast forms that move fantastically
　　To a discordant melody;
While, like a ghastly rapid river,
　　Through the pale door
A hideous throng rush out forever,
　　And laugh—but smile no more.

from The Fall of the House of Usher

Roderick Usher sings what the narrator of "The Fall of the House of Usher" variously calls a rhapsody, an improvisation, a fantasia, and a ballad. A poem about a palace in a story about a house, with both structures patently symbolic and human, is an obvious case of an inner text that repeats and validates an outer. Such texts-within-texts are common in horror stories, all the way from Frankenstein *to* Wuthering Heights *and beyond.*

Alfred Tennyson, 1st Baron Tennyson 1809–1892

Tennyson is one of the greatest poets to hold the Laureateship; his tenure in that position continued for forty-two years, from 1850 until his death. He was born in Lincolnshire and educated at Cambridge. A friend there was the brilliant Arthur Hallam, whose death in 1833 stimulated Tennyson to write the noble and eloquent elegy *In Memoriam* (published in 1850). Tennyson excelled in the short musical lyric, the dramatic monologue, the long narrative, and certain boldly mixed forms for which we still lack accurate names, such as in "The Princess" and "Maud."

The Splendor Falls

The splendor falls on castle walls
    And snowy summits old in story;
The long light shakes across the lakes,
    And the wild cataract leaps in glory.
Blow, bugle, blow, set the wild echoes flying,
Blow, bugle; answer, echoes, dying, dying, dying.

O, hark, O, hear! how thin and clear,
    And thinner, clearer, farther going!
O, sweet and far from cliff and scar
    The horns of Elfland faintly blowing!
Blow, let us hear the purple glens replying,
Blow, bugle; answer, echoes, dying, dying, dying.

O love, they die in yon rich sky,
  They faint on hill or field or river;
Our echoes roll from soul to soul,
  And grow for ever and for ever.
Blow, bugle, blow, set the wild echoes flying,
And answer, echoes, answer, dying, dying, dying.

from The Princess

The subtitle of Tennyson's "Princess" is "A Medley"—and that is accurate: there are varying narrative levels along with several memorable songs (added in the third edition) that have achieved independent celebrity. This poem, "Tears, Idle Tears" (p. 649), and "Now Sleeps the Crimson Petal" (p. 650), along with "Sweet and Low," are known to many who do not know "The Princess" and to some who may not even know Tennyson.

Break, Break, Break

Break, break, break,
　　On thy cold gray stones, O Sea!
And I would that my tongue could utter
　　The thoughts that arise in me.

O, well for the fisherman's boy,
　　That he shouts with his sister at play!
O, well for the sailor lad,
　　That he sings in his boat on the bay!

And the stately ships go on
　　To their haven under the hill;
But O for the touch of a vanished hand,
　　And the sound of a voice that is still!

Break, break, break,
　　At the foot of thy crags, O Sea!
But the tender grace of a day that is dead
　　Will never come back to me.

Lord Byron, one of Tennyson's earliest exemplars, had addressed the ocean memorably in Childe Harold's Pilgrimage *(p. 486), and we accept the appropriateness of the gesture, although it may seem fruitless to command an inanimate object to do what it can't help doing anyway. It is probable that Tennyson's poem refers to the death of his friend Arthur Henry Hallam, also the subject of the great elegy* In Memoriam.

Crossing the Bar

Sunset and evening star,
  And one clear call for me!
And may there be no moaning of the bar,
  When I put out to sea,

But such a tide as moving seems asleep,
  Too full for sound and foam,
When that which drew from out the boundless deep
  Turns again home.

Twilight and evening bell,
  And after that the dark!
And may there be no sadness of farewell,
  When I embark;

For though from out our bourne of Time and Place
  The flood may bear me far,
I hope to see my Pilot face to face
  When I have crossed the bar.

Tennyson wrote this when he was eighty and, although he wrote other poems afterwards, asked that this one be placed at the end of all collections of his poetry. He showed a fine sense of fitness in writing the poem in the first place, with its noble stoicism and good Britannic sea imagery, and also in dictating its appropriate placement.

Ulysses

It little profits that an idle king,
By this still hearth, among these barren crags,
Matched with an agèd wife, I mete and dole
Unequal laws unto a savage race
That hoard, and sleep, and feed, and know not me.
I cannot rest from travel; I will drink
Life to the lees. All times I have enjoyed
Greatly, have suffered greatly, both with those
That loved me, and alone; on shore, and when
Through scudding drifts the rainy Hyades
Vexed the dim sea. I am become a name;
For always roaming with a hungry heart
Much have I seen and known—cities of men
And manners, climates, councils, governments,
Myself not least, but honored of them all—
And drunk delight of battle with my peers,
Far on the ringing plains of windy Troy.
I am a part of all that I have met;
Yet all experience is an arch wherethrough
Gleams that untraveled world whose margin fades
Forever and forever when I move.
How dull it is to pause, to make an end,
To rust unburnished, not to shine in use!
As though to breathe were life! Life piled on life
Were all too little, and of one to me
Little remains; but every hour is saved
From that eternal silence, something more,
A bringer of new things; and vile it were
For some three suns to store and hoard myself,
And this gray spirit yearning in desire
To follow knowledge like a sinking star,
Beyond the utmost bound of human thought.
  This is my son, mine own Telemachus,
To whom I leave the scepter and the isle—

Well-loved of me, discerning to fulfill
This labor, by slow prudence to make mild
A rugged people, and through soft degrees
Subdue them to the useful and the good.
Most blameless is he, centered in the sphere
Of common duties, decent not to fail
In offices of tenderness, and pay
Meet adoration to my household gods,
When I am gone. He works his work, I mine.
   There lies the port; the vessel puffs her sail;
There gloom the dark, broad seas. My mariners,
Souls that have toiled, and wrought, and thought with me—
That ever with a frolic welcome took
The thunder and the sunshine, and opposed
Free hearts, free foreheads—you and I are old;
Old age hath yet his honor and his toil.
Death closes all; but something ere the end,
Some work of noble note, may yet be done,
Not unbecoming men that strove with Gods.
The lights begin to twinkle from the rocks;
The long day wanes, the slow moon climbs; the deep
Moans round with many voices. Come, my friends,
'Tis not too late to seek a newer world.
Push off, and sitting well in order smite
The sounding furrows; for my purpose holds
To sail beyond the sunset, and the baths
Of all the western stars, until I die.
It may be that the gulfs will wash us down;
It may be we shall touch the Happy Isles,
And see the great Achilles, whom we knew.
Though much is taken, much abides; and though
We are not now that strength which in old days
Moved earth and heaven, that which we are, we are—
One equal temper of heroic hearts,
Made weak by time and fate, but strong in will
To strive, to seek, to find, and not to yield.

This complex Ulysses owes as much to Dante as to Homer, with further debt to Milton, whose Satan in Paradise Lost *makes speeches including "will" and "not to yield." Ambiguities notwithstanding, Tennyson's poem remains inspirational, and its last line is carved on the memorial to the heroic members of Robert Falcon Scott's expedition to the Antarctic.*

The Eagle

He clasps the crag with crooked hands;
Close to the sun in lonely lands,
Ringed with the azure world, he stands.

The wrinkled sea beneath him crawls;
He watches from his mountain walls,
And like a thunderbolt he falls.

A brief, flawless, heraldic realization of a creature in all the spikily tangible properties of his creatureliness.

Tears, Idle Tears

❖❖❖❖❖

Tears, idle tears, I know not what they mean,
Tears from the depth of some divine despair
Rise in the heart, and gather to the eyes,
In looking on the happy autumn-fields,
And thinking of the days that are no more.

Fresh as the first beam glittering on a sail,
That brings our friends up from the underworld,
Sad as the last which reddens over one
That sinks with all we love below the verge;
So sad, so fresh, the days that are no more.

Ah, sad and strange as in dark summer dawns
The earliest pipe of half-awakened birds
To dying ears, when unto dying eyes
The casement slowly grows a glimmering square;
So sad, so strange, the days that are no more.

Dear as remembered kisses after death,
And sweet as those by hopeless fancy feigned
On lips that are for others; deep as love,
Deep as first love, and wild with all regret;
O Death in Life, the days that are no more.

from The Princess

Extraordinary: an unrhymed song, although the terminal phrase in every fifth line returns as a refrain. There are a few other unrhymed songs in "The Princess," including "Now Sleeps the Crimson Petal" (p. 650). Tennyson said that he had written "Tears, Idle Tears" at Tintern Abbey (see Wordsworth's poem, p. 407).

Now Sleeps the Crimson Petal

Now sleeps the crimson petal, now the white;
Nor waves the cypress in the palace walk;
Nor winks the gold fin in the porphyry font.
The firefly wakens; waken thou with me.

Now droops the milk-white peacock like a ghost,
And like a ghost she glimmers on to me.

Now lies the Earth all Danaë to the stars,
And all thy heart lies open unto me.

Now slides the silent meteor on, and leaves
A shining furrow, as thy thoughts in me.

Now folds the lily all her sweetness up,
And slips into the bosom of the lake.
So fold thyself, my dearest, thou, and slip
Into my bosom and be lost in me.

from The Princess

---

*Like "Tears, Idle Tears" (p. 649), this is a remarkable "blank verse lyric"
(Tennyson's phrase), with a repeated word functioning as a refrain.*

The Charge of the Light Brigade

>>>>>>

I

Half a league, half a league,
Half a league onward,
All in the valley of Death
　Rode the six hundred.
"Forward the Light Brigade!
Charge for the guns!" he said.
Into the valley of Death
　Rode the six hundred.

II

"Forward, the Light Brigade!"
Was there a man dismayed?
Not though the soldier knew
　Someone had blundered.
Theirs not to make reply,
Theirs not to reason why,
Theirs but to do and die.
Into the valley of Death
　Rode the six hundred.

III

Cannon to right of them,
Cannon to left of them,
Cannon in front of them
　Volleyed and thundered;
Stormed at with shot and shell,
Boldly they rode and well,
Into the jaws of Death,
Into the mouth of hell
　Rode the six hundred.

IV

Flashed all their sabres bare,
Flashed as they turned in air
Sabring the gunners there,
Charging an army, while
 All the world wondered.
Plunged in the battery-smoke
Right through the line they broke;
Cossack and Russian
Reeled from the sabre-stroke
 Shattered and sundered.
Then they rode back, but not,
 Not the six hundred.

V

Cannon to right of them,
Cannon to left of them,
Cannon behind them
 Volleyed and thundered;
Stormed at with shot and shell,
While horse and hero fell.
They that had fought so well
Came through the jaws of Death,
Back from the mouth of hell,
All that was left of them,
 Left of six hundred.

VI

When can their glory fade?
O the wild charge they made!
 All the world wondered.
Honor the charge they made!
Honor the Light Brigade,
 Noble six hundred!

Of the 673 soldiers who, on October 25, 1854, charged into the North Valley above Balaclava in the Crimea, 113 were killed, 134 were wounded, and 231 were missing and presumed captured. The order, scribbled in pencil by General Richard Airey, was perhaps unclear: "Lord Raglan the Commander-in-Chief wishes the cavalry to advance rapidly to the front, and try to prevent the enemy carrying away the guns . . . ." This poem has enjoyed much celebrity—or notoriety; its title was given to at least two films: Michael Curtiz's in 1936, starring Errol Flynn and having little to do with history, and Tony Richardson's in 1968.

Mariana

With blackest moss the flower-pots
  Were thickly crusted, one and all:
The rusted nails fell from the knots
  That held the pear to the gable-wall.
The broken sheds looked sad and strange:
  Unlifted was the clinking latch;
  Weeded and worn the ancient thatch
Upon the lonely moated grange.
    She only said, "My life is dreary,
      He cometh not," she said;
    She said, "I am aweary, aweary,
      I would that I were dead!"

Her tears fell with the dews at even;
  Her tears fell ere the dews were dried;
She could not look on the sweet heaven,
  Either at morn or eventide.
After the flitting of the bats,
  When thickest dark did trance the sky,
  She drew her casement-curtain by,
And glanced athwart the glooming flats.
    She only said, "The night is dreary,
      He cometh not," she said;
    She said, "I am aweary, aweary,
      I would that I were dead!"

Upon the middle of the night,
  Waking she heard the night-fowl crow:
The cock sung out an hour ere light:
  From the dark fen the oxen's low
Came to her: without hope of change,
  In sleep she seemed to walk forlorn,
  Till cold winds woke the gray-eyed morn

About the lonely moated grange.
    She only said, "The day is dreary,
      He cometh not," she said;
    She said, "I am aweary, aweary,
      I would that I were dead!"

About a stone-cast from the wall
    A sluice with blackened waters slept,
And o'er it many, round and small,
    The clustered marish-mosses crept.
Hard by a poplar shook alway,
    All silver-green with gnarlèd bark:
    For leagues no other tree did mark
The level waste, the rounding gray.
    She only said, "My life is dreary,
      He cometh not," she said;
    She said, "I am aweary, aweary,
      I would that I were dead!"

And ever when the moon was low,
    And the shrill winds were up and away,
In the white curtain, to and fro,
    She saw the gusty shadow sway.
But when the moon was very low,
    And wild winds bound within their cell,
    The shadow of the poplar fell
Upon her bed, across her brow.
    She only said, "The night is dreary,
      He cometh not," she said;
    She said, "I am aweary, aweary,
      I would that I were dead!"

All day within the dreamy house,
    The doors upon their hinges creaked;
The blue fly sung in the pane; the mouse
    Behind the mouldering wainscot shrieked,
Or from the crevice peered about.
    Old faces glimmered through the doors,

Old footsteps trod the upper floors,
Old voices called her from without.
　　She only said, "My life is dreary,
　　　He cometh not," she said;
　　She said, "I am aweary, aweary,
　　　I would that I were dead!"

The sparrow's chirrup on the roof,
　The slow clock ticking, and the sound
Which to the wooing wind aloof
　The poplar made, did all confound
Her sense; but most she loathed the hour
　When the thick-moted sunbeam lay
　Athwart the chambers, and the day
Was sloping toward his western bower.
　　Then, said she, "I am very dreary,
　　　He will not come," she said;
　　She wept, "I am aweary, aweary,
　　　Oh God, that I were dead!"

This early poem, published when Tennyson was twenty-one, is about a subject that Tennyson was to devote many more poems to: the abandoned and the bereft. (See also Shakespeare's Measure for Measure, *Act III, scene 1.)*

The Lady of Shalott

PART I

On either side the river lie
Long fields of barley and of rye,
That clothe the wold and meet the sky;
And through the field the road runs by
　To many-towered Camelot;
And up and down the people go,
Gazing where the lilies blow
Round an island there below,
　The island of Shalott.

Willows whiten, aspens quiver,
Little breezes dusk and shiver
Through the wave that runs for ever
By the island in the river
　Flowing down to Camelot.
Four gray walls, and four gray towers,
Overlook a space of flowers,
And the silent isle imbowers
　The Lady of Shalott.

By the margin, willow-veiled,
Slide the heavy barges trailed
By slow horses; and unhailed
The shallop flitteth silken-sailed
　Skimming down to Camelot:
But who hath seen her wave her hand?
Or at the casement seen her stand?
Or is she known in all the land,
　The Lady of Shalott?

Only reapers, reaping early
In among the bearded barley,
Hear a song that echoes cheerly
From the river winding clearly,
   Down to towered Camelot:
And by the moon the reaper weary,
Piling sheaves in uplands airy,
Listening, whispers " 'Tis the fairy
   Lady of Shalott."

PART II

There she weaves by night and day
A magic web with colours gay.
She has heard a whisper say,
A curse is on her if she stay
   To look down to Camelot.
She knows not what the curse may be,
And so she weaveth steadily,
And little other care hath she,
   The Lady of Shalott.

And moving through a mirror clear
That hangs before her all the year,
Shadows of the world appear.
There she sees the highway near
   Winding down to Camelot:
There the river eddy whirls,
And there the surly village-churls,
And the red cloaks of market girls,
   Pass onward from Shalott.

Sometimes a troop of damsels glad,
An abbot on an ambling pad,
Sometimes a curly shepherd-lad,
Or long-haired page in crimson clad,
   Goes by to towered Camelot;
And sometimes through the mirror blue
The knights come riding two and two:
She hath no loyal knight and true,
   The Lady of Shalott.

But in her web she still delights
To weave the mirror's magic sights,
For often through the silent nights
A funeral, with plumes and lights
   And music, went to Camelot:
Or when the moon was overhead,
Came two young lovers lately wed;
"I am half sick of shadows," said
   The Lady of Shalott.

PART III

A bow-shot from her bower-eaves,
He rode between the barley-sheaves,
The sun came dazzling through the leaves,
And flamed upon the brazen greaves
   Of bold Sir Lancelot.
A red-cross knight for ever kneeled
To a lady in his shield,
That sparkled on the yellow field,
   Beside remote Shalott.

The gemmy bridle glittered free,
Like to some branch of stars we see
Hung in the golden Galaxy.
The bridle bells rang merrily
  As he rode down to Camelot:
And from his blazoned baldric slung
A mighty silver bugle hung,
And as he rode his armour rung,
  Beside remote Shalott.

All in the blue unclouded weather
Thick-jewelled shone the saddle-leather,
The helmet and the helmet-feather
Burned like one burning flame together,
  As he rode down to Camelot.
As often through the purple night,
Below the starry clusters bright,
Some bearded meteor, trailing light,
  Moves over still Shalott.

His broad clear brow in sunlight glowed;
On burnished hooves his war-horse trode;
From underneath his helmet flowed
His coal-black curls as on he rode,
  As he rode down to Camelot.
From the bank and from the river
He flashed into the crystal mirror,
"Tirra lirra," by the river
  Sang Sir Lancelot.

She left the web, she left the loom,
She made three paces through the room,
She saw the water-lily bloom,
She saw the helmet and the plume,
　　She looked down to Camelot.
Out flew the web and floated wide;
The mirror cracked from side to side;
"The curse is come upon me," cried
　　The Lady of Shalott.

PART IV

In the stormy east-wind straining,
The pale yellow woods were waning,
The broad stream in his banks complaining,
Heavily the low sky raining
　　Over towered Camelot;
Down she came and found a boat
Beneath a willow left afloat,
And round about the prow she wrote
　　The Lady of Shalott.

And down the river's dim expanse
Like some bold seër in a trance,
Seeing all his own mischance—
With a glassy countenance
　　Did she look to Camelot.
And at the closing of the day
She loosed the chain, and down she lay;
The broad stream bore her far away,
　　The Lady of Shalott.

Lying, robed in snowy white
That loosely flew to left and right—
The leaves upon her falling light—
Through the noises of the night
   She floated down to Camelot:
And as the boat-head wound along
The willowy hills and fields among,
They heard her singing her last song,
   The Lady of Shalott.

Heard a carol, mournful, holy,
Chanted loudly, chanted lowly,
Till her blood was frozen slowly,
And her eyes were darkened wholly,
   Turned to towered Camelot.
For ere she reached upon the tide
The first house by the water-side,
Singing in her song she died,
   The Lady of Shalott.

Under tower and balcony,
By garden-wall and gallery,
A gleaming shape she floated by,
Dead-pale between the houses high,
   Silent into Camelot.
Out upon the wharfs they came,
Knight and burgher, lord and dame,
And round the prow they read her name,
   The Lady of Shalott.

Who is this? and what is here?
And in the lighted palace near
Died the sound of royal cheer;
And they crossed themselves for fear,
   All the knights at Camelot:
But Lancelot mused a little space;
He said, "She has a lovely face;
God in his mercy lend her grace,
   The lady of Shalott."

Tennyson later used the same material in "Lancelot and Elaine" in The Idylls
of the King.

Flower in the Crannied Wall

Flower in the crannied wall,
I pluck you out of the crannies,
I hold you here, root and all, in my hand,
Little flower—but *if* I could understand
What you are, root and all, and all in all,
I should know what God and man is.

This poem is sometimes labelled a "fragment." Many works, especially those from 1800 on, concentrate on a single small creature to ponder large meanings.

Browning was a varied poet for all of his long career,
but his modern reputation owes most to his perfection
of the dramatic monologue (although that designation
applies to only two of his poems in this anthology: "My
Last Duchess" and "The Bishop Orders His Tomb at
St. Praxed's Church"). After their sensational elope-
ment in 1846, he and his wife lived in Florence, Italy,
until her death in 1861. He then returned to England,
where he spent most of his remaining days.

My Last Duchess

Ferrara

That's my last Duchess painted on the wall,
Looking as if she were alive. I call
That piece a wonder, now: Frà Pandolf's hands
Worked busily a day, and there she stands.
Will 't please you sit and look at her? I said
"Frà Pandolf" by design, for never read
Strangers like you that pictured countenance,
The depth and passion of its earnest glance,
But to myself they turned (since none puts by
The curtain I have drawn for you, but I)
And seemed as they would ask me, if they durst,
How such a glance came there; so, not the first
Are you to turn and ask thus. Sir, 't was not
Her husband's presence only, called that spot
Of joy into the Duchess' cheek: perhaps
Frà Pandolf chanced to say "Her mantle laps
Over my lady's wrist too much," or "Paint
Must never hope to reproduce the faint
Half-flush that dies along her throat": such stuff
Was courtesy, she thought, and cause enough
For calling up that spot of joy. She had

A heart—how shall I say?— too soon made glad,
Too easily impressed; she liked whate'er
She looked on, and her looks went everywhere.
Sir, 't was all one! My favour at her breast,
The dropping of the daylight in the West,
The bough of cherries some officious fool
Broke in the orchard for her, the white mule
She rode with round the terrace—all and each
Would draw from her alike the approving speech,
Or blush, at least. She thanked men,—good! but
    thanked
Somehow—I know not how—as if she ranked
My gift of a nine-hundred-years-old name
With anybody's gift. Who'd stoop to blame
This sort of trifling? Even had you skill
In speech—(which I have not)—to make your will
Quite clear to such an one, and say, "Just this
Or that in you disgusts me; here you miss,
Or there exceed the mark"—and if she let
Herself be lessoned so, nor plainly set
Her wits to yours, forsooth, and made excuse,
—E'en then would be some stooping; and I choose
Never to stoop. Oh sir, she smiled, no doubt,
Whene'er I passed her; but who passed without
Much the same smile? This grew; I gave
    commands;
Then all smiles stopped together. There she stands
As if alive. Will 't please you rise? We'll meet
The company below, then. I repeat,
The Count your master's known munificence
Is ample warrant that no just pretense
Of mine for dowry will be disallowed;
Though his fair daughter's self, as I avowed
At starting, is my object. Nay, we'll go
Together down, sir. Notice Neptune, though,
Taming a sea horse, thought a rarity,
Which Claus of Innsbruck cast in bronze for me!

It has been observed that the Duke's admiration for a bronze of Neptune Taming a Sea Horse shows his dedication to bullying. Just as he tried to dominate the earlier Duchess, he is trying now to monopolize his negotiations with the envoy. And now you can answer half of the famous English literature exam question: Name two works in which an Italian duchess is offered fruit. (The other is John Webster's Duchess of Malfi, *where the duchess is offered the fruit of the apricot tree.)*

Home Thoughts from Abroad

I

Oh, to be in England
Now that April's there,
And whoever wakes in England
Sees, some morning, unaware,
That the lowest boughs and the brushwood sheaf
Round the elm-tree bole are in tiny leaf,
While the chaffinch sings on the orchard bough
In England—now!

II

And after April, when May follows,
And the whitethroat builds, and all the swallows!
Hark, where my blossomed pear-tree in the hedge
Leans to the field and scatters on the clover
Blossoms and dewdrops—at the bent spray's edge—
That's the wise thrush; he sings each song twice over,
Lest you should think he never could recapture
The first fine careless rapture!
And though the fields look rough with hoary dew,
All will be gay when noontide wakes anew
The buttercups, the little children's dower
—Far brighter than this gaudy melon-flower!

Browning published this poem and a companion piece, "Home-Thoughts, from the Sea," in 1845, both imagined from the viewpoint of an Englishman in or near the southwest corner of the Continent. Even the wording "Home-Thoughts" is peculiarly English (or Germanic), different from a corresponding expression in a Romance language.

Meeting at Night

❖❖❖❖

1

The gray sea and the long black land;
And the yellow half-moon large and low;
And the startled little waves that leap
In fiery ringlets from their sleep,
As I gain the cove with pushing prow,
And quench its speed i' the slushy sand.

2

Then a mile of warm sea-scented beach;
Three fields to cross till a farm appears;
A tap at the pane, the quick sharp scratch
And blue spurt of a lighted match,
And a voice less loud, through its joys and fears,
Then the two hearts beating each to each!

In Dramatic Romances *(1845), this poem and "Parting at Morning" (p. 675) were printed together as one work entitled "Night and Morning." The parts were separated and re-titled in 1849.*

The Year's at the Spring

The year's at the spring,
And day's at the morn;
Morning's at seven;
The hillside's dew-pearled;
The lark's on the wing;
The snail's on the thorn:
God's in His Heaven —
All's right with the world!

from Pippa Passes

Although Pippa's song, which comes in the first scene ("Morning") of the drama Pippa Passes, *may seem ridiculously optimistic, Pippa is no Pollyanna, and her song is far from simple. The* abcdabcd *rhyme-scheme itself bears the stamp of complexity.*

The Bishop Orders His Tomb
at St. Praxed's Church

>>>>>>>

Vanity, saith the preacher, vanity!
Draw round my bed: is Anselm keeping back?
Nephews—sons mine . . . ah, God, I know not! Well—
She, men would have to be your mother once,
Old Gandolf envied me, so fair she was!
What's done is done, and she is dead beside,
Dead long ago, and I am Bishop since,
And as she died so must we die ourselves,
And thence ye may perceive the world's a dream.
Life, how and what is it? As here I lie
In this state-chamber, dying by degrees,
Hours and long hours in the dead night, I ask
'Do I live, am I dead?' Peace, peace seems all.
Saint Praxed's ever was the church for peace;
And so, about this tomb of mine. I fought
With tooth and nail to save my niche, ye know:
—Old Gandolf cozened me, despite my care;
Shrewd was that snatch from out the corner South
He graced his carrion with, God curse the same!
Yet still my niche is not so cramped but thence
One sees the pulpit o' the epistle-side,
And somewhat of the choir, those silent seats,
And up into the aery dome where live
The angels, and a sunbeam's sure to lurk:
And I shall fill my slab of basalt there,
And 'neath my tabernacle take my rest,
With those nine columns round me, two and two,
The odd one at my feet where Anselm stands:
Peach-blossom marble all, the rare, the ripe
As fresh-poured red wine of a mighty pulse.
—Old Gandolf with his paltry onion-stone,
Put me where I may look at him! True peach,

Rosy and flawless: how I earned the prize!
Draw close: that conflagration of my church
—What then? So much was saved if aught were missed!
My sons, ye would not be my death? Go dig
The white-grape vineyard where the oil-press stood,
Drop water gently till the surface sink,
And if ye fine . . . Ah God, I know not, I! . . .
Bedded in store of rotten fig-leaves soft,
And corded up in a tight olive-frail,
Some lump, ah God, of *lapis lazuli*,
Big as a Jew's head cut off at the nape,
Blue as a vein o'er the Madonna's breast . . .
Sons, all have I bequeathed you, villas, all,
That brave Frascati villa with its bath,
So, let the blue lump poise between my knees,
Like God the Father's globe on both his hands
Ye worship in the Jesu Church so gay,
For Gandolf shall not choose but see and burst!
Swift as a weaver's shuttle fleet our years:
Man goeth to the grave, and where is he?
Did I say basalt for my slab, sons? Black—
'Twas ever antique-black I meant! How else
Shall ye contrast my frieze to come beneath?
The bas-relief in bronze ye promised me,
Those Pans and Nymphs ye wot of, and perchance
Some tripod, thyrsus, with a vase or so,
The Saviour at his sermon on the mount,
Saint Praxed in a glory, and one Pan
Ready to twitch the Nymph's last garment off,
And Moses with the tables . . . but I know
Ye mark me not! What do they whisper thee,
Child of my bowels, Anselm? Ah, ye hope
To revel down my villas while I gasp
Bricked o'er with beggar's mouldy travertine
Which Gandolf from his tomb-top chuckles at!
Nay, boys, ye love me—all of jasper, then!
'Tis jasper ye stand pledged to, lest I grieve
My bath must needs be left behind, alas!

One block, pure green as a pistachio-nut,
There's plenty jasper somewhere in the world—
And have I not Saint Praxed's ear to pray
Horses for ye, and brown Greek manuscripts,
And mistresses with great smooth marbly limbs?
—That's if ye carve my epitaph aright,
Choice Latin, picked phrase, Tully's every word,
No gaudy ware like Gandolf's second line—
Tully, my masters? Ulpian serves his need!
And then how I shall lie through centuries,
And hear the blessed mutter of the mass,
And see God made and eaten all day long,
And feel the steady candle-flame, and taste
Good strong thick stupefying incense-smoke!
For as I lie here, hours of the dead night,
Dying in state and by such slow degrees,
I fold my arms as if they clasped a crook,
And stretch my feet forth straight as stone can point,
And let the bedclothes, for a mortcloth, drop
Into great laps and folds of sculptor's-work:
And as yon tapers dwindle, and strange thoughts
Grow, with a certain humming in my ears,
About the life before I lived this life,
And this life too, popes, cardinals and priests,
Saint Praxed at his sermon on the mount,
Your tall pale mother with her talking eyes,
And new-found agate urns as fresh as day,
And marble's language, Latin pure, discreet,
—Aha, ELUCESCEBAT quoth our friend?
No Tully, said I, Ulpian at the best!
Evil and brief hath been my pilgrimage.
All *lapis*, all, sons! Else I give the Pope
My villas! Will ye ever eat my heart?
Ever your eyes were as a lizard's quick
They glitter like your mother's for my soul,
Or ye would heighten my impoverished frieze,
Piece out its starved design, and fill my vase
With grapes, and add a vizor and a Term,

And to the tripod ye would tie a lynx
That in his struggle throws the thyrsus down,
To comfort me on my entablature
Whereon I am to lie till I must ask
"Do I live, am I dead?" There, leave me, there!
For ye have stabbed me with ingratitude
To death—ye wish it—God, ye wish it! Stone—
Gritstone, a-crumble! Clammy squares which sweat
As if the corpse they keep were oozing through—
And no more *lapis* to delight the world!
Well go! I bless ye. Fewer tapers there,
But in a row: and, going, turn your backs
—Ay, like departing altar-ministrants,
And leave me in my church, the church for peace,
That I may watch at leisure if he leers—
Old Gandolf, at me, from his onion-stone,
As still he envied me, so fair she was!

Browning's Bishop remains a vivacious and compelling preacher to the end. In a mixture that may impress the innocent as hypocritical, he is a theologian, an aesthete, a politician, and an ardent lover of the physical.

Parting at Morning

Round the cape of a sudden came the sea,
And the sun looked over the mountain's rim:
And straight was a path of gold for him,
And the need of a world of men for me.

This poem and "Meeting at Night" (p. 669) were originally printed together as one work in Dramatic Romances *(1845). "Him" in the third line refers to the sun.*

Two in the Campagna

I wonder do you feel to-day
  As I have felt, since, hand in hand,
We sat down on the grass, to stray
  In spirit better through the land,
This morn of Rome and May?

For me, I touched a thought, I know,
  Has tantalised me many times,
(Like turns of thread the spiders throw
  Mocking across our path) for rhymes
To catch at and let go.

Help me to hold it! First it left
  The yellowing fennel, run to seed
There, branching from the brickwork's cleft,
  Some old tomb's ruin: yonder weed
Took up the floating weft,

Where one small orange cup amassed
  Five beetles,—blind and green they grope
Among the honey-meal; and last,
  Everywhere on the grassy slope
I traced it. Hold it fast!

The champaign with its endless fleece
  Of feathery grasses everywhere!
Silence and passion, joy and peace,
  An everlasting wash of air—
Rome's ghost since her decease.

Such life there, through such lengths of hours,
  Such miracles performed in play,
Such primal naked forms of flowers,
  Such letting nature have her way
While heaven looks from its towers.

How say you? Let us, O my dove,
  Let us be unashamed of soul,
As earth lies bare to heaven above!
  How is it under our control
To love or not to love?

I would that you were all to me,
  You that are just so much, no more—
Nor yours, nor mine, nor slave nor free!
  Where does the fault lie? what the core
Of the wound, since wound must be?

I would I could adopt your will,
  See with your eyes, and set my heart
Beating by yours, and drink my fill
  At your soul's springs,—your part my part
In life, for good and ill.

No. I yearn upward, touch you close,
  Then stand away. I kiss your cheek,
Catch your soul's warmth,—I pluck the rose
  And love it more than tongue can speak—
Then the good minute goes.

Already how am I so far
  Out of that minute? Must I go
Still like the thistle-ball, no bar,
  Onward, whenever light winds blow,
Fixed by no friendly star?

Just when I seemed about to learn!
   Where is the thread now? Off again!
   The old trick! Only I discern—
   Infinite passion, and the pain
Of finite hearts that yearn.

The Brownings visited the Campagna di Roma—an 800-square-mile "champaign" or waste plain with thought-provoking ruins and relics. The speaker of the poem does not have to be Robert Browning himself or, indeed, any man.

EDWARD LEAR 1812-1888

Lear was an observant traveler and a gifted draftsman who began writing to add some text to drawings for children. He belonged to about the same generation as "Lewis Carroll" and Sir William Schwenck Gilbert, writers of humorous verse that reaches genuine nonsense on one side but also touches the realms of travesty, parody, and satire, and even now and then some horror and pathos.

The Owl and the Pussy-Cat

The Owl and the Pussy-cat went to sea
  In a beautiful pea-green boat,
They took some honey, and plenty of money,
  Wrapped up in a five-pound note.
The Owl looked up to the stars above,
  And sang to a small guitar,
"O lovely Pussy! O Pussy, my love,
  What a beautiful Pussy you are,
    You are,
    You are!
  What a beautiful Pussy you are!"

Pussy said to the Owl, "You elegant fowl!
  How charmingly sweet you sing!
O let us be married! too long we have tarried:
  But what shall we do for a ring?"
They sailed away, for a year and a day,
  To the land where the Bong-Tree grows,
And there in a wood a Piggy-wig stood,
  With a ring at the end of his nose,
    His nose,
    His nose,
  With a ring at the end of his nose.

"Dear Pig, are you willing to sell for one shilling
   Your ring?" Said the Piggy, "I will."
So they took it away, and were married next day
   By the Turkey who lives on the hill.
They dined on mince, and slices of quince,
   Which they ate with a runcible spoon;
And hand in hand, on the edge of the sand,
   They danced by the light of the moon,
     The moon,
     The moon,
   They danced by the light of the moon.

Nonsense notwithstanding, Lear somehow puts a good deal of compassion and a great deal of charm into a little song. In this love story with a happy ending, one may hear echoes of moon-music from Byron's "So We'll Go No More a-Roving" (p. 479) and Poe's "Annabel Lee" (p. 631). Lear uses his favorite made-up word "runcible" here for the first time; it later modifies a cat and a hat. It meant nothing special then but has come to be the name of a kind of pickle-fork.

The Jumblies

I

They went to sea in a Sieve, they did,
   In a Sieve they went to sea:
In spite of all their friends could say,
On a winter's morn, on a stormy day,
   In a Sieve they went to sea!
And when the Sieve turned round and round,
And every one cried, "You'll all be drowned!"
They called aloud, "Our Sieve ain't big,
But we don't care a button! we don't care a fig!
   In a Sieve we'll go to sea!"
      Far and few, far and few,
         Are the lands where the Jumblies live;
         Their heads are green, and their hands are blue,
         And they went to sea in a Sieve.

II

They sailed away in a Sieve, they did,
   In a Sieve they sailed so fast,
With only a beautiful pea-green veil
Tied with a riband by way of a sail,
   To a small tobacco-pipe mast;
And every one said, who saw them go,
"O won't they be soon upset, you know!
For the sky is dark, and the voyage is long,
And happen what may, it's extremely wrong
   In a Sieve to sail so fast!"
      Far and few, far and few,
         Are the lands where the Jumblies live;
         Their heads are green, and their hands are blue,
         And they went to sea in a Sieve.

III

The water it soon came in, it did,
  The water it soon came in;
So to keep them dry, they wrapped their feet
In a pinky paper all folded neat,
  And they fastened it down with a pin.
And they passed the night in a crockery-jar,
And each of them said, "How wise we are!
Though the sky be dark, and the voyage be long,
Yet we never can think we were rash or wrong,
While round in our Sieve we spin!"
    Far and few, far and few,
      Are the lands where the Jumblies live;
      Their heads are green, and their hands are blue,
      And they went to sea in a Sieve.

IV

And all night long they sailed away;
  And when the sun went down,
They whistled and warbled a moony song
To the echoing sound of a coppery gong,
  In the shade of the mountains brown.
  "O Timballo! How happy we are,
When we live in a sieve and a crockery-jar;
And all night long in the moonlight pale,
We sail away with a pea-green sail,
  In the shade of the mountains brown!"
    Far and few, far and few,
      Are the lands where the Jumblies live;
      Their heads are green, and their hands are blue,
      And they went to sea in a Sieve.

V

They sailed to the Western Sea, they did,
  To a land all covered with trees,
And they bought an Owl, and a useful Cart,
And a pound of Rice, and a Cranberry Tart,
  And a hive of silvery Bees.

And they bought a Pig, and some green Jack-daws,
And a lovely Monkey with lollipop paws,
And forty bottles of Ring-Bo-Ree,
  And no end of Stilton Cheese.
    Far and few, far and few,
      Are the lands where the Jumblies live;
    Their heads are green, and their hands are blue,
      And they went to sea in a Sieve.

VI

And in twenty years they all came back,
  In twenty years or more,
And every one said, 'How tall they've grown!
For they've been to the Lakes, and the Torrible Zone,
  And the hills of the Chankly Bore;
And they drank their health, and gave them a feast
Of dumplings made of beautiful yeast;
And every one said, "If we only live,
We too will go to sea in a Sieve,—
  To the hills of the Chankly Bore!"
    Far and few, far and few,
      Are the lands where the Jumblies live;
    Their heads are green, and their hands are blue,
      And they went to sea in a Sieve.

Is there not something heroic about the Jumblies' pluck as they sail out in bad weather in an unfit vessel "In spite of all their friends could say"? (See also "Sir Patrick Spens," p. 10.) Like Odysseus, they come home after twenty years of adventures in exotic-sounding places. Lear's two poems in this anthology begin to show how much he liked certain combinations, such as "beautiful pea-green."

EMILY BRONTË 1818–1848

Emily Brontë will always be known more for *Wuthering Heights* than for her poetry, but that is only because the novel is one of the greatest books in the language. She was an accomplished and versatile poet, and it is a pity that she died so young. Her older sister Charlotte is famous for *Jane Eyre*, their younger sister Anne for *Agnes Grey* and *The Tenant of Wildfell Hall.*

Remembrance

Cold in the earth—and the deep snow piled above thee,
Far, far removed, cold in the dreary grave!
Have I forgot, my only Love, to love thee,
Severed at last by Time's all-severing wave?

Now, when alone, do my thoughts no longer hover
Over the mountains, on that northern shore,
Resting their wings where heath and fern-leaves cover
That noble heart for ever, ever more?

Cold in the earth—and fifteen wild Decembers
From those brown hills, have melted into spring—
Faithful indeed is the spirit that remembers
After such years of change and suffering!

Sweet Love of youth, forgive if I forget thee,
While the world's tide is bearing me along:
Other desires and darker hopes beset me,
Hopes which obscure, but cannot do thee wrong!

No later light has lightened up my heaven;
No second morn has ever shone for me:
All my life's bliss from thy dear life was given—
All my life's bliss is in the grave with thee.

But, when the days of golden dreams had perished,
And even Despair was powerless to destroy,
Then did I learn how existence could be cherished,
Strengthened, and fed without the aid of joy;

Then did I check the tears of useless passion,
Weaned my young soul from yearning after thine;
Sternly denied its burning wish to hasten
Down to that tomb already more than mine!

And, even yet, I dare not let it languish,
Dare not indulge in memory's rapturous pain;
Once drinking deep of that divinest anguish,
How could I seek the empty world again?

---

*For more than half of her thirty years, Emily Brontë, along with her younger
sister Anne, wrote prose and verse about an imaginary northern realm they called
Gondal. "Remembrance" contains passion, memory, dream, Time, and winter:
the same elements that animate* Wuthering Heights.

One of Clough's poems in this anthology is gravely earnest, the other flippantly light, but both are about conduct, morality, and belief. Clough was a friend of Matthew Arnold and had the same Rugby-Oxford orientation; although he early gave up Oxford and went his own way. Arnold addressed "To a Republican Friend, 1848" to Clough and commemorated Clough in the pastoral "Thyrsis."

Say Not the Struggle Nought Availeth

Say not the struggle nought availeth,
   The labor and the wounds are vain,
The enemy faints not, nor faileth,
   And as things have been they remain.

If hopes were dupes, fears may be liars;
   It may be, in yon smoke concealed,
Your comrades chase e'en now the fliers,
   And, but for you, possess the field.

For while the tired waves, vainly breaking,
   Seem here no painful inch to gain,
Far back through creeks and inlets making,
   Comes silent, flooding in, the main.

And not by eastern windows only,
   When daylight comes, comes in the light,
In front the sun climbs slow, how slowly,
   But westward, look, the land is bright.

Clough sounds here like one of Charles Kingsley's brigadiers of Muscular Christianity.

The Latest Decalogue

Thou shalt have one God only; who
Would be at the expense of two?
No graven images may be
Worshipped, except the currency:
Swear not at all; for, for thy curse
Thine enemy is none the worse:
At church on Sunday to attend
Will serve to keep the world thy friend:
Honour thy parents; that is, all
From whom advancement may befall:
Thou shalt not kill; but need'st not strive
Officiously to keep alive:
Do not adultery commit;
Advantage rarely comes of it:
Thou shalt not steal; an empty feat,
When it's so lucrative to cheat:
Bear not false witness; let the lie
Have time on its own wings to fly:
Thou shalt not covet, but tradition
Approves all forms of competition.

Clough could write a poem as wholesomely inspiring as "Say Not the Struggle Nought Availeth" (p. 686), but he was also capable of producing a telling satire as sharp and witty as attacks by Swift and Byron.

JULIA WARD HOWE 1819–1910

With her husband, Samuel G. Howe, Julia Ward
Howe edited an antislavery newspaper and was active
as a writer and lecturer in support of women's rights
and the abolition of slavery.

The Battle Hymn of the Republic

Mine eyes have seen the glory of the coming of the Lord;
He is trampling out the vintage where the grapes of wrath are
    stored;
He hath loosed the fateful lightning of His terrible swift sword;
His truth is marching on.
    Glory! Glory! Hallelujah!
    Glory! Glory! Hallelujah!
    Glory! Glory! Hallelujah!
    His truth is marching on.

I have seen Him in the watch fires of a hundred circling camps
They have builded Him an altar in the evening dews and damps;
I can read His righteous sentence by the dim and flaring lamps;
His day is marching on.
    Glory! Glory! Hallelujah!
    Glory! Glory! Hallelujah!
    Glory! Glory! Hallelujah!
    His day is marching on.

He has sounded forth the trumpet that shall never call retreat;
He is sifting out the hearts of men before His judgment seat;
Oh, be swift, my soul, to answer Him; be jubilant, my feet;
Our God is marching on.
    Glory! Glory! Hallelujah!
    Glory! Glory! Hallelujah!
    Glory! Glory! Hallelujah!
    Our God is marching on.

In the beauty of the lilies Christ was born across the sea,
With a glory in His bosom that transfigures you and me;
As He died to make men holy, let us die to make men free;
While God is marching on.
    Glory! Glory! Hallelujah!
    Glory! Glory! Hallelujah!
    Glory! Glory! Hallelujah!
    While God is marching on.

Early in the American Civil War, Julia Ward Howe wrote these stirring new words to the tune (and somewhat to the spirit) of "John Brown's Body," an antebellum song about the abolitionist leader who was hanged in 1859. This battle hymn, published in a magazine in 1862, has long been associated with the Union side in the Civil War, although it has lost a good deal of its partisan or regional significance.

Whitman wrote a lot about himself, and most readers are familiar with the outlines of his history: born on Long Island, worked as a printer and journalist, especially for Democrat organs, travelled to New Orleans, served as a wound-dresser during the Civil War, stayed on in Washington for some years after the war, moving finally to Camden, New Jersey, where he spent the last 19 years of his life. Whitman was uncommonly susceptible to influences of every sort. In creating his prodigiously capacious idiom for American poetry, he used slang, opera, phrenology, all religions and philosophies, the oratorical manners of preachers and lecturers, free association, the cutting-pasting assemblage of newspapers—in short, anything. He was always a democrat (although during the Civil War changed his party allegiance from Democrat to Republican). He was hailed by Emerson on the first appearance of *Leaves of Grass* in 1855; praise also came from W. M. Rossetti and Algernon Charles Swinburne.

A Noiseless Patient Spider

A noiseless patient spider,
I mark'd where on a little promontory it stood isolated,
Mark'd how to explore the vacant vast surrounding,
It launch'd forth filament, filament, filament, out of itself,
Ever unreeling them, ever tirelessly speeding them.

And you O my soul where you stand,
Surrounded, detached, in measureless oceans of space,
Ceaselessly musing, venturing, throwing, seeking the spheres to
    connect them,
Till the bridge you will need be form'd, till the ductile anchor
    hold,
Till the gossamer thread you fling catch somewhere, O, my
    soul.

Both Oliver Wendell Holmes's "Chambered Nautilus" (p. 620) of 1858 and Whitman's "Noiseless Patient Spider" of 1868 carefully observe the structure or behavior of a creature simpler than ourselves and go on to apply the zoological message with a moral "O my soul."

O Captain! My Captain!

O Captain! my Captain! our fearful trip is done,
The ship has weather'd every rack, the prize we sought is won,
The port is near, the bells I hear, the people all exulting,
While follow eyes the steady keel, the vessel grim and daring;
But O heart! heart! heart!
O the bleeding drops of red,
Where on the deck my Captain lies,
Fallen cold and dead.

O Captain! my Captain! rise up and hear the bells;
Rise up—for you the flag is flung—for you the bugle trills,
For you bouquets and ribbon'd wreaths—for you the shores
a-crowding,
For you they call, the swaying mass, their eager faces turning;
Here Captain! dear father!
This arm beneath your head!
It is some dream that on the deck,
You've fallen cold and dead.

My Captain does not answer, his lips are pale and still,
My father does not feel my arm, he has no pulse nor will,
The ship is anchor'd safe and sound, its voyage closed and done,
From fearful trip the victor ship comes in with object won;
Exult O shores, and ring O bells!
But I with mournful tread,
Walk the deck my Captain lies,
Fallen cold and dead.

from Memories of President Lincoln

Whitman's sheaf called Memories of President Lincoln *contains this poem and three others: "When Lilacs Last in the Dooryard Bloomed" (p. 694), "Hush'd Be the Camps Today," and "This Dust Was Once the Man." Although "O Captain! My Captain!" may seem to regress to a simple mode of allegory characteristic more of Holmes and Longfellow, and although some critics regard the poem as among Whitman's worst and least typical, it may be in these tormented lines that Whitman best achieves the status he desired of a genuinely popular writer.*

When Lilacs Last in the Dooryard Bloom'd

1

When lilacs last in the dooryard bloom'd
And the great star early drooped in the western sky in the night,
I mourned, and yet shall mourn with ever-returning spring.

Ever-returning spring, trinity sure to me you bring,
Lilac blooming perennial and drooping star in the west,
And thought of him I love.

2

O powerful western fallen star!
O shades of night—O moody, tearful night!
O great star disappeared—O the black murk that hides the star!
O cruel hands that hold me powerless—O helpless soul of me!
O harsh surrounding cloud that will not free my soul.

3

In the dooryard fronting an old farmhouse near the whitewashed
  palings
Stands the lilac-bush tall-growing with heart-shaped leaves of rich
  green,
With many a pointed blossom rising delicate, with the perfume
  strong I love,
With every leaf a miracle—and from this bush in the dooryard,
With delicate-colored blossoms and heart-shaped leaves of rich
  green,
A sprig with its flower I break.

4

In the swamp in secluded recesses,
A shy and hidden bird is warbling a song.

Solitary the thrush,
The hermit withdrawn to himself, avoiding the settlements,
Sings by himself a song.

Song of the bleeding throat,
Death's outlet song of life, (for well dear brother I know,
If thou wast not granted to sing thou would'st surely die.)

5

Over the breast of the spring, the land, amid cities,
Amid lanes and through old woods, where lately the violets
    peeped from the ground, spotting the grey debris,
Amid the grass in the fields each side of the lanes, passing the
    endless grass,
Passing the yellow-speared wheat, every grain from its shroud in
    the dark-brown fields uprisen,
Passing the apple-tree blows of white and pink in the orchards,
Carrying a corpse to where it shall rest in the grave,
Night and day journeys a coffin.

6

Coffin that passes through lanes and streets,
Through day and night with the great cloud darkening the land,
With the pomp of the inlooped flags, with the cities draped in
    black,
With the show of the States themselves as of crape-veiled women
    standing,
With processions long and winding and the flambeaus of the
    night,
With the countless torches lit, with the silent sea of faces and the
    unbared heads,
With the waiting depot, the arriving coffin, and the sombre faces,
With dirges through the night, with the thousand voices rising
    strong and solemn,

With the mournful voices of the dirges poured around the coffin,
The dim-lit churches and the shuddering organs—where amid
these you journey,
With the tolling tolling bells' perpetual clang,
Here, coffin that slowly passes,
I give you my sprig of lilac.

7

(Nor for you, for one alone,
Blossoms and branches green to coffins all I bring,

For fresh as the morning, thus would I chant a song for you, O
sane and sacred death.

All over bouquets of roses,
O death, I cover you over with roses and early lilies,
But mostly and now the lilac that blooms the first,
Copious I break, I break the sprigs from the bushes,
With loaded arms I come, pouring for you,
For you and the coffins all of you, O death.)

8

O western orb sailing the heaven,
Now I know what you must have meant as a month since I
walked,
As I walked in silence the transparent shadowy night,
As I saw you had something to tell as you bent to me night after
night,
As you drooped from the sky low down as if to my side, (while
the other stars all looked on,)
As we wandered together the solemn night, (for something I
know not what kept me from sleep,)
As the night advanced, and I saw on the rim of the west how
full you were of woe,
As I stood on the rising ground in the breeze in the cool
transparent night,
As I watched where you passed and was lost in the netherward
black of the night,

As my soul in its trouble dissatisfied sank, as where you, sad
    orb,
Concluded, dropped in the night, and was gone.

9

Sing on there in the swamp,
O singer bashful and tender, I hear your notes, I hear your call,
I hear, I come presently, I understand you,
But a moment I linger, for the lustrous star has detained me,
The star my departing comrade holds and detains me.

10

O how shall I warble myself for the dead one there I loved?
And how shall I deck my song for the large sweet soul that has
    gone?
And what shall my perfume be for the grave of him I love?

Sea-winds blown from east and west,
Blown from the Eastern sea and blown from the Western sea, till
there on the prairies meeting,
These and with these and the breath of my chant,
I'll perfume the grave of him I love.

11

O what shall I hang on the chamber walls?
And what shall the pictures be that I hang on the walls,
To adorn the burial-house of him I love?

Pictures of growing spring and farms and homes,
With the Fourth-month eve at sundown, and the grey smoke
    lucid and bright,
With floods of yellow gold of the gorgeous, indolent, sinking sun,
    burning, expanding the air,
With the fresh sweet herbage underfoot, and the pale green
    leaves of the trees prolific,
In the distance the flowing glaze, the breast of the river, with a
    wind-dapple here and there,

With ranging hills on the banks, with many a line against the
    sky, and shadows,
And the city at hand with dwellings so dense, and stacks of
    chimneys,
And all the scenes of life and the workshops, and the workmen
    homeward returning.

12

Lo, body and soul—this land,
My own Manhattan with spires, and the sparkling and hurrying
    tides, and the ships,
The varied and ample land, the South and the North in the light,
Ohio's shores and flashing Missouri,
And ever the far-spreading prairies covered with grass and corn.

Lo, the most excellent sun so calm and haughty,
The violet and purple morn with just-felt breezes,
The gentle soft-born measureless light,
The miracle spreading bathing all, the fulfilled noon,
The coming eve delicious, the welcome night and the stars,
Over my cities shining all, enveloping man and land.

13

Sing on, sing on you grey-brown bird,
Sing from the swamps, the recesses, pour your chant from the
    bushes,
Limitless out of the dusk, out of the cedars and pines.

Sing on dearest brother, warble your reedy song,
Loud human song, with voice of uttermost woe.

O liquid and free and tender!
O wild and loose to my soul—O wondrous singer!
You only I hear—yet the star holds me, (but will soon depart,)
Yet the lilac with mastering odor holds me.

14

Now while I sat in the day and looked forth,
In the close of the day with its light and the fields of spring, and
the farmers preparing their crops,
In the large unconscious scenery of my land with its lakes and
forests,
In the heavenly aerial beauty, (after the perturbed winds and the
storms,)
Under the arching heavens of the afternoon swift passing, and
the voices of children and women,
The many-moving sea-tides, and I saw the ships how they sailed,
And the summer approaching with richness, and the fields all
busy with labor,
And the infinite separate houses, how they all went on, each with
its meals and minutia of daily usages,
And the streets how their throbbings throbbed, and the cities
pent—lo, then and there,
Falling upon them all and among them all, enveloping me with
the rest,
Appeared the cloud, appeared the long black trail;
And I knew death, its thought, and the sacred knowledge of
death.

Then with the knowledge of death as walking one side of me,
And the thought of death close-walking the other side of me,
And I in the middle as with companions, and as holding the
hands of companions,
I fled forth to the hiding receiving night that talks not,
Down to the shores of the water, the path by the swamp in the
dimness,
To the solemn shadowy cedars and ghostly pines so still.

And the singer so shy to the rest received me,
The grey-brown bird I know received us comrades three,
And he sang the carol of death, and a verse for him I love.

From deep secluded recesses,
From the fragrant cedars and the ghostly pines so still,
Came the carol of the bird.

And the charm of the carol rapt me,
As I held as if by their hands my comrades in the night,
And the voice of my spirit tallied the song of the bird.

Come lovely and soothing death,
Undulate round the world, serenely arriving, arriving,
In the day, in the night, to all, to each,
Sooner or later delicate death.

Praised be the fathomless universe,
For life and joy, and for objects and knowledge curious,
And for love, sweet love—but praise! praise! praise!
For the sure-enwinding arms of cool-enfolding death.

Dark mother always gliding near with soft feet,
Have none chanted for thee a chant of fullest welcome?
Then I chant it for thee, I glorify thee above all,
I bring thee a song that when thou must indeed come, come unfalteringly.

Approach strong deliveress,
When it is so, when thou hast taken them I joyously sing the dead,
Lost in the loving floating ocean of thee,
Laved in the flood by thy bliss O death.

From me to thee glad serenades,
Dances for thee I propose saluting thee, adornments and feastings for
*   thee,*
And the sights of the open landscape and the high-spread sky are fitting,
And life and the fields, and the huge and thoughtful night.

The night in silence under many a star,
The ocean shore and the husky whispering wave whose voice I know,
And the soul turning to thee, O vast and well-veiled death,
And the body gratefully nestling close to thee.

Over the tree-topsI float thee a song,
Over the rising and sinking waves,over the myriad fields and the prairies
wide,
Over the dense-packed cities all and the teeming wharves and ways,
I float this carol with joy, with joy to thee, O death,

15

To the tally of my soul,
Loud and strong kept up the grey-brown bird,
With pure, deliberate notes spreading filling the night.

Loud in the pines and cedars dim,
Clear in the freshness moist and the swamp-perfume,
And I with my comrades there in the night.
While my sight that was bound in my eyes unclosed,
As to long panoramas of visions.

And I saw askant the armies,
I saw as in noiseless dreams hundreds of battle-flags,
Born through the smoke of the battles and pierced with missiles I
   saw them,
And carried hither and yon through the smoke, and torn and
   bloody,
And at last but a few shreds left on the staffs, (and all in
   silence,)
And the staffs all splintered and broken.

I saw battle-corpses, myriads of them,
And the white skeletons of young men, I saw them,
I saw the debris and debris of all the slain soldiers of war,
But I saw they were not as was thought,
They themselves were fully at rest, they suffered not,
The living remained and suffered, the mother suffered,
And the wife and the child and the musing comrade suffered,
And the armies that remained suffered.

16

Passing the visions, passing the night,
Passing, unloosing the hold of my comrades' hands,
Passing the song of the hermit bird and the tallying song of my
 soul,
Victorious song, death's outlet song, yet varying ever-altering
 song,
As low and wailing, yet clear the notes, rising and falling,
 flooding the night,
Sadly sinking and fainting, as warning and warning, and yet
 again bursting with joy,
Covering the earth and filling the spread of the heaven,
As that powerful psalm in the night I heard from recesses,
Passing, I leave thee lilac with heart-shaped leaves,
I leave thee there in the dooryard, blooming, returning with
 spring.

I cease my song for thee,
From my gaze on thee in the west, fronting the west, communing
 with thee,
O comrade lustrous with silver face in the night.
Yet each to keep and all, retrievements out of the night,
The song, the wondrous chant of the grey-brown bird,
And the tallying chant, the echo aroused in my soul,
With the lustrous and drooping star with the countenance full of
 woe,
With the holders holding my hand nearing the call of the bird,
Comrades mine and I in the midst, and their memory ever to
 keep, for the dead I loved so well,
For the sweetest, wisest soul of all my days and lands—and this
 for his dear sake,
Lilac and star and bird twined with the chant of my soul,
There in the fragrant pines and the cedars dusk and dim.
from Memories of President Lincoln

It is hard to believe that the same poet wrote "O Captain! My Captain!" — with its simple rhyming and allegorizing — and "When Lilacs Last in the Dooryard Bloom'd," so much more powerful, eloquent, and artistic. The threefold symbols of star, bird, and plant contain a profound awareness of grief within an even profounder awareness of the ever-returning seasons. Other great "April elegies" in this anthology are Milton's "On the Late Massacre in Piedmont" (p. 211), Hardy's "Convergence of the Twain" (p. 777), Yeats's "Easter, 1916" (p. 864), and Eliot's "Waste Land" (p. 968).

I Hear America Singing

I hear America singing, the varied carols I hear,
Those of mechanics, each one singing his as it should be blithe
and strong,
The carpenter singing his as he measures his plank or beam,
The mason singing his as he makes ready for work, or leaves off
work,
The boatman singing what belongs to him in his boat, the deck-
hand singing on the steamboat deck,
The shoemaker singing as he sits on his bench, the hatter singing
as he stands,
The wood-cutter's song, the plowboy's on his way in the
morning, or at noon intermission or at sundown,
The delicious singing of the mother, or of the young wife at
work, or of the girl sewing or washing,
Each singing what belongs to him or her and to none else,
The day what belongs to the day—at night the party of young
fellows, robust, friendly,
Singing with open mouths their strong melodious songs.

In various editions of Leave of Grass *between 1860 and 1881, Whitman moved
this poem around and even changed its first line and its title, which was orig-
inally "American mouth-songs!"*

Cavalry Crossing a Ford

A line in long array, where they wind betwixt green islands;
They take a serpentine course— their arms flash in the sun—
    hark to the musical clank;
Behold the silvery river—in it the splashing horses, loitering, stop
    to drink;
Behold the brown-faced men—each group, each person, a
    picture—the negligent rest on the saddles;
Some emerge on the opposite bank—others are just entering the
    ford—while,
Scarlet, and blue, and snowy white,
The guidon flags flutter gaily in the wind.

---

*With the clarity of documentary photography, Whitman renders an unadorned
wartime scene. All the implicit horror of war is held in abeyance, however, while
the artist concentrates on the elaborate interplay of elements and colors. The
poem begins and ends with simple description; between, in the second, third, and
fourth lines, the reader is invited into the action: "hark . . . Behold . . . Be-
hold . . . ."*

The son of Dr. Thomas Arnold (headmaster of Rugby),
Matthew Arnold was appointed an inspector of schools
in 1851 and later held the Chair of Poetry at Oxford for
ten years. His aesthetic and cultural criticism is almost
as influential as his poetry.

Dover Beach

The sea is calm tonight.
The tide is full, the moon lies fair
Upon the straits; — on the French coast the light
Gleams and is gone; the cliffs of England stand,
Glimmering and vast, out in the tranquil bay.
Come to the window, sweet is the night-air!
Only, from the long line of spray
Where the sea meets the moon-blanched land,
Listen! you hear the grating roar
Of pebbles which the waves draw back, and fling,
At their return, up the high strand,
Begin, and cease, and then again begin,
With tremulous cadence slow, and bring
The eternal note of sadness in.

Sophocles long ago
Heard it on the Ægæan, and it brought
Into his mind the turbid ebb and flow
Of human misery; we
Find also in the sound a thought,
Hearing it by this distant northern sea.

The Sea of Faith
Was once, too, at the full, and round earth's shore
Lay like the folds of a bright girdle furled.
But now I only hear
Its melancholy, long, withdrawing roar,
Retreating, to the breath
Of the night-wind, down the vast edges drear
And naked shingles of the world.

Ah, love, let us be true
To one another! for the world, which seems
To lie before us like a land of dreams,
So various, so beautiful, so new,
Hath really neither joy, nor love, nor light,
Nor certitude, nor peace, nor help for pain;
And we are here as on a darkling plain
Swept with confused alarms of struggle and flight,
Where ignorant armies clash by night.

Written in the middle of the nineteenth century, "Dover Beach" has some claim to be the first distinctly modern poem, perhaps even qualifying as "modernist" in the way it places an isolated neurotic on the edge of a highly charged symbolic scene. The lines are broken and uneven; some of the transitions are abrupt, almost surrealist.

The Scholar-Gipsy

Go, for they call you, shepherd, from the hill;
  Go, shepherd, and untie the wattled cotes!
    No longer leave thy wistful flock unfed,
  Nor let thy bawling fellows rack their throats,
    Nor the cropped herbage shoot another head.
      But when the fields are still,
  And the tired men and dogs all gone to rest,
    And only the white sheep are sometimes seen
    Cross and recross the strips of moon-blanched green,
  Come, shepherd, and again begin the quest!

Here, where the reaper was at work of late—
  In this high field's dark corner, where he leaves
    His coat, his basket, and his earthen cruse,
  And in the sun all morning binds the sheaves,
    Then here, at noon, comes back his stores to use—
      Here will I sit and wait,
  While to my ear from uplands far away
    The bleating of the folded flocks is borne,
    With distant cries of reapers in the corn—
  All the live murmur of a summer's day.

Screened is this nook o'er the high, half-reaped field,
  And here till sundown, shepherd! will I be.
    Through the thick corn the scarlet poppies peep,
  And round green roots and yellowing stalks I see
    Pale pink convolvulus in tendrils creep;
      And air-swept lindens yield
  Their scent, and rustle down their perfumed showers
    Of bloom on the bent grass where I am laid,
    And bower me from the August sun with shade;
  And the eye travels down to Oxford's towers.

And near me on the grass lies Glanvil's book—
   Come, let me read the oft-read tale again!
      The story of the Oxford scholar poor,
   Of pregnant parts and quick inventive brain,
      Who, tired of knocking at preferment's door,
         One summer-morn forsook
   His friends, and went to learn the gipsy-lore,
      And roamed the world with that wild brotherhood,
      And came, as most men deemed, to little good,
   But came to Oxford and his friends no more.

But once, years after, in the country-lanes,
   Two scholars, whom at college erst he knew,
      Met him, and of his way of life enquired;
   Whereat he answered, that the gipsy-crew,
      His mates, had arts to rule as they desired
         The workings of men's brains,
   And they can bind them to what thoughts they will.
      "And I," he said, "the secret of their art,
      When fully learned, will to the world impart;
   But it needs heaven-sent moments for this skill."

This said, he left them, and returned no more.—
   But rumors hung about the country-side,
      That the lost Scholar long was seen to stray,
   Seen by rare glimpses, pensive and tongue-tied,
      In hat of antique shape, and cloak of gray.
         The same the gipsies wore.
   Shepherds had met him on the Hurst in spring;
      At some lone alehouse in the Berkshire moors,
      On the warm ingle-bench, the smock-frocked boors
   Had found him seated at their entering,

But, 'mid their drink and clatter, he would fly.
   And I myself seem half to know thy looks,
      And put the shepherds, wanderer! on thy trace;
    And boys who in lone wheatfields scare the rooks
      I ask if thou hast passed their quiet place;
         Or in my boat I lie
   Moored to the cool bank in the summer-heats,
      'Mid wide grass meadows which the sunshine fills,
      And watch the warm, green-muffled Cumner hills,
   And wonder if thou haunt'st their shy retreats.

For most, I know, thou lov'st retired ground!
   Thee at the ferry Oxford riders blithe,
      Returning home on summer-nights, have met
   Crossing the stripling Thames at Bab-lock-hithe,
      Trailing in the cool stream thy fingers wet,
        As the punt's rope chops round;
   And leaning backward in a pensive dream,
      And fostering in thy lap a heap of flowers
      Plucked in shy fields and distant Wychwood bowers,
   And thine eyes resting on the moonlit stream.

And then they land, and thou art seen no more!
   Maidens, who from the distant hamlets come
      To dance around the Fyfield elm in May,
   Oft through the darkening fields have seen thee roam,
      Or cross a stile into the public way.
        Oft thou hast given them store
   Of flowers—the frail-leafed, white anemone,
      Dark bluebells drenched with dews of summer eves,
      And purple orchises with spotted leaves—
   But none hath words she can report of thee.

And, above Godstow Bridge, when hay-time's here
   In June, and many a scythe in sunshine flames,
      Men who through those wide fields of breezy grass
   Where black-winged swallows haunt the glittering Thames,
      To bathe in the abandoned lasher pass,
         Have often passed thee near
   Sitting upon the river bank o'ergrown;
      Marked thine outlandish garb, thy figure spare,
      Thy dark vague eyes, and soft abstracted air—
   But, when they came from bathing, thou wast gone!

At some lone homestead in the Cumner hills,
   Where at her open door the housewife darns,
      Thou hast been seen, or hanging on a gate
   To watch the threshers in the mossy barns.
      Children, who early range these slopes and late
         For cresses from the rills,
   Have known thee eying, all an April-day,
      The springing pastures and the feeding kine;
      And marked thee, when the stars come out and shine,
   Through the long dewy grass move slow away.

In autumn, on the skirts of Bagley Wood—
   Where most the gipsies by the turf-edged way
      Pitch their smoked tents, and every bush you see
   With scarlet patches tagged and shreds of gray,
      Above the forest-ground called Thessaly—
         The blackbird, picking food,
   Sees thee, nor stops his meal, nor fears at all;
      So often has he known thee past him stray,
      Rapt, twirling in thy hand a withered spray,
   And waiting for the spark from heaven to fall.

And once, in winter, on the causeway chill
  Where home through flooded fields foot-travelers go,
    Have I not passed thee on the wooden bridge,
  Wrapped in thy cloak and battling with the snow,
    Thy face tow'rd Hinksey and its wintry ridge?
      And thou hast climbed the hill,
  And gained the white brow of the Cumner range;
    Turned once to watch, while thick the snowflakes fall,
    The line of festal light in Christ-Church hall—
  Then sought thy straw in some sequestered grange.

But what—I dream! Two hundred years are flown
  Since first thy story ran through Oxford halls,
    And the grave Glanvil did the tale inscribe
  That thou wert wandered from the studious walls
    To learn strange arts, and join a gipsy-tribe;
      And thou from earth art gone
  Long since, and in some quiet churchyard laid—
    Some country-nook, where o'er thy unknown grave
    Tall grasses and white flowering nettles wave,
  Under a dark, red-fruited yew-tree's shade.

—No, no, thou hast not felt the lapse of hours!
  For what wears out the life of mortal men?
    'Tis that from change to change their being rolls;
  'Tis that repeated shocks, again, again,
    Exhaust the energy of strongest souls
      And numb the elastic powers.
  Till having used our nerves with bliss and teen,
    And tired upon a thousand schemes our wit,
    To the just-pausing Genius we remit
  Our worn-out life, and are—what we have been.

Thou hast not lived, why should'st thou perish, so?
  Thou hadst *one* aim, *one* business, *one* desire;
    Else wert thou long since numbered with the dead!
  Else hadst thou spent, like other men, thy fire!
    The generations of thy peers are fled.
      And we ourselves shall go;
  But thou possessest an immortal lot,
    And we imagine thee exempt from age
    And living as thou liv'st on Glanvil's page,
  Because thou hadst—what we, alas! have not.

For early didst thou leave the world, with powers
  Fresh, undiverted to the world without,
    Firm to their mark, not spent on other things;
  Free from the sick fatigue, the languid doubt,
    Which much to have tried, in much been baffled, brings.
      O life unlike to ours!
  Who fluctuate idly without term or scope,
    Of whom each strives, nor knows for what he strives,
    And each half lives a hundred different lives;
  Who wait like thee, but not, like thee, in hope.

Thou waitest for the spark from heaven! and we,
  Light half-believers of our casual creeds,
    Who never deeply felt, nor clearly willed,
  Whose insight never has borne fruit in deeds,
    Whose vague resolves never have been fulfilled;
      For whom each year we see
  Breeds new beginnings, disappointments new;
    Who hesitate and falter life away,
    And lose tomorrow the ground won today—
  Ah! do not we, wanderer! await it too?

Yes, we await it! but it still delays,
  And then we suffer! and amongst us one,
    Who most has suffered, takes dejectedly
  His seat upon the intellectual throne;
    And all his store of sad experience he
      Lays bare of wretched days;
  Tells us his misery's birth and growth and signs,
    And how the dying spark of hope was fed,
    And how the breast was soothed, and how the head,
  And all his hourly varied anodynes.

This for our wisest! and we others pine,
  And wish the long unhappy dream would end,
    And waive all claim to bliss, and try to bear;
  With close-lipped patience for our only friend,
    Sad patience, too near neighbor to despair—
      But none has hope like thine!
  Thou through the fields and through the woods dost stray,
    Roaming the countryside, a truant boy,
    Nursing thy project in unclouded joy,
  And every doubt long blown by time away.

O born in days when wits were fresh and clear,
  And life ran gaily as the sparkling Thames;
    Before this strange disease of modern life,
  With its sick hurry, its divided aims,
    Its head o'ertaxed, its palsied hearts, was rife—
      Fly hence, our contact fear!
  Still fly, plunge deeper in the bowering wood!
    Averse, as Dido did with gesture stern
    From her false friend's approach in Hades turn,
  Wave us away, and keep thy solitude!

Still nursing the unconquerable hope,
  Still clutching the inviolable shade,
    With a free, onward impulse brushing through,
  By night, the silvered branches of the glade—
    Far on the forest-skirts, where none pursue,
      On some mild pastoral slope
  Emerge, and resting on the moonlit pales
    Freshen thy flowers as in former years
    With dew, or listen with enchanted ears,
  From the dark dingles, to the nightingales!

But fly our paths, our feverish contact fly!
  For strong the infection of our mental strife,
    Which, though it gives no bliss, yet spoils for rest;
  And we should win thee from thy own fair life,
    Like us distracted, and like us unblest.
      Soon, soon thy cheer would die,
  Thy hopes grow timorous, and unfixed thy powers,
    And thy clear aims be cross and shifting made;
    And then thy glad perennial youth would fade,
  Fade, and grow old at last, and die like ours.

Then fly our greetings, fly our speech and smiles!
  —As some grave Tyrian trader, from the sea,
    Described at sunrise and emerging prow
  Lifting the cool-haired creepers stealthily,
    The fringes of a southward-facing brow
      Among the Aegean isles;
  And saw the merry Grecian coaster come,
    Freighted with amber grapes, and Chian wine,
    Green, bursting figs, and tunnies steeped in brine—
  And knew the intruders on his ancient home,

The young light-hearted masters of the waves —
    And snatched his rudder, he shook out more sail;
    And day and night held on indignantly
O'er the blue Midland waters with the gale,
    Betwixt the Syrtes and soft Sicily,
        To where the Atlantic raves
Outside the western straits; and unbent sails
    There, where down cloudy cliffs, through sheets of foam,
    Shy traffickers, the dark Iberians come;
And on the beach undid his corded bales.

Arnold's notes make clear that this poem was inspired by a passage from Joseph Glanvil's Vanity of Dogmatizing *(1661). Arnold used the same stanza (meter and rhyme) later in "Thyrsis," his pastoral elegy on the death of his friend and fellow-poet Arthur Hugh Clough. Arnold seems to have modelled the stanza on that in some of Keats's odes.*

Allingham was known mostly as a poet and anthologist. He was also a notable diarist, in which role he provides information about many of his literary friends, including D. G. Rossetti and Tennyson.

The Fairies

Up the airy mountain,
    Down the rushy glen,
We daren't go a-hunting
    For fear of little men;
Wee folk, good folk,
    Trooping all together;
Green jacket, red cap,
    And white owl's feather!

Down along the rocky shore
    Some make their home,
They live on crispy pancakes
    Of yellow tide-foam;
Some in the reeds
    Of the black mountain lake,
With frogs for their watch-dogs,
    All night awake.

High on the hill-top
    The old King sits;
He is now so old and gray
    He's nigh lost his wits.
With a bridge of white mist
    Columbkill he crosses,
On his stately journeys
    From Slieveleague to Rosses;

Or going up with music
    On cold starry nights
To sup with the Queen
    Of the gay Northern Lights.

They stole little Bridget
    For seven years long;
When she came down again
    Her friends were all gone.
They took her lightly back,
    Between the night and morrow,
They thought that she was fast asleep,
    But she was dead with sorrow.
They have kept her ever since
    Deep within the lake,
On a bed of flag-leaves,
    Watching till she wake.

By the craggy hill-side,
    Through the mosses bare,
They have planted thorn-trees
    For pleasure here and there.
Is any man so daring
    As dig them up in spite,
He shall find their sharpest thorns
    In his bed at night.

Up the airy mountain,
    Down the rushy glen,
We daren't go a-hunting
    For fear of little men;
Wee folk, good folk,
    Trooping all together;
Green jacket, red cap,
    And white owl's feather!

Legends of wee folk persist everywhere, a survival or atavism that predates most of the modern religions.

GEORGE MEREDITH 1828–1909

Meredith stands higher among the novelists than among the poets, and most readers who know of him will think of him as the author of such novels as *The Ordeal of Richard Feverel* and *The Egoist*. But Meredith's poetry deserves as much respect: it is varied, animated, witty, humane, and consistently dramatic.

Lucifer in Starlight

On a starred night Prince Lucifer uprose.
 Tired of his dark dominion, swung the fiend
 Above the rolling ball in cloud part screened,
Where sinners hugged their specter of repose.
Poor prey to his hot fit of pride were those.
 And now upon his western wing he leaned,
 Now his huge bulk o'er Afric's sands careened,
Now the black planet shadowed Arctic snows.
Soaring through wider zones that pricked his scars
 With memory of the old revolt from Awe,
He reached a middle height, and at the stars,
Which are the brain of heaven, he looked, and sank.
Around the ancient track marched, rank on rank,
 The army of unalterable law.

Meredith excelled in prose and poetry, in some moods looking forward to modernist realism and skepticism. In this powerful sonnet he assumes, however, the grand manner of a Victorian Milton—soon to be mocked by T. S. Eliot, whose "Cousin Nancy," written at about the time of Meredith's death, ends:

> *Upon the glazen shelves kept watch*
> *Matthew and Waldo, guardians of the faith,*
> *The army of unalterable law.*

Thus Piteously
Love Closed What He Begat

>>>>>>>

Thus piteously Love closed what he begat:
The union of this ever-diverse pair!
These two were rapid falcons in a snare,
Condemned to do the flitting of the bat.
Lovers beneath the singing sky of May,
They wandered once, clear as the dew on flowers:
But they fed not on the advancing hours:
Their hearts held cravings for the buried day.
Then each applied to each that fatal knife,
Deep questioning, which probes to endless dole.
Ah, what a dusty answer gets the soul
When hot for certainties in this our life! —
In tragic hints here see what evermore
Moves dark as yonder midnight ocean's force,
Thundering like ramping hosts of warrior horse,
To throw that faint thin line upon the shore!

from Modern Love

Meredith's forward-looking "Modern Love," in sixteen-line variations on the son-net, tells the sternly honest story of the all-too-familiar failure of his own miserable first marriage to the widowed daughter of Thomas Love Peacock.

A painter as well as a poet, Dante Gabriel Rossetti was
one of the founders of the Pre-Raphaelite Brotherhood,
a movement that had broad influence on English liter-
ature, criticism, painting, architecture, and design.
Dante Gabriel Rossetti was the older brother of Chris-
tina Georgina Rossetti. He is the only poet in this an-
thology whose sister is also here.

The Blessed Damozel

The blessed damozel leaned out
    From the gold bar of Heaven;
Her eyes were deeper than the depth
    Of waters stilled at even;
She had three lilies in her hand,
    And the stars in her hair were seven.

Her robe, ungirt from clasp to hem,
    No wrought flowers did adorn,
But a white rose of Mary's gift,
    For service meetly worn;
Her hair that lay along her back
    Was yellow like ripe corn.

Herseemed she scarce had been a day
    One of God's choristers;
The wonder was not yet quite gone
    From that still look of hers;
Albeit, to them she left, her day
    Had counted as ten years.

(To one, it is ten years of years.
    . . . Yet now, and in this place,
Surely she leaned o'er me—her hair
    Fell all about my face . . .
Nothing: the autumn fall of leaves.
    The whole year sets apace.)

It was the rampart of God's house
    That she was standing on;
By God built over the sheer depth
    The which is Space begun;
So high, that looking downward thence
    She scarce could see the sun.

It lies in Heaven, across the flood
    Of ether, as a bridge.
Beneath, the tides of day and night
    With flame and darkness ridge
The void, as low as where this earth
    Spins like a fretful midge.

Around her, lovers, newly met
    'Mid deathless love's acclaims,
Spoke evermore among themselves
    Their heart remembered names;
And the souls mounting up to God
    Went by her like thin flames.

And still she bowed herself and stooped
    Out of the circling charm;
Until her bosom must have made
    The bar she leaned on warm,
And the lilies lay as if asleep
    Along her bended arm.

From the fixed place of Heaven she saw
   Time like a pulse shake fierce
Through all the worlds. Her gaze still strove
   Within the gulf to pierce
Its path; and now she spoke as when
   The stars sang in their spheres.

The sun was gone now; the curled moon
   Was like a little feather
Fluttering far down the gulf; and now
   She spoke through the still weather.
Her voice was like the voice the stars
   Had when they sang together.

(Ah sweet! Even now, in that bird's song,
   Strove not her accents there,
Fain to be hearkened? When those bells
   Possessed the mid-day air,
Strove not her steps to reach my side
   Down all the echoing stair?)

"I wish that he were come to me,
   For he will come," she said.
"Have I not prayed in Heaven? —on earth,
   Lord, Lord, has he not prayed?
Are not two prayers a perfect strength?
   And shall I feel afraid?

"When round his head the aureole clings,
   And he is clothed in white,
I'll take his hand and go with him
   To the deep wells of light;
As unto a stream we will step down
   And bathe there in God's sight.

"We two will stand beside that shrine,
　　Occult, withheld, untrod,
Whose lamps are stirred continually
　　With prayer sent up to God;
And see our old prayers, granted, melt
　　Each like a little cloud.

"We two will lie i' the shadow of
　　That living mystic tree
Within whose secret growth the Dove
　　Is sometimes felt to be,
While every leaf that His plumes touch
　　Saith His Name audibly.

"And I myself will teach to him,
　　I myself, lying so,
The songs I sing here; which his voice
　　Shall pause in, hushed and slow,
And find some knowledge at each pause,
　　Or some new thing to know."

(Alas! We two, we two, thou sayst!
　　Yea, one wast thou with me
That once of old. But shall God lift
　　To endless unity
The soul whose likeness with thy soul
　　Was but its love for thee?)

"We two," she said, "will seek the groves
　　Where the lady Mary is,
With her five handmaidens, whose names
　　Are five sweet symphonies,
Cecily, Gertrude, Magdalen,
　　Margaret and Rosalys.

"Circlewise sit they, with bound locks
    And foreheads garlanded;
Into the fine cloth white like flame
    Weaving the golden thread,
To fashion the birth-robes for them
    Who are just born, being dead.

"He shall fear, haply, and be dumb:
    Then will I lay my cheek
To his, and tell about our love,
    Not once abashed or weak:
And the dear Mother will approve
    My pride, and let me speak.

"Herself shall bring us, hand in hand,
    To Him round whom all souls
Kneel, the clear-ranged unnumbered heads
    Bowed with their aureoles:
And angels meeting us shall sing
    To their citherns and citoles.

"There will I ask of Christ the Lord
    Thus much for him and me: —
Only to live as once on earth
    With Love, — only to be,
As then awhile, for ever now
    Together, I and he."

She gazed and listened and then said,
    Less sad of speech than mild, —
"All this is when he comes." She ceased.
    The light thrilled towards her, filled
With angels in strong level flight.
    Her eyes prayed, and she smiled.

(I saw her smile.) But soon their path
  Was vague in distant spheres:
And then she cast her arms along
  The golden barriers,
And laid her face between her hands,
  And wept. (I heard her tears.)

Of "The Raven" (p. 625), Rossetti supposedly said, "I saw that Poe had done the utmost it was possible to do with grief of the lover on earth, and I determined to reverse the conditions." This poem, along with some of Blake's, has the uncommon distinction of possessing a companion-painting by the same artist.

The Woodspurge

The wind flapped loose, the wind was still,
Shaken out dead from tree and hill:
I had walked on at the wind's will, —
I sat now, for the wind was still.

Between my knees my forehead was, —
My lips, drawn in, said not Alas!
My hair was over in the grass,
My naked ears heard the day pass.

My eyes, wide open, had the run
Of some ten weeds to fix upon;
Among those few, out of the sun,
The woodspurge flowered, three cups in one.

From perfect grief there need not be
Wisdom or even memory:
One thing then learnt remains to me, —
The woodspurge has a cup of three.

Byron, who remarked tartly that Keats could not look at an oak tree without seeing a dryad, might have admired Rossetti's lucidity in looking at a woodspurge and seeing — a woodspurge. (Cups and threes can mean much to pagan and Christian interpreters alike, and spurge is, by definition, an instrument of purgation; but Rossetti is above all that — or below it.)

EMILY DICKINSON 1830–1886

Dickinson spent most of her strange life in Amherst,
Massachusetts, where she had been born. Her father
was a lawyer who served in the United States House of
Representatives. She seems to have been gregarious
when young but became reclusive as time passed. Of
her many poems—upwards of 1,800—only eight or so
were published in her lifetime. Since she was such a
great and eloquent poet, people have naturally been cu-
rious about her, but biographical speculations have en-
countered many barriers, and the poetry itself continues
to present inconsistencies, enigmas, anomalies, and
opacities. Whatever the truth about her life, she re-
mains a poet of unmatched strength and vitality. The
primitive simplicity of some of her stanzas is balanced
by the audacious complexity of syntax and rhythm,
along with eccentric rhymes.

"Because I could not stop for Death"

Because I could not stop for Death—
He kindly stopped for me—
The Carriage held but just Ourselves—
And Immortality.

We slowly drove—He knew no haste
And I had put away
My labor and my leisure too,
For His Civility—

We passed the School, where Children strove
At Recess—in the Ring—
We passed the Fields of Gazing Grain—
We passed the Setting Sun—

Or rather—He passed Us—
The Dews drew quivering and chill—
For only Gossamer, my Gown—
My Tippet—only Tulle—

We paused before a House that seemed
A Swelling of the Ground—
The Roof was scarcely visible—
The Cornice—in the Ground—

Since then—'tis Centuries—and yet
Feels shorter than the Day
I first surmised the Horses' Heads
Were toward Eternity—

Dickinson, a generation younger than Poe, came along just in time to witness a mass-movement in obituary poetry so widespread and so bathetically lugubrious that it became a joke. Mark Twain and others repeatedly made fun of the death poems of Julia A. Moore, who appears as Emmeline Grangerford in Huckle-berry Finn. "Because I could not stop for Death" personifies Death as a civil gentleman, not so different from Whitman's "lovely and soothing death" ("When Lilacs Last in the Dooryard Bloom'd," p. 694) or even Keats's "easeful death" ("Ode to a Nightingale," p. 542).

"I heard a Fly buzz—when I died"

✕✕✕✕✕

I heard a Fly buzz—when I died—
The Stillness in the Room
Was like the Stillness in the Air—
Between the Heaves of Storm—

The Eyes around—had wrung them dry—
And Breaths were gathering firm
For that last Onset—when the King
Be witnessed—in the Room—

I willed my Keepsakes—Signed away
What portion of me be
Assignable—and then it was
There interposed a Fly—

With Blue—uncertain stumbling Buzz—
Between the light—and me—
And then the Windows failed—and then
I could not see to see—

In Dickinson's time, improvements in public health favored large families, but illness and death were all around. Dickinson, born in 1830, probably had more firsthand experience of death than most people born in 1930. Dickinson's fly has more tangible, terrifying reality than Melville's whale or Poe's raven. It is rendered in its full fly-hood of things seen and heard, as well as with "Blue— uncertain stumbling Buzz."

"A narrow Fellow in the Grass"

()◀▶()

A narrow Fellow in the Grass
Occasionally rides—
You may have met Him—did you not
His notice sudden is—

The Grass divides as with a Comb—
A spotted shaft is seen—
And then it closes at your feet
And opens further on—

He likes a Boggy Acre
A Floor to cool for Corn—
Yet when a Boy, and Barefoot—
I more than once at Noon
Have passed, I thought, a Whip lash
Unbraiding in the Sun
When stooping to secure it
It wrinkled, and was gone—

Several of Nature's People
I know, and they know me—
I feel for them a transport
Of cordiality—

But never met this Fellow
Attended, or alone
Without a tighter breathing
And Zero at the Bone—

Charms and riddles are among the oldest poems, and they are also, in a sense, the "oldest" or earliest poems for many readers. The point is to describe something without naming it. There are riddles in the Bible, in Homer, in Old English literature, and in any schoolyard or workplace.

"There's a certain Slant of light"

There's a certain Slant of light,
Winter Afternoons—
That oppresses, like the Heft
Of Cathedral Tunes—

Heavenly Hurt, it gives us—
We can find no scar,
But internal difference,
Where the Meanings, are—

None may teach it—Any—
'Tis the Seal Despair—
An imperial affliction
Sent us of the Air—

When it comes, the Landscape listens—
Shadows—hold their breath—
When it goes, 'tis like the Distance
On the look of Death—

Dickinson was a generation ahead of Ferdinand de Saussure and a century ahead of Jacques Derrida in recognizing that "internal difference" is "Where the Meanings, are." Neither dot nor dash means anything; it is the difference between that makes the Morse code possible.

"A Bird came down the Walk"

❖❖❖❖

A Bird came down the Walk—
He did not know I saw—
He bit an Angleworm in halves
And ate the fellow, raw,

And then he drank a Dew
From a convenient Grass—
And then hopped sidewise to the Wall
To let a Beetle pass—

He glanced with rapid eyes
That hurried all around—
They looked like frightened Beads, I thought—
He stirred his Velvet Head

Like one in danger, Cautious,
I offered him a Crumb
And he unrolled his feathers
And rowed him softer home—

Than Oars divide the Ocean,—
Too silver for a seam—
Or Butterflies, off Banks of Noon
Leap, plashless as they swim.

Dickinson's life was reduced to a few essentials (Thoreau, in comparison, was a boulevardier and globetrotter). She had the leisure to compose hundreds of poems and the patience to devote herself to detailed observation of the minute particulars of the world.

"The Soul selects her own Society"

❦❦❦

The Soul selects her own Society—
Then—shuts the Door—
To her divine Majority—
Present no more—

Unmoved—she notes the Chariots—pausing—
At her low Gate—
Unmoved—an Emperor be kneeling
Upon her Mat—

I've known her—from an ample nation—
Choose One—
Then—close the Valves of her attention—
Like Stone—

As in so many of her lyrics, Dickinson here adapts an idiom peculiar to American politics, which stresses the Majority and rejects any Emperor, to the requirements of a wholly personal poem.

"I like to see it lap the Miles"

>>>>>>>

I like to see it lap the Miles—
And lick the Valleys up—
And stop to feed itself at Tanks—
And then—prodigious step

Around a Pile of Mountains—
And supercilious peer
In Shanties—by the sides of Roads—
And then a Quarry pare

To fit its Ribs
And crawl between
Complaining all the while
In horrid—hooting stanza—
Then chase itself down Hill—

And neigh like Boanerges—
Then—punctual as a Star
Stop—docile and omnipotent
At its own stable door—

Many poets recoiled in horror and anxiety from the new machinery of the nineteenth century, but the locomotive found adherents in Whitman (who wrote a poem called "To a Locomotive in Winter") and Dickinson, who needed the figurative arsenal of the New Testament to reinforce the metaphor of the Iron Horse.

"My life closed twice before its close"

My life closed twice before its close—
It yet remains to see
If Immortality unveil
A third event to me

So huge, so hopeless to conceive
As these that twice befell.
Parting is all we know of heaven,
And all we need of hell.

Closure, partition, separation—all are kinds of death. After the final death, the departure is all we know of those headed for heaven; parting itself is so painful that no other news of hell is needed to make it hellish.

"Success is counted sweetest"

Success is counted sweetest
By those who ne'er succeed.
To comprehend a nectar
Requires sorest need.

Not one of all the purple Host
Who took the Flag today
Can tell the definition
So clear of Victory

As he defeated — dying —
On whose forbidden ear
The distant strains of triumph
Burst agonized and clear!

One wise moment in J. D. Salinger's Catcher in the Rye *comes with the suggestion (made by Holden Caulfield's older brother) that Emily Dickinson was a great war poet, even though she did not fight in a war.*

"I taste a liquor never brewed"

I taste a liquor never brewed—
From Tankards scooped in Pearl—
Not all the Vats upon the Rhine
Yield such an Alcohol!

Inebriate of Air—am I—
And Debauchee of Dew—
Reeling—thro endless summer days—
From inns of Molten Blue—

When "Landlords" turn the drunken Bee
Out of the Foxglove's door—
When Butterflies—renounce their "drams"—
I shall but drink the more!

Till Seraphs swing their snowy Hats—
And Saints—to windows run—
To see the little Tippler
Leaning against the—Sun—

The highest annual per capita consumption of alcoholic beverages in the United States was in 1830, the year of Dickinson's birth. Drinking was only casually disciplined by law, and quality control was so quixotic that the drinker might feel either nothing or a 200-proof belt. The environment favored the immemorial metaphors of intoxication.

"After great pain, a formal feeling comes"

After great pain, a formal feeling comes—
The Nerves sit ceremonious, like Tombs—
The stiff Heart questions was it He, that bore,
And Yesterday, or Centuries before?

The Feet, mechanical, go round—
Of Ground, or Air, or Ought—
A Wooden way
Regardless grown,
A Quartz contentment, like a stone—

This is the Hour of Lead—
Remembered, if outlived,
As Freezing persons, recollect the Snow—
First—Chill—then Stupor—then the letting go—

Like Poe before her, Dickinson could imagine death from the inside and from the far side. Her subject was that of the oldest scriptures, but her idiom included such state-of-the-art locutions as "Nerves" and "mechanical."

"I felt a Funeral, in my Brain"

I felt a Funeral, in my Brain,
And Mourners to and fro
Kept treading—treading—till it seemed
That Sense was breaking through—

And when they all were seated,
A Service, like a Drum—
Kept beating—beating—till I thought
My Mind was going numb—

And then I heard them lift a Box
And creak across my Soul
With those same Boots of Lead, again,
Then Space—began to toll,

As all the Heavens were a Bell,
And Being, but an Ear,
And I, and Silence, some strange Race
Wrecked, solitary, here—

And then a Plank in Reason, broke,
And I dropped down, and down—
And hit a World, at every plunge,
And Finished knowing—then—

One hallmark of Dickinson's genius is her skill in capturing extremes of extraordinary vision and horror by means of the simplest verbal traps: "And then . . . And . . . And . . . And . . . ."

"I never saw a Moor"

I never saw a Moor—
I never saw the Sea—
Yet know I how the Heather looks
And what a Billow be.

I never spoke with God
Nor visited in Heaven—
Yet certain am I of the spot
As if the Checks were given—

One hears about a cult of hands-on experience in America, but Dickinson shows again and again that the imagination can function magnificently in a person who seldom leaves the house.

"Much Madness is divinest Sense"

Much madness is divinest sense
To a discerning eye;
Much sense the starkest madness.
'T is the majority
In this, as all, prevails.
Assent, and you are sane;
Demur,—you're straightway dangerous,
And handled with a chain.

Dickinson could sound like an American Blake, insisting on individual liberty so emphatically that collective standards ("manacles," according to Blake; "a Chain," according to Dickinson) counted for nothing.

CHRISTINA GEORGINA ROSSETTI 1830–1894

Christina Rossetti is the only woman represented in this anthology who also has a brother (Dante Gabriel Rossetti) represented. (Another brother, William Michael Rossetti, was also important as a writer.) Although the Rossettis shared an Italian heritage, Christina Rossetti was a devout Anglican; and much of her poetry is religious. In some more personal lyrics, she shows a persistent melancholy but an equally persistent stoicism. Two men proposed marriage to her, but she remained single.

When I Am Dead

When I am dead, my dearest,
    Sing no sad songs for me;
Plant thou no roses at my head,
    Nor shady cypress tree:
Be the green grass above me
    With showers and dewdrops wet;
And if thou wilt, remember,
    And if thou wilt, forget.

I shall not see the shadows,
    I shall not feel the rain;
I shall not hear the nightingale
    Sing on, as if in pain:
And dreaming through the twilight
    That doth not rise nor set,
Haply I may remember,
    And haply may forget.

These tough verses gain in power when compared with Rupert Brooke's "Soldier" (p. 951). Christina Rossetti's sentiment will probably strike the modern reader as the more genuine of the two.

Up-Hill

>>>>>>>

Does the road wind uphill all the way?
   Yes, to the very end.
Will the day's journey take the whole long day?
   From morn to night, my friend.

But is there for the night a resting-place?
   A roof for when the slow, dark hours begin,
May not the darkness hide it from my face?
   You cannot miss that inn.

Shall I meet other wayfarers at night?
   Those who have gone before.
Then must I knock, or call when just in sight?
   They will not keep you waiting at that door.

Shall I find comfort, travel-sore and weak?
   Of labour you shall find the sum.
Will there be beds for me and all who seek?
   Yea, beds for all who come.

Reminiscent in some ways of old ballads and in some ways of seventeenth-century religious lyrics, "Up-Hill" also seems to be a prelude to A. E. Housman's meditative poems a generation later.

A Birthday

My heart is like a singing bird
  Whose nest is in a watered shoot;
My heart is like an apple-tree
  Whose boughs are bent with thickset fruit;
My heart is like a rainbow shell
  That paddles in a halcyon sea;
My heart is gladder than all these
  Because my love is come to me.

Raise me a dais of silk and down;
  Hang it with vair and purple dyes;
Carve it in doves and pomegranates,
  And peacocks with a hundred eyes;
Work it in gold and silver grapes,
  In leaves and silver fleurs-de-lys;
Because the birthday of my life
  Is come, my love is come to me.

The poet's brother William Michael Rossetti was unable to account for the happiness of this birthday poem, at least on the basis of any happiness in the author's actual life.

Remember

Remember me when I am gone away,
   Gone far away into the silent land;
   When you can no more hold me by the hand,
Nor I half turn to go yet turning stay.
Remember me when no more day by day
   You tell me of our future that you planned:
   Only remember me; you understand
It will be late to counsel then or pray.
Yet if you should forget me for a while
   And afterwards remember, do not grieve:
   For if the darkness and corruption leave
A vestige of the thoughts that once I had,
Better by far you should forget and smile
   Than that you should remember and be sad.

The sentiments here expressed are said to be associated with the Pre-Raphaelite painter James Collinson, to whom Christina Rossetti was briefly engaged.

"LEWIS CARROLL" (CHARLES LUTWIDGE DODGSON) 1832–1898

"Lewis Carroll" was an ordained minister, a talented amateur photographer, and an accomplished mathematician and classicist. A deeper, and perhaps darker, self communicated with children, mostly little girls. To amuse Alice Liddell, he wrote something first called "Alice's Adventures Underground," eventually published as *Alice's Adventures in Wonderland* (1865), followed by *Through the Looking-Glass and What Alice Found There* (1871).

Jabberwocky

'Twas brillig, and the slithy toves
   Did gyre and gimble in the wabe;
All mimsy were the borogoves,
   And the mome raths outgrabe.

"Beware the Jabberwock, my son!
   The jaws that bite, the claws that catch!
Beware the Jubjub bird, and shun
   The frumious Bandersnatch!"

He took his vorpal sword in hand:
   Long time the manxome foe he sought—
So rested he by the Tumtum tree,
   And stood awhile in thought.

And as in uffish thought he stood,
   The Jabberwock, with eyes of flame,
Came whiffling through the tulgey wood,
   And burbled as it came!

One, two! One, two! And through and through
   The vorpal blade went snicker-snack!
He left it dead, and with its head
   He went galumphing back.

"And hast thou slain the Jabberwock!
   Come to my arms, my beamish boy!
O frabjous day! Callooh! Callay!"
   He chortled in his joy.

'Twas brillig, and the slithy toves
   Did gyre and gimble in the wabe;
All mimsy were the borogoves,
   And the mome raths outgrabe.

from Through the Looking-Glass

This poem—a version of which was published earlier as a joke "Stanza of Anglo-Saxon Poetry"—is in Through the Looking-Glass, *where it is read by Alice and explicated by Humpty Dumpty. Formation of words by the blend or "portmanteau" device has become common, as in "motel," "smog," "palimony," and "modem." "Chortle," coined here by Carroll, is now a part of the language.*

The Walrus and the Carpenter

The sun was shining on the sea,
  Shining with all his might:
He did his very best to make
  The billows smooth and bright—
And this was odd, because it was
  The middle of the night.

The moon was shining sulkily,
  Because she thought the sun
Had got no business to be there
  After the day was done—
"It's very rude of him," she said,
  "To come and spoil the fun!"

The sea was wet as wet could be,
  The sands were dry as dry.
You could not see a cloud, because
  No cloud was in the sky:
No birds were flying overhead—
  There were no birds to fly.

The Walrus and the Carpenter
  Were walking close at hand:
They wept like anything to see
  Such quantities of sand:
"If this were only cleared away,"
  They said, "it would be grand!"

"If seven maids with seven mops
  Swept it for half a year,
Do you suppose," the Walrus said,
  "That they could get it clear?"
"I doubt it," said the Carpenter,
  And shed a bitter tear.

"O Oysters, come and walk with us!"
   The Walrus did beseech.
"A pleasant walk, a pleasant talk,
   Along the briny beach:
We cannot do with more than four,
   To give a hand to each."

The eldest Oyster looked at him,
   But never a word he said:
The eldest Oyster winked his eye,
   And shook his heavy head—
Meaning to say he did not choose
   To leave the oyster-bed.

But four young Oysters hurried up,
   All eager for the treat:
Their coats were brushed, their faces washed,
   Their shoes were clean and neat—
And this was odd, because, you know,
   They hadn't any feet.

Four other Oysters followed them,
   And yet another four;
And thick and fast they came at last,
   And more, and more, and more—
All hopping through the frothy waves,
   And scrambling to the shore.

The Walrus and the Carpenter
   Walked on a mile or so,
And then they rested on a rock
   Conveniently low:
And all the little Oysters stood
   And waited in a row.

"The time has come," the Walrus said,
    "To talk of many things:
Of shoes—and ships—and sealing wax—
    Of cabbages—and kings—
And why the sea is boiling hot—
    And whether pigs have wings."

"But wait a bit," the Oysters cried,
    "Before we have our chat;
For some of us are out of breath,
    And all of us are fat!"
"No hurry!" said the Carpenter.
    They thanked him much for that.

"A loaf of bread," the Walrus said,
    "Is what we chiefly need:
Pepper and vinegar besides
    Are very good indeed—
Now, if you're ready, Oysters dear,
    We can begin to feed."

"But not on us!" the Oysters cried,
    Turning a little blue.
"After such kindness, that would be
    A dismal thing to do!"
"The night is fine," the Walrus said.
    "Do you admire the view?

"It was so kind of you to come!
    And you are very nice!"
The Carpenter said nothing but
    "Cut us another slice.
I wish you were not quite so deaf—
    I've had to ask you twice!"

"It seems a shame," the Walrus said,
   "To play them such a trick,
After we've brought them out so far,
   And made them trot so quick!"
The Carpenter said nothing but
   "The butter's spread too thick!"

"I weep for you," the Walrus said:
   "I deeply sympathize."
With sobs and tears he sorted out
   Those of the largest size,
Holding his pocket-handkerchief
   Before his streaming eyes.

"O Oysters," said the Carpenter,
   "You've had a pleasant run!
Shall we be trotting home again?"
   But answer came there none—
And this was scarcely odd, because
   They'd eaten every one.

from Through the Looking-Glass

Tweedledee recites this lighthearted horror story in an augmented ballad stanza that had been used earlier by Coleridge (intermittently in "The Rime of the Ancient Mariner," p. 433) and by Thomas Hood; the form would be used later by Oscar Wilde in "The Ballad of Reading Gaol" (p. 810). The measure seems rather simple, but danger of some sort lurks just under the surface.

Father William

○◄──►○

"You are old, Father William," the young man said,
  "And your hair has become very white;
And yet you incessantly stand on your head—
  Do you think, at your age, it is right?"

"In my youth," Father William replied to his son,
  "I feared it might injure the brain;
But now that I'm perfectly sure I have none,
  Why, I do it again and again."

"You are old," said the youth, "as I mentioned before,
  And have grown most uncommonly fat;
Yet you turned a back somersault in at the door—
  Pray, what is the reason of that?"

"In my youth," said the sage, as he shook his gray locks,
  "I kept all my limbs very supple
By the use of this ointment—one shilling the box—
  Allow me to sell you a couple."

"You are old," said the youth, "and your jaws are too weak
  For anything tougher than suet;
Yet you finished the goose, with the bones and the beak—
  Pray, how did you manage to do it?"

"In my youth,"said his father, "I took to the law,
  And argued each case with my wife;
And the muscular strength, which it gave to my jaw,
  Has lasted the rest of my life."

"You are old," said the youth, "one would hardly suppose
   That your eye was as steady as ever;
Yet you balanced an eel on the end of your nose—
   What made you so awfully clever?"

"I have answered three questions, and that is enough,"
   Said his father; "don't give yourself airs!
Do you think I can listen all day to such stuff?
   Be off, or I'll kick you downstairs!"

                    from Alice's Adventures in Wonderland

Only two or three of the 500 poems in this anthology qualify as proper parodies, aimed immediately at another poem. "Father William" parodies Robert Southey's "Old Man's Comforts" and follows its pattern of a dialogue in quatrains between "the young man" and Father William. Oddly for a parody, "Father William" is two stanzas longer than Southey's original.

I'll Tell Thee Everything I Can

"I'll tell thee everything I can;
   There's little to relate.
I saw an aged aged man,
   A-sitting on a gate.
'Who are you, aged man?' I said,
   'And how is it you live?'
And his answer trickled through my head
   Like water through a sieve.

He said, 'I look for butterflies
   That sleep among the wheat:
I make them into mutton-pies
   And sell them in the street.
I sell them unto men,' he said,
   'Who sail on stormy seas;
And that's the way I get my bread—
   A trifle, if you please.'

But I was thinking of a plan
   To dye one's whiskers green,
And always use so large a fan
   That they could not be seen.
So, having no reply to give
   To what the old man said,
I cried, 'Come, tell me how you live!'
   And thumped him on the head.

His accents mild took up the tale:
   He said, 'I go my ways,
And when I find a mountain rill,
   I set it in a blaze:
And thence they make a stuff they call
   Rowland's Macassar-Oil —
Yet twopence-halfpenny is all
   They give me for my toil.'

But I was thinking of a way
   To feed oneself on batter,
And so go on from day to day
   Getting a little fatter.
I shook him well from side to side,
   Until his face was blue:
'Come, tell me how you live,' I cried,
   'And what it is you do!'

He said, 'I hunt for haddocks' eyes
   Among the heather bright,
And work them into waistcoat buttons
   In the silent night.
And these I do not sell for gold
   Or coin of silvery shine,
But for a copper halfpenny,
   And that will purchase nine.

I sometimes dig for buttered rolls.
   Or set limed twigs for crabs;
I sometimes search the grassy knolls
   For wheels of hansom-cabs.
And that's the way' (he gave a wink)
   'By which I get my wealth —
And very gladly will I drink
   Your Honor's noble health.'

I heard him then, for I had just
    Completed my design
To keep the Menai bridge from rust
    By boiling it in wine.
I thanked him much for telling me
    The way he got his wealth,
But chiefly for his wish that he
    Might drink my noble health.

And now, if e'er by chance I put
    My fingers into glue,
Or madly squeeze a right-hand foot
    Into a left-hand shoe,
Or if I drop upon my toe
    A very heavy weight,
I weep, for it reminds me so
Of that old man I used to know—
Whose look was mild, whose speech was slow,
Whose hair was whiter than the snow,
Whose face was very like a crow,
With eyes, like cinders, all aglow,
Who seemed distracted with his woe,
Who rocked his body to and fro,
And muttered mumblingly and low,
As if his mouth were full of dough,
Who snorted like a buffalo—
That summer evening long ago
    A-sitting on a gate."

              from Through the Looking-Glass

An early version of this travesty of Wordsworth's "Resolution and Independence" (p. 421) was published anonymously in a magazine before the Alice books.

How Doth the Little Crocodile

◆◆◆◆

How doth the little crocodile
　　Improve his shining tail,
And pour the waters of the Nile
　　On every golden scale!

How cheerfully he seems to grin,
　　How neatly spreads his claws,
And welcomes little fishes in
　　With gently smiling jaws!

from Alice's Adventures in Wonderland

For many readers, this expert parody has so eclipsed the original (Isaac Watts's "Against Idleness and Mischief") that they may need to be reminded of it—at least of its first two stanzas:

How doth the little busy bee
*　　Improve each shining hour,*
And gather honey all the day
*　　From every opening flower?*

How skillfully she builds her cell!
*　　How neat she spreads the wax!*
And labours hard to store it well
*　　With the sweet food she makes.*

SIR WILLIAM SCHWENCK
GILBERT 1836-1911

Gilbert's early career was as a writer and illustrator of comic verse (such as the ballad in this anthology), and he also wrote verse dramas. He is, however, much better known as the collaborator with Sir Arthur Sullivan on more than a dozen sparkling operettas.

The Yarn of the Nancy Bell

'Twas on the shores that round our coast
  From Deal to Ramsgate span,
That I found alone on a piece of stone
  An elderly naval man.

His hair was weedy, his beard was long,
  And weedy and long was he,
And I heard this wight on the shore recite
  In a singular minor key:

"Oh, I am a cook and a captain bold,
  And the mate of the *Nancy* brig,
And a bo'sun tight, and a midshipmite,
  And the crew of the captain's gig."

And he shook his fists, and he tore his hair,
  Till I really felt afraid,
For I couldn't help thinking the man had been drinking,
  And so I simply said:

"Oh elderly man, it's little I know
  Of the duties of men of the sea,
And I'll eat my hand if I understand
  However you can be

At once a cook, and a captain bold,
  And the mate of the *Nancy* brig,
And a bo'sun tight, and a midshipmite,
  And the crew of the captain's gig."

Then he gave a hitch to his trousers, which
  Is a trick all seamen larn,
And having got rid of a thumping quid,
  He spun this painful yarn:

" 'Twas in the good ship *Nancy Bell*
  That we sailed to the Indian Sea,
And there on a reef we came to grief,
  Which has often occurred to me.

And pretty nigh all the crew was drowned
  (There was seventy-seven o'soul),
And only ten of the *Nancy's* men
  Said "Here!" to the muster-roll.

There was me and the cook and the captain bold,
  And the mate of the *Nancy* brig,
And the bo'sun tight, and a midshipmite,
  And the crew of the captain's gig.

For a month we'd neither wittles nor drink,
  Till a-hungry we did feel,
So we drawed a lot, and, accordin' shot
  The captain for our meal.

The next lot fell to the *Nancy's* mate,
  And a delicate dish he made;
Then our appetite with the midshipmite
  We seven survivors stayed.

And then we murdered the bo'sun tight,
   And he much resembled the pig;
Then we wittled free, did the cook and me,
   On the crew of the captain's gig.

Then only the cook and me was left,
   And the delicate question, "Which
Of us two goes to the kettle?" arose,
   And we argued it out as sich.

For I loved that cook as a brother, I did,
   And the cook he worshiped me;
But we'd both be blowed if we'd either be stowed
   In the other chap's hold, you see.

"I'll be eat if you dines off me," says Tom;
   "Yes, that" says I "you'll be—"
"I'm boiled if I die, my friend," quoth I;
   And "Exactly so," quoth he.

Says he, "Dear James, to murder me
   Were a foolish thing to do,
For don't you see that you can't cook *me*,
   While I can—and will—cook *you!*"

So he boils the water, and takes the salt
   And the pepper in portions true
(Which he never forgot) and some chopped shallot,
   And some sage and parsley too.

"Come here," says he, with a proper pride
   Which his smiling features tell,
" 'Twill soothing be if I let you see
   How extremely nice you'll smell."

And he stirred it round and round and round,
    And he sniffed at the foaming froth;
When I ups with his heels, and smothers his squeals
    In the scum of the boiling broth.

And I eat that cook in a week or less,
    And—as I eating be
The last of his chops, why, I almost drops,
    For a wessel in sight I see!
    . . . .

And I never larf, and I never smile,
    And I never lark nor play,
But sit and croak, a single joke
    I have—which is to say:

"Oh, I am a cook and a captain bold,
    And the mate of the *Nancy* brig,
And a bos'sun tight, and a midshipmite,
    And the crew of the captain's gig!"

Gilbert said that this Victorian demonstration that you are indeed what you eat was the first of his "Bab" Ballads. It was offered to Punch, *whose editor declined it "on the ground that it was 'too cannibalistic for his readers' tastes.' " Note how the "elderly naval man" resembles an "ancient mariner" (p. 433).*

ALGERNON CHARLES SWINBURNE 1837–1909

Although he was associated with D. G. Rossetti and others of the Pre-Raphaelite group, Swinburne stood alone with his gift for gorgeous music and trenchant caricature (which includes a brilliant parody of his own poetry). He was a controversial figure in the last third of the nineteenth century, causing ripples of disapproval with his anti-Christian attitude, political idealism, devotion to masochism, and fondness for strong drink. But he was a fine critic (as his work on Chapman and Marlowe testifies), and he was a loyal supporter of worthy fellow-artists (as the tribute of Thomas Hardy eloquently demonstrates).

When the Hounds of Spring Are on Winter's Traces

>>>>>>>

When the hounds of spring are on winter's traces,
   The mother of months in meadow or plain
Fills the shadows and windy places
   With lisp of leaves and ripple of rain;
And the brown bright nightingale amorous
Is half assuaged for Itylus,
For the Thracian ships and the foreign faces,
   The tongueless vigil, and all the pain.

Come with bows bent and with emptying of quivers,
   Maiden most perfect, lady of light,
With a noise of winds and many rivers,
   With a clamour of waters, and with might;
Bind on thy sandals, O thou most fleet,
Over the splendour and speed of thy feet;
For the faint east quickens, the wan west shivers,
   Round the feet of the day and the feet of the night.

Where shall we find her, how shall we sing to her,
　Fold our hands round her knees, and cling?
O that man's heart were as fire and could spring to her,
　Fire, or the strength of the streams that spring!
For the stars and the winds are unto her
As raiment, as songs of the harp-player;
For the risen stars and the fallen cling to her,
　And the southwest-wind and the west-wind sing.

For winter's rains and ruins are over,
　And all the season of snows and sins;
The days dividing lover and lover,
　The light that loses, the night that wins;
And time remembered is grief forgotten,
And frosts are slain and flowers begotten,
And in green underwood and cover
　Blossom by blossom the spring begins.

The full streams feed on flower of rushes,
　Ripe grasses trammel a travelling foot,
The faint fresh flame of the young year flushes
　From leaf to flower and flower to fruit;
And fruit and leaf are as gold and fire,
And the oat is heard above the lyre,
And the hoofèd heel of a satyr crushes
　The chestnut-husk at the chestnut-root.

And Pan by noon and Bacchus by night,
　Fleeter of foot than the fleet-foot kid,
Follows with dancing and fills with delight
　The Mænad and the Bassarid;
And soft as lips that laugh and hide
The laughing leaves of the trees divide,
And screen from seeing and leave in sight
　The god pursuing, the maiden hid.

The ivy falls with the Bacchanal's hair
  Over her eyebrows hiding her eyes;
The wild vine slipping down leaves bare
  Her bright breast shortening into sighs;
The wild vine slips with the weight of its leaves,
But the berried ivy catches and cleaves
To the limbs that glitter, the feet that scare
  The wolf that follows, the fawn that flies.

from Atalanta in Calydon

This is the first of several choruses in Atalanta in Calydon, *Swinburne's early attempt at Greek-style verse-tragedy. The chorus uses both vigorous rhythm and vivid image to catch the spirit of pagan spring. The percussive alliteration, more like Old English than Greek, is one of Swinburne's most characteristic flourishes (a device that he was to mock in his self-caricaturing "Nephelidia": "From the depth of the dreamy decline of the dawn through a notable nimbus of nebulous noonshine . . .").*

The Garden of Proserpine

Here, where the world is quiet;
Here, where all trouble seems
Dead winds' and spent waves' riot
In doubtful dreams of dreams;
I watch the green field growing
For reaping folk and sowing
For harvest-time and mowing,
A sleepy world of streams.

I am tired of tears and laughter,
And men that laugh and weep;
Of what may come hereafter
For men that sow to reap:
I am weary of days and hours,
Blown buds of barren flowers,
Desires and dreams and powers
And everything but sleep.

Here life has death for neighbour,
    And far from eye or ear
Wan waves and wet winds labour,
    Weak ships and spirits steer;
They drive adrift, and whither
They wot not who make thither;
But no such winds blow hither,
    And no such things grow here.

No growth of moor or coppice,
  No heather-flower or vine,
But bloomless buds of poppies,
  Green grapes of Proserpine,
Pale beds of blowing rushes
Where no leaf blooms or blushes
Save this whereout she crushes
  For dead men deadly wine.

Pale, without name or number,
  In fruitless fields of corn,
They bow themselves and slumber
  All night till light is born;
And like a soul belated,
In hell and heaven unmated,
By cloud and mist abated
  Comes out of darkness morn.

Though one were strong as seven,
  He too with death shall dwell,
Nor wake with wings in heaven,
  Nor weep for pains in hell;
Though one were fair as roses,
His beauty clouds and closes;
And well though love reposes,
  In the end it is not well.

Pale, beyond porch and portal,
  Crowned with calm leaves, she stands
Who gathers all things mortal
  With cold immortal hands;
Her languid lips are sweeter
Than love's who fears to greet her
To men that mix and meet her
  From many times and lands.

She waits for each and other,
  She waits for all men born;
Forgets the earth her mother,
  The life of fruits and corn;
And spring and seed and swallow
Take wing for her and follow
Where summer song rings hollow
  And flowers are put to scorn.

There go the loves that wither,
  The old loves with wearier wings;
And all dead years draw thither,
  And all disastrous things;
Dead dreams of days forsaken,
Blind buds that snows have shaken,
Wild leaves that winds have taken,
  Red strays of ruined springs.

We are not sure of sorrow,
  And joy was never sure;
To-day will die to-morrow;
  Time stoops to no man's lure;
And love, grown faint and fretful,
With lips but half regretful
Sighs, and with eyes forgetful
Weeps that no loves endure.

From too much love of living,
From hope and fear set free,
We thank with brief thanksgiving
Whatever gods may be
That no life lives for ever;
That dead men rise up never;
That even the weariest river
Winds somewhere safe to sea.

Then star nor sun shall waken,
Nor any change of light:
Nor sound of waters shaken,
Nor any sound or sight;
Nor wintry leaves nor vernal,
Nor days nor things diurnal;
Only the sleep eternal
In an eternal night.

Swinburne's passion and learning were equally remarkable, and he was inspired in this poem by a still-potent nature myth that was attractive to the great adherents of classical stoicism, a myth associated with the cyclical recurrence of life. Proserpine—also called Proserpina, Persephone, and Kore—was the daughter of the earth goddess Demeter (Ceres). She spent part of her year aboveground and part in the underworld, where she was queen of the dead land. Her garden was in the world beyond. The key rhyme between "ever" and "river" is also found in Shelley's "Hellas."

After some years as an architectural apprentice, Hardy began writing fiction and, over a thirty-year period, produced fourteen novels and several stories. Then, from 1898, in another thirty-year career, he produced eight volumes of poetry as well as the epic drama *The Dynasts*. Hardy is among the very few English-speaking writers who have any serious claim to superlative distinction in both fiction and poetry.

The Darkling Thrush

I leant upon a coppice gate
   When Frost was specter-gray,
And Winter's dregs made desolate
   The weakening eye of day.
The tangled bine-stems scored the sky
   Like strings of broken lyres,
And all mankind that haunted nigh
   Had sought their household fires.

The land's sharp features seemed to be
   The Century's corpse outleant,
His crypt the cloudy canopy,
   The wind his death-lament.
The ancient pulse of germ and birth
   Was shrunken hard and dry,
And every spirit upon earth
   Seemed fervorless as I.

At once a voice arose among
  The bleak twigs overhead
In a full-hearted evensong
  Of joy illimited;
An aged thrush, frail, gaunt, and small,
  In blast-beruffled plume,
Had chosen thus to fling his soul
  Upon the growing gloom.

So little cause for carolings
  Of such ecstatic sound
Was written on terrestrial things
  Afar or nigh around,
That I could think there trembled through
  His happy good-night air
Some blessed Hope, whereof he knew
  And I was unaware.

"The Darkling Thrush" is dated "31st December 1900": it is set on the last day of the nineteenth century (actually, it was published in a magazine a few days before that date). It is the evening of the end of the month, year, century; the author is sixty. The poem is also poised on a liminal gate, and it mentions two acts of leaning.

The Oxen

Christmas Eve, and twelve of the clock.
   "Now they are all on their knees,"
An elder said as we sat in a flock
   By the embers in hearthside ease.

We pictured the meek and mild creatures where
   They dwelt in their strawy pen,
Nor did it occur to one of us there
   To doubt they were kneeling then.

So fair a fancy few would weave
   In these years! Yet, I feel,
If someone said on Christmas Eve,
   "Come; see the oxen kneel,

"In the lonely barton by yonder coomb
   Our childhood used to know,"
I should go with him in the gloom,
   Hoping it might be so.

As with "The Darkling Thrush" (p. 770), we see here a poem set on a holiday and ending on a conditional note of hope somehow stimulated by the behavior of animals.

In Time of "The Breaking of Nations"

Only a man harrowing clods
  In a slow silent walk
With an old horse that stumbles and nods
  Half asleep as they stalk.

Only thin smoke without flame
  From the heaps of couch-grass;
Yet this will go onward the same
  Though Dynasties pass.

Yonder a maid and her wight
  Come whispering by:
War's annals will cloud into night
  Ere their story die.

The title comes from the account in Jeremiah in the Bible of God's judgment against Babylon. The immediate occasion of the poem is the First World War, but Hardy claimed to have planned the poem as early as 1870, the time of the Franco-Prussian War. The lovely stanza, graced by the long third line, recalls that in Tennyson's "Crossing the Bar" (p. 644).

Channel Firing

()◀▶()

That night your great guns, unawares,
Shook all our coffins as we lay,
And broke the chancel window-squares,
We thought it was the Judgment-day

And sat upright. While drearisome
Arose the howl of wakened hounds:
The mouse let fall the altar-crumb,
The worms drew back into the mounds,

The glebe cow drooled. Till God called, "No;
It's gunnery practice out at sea
Just as before you went below;
The world is as it used to be:

"All nations striving strong to make
Red war yet redder. Mad as hatters
They do no more for Christés sake
Than you who are helpless in such matters.

"That this is not the judgment-hour
For some of them's a blessed thing,
For if it were they'd have to scour
Hell's floor for so much threatening. . . .

"Ha, ha. It will be warmer when
I blow the trumpet (if indeed
I ever do; for you are men,
And rest eternal sorely need)."

So down we lay again. "I wonder,
Will the world ever saner be,"
Said one, "than when He sent us under
In our indifferent century!"

And many a skeleton shook his head.
"Instead of preaching forty year,"
My neighbor Parson Thirdly said,
"I wish I had stuck to pipes and beer."

Again the guns disturbed the hour,
Roaring their readiness to avenge,
As far inland as Stourton Tower,
And Camelot, and starlit Stonehenge.

A flat expression — "Loud enough to wake the dead" — is given new life and depth here in a poem that eccentrically but convincingly mixes humor and pathos. The reader of Hardy's greatest novel, Tess of the d'Urbervilles, *will remember how that book, set about thirty years before this poem, places the capture of Tess at Stonehenge, on Salisbury Plain in Hardy's native Wessex. Even in 1914, it was technically possible for the sound of naval gunfire in the Channel to be heard many miles inland.*

Afterwards

When the Present has latched its postern behind my tremulous
    stay,
  And the May month flaps its glad green leaves like wings,
Delicate-filmed as new-spun silk, will the neighbors say,
  "He was a man who used to notice such things"?

If it be in the dusk when, like an eyelid's soundless blink,
  The dewfall-hawk comes crossing the shades to alight
Upon the wind-warped upland thorn, a gazer may think,
  "To him this must have been a familiar sight."

If I pass during some nocturnal blackness, mothy and warm,
  When the hedgehog travels furtively over the lawn,
One may say, "He strove that such innocent creatures should
    come to no harm,
  But he could do little for them; and now he is gone."

If, when hearing that I have been stilled at last, they stand at the
    door,
  Watching the full-starred heavens that winter sees,
Will this thought rise on those who will meet my face no more,
  "He was one who had an eye for such mysteries"?

And will any say when my bell of quittance is heard in the
    gloom,
  And a crossing breeze cuts a pause in its outrollings,
Till they rise again, as they were a new bell's bloom,
  "He hears it not now, but used to notice such things"?

As the fourteen novels, eight volumes of poetry, and several other works over-whelmingly testify, Hardy did notice things and did devote his genius to setting down the truth about innocent creatures.

The Convergence of the Twain

❖·❖·❖·❖

(Lines on the loss of the *Titanic*)

1

In a solitude of the sea
Deep from human vanity,
And the Pride of Life that planned her, stilly couches she.

2

Steel chambers, late the pyres
Of her salamandrine fires,
Cold currents thrid, and turn to rhythmic tidal lyres.

3

Over the mirrors meant
To glass the opulent
The sea-worm crawls—grotesque, slimed, dumb, indifferent.

4

Jewels in joy designed
To ravish the sensuous mind
Lie lightless, all their sparkles bleared and black and blind.

5

Dim moon-eyed fishes near
Gaze at the gilded gear
And query: "What does this vaingloriousness down here?" . . .

6

Well: while was fashioning
This creature of cleaving wing,
The Immanent Will that stirs and urges everything

7

Prepared a sinister mate
For her—so gaily great—
A Shape of Ice, for the time far and dissociate.

8

And as the smart ship grew
In stature, grace, and hue,
In shadowy silent distance grew the Iceberg too.

9

Alien they seemed to be:
No mortal eye could see
The intimate welding of their later history,

10

Or sign that they were bent
By paths coincident
On being anon twin halves of one august event,

11

Till the Spinner of the Years
Said "Now!" And each one hears,
And consummation comes, and jars two hemispheres.

Whitman's "When Lilacs Last in the Dooryard Bloomed" (p. 694), Yeats's "Easter 1916" (p. 864), and Eliot's "Waste Land" (p. 968), like this poem from Hardy's Satires of Circumstance, could all be classified as "April elegies." The irony is right on the surface: the ship had a divine name, was advertised as unsinkable, and sank on her maiden voyage. The stanza (meter and rhyme) seems to be adapted from that in Robert Browning's "Rabbi ben Ezra."

The Man He Killed

‹‹‹-‹‹‹-‹‹‹

"Had he and I but met
    By some old ancient inn,
We should have sat us down to wet
    Right many a nipperkin!

"But ranged as infantry,
    And staring face to face,
I shot at him as he at me,
    And killed him in his place.

"I shot him dead because—
    Because he was my foe,
Just so: my foe of course he was;
    That's clear enough; although

"He thought he'd 'list, perhaps,
    Off-hand—just as I—
Was out of work—had sold his traps—
    No other reason why.

"Yes; quaint and curious war is!
    You shoot a fellow down
You'd treat if met where any bar is,
    Or help to half-a-crown."

The date 1902 attaches the poem to the Boer War, about which Hardy wrote several poems. The stanza (meter and rhyme) is what hymnals call Short Measure; it was used by few poets except Hardy and Dickinson, who was ten years his senior. (See "There's a certain Slant of light," p. 732, "A Bird Came down the Walk," p. 733, and "I never saw a Moor," p. 741). The stanza seems best adapted for use in elementary situations like war and peace, life and death.

Neutral Tones

≫≫≫≫≫≫

We stood by a pond that winter day,
And the sun was white, as though chidden of God,
And a few leaves lay on the starving sod;
   —They had fallen from an ash, and were gray.

Your eyes on me were as eyes that rove
Over tedious riddles of years ago;
And some words played between us to and fro
   On which lost the more by our love.

The smile on your mouth was the deadest thing
Alive enough to have strength to die;
And a grin of bitterness swept thereby
   Like an ominous bird a-wing. . . .

Since then, keen lessons that love deceives,
And wrings with wrong, have shaped to me
Your face, and the God-curst sun, and a tree,
   And a pond edged with grayish leaves.

A sonnet called "Hap" (dated 1866) and this poem (dated 1867) are both recalled in "He Never Expected Much," written about sixty years later. The World tells the aged speaker:

   "I do not promise overmuch,
      Child, overmuch;
   Just neutral-tinted haps and such."

The Ruined Maid

"O 'Melia, my dear, this does everything crown!
Who could have supposed I should meet you in Town?
And whence such fair garments, such prosperi-ty?"
—"O didn't you know I'd been ruined?" said she.

—"You left us in tatters, without shoes or socks,
Tired of digging potatoes, and spudding up docks;
—And now you've gay bracelets and bright feathers three!"
"Yes: that's how we dress when we we're ruined," said she.

—"At home in the barton you said 'thee' and 'thou,'
And 'thik oon,' and 'theas oon,' and 't'other'; but now
Your talking quite fits 'ee for high compa-ny!"—
"Some polish is gained with one's ruin," said she.

—"Your hands were like paws then, your face blue and bleak
But now I'm bewitched by your delicate cheek,
And your little gloves fit as on any la-dy!"
—"We never do work when we're ruined," said she.

—"You used to call home-life a hag-ridden dream,
And you'd sigh, and you'd sock; but at present you seem
To know not of megrims or melancho-ly!"—
"True. One's pretty lively when ruined," said she.

—"I wish I had feathers, a fine sweeping gown,
And a delicate face, and could strut about Town!"
—"My dear—a raw country girl, such as you be,
Cannot quite expect that. You ain't ruined," said she.

Hardy had a humorous side and could produce a mock-ballad in which a whole story (not so different from that of Tess Durbeyfield, after all) is told purely by a dialogue between two speakers who repeat the same rhyme-word, like a refrain. Hardy's "blue and bleak" here and Hopkins's "blue-bleak" in "The Windhover" (p. 790) seem to have been written independently.

The Voice

Woman much missed, how you call to me, call to me,
Saying that now you are not as you were
When you had changed from the one who was all to me,
But as at first, when our day was fair.

Can it be you that I hear? Let me view you, then,
Standing as when I drew near to the town
Where you would wait for me: yes, as I knew you then,
Even to the original air-blue gown!

Or is it only the breeze, in its listlessness
Travelling across the wet mead to me here,
You being ever dissolved to wan wistlessness,
Heard no more again far or near?

    Thus I; faltering forward,
    Leaves around me falling,
Wind oozing thin through the thorn from norward,
    And the woman calling.

As Catherine Frank notes, the twenty-one works that make up Poems of
1912–13 *are all in different forms. "The Voice" complements "The Haunter,"
which is spoken by the woman addressed here. Hardy and his first wife, Emma,
seemed to be living a bitterly strained existence for many years, at least for the
last twenty years of their marriage, but, when she died in November 1912, he let
all the bitterness go and returned most touchingly to their earliest days together,
more than forty years before.*

During Wind and Rain

They sing their dearest songs—
He, she, all of them—yea,
Treble and tenor and bass,
   And one to play;
With the candles mooning each face. . . .
   Ah, no; the years O!
How the sick leaves reel down in throngs!

They clear the creeping moss—
Elders and juniors—aye,
Making the pathways neat
   And the garden gay;
And they build a shady seat. . . .
   Ah, no; the years, the years;
See, the white storm-birds wing across!

They are blithely breakfasting all—
Men and maidens—yea,
Under the summer tree,
   With a glimpse of the bay,
While pet fowl come to the knee. . . .
   Ah, no; the years O!
And the rotten rose is ript from the wall.

They change to a high new house,
He, she, all of them—aye,
Clocks and carpets and chairs
   On the lawn all day,
And brightest things that are theirs. . . .
   Ah, no; the years, the years;
Down their carved names the rain-drop ploughs.

The weather here, as well as the songs, may come from Shakespeare's "When That I Was and a Little Tiny Boy" (p. 103). Robert Frost's late poem called "The Wind and the Rain" owes a debt to Shakespeare and to Hardy and to many other bards who were weather-wise.

ROBERT BRIDGES 1844–1930

Trained in medicine, Bridges was an admirable versifier and an influential student of prosody (particularly Milton's). He was the first editor of the poems of Gerard Manley Hopkins, who had been a good friend and robust correspondent. Bridges's long tenure as Poet Laureate covered an important period of the twentieth century (1913–1930).

London Snow

When men were all asleep the snow came flying,
In large white flakes falling on the city brown,
Stealthily and perpetually settling and loosely lying,
  Hushing the latest traffic of the drowsy town;
Deadening, muffling, stifling its murmurs failing;
Lazily and incessantly floating down and down:
  Silently sifting and veiling road, roof and railing;
Hiding difference, making unevenness even,
Into angles and crevices softly drifting and sailing.
  All night it fell, and when full inches seven
It lay in the depth of its uncompacted lightness,
The clouds blew off from a high and frosty heaven;
  And all woke earlier for the unaccustomed brightness
Of the winter dawning, the strange unheavenly glare:
The eye marvelled—marvelled at the dazzling whiteness;
  The ear hearkened to the stillness of the solemn air;
No sound of wheel rumbling nor of foot falling,
And the busy morning cries came thin and spare.
  Then boys I heard, as they went to school, calling,
They gathered up the crystal manna to freeze
Their tongues with tasting, their hands with snowballing;
  Or rioted in a drift, plunging up to the knees;
Or peering up from under the white-mossed wonder,

"O look at the trees!" they cried, "O look at the trees!"
  With lessened load a few carts creak and blunder,
Following along the white deserted way,
A country company long dispersed asunder:
  When now already the sun, in pale display
Standing by Paul's high dome, spread forth below
His sparkling beams, and awoke the stir of the day.

  For now doors open, and war is waged with the snow;
And trains of sombre men, past tale of number,
Tread long brown paths, as toward their toil they go:
  But even for them awhile no cares encumber
Their minds diverted; the daily word is unspoken,
The daily thoughts of labour and sorrow slumber
At the sight of the beauty that greets them, for the charm they
  have broken.

Bridges, a bold experimenter if not an avant-garde iconoclast, here seems to be testing how much ongoing activity a poem can register with words ending in -ing. (See also Emerson's "Snow-Storm," p. 574, and Whittier's "Snow-Bound," p. 593, for American versions of the same sort of picture.)

Nightingales

()◀━()

Beautiful must be the mountains whence ye come,
And bright in the fruitful valleys the streams, wherefrom
    Ye learn your song:
Where are those starry woods? O might I wander there,
  Among the flowers, which in that heavenly air
    Bloom the year long!

Nay, barren are those mountains and spent the streams:
Our song is the voice of desire, that haunts our dreams,
    A throe of the heart,
Whose pining visions dim, forbidden hopes profound,
  No dying cadence nor long sigh can sound,
    For all our art.

Alone, aloud in the raptured ear of men
  We pour our dark nocturnal secret; and then,
    As night is withdrawn
From these sweet-springing meads and bursting boughs of May,
  Dream, while the innumerable choir of day
    Welcome the dawn.

The human speaker says only the first stanza. By imagining that nightingales can respond to our speculative addresses, Bridges gives a new interpretation to the "selfsame song" that Keats heard in an earlier May (p. 542).

GERARD MANLEY HOPKINS 1844–1889

Hopkins converted to Catholicism while an Oxford undergraduate and became a Jesuit priest in 1877. He wrote little, and none of his poetry was published in his lifetime. Idiosyncrasies of diction and prosody set his poems apart from those of his contemporaries and delayed the appreciation of his genius for many decades. Even now we are still learning to appreciate his innovations, which are testimony to the authenticity of Hopkins's enormous feeling—ecstasy in many cases, desperation in a few.

Pied Beauty

Glory be to God for dappled things—
  For skies of couple-colour as a brinded cow;
    For rose-moles all in stipple upon trout that swim;
Fresh-firecoal chestnut-falls; finches' wings;
  Landscape plotted and pieced—fold, fallow, and plough;
    And áll trádes, their gear and tackle and trim.
All things counter, original, spare, strange;
  Whatever is fickle, freckled (who knows how?)
    With swift, slow; sweet, sour; adazzle, dim;
He fathers-forth whose beauty is past change:
        Praise him.

The first words of this poem echo the motto of the Society of Jesus: Ad maiorem Dei gloriam, *"To the greater glory of God." Just as "The Windhover" (p. 790) puts a dangerous predator in the place of the meek Dove of conventional Christian symbolism, "Pied Beauty" puts changeable nature, freckled and fickle, in the place of the immutable spotlessness of a remote Platonic ideal.*

The Windhover

To Christ Our Lord

I caught this morning morning's minion, king-
  dom of daylight's dauphin, dapple-dawn-drawn
     Falcon, in his riding
Of the rolling level underneath him steady
  air, and striding
High there, how he rung upon the rein of a wimpling
  wing
In his ecstasy! then, off, off forth on swing,
  As a skate's heel sweeps smooth on a bow-bend:
    the hurl and gliding
  Rebuffed the big wind. My heart in hiding
Stirred for a bird,—the achieve of, the mastery of the
  thing!

Brute beauty and valour and act, oh, air, pride,
  plume, here
  Buckle! AND the fire that breaks from thee then, a
    billion
Times told lovelier, more dangerous, O my chevalier!

  No wonder of it: shéer plód makes plough down
    sillion
Shine, and blue-bleak embers, ah my dear,
  Fall, gall themselves, and gash gold-vermilion.

After the fantastic description of the bird in the first nine lines, Hopkins turns to the poem's divine addressee and asserts that His glory is a billion times greater (a British billion: 1,000,000,000,000). The comparison of Christ to a million-million predators is breathtaking enough, to be sure, but the final three lines are even more spectacular. In imagery drawn from accounts of the Crucifixion ("gall" and "gash") and the Eucharist (gold-vermilion parallel to bread-wine, in turn parallel to flesh-blood), the ember sends out brilliant light. (Note that: "sillion" is "ridge between furrows.")

God's Grandeur

>>>>>>>

The world is charged with the grandeur of God.
 It will flame out, like shining from shook foil;
 It gathers to a greatness, like the ooze of oil
Crushed. Why do men then now not reck his rod?
Generations have trod, have trod, have trod;
 And all is seared with trade; bleared, smeared with toil;
 And wears man's smudge and shares man's smell: the soil
Is bare now, nor can foot feel, being shod.

And for all this, nature is never spent;
 There lives the dearest freshness deep down things;
And though the last lights off the black West went
 Oh, morning, at the brown brink eastward, springs—
Because the Holy Ghost over the bent
 World broods with warm breast and with ah! bright wings.

As we see with "Pied Beauty" (p. 789), a good deal of Hopkins's practice as a poet was devoted to living up to the motto of the Jesuit order to which he belonged: "To the greater glory of God."

Spring and Fall

Márgarét, áre you gríeving
Over Goldengrove unleaving?
Leáves, líke the things of man, you
With your fresh thoughts care for, can you?
Ah! ás the heart grows older
It will come to such sights colder
By and by, nor spare a sigh
Though worlds of wanwood leafmeal lie;
And yet you *will* weep and know why.
Now no matter, child, the name:
Sórrow's spríngs áre the same.
Nor mouth had, no nor mind, expressed
What heart heard of, ghost guessed:
It ís the blight man was born for,
It is Margaret you mourn for.

All but three of the words in this poem are of Germanic extraction, and Hopkins uses the Germanic "sprung" rhythm that counts only stressed syllables. He also makes up words like "wanwood" and "leafmeal" on a Germanic basis—all with the effect of primal strangeness but also of undeniable originality and sincerity.

Felix Randal

Felix Randal the farrier, O he is dead then? my duty all ended,
Who have watched his mold of man, big-boned and hardy-
    handsome
Pining, pining, till time when reason rambled in it and some
Fatal four disorders, fleshed there, all contended?

Sickness broke him. Impatient he cursed at first, but mended
Being anointed and all; though a heavenlier heart began some
Months earlier, since I had our sweet reprieve and ransom
Tendered to him. Ah, well, God rest him all road ever he
    offended!

This seeing the sick endears them to us, us too it endears.
My tongue had taught the comfort, touch had quenched thy
    tears,
Thy tears that touched my heart, child, Felix, poor Felix
    Randal;

How far from then forethought of, all thy more boisterous
    years,
When thou at the random grim forge, powerful amidst peers,
Didst fettle for the great gray drayhorse his bright and
    battering sandal!

---

*The Latin for "iron," ferrum, gives us "farrier," which means "blacksmith."
Here Hopkins uses language with great physical force to represent a man and a
job of great physical force. A fifteenth-century poem called "The Smiths" begins,
"Swarte-smeked smethes, smatered with smoke" ("Swart-smocked smiths,
smirched with smoke"). Nowadays, a century after Hopkins's death, few people
have ever seen a smith at work.*

No Worst, There Is None

No worst, there is none. Pitched past pitch of grief,
More pangs will, schooled at forepangs, wilder wring.
Comforter, where, where is your comforting?
Mary, mother of us, where is your relief?
My cries heave, herds-long; huddle in a main, a chief-
woe, world-sorrow; on an age-old anvil wince and sing—
Then lull, then leave off. Fury had shrieked "No ling-
ering! Let me be fell: force I must be brief."
O the mind, mind has mountains; cliffs of fall
Frightful, sheer, no-man-fathomed. Hold them cheap
May who ne'er hung there. Nor does long our small
Durance deal with that steep or deep. Here! creep,
Wretch, under a comfort serves in a whirlwind: all
Life death does end and each day dies with sleep.

This poem, the next poem, and "Carrion Comfort" (p. 802) belong to the group called "Terrible Sonnets" that Hopkins wrote towards the end of his life. The diction of these poems is somewhat more restrained and chastened than that in Hopkins's earlier poems.

Thou Art Indeed Just, Lord

✕✕✕✕✕

Justus quidem tu es, Domine, si disputem tecum;
verumtamen justa loquar ad te: Quare via impiorum
prosperatur? &c.

Thou art indeed just, Lord, if I contend
With thee; but, sir, so what I plead is just.
Why do sinners' ways prosper? and why must
Disappointment all I endeavour end?

Wert thou my enemy, O thou my friend,
How wouldst thou worse, I wonder, than thou dost
Defeat, thwart me? Oh, the sots and thralls of lust
Do in spare hours more thrive than I that spend,

Sir, life upon thy cause. See, banks and brakes
Now, leavèd how thick! lacèd they are again
With fretty chervil, look, and fresh wind shakes

Them; birds build—but not I build; no, but strain,
Time's eunuch, and not breed one work that wakes.
Mine, O thou lord of life, send my roots rain.

Manuscripts of this spare sonnet are dated March 17, 1889, and Hopkins died
less than three months later, on June 8, seven weeks short of his forty-fifth
birthday. Much of the poem translates and extends the twelfth chapter of Jer-
emiah.

Spring

Nothing is so beautiful as Spring—
  When weeds, in wheels, shoot long and lovely and lush;
  Thrush's eggs look little low heavens, and thrush
Through the echoing timber does so rinse and wring
The ear, it strikes like lightnings to hear him sing;
  The glassy peartree leaves and blooms, they brush
  The descending blue; that blue is all in a rush
With richness; the racing lambs too have fair their fling.

What is all this juice and all this joy?
  A strain of the earth's sweet being in the beginning
In Eden garden.—Have, get, before it cloy,

  Before it cloud, Christ, lord, and sour with sinning,
Innocent mind and Mayday in girl and boy,
  Most, O maid's child, thy choice and worthy the winning.

Manuscripts of this poem are dated "May 1877." Hopkins says in "The May Magnificat" that "May is Mary's month." "Spring" recalls the association of Mary's month with that of Maia, a Roman earth goddess. Also present, possibly, is the tradition that the Creation, the Fall, and the Crucifixion all happened in the spring (usually in April).

Heaven-Haven

I have desired to go
    Where springs not fail,
To fields where flies no sharp and sided hail
    And a few lilies blow.

And I have asked to be
    Where no storms come,
Where the green swell is in the havens dumb,
    And out of the swing of the sea.

The consonance of "heaven" and "haven," though audible to any speaker of English, is traceable to a poem by George Herbert called "The Size." The quatrain with a gracefully prolonged third line is also used in Tennyson's "Crossing the Bar" (p. 644) and Hardy's "In Time of 'The Breaking of Nations' " (p. 773).

Inversnaid

◆◇◆◇◆

This darksome burn, horseback brown,
His rollrock highroad roaring down,
In coop and in comb the fleece of his foam
Flutes and low to the lake falls home.

A windpuff-bonnet of fáwn-fróth
Turns and twindles over the broth
Of a pool so pitchblack, féll frówning,
It rounds and rounds Despair to drowning.

Degged with dew, dappled with dew
Are the groins of the braes that the brook treads through,
Wiry heathpacks, flitches of fern,
And the beadbonny ash that sits over the burn.

What would the world be, once bereft
Of wet and of wildness? Let them be left,
O let them be left, wildness and wet;
Long live the weeds and the wilderness yet.

Here is Hopkins at his wittiest. Unlike the grandeur and beauty celebrated in many of his more popular poems, "Inversnaid"—even the name is unattractive—could be called "Pied Ugliness." The landscape and history of Scotland are fearsome: "one fell swoop" comes from Macbeth; but this pitchblack pool is so absurdly "fell-frowning" that it cheers one up. No one claims that Hopkins invented Rock n' Roll, but in his coinage "rollrock" the two key terms are combined for the first time.

The Habit of Perfection

Elected Silence, sing to me
And beat upon my whorlèd ear,
Pipe me to pastures still and be
The music that I care to hear.

Shape nothing, lips; be lovely-dumb:
It is the shut, the curfew sent
From there where all surrenders come
Which only makes you eloquent.

Be shellèd, eyes, with double dark
And find the uncreated light:
This ruck and reel which you remark
Coils, keeps, and teases simple sight.

Palate, the hutch of tasty lust,
Desire not to be rinsed with wine:
The can must be so sweet, the crust
So fresh that come in fasts divine!

Nostrils, your careless breath that spend
Upon the stir and keep of pride,
What relish shall the censers send
Along the sanctuary side!

O feel-of-primrose hands, O feet
That want the yield of plushy sward,
But you shall walk the golden street
And you unhouse and house the Lord.

And, Poverty, be thou the bride
And now the marriage feast begun,
And lily-coloured clothes provide
Your spouse not laboured-at nor spun.

Readers are accustomed to erotic poems that systematically itemize the beloved's physical charms: Shakespeare's Sonnet CXXX (p. 99), Campion's "There Is a Garden in Her Face" (p. 116), and Herrick's "Delight in Disorder" (p. 174) are distinguished examples. Here, however, the austere Jesuit Hopkins converts the erotic conventions to a catalogue of asceticism, which, in its way, can be as rewarding.

Carrion Comfort

>>>>>>>

Not, I'll not, carrion comfort, Despair, not feast on thee:
Not untwist—slack they may be—these last strands of man
In me ór, most weary, cry *I can no more.* I can;
Can something, hope, wish day come, not choose not to be.

But ah, but O thou terrible, why wouldst thou rude on me
Thy wring-world right foot rock? lay a lionlimb against me? scan
With darksome devouring eyes my bruisèd bones? and fan,
O in turns of tempest, me heaped there; me frantic to avoid thee
    and flee?

Why? That my chaff might fly; my grain lie, sheer and clear.
Nay in all that toil, that coil, since (seems) I kissed the rod,
Hand rather, my heart lo! lapped strength, stole joy, would
    laugh, chéer.
Cheer whom though? The hero whose heaven-handling flung me,
    fóot tród
Me? or me that fought him? O which one? is it each one? That
    night, that year
Of now done darkness I wretch lay wrestling with (my God!)
    my God.

This poem, untitled by Hopkins, is grouped with six or seven others called Terrible Sonnets, Dark Sonnets, or Sonnets of Desolation (see also "No Worst, There Is None," p. 795). The rejection of Despair resembles the drowning of Despair in "Inversnaid" (p. 799). Significantly, the earlier parts of the poem echo the Old Testament, while the later echo the New Testament.

EUGENE FIELD 1850-1895

For more than a quarter of his short life, Field was a
Chicago newspaper columnist in the old style, writing
anecdotes and verses, some in the so-called dialect that
was immensely popular at the time. Some of his poems
for the juvenile market gained added popularity by be-
ing set to music.

Wynken, Blynken, and Nod

Wynken, Blynken, and Nod one night
   Sailed off in a wooden shoe—
Sailed on a river of crystal light,
   Into a sea of dew.
"Where are you going, and what do you wish?"
   The old moon asked the three.
"We have come to fish for the herring fish
   That live in this beautiful sea;
   Nets of silver and gold have we!"
Said Wynken,
Blynken,
And Nod.

The old moon laughed and sang a song,
   As they rocked in the wooden shoe,
And the wind that sped them all night long
   Ruffled the waves of dew.
The little stars were the herring fish
   That lived in that beautiful sea———
"Now cast your nets wherever you wish———
   Never afeard are we";
   So cried the stars to the fishermen three:
Wynken,
Blynken,
And Nod.

All night long their nets they threw
  To the stars in the twinkling foam ― ― ―
Then down from the skies came the wooden shoe,
  Bringing the fishermen home;
'T was all so pretty a sail it seemed
  As if it could not be,
And some folks thought 'twas a dream they'd dreamed
  Of sailing that beautiful sea ― ― ―
  But I shall name you the fishermen three:
Wynken,
Blynken,
And Nod.

Wynken and Blynken are two little eyes,
  And Nod is a little head,
And the wooden shoe that sailed the skies
  Is a wee one's trundle-bed.
So shut your eyes while your mother sings
  Of wonderful sights that be,
And you shall see the beautiful things
  As you rock in the misty sea,
  Where the old shoe rocked the fishermen three:
Wynken,
Blynken,
And Nod.

People charged with the care of small children will recognize the functional tendency of children's stories to be sleep-inducing. Field cleverly added the Knickerbocker-Dutch element (and "Wynken" is close to a real Dutch name) and the anatomical allegory of winkin', blinkin', and nod.

The Duel

The gingham dog and the calico cat
Side by side on the table sat;
'Twas half-past twelve, and (what do you think!)
Nor one nor t' other had slept a wink!
   The old Dutch clock and the Chinese plate
   Appeared to know as sure as fate
There was going to be a terrible spat.

     (I wasn't there; I simply state
     What was told to me by the Chinese plate!)

The gingham dog went "bow-wow-wow!"
And the calico cat replied "mee-ow!"
The air was littered, an hour or so,
With bits of gingham and calico,
   While the old Dutch clock in the chimney-place
   Up with its hands before its face,
For it always dreaded a family row!

     (Now mind: I'm only telling you
     What the old Dutch clock declares is true!)

The Chinese plate looked very blue,
And wailed, "Oh, dear! what shall we do!"
But the gingham dog and the calico cat
Wallowed this way and tumbled that,
   Employing every tooth and claw
   In the awfullest way you ever saw—
And, oh! how the gingham and calico flew!

(*Don't fancy I exaggerate —*
I got my news from the Chinese plate!)

Next morning, where the two had sat
They found no trace of dog or cat;
And some folks think unto this day
That burglars stole that pair away!
    But the truth about the cat and pup
    Is this: they ate each other up!
Now what do you really think of that!

(*The old Dutch clock it told me so,*
And that is how I came to know.)

Folklore contains innumerable tales of a vicious fight between mutually destructive adversaries. Children still get a kick out of re-staging the great bout.

ROBERT LOUIS STEVENSON 1850–1894

Stevenson belongs in the company of Scott, Poe, and Wilde, whose works in prose and verse have appealed to a mass audience and continue to do so via movies, radio, television, and the vernacular. Thanks to Stevenson, we can talk about "Jekyll-Hyde" personalities, and recent congressional hearings touched on a vulgar variant of "Long John Silver." In addition to his poetry and fiction, Stevenson wrote many essays and travel books.

Requiem

Under the wide and starry sky,
Dig the grave and let me lie.
Glad did I live and gladly die,
    And I laid me down with a will.

This be the verse you grave for me:
Here he lies where he longed to be;
Home is the sailor, home from the sea,
    And the hunter home from the hill.

T. S. Eliot recollected one part of Stevenson's little poem in the third part of "The Waste Land" (p. 968). Philip Larkin borrowed another part for the title of the late poem "This Be the Verse."

Markham was born in Oregon and lived more than half of his life in California, where he was a schoolteacher. His poetry, which was extremely popular, recorded genuine sentiments of pity and patriotism.

The Man with the Hoe

God made man in His own image,
in the image of God he made him.

                    Genesis

Bowed by the weight of centuries he leans
Upon his hoe and gazes on the ground,
The emptiness of ages in his face,
And on his back the burden of the world.
Who made him dead to rapture and despair,
A thing that grieves not and that never hopes,
Stolid and stunned, a brother to the ox?
Who loosened and let down this brutal jaw?
Whose was the hand that slanted back this brow?
Whose breath blew out the light within this brain?

Is this the Thing the Lord God made and gave
To have dominion over sea and land?
To trace the stars and search the heavens for power;
To feel the passion of Eternity?
Is this the dream He dreamed who shaped the suns
And marked their ways upon the ancient deep?
Down all the caverns of Hell to their last gulf
There is no shape more terrible than this—
More tongued with censure of the world's blind greed—
More filled with signs and portents for the soul—
More packt with danger to the universe.

What gulfs between him and the seraphim!
Slave of the wheel of labor, what to him
Are Plato and the swing of Pleiades?
What the long reaches of the peaks of song,
The rift of dawn, the reddening of the rose?
Through this dread shape the suffering ages look;
Time's tragedy is in that aching stoop;
Through this dread shape humanity betrayed,
Plundered, profaned and disinherited,
Cries protest to the Powers that made the world,
A protest that is also prophecy.

O masters, lords and rulers in all lands,
Is this the handiwork you give to God,
This monstrous thing distorted and soul-quencht?
How will you ever straighten up this shape;
Touch it again with immortality;
Give back the upward looking and the light;
Rebuild in it the music and the dream;
Make right the immemorial infamies,
Perfidious wrongs, immedicable woes?

O masters, lords and rulers in all lands,
How will the future reckon with this Man?
How answer his brute question in that hour
When whirlwinds of rebellion shake all shores?
How will it be with kingdoms and with kings —
With those who shaped him to the thing he is —
When this dumb Terror shall rise to judge the world,
After the silence of the centuries?

For at least a quarter of a century after its first appearance in 1899, Markham's poem enjoyed a good deal of respect and celebrity. It can still appeal to instincts of Art History and Aesthetic Moralizing. The fame of Markham's poem reflected back on Millet's painting that inspired it. (Gertrude Stein reports that her no-nonsense brother Michael looked at a reproduction of the painting and said, "A hell of a hoe"; later, seeing the painting with another brother, Leo, Gertrude agreed that it was a hell of a hoe.)

OSCAR WILDE 1854–1900

Wilde's genius illuminated every sort of literature: comedy, farce, lyric tragedy, symbolic fiction, poetry, critical essays and dialogues, and some of the greatest letters in the language. He was both audacious and humane, and he seems never to have been at a loss for a witty and true thing to say. There is no doubt that his two years in prison (1895–1897) for indecent conduct brought about his early death, right at the end of the nineteenth century. He passed on a marvelous legacy to many modern Irish writers, including James Joyce and Brendan Behan, and his plays are still being performed all over the world.

The Ballad of Reading Gaol

I

He did not wear his scarlet coat,
  For blood and wine are red,
And blood and wine were on his hands
  When they found him with the dead,
The poor dead woman whom he loved,
  And murdered in her bed.

He walked amongst the Trial Men
  In a suit of shady grey;
A cricket cap was on his head,
  And his step seemed light and gay;
But I never saw a man who looked
  So wistfully at the day.

I never saw a man who looked
    With such a wistful eye
Upon that little tent of blue
    Which prisoners call the sky,
And at every drifting cloud that went
    With sails of silver by.

I walked, with other souls in pain,
    Within another ring,
And was wondering if the man had done
    A great or little thing,
When a voice behind me whispered low,
    "That fellow's got to swing."

Dear Christ! the very prison walls
    Suddenly seemed to reel,
And the sky above my head became
    Like a casque of scorching steel;
And, though I was a soul in pain,
    My pain I could not feel.

I only knew what hunted thought
    Quickened his step, and why
He looked upon the garish day
    With such a wistful eye;
The man had killed the thing he loved,
    And so he had to die.

. . . .

Yet each man kills the thing he loves,
    By each let this be heard,
Some do it with a bitter look,
    Some with a flattering word,
The coward does it with a kiss,
    The brave man with a sword!

Some kill their love when they are young,
  And some when they are old;
Some strangle with the hands of Lust,
  Some with the hands of Gold:
The kindest use a knife, because
  The dead so soon grow cold.

Some love too little, some too long,
  Some sell, and others buy;
Some do the deed with many tears,
  And some without a sigh:
For each man kills the thing he loves,
  Yet each man does not die.

He does not die a death of shame
  On a day of dark disgrace,
Nor have a noose about his neck,
  Nor a cloth upon his face,
Nor drop feet foremost through the floor
  Into an empty space.

He does not sit with silent men
  Who watch him night and day;
Who watch him when he tries to weep,
  And when he tries to pray;
Who watch him lest himself should rob
  The prison of its prey.

He does not wake at dawn to see
  Dread figures throng his room,
The shivering Chaplain robed in white,
  The Sheriff stern with gloom,
And the Governor all in shiny black,
  With the yellow face of Doom.

He does not rise in piteous haste
  To put on convict-clothes,
While some coarse-mouthed Doctor gloats, and notes
  Each new and nerve-twitched pose,
Fingering a watch whose little ticks
  Are like horrible hammer-blows.

He does not know that sickening thirst
  That sands one's throat, before
The hangman with his gardener's gloves
  Slips through the padded door,
And binds one with three leathern thongs,
  That the throat may thirst no more.

He does not bend his head to hear
  The Burial Office read,
Nor, while the terror of his soul
  Tells him he is not dead,
Cross his own coffin, as he moves
  Into the hideous shed.

He does not stare upon the air
  Through a little roof of glass:
He does not pray with lips of clay
  For his agony to pass;
Nor feel upon his shuddering cheek
  The kiss of Caiaphas.

II

Six weeks our guardsman walked the yard,
  In the suit of shabby grey:
His cricket cap was on his head,
  And his step seemed light and gay,
But I never saw a man who looked
  So wistfully at the day.

I never saw a man who looked
  With such a wistful eye
Upon that little tent of blue
  Which prisoners call the sky,
And at every wandering cloud that trailed
  Its ravelled fleeces by.

He did not wring his hands, as do
  Those witless men who dare
To try to rear the changeling Hope
  In the cave of black Despair:
He only looked upon the sun,
  And drank the morning air.

He did not wring his hands nor weep,
  Nor did he peek or pine,
But he drank the air as though it held
  Some healthful anodyne;
With open mouth he drank the sun
  As though it had been wine!

And I and all the souls in pain,
  Who tramped the other ring,
Forgot if we ourselves had done
  A great or little thing,
And watched with gaze of dull amaze
  The man who had to swing.

And strange it was to see him pass
  With a step so light and gay,
And strange it was to see him look
  So wistfully at the day,
And strange it was to think that he
  Had such a debt to pay.

For oak and elm have pleasant leaves
  That in the spring-time shoot:
But grim to see is the gallows-tree,
  With its adder-bitten root,
And, green or dry, a man must die
  Before it bears its fruit!

The loftiest place is that seat of grace
  For which all worldlings try:
But who would stand in hempen band
  Upon a scaffold high,
And through a murderer's collar take
  His last look at the sky?

It is sweet to dance to violins
  When Love and Life are fair:
To dance to flutes, to dance to lutes
  Is delicate and rare:
But it is not sweet with nimble feet
  To dance upon the air!

So with curious eyes and sick surmise
  We watched him day by day,
And wondered if each one of us
  Would end the self-same way,
For none can tell to what red Hell
  His sightless soul may stray.

At last the dead man walked no more
  Amongst the Trial Men,
And I knew that he was standing up
  In the black dock's dreadful pen,
And that never would I see his face
  In God's sweet world again.

Like two doomed ships that pass in storm
　　We had crossed each other's way:
But we made no sign, we said no word,
　　We had no word to say;
For we did not meet in the holy night,
　　But in the shameful day.

A prison wall was round us both,
　　Two outcast men we were:
The world had thrust us from its heart,
　　And God from out His care:
And the iron gin that waits for Sin
　　Had caught us in its snare.

III

In Debtors' Yard the stones are hard,
　　And the dripping wall is high,
So it was there he took the air
　　Beneath the leaden sky,
And by each side a Warder walked,
　　For fear the man might die.

Or else he sat with those who watched
　　His anguish night and day;
Who watched him when he rose to weep,
　　And when he crouched to pray;
Who watched him lest himself should rob
　　Their scaffold of its prey.

The Governor was strong upon
　　The Regulations Act:
The Doctor said that Death was but
　　A scientific fact:
And twice a day the Chaplain called,
　　And left a little tract.

And twice a day he smoked his pipe,
   And drank his quart of beer:
His soul was resolute, and held
   No hiding-place for fear;
He often said that he was glad
   The hangman's hands were near.

But why he said so strange a thing
   No Warder dared to ask:
For he to whom a watcher's doom
   Is given as his task,
Must set a lock upon his lips,
   And make his face a mask.

Or else he might be moved, and try
   To comfort or console:
And what should Human Pity do
   Pent up in Murderers' Hole?
What word of grace in such a place
   Could help a brother's soul?

     . . . .

With slouch and swing around the ring
   We trod the Fool's Parade!
We did not care: we knew we were
   The Devil's Own Brigade;
And shaven head and feet of lead
   Make a merry masquerade.

We tore the tarry rope to shreds
   With blunt and bleeding nails;
We rubbed the doors, and scrubbed the floors,
   And cleaned the shining rails:
And, rank by rank, we soaped the plank,
   And clattered with the pails.

We sewed the sacks, we broke the stones,
  We turned the dusty drill:
We banged the tins, and bawled the hymns,
  And sweated on the mill:
But in the heart of every man
  Terror was lying still.

So still it lay that every day
  Crawled like a weed-clogged wave:
And we forgot the bitter lot
  That waits for fool and knave,
Till once, as we tramped in from work,
  We passed an open grave.

With yawning mouth the yellow hole
  Gaped for a living thing;
The very mud cried out for blood
  To the thirsty asphalt ring:
And we knew that ere one dawn grew fair
  Some prisoner had to swing.

Right in we went, with soul intent
  On Death and Dread and Doom:
The hangman, with his little bag,
  Went shuffling through the gloom:
And each man trembled as he crept
  Into his numbered tomb.

. . . .

That night the empty corridors
  Were full of forms of Fear,
And up and down the iron town
  Stole feet we could not hear,
And through the bars that hide the stars
  White faces seemed to peer.

He lay as one who lies and dreams
   In a pleasant meadow-land,
The watchers watched him as he slept,
   And could not understand
How one could sleep so sweet a sleep
   With a hangman close at hand.

But there is no sleep when men must weep
   Who never yet have wept:
So we—the fool, the fraud, the knave—
   That endless vigil kept,
And through each brain on hands of pain
   Another's terror crept.

Alas! it is a fearful thing
   To feel another's guilt!
For, right within, the sword of Sin
   Pierced to its poisoned hilt,
And as molten lead were the tears we shed
   For the blood we had not spilt.

The Warders with their shoes of felt
   Crept by each padlocked door,
And peeped and saw, with eyes of awe,
   Grey figures on the floor,
And wondered why men knelt to pray
   Who never prayed before.

All through the night we knelt and prayed,
   Mad mourners of a corse!
The troubled plumes of midnight were
   The plumes upon a hearse:
And bitter wine upon a sponge
   Was the savour of Remorse.

. . . .

The grey cock crew, the red cock crew,
  But never came the day:
And crooked shapes of Terror crouched,
  In the corners where we lay:
And each evil sprite that walks by night
  Before us seemed to play.

They glided past, they glided fast,
  Like travellers through a mist:
They mocked the moon in a rigadoon
  Of delicate turn and twist,
And with formal pace and loathsome grace
  The phantoms kept their tryst.

With mop and mow, we saw them go,
  Slim shadows hand in hand:
About, about, in ghostly rout
  They trod a saraband:
And the damned grotesques made arabesques,
  Like the wind upon the sand!

With the pirouettes of marionettes,
  They tripped on pointed tread:
But with flutes of Fear they filled the ear,
  As their grisly masque they led,
And loud they sang, and long they sang,
  For they sang to wake the dead.

"*Oho!*" they cried, "*The world is wide,*
  But fettered limbs go lame!
And once, or twice, to throw the dice
  Is a gentlemanly game,
But he does not win who plays with Sin
  In the secret House of Shame."

No things of air these antics were,
    That frolicked with such glee:
To men whose lives were held in gyves,
    And whose feet might not go free,
Ah! wounds of Christ! they were living things,
    Most terrible to see.

Around, around, they waltzed and wound;
    Some wheeled in smirking pairs;
With the mincing step of a demirep
    Some sidled up the stairs:
And with subtle sneer, and fawning leer,
    Each helped us at our prayers.

The morning wind began to moan,
    But still the night went on:
Through its giant loom the web of gloom
    Crept till each thread was spun:
And, as we prayed, we grew afraid
    Of the Justice of the Sun.

The moaning wind went wandering round
    The weeping prison-wall:
Till like a wheel of turning steel
    We felt the minutes crawl:
O moaning wind! what had we done
    To have such a seneschal?

At last I saw the shadowed bars,
    Like a lattice wrought in lead,
Move right across the whitewashed wall
    That faced my three-plank bed,
And I knew that somewhere in the world
    God's dreadful dawn was red.

At six o'clock we cleaned our cells,
   At seven all was still,
But the sough and swing of a mighty wing
   The prison seemed to fill,
For the Lord of Death with icy breath
   Had entered in to kill.

He did not pass in purple pomp,
   Nor ride a moon-white steed.
Three yards of cord and a sliding board
   Are all the gallows' need:
So with rope of shame the Herald came
   To do the secret deed.

We were as men who through a fen
   Of filthy darkness grope:
We did not dare to breathe a prayer,
   Or to give our anguish scope:
Something was dead in each of us,
   And what was dead was Hope.

For Man's grim Justice goes its way,
   And will not swerve aside:
It slays the weak, it slays the strong,
   It has a deadly stride:
With iron heel it slays the strong,
   The monstrous parricide!

We waited for the stroke of eight:
   Each tongue was thick with thirst:
For the stroke of eight is the stroke of Fate
   That makes a man accursed,
And Fate will use a running noose
   For the best man and the worst.

We had no other thing to do,
    Save to wait for the sign to come:
So, like things of stone in a valley lone,
    Quiet we sat and dumb:
But each man's heart beat thick and quick,
    Like a madman on a drum!

With sudden shock the prison-clock
    Smote on the shivering air,
And from all the gaol rose up a wail
    Of impotent despair,
Like the sound that frightened marshes hear
    From some leper in his lair.

And as one sees most fearful things
    In the crystal of a dream,
We saw the greasy hempen rope
    Hooked to the blackened beam,
And heard the prayer the hangman's snare
    Strangled into a scream.

And all the woe that moved him so
    That he gave that bitter cry,
And the wild regrets, and the bloody sweats,
    None knew so well as I:
For he who lives more lives than one
    More deaths than one must die.

IV

There is no chapel on the day
    On which they hang a man:
The Chaplain's heart is far too sick,
    Or his face is far too wan,
Or there is that written in his eyes
    Which none should look upon.

So they kept us close till nigh on noon,
  And then they rang the bell,
And the Warders with their jingling keys
  Opened each listening cell,
And down the iron stair we tramped,
  Each from his separate Hell.

Out into God's sweet air we went,
  But not in wonted way,
For this man's face was white with fear,
  And that man's face was grey,
And I never saw sad men who looked
  So wistfully at the day.

I never saw sad men who looked
  With such a wistful eye
Upon that little tent of blue
  We prisoners called the sky,
And at every careless cloud that passed
  In happy freedom by.

But there were those amongst us all
  Who walked with downcast head,
And knew that, had each got his due,
  They should have died instead:
He had but killed a thing that lived,
  Whilst they had killed the dead.

For he who sins a second time
  Wakes a dead soul to pain,
And draws it from its spotted shroud,
  And makes it bleed again,
And makes it bleed great gouts of blood,
  And makes it bleed in vain!

Like ape or clown, in monstrous garb
  With crooked arrows starred,
Silently we went round and round,
  The slippery asphalt yard;
Silently we went round and round
  And no man spoke a word.

Silently we went round and round,
  And through each hollow mind
The Memory of dreadful things
  Rushed like a dreadful wind,
And Horror stalked before each man,
  And Terror crept behind.

The Warders strutted up and down,
  And kept their herd of brutes,
Their uniforms were spick and span,
  And they wore their Sunday suits,
But we knew the work they had been at,
  By the quicklime on their boots.

For where a grave had opened wide,
  There was no grave at all:
Only a stretch of mud and sand
  By the hideous prison-wall,
And a little heap of burning lime,
  That the man should have his pall.

For he has a pall, this wretched man,
  Such as few men can claim:
Deep down below a prison-yard,
  Naked for greater shame,
He lies, with fetters on each foot,
  Wrapt in a sheet of flame!

And all the while the burning lime
    Eats flesh and bone away,
It eats the brittle bone by night,
    And the soft flesh by day,
It eats the flesh and bone by turns,
    But it eats the heart alway.

For three long years they will not sow
    Or root or seedling there:
For three long years the unblessed spot
    Will sterile be and bare,
And look upon the wondering sky
    With unreproachful stare.

They think a murderer's heart would taint
    Each simple seed they sow.
It is not true! God's kindly earth
    Is kindlier than men know,
And the red rose would but blow more red,
    The white rose whiter blow.

Out of his mouth a red, red rose!
    Out of his heart a white!
For who can say by what strange way,
    Christ brings His will to light,
Since the barren staff the pilgrim bore
    Bloomed in the great Pope's sight?

But neither milk-white rose nor red
    May bloom in prison air;
The shard, the pebble, and the flint,
    Are what they give us there:
For flowers have been known to heal
    A common man's despair.

So never will wine-red rose or white,
  Petal by petal, fall
On that stretch of mud and sand that lies
  By the hideous prison-wall,
To tell the men who tramp the yard
  That God's Son died for all.

Yet though the hideous prison-wall
  Still hems him round and round,
And a spirit may not walk by night
  That is with fetters bound,
And a spirit may but weep that lies
  In such unholy ground,

He is at peace—this wretched man—
  At peace, or will be soon:
There is no thing to make him mad,
  Nor does Terror walk at noon,
For the lampless Earth in which he lies
  Has neither Sun nor Moon.

They hanged him as a beast is hanged:
  They did not even toll
A requiem that might have brought
  Rest to his startled soul,
But hurriedly they took him out,
  And hid him in a hole.

They stripped him of his canvas clothes,
  And gave him to the flies:
They mocked the swollen purple throat,
  And the stark and staring eyes:
And with laughter loud they heaped the shroud
  In which their convict lies.

The Chaplain would not kneel to pray
   By his dishonoured grave:
Nor mark it with that blessed Cross
   That Christ for sinners gave,
Because the man was one of those
   Whom Christ came down to save.

Yet all is well; he has but passed
   To Life's appointed bourne:
And alien tears will fill for him
   Pity's long-broken urn,
For his mourners will be outcast men,
   And outcasts always mourn.

V

I know not whether Laws be right,
   Or whether Laws be wrong;
All that we know who lie in gaol
   Is that the wall is strong;
And that each day is like a year,
   A year whose days are ong.

But this I know, that every Law
   That men have made for Man,
Since first Man took his brother's life,
   And the sad world began,
But straws the wheat and saves the chaff
   With a most evil fan.

This too I know—and wise it were
   If each could know the same—
That every prison that men build
   Is built with bricks of shame,
And bound with bars lest Christ should see
   How men their brothers maim.

With bars they blur the gracious moon,
　　And blind the goodly sun:
And they do well to hide their Hell,
　　For in it things are done
That Son of God nor son of Man
　　Ever should look upon!

The vilest deeds like poison weeds,
　　Bloom well in prison-air;
It is only what is good in Man
　　That wastes and withers there:
Pale Anguish keeps the heavy gate,
　　And the Warder is Despair.

For they starve the little frightened child
　　Till it weeps both night and day:
And they scourge the weak, and flog the fool,
　　And gibe the old and grey,
And some grow mad, and all grow bad,
　　And none a word may say.

Each narrow cell in which we dwell
　　Is a foul and dark latrine,
And the fetid breath of living Death
　　Chokes up each grated screen,
And all, but Lust, is turned to dust
　　In Humanity's machine.

The brackish water that we drink
　　Creeps with a loathsome slime,
And the bitter bread they weigh in scales
　　Is full of chalk and lime,
And Sleep will not lie down, but walks
　　Wild-eyed, and cries to Time.

But though lean Hunger and green Thirst
　Like asp with adder fight,
We have little care of prison fare,
　For what chills and kills outright
Is that every stone one lifts by day
　Becomes one's heart by night.

With midnight always in one's heart,
　And twilight in one's cell,
We turn the crank, or tear the rope,
　Each in his separate Hell,
And the silence is more awful far
　Than the sound of a brazen bell.

And never a human voice comes near
　To speak a gentle word:
And the eye that watches through the door
　Is pitiless and hard:
And by all forgot, we rot and rot,
　With soul and body marred.

And thus we rust Life's iron chain
　Degraded and alone:
And some men curse, and some men weep,
　And some men make no moan:
But God's eternal Laws are kind
　And break the heart of stone:

And every human heart that breaks,
　In prison-cell or yard,
Is as that broken box that gave
　Its treasure to the Lord,
And filled the unclean leper's house
　With the scent of costliest nard.

Ah! happy they whose hearts can break
  And peace of pardon win!
How else may man make straight his plan
  And cleanse his soul from Sin?
How else but through a broken heart
  May Lord Christ enter in?

And he of the swollen purple throat,
  And the stark and staring eyes,
Waits for the holy hands that took
  The Thief to Paradise;
And a broken and a contrite heart
  The Lord will not despise.

The man in red who reads the Law
  Gave him three weeks of life,
Three little weeks in which to heal
  His soul of his soul's strife,
And cleanse from every blot of blood
  The hand that held the knife.

And with tears of blood he cleansed the hand,
  The hand that held the steel:
For only blood can wipe out blood,
  And only tears can heal:
And the crimson stain that was of Cain
  Became Christ's snow-white seal.

VI

In Reading gaol by Reading town
  There is a pit of shame,
  And in it lies a wretched man
  Eaten by teeth of flame,
In a burning winding-sheet he lies,
  And his grave has got no name.

And there, till Christ call forth the dead,
  In silence let him lie:
No need to waste the foolish tear,
  Or heave the windy sigh:
The man had killed the thing he loved,
  And so he had to die.

And all men kill the thing they love,
  By all let this be heard,
Some do it with a bitter look,
  Some with a flattering word,
The coward does it with a kiss,
  The brave man with a sword!

In 1895, by a grotesque tissue of ironies, Wilde was found guilty of having done something that had not been a crime ten years earlier and subjected to two years of imprisonment of a kind (accompanied by genuinely hard labor) that would be much softened by prison reforms just ten years later. Wilde's prison experience led to his two final works, which could hardly differ more from each other: the unique letter called De Profundis *that is one of the great personal documents in the language; and this Ballad, which uses a haunting stanza found here and there in Coleridge's "Rime of the Ancient Mariner" (p. 433) and also in some verses by Thomas Hood. Wilde, always the wit and always the self-conscious critic, said, "I am out-Henleying Kipling!"—referring to Kipling's "Danny Deever" (p. 851), also about a soldier hanged for murder, which was first published in a magazine that W. E. Henley edited. At the Paris Exposition of 1900, not long before his death at forty-six, Wilde made a recording of his own reading of some stanzas from the Ballad.*

ALFRED EDWARD HOUSMAN 1859–1936

Although the book for which he is most famous is called *A Shropshire Lad*, A. E. Housman did not come from Shropshire and was hardly a lad when the book was published in 1896. He was born in Worcestershire, near Shropshire, and spent a melancholy and undistinguished time at Oxford before taking a clerical job in 1882. In time, however, he joined the faculty of University College, London, as a teacher of Latin and later went on to Cambridge. He was a distinguished and acerbic editor of classical texts. Housman was old-fashioned, patriotic, conservative, and conventional in literature; but he was also adventuresome enough to be one of the first people to fly commercially!

Loveliest of Trees

Loveliest of trees, the cherry now
Is hung with bloom along the bough,
And stands about the woodland ride
Wearing white for Eastertide.

Now, of my threescore years and ten,
Twenty will not come again,
And take from seventy springs a score,
It only leaves me fifty more.

And since to look at things in bloom
Fifty springs are little room,
About the woodlands I will go
To see the cherry hung with snow.

from A Shropshire Lad

Housman used a persona called Terence Hearsay to express many of the Romantic sentiments of the late nineteenth century, as though in conscious continuation of Byron's "So, We'll Go No More a-Roving" (p. 479), although Housman adds a tender stoicism not explicit in Byron.

To an Athlete Dying Young

The time you won your town the race
We chaired you through the market-place;
Man and boy stood cheering by,
And home we brought you shoulder-high.

To-day, the road all runners come,
Shoulder-high we bring you home,
And set you at your threshold down,
Townsman of a stiller town.

Smart lad, to slip betimes away
From fields where glory does not stay
And early though the laurel grows
It withers quicker than the rose.

Eyes the shady night has shut
Cannot see the record cut,
And silence sounds no worse than cheers
After earth has stopped the ears:

Now you will not swell the rout
Of lads that wore their honours out,
Runners whom renown outran
And the name died before the man.

So set, before its echoes fade,
The fleet foot on the sill of shade,
And hold to the low lintel up
The still-defended challenge-cup.

And round that early-laurelled head
Will flock to gaze the strengthless dead,
And find unwithered on its curls
The garland briefer than a girl's.

Housman could approach a modern subject with the humble simplicity of folk art but, at the same time, with matchless sophistication and learning. This elegy was published in 1896, but, with a change of language, it could have been written in 1896 B.C.

With Rue My Heart Is Laden

With rue my heart is laden
  For golden friends I had,
For many a rose-lipt maiden
  And many a lightfoot lad.

By brooks too broad for leaping
  The lightfoot boys are laid;
The rose-lipt girls are sleeping
  In fields where roses fade.

from A Shropshire Lad

Housman seems to have challenged himself to try the discipline of making do with minimal materials—here, just a handful of related sounds: "laden . . . lad . . . laid . . ." and the story is told.

When I Was One-and-Twenty

>>>>>>>

When I was one-and-twenty
   I heard a wise man say,
"Give crowns and pounds and guineas
   But not your heart away;
Give pearls away and rubies
   But keep your fancy free."
But I was one-and-twenty,
   No use to talk to me.

When I was one-and-twenty
   I heard him say again,
"The heart out of the bosom
   Was never given in vain;
'Tis paid with sighs a plenty
   And sold for endless rue."
And I am two-and-twenty,
   And oh, 'tis true, 'tis true.

from A Shropshire Lad

What remains, after a hundred years, so surprising about this delightful and moving poem is the disclosure, right at the end, that our perspective on life at twenty-one has come from a philosopher of twenty-two.

Terence, This Is Stupid Stuff

"Terence, this is stupid stuff:
You eat your victuals fast enough;
There can't be much amiss, 'tis clear,
To see the rate you drink your beer.
But oh, good Lord, the verse you make,
It gives a chap the belly-ache.
The cow, the old cow, she is dead;
It sleeps well, the hornèd head:
We poor lads, 'tis our turn now
To hear such tunes as killed the cow.
Pretty friendship 'tis to rhyme
Your friends to death before their time
Moping melancholy mad:
Come, pipe a tune to dance to, lad."

Why, if 'tis dancing you would be,
There's brisker pipes than poetry.
Say, for what were hop-yards meant,
Or why was Burton built on Trent?
Oh many a peer of England brews
Livelier liquor than the Muse,
And malt does more than Milton can
To justify God's ways to man.
Ale, man, ale's the stuff to drink
For fellows whom it hurts to think:
Look into the pewter pot
To see the world as the world's not.
And faith, 'tis pleasant till 'tis past:
The mischief is that 'twill not last.
Oh I have been to Ludlow fair
And left my necktie God knows where,
And carried half-way home, or near,
Pints and quarts of Ludlow beer:

Then the world seemed none so bad,
And I myself a sterling lad;
And down in lovely muck I've lain,
Happy till I woke again.
Then I saw the morning sky:
Heigho, the tale was all a lie;
The world, it was the old world yet,
I was I, my things were wet,
And nothing now remained to do
But begin the game anew.

Therefore, since the world has still
Much good, but much less good than ill,
And while the sun and moon endure
Luck's a chance, but trouble's sure,
I'd face it as a wise man would,
And train for ill and not for good.
'Tis true, the stuff I bring for sale
Is not so brisk a brew as ale:
Out of a stem that scored the hand
I wrung it in a weary land.
But take it: if the smack is sour,
The better for the embittered hour;
It should do good to heart and head
When your soul is in my soul's stead;
And I will friend you, if I may,
In the dark and cloudy day.

There was a king reigned in the East:
There, when kings will sit to feast,
They get their fill before they think
With poisoned meat and poisoned drink.
He gathered all that springs to birth
From the many-venomed earth;
First a little, thence to more,
He sampled all her killing store;
An easy, smiling, seasoned sound,
Sate the king when healths went round.

They put arsenic in his meat
And stared aghast to watch him eat;
They poured strychnine in his cup
And shook to see him drink it up:
They shook, they stared as white's their shirt:
Them it was their poison hurt.
—I tell the tale that I heard told.
Mithridates, he died old.

from A Shropshire Lad

Housman had planned to call his first volume The Poems of Terence Hearsay *but settled finally on* A Shropshire Lad. *The Terence in this poem is a good-enough representation of certain sides of Housman's complex character: the classical learning, the stoicism, the wit.*

Into My Heart an Air That Kills

Into my heart an air that kills
  From yon far country blows:
What are those blue remembered hills,
  What spires, what farms are those?

That is the land of lost content,
  I see it shining plain,
The happy highways where I went
  And cannot come again.

from A Shropshire Lad

---

*From Housman's native Worcestershire (now Hereford and Worcester), Shrop-
shire was a "far country" with hills and spires visible to westward. Like Hardy,
whose work he admired, Housman made a local landscape an abstract symbol as
well as a concrete setting. For mysterious reasons, it is much more effective to
say "blue remembered hills," with the words seemingly out of order, than the
expected "remembered blue hills."*

On Wenlock Edge

On Wenlock Edge the wood's in trouble;
   His forest fleece the Wrekin heaves;
The gale, it plies the saplings double,
   And thick on Severn snow the leaves.

'Twould blow like this through holt and hanger
   When Uricon the city stood:
'Tis the old wind in the old anger,
   But then it threshed another wood.

Then, 'twas before my time, the Roman
   At yonder heaving hill would stare:
The blood that warms an English yeoman,
   The thoughts that hurt him, they were there.

There, like the wind through woods in riot,
   Through him the gale of life blew high;
The tree of man was never quiet:
   Then 'twas the Roman, now 'tis I.

The gale, it plies the saplings double,
   It blows so hard, 'twill soon be gone:
To-day the Roman and his trouble
   Are ashes under Uricon.

from A Shropshire Lad

With Housman, as with Hardy, Kipling, Chesterton, and some other late Victorians, one is aware of eons of history underfoot almost anywhere in Britain: a Catholic Christianity under the Protestant surface, Roman and Druid layers of paganism under the Christian layers, millions of centuries of prehistory under any human time. Roman Uricon (Uriconium or Viroconium) is the modern Wroxeter.

Poverty, failure, illness, and drug addiction almost destroyed Thompson until, in about 1888, he was rescued by Wilfred and Alice Meynell, who took care of him and gave him some literary connections. He published three volumes of verse during the 1890s, along with a good deal of literary journalism.

The Hound of Heaven

><>><><

I fled Him, down the nights and down the days;
  I fled Him, down the arches of the years;
I fled Him, down the labyrinthine ways
    Of my own mind; and in the midst of tears
I hid from Him, and under running laughter.
        Up vistaed hopes I sped;
        And shot, precipitated,
Adown Titanic glooms of chasmèd fears,
  From those strong Feet that followed, followed after.
        But with unhurrying chase,
        And unperturbèd pace,
    Deliberate speed, majestic instancy,
      They beat—and a Voice beat
      More instant than the Feet—
"All things betray thee, who betrayest Me."

      I pleaded, outlaw-wise,
By many a hearted casement, curtained red,
  Trellised with intertwining charities;
(For, though I knew His love Who followèd,
      Yet was I sore adread
Lest, having Him, I must have naught beside);
But, if one little casement parted wide,
  The gust of His approach would clash it to.
  Fear wist not to evade, as Love wist to pursue.

Across the margent of the world I fled,
  And troubled the gold gateways of the stars,
  Smiting for shelter on their clangèd bars;
    Fretted to dulcet jars
And silvern chatter the pale ports o' the moon.
I said to Dawn: Be sudden—to Eve: Be soon;
  With thy young skiey blossoms heap me over
    From this tremendous Lover!
Float thy vague veil about me, lest He see!
  I tempted all His servitors, but to find
My own betrayal in their constancy,
In faith to Him their fickleness to me,
  Their traitorous trueness, and their loyal deceit.
To all swift things for swiftness did I sue;
  Clung to the whistling mane of every wind.
    But whether they swept, smoothly fleet,
    The long savannahs of the blue;
      Or whether, Thunder-driven,
    They clanged his chariot 'thwart a heaven
Plashy with flying lightnings round the spurn o' their feet: —
  Fear wist not to evade as Love wist to pursue.
    Still with unhurrying chase,
    And unperturbèd pace,
  Deliberate speed, majestic instancy,
    Came on the following Feet,
    And a Voice above their beat—
" Naught shelters thee, who wilt not shelter Me."

I sought no more that after which I strayed
    In face of man or maid;
But still within the little children's eyes
    Seems something, something that replies,
They at least are for me, surely for me!
I turned me to them very wistfully;
But just as their young eyes grew sudden fair
    With dawning answers there,
Their angel plucked them from me by the hair.
"Come then, ye other children, Nature's—share

With me" (said I) "your delicate fellowship;
    Let me greet you lip to lip,
    Let me twine with you caresses,
      Wantoning
    With our Lady-Mother's vagrant tresses,
      Banqueting
    With her in her wind-walled palace,
    Underneath her azured daïs,
    Quaffing, as your taintless way is,
      From a chalice
Lucent-weeping out of the dayspring."
      So it was done:
I in their delicate fellowship was one —
Drew the bolt of Nature's secrecies.
    I knew all the swift importings
    On the willful face of skies;
    I knew how the clouds arise
    Spumèd of the wild sea-snortings;
      All that's born or dies
    Rose and drooped with; made the shapers
Of mine own moods, or wailful or divine;
    With them joyed and was bereaven.
    I was heavy with the even,
    When she lit her glimmering tapers
    Round the day's dead sanctities.
    I laughed in the morning's eyes.
I triumphed and I saddened with all weather,
    Heaven and I wept together,
And its sweet tears were salt with mortal mine.
Against the red throb of its sunset-heart
    I laid my own to beat,
    And share commingling heat;
But not by that, by that, was eased my human smart.
In vain my tears were wet on Heaven's grey cheek.
For ah! we know not what each other says,
    These things and I; in sound *I* speak —

Their sound is but their stir, they speak by silences.
Nature, poor stepdame, cannot slake my drouth;
      Let her, if she would owe me,
Drop yon blue bosom-veil of sky, and show me
      The breasts o' her tenderness:
Never did any milk of hers once bless
      My thirsting mouth.
      Nigh and nigh draws the chase,
      With unperturbèd pace,
      Deliberate speed, majestic instancy;
      And past those noisèd Feet
      A Voice comes yet more fleet—
"Lo! naught contents thee, who content'st not Me."

Naked I wait Thy love's uplifted stroke!
My harness piece by piece Thou hast hewn from me,
      And smitten me to my knee;
      I am defenceless utterly.
      I slept, methinks, and woke,
And, slowly gazing, find me stripped in sleep.
In the rash lustihead of my young powers,
      I shook the pillaring hours
And pulled my life upon me; grimed with smears,
I stand amid the dust o' the mounded years—
My mangled youth lies dead beneath the heap,
My days have crackled and gone up in smoke,
Have puffed and burst as sun-starts on a stream.
      Yea, faileth now even dream
The dreamer, and the lute the lutanist;
Even the linked fantasies, in whose blossomy twist
I swung the earth a trinket at my wrist,
Are yielding; cords of all too weak account
For earth with heavy griefs so overplussed.
      Ah! is Thy love indeed
A weed, albeit an amaranthine weed,
Suffering no flowers except its own to mount?
      Ah! must—
      Designer infinite!—

Ah! must Thou char the wood ere Thou canst limn with it?
My freshness spent its wavering shower i' the dust;
And now my heart is as a broken fount,
Wherein tear-drippings stagnate, spilt down ever
    From the dank thoughts that shiver
Upon the sighful branches of my mind.
    Such is; what is to be?
The pulp so bitter, how shall taste the rind?
I dimly guess what Time in mists confounds;
Yet ever and anon a trumpet sounds
From the hid battlements of Eternity;
Those shaken mists a space unsettle, then
Round the half-glimpsèd turrets slowly wash again.
    But not ere him who summoneth
    I first have seen, enwound
With glooming robes purpureal, cypress-crowned;
His name I know, and what his trumpet saith.
Whether man's heart or life it be which yields
    Thee harvest, must Thy harvest-fields
    Be dunged with rotten death?
    Now of that long pursuit
    Comes at hand the bruit;
    That Voice is round me like a bursting sea:
    "And is thy earth so marred,
    Shattered in shard on shard?
    Lo, all things fly thee, for thou fliest Me!
    Strange, piteous, futile thing!
Wherefore should any set thee love apart?
Seeing none but I make much of naught" (He said),
"And human love needs human meriting:
    How hast thou merited —
Of all man's clotted clay the dingiest clot?
    Alack, thou knowest not
How little worthy of any love thou art!
Whom wilt thou find to love ignoble thee
    Save Me, save only Me?
All which I took from thee I did but take,
    Not for thy harms,

But just that thou might'st seek it in My arms.
    All which thy child's mistake
Fancies as lost, I have stored for thee at home: ·
    Rise, clasp My hand, and come!"
  Halts by me that footfall:

  Is my gloom, after all,
Shade of His hand, outstretched caressingly?
    "Ah, fondest, blindest, weakest,
    I am He Whom thou seekest!
Thou dravest love from thee, who dravest Me."

Thompson's tormented verse takes the characteristically emotional idiom of the 1890s back to the agonies and ecstasies of certain religious poets of the seventeenth century, including George Herbert (pp. 186–195) and Henry Vaughan (pp. 247–254), along with Abraham Cowley and Richard Crashaw. Thompson's canine pursuer shocked some Victorian readers who were more accustomed to Cecil Frances Alexander's holy "Child so dear and gentle" who "leads his children on / To the place where he is gone."

It may surprise some former Cub Scouts to learn that
much of the lore and law of their movement is drawn
from *The Jungle Book* by Kipling (who also suspected
Edgar Rice Burroughs of felonious plagarism, since
Tarzan is so much like Mowgli). Kipling's stories, nov-
els, and poems remain unforgettable for many readers,
especially those who were exposed to his influence as
children—if not through Cub Scouts then maybe in the
form of stirring musical settings and movie adaptations.
Before he died, Kipling seemed awfully right-wing, par-
ticularly to left-wing critics of his day; but efforts of
redemption on the parts of T. S. Eliot and W. H. Au-
den did much to restore the luster to Kipling's reputa-
tion, which had never faded for many younger readers.

Recessional

1897

God of our fathers, known of old,
  Lord of our far-flung battle-line,
Beneath whose awful Hand we hold
  Dominion over palm and pine—
Lord God of Hosts, be with us yet,
Lest we forget—lest we forget!

The tumult and the shouting dies;
  The Captains and the Kings depart:
Still stands Thine ancient sacrifice,
  An humble and a contrite heart.
Lord God of Hosts, be with us yet,
Lest we forget—lest we forget!

Far-called, our navies melt away;
   On dune and headland sinks the fire:
Lo, all our pomp of yesterday
   Is one with Nineveh and Tyre!
Judge of the Nations, spare us yet,
Lest we forget—lest we forget!

If, drunk with sight of power, we loose
   Wild tongues that have not Thee in awe,
Such boastings as the Gentiles use,
   Or lesser breeds without the Law—
Lord God of Hosts, be with us yet,
Lest we forget—lest we forget!

For heathen heart that puts her trust
   In reeking tube and iron shard,
All valiant dust that builds on dust,
   And guarding, calls not Thee to guard,
For frantic boast and foolish word—
Thy mercy on Thy People, Lord!

Victoria became Queen in 1837 and ruled until she died in 1901. During the Jubilee of 1897 that celebrated her first sixty years on the throne, Kipling wrote a touchingly cautionary hymn of receding: recessionals come at the end of a service or ceremony, when people are leaving.

Danny Deever

"What are the bugles blowin' for?" said Files-on-Parade.
"To turn you out, to turn you out," the Color-Sergeant said.
"What makes you look so white, so white?" said Files-on-
 Parade.
"I'm dreadin' what I've got to watch," the Color-Sergeant said.
 For they're hangin' Danny Deever, you can hear the Dead
  March play,
 The Regiment's in 'ollow square—they're hangin' him
  today;
 They've taken of his buttons off an' cut his stripes away,
An' they're hangin' Danny Deever in the mornin'.

"What makes the rear-rank breathe so 'ard?" said Files-on-
 Parade.
"It's bitter cold, it's bitter cold," the Color-Sergeant said.
"What makes that front-rank man fall down?" said Files-on-
 Parade.
"A touch o' sun, a touch o' sun," the Color-Sergeant said.
 They are hangin' Danny Deever, they are marchin' of 'im
  round.
 They 'ave 'alted Danny Deever by 'is coffin on the
  ground;
 And 'e'll swing in 'arf a minute for a sneakin' shootin'
  hound—
 O they're hangin' Danny Deever in the mornin'!

" 'Is cot was right-'and cot to mine," said Files-on-Parade.
" 'E's sleepin' out an' far tonight," the Color-Sergeant said.
"I've drunk 'is beer a score o' times," said Files-on-Parade.
" 'E's drinkin' bitter beer alone," the Color-Sergeant said.
> They are hangin' Danny Deever, you must mark 'im to 'is
> place,
> For 'e shot a comrade sleepin'—you must look 'im in the
> face;
> Nine 'undred of 'is county an' the Regiment's disgrace,
> While they're hangin' Danny Deever in the mornin'.

"What's that so black agin the sun?" said Files-on-Parade.
"It's Danny fightin' 'ard for life," the Color-Sergeant said.
"What's that that whimpers over'ead?" said Files-on-Parade.
"It's Danny's soul that's passin' now," the Color-Sergeant said.
> For they're done with Danny Deever, you can 'ear the
> quickstep play,
> The Regiment's in column, an' they're marchin' us away;
> Ho! the young recruits are shakin', an' they'll want their
> beer today,
> After hangin' Danny Deever in the mornin'!

---

*Writing of "The Ballad of Reading Gaol" (p. 810), Oscar Wilde said in a letter,
"I am out-Henleying Kipling!" He was most probably thinking of "Danny
Deever," which also concerns the public hanging of an enlisted soldier convicted
of murder. (Kipling's poem first appeared, only a few years before Wilde's, in
a magazine edited by W. E. Henley.)*

WILLIAM BUTLER YEATS 1865-1939

William Butler Yeats first studied art (his father was a celebrated painter), but he soon turned to literature and produced a succession of lovely works in many modes: romantic lyric, political satire, mythic metamorphosis (transforming one of his great loves, Maud Gonne, into a Helen), verse drama, aesthetic criticism, visionary history, and some of the deepest and most entertaining autobiographical writing of the modern age. He remained single until his fifties, when he married the young Georgie Hyde Lees, with whom he had a son and a daughter, for both of whom he wrote engaging prayers. Many readers consider Yeats the greatest English-speaking poet of the twentieth century.

The Second Coming

Turning and turning in the widening gyre
The falcon cannot hear the falconer;
Things fall apart; the center cannot hold;
Mere anarchy is loosed upon the world,
The blood-dimmed tide is loosed, and everywhere
The ceremony of innocence is drowned;
The best lack all conviction, while the worst
Are full of passionate intensity.

Surely some revelation is at hand;
Surely the Second Coming is at hand.
The Second Coming! Hardly are those words out
When a vast image out of *Spiritus Mundi*
Troubles my sight: somewhere in the sands of the desert
A shape with lion body and the head of a man,
A gaze blank and pitiless as the sun,
Is moving its slow thighs, while all about it
Reel shadows of the indignant desert birds.

The darkness drops again; but now I know
That twenty centuries of stony sleep
Were vexed to nightmare by a rocking cradle,
And what rough beast, its hour come round at last,
Slouches towards Bethlehem to be born?

"The Second Coming" feints in the direction of mumbo jumbo in its reference to Spiritus Mundi, *but, against this farfetched realm of sphinxes and poppycock, there is a picture of Yeats struggling with the greatest problem of the modern world: war. The irony is that this second coming is hardly the peace-bringing Second Coming of Christ but rather the reappearance of a terrible beast.*

Sailing to Byzantium

I

That is no country for old men. The young
In one another's arms, birds in the trees
—Those dying generations—at their song,
The salmon-falls, the mackerel-crowded seas,
Fish, flesh, or fowl, commend all summer long
Whatever is begotten, born, and dies.
Caught in that sensual music all neglect
Monuments of unageing intellect.

II

An aged man is but a paltry thing,
A tattered coat upon a stick, unless
Soul clap its hands and sing, and louder sing
For every tatter in its mortal dress,
Nor is there singing school but studying
Monuments of its own magnificence;
And therefore I have sailed the seas and come
To the holy city of Byzantium.

III

O sages standing in God's holy fire
As in the gold mosaic of a wall,
Come from the holy fire, perne in a gyre,
And be the singing-masters of my soul.
Consume my heart away; sick with desire
And fastened to a dying animal
It knows not what it is; and gather me
Into the artifice of eternity.

IV

Once out of nature I shall never take
My bodily form from any natural thing,
But such a form as Grecian goldsmiths make
Of hammered gold and gold enamelling
To keep a drowsy Emperor awake;
Or set upon a golden bough to sing
To lords and ladies of Byzantium
Of what is past, or passing, or to come.

What is sought is not the rural peace of a small island in a beautiful lake (see "The Lake Isle of Innisfree," p. 858) but the concentrated unity of life in an ideal city, medieval Byzantium (which was the name of the place until A.D. 330, when it became Constantinople, changed in 1930 to Istanbul—but a note by Yeats suggests that he has in mind the city as it might have been in the sixth century). (Note that: "perne" is "spin.")

Leda and the Swan

>>>>>>>

A sudden blow: the great wings beating still
Above the staggering girl, her thighs caressed
By the dark webs, her nape caught in his bill,
He holds her helpless breast upon his breast.

How can those terrified vague fingers push
The feathered glory from her loosening thighs?
And how can body, laid in that white rush,
But feel the strange heart beating where it lies?

A shudder in the loins engenders there
The broken wall, the burning roof and tower
And Agamemnon dead.
                    Being so caught up,
So mastered by the brute blood of the air,
Did she put on his knowledge with his power
Before the indifferent beak could let her drop?

Hopkins's "Windhover" (p. 790) was first published in 1918. It included "mastery of the thing" and "Brute beauty and valour and act, oh, air . . .," and Yeats writes here, in another poem about a terrifying bird, almost the same words in the same order: "So mastered by the brute blood of the air."

The Lake Isle of Innisfree

I will arise and go now, and go to Innisfree,
And a small cabin build there, of clay and wattles made:
Nine bean-rows will I have there, a hive for the honey-bee,
And live alone in the bee-loud glade.

And I shall have some peace there, for peace comes dropping
    slow,
Dropping from the veils of the morning to where the cricket
    sings;
There midnight's all a glimmer, and noon a purple glow,
And evening full of the linnet's wings.

And I will arise and go now, for always night and day
I hear lake water lapping with low sounds by the shore;
While I stand on the roadway, or on the pavements gray,
I hear it in the deep heart's core.

---

*Yeats's celebrated poem of nostalgia was apparently inspired—not by a genuine
desire to lead a simple agricultural life—but by falling asleep over Thoreau's
Walden. The poem is parodied in Ezra Pound's "Mauberley."*

When You Are Old

When you are old and gray and full of sleep,
And nodding by the fire, take down this book,
And slowly read, and dream of the soft look
Your eyes had once, and of their shadows deep;

How many loved your moments of glad grace,
And loved your beauty with love false or true,
But one man loved the pilgrim soul in you,
And loved the sorrows of your changing face;

And bending down beside the glowing bars,
Murmur, a little sadly, how love fled
And paced upon the mountains overhead
And hid his face amid a crowd of stars.

Yeats wrote few translations, and in fact there are not many translations or adaptations in this book. "When You Are Old," represents a reworking by the young Yeats (in 1892) of a poem by the sixteenth-century French poet Pierre Ronsard, "Quand vous serez bien vielle, au soir à la chandelle."

Among School Children

I

I walk through the long schoolroom questioning;
A kind old nun in a white hood replies;
The children learn to cipher and to sing,
To study reading-books and history,
To cut and sew, be neat in everything
In the best modern way—the children's eyes
In momentary wonder stare upon
A sixty-year-old smiling public man.

II

I dream of a Ledaean body, bent
Above a sinking fire, a tale that she
Told of a harsh reproof, or trivial event
That changed some childish day to tragedy—
Told, and it seemed that our two natures blent
Into a sphere from youthful sympathy,
Or else, to alter Plato's parable,
Into the yolk and white of the one shell.

III

And thinking of that fit of grief or rage
I look upon one child or t'other there
And wonder if she stood so at that age—
For even daughters of the swan can share
Something of every paddler's heritage—
And had that colour upon cheek or hair,
And thereupon my heart is driven wild:
She stands before me as a living child.

IV

Her present image floats into the mind—
Did Quattrocento finger fashion it
Hollow of cheek as though it drank the wind
And took a mess of shadows for its meat?
And I though never of Ledaean kind
Had pretty plumage once—enough of that,
Better to smile on all that smile, and show
There is a comfortable kind of old scarecrow.

V

What youthful mother, a shape upon her lap
Honey of generation had betrayed,
And that must sleep, shriek, struggle to escape
As recollection or the drug decide,
Would think her son, did she but see that shape
With sixty or more winters on its head,
A compensation for the pang of his birth,
Or the uncertainty of his setting forth?

VI

Plato thought nature but a spume that plays
Upon a ghostly paradigm of things;
Solider Aristotle played the taws
Upon the bottom of a king of kings;
World-famous golden-thighed Pythagoras
Fingered upon a fiddle-stick or strings
What a star sang and careless Muses heard:
Old clothes upon old sticks to scare a bird.

VII

Both nuns and mothers worship images,
But those the candles light are not as those
That animate a mother's reveries,
But keep a marble or a bronze repose.
And yet they too break hearts—O Presences
That passion, piety or affection knows,
And that all heavenly glory symbolise—
O self-born mockers of man's enterprise;

VIII

Labour is blossoming or dancing where
The body is not bruised to pleasure soul,
Nor beauty born out of its own despair,
Nor blear-eyed wisdom out of midnight oil.
O chestnut tree, great rooted blossomer,
Are you the leaf, the blossom or the bole?
O body swayed to music, O brightening glance,
How can we know the dancer from the dance?

In eight eight-line stanzas, the poet moves from a literally pedestrian statement about bureaucratic walking to a literally ecstatic question about charismatic dancing. Within this orbit, there is room for personal considerations and for the grandest philosophical and theological speculation.

An Irish Airman Foresees His Death

I know that I shall meet my fate
Somewhere among the clouds above;
Those that I fight I do not hate,
Those that I guard I do not love;
My country is Kiltartan Cross,
My countrymen Kiltartan's poor,
No likely end could bring them loss
Or leave them happier than before.
Nor law, nor duty bade me fight,
Nor public men, nor cheering crowds,
A lonely impulse of delight
Drove to this tumult in the clouds;
I balanced all, brought all to mind,
The years to come seemed waste of breath,
A waste of breath the years behind
In balance with this life, this death.

Major Robert Gregory was the son of Lady Augusta Gregory, Yeats's friend and co-founder of the Abbey Theatre. He was killed in early 1918.

Easter, 1916

I have met them at close of day
Coming with vivid faces
From counter or desk among grey
Eighteenth-century houses.
I have passed with a nod of the head
Or polite meaningless words,
Or have lingered awhile and said
Polite meaningless words,
And thought before I had done
Of a mocking tale or a gibe
To please a companion
Around the fire at the club,
Being certain that they and I
But lived where motley is worn:
All changed, changed utterly:
A terrible beauty is born.

That woman's days were spent
In ignorant good-will,
Her nights in argument
Until her voice grew shrill.
What voice more sweet than hers
When, young and beautiful,
She rode to harriers?
This man had kept a school
And rode our wingèd horse;
This other his helper and friend
Was coming into his force;
He might have won fame in the end,
So sensitive his nature seemed,
So daring and sweet his thought.
This other man I had dreamed
A drunken, vainglorious lout.
He had done most bitter wrong

To some who are near my heart,
Yet I number him in the song;
He, too, has resigned his part
In the casual comedy;
He, too, has been changed in his turn,
Transformed utterly:
A terrible beauty is born.
Hearts with one purpose alone
Through summer and winter seem
Enchanted to a stone
To trouble the living stream.
The horse that comes from the road,
The rider, the birds that range
From cloud to tumbling cloud,
Minute by minute they change;
A shadow of cloud on the stream
Changes minute by minute;
A horse-hoof slides on the brim,
And a horse plashes within it;
The long-legged moor-hens dive,
And hens to moor-cocks call;
Minute by minute they live:
The stone's in the midst of all.

Too long a sacrifice
Can make a stone of the heart.
O when may it suffice?
That is Heaven's part, our part
To murmur name upon name,
As a mother names her child
When sleep at last has come
On limbs that had run wild.
What is it but nightfall?
No, no, not night but death;
Was it needless death after all?
For England may keep faith
For all that is done and said.
We know their dream; enough

To know they dreamed and are dead;
And what if excess of love
Bewildered them till they died?
I write it out in a verse—
MacDonagh and MacBride
And Connolly and Pearse
Now and in time to be,
Wherever green is worn,
Are changed, changed utterly:
A terrible beauty is born.

In "September 1913" Yeats had announced the death of Romantic Ireland. After the failure of the Easter Rebellion and the execution of sixteen of the Irish leaders in late April and early May of 1916, the Irish-American Joyce Kilmer wrote a lament that began by mocking Yeats's earlier "Romantic Ireland's dead and gone." In September 1916, as though in answer to Kilmer, from whom he borrowed some verbiage and rhetoric, Yeats produced one of the great political elegies of all time.

The Wild Swans at Coole

The trees are in their autumn beauty,
The woodland paths are dry,
Under the October twilight the water
Mirrors a still sky;
Upon the brimming water among the stones
Are nine-and-fifty swans.

The nineteenth autumn has come upon me
Since I first made my count;
I saw, before I had well finished,
All suddenly mount
And scatter wheeling in great broken rings
Upon their clamorous wings.

I have looked upon those brilliant creatures,
And now my heart is sore.
All's changed since I, hearing at twilight,
The first time on this shore,
The bell-beat of their wings above my head,
Trod with a lighter tread.

Unwearied still, lover by lover,
They paddle in the cold
Companionable streams or climb the air;
Their hearts have not grown old;
Passion or conquest, wander where they will,
Attend upon them still.

But now they drift on the still water,
Mysterious, beautiful;
Among what rushes will they build,
By what lake's edge or pool
Delight men's eyes when I awake some day
To find they have flown away?

Yeats seems to have produced a touchstone poem for certain lower slopes of the postmodern mentality. Clive James has ironically entitled a book Brilliant Creatures; *the teacher in the movie* Educating Rita *cites "stones"/"swans" as an instance of consonance (which Rita explains as "The rhyme's not right"). Like many of Yeats's poems, this one ends with a question.*

The Circus Animals' Desertion

I

I sought a theme and sought for it in vain,
I sought it daily for six weeks or so.
Maybe at last, being but a broken man,
I must be satisfied with my heart, although
Winter and summer till old age began
My circus animals were all on show,
Those stilted boys, that burnished chariot,
Lion and woman and the Lord knows what.

II

What can I but enumerate old themes?
First that sea-rider Oisin led by the nose
Through three enchanted islands, allegorical dreams,
Vain gaiety, vain battle, vain repose,
Themes of the embittered heart, or so it seems,
That might adorn old songs or courtly shows;
But what cared I that set him on to ride,
I, starved for the bosom of his faery bride?
And then a counter-truth filled out its play,
The Countess Cathleen was the name I gave it;
She, pity-crazed, had given her soul away,
But masterful Heaven had intervened to save it.
I thought my dear must her own soul destroy,
So did fanaticism and hate enslave it,
And this brought forth a dream and soon enough
This dream itself had all my thought and love.

And when the Fool and Blind Man stole the bread
Cuchulain fought the ungovernable sea;
Heart-mysteries there, and yet when all is said
It was the dream itself enchanted me:
Character isolated by a deed
To engross the present and dominate memory.
Players and painted stage took all my love,
And not those things that they were emblems of.

III

Those masterful images because complete
Grew in pure mind, but out of what began?
A mound of refuse or the sweepings of a street,
Old kettles, old bottles, and a broken can,
Old iron, old bones, old rags, that raving slut
Who keeps the till. Now that my ladder's gone,
I must lie down where all the ladders start,
In the foul rag-and-bone shop of the heart.

---

*In this late poem, Yeats looks back on his earliest works, some of them fifty and more years in the past. The references are to a long allegorical poem (*The Wanderings of Oisin*) and two plays (*The Countess Cathleen *and* On Baile's Strand*) as well as to his long-standing vexatious relationship with Maud Gonne, the most important personage in Yeats's work from beginning to end.*

A Prayer for My Daughter

Once more the storm is howling, and half hid
Under this cradle-hood and coverlid
My child sleeps on. There is no obstacle
But Gregory's wood and one bare hill
Whereby the haystack- and roof-levelling wind,
Bred on the Atlantic, can be stayed;
And for an hour I have walked and prayed
Because of the great gloom that is in my mind.

I have walked and prayed for this young child an hour
And heard the sea-wind scream upon the tower,
And under the arches of the bridge, and scream
In the elms above the flooded stream;
Imagining in excited reverie
That the future years had come,
Dancing to a frenzied drum,
Out of the murderous innocence of the sea.

May she be granted beauty and yet not
Beauty to make a stranger's eye distraught,
Or hers before a looking-glass, for such,
Being made beautiful overmuch,
Consider beauty a sufficient end,
Lose natural kindness and maybe
The heart-revealing intimacy
That chooses right, and never find a friend.

Helen being chosen found life flat and dull
And later had much trouble from a fool,
While that great Queen, that rose out of the spray,
Being fatherless could have her way
Yet chose a bandy-leggèd smith for man.
It's certain that fine women eat
A crazy salad with their meat
Whereby the Horn of Plenty is undone.

In courtesy I'd have her chiefly learned;
Hearts are not had as a gift but hearts are earned
By those that are not entirely beautiful;
Yet many, that have played the fool
For beauty's very self, has charm made wise,
And many a poor man that has roved,
Loved and thought himself beloved,
From a glad kindness cannot take his eyes.

May she become a flourishing hidden tree
That all her thoughts may like the linnet be,
And have no business but dispensing round
Their magnanimities of sound,
Nor but in merriment begin a chase,
Nor but in merriment a quarrel.
O may she live like some green laurel
Rooted in one dear perpetual place.

My mind, because the minds that I have loved,
The sort of beauty that I have approved,
Prosper but little, has dried up of late,
Yet knows that to be choked with hate
May well be of all evil chances chief.
If there's no hatred in a mind
Assault and battery of the wind
Can never tear the linnet from the leaf.

An intellectual hatred is the worst,
So let her think opinions are accursed.
Have I not seen the loveliest woman born
Out of the mouth of Plenty's horn,
Because of her opinionated mind
Barter that horn and every good
By quiet natures understood
For an old bellows full of angry wind?

Considering that, all hatred driven hence,
The soul recovers radical innocence
And learns at last that it is self-delighting,
Self-appeasing, self-affrighting,
And that its own sweet will is Heaven's will;
She can, though every face should scowl
And every windy quarter howl
Or every bellows burst, be happy still.

And may her bridegroom bring her to a house
Where all's accustomed, ceremonious;
For arrogance and hatred are the wares
Peddled in the thoroughfares.
How but in custom and in ceremony
Are innocence and beauty born?
Ceremony's a name for the rich horn,
And custom for the spreading laurel tree.

Some readers, including some feminists, find it strange and even objectionable that Yeats should seemingly ask so little in a prayer for his only daughter. But Yeats bases his prayer for courtesy and modesty on experience (he was already fifty-three when she was born); he had seen the terrible damage that too much beauty can wreak.

Lapis Lazuli

For Harry Clifton

I have heard that hysterical women say
They are sick of the palette and fiddle-bow,
Of poets that are always gay,
For everybody knows or else should know
That if nothing drastic is done
Aeroplane and Zeppelin will come out,
Pitch like King Billy bomb-balls in
Until the town lie beaten flat.

All perform their tragic play,
There struts Hamlet, there is Lear,
That's Ophelia, that Cordelia;
Yet they, should the last scene be there,
The great stage curtain about to drop,
If worthy their prominent part in the play,
Do not break up their lines to weep.
They know that Hamlet and Lear are gay;
Gaiety transfiguring all that dread.
All men have aimed at, found and lost;
Black out; Heaven blazing into the head:
Tragedy wrought to its uttermost.
Though Hamlet rambles and Lear rages,
And all the drop-scenes drop at once
Upon a hundred thousand stages,
It cannot grow by an inch or an ounce.

On their own feet they came, or on shipboard,
Camelback, horseback, ass-back, mule-back,
Old civilizations put to the sword.
Then they and their wisdom went to rack:
No handiwork of Callimachus,
Who handled marble as if it were bronze,

Made draperies that seemed to rise
When sea-wind swept the corner, stands;
His long lamp-chimney shaped like the stem
Of a slender palm, stood but a day;
All things fall and are built again,
And those that build them again are gay.

Two Chinamen, behind them a third,
Are carved in lapis lazuli,
Over them flies a long-legged bird,
A symbol of longevity;
The third, doubtless a serving-man,
Carries a musical instrument.

Every discoloration of the stone,
Every accidental crack or dent,
Seems a water-course or an avalanche,
Or lofty slope where it still snows
Though doubtless plum or cherry-branch
Sweetens the little half-way house
Those Chinamen climb towards, and I
Delight to imagine them seated there;
There, on the mountain and the sky,
On all the tragic scene they stare.
One asks for mournful melodies;
Accomplished fingers begin to play.
Their eyes mid many wrinkles, their eyes,
Their ancient, glittering eyes, are gay.

Such a theatrical poem about tragedy and gaiety deserves the full theatrical treatment. Kingsley Amis, among others, reports that Dylan Thomas would read "Lapis Lazuli" with all the tricks at his command, including a ten-second pause before the last two words. Amis may mean to disparage or ridicule both Thomas's performance and Yeats's poem, but for some readers Amis's account just raises both to an even grander level.

The Song of Wandering Aengus

I went out to the hazel wood,
Because a fire was in my head,
And cut and peeled a hazel wand,
And hooked a berry to a thread;
And when white moths were on the wing,
And moth-like stars were flickering out,
I dropped the berry in a stream
And caught a little silver trout.

When I had laid it on the floor
I went to blow the fire aflame,
But something rustled on the floor,
And some one called me by my name:
It had become a glimmering girl
With apple blossoms in her hair
Who called me by my name and ran
And faded through the brightening air.

Though I am old with wandering
Through hollow lands and hilly lands,
I will find out where she has gone,
And kiss her lips and take her hands;
And walk among long dappled grass,
And pluck till time and times are done
The silver apples of the moon,
The golden apples of the sun.

Yeats was inspired by an ancient story of Aengus (or Óengus, also called the Macc Óc, "great son") who "was asleep one night when he saw something like a young girl . . . and she was the most beautiful woman in Ériu" (Gantz, Early Irish Myths and Sagas). *He wandered for years in search of her.*

No Second Troy

Why should I blame her that she filled my days
With misery, or that she would of late
Have taught to ignorant men most violent ways,
Or hurled the little streets upon the great,
Had they but courage equal to desire?
What could have made her peaceful with a mind
That nobleness made simple as a fire,
With beauty like a tightened bow, a kind
That is not natural in an age like this,
Being high and solitary and most stern?
Why, what could she have done, being what she is?
Was there another Troy for her to burn?

In a poem made exclusively of rhetorical questions, Yeats likens Maud Gonne to Helen: a superlatively beautiful and charismatic woman who also causes terrible trouble. The likeness turns up in many other poems by Yeats, including "A Prayer for My Daughter" (p. 871) and "Among School Children" (p. 860).

Burgess is a lot like Ernest Lawrence Thayer (1863–1940), the author of "Casey at the Bat": born in the East, associated with California in its first heyday in the late nineteenth century, and remembered almost exclusively for a single piece of light verse.

The Purple Cow

I never saw a Purple Cow,
I never hope to see one;
But I can tell you, anyhow,
I'd rather see than be one.

Some poets live to regret having written wildly successful poems. Five years (presumably) after writing "The Purple Cow," Burgess offered "Cinq Ans Après":

Ah, yes! I wrote the "Purple Cow"—
I'm Sorry, now, I Wrote it!
But I can Tell you, Anyhow,
I'll Kill you if you Quote it!

ERNEST DOWSON 1867–1900

Although Dowson was born in Kent and schooled at Oxford, he spent much of his short life in France, the incarnation of dissipation and decadence. He was consumptive and made his condition worse by drinking. While living in the slums of London's East End, he met his "Cynara," a café-owner's daughter who was to marry a waiter.

Non Sum Qualis Eram Bonae sub Regno Cynarae

Last night, ah, yesternight, betwixt her lips and mine
There fell thy shadow, Cynara! thy breath was shed
Upon my soul between the kisses and the wine;
And I was desolate and sick of an old passion,
   Yea, I was desolate and bowed my head:
I have been faithful to thee, Cynara! in my fashion.

All night upon mine heart I felt her warm heart beat,
Night-long within mine arms in love and sleep she lay;
Surely the kisses of her bought red mouth were sweet;
But I was desolate and sick of an old passion,
   When I awoke and found the dawn was gray:
I have been faithful to thee, Cynara! in my fashion.

I have forgot much, Cynara! gone with the wind,
Flung roses, roses riotously with the throng,
Dancing, to put thy pale, lost lilies out of mind;
But I was desolate and sick of an old passion,
   Yea, all the time, because the dance was long:
I have been faithful to thee, Cynara! in my fashion.

I cried for madder music and for stronger wine,
But when the feast is finished and the lamps expire,
Then falls thy shadow, Cynara! the night is thine;
And I am desolate and sick of an old passion,
   Yea, hungry for the lips of my desire:
I have been faithful to thee, Cynara! in my fashion.

"I am not what I was under the rule of the kind Cynara" (Horace, Odes, I.iv). This modest poem provides the model for a memorable Cole Porter song and the phrase "Gone with the wind" that turns up in Joyce's Ulysses and elsewhere.

Vitae Summa Brevis
Spem Nos Vetat Incohare Longam

()◀▶()

They are not long, the weeping and the laughter,
   Love and desire and hate:
I think they have no portion in us after
     We pass the gate.

They are not long, the days of wine and roses:
   Out of a misty dream
Our path emerges for a while, then closes
     Within a dream.

The title comes from Horace: "The brief sum of life forbids us the hope of enduring long." Dowson's poem furnished the title of a movie about alcoholics, Days of Wine and Roses.

EDGAR LEE MASTERS 1868–1950

Although Masters wrote history, biography, fiction, and poetry of many sorts in many styles, he is remembered only for one volume, *The Spoon River Anthology*, in which free-verse epitaphs are spoken by the miscellaneous dead (a few of whom had been real people) of a typical midwestern village. The themes are those of Midwestern populism, but the form is in some ways classical, based on the *Greek Anthology*, much of which is epitaphs spoken by the dead themselves.

Anne Rutledge

Out of me unworthy and unknown
The vibrations of deathless music;
"With malice toward none, with charity for all."
Out of me the forgiveness of millions toward millions,
And the beneficent face of a nation
Shining with justice and truth.
I am Anne Rutledge who sleep beneath these weeds,
Beloved in life of Abraham Lincoln,
Wedded to him, not through union,
But through separation.
Bloom forever, O Republic,
From the dust of my bosom!

from Spoon River Anthology

Masters's Spoon River Anthology, *consists of epitaphs, also spoken by the dead. In most cases, Masters's characters are fictional and typical; Anne Rutledge, however, is real, with plangent meaning for Americans and especially for Midwesterners like Masters.*

[881]

Robinson's early books were not successful, but for the last twenty years of his life he was among the most honored American poets, receiving three Pulitzer Prizes. In addition to the quick, incisive sketches of the blighted lives of those doomed to a small-town existence—such as the poems of Robinson's that have made it into this anthology—he also wrote ambitious philosophical poems and, in his final years, Arthurian narratives, including *Merlin, Lancelot,* and *Tristram.*

Mr. Flood's Party

Old Eben Flood, climbing alone one night
Over the hill between the town below
And the forsaken upland hermitage
That held as much as he should ever know
On earth again of home, paused warily.
The road was his with not a native near;
And Eben, having leisure, said aloud,
For no man else in Tilbury Town to hear:

"Well, Mr. Flood, we have the harvest moon
Again, and we may not have many more;
The bird is on the wing, the poet says,
And you and I have said it here before.
Drink to the bird." He raised up to the light
The jug that he had gone so far to fill,
And answered huskily: "Well, Mr. Flood,
Since you propose it, I believe I will."

Alone, as if enduring to the end
A valiant armor of scarred hopes outworn,
He stood there in the middle of the road
Like Roland's ghost winding a silent horn.
Below him, in the town among the trees,
Where friends of other days had honored him,
A phantom salutation of the dead
Rang thinly till old Eben's eyes were dim.

Then, as a mother lays her sleeping child
Down tenderly, fearing it may awake,
He set the jug down slowly at his feet
With trembling care, knowing that most things break;
And only when assured that on firm earth
It stood, as the uncertain lives of men
Assuredly did not, he paced away,
And with his hand extended paused again:

"Well, Mr. Flood, we have not met like this
In a long time; and many a change has come
To both of us, I fear, since last it was
We had a drop together. Welcome home!"
Convivially returning with himself,
Again he raised the jug up to the light;
And with an acquiescent quaver said:
"Well, Mr. Flood, if you insist, I might.

"Only a very little, Mr. Flood —
For auld lang syne. No more, sir; that will do."
So, for the time, apparently it did,
And Eben evidently thought so too;
For soon amid the silver loneliness
Of night he lifted up his voice and sang,
Secure, with only two moons listening,
Until the whole harmonious landscape rang —

"For auld lang syne." The weary throat gave out,
The last word wavered; and the song being done,
He raised again the jug regretfully
And shook his head, and was again alone.
There was not much that was ahead of him,
And there was nothing in the town below—
Where strangers would have shut the many doors
That many friends had opened long ago.

By simply asserting the presence of two moons (instead of belaboring the point that drunkenness caused Mr. Flood to see double), the poem enters into the character's consciousness. The comparisons to a mother and to the heroic knight Roland also add sympathy.

Miniver Cheevy

Miniver Cheevy, child of scorn,
  Grew lean while he assailed the seasons;
He wept that he was ever born,
  And he had reasons.

Miniver loved the days of old
  When swords were bright and steeds were prancing;
The vision of a warrior bold
  Would set him dancing.

Miniver sighed for what was not,
  And dreamed, and rested from his labors;
He dreamed of Thebes and Camelot,
  And Priam's neighbors.

Miniver mourned the ripe renown
  That made so many a name so fragrant;
He mourned Romance, now on the town,
  And Art, a vagrant.

Miniver loved the Medici,
  Albeit he had never seen one;
He would have sinned incessantly
  Could he have been one.

Miniver cursed the commonplace
  And eyed a khaki suit with loathing;
He missed the medieval grace
  Of iron clothing.

Miniver scorned the gold he sought,
  But sore annoyed was he without it;
Miniver thought, and thought, and thought,
  And thought about it.

Miniver Cheevy, born too late,
   Scratched his head and kept on thinking;
Miniver coughed, and called it fate,
   And kept on drinking.

"Miniver Cheevy" is partly a lucid, ironic caricature of a common village type ridiculously in love with Middle Ages that never existed, but it is partly a self-portrait as well: Robinson himself certainly "kept on drinking" and came to write some notoriously inert poems on Arthurian subjects.

Richard Cory

>>>>>>>

Whenever Richard Cory went down town,
We people on the pavement looked at him:
He was a gentleman from sole to crown,
Clean favored, and imperially slim.

And he was always quietly arrayed,
And he was always human when he talked;
But still he fluttered pulses when he said,
"Good-morning," and he glittered when he walked.

And he was rich—yes, richer than a king—
And admirably schooled in every grace:
In fine, we thought that he was everything
To make us wish that we were in his place.

So on we worked, and waited for the light,
And went without the meat, and cursed the bread;
And Richard Cory, one calm summer night,
Went home and put a bullet through his head.

---

*Robinson takes over the heroic quatrain of Gray's "Elegy Written in a Country
Churchyard" (p. 327) to fashion a modern ironic epitaph. You can probably read
an obituary for a Richard Cory in a local newspaper within the next twelve-
month.*

Eros Turannos

She fears him, and will always ask
　　What fated her to choose him;
She meets in his engaging mask
　　All reasons to refuse him;
But what she meets and what she fears
Are less than are the downward years,
Drawn slowly to the foamless weirs
　　Of age, were she to lose him.

Between a blurred sagacity
　　That once had power to sound him,
And Love, that will not let him be
　　The Judas that she found him,
Her pride assuages her almost,
As if it were alone the cost. —
He sees that he will not be lost,
　　And waits and looks around him.

A sense of ocean and old trees
　　Envelopes and allures him;
Tradition, touching all he sees,
　　Beguiles and reassures him;
And all her doubts of what he says
Are dimmed with what she knows of days —
Till even prejudice delays
　　And fades, and she secures him.

The falling leaf inaugurates
   The reign of her confusion;
The pounding wave reverberates
   The dirge of her illusion;
And home, where passion lived and died,
Becomes a place where she can hide,
While all the town and harbor side
   Vibrate with her seclusion.

We tell you, tapping on our brows,
   The story as it should be,
As if the story of a house
   Were told, or ever could be;
We'll have no kindly veil between
Her visions and those we have seen,
As if we guessed what hers have been,
   Or what they are or would be.

Meanwhile we do no harm; for they
   That with a god have striven,
Not hearing much of what we say,
   Take what the god has given;
Though like waves breaking it may be,
Or like a changed familiar tree,
Or like a stairway to the sea
   Where down the blind are driven.

---

*In a stanza form that seems to owe something to Swinburne's "Garden of
Proserpine" (p. 766), Robinson locates the outline of a sad but familiar domestic
story in a setting of pagan realism and irony, underscored by the Greek title
("Love the King" or "Love the Tyrant").*

For a Dead Lady

No more with overflowing light
Shall fill the eyes that now are faded,
Nor shall another's fringe with night
Their woman-hidden world as they did.
No more shall quiver down the days
The flowing wonder of her ways,
Whereof no language may requite
The shifting and the many-shaded.

The grace, divine, definitive,
Clings only as a faint forestalling;
The laugh that love could not forgive
Is hushed, and answers to no calling;
The forehead and the little ears
Have gone where Saturn keeps the years;
The breast where roses could not live
Has done with rising and with falling.

The beauty, shattered by the laws
That have creation in their keeping,
No longer trembles at applause,
Or over children that are sleeping;
And we who delve in beauty's lore
Know all that we have known before
Of what inexorable cause
Makes Time so vicious in his reaping.

It is typical of Robinson's iron discipline that he says that we "Know all that we have known before" but leaves the reader to figure out that all we know is nothing. It is typical of his fine craft that the fifth line of each stanza contains a word with an "-ore" sound, as though a mournful note were being softly repeated.

Luke Havergal

Go to the western gate, Luke Havergal,
There where the vines cling crimson on the wall,
And in the twilight wait for what will come.
The leaves will whisper there of her, and some,
Like flying words, will strike you as they fall;
But go, and if you listen she will call.
Go to the western gate, Luke Havergal —
Luke Havergal.

No, there is not a dawn in eastern skies
To rift the fiery night that's in your eyes;
But there, where western glooms are gathering,
The dark will end the dark, if anything:
God slays Himself with every leaf that flies,
And hell is more than half of paradise.
No, there is not a dawn in eastern skies —
In eastern skies.

Out of a grave I come to tell you this,
Out of a grave I come to quench the kiss
That flames upon your forehead with a glow
That blinds you to the way that you must go.
Yes, there is yet one way to where she is,
Bitter, but one that faith may never miss.
Out of a grave I come to tell you this —
To tell you this.

There is the western gate, Luke Havergal,
There are the crimson leaves upon the wall.
Go, for the winds are tearing them away, —
Nor think to riddle the dead words they say,
Nor any more to feel them as they fall;
But go, and if you trust her she will call.
There is the western gate, Luke Havergal —
Luke Havergal.

The unobtrusive general imagery, powerful feeling, and subtle repetitions of words and rhythms all locate Robinson somewhere between Poe and Hardy.

The title of W. H. Davies's autobiography tells more of his story than the titles of most such books: *The Autobiography of a Super-Tramp* (1908). Of his years as a wanderer, several were spent in America.

Leisure

What is this life if, full of care,
We have no time to stand and stare.

No time to stand beneath the boughs
And stare as long as sheep or cows.

No time to see, when woods we pass,
Where squirrels hide their nuts in grass.

No time to see, in broad daylight,
Streams full of stars like skies at night.

No time to turn at Beauty's glance,
And watch her feet, how they can dance.

No time to wait till her mouth can
Enrich that smile her eyes began.

A poor life this if, full of care,
We have no time to stand and stare.

Davies gives us some idea of what Joyce Kilmer might have done had he been a somewhat better writer.

Walter de la Mare, born in Kent, was too poor to go to school beyond adolescence and worked for many years as a bookkeeper for a petroleum conglomerate. It was not until middle age that he could spend all his time as a writer. He is best known for his fanciful poetry (praised by Hardy, Eliot, and Auden), but he also wrote fiction, including the celebrated *Memoirs of a Midget* (1931).

The Listeners

"Is there anybody there?" said the Traveler,
　Knocking on the moonlit door;
And his horse in the silence champed the grasses
　Of the forest's ferny floor:
And a bird flew up out of the turret,
　Above the Traveler's head:
And he smote upon the door again a second time;
　"Is there anybody there?" he said.
But no one descended to the Traveler;
　No head from the leaf-fringed sill
Leaned over and looked into his gray eyes,
　Where he stood perplexed and still.
But only a host of phantom listeners
　That dwelt in the lone house then
Stood listening in the quiet of the moonlight
　To that voice from the world of men:
Stood thronging the faint moonbeams on the dark stair,
　That goes down to the empty hall,
Hearkening in an air stirred and shaken
　By the lonely Traveler's call.
And he felt in his heart their strangeness,
　Their stillness answering his cry,
While his horse moved, cropping the dark turf,
　'Neath the starred and leafy sky;

For he suddenly smote on the door, even
    Louder, and lifted his head: —
"Tell them I came, and no one answered,
    That I kept my word," he said.
Never the least stir made the listeners,
    Though every word he spake
Fell echoing through the shadowiness of the still house
    From the one man left awake:
Ay, they heard his foot upon the stirrup,
    And the sound of iron on stone,
And how the silence surged softly backward,
    When the plunging hoofs were gone.

Thomas Hardy, according to his widow's account of his last days, at the end "could no longer listen to the reading of prose, though a short poem now and again interested him." In the middle of one night he asked his wife to read "The Listeners" aloud to him.

ROBERT FROST 1874–1963

Although Frost was born in California and named for
the Confederate general Robert E. Lee, he was associ-
ated for most of his long life with New England, where
he was raised. Frost lived mostly in New Hampshire
and Vermont but also spent significant periods in Mich-
igan and Florida. He was unique in his power to com-
bine a modernist sensibility and learning with a knack
for the genuinely popular.

Stopping by Woods on a Snowy Evening

Whose woods these are I think I know.
His house is in the village, though;
He will not see me stopping here
To watch his woods fill up with snow.

My little horse must think it queer
To stop without a farmhouse near
Between the woods and frozen lake
The darkest evening of the year.

He gives his harness bells a shake
To ask if there is some mistake.
The only other sound's the sweep
Of easy wind and downy flake.

The woods are lovely, dark and deep,
But I have promises to keep,
And miles to go before I sleep,
And miles to go before I sleep.

---

*The arrangement of the adjectives in the thirteenth line may be puzzling: the
woods are lovely and dark and deep, or they are lovely because they are dark and
deep. The second reading lends a measure of subtlety not evident in the simpler
sequence.*

Mending Wall

•◇•◇•◇•◇•

Something there is that doesn't love a wall,
That sends the frozen-ground-swell under it
And spills the upper boulders in the sun,
And makes gaps even two can pass abreast.
The work of hunters is another thing:
I have come after them and made repair
Where they have left not one stone on a stone,
But they would have the rabbit out of hiding,
To please the yelping dogs. The gaps I mean,
No one has seen them made or heard them made,
But at spring mending-time we find them there.
I let my neighbor know beyond the hill;
And on a day we meet to walk the line
And set the wall between us once again.
We keep the wall between us as we go.
To each the boulders that have fallen to each.
And some are loaves and some so nearly balls
We have to use a spell to make them balance:
"Stay where you are until our backs are turned!"
We wear our fingers rough with handling them.
Oh, just another kind of outdoor game,
One on a side. It comes to little more:
There where it is we do not need the wall:
He is all pine and I am apple orchard.
My apple trees will never get across
And eat the cones under his pines, I tell him.
He only says, "Good fences make good neighbors."
Spring is the mischief in me, and I wonder
If I could put a notion in his head:
"Why do they make good neighbors? Isn't it
Where there are cows? But here there are no cows.
Before I built a wall I'd ask to know
What I was walling in or walling out,
And to whom I was like to give offense.

Something there is that doesn't love a wall,
That wants it down." I could say "Elves" to him,
But it's not elves exactly, and I'd rather
He said it for himself. I see him there,
Bringing a stone grasped firmly by the top
In each hand, like an old-stone savage armed.
He moves in darkness as it seems to me,
Not of woods only and the shade of trees.
He will not go behind his father's saying,
And he likes having thought of it so well
He says again, "Good fences make good neighbors."

The sentiment can be traced back to Poor Richard's Almanac, *but the wording is Frost's own, so that he is alone among modern poets distinguished by having composed a genuine proverb. One can read the poem as a justification for verse form, which itself is a fence, wall, or net for containing the unruly fears and desires that motivate us.*

Fire and Ice

Some say the world will end in fire,
Some say in ice.
From what I've tasted of desire
I hold with those who favor fire.
But if it had to perish twice,
I think I know enough of hate
To say that for destruction ice
Is also great
And would suffice.

Frost's treatment of elementary emblems matches the grace if not the depth of Eliot's "Little Gidding" (p. 987).

The Road Not Taken

>>>>>>>

Two roads diverged in a yellow wood,
And sorry I could not travel both
And be one traveler, long I stood
And looked down one as far as I could
To where it bent in the undergrowth;

Then took the other, as just as fair,
And having perhaps the better claim,
Because it was grassy and wanted wear;
Though as for that the passing there
Had worn them really about the same,

And both that morning equally lay
In leaves no step had trodden black.
Oh, I kept the first for another day!
Yet knowing how way leads on to way,
I doubted if I should ever come back.

I shall be telling this with a sigh
Somewhere ages and ages hence:
Two roads diverged in a wood, and I—
I took the one less traveled by,
And that has made all the difference.

This was the opening poem in Frost's third book, Mountain Interval *(1916).
It is said that Frost was thinking mainly of his friend and fellow-poet Edward
Thomas (see p. 917).*

Birches

When I see birches bend to left and right
Across the line of straighter darker trees,
I like to think some boy's been swinging them.
But swinging doesn't bend them down to stay.
Ice-storms do that. Often you must have seen them
Loaded with ice a sunny winter morning
After a rain. They click upon themselves
As the breeze rises, and turn many-colored
As the stir cracks and crazes their enamel.
Soon the sun's warmth makes them shed crystal shells
Shattering and avalanching on the snow-crust—
Such heaps of broken glass to sweep away
You'd think the inner dome of heaven had fallen.
They are dragged to the withered bracken by the load,
And they seem not to break; though once they are bowed
So low for long, they never right themselves:
You may see their trunks arching in the woods
Years afterwards, trailing their leaves on the ground
Like girls on hands and knees that throw their hair
Before them over their heads to dry in the sun.
But I was going to say when Truth broke in
With all her matter-of-fact about the ice-storm
I should prefer to have some boy bend them
As he went out and in to fetch the cows—
Some boy too far from town to learn baseball,
Whose only play was what he found himself,
Summer or winter, and could play alone.
One by one he subdued his father's trees
By riding them down over and over again
Until he took the stiffness out of them,
And not one but hung limp, not one was left
For him to conquer. He learned all there was
To learn about not launching out too soon
And so not carrying the tree away

Clear to the ground. He always kept his poise
To the top branches, climbing carefully
With the same pains you use to fill a cup
Up to the brim, and even above the brim.
Then he flung outward, feet first, with a swish,
Kicking his way down through the air to the ground.

So was I once myself a swinger of birches;
And so I dream of going back to be.
It's when I'm weary of considerations,
And life is too much like a pathless wood
Where your face burns and tickles with the cobwebs
Broken across it, and one eye is weeping
From a twig's having lashed across it open.
I'd like to get away from earth awhile
And then come back to it and begin over.
May no fate willfully misunderstand me
And half grant what I wish and snatch me away
Not to return. Earth's the right place for love:
I don't know where it's likely to go better.
I'd like to go by climbing a birch tree,
And climb black branches up a snow-white trunk
Toward heaven, till the tree could bear no more,
But dipped its top and set me down again.
That would be good both going and coming back.
One could do worse than be a swinger of birches.

"Birches" came out in 1915, a year after Joyce Kilmer's extraordinarily popular "Trees" appeared in Poetry *(Chicago). It is as though Frost were saying, "If you want to write a real poem about trees, start with a specific tree, then report some personal experience, then . . . ."*

After Apple-Picking

◆◆◆◆◆

My long two-pointed ladder's sticking through a tree
Toward heaven still,
And there's a barrel that I didn't fill
Beside it, and there may be two or three
Apples I didn't pick upon some bough.
But I am done with apple-picking now.
Essence of winter sleep is on the night,
The scent of apples: I am drowsing off.
I cannot rub the strangeness from my sight
I got from looking through a pane of glass
I skimmed this morning from the drinking trough
And held against the world of hoary grass.
It melted, and I let it fall and break.
But I was well
Upon my way to sleep before it fell,
And I could tell
What form my dreaming was about to take.
Magnified apples appear and disappear,
Stem end and blossom end,
And every fleck of russet showing clear.
My instep arch not only keeps the ache,
It keeps the pressure of a ladder-round.
I feel the ladder sway as the boughs bend.
And I keep hearing from the cellar bin
The rumbling sound
Of load on load of apples coming in.
For I have had too much
Of apple-picking: I am overtired
Of the great harvest I myself desired.
There were ten thousand thousand fruit to touch,
Cherish in hand, lift down, and not let fall.
For all
That struck the earth,
No matter if not bruised or spiked with stubble,

Went surely to the cider-apple heap
As of no worth.
One can see what will trouble
This sleep of mine, whatever sleep it is.
Were he not gone,
The woodchuck could say whether it's like his
Long sleep, as I describe its coming on,
Or just some human sleep.

Frost gives enough anecdotal detail about actual apple-picking to invite the reader along on a symbolic interpretation, especially when the poem mentions heaven and earth outright and talks about the damnation of the fallen, even if blameless. (Such apples are still called "drops.") But there's no heavy lesson.

Acquainted with the Night

I have been one acquainted with the night.
I have walked out in rain—and back in rain.
I have outwalked the furthest city light.

I have looked down the saddest city lane.
I have passed by the watchman on his beat
And dropped my eyes, unwilling to explain.

I have stood still and stopped the sound of feet
When far away an interrupted cry
Came over houses from another street,

But not to call me back or say good-by;
And further still at an unearthly height
One luminary clock against the sky

Proclaimed the time was neither wrong nor right.
I have been one acquainted with the night.

Frost here shows his virtuosity in one of the rarest of verse forms, the "terza rima sonnet" that is also used in Shelley's "Ode to the West Wind" (p. 497).

Provide, Provide

The witch that came (the withered hag)
To wash the steps with pail and rag,
Was once the beauty Abishag,

The picture pride of Hollywood.
Too many fall from great and good
For you to doubt the likelihood.

Die early and avoid the fate.
Or if predestined to die late,
Make up your mind to die in state.

Make the whole stock exchange your own!
If need be occupy a throne,
Where nobody can call *you* crone.

Some have relied on what they knew;
Others on being simply true.
What worked for them might work for you.

No memory of having starred
Atones for later disregard,
Or keeps the end from being hard.

Better to go down dignified
With boughten friendship at your side
Than none at all. Provide, provide!

The sad end of Rita Hayworth's life reminded some of this poem; such falls from greatness happen all the time, as the weekly tabloids are all-too-eager to document. One may object that the dialectical word "boughten" hints that Frost is not sincerely urging the reader to try to buy friendship, but the poem certainly sounds earnest. In public readings, Frost changed "Atones" to "Makes up," an earthier wording that adds to the credibility of the poem.

The Gift Outright

The land was ours before we were the land's.
She was our land more than a hundred years
Before we were her people. She was ours
In Massachusetts, in Virginia,
But we were England's, still colonials,
Possessing what we still were unpossessed by,
Possessed by what we now no more possessed.
Something we were withholding made us weak
Until we found it was ourselves
We were withholding from our land of living,
And forthwith found salvation in surrender.
Such as we were we gave ourselves outright
(The deed of gift was many deeds of war)
To the land vaguely realizing westward,
But still unstoried, artless, unenhanced,
Such as she was, such as she would become.

At the request of John F. Kennedy, Frost read this poem at the Inauguration of the President in 1961. Kennedy requested that the "would" in the last line be changed to "will," and Frost went along with the President, although the printed text was unchanged.

Directive

Back out of all this now too much for us,
Back in a time made simple by the loss
Of detail, burned, dissolved, and broken off
Like graveyard marble sculpture in the weather,
There is a house that is no more a house
Upon a farm that is no more a farm
And in a town that is no more a town.
The road there, if you'll let a guide direct you
Who only has at heart your getting lost,
May seem as if it should have been a quarry—
Great monolithic knees the former town
Long since gave up pretense of keeping covered.
And there's a story in a book about it:
Besides the wear of iron wagon wheels
The ledges show lines ruled southeast northwest,
The chisel work of an enormous Glacier
That braced his feet against the Arctic Pole.
You must not mind a certain coolness from him
Still said to haunt this side of Panther Mountain.
Nor need you mind the serial ordeal
Of being watched from forty cellar holes
As if by eye pairs out of forty firkins.
As for the woods' excitement over you
That sends light rustle rushes to their leaves,
Charge that to upstart inexperience.
Where were they all not twenty years ago?
They think too much of having shaded out
A few old pecker-fretted apple trees.
Make yourself up a cheering song of how
Someone's road home from work this once was,
Who may be just ahead of you on foot
Or creaking with a buggy load of grain.
The height of the adventure is the height
Of country where two village cultures faded

Into each other. Both of them are lost.
And if you're lost enough to find yourself
By now, pull in your ladder road behind you
And put a sign up CLOSED to all but me.
Then make yourself at home. The only field
Now left's no bigger than a harness gall.
First there's the children's house of make believe,
Some shattered dishes underneath a pine,
The playthings in the playhouse of the children.
Weep for what little things could make them glad.
Then for the house that is no more a house,
But only a belilaced cellar hole,
Now slowly closing like a dent in dough.
This was no playhouse but a house in earnest.
Your destination and your destiny's
A brook that was the water of the house,
Cold as a spring as yet so near its source,
Too lofty and original to rage.
(We know the valley streams that when aroused
Will leave their tatters hung on barb and thorn.)
I have kept hidden in the instep arch
Of an old cedar at the waterside
A broken drinking goblet like the Grail
Under a spell so the wrong ones can't find it,
So can't get saved, as Saint Mark says they mustn't.
(I stole the goblet from the children's playhouse.)
Here are your waters and your watering place.
Drink and be whole again beyond confusion.

As with Williams's "Spring and All" (p. 937), Frost's "Directive" can be read as an answer to Eliot's "Waste Land" (p. 968). Or one could say that Frost joins Eliot in writing modern extensions of Oliver Goldsmith's "Deserted Village" (p. 341). As with "The Waste Land," "Directive" includes lilacs, a rock-water contrast, and reference to the legend of the Grail.

Design

I found a dimpled spider, fat and white,
On a white heal-all, holding up a moth
Like a white piece of rigid satin cloth—
Assorted characters of death and blight
Mixed ready to begin the morning right,
Like the ingredients of a witches' broth—
A snow-drop spider, a flower like a froth,
And dead wings carried like a paper kite.

What had that flower to do with being white,
The wayside blue and innocent heal-all?
What brought the kindred spider to that height,
Then steered the white moth thither in the night?
What but design of darkness to appall?—
If design govern in a thing so small.

Stevens's "Thirteen Ways of Looking at a Blackbird" (p. 932) furnishes several new meanings of blackness, and Frost's "Design" makes whiteness—the outcome of the process of appalling, after all—a sign of (anticlimactic) death and blight.

JOHN MASEFIELD 1878–1967

Like W. H. Davies and Vachel Lindsay (who were also born in the 1870s), Masefield spent some of his early years in what is politely known as vagrancy. In time, Masefield turned to journalism and the steady production of poetry, more than fifty volumes all told. From 1930 until his death, Masefield was Poet Laureate, an honor that recognized his excellence in recording so much of British life, including the nautical experience and the country life.

Cargoes

Quinquireme of Nineveh from distant Ophir
Rowing home to haven in sunny Palestine,
With a cargo of ivory,
And apes and peacocks,
Sandalwood, cedarwood, and sweet white wine.

Stately Spanish galleon coming from the Isthmus,
Dipping through the Tropics by the palm-green shores,
With a cargo of diamonds,
Emeralds, amethysts,
Topazes, and cinnamon, and gold moidores.

Dirty British coaster with a salt-caked smoke stack
Butting through the Channel in the mad March days,
With a cargo of Tyne coal,
Road-rail, pig-lead,
Firewood, iron-ware, and cheap tin trays.

Masefield was one of the finest English poets of the sea, in a noble tradition going back to the Middle Ages. As Joseph Conrad demonstrates in the opening of Heart of Darkness, *following the sea gives one a sense of a continuous maritime effort from prehistory to the present.*

CARL SANDBURG 1878-1967

Sandburg was first recognized as a substantial poet with the publication of *Chicago Poems* in 1916. He continued to produce short, free-verse poems, later writing also a much longer evocation of America called *The People, Yes* and a six-volume biography of Abraham Lincoln.

Chicago

>>>>>>>

Hog Butcher for the World,
Tool Maker, Stacker of Wheat,
Player with Railroads and the Nation's Freight Handler;
Stormy, husky, brawling,
City of the Big Shoulders:

They tell me you are wicked and I believe them, for I have seen
   your painted women under the gas lamps luring the farm
   boys.
And they tell me you are crooked and I answer: Yes, it is true I
   have seen the gunman kill and go free to kill again.
And they tell me you are brutal and my reply is: On the faces
   of women and children I have seen the marks of wanton
   hunger.
And having answered so I turn once more to those who sneer at
   this my city, and I give them back the sneer and say to
   them:
Come and show me another city with lifted head singing so
   proud to be alive and coarse and strong and cunning.
Flinging magnetic curses amid the toil of piling job on job, here
   is a tall bold slugger set vivid against the little soft cities;
Fierce as a dog with tongue lapping for action, cunning as a
   savage pitted against the wilderness,
      Bareheaded,
      Shoveling,

Wrecking,
Planning,
Building, breaking, rebuilding,
Under the smoke, dust all over his mouth, laughing with white
   teeth,
Under the terrible burden of destiny laughing as a young man
   laughs,
Laughing even as an ignorant fighter laughs who has never lost
   a battle,
Bragging and laughing that under his wrist is the pulse, and
   under his ribs the heart of the people,
      Laughing!
Laughing the stormy, husky, brawling laughter of Youth, half-
   naked, sweating, proud to be Hog Butcher, Tool Maker,
   Stacker of Wheat, Player with Railroads and Freight
   Handler to the Nation.

---

*Chicago was long known as the second city (after New York). It was and is a
tough town, especially in the winter, and the stockyards are still there. But, early
in Sandburg's lifetime, energetic Chicago was also the home of some of America's
most distinguished architecture, its most advanced poetry magazine, and one of
its greatest universities.*

Fog

The fog comes
on little cat feet.

It sits looking
over harbor and city
on silent haunches
and then, moves on.

Sandburg is content to let a single metaphoric equation carry a whole poem; the same fog-cat image appears in Eliot's "Love Song of J. Alfred Prufrock" (p. 961).

Cool Tombs

When Abraham Lincoln was shoveled into the tombs he forgot
 the copperheads and the assassin . . . in the dust, in the
 cool tombs.

And Ulysses Grant lost all thought of con men and Wall Street,
 cash and collateral turned ashes . . . in the dust, in the cool
 tombs.

Pocahontas' body, lovely as a poplar, sweet as a red haw in
 November or a pawpaw in May, did she wonder? does she
 remember? . . . in the dust, in the cool tombs?

Take any streetful of people buying clothes and groceries,
 cheering a hero or throwing confetti and blowing tin
 horns . . . tell me if the lovers are losers . . . tell me if any
 get more than the lovers . . . in the dust . . . in the cool
 tombs.

---

*Like Edgar Lee Masters (see p. 882) and Vachel Lindsay (see pp. 918–919),
Sandburg was a Midwestern modernist taking advantage of the surge of energy
radiating from Chicago after 1890. For such poets, Lincoln and Grant were local
heroes of historic resonances, capable of being given a place among the other great
figures (Pocahontas . . . Cleopatra . . .) in a catalogue of oblivion.*

Grass

Pile the bodies high at Austerlitz and Waterloo.
Shovel them under and let me work—
   I am the grass; I cover all.

And pile them high at Gettysburg
And pile them high at Ypres and Verdun.
Shovel them under and let me work.
Two years, ten years, and passengers ask the conductor:
   What place is this?
   Where are we now?

   I am the grass.
   Let me work.

The original 1918 version of "Grass" catalogued battles from the Napoleonic Wars, the American Civil War, and the First World War. Later, in phonograph recordings made in the 1940s, Sandburg would add "Stalingrad" after "Verdun."

EDWARD THOMAS 1878–1917

In his early maturity, up to about the age of thirty-two, Thomas was content to write prose, including a biography of the fascinating Victorian naturalist Richard Jefferies. At the urging of his American friend Robert Frost, however, Thomas turned to poetry, for which he had a genuine calling. He belonged in the age-old, English rural-pastoral tradition, which has survived any number of revolutions and vicissitudes since the Middle Ages. Thomas enlisted in the army in 1915 and was killed in Flanders.

The Owl

Downhill I came, hungry, and yet not starved;
Cold, yet had heat within me that was proof
Against the North wind; tired, yet so that rest
Had seemed the sweetest thing under a roof.

Then at the inn I had food, fire, and rest,
Knowing how hungry, cold, and tired was I.
All of the night was quite barred out except
An owl's cry, a most melancholy cry

Shaken out long and clear upon the hill,
No merry note, nor cause of merriment,
But one telling me plain what I escaped
And others could not, that night, as in I went.

And slated was my food, and my repose,
Salted and sobered, too, by the bird's voice
Speaking for all who lay under the stars,
Soldiers and poor, unable to rejoice.

As Robert Frost recognized, Edward Thomas belonged to an English tradition of bucolic realists with heightened sensitivity but without heightened rhetoric.

VACHEL LINDSAY 1879-1931

Externally, Lindsay's life resembles that of his contemporary, W. H. Davies; both men were poets who also spent time as tramps. Lindsay has forebears in a number of American traditions, including vaudeville, Whitman, revival meetings, and political oratory. He seemed always to be trying to live up to his heritage as a child of Springfield, Illinois, where Abraham Lincoln had lived and where he practiced law.

Abraham Lincoln Walks at Midnight

In Springfield, Illinois

It is portentous, and a thing of state
That here at midnight, in our little town
A mourning figure walks, and will not rest,
Near the old court-house pacing up and down,
Or by his homestead, or in shadowed yards
He lingers where his children used to play,
Or through the market, on the well-worn stones
He stalks until the dawn-stars burn away.

A bronzed, lank man! His suit of ancient black,
A famous high top-hat and plain worn shawl
Make him the quaint great figure that men love,
The prairie-lawyer, master of us all.

He cannot sleep upon his hillside now.
He is among us:—as in times before!
And we who toss and lie awake for long
Breathe deep, and start, to see him pass the door.

His head is bowed. He thinks on men and kings.
Yea, when the sick world cries, how can he sleep?
Too many peasants fight, they know not why,
Too many homesteads in black terror weep.

The sins of all the war-lords burn his heart.
He sees the dreadnaughts scouring every main.
He carries on his shawl-wrapped shoulders now
The bitterness, the folly and the pain.

He cannot rest until a spirit-dawn
Shall come;—the shining hope of Europe free:
The league of sober folk, the Workers' Earth,
Bringing long peace to Cornland, Alp and Sea.

It breaks his heart that kings must murder still,
That all his hours of travail here for men
Seem yet in vain. And who will bring white peace
That he may sleep upon his hill again?

Lindsay came from Springfield, Illinois, where Lincoln had practiced law before being elected to the Presidency in 1860. As with Masters's "Anne Rutledge" (p. 881), this is a poem by a Midwesterner about a Midwestern hero. From the perspective of the twentieth century's end, the ideal of "the Worker's Earth" may indeed sound quaint.

Stevens, a lawyer, worked most of his adult life as an officer of a major insurance company (now called The Hartford). He did not publish his first book, *Harmonium*, until 1923, when he was in his middle forties. Thereafter at irregular intervals he published a succession of volumes of increasing solemnity and profundity. He was relegated to the margins of dandyism during most of his writing career but, since his death, has been recognized as uniquely central and important.

Sunday Morning

I

Complacencies of the peignoir, and late
Coffee and oranges in a sunny chair,
And the green freedom of a cockatoo
Upon a rug mingle to dissipate
The holy hush of ancient sacrifice.
She dreams a little, and she feels the dark
Encroachment of that old catastrophe,
As a calm darkens among water-lights.
The pungent oranges and bright, green wings
Seem things in some procession of the dead,
Winding across wide water, without sound.
The day is like wide water, without sound,
Stilled for the passing of her dreaming feet
Over the seas, to silent Palestine,
Dominion of the blood and sepulchre.

II

Why should she give her bounty to the dead?
What is divinity if it can come
Only in silent shadows and in dreams?
Shall she not find in comforts of the sun,
In pungent fruit and bright, green wings, or else
In any balm or beauty of the earth,
Things to be cherished like the thought of heaven,
Divinity must live within herself:
Passions of rain, or moods in falling snow;
Grievings in loneliness, or unsubdued
Elations when the forest blooms; gusty
Emotions on wet roads on autumn nights;
All pleasures and all pains, remembering
The bough of summer and the winter branch.
These are the measures destined for her soul.

III

Jove in the clouds had his inhuman birth.
No mother suckled him, no sweet land gave
Large-mannered motions to his mythy mind.
He moved among us, as a muttering king,
Magnificent, would move among his hinds,
Until our blood, commingling, virginal,
With heaven, brought such requital to desire
The very hinds discerned it, in a star.
Shall our blood fail? Or shall it come to be
The blood of paradise? And shall the earth
Seem all of paradise that we shall know?
The sky will be much friendlier then than now,
A part of labor and a part of pain,
And next in glory to enduring love,
Not this dividing and indifferent blue.

IV

She says, "I am content when wakened birds,
Before they fly, test the reality
Of misty fields, by their sweet questionings;
But when the birds are gone, and their warm field
Return no more, where, then, is paradise?"
There is not any haunt of prophecy,
Nor any old chimera of the grave,
Neither the golden underground, nor isle
Melodious, where spirits gat them home,
Nor visionary south, nor cloudy palm
Remote on heaven's hill, that has endured
As April's green endures; or will endure
Like her remembrance of awakened birds,
Or her desire for June and evening, tipped
By the consummation of the swallow's wings.

V

She says, "But in contentment I still feel
The need of some imperishable bliss."
Death is the mother of beauty; hence from her,
Alone, shall come fulfilment to our dreams
And our desires. Although she strews the leaves
Of sure obliteration on our paths,
The path sick sorrow took, the many paths
Where triumph rang its brassy phrase, or love
Whispered a little out of tenderness,
She makes the willow shiver in the sun
For maidens who were wont to sit and gaze
Upon the grass, relinquished to their feet.
She causes boys to pile new plums and pears
On disregarded plate. The maidens taste
And stray impassioned in the littering leaves.

VI

Is there no change of death in paradise?
Does ripe fruit never fall? Or do the boughs
Hang always heavy in that perfect sky,
Unchanging, yet so like our perishing earth,
With rivers like our own that seek for seas
They never find, the same receding shores
That never touch with inarticulate pang?
Why set the pear upon those river-banks
Or spice the shores with odors of the plum?
Alas, that they should wear our colors there,
The silken weavings of our afternoons,
And pick the strings of our insipid lutes!
Death is the mother of beauty, mystical,
Within whose burning bosom we devise
Our earthly mothers waiting, sleeplessly.

VII

Supple and turbulent, a ring of men
Shall chant in orgy on a summer morn
Their boisterous devotion to the sun,
Not as a god, but as a god might be,
Naked among them, like a savage source.
Their chant shall be a chant of paradise,
Out of their blood, returning to the sky;
And in their chant shall enter, voice by voice,
The windy lake wherein their lord delights,
The trees, like serafin, and echoing hills,
That choir among themselves long afterward.
They shall know well the heavenly fellowship
Of men that perish and of summer morn.
And whence they came and whither they shall go
The dew upon their feet shall manifest.

VIII

She hears, upon that water without sound,
A voice that cries, "The tomb in Palestine
Is not the porch of spirits lingering.
It is the grave of Jesus, where he lay."
We live in an old chaos of the sun,
Or old dependency of day and night,
Or island solitude, unsponsored, free,
Of that wide water, inescapable.
Deer walk upon our mountains, and the quail
Whistle about us their spontaneous cries;
Sweet berries ripen in the wilderness;
And, in the isolation of the sky,
At evening, casual flocks of pigeons make
Ambiguous undulations as they sink,
Downward to darkness, on extended wings.

In some ways the most secular of poets, Stevens could write great poems of the earth by transforming the dignified idiom of the great poems of heaven and hell. Stevens emerged, by the time of his centennial in 1979, a central visionary of depth and substance, although, for him, as for Oscar Wilde, the aesthetic surface is the profoundest substance that we know.

Anecdote of the Jar

❖❖❖❖❖

I placed a jar in Tennessee,
And round it was, upon a hill.
It made the slovenly wilderness
Surround that hill.

The wilderness rose up to it,
And sprawled around, no longer wild.
The jar was round upon the ground
And tall and of a port in air.

It took dominion everywhere.
The jar was gray and bare.
It did not give of bird or bush,
Like nothing else in Tennessee.

We seem to have here not only Stevens's but the whole twentieth century's version of Keats's "Ode on a Grecian Urn" (p. 546) —a poem that is about the power of a symmetrical and useful artifact to tame a wilderness.

The Emperor of Ice-Cream

Call the roller of big cigars,
The muscular one, and bid him whip
In kitchen cups concupiscent curds.
Let the wenches dawdle in such dress
As they are used to wear, and let the boys
Bring flowers in last month's newspapers.
Let be be finale of seem.
The only emperor is the emperor of ice-cream.

Take from the dresser of deal,
Lacking the three glass knobs, that sheet
On which she embroidered fantails once
And spread it so as to cover her face.
If her horny feet protrude, they come
To show how cold she is, and dumb.
Let the lamp affix its beam.
The only emperor is the emperor of ice-cream.

Stevens enlarges on a joke in Hamlet: *"Your worm is your only emperor for diet." Romance and ritual gloss over certain facts that an honest obituary needs to face. As palpably physical objects inviting attention to their own visible and audible reality, all poems remind us of our own mortality, which has an up-side as well as a down. The cold splendor of ice-cream is a function of our limitations, and, as Stevens says in "Sunday Morning" (p. 920), "Death is the mother of beauty."*

The Idea of Order at Key West

>>>>>>>

She sang beyond the genius of the sea.
The water never formed to mind or voice,
Like a body wholly body, fluttering
Its empty sleeves; and yet its mimic motion
Made constant cry, caused constantly a cry,
That was not ours although we understood,
Inhuman, of the veritable ocean.

The sea was not a mask. No more was she.
The song and water were not medleyed sound
Even if what she sang was what she heard,
Since what she sang was uttered word by word.
It may be that in all her phrases stirred
The grinding water and the gasping wind;
But it was she and not the sea we heard.

For she was the maker of the song she sang.
The ever-hooded, tragic-gestured sea
Was merely a place by which she walked to sing.
Whose spirit is this? we said, because we knew
It was the spirit that we sought and knew
That we should ask this often as she sang.

If it was only the dark voice of the sea
That rose, or even colored by many waves;
If it was only the outer voice of sky
And cloud, of the sunken coral water-walled,
However clear, it would have been deep air,
The heaving speech of air, a summer sound
Repeated in a summer without end
And sound alone. But it was more than that,
More even than her voice, and ours, among
The meaningless plungings of water and the wind,
Theatrical distances, bronze shadows heaped

On high horizons, mountainous atmospheres
Of sky and sea.
                    It was her voice that made
The sky acutest at its vanishing.
She measured to the hour its solitude.
She was the single artificer of the world
In which she sang. And when she sang, the sea,
Whatever self it had, became the self
That was her song, for she was the maker. Then we,
As we beheld her striding there alone,
Knew that there never was a world for her
Except the one she sang and, singing, made.

Ramon Fernandez, tell me, if you know,
Why, when the singing ended and we turned
Toward the town, tell why the glassy lights,
The lights in the fishing boats at anchor there,
As the night descended, tilting in the air,
Mastered the night and portioned out the sea,
Fixing emblazoned zones and fiery poles,
Arranging, deepening, enchanting night.

Oh! Blessed rage for order, pale Ramon,
The maker's rage to order words of the sea,
Words of the fragrant portals, dimly-starred,
And of ourselves and of our origins,
In ghostlier demarcations, keener sounds.

If "Anecdote of the Jar" (p. 925) is the counterpart of Keats's "Ode on a Grecian Urn" (p. 546), then "The Idea of Order at Key West" is one of many modern avatars of Matthew Arnold's "Dover Beach" (p. 706).

Peter Quince at the Clavier

1

Just as my fingers on these keys
Make music, so the selfsame sounds
On my spirit make a music, too.

Music is feeling, then, not sound;
And thus it is that what I feel,
Here in this room, desiring you,

Thinking of your blue-shadowed silk,
Is music. It is like the strain
Waked in the elders by Susanna.

Of a green evening, clear and warm,
She bathed in her still garden, while
The red-eyed elders watching, felt

The basses of their beings throb
In witching chords, and their thin blood
Pulse pizzicati of Hosanna.

2

In the green water, clear and warm,
Susanna lay.
She searched
The touch of springs,
And found
Concealed imaginings.
She sighed,
For so much melody.

Upon the bank, she stood
In the cool
Of spent emotions.
She felt, among the leaves,
The dew
Of old devotions.

She walked upon the grass,
Still quavering.
The winds were like her maids,
On timid feet,
Fetching her woven scarves,
Yet wavering.

A breath upon her hand
Muted the night.
She turned—
A cymbal crashed,
And roaring horns.

3

Soon, with a noise like tambourines,
Came her attendant Byzantines.
They wondered why Susanna cried
Against the elders by her side;

And as they whispered, the refrain
Was like a willow swept by rain.

Anon, their lamps' uplifted flame
Revealed Susanna and her shame.

And then, the simpering Byzantines
Fled, with a noise like tambourines.

4

Beauty is momentary in the mind—
The fitful tracing of a portal;
But in the flesh it is immortal.

The body dies; the body's beauty lives.
So evenings die, in their green going,
A wave, interminably flowing.
So gardens die, their meek breath scenting
The cowl of winter, done repenting.
So maidens die, to the auroral
Celebration of a maiden's choral.
Susanna's music touched the bawdy strings
Of those white elders; but, escaping,
Left only Death's ironic scraping.
Now, in its immortality, it plays
On the clear viol of her memory,
And makes a constant sacrament of praise.

A Midsummer Night's Dream, *in which Peter Quince is a clownish carpenter, contains four levels of romantic love: proletarian, aristocratic, heroic, and supernatural. The four parts of this poem can be matched up with that quartet of loves, along with autoerotism and religious devotion such as that in the Apocryphal Book of Susannah. As a formal encomium, Stevens's poem ends with "praise," as does Auden's "In Memory of W. B. Yeats" (p. 1028).*

Thirteen Ways
of Looking at a Blackbird

I

Among twenty snowy mountains
The only moving thing
Was the eye of the blackbird.

II

I was of three minds,
Like a tree
In which there are three blackbirds.

III

The blackbird whirled in the autumn winds.
It was a small part of the pantomime.

IV

A man and a woman
Are one.
A man and a woman and a blackbird
Are one.

V

I do not know which to prefer,
The beauty of inflexions
Or the beauty of innuendos,
The blackbird whistling
Or just after.

VI

Icicles filled the long window
With barbaric glass.
The shadow of the blackbird
Crossed it, to and fro.
The mood
Traced in the shadow
An indecipherable cause.

VII

O thin men of Haddam,
Why do you imagine golden birds?
Do you not see how the blackbird
Walks around the feet
Of the women about you?

VIII

I know noble accents
And lucid, inescapable rhythms;
But I know, too,
That the blackbird is involved
In what I know.

IX

When the blackbird flew out of sight,
It marked the edge
Of one of many circles.

X

At the sight of blackbirds
Flying in a green light
Even the bawds of euphony
Would cry out sharply.

XI

He road over Connecticut
In a glass coach.
Once, a fear pierced him,
In that he mistook
The shadow of his equipage
For blackbirds.

XII

The river is moving.
The blackbird must be flying.

XIII

It was evening all afternoon.
It was snowing
And it was going to snow.
The blackbird sat
In the cedar limbs.

Poe's "Raven" (p. 625) seems to have laid down a reverberating challenge: the world distilled into the negative message of a single black bird at midnight. Stevens multiplies the single to thirteen—another loaded symbol—but suggests that neither thirteen nor black necessarily mean anything negative.

WILLIAM CARLOS WILLIAMS 1883–1963

Williams went straight from high school to medical school and then spent the bulk of his long life as a physician in Rutherford, New Jersey, not far from New York City. In his youth he knew both Ezra Pound and Hilda Doolittle, and his poetry grew and developed in much the same way theirs did: from mannered derivative romanticism to a tougher poetry of colloquial language and homely image.

The Red Wheelbarrow

so much depends
upon

a red wheel
barrow

glazed with rain
water

beside the white
chickens

See *Stevens's "Thirteen Ways of Looking at a Blackbird"* (p. 932). *Williams takes up Poe's challenge and metamorphoses the Raven into many white domestic birds by daylight; and, as with Stevens, the meaning is obscure but affirmative.*

The Dance

〰〰〰

In Breughel's great picture, The Kermess,
the dancers go round, they go round and
around, the squeal and the blare and the
tweedle of bagpipes, a bugle and fiddles
tipping their bellies (round as the thick-
sided glasses whose wash they impound)
their hips and their bellies off balance
to turn them. Kicking and rolling about
the Fair Grounds, swinging their butts, those
shanks must be sound to bear up under such
rollicking measures, prance as they dance
in Breughel's great picture, The Kermess.

Williams must have loved Brueghel's paintings. In addition to this poem (one of few by Williams that take advantage of the powers of rhyme and regular rhythm), he wrote a dozen others about them, collected in a volume called Pictures from Brueghel.

Spring and All

() ◀▶ ()

By the road to the contagious hospital
under the surge of the blue
mottled clouds driven from the
northeast—a cold wind. Beyond, the
waste of broad, muddy fields
brown with dried weeds, standing and fallen

patches of standing water
the scattering of tall trees

All along the road the reddish
purplish, forked, upstanding, twiggy
stuff of bushes and small trees
with dead, brown leaves under them
leafless vines—

Lifeless in appearance, sluggish
dazed spring approaches—

They enter the new world naked,
cold, uncertain of all
save that they enter. All about them
the cold, familiar wind—

Now the grass, tomorrow
the stiff curl of wildcarrot leaf
One by one objects are defined—
It quickens: clarity, outline of leaf

But now the stark dignity of
entrance — Still, the profound change
has come upon them: rooted, they
grip down and begin to awaken

"The Waste Land" (p. 968) challenged others to defend the idea of the good place (as Frost did in his New Hampshire *in 1923) and the idea of the good season, as Williams did with* Spring and All, *also in 1923. The very word "waste" strengthens the similarity with Eliot's poem. Originally, this poem was untitled.*

The Yachts

contend in a sea which the land partly encloses
shielding them from the too-heavy blows
of an ungoverned ocean which when it chooses

tortures the biggest hulls, the best man knows
to pit against its beatings, and sinks them pitilessly.
Mothlike in mists, scintillant in the minute

brilliance of cloudless days, with broad bellying sails
they glide to the wind tossing green water
from their sharp prows while over them the crew crawls

ant-like, solicitously grooming them, releasing,
making fast as they turn, lean far over and having
caught the wind again, side by side, head for the mark.

In a well guarded arena of open water surrounded by
lesser and greater craft which, sycophant, lumbering
and flittering follow them, they appear youthful, rare

as the light of a happy eye, live with the grace
of all that in the mind is feckless, free and
naturally to be desired. Now the sea which holds them

is moody, lapping their glossy sides, as if feeling
for some slightest flaw but fails completely.
Today no race. Then the wind comes again. The yachts

move, jockeying for a start, the signal is set and they
are off. Now the waves strike at them but they are too
well made, they slip through, though they take in canvas.

Arms with hands grasping seek to clutch at the prows.
Bodies thrown recklessly in the way are cut aside.
It is a sea of faces about them in agony, in despair

until the horror of the race dawns staggering the mind,
the whole sea become an entanglement of watery bodies
lost to the world bearing what they cannot hold. Broken,

beaten, desolate, reaching from the dead to be taken up
they cry out, failing, failing! their cries rising
in waves still as the skillful yachts pass over.

Still a mysterious poem and, for Williams, an obscure one, beginning like Manet and ending like Dante. Yachts are superlative works of engineering, shaped with beautiful economy to engage the forces of wind and water. Racing yachts con- tend, *among themselves and also with nature—perhaps the "horror of the race" means that of the human "race," for whom life is a supremely dangerous contest.*

DAVID HERBERT LAWRENCE 1885-1930

It seems improbable that D. H. Lawrence will ever be more respected for his poetry than for his fiction, but stranger vicissitudes have befallen literary reputations. Lawrence came from a working-class Nottinghamshire family and worked briefly as a clerk and a schoolmaster. He eloped spectacularly with the wife of one of his Nottingham professors (she was six years older than he and had three young children) and set off on a life of wandering around the world, producing stories and novels that passionately explore the meaning of life and love. It was only after his death that the world had a chance to realize what an accomplished poet he had been, never more so than towards the end of his life when he produced a succession of powerful and moving elegies.

Piano

Softly, in the dusk, a woman is singing to me;
Taking me back down the vista of years, till I see
A child sitting under the piano, in the boom of the tingling
    strings
And pressing the small, poised feet of a mother who smiles as she
    sings.

In spite of myself, the insidious mastery of song
Betrays me back, till the heart of me weeps to belong
To the old Sunday evenings at home, with winter outside
And hymns in the cozy parlor, the tinkling piano our guide.

So now it is vain for the singer to burst into clamor
With the great black piano appassionato. The glamour
Of childish days is upon me, my manhood is cast
Down in the flood of remembrance, I weep like a child for the
    past.

Lawrence sounds like a combination of Walt Whitman and Marcel Proust. The "glamour" here is the magic revived by Sir Walter Scott, not the later cosmetic debasement.

Snake

A snake came to my water-trough
On a hot, hot day, and I in pajamas for the heat,
To drink there.
In the deep, strange-scented shade of the great dark carob tree
I came down the steps with my pitcher
And must wait, must stand and wait, for there he was at the
    trough before me.

He reached down from a fissure in the earth-wall in the gloom
And trailed his yellow-brown slackness soft-bellied down, over
    the edge of the stone trough
And rested his throat upon the stone bottom,
And where the water had dripped from the tap, in a small
    clearness,
He sipped with his straight mouth,
Softly drank through his straight gums, into his slack long
    body,
Silently.

Someone was before me at my water-trough,
And I, like a second comer, waiting.

He lifted his head from his drinking, as cattle do,
And looked at me vaguely, as drinking cattle do,
And flickered his two-forked tongue from his lips, and mused a
    moment,
And stooped and drank a little more,
Being earth-brown, earth-golden from the burning bowels of the
    earth
On the day of Sicilian July, with Etna smoking.

The voice of my education said to me
He must be killed,
For in Sicily the black, black snakes are innocent, the gold are
    venomous.

And voices in me said, If you were a man
You would take a stick and break him now, and finish him off.

But must I confess how I liked him,
How glad I was he had come like a guest in quiet, to drink at
    my water-trough
And depart peaceful, pacified, and thankless,
Into the burning bowels of this earth?

Was it cowardice, that I dared not kill him?
Was it perversity, that I longed to talk to him?
Was it humility, to feel so honored?
I felt so honored.

And yet those voices:
If you were not afraid, you would kill him!

And truly I was afraid, I was most afraid,
But even so, honored still more
That he should seek my hospitality
From out the dark door of the secret earth.

He drank enough
And lifted his head, dreamily, as one who has drunken,
And flickered his tongue like a forked night on the air, so
    black,
Seeming to lick his lips,
And looked around like a god, unseeing, into the air,
And slowly turned his head,
And slowly, very slowly, as if thrice adream,
Proceeded to draw his slow length curving round
And climb again the broken bank of my wall-face.

And as he put his head into that dreadful hole,
And as he slowly drew up, snake-easing his shoulders, and
    entered farther,
A sort of horror, a sort of protest against his withdrawing into
    that horrid black hole,
Deliberately going into the blackness, and slowly drawing
    himself after,
Overcame me now his back was turned.

I looked round, I put down my pitcher,
I picked up a clumsy log
And threw it at the water-trough with a clatter.

I think it did not hit him,
But suddenly that part of him that was left behind convulsed in
    undignified haste,
Writhed like lightning, and was gone
Into the black hole, the earth-lipped fissure in the wall-front,
At which, in the intense still noon, I stared with fascination.

And immediately I regretted it.
I thought how paltry, how vulgar, what a mean act!
I despised myself and the voices of my accursed human
    education.

And I thought of the albatross,
And I wished he would come back, my snake.

For he seemed to me again like a king,
Like a king in exile, uncrowned in the underworld,
Now due to be crowned again.

And so, I missed my chance with one of the lords
Of life.
And I have something to expiate;
A pettiness.

Not "A Snake" or "The Snake," "Snake" has to do with an archetypal snake at once real and symbolic. The biblical serpent remains an object of fear and evil. Some serpents can, however, be symbols of health (as on the caduceus) and good luck (as with certain dragons).

Bavarian Gentians

>>>>>>>

Not every man has gentians in his house
in soft September, at slow, sad Michaelmas.

Bavarian gentians, big and dark, only dark
darkening the daytime, torch-like with the smoking blueness of
    Pluto's gloom,
ribbed and torch-like, with their blaze of darkness spread blue
down flattening into points, flattened under the sweep of white
    day
torch-flower of the blue-smoking darkness, Pluto's dark-blue
    daze,
black lamps from the halls of Dis, burning dark blue,
giving off darkness, blue darkness, as Demeter's pale lamps give
    off light,
lead me then, lead the way.

Reach me a gentian, give me a torch!
let me guide myself with the blue, forked torch of this flower
down the darker and darker stairs, where blue is darkened on
    blueness
even where Persephone goes, just now, from the frosted
    September
to the sightless realm where darkness is awake upon the dark
and Persephone herself is but a voice
or a darkness invisible enfolded in the deeper dark
of the arms Plutonic, and pierced with the passion of dense
    gloom,
among the splendor of torches of darkness, shedding darkness on
the lost bride and her groom.

Looking at blue autumn flowers made Lawrence think of the year's death in late September, when Persephone must return to the underworld ruled by Pluto (Dis). Lawrence probably thought also of William Cullen Bryant's well-known poem "To the Fringed Gentian," which emphasizes the blueness of the flower and the frostiness of its season; and, as Lawrence would also be, Bryant was put in mind of his own "hour of death."

Ezra Pound 1885–1972

Pound was born in Idaho, educated in Pennsylvania and New York, employed briefly in Indiana, and was an expatriate for many years in England, France, and Italy. During World War II he made scores of radio broadcasts from Rome defending the Fascist powers and attacking the Allies, including the United States. He was indicted for treason but adjudged insane and unfit for trial. He was held in the prison wing of a federal mental hospital for more than a dozen years but was finally released, too old any longer to threaten anyone. He returned to Italy in 1959 and lived on for thirteen more years, lapsing toward the end into humility and silence after a long life of obstreperous racket, much of it silly, some of it insane, but some of it of matchless brilliance.

The River-Merchant's Wife: A Letter

While my hair was still cut straight across my forehead
I played about the front gate, pulling flowers.
You came by on bamboo stilts, playing horse,
You walked about my seat, playing with blue plums.
And we went on living in the village of Chokan:
Two small people, without dislike or suspicion.

At fourteen I married My Lord you.
I never laughed, being bashful.
Lowering my head, I looked at the wall.
Called to, a thousand times, I never looked back.

At fifteen I stopped scowling,
I desired my dust to be mingled with yours
Forever and forever and forever.
Why should I climb the look out?

At sixteen you departed,
You went into far Ku-to-yen, by the river of swirling eddies,
And you have been gone five months.
The monkeys make sorrowful noise overhead.
You dragged your feet when you went out.
By the gate now, the moss is grown, the different mosses,
Too deep to clear them away!
The leaves fall early this autumn, in wind.
The paired butterflies are already yellow with August
Over the grass in the West garden;
They hurt me. I grow older.
If you are coming down through the narrows of the river Kiang,
Please let me know beforehand,
And I will come out to meet you
          As far as Cho-fu-Sa.

Maybe because of his amateur standing as a sinologist (abetted by genius), Pound simplified the subtle style of Li Po's verse to a flat and rather commercial prose (the addressee is a merchant, after all) concentrating on visual images of objects with primary colors, like a woodblock print.

In a Station of the Metro

The apparition of these faces in the crowd;
Petals on a wet, black bough.

The quintessential distillation of the principle of the Image. For poets of the Imagist school, which flourished between 1910 and 1920, the ideal of poetry is a clear presentation of the visual.

RUPERT BROOKE 1887–1915

Brooke, one of the most talented and attractive members of his generation, has been anthologized mostly as a war poet, but he is also recognized as a playwright and as the author of some very fine light verse.

The Soldier

If I should die, think only this of me;
  That there's some corner of a foreign field
That is for ever England. There shall be
  In that rich earth a richer dust concealed;
A dust whom England bore, shaped, and made aware,
  Gave, once, her flowers to love, her ways to roam
A body of England's, breathing English air,
  Washed by the rivers, blest by the aura of home.

And think, this heart, all evil shed away,
  A pulse in the eternal mind, no less
    Gives somewhere back the thoughts by England given;
Her sights and sounds; dreams happy as her day;
  And laughter, learnt of friends; and gentleness,
    In hearts at peace, under an English heaven.

Three poets in this anthology were killed in action in the First World War: Edward Thomas, Isaac Rosenberg, and Wilfred Owen. Brooke died of blood poisoning while en route to the Dardanelles but had earlier been involved in military operations and would certainly have seen action later if he had lived. "The Soldier," one of five war sonnets that Brooke wrote in 1914, cannot be interpreted as strictly autobiographical, since Brooke was not a soldier but a sailor. In any event, he is buried in a foreign field, on the Greek island of Scyros.

Rather theatrically, Jeffers situated himself and his po-
etry in a stark landscape with inhospitable rocks, con-
temptuous hawks, and as few people as possible. He
was not always capable of living up to his stoical atti-
tudes, but he was consistent and stubborn, and once in
a while his language works like a harpoon. He is still
honored by such younger poets as William Everson,
James Tate, and Alan Williamson.

Hurt Hawks

I

The broken pillar of the wing jags from the clotted shoulder,
The wing trails like a banner in defeat,
No more to use the sky forever but live with famine
And pain a few days: cat nor coyote
Will shorten the week of waiting for death, there is game
    without talons.
He stands under the oak-bush and waits
The lame feet of salvation; at night he remembers freedom
And flies in a dream, the dawns ruin it.
He is strong and pain is worse to the strong, incapacity is
    worse.
The curs of the day come and torment him
At distance, no one but death the redeemer will humble that
    head,
The intrepid readiness, the terrible eyes.
The wild God of the world is sometimes merciful to those
That ask mercy, not often to the arrogant.
You do not know him, you communal people, or you have
    forgotten him;
Intemperate and savage, the hawk remembers him;
Beautiful and wild, the hawks, and men that are dying,
    remember him.

II

I'd sooner, except the penalties, kill a man than a hawk; but the
    great redtail
Had nothing left but unable misery
From the bone too shattered for mending, the wing that trailed
    under his talons when he moved.
We had fed him six weeks, I gave him freedom,
He wandered over the foreland hill and returned in the evening,
    asking for death,
Not like a beggar, still eyed with the old
Implacable arrogance. I gave him the lead gift in the twilight.
    What fell was relaxed,
Owl-downy, soft feminine feathers; but what
Soared: the fierce rush: the night-herons by the flooded river
    cried fear at its rising
Before it was quite unsheathed from reality.

---

*Some readers may find Jeffers somewhat too melodramatic, too willing to identify
himself with an arrogant individualist bird, but, for many, he remains a pow-
erfully eloquent champion of life away from "communal people." William Ever-
son's "Poet Is Dead," which is a memorial for Jeffers, includes a reference to a
structure called Hawk Tower that Jeffers himself built: "On the top of the tower
/ The hawk will not perch tomorrow."*

Shine, Perishing Republic

While this America settles in the mould of its vulgarity, heavily
    thickening to empire,
And protest, only a bubble in the molten mass, pops and sighs
    out, and the mass hardens,

I sadly smiling remember that the flower fades to make fruit, the
    fruit rots to make earth.
Out of the mother; and through the spring exultances, ripeness
    and decadence; and home to the mother.

You making haste haste on decay: not blameworthy; life is
    good, be it stubbornly long or suddenly
A mortal splendor: meteors are not needed less than mountains:
    shine, perishing republic.

But for my children, I would have them keep their distance
    from the thickening center; corruption
Never has been compulsory, when the cities lie at the monster's
    feet there are left the mountains.

And boys, be in nothing so moderate as in love of man, a clever
    servant, insufferable master.
There is the trap that catches noblest spirits, that caught—they
    say—God, when he walked on earth.

---

*One of Robert Frost's last poems is called "Our Doom to Bloom," and its
epigraph is "Shine, perishing republic." Frost's poem is much lighter-hearted
than Jeffers's.*

MARIANNE MOORE 1887–1972

Marianne Moore was born in St. Louis, Missouri, the year before T. S. Eliot was born in the same city. After graduation from Bryn Mawr, she lived most of her long life in New York City, much of the time in Brooklyn. She was an editor of *The Dial* during the 1920s. In 1921, she began publication of a succession of distinguished books of poetry marked by scrupulous observation of nature, a plucky spirit, and technical wizardry.

Poetry

I, too, dislike it: there are things that are important beyond all
   this fiddle.
  Reading it, however, with a perfect contempt for it, one
    discovers in
 it after all, a place for the genuine.
   Hands that can grasp, eyes
    that can dilate, hair that can rise
     if it must, these things are important not because a

high-sounding interpretation can be put upon them but because
  they are
 useful. When they become so derivative as to become
   unintelligible,
 the same thing may be said for all of us, that we
   do not admire what
    we cannot understand: the bat
     holding on upside down or in quest of something to

eat, elephants pushing, a wild horse taking a roll, a tireless wolf under
    a tree, the immovable critic twitching his skin like a horse that feels a
        flea, the base-
    ball fan, the statistician—
    nor is it valid
        to discriminate against 'business documents and

school-books'; all these phenomena are important. One must make a distinction
    however: when dragged into prominence by half poets, the result is not poetry,
    nor till the poets among us can be
        'literalists of
    the imagination'—above
        insolence and triviality and can present

for inspection, 'imaginary gardens with real toads in them', shall we have
    it. In the meantime, if you demand on the one hand,
    the raw material of poetry in
        all its rawness and
    that which is on the other hand
        genuine, you are interested in poetry.

A fastidious reviser, Marianne Moore produced several different versions of this poem, the last with just a few lines, ending with "genuine." Since the longer versions were the works represented in anthologies, however, the 1921 version that appeared in Poetry *is given here.*

A Grave

Man looking into the sea,
taking the view from those who have as much right to it as you
    have to it yourself,
it is human nature to stand in the middle of a thing,
but you cannot stand in the middle of this;
the sea has nothing to give but a well excavated grave.
The firs stand in a procession, each with an emerald turkey foot
    at the top,
reserved as their contours, saying nothing;
repression, however, is not the most obvious characteristic of
    the sea;
the sea is a collector, quick to return a rapacious look.
There are others besides you who have worn that look—
whose expression is no longer a protest; the fish no longer
    investigate them
for their bones have not lasted:
men lower nets, unconscious of the fact that they are
    desecrating a grave,
and row quickly away—the blades of the oars
moving together like the feet of water spiders as if there were
    no such thing as death.
The wrinkles progress among themselves in a phalanx—beautiful
    under networks of foam,
and fade breathlessly while the sea rustles in and out of the
    seaweed;
the birds swim through the air at top speed, emitting catcalls as
    heretofore—
the tortoise shell scourges about the feet of the cliffs, in motion
    beneath them;
and the ocean, under the pulsation of lighthouses and noise of
    bell buoys,
advances as usual, looking as if it were not that ocean in which
    dropped things are bound to sink—

in which if they turn and twist, it is neither with volition nor consciousness.

Marianne Moore here gave up her syllabic stanzas for an elegantly undulating look at much the same ocean as that addressed in Byron's Childe Harold's Pilgrimage *(p. 486). Both pieces end with a sinking motion.*

The Sitwells have been a twentieth-century literary family, much as the Rossettis were a nineteenth-century literary family. For the purposes of this book, however, neither of Dame Edith's writing brothers (Sacheverell and Sir Osbert) are qualified for inclusion. At the time of World War I, Dame Edith edited a magazine called *Wheels*, in which Wilfred Owen's poems were first published. Her own earlier poems were gaudy and experimental, bristling with outlandish images and hyperkinetic syncopations, but, by the time of World War II, her tone had deepened into a most moving solemnity, achieving scriptural eloquence in many lines.

Still Falls the Rain

(The Raids, 1940. Night and Dawn)

Still falls the Rain—
Dark as the world of man, black as our loss—
Blind as the nineteen hundred and forty nails
Upon the Cross.

Still falls the Rain
With a sound like the pulse of the heart that is changed to the
    hammerbeat
In the Potters' Field, and the sound of the impious feet
On the Tomb:
      Still falls the Rain
In the Field of Blood where the small hopes breed and the
    human brain
Nurtures its greed, that worm with the brow of Cain.

Still falls the Rain
At the feet of the Starved Man hung upon the Cross.
Christ that each day, each night, nails there, have mercy on us—
On Dives and on Lazarus:
Under the Rain the sore and the gold are as one.

Still falls the Rain—
Still falls the Blood from the Starved Man's wounded Side
He bears in his Heart all wounds,—those of the light that died,
The last faint spark
In the self-murdered heart, the wounds of the sad
    uncomprehending dark,
The wounds of the baited bear,—
The blind and weeping bear whom the keepers beat
On his helpless flesh . . . the tears of the hunted hare.

Still falls the Rain—
Then—O Ile leape up to my God: who pulles me doune—
See, see where Christ's blood streames in the firmament:
It flows from the Brow we nailed upon the tree
Deep to the dying, to the thirsting heart
That holds the fires of the world,—dark-smirched with pain
As Caesar's laurel crown.

Then sounds the voice of One who like the heart of man
Was once a child who among beasts has lain—
'Still do I love, still shed my innocent light, my Blood, for thee.'

Her earlier poetry, published in the 1920s, was jazzy, and playful, but, with the coming of age Sitwell changed her style completely and achieved a level of dignity reminiscent of the great poets of the sixteenth and seventeenth centuries.

Eliot emigrated to England in 1914 and became a British subject in 1927, but he retained an attachment to his native Saint Louis, Missouri, on the banks of the Mississippi, and to coastal Massachusetts, where his family had a summer home near Gloucester. His education was more in philosophy than in literature, and he all-but-finished the work for a Harvard doctorate. He worked for a time as an officer of a bank and then became a valued member of the directorate of Faber and Faber, publishers. In the 1920s he established a potent reputation as a poet and critic, and for many years he edited the influential magazine *The Criterion*. Like Thomas Hardy, he was given the Order of Merit; like W. B. Yeats, he was awarded the Nobel Prize for Literature.

The Love Song of J. Alfred Prufrock

⟫⟫⟫⟫⟫

S'io credessi che mia risposta fosse
a persona che mai tornasse al mondo,
questa fiamma staria senza più scosse.
Ma per ciò che giammai di questo fondo
non tornò vivo alcun, s'i' odo il vero,
senza tema d'infamia ti rispondo.

Dante Alighieri
Inferno

Let us go then, you and I,
When the evening is spread out against the sky
Like a patient etherised upon a table;
Let us go, through certain half-deserted streets,
The muttering retreats
Of restless nights in one-night cheap hotels
And sawdust restaurants with oyster-shells:
Streets that follow like a tedious argument
Of insidious intent
To lead you to an overwhelming question . . .
Oh, do not ask, "What is it?"
Let us go and make our visit.

In the room the women come and go
Talking of Michelangelo.

The yellow fog that rubs its back upon the window-panes,
The yellow smoke that rubs its muzzle on the window-panes,
Licked its tongue into the corners of the evening,
Lingered upon the pools that stand in drains,
Let fall upon its back the soot that falls from chimneys,
Slipped by the terrace, made a sudden leap,
And seeing that it was a soft October night,
Curled once about the house, and fell asleep.

And indeed there will be time
For the yellow smoke that slides along the street
Rubbing its back upon the window-panes;
There will be time, there will be time
To prepare a face to meet the faces that you meet;
There will be time to murder and create,
And time for all the works and days of hands
That lift and drop a question on your plate;
Time for you and time for me,
And time yet for a hundred indecisions,
And for a hundred visions and revisions,
Before the taking of a toast and tea.

In the room the women come and go
Talking of Michelangelo.

And indeed there will be time
To wonder, "Do I dare?" and, "Do I dare?"
Time to turn back and descend the stair,
With a bald spot in the middle of my hair—
(They will say: "How his hair is growing thin!")
My morning coat, my collar mounting firmly to the chin,
My necktie rich and modest, but asserted by a simple pin—
(They will say: "But how his arms and legs are thin!")
Do I dare
Disturb the universe?

In a minute there is time
For decisions and revisions which a minute will reverse.

For I have known them all already, known them all—
Have known the evenings, mornings, afternoons,
I have measured out my life with coffee spoons;
I know the voices dying with a dying fall
Beneath the music from a farther room.
　　So how should I presume?

And I have known the eyes already, known them all—
The eyes that fix you in a formulated phrase,
And when I am formulated, sprawling on a pin,
When I am pinned and wriggling on the wall,
Then how should I begin
To spit out all the butt-ends of my days and ways?
　　And how should I presume?

And I have known the arms already, known them all—
Arms that are braceleted and white and bare
(But in the lamplight, downed with light brown hair!)
Is it perfume from a dress
That makes me so digress?
Arms that lie along a table, or wrap about a shawl.
　　And should I then presume?
　　And how should I begin?

　　　　. . . . .

Shall I say, I have gone at dusk through narrow streets
And watched the smoke that rises from the pipes
Of lonely men in shirt-sleeves, leaning out of windows? . . .

I should have been a pair of ragged claws
Scuttling across the floors of silent seas.

　　　　. . . . .

And the afternoon, the evening, sleeps so peacefully!
Smoothed by long fingers,
Asleep . . . tired . . . or it malingers,
Stretched on the floor, here beside you and me.
Should I, after tea and cakes and ices,
Have the strength to force the moment to its crisis?
But though I have wept and fasted, wept and prayed,
Though I have seen my head (grown slightly bald) brought in
    upon a platter,
I am no prophet—and here's no great matter;
I have seen the moment of my greatness flicker,
And I have seen the eternal Footman hold my coat, and
    snicker,
And in short, I was afraid.

And would it have been worth it, after all,
After the cups, the marmalade, the tea,
Among the porcelain, among some talk of you and me,
Would it have been worth while,
To have bitten off the matter with a smile,
To have squeezed the universe into a ball
To roll it towards some overwhelming question,
To say: "I am Lazarus, come from the dead,
Come back to tell you all, I shall tell you all"—
If one, settling a pillow by her head,
    Should say: "That is not what I meant at all.
    That is not it, at all."

And would it have been worth it, after all,
Would it have been worth while,
After the sunsets and the dooryards and the sprinkled streets,
After the novels, after the teacups, after the skirts that trail
    along the floor—
And this, and so much more?—
It is impossible to say just what I mean!
But as if a magic lantern threw the nerves in patterns on a
    screen:
Would it have been worth while

If one, settling a pillow or throwing off a shawl,
And turning toward the window, should say:
   "That is not it, at all,
   That is not what I meant, at all."

    . . . .

No! I am not Prince Hamlet, nor was meant to be;
Am an attendant lord, one that will do
To swell a progress, start a scene or two,
Advise the prince; no doubt, an easy tool,
Deferential, glad to be of use,
Politic, cautious, and meticulous;
Full of high sentence, but a bit obtuse;
At times, indeed, almost ridiculous—
Almost, at times, the Fool.

I grow old . . . I grow old . . .
I shall wear the bottoms of my trousers rolled.

Shall I part my hair behind? Do I dare to eat a peach?
I shall wear white flannel trousers, and walk upon the beach.
I have heard the mermaids singing, each to each.

I do not think that they will sing to me.

I have seen them riding seaward on the waves
Combing the white hair of the waves blown back
When the wind blows the water white and black.

We have lingered in the chambers of the sea
By sea-girls wreathed with seaweed red and brown
Till human voices wake us, and we drown.

Although it remains the last word in tired modernist irony and sophistication, "The Love Song of J. Alfred Prufrock" was written by an uncommonly robust twenty-year-old. The title is off-target, since this is a non-song about unlove, an affair of inversions and subversions.

Journey of the Magi

"A cold coming we had of it,
Just the worst time of the year
For a journey, and such a long journey:
The ways deep and the weather sharp,
The very dead of winter."
And the camels galled, sore-footed, refractory,
Lying down in the melting snow.
There were times we regretted
The summer palaces on slopes, the terraces,
And the silken girls bringing sherbet.
Then the camel men cursing and grumbling
And running away, and wanting their liquor and women,
And the night-fires going out, and the lack of shelters,
And the cities hostile and the towns unfriendly
And the villages dirty and charging high prices:
A hard time we had of it.
At the end we preferred to travel all night,
Sleeping in snatches,
With the voices singing in our ears, saying
That this was all folly.

Then at dawn we came down to a temperate valley,
Wet, below the snow line, smelling of vegetation,
With a running stream and a water-mill beating the darkness,
And three trees on the low sky.
And an old white horse galloped away in the meadow.
Then we came to a tavern with vine-leaves over the lintel,
Six hands at an open door dicing for pieces of silver,
And feet kicking the empty wine-skins.
But there was no information, and so we continued
And arrived at evening, not a moment too soon
Finding the place; it was (you may say) satisfactory.

All this was a long time ago, I remember.
And I would do it again, but set down
This set down
This: were we led all that way for
Birth or Death? There was a Birth, certainly,
We had evidence and no doubt. I had seen birth and death,
But had thought they were different; this Birth was
Hard and bitter agony for us, like Death, our death.
We returned to our places, these Kingdoms,
But no longer at ease here, in the old dispensation,
With an alien people clutching their gods.
I should be glad of another death.

This is the first of the five "Ariel Poems" that Eliot wrote after becoming an Anglo-Catholic in 1927. It is spoken by one of the Wise Men. The first five lines are quoted from a Jacobean sermon by Lancelot Andrewes (1555–1626), a preacher much admired by Eliot.

The Waste Land

Nam Sibyllam quidem Cumis ego ipse oculis meis vidi in ampulla
pendere, et cum illi pueri dicerent: Σίβυλλα τί θέλεις; respondebat
illa: ἀποθανεῖν θέλω.

Petronius
Satyricon

For Ezra Pound
il miglior fabbro.

I. THE BURIAL OF THE DEAD

April is the cruellest month, breeding
Lilacs out of the dead land, mixing
Memory and desire, stirring
Dull roots with spring rain.
Winter kept us warm, covering
Earth in forgetful snow, feeding
A little life with dried tubers.
Summer surprised us, coming over the Starnbergersee
With a shower of rain; we stopped in the colonnade,
And went on in sunlight, into the Hofgarten,
And drank coffee, and talked for an hour.
Bin gar keine Russin, stamm' aus Litauen, echt deutsch.
And when we were children, staying at the arch-duke's,
My cousin's, he took me out on a sled,
And I was frightened. He said, Marie,
Marie, hold on tight. And down we went.
In the mountains, there you feel free.
I read, much of the night, and go south in the winter.

What are the roots that clutch, what branches grow
Out of this stony rubbish? Son of man,
You cannot say, or guess, for you know only
A heap of broken images, where the sun beats,
And the dead tree gives no shelter, the cricket no relief,
And the dry stone no sound of water. Only
There is shadow under this red rock,

(Come in under the shadow of this red rock),
And I will show you something different from either
Your shadow at morning striding behind you
Or your shadow at evening rising to meet you;
I will show you fear in a handful of dust.

      Frisch weht der Wind
      Der Heimat zu
      Mein Irisch Kind,
      Wo weilest du?

"You gave me hyacinths first a year ago;
"They called me the hyacinth girl."
—Yet when we came back, late, from the hyacinth garden,
Your arms full, and your hair wet, I could not
Speak, and my eyes failed, I was neither
Living nor dead, and I knew nothing,
Looking into the heart of light, the silence.
Oed' und leer das Meer.

Madame Sosostris, famous clairvoyante,
Had a bad cold, nevertheless
Is known to be the wisest woman in Europe,
With a wicked pack of cards. Here, said she,
Is your card, the drowned Phoenician Sailor,
(Those are pearls that were his eyes. Look!)
Here is Belladonna, the Lady of the Rocks,
The lady of situations.
Here is the man with three staves, and here the Wheel,
And here is the one-eyed merchant, and this card,
Which is blank, is something he carries on his back,
Which I am forbidden to see. I do not find
The Hanged Man. Fear death by water.
I see crowds of people, walking round in a ring.
Thank you. If you see dear Mrs. Equitone,
Tell her I bring the horoscope myself:
One must be so careful these days.

Unreal city,
Under the brown fog of a winter dawn,
A crowd flowed over London Bridge, so many,
I had not thought death had undone so many.
Sighs, short and infrequent, were exhaled,
And each man fixed his eyes before his feet.
Flowed up the hill and down King William Street,
To where Saint Mary Woolnoth kept the hours
With a dead sound on the final stroke of nine.
There I saw one I knew, and stopped him, crying: "Stetson!
"You who were with me in the ships at Mylae!
"That corpse you planted last year in your garden,
"Has it begun to sprout? Will it bloom this year?
"Or has the sudden frost disturbed its bed?
"O keep the Dog far hence, that's friend to men,
"Or with his nails he'll dig it up again!
"You! hypocrite lecteur!—mon semblable,—mon frère!"

II. A GAME OF CHESS

The Chair she sat in, like a burnished throne,
Glowed on the marble, where the glass
Held up by standards wrought with fruited vines
From which a golden Cupidon peeped out
(Another hid his eyes behind his wing)
Doubled the flames of sevenbranched candelabra
Reflecting light upon the table as
The glitter of her jewels rose to meet it,
From satin cases poured in rich profusion.
In vials of ivory and coloured glass
Unstoppered, lurked her strange synthetic perfumes,
Unguent, powdered, or liquid—troubled, confused
And drowned the sense in odours; stirred by the air
That freshened from the window, these ascended
In fattening the prolonged candle-flames,
Flung their smoke into the laquearia,
Stirring the pattern on the coffered ceiling.
Huge sea-wood fed with copper
Burned green and orange, framed by the coloured stone,

In which sad light a carvèd dolphin swam.
Above the antique mantel was displayed
As though a window gave upon the sylvan scene
The change of Philomel, by the barbarous king
So rudely forced; yet there the nightingale
Filled all the desert with inviolable voice
And still she cried, and still the world pursues,
"Jug Jug" to dirty ears.
And other withered stumps of time
Were told upon the walls; staring forms
Leaned out, leaning, hushing the room enclosed.
Footsteps shuffled on the stair.
Under the firelight, under the brush, her hair
Spread out in fiery points
Glowed into words, then would be savagely still.

"My nerves are bad to-night. Yes, bad. Stay with me.
"Speak to me. Why do you never speak. Speak.
    "What are you thinking of? What thinking? What?
"I never know what you are thinking. Think."

I think we are in rats' alley
Where the dead men lost their bones.
"What is that noise?"
                    The wind under the door.
"What is that noise now? What is the wind doing?"
                    Nothing again nothing.
                         "Do
"You know nothing? Do you see nothing? Do you remember
"Nothing?"

    I remember
Those are pearls that were his eyes.
"Are you alive, or not? Is there nothing in your head?"

                                            But
O O O O that Shakespeherian Rag—
It's so elegant
So intelligent
"What shall I do now? What shall I do?
"I shall rush out as I am, and walk the street
"With my hair down, so. What shall we do tomorrow?
What shall we ever do?"
                              The hot water at ten.
And if it rains, a closed car at four.
And we shall play a game of chess,
Pressing lidless eyes and waiting for a knock upon the door.

When Lil's husband got demobbed, I said—
I didn't mince my words, I said to her myself,
HURRY UP PLEASE ITS TIME
Now Albert's coming back, make yourself a bit smart.
He'll want to know what you done with that money he gave
      you
To get yourself some teeth. He did, I was there.
You have them all out, Lil, and get a nice set,
He said, I swear, I can't bear to look at you.
And no more can't I, I said, and think of poor Albert,
He's been in the army four years, he wants a good time,
And if you don't give it him, there's others will, I said.
Oh is there, she said. Something o' that, I said.
Then I'll know who to thank, she said, and give me a straight
      look.
HURRY UP PLEASE ITS TIME
If you don't like it you can get on with it, I said.
Others can pick and choose if you can't.
But if Albert makes off, it won't be for lack of telling.
You ought to be ashamed, I said, to look so antique.
(And her only thirty-one.)
I can't help it, she said, pulling a long face,

It's them pills I took, to bring it off, she said.
(She's had five already, and nearly died of young George.)
The chemist said it would be all right, but I've never been the
    same.
You *are* a proper fool, I said.
Well, if Albert won't leave you alone, there it is, I said,
What you get married for if you don't want children?
HURRY UP PLEASE ITS TIME
Well, that Sunday Albert was home, they had a hot gammon,
And they asked me in to dinner, to get the beauty of it hot—
HURRY UP PLEASE ITS TIME
HURRY UP PLEASE ITS TIME
Goonight Bill. Goonight Lou. Goonight May. Goonight.
Ta ta. Goonight. Goonight.
Good night, ladies, good night, sweet ladies, good night, good
    night.

III. THE FIRE SERMON

The river's tent is broken; the last fingers of leaf
Clutch and sink into the wet bank. The wind
Crosses the brown land, unheard. The nymphs are departed.
Sweet Thames, run softly, till I end my song.
The river bears no empty bottles, sandwich papers,
Silk handkerchiefs, cardboard boxes, cigarette ends
Or other testimony of summer nights. The nymphs are
    departed.
And their friends, the loitering heirs of City directors;
Departed, have left no addresses.
By the waters of Leman I sat down and wept . . .
Sweet Thames, run softly, till I end my song,
Sweet Thames, run softly, for I speak not loud or long.
But at my back in a cold blast I hear
The rattle of the bones, and chuckle spread from ear to ear.

A rat crept softly through the vegetation
Dragging its slimy belly on the bank
While I was fishing in the dull canal
On a winter evening round behind the gashouse

Musing upon the king my brother's wreck
And on the king my father's death before him.
White bodies naked on the low damp ground
And bones cast in a little low dry garret,
Rattled by the rat's foot only, year to year.
But at my back from time to time I hear
The sound of horns and motors, which shall bring
Sweeney to Mrs. Porter in the spring.
O the moon shone bright on Mrs. Porter
And on her daughter
They wash their feet in soda water
Et O ces voix d'enfants, chantant dans la coupole!

Twit twit twit
Jug jug jug jug jug jug
So rudely forc'd.
Tereu

Unreal City
Under the brown fog of a winter noon
Mr. Eugenides, the Smyrna merchant
Unshaven, with a pocket full of currants
C.i.f. London: documents at sight,
Asked me in demotic French
To luncheon at the Cannon Street Hotel
Followed by a weekend at the Metropole.

At the violet hour, when the eyes and back
Turn upward from the desk, when the human engine waits
Like a taxi throbbing waiting,
I Tiresias, though blind, throbbing between two lives,
Old man with wrinkled female breasts, can see
At the violet hour, the evening hour that strives
Homeward, and brings the sailor home from sea,
The typist home at teatime, clears her breakfast, lights
Her stove, and lays out food in tins.
Out of the window perilously spread
Her drying combinations touched by the sun's last rays,

On the divan are piled (at night her bed)
Stockings, slippers, camisoles, and stays.
I Tiresias, old man with wrinkled dugs
Perceived the scene, and foretold the rest—
I too awaited the expected guest.
He, the young man carbuncular, arrives,
A small house agent's clerk, with one bold stare,
One of the low on whom assurance sits
As a silk hat on a Bradford millionaire.
The time is now propitious, as he guesses,
The meal is ended, she is bored and tired,
Endeavours to engage her in caresses
Which still are unreproved, if undesired..
Flushed and decided, he assaults at once;
Exploring hands encounter no defence;
His vanity requires no response,
And makes a welcome of indifference.
(And I Tiresias have foresuffered all
Enacted on this same divan or bed;
I who have sat by Thebes below the wall
And walked among the lowest of the dead.)
Bestows one final patronising kiss,
And gropes his way, finding the stairs unlit . . .

She turns and looks a moment in the glass,
Hardly aware of her departed lover;
Her brain allows one half-formed thought to pass:
"Well now that's done: and I'm glad it's over."
When lovely woman stoops to folly and
Paces about her room again, alone,
She smoothes her hair with automatic hand,
And puts a record on the gramophone.
"This music crept by me upon the waters"
And along the Strand, up Queen Victoria Street.
O City city, I can sometimes hear
Beside a public bar in Lower Thames Street,
The pleasant whining of a mandoline
And a clatter and a chatter from within

Where fishmen lounge at noon: where the walls
Of Magnus Martyr hold
Inexplicable splendour of Ionian white and gold.

> The river sweats
> Oil and tar
> The barges drift
> With the turning tide
> Red sails
> Wide
> To leeward, swing on the heavy spar.
> The barges wash
> Drifting logs
> Down Greenwich reach
> Past the Isle of Dogs.
>> Weialala leia
>> Wallala leialala

> Elizabeth and Leicester
> Beating oars
> The stern was formed
> A gilded shell
> Red and gold
> The brisk swell
> Rippled both shores
> Southwest wind
> Carried down stream
> The peal of bells
> White towers
>> Weialala leia
>> Wallala leialala

"Trams and dusty trees.
Highbury bore me. Richmond and Kew
Undid me. By Richmond I raised my knees
Supine on the floor of a narrow canoe."

"My feet are at Moorgate, and my heart
Under my feet. After the event
He wept. He promised 'a new start.'
I made no comment. What should I resent?"
"On Margate Sands.
I can connect
Nothing with nothing.
The broken fingernails of dirty hands.
My people humble people who expect
Nothing."
    la la

To Carthage then I came

Burning burning burning burning
O Lord Thou pluckest me out
O Lord Thou pluckest

burning

IV. DEATH BY WATER

Phlebas the Phoenician, a fortnight dead,
Forgot the cry of gulls, and the deep sea swell
And the profit and loss.
        A current under sea
Picked his bones in whispers. As he rose and fell
He passed the stages of his age and youth
Entering the whirlpool.
        Gentile or Jew
O you who turn the wheel and look to windward,
Consider Phlebas, who was once handsome and tall as you.

V. WHAT THE THUNDER SAID

After the torchlight red on sweaty faces
After the frosty silence in the gardens
After the agony in stony places
The shouting and the crying

Prison and palace and reverberation
Of thunder of spring over distant mountains
He who was living is now dead
We who were living are now dying
With a little patience

Here is no water but only rock
Rock and no water and the sandy road
The road winding above among the mountains
Which are mountains of rock without water
If there were water we should stop and drink
Amongst the rock one cannot stop or think
Sweat is dry and feet are in the sand
If there were only water amongst the rock
Dead mountain mouth of carious teeth that cannot spit
Here one can neither stand nor lie nor sit
There is not even silence in the mountains
But dry sterile thunder without rain
There is not even solitude in the mountains
But red sullen faces sneer and snarl
From doors of mudcracked houses
                        If there were water
   And no rock
   If there were rock
   And also water
   And water
   A spring
   A pool among the rock
   If there were the sound of water only
   Not the cicada
   And dry grass singing
   But sound of water over a rock
   Where the hermit-thrush sings in the pine trees
   Drip drop drip drop drop drop drop
   But there is no water

Who is the third who walks always beside you?
When I count, there are only you and I together
But when I look ahead up the white road
There is always another one walking beside you
Gliding wrapt in a brown mantle, hooded
I do not know whether a man or a woman
—But who is that on the other side of you?
What is that sound high in the air
Murmur of maternal lamentation
Who are those hooded hordes swarming
Over endless plains, stumbling in cracked earth
Ringed by the flat horizon only
What is the city over the mountains
Cracks and reforms and bursts in the violet air
Falling towers
Jerusalem Athens Alexandria
Vienna London
Unreal

A woman drew her long black hair out tight
And fiddled whisper music on those strings
And bats with baby faces in the violet light
Whistled, and beat their wings
And crawled head downward down a blackened wall
And upside down in air were towers
Tolling reminiscent bells, that kept the hours
And voices singing out of empty cisterns and exhausted wells

In this decayed hole among the mountains
In the faint moonlight, the grass is singing
Over the tumbled graves, about the chapel
There is the empty chapel, only the wind's home.
It has no windows, and the door swings,
Dry bones can harm no one.

Only a cock stood on the rooftree
Co co rico co co rico
In a flash of lightning. Then a damp gust
Bringing rain

Ganga was sunken, and the limp leaves
Waited for rain, while the black clouds
Gathered far distant, over Himavant.
The jungle crouched, humped in silence.
Then spoke the thunder
DA
Datta: what have we given?
My friend, blood shaking my heart
The awful daring of a moment's surrender
Which an age of prudence can never retract
By this, and this only, we have existed
Which is not to be found in our obituaries
Or in memories draped by the beneficent spider
Or under seals broken by the lean solicitor
In our empty rooms
DA
Dayadhvam: I have heard the key
Turn in the door once and turn once only
We think of the key, each in his prison
Thinking of the key, each confirms a prison
Only at nightfall, aethereal rumours
Revive for a moment a broken Coriolanus
DA
Damyata: The boat responded
Gaily, to the hand expert with sail and oar
The sea was calm, your heart would have responded
Gaily, when invited, beating obedient
To controlling hands

I sat upon the shore
Fishing, with the arid plain behind me
Shall I at least set my lands in order?
London Bridge is falling down falling down falling down
Poi s'ascose nel foco che gli affina
Quando fiam uti chelidon — O swallow swallow
Le Prince d'Aquitaine à la tour abolie
These fragments I have shored against my ruins
Why then Ile fit you. Hieronymo's mad againe.
Datta. Dayadhvam. Damyata.
      Shantih   shantih   shantih

After seventy years, "The Waste Land" remains the most influential poem of the twentieth century. Although obscure in many places and even opaque in some, it appeals to a great audience by the force of its images, rhythms, and overall design, which owes something to the five-act structure of Senecan and Elizabethan plays.

Sweeney among the Nightingales

ὤμοι, πέπληγμαι καιρίαν πληγὴν ἔσω.
Aeschylus
Agamemnon

Apeneck Sweeney spreads his knees
Letting his arms hang down to laugh,
The zebra stripes along his jaw
Swelling to maculate giraffe.

The circles of the stormy moon
Slide westward toward the River Plate,
Death and the Raven drift above
And Sweeney guards the hornèd gate.

Gloomy Orion and the Dog
Are veiled; and hushed the shrunken seas;
The person in the Spanish cape
Tries to sit on Sweeney's knees

Slips and pulls the table cloth
Overturns a coffee-cup,
Reorganized upon the floor
She yawns and draws a stocking up;

The silent man in mocha brown
Sprawls at the window-sill and gapes;
The waiter brings in oranges
Bananas figs and hothouse grapes;

The silent vertebrate in brown
Contracts and concentrates, withdraws;
Rachel *née* Rabinovitch
Tears at the grapes with murderous paws;

She and the lady in the cape
Are suspect, thought to be in league;
Therefore the man with heavy eyes
Declines the gambit, shows fatigue,

Leaves the room and reappears
Outside the window, leaning in,
Branches of wistaria
Circumscribe a golden grin;

The host with someone indistinct
Converses at the door apart,
The nightingales are singing near
The Convent of the Sacred Heart,

And sang within the bloody wood
When Agamemnon cried aloud,
And let their liquid siftings fall
To stain the stiff dishonoured shroud.

Eliot, a reader of Thackeray, here adapts the two charades acted out in Vanity
Fair: *Agamemnon and Nightingale. As with Thackeray's, Eliot's handling of the
myths brings out their depth and brutality.*

Gerontion

❧❧❧❧❧

Thou hast nor youth nor age
But as it were an after dinner sleep
Dreaming of both.

Here I am, an old man in a dry month,
Being read to by a boy, waiting for rain.
I was neither at the hot gates
Nor fought in the warm rain
Nor knee deep in the salt marsh, heaving a cutlass,
Bitten by flies, fought.
My house is a decayed house,
And the jew squats on the window sill, the owner,
Spawned in some estaminet of Antwerp,
Blistered in Brussels, patched and peeled in London.
The goat coughs at night in the field overhead;
Rocks, moss, stonecrop, iron, merds.
The woman keeps the kitchen, makes tea,
Sneezes at evening, poking the peevish gutter.
                    I an old man,
A dull head among windy spaces.

Signs are taken for wonders. "We would see a sign!"
The word within a word, unable to speak a word,
Swaddled with darkness. In the juvescence of the year
Came Christ the tiger
In depraved May, dogwood and chestnut flowering judas,
To be eaten, to be divided, to be drunk
Among whispers; by Mr. Silvero
With caressing hands, at Limoges
Who walked all night in the next room;

By Hakagawa, bowing among the Titians;
By Madame de Tornquist, in the dark room
Shifting the candles; Fräulein von Kulp
Who turned in the hall, one hand on the door. Vacant shuttles
Weave the wind. I have no ghosts,
An old man in a draughty house
Under a windy knob.

After such knowledge, what forgiveness? Think now
History has many cunning passages, contrived corridors
And issues, deceives with whispering ambitions,
Guides us by vanities. Think now
She gives when our attention is distracted
And what she gives, gives with such supple confusions
That the giving famishes the craving. Gives too late
What's not believed in, or if still believed,
In memory only, reconsidered passion. Gives too soon
Into weak hands, what's thought can be dispensed with
Till the refusal propagates a fear. Think
Neither fear nor courage saves us. Unnatural vices
Are fathered by our heroism. Virtues
Are forced upon us by our impudent crimes.
These tears are shaken from the wrath-bearing tree.

The tiger springs in the new year. Us he devours. Think at last
We have not reached conclusions, when I
Stiffen in a rented house. Think at last
I have not made this show purposelessly
And it is not by any concitation
Of the backward devils.
I would meet you upon this honestly.
I that was near your heart was removed therefrom
To lose beauty in terror, terror in inquisition.
I have lost my passion: why should I need to keep it
Since what is kept must be adulterated?
I have lost my sight, smell, hearing, taste and touch:
How should I use them for your closer contact?

[985]

These with a thousand small deliberations
Protract the profit of their chilled delirium,
Excite the membrane, when the sense has cooled,
With pungent sauces, multiply variety
In a wilderness of mirrors. What will the spider do,
Suspend its operations, will the weevil
Delay? De Bailhache, Fresca, Mrs. Cammel, whirled
Beyond the circuit of the shuddering Bear
In fractured atoms. Gull against the wind, in the windy straits
Of Belle Isle, or running on the Horn,
White feathers in the snow, the Gulf claims,
And an old man driven by the Trades
To a sleepy corner.
                   Tenants of the house,
Thoughts of a dry brain in a dry season.

Planned at one time to serve as the prologue to "The Waste Land," "Gerontion" seems to be a cross-section or core-sample of the Western mind since the Persian Wars. This "little old man" in a "dry month" was created by a thirty-year-old poet in May and June of 1919, when there was a record drought in England.

Little Gidding

()◄━━► ()

I

Midwinter spring is its own season
Sempiternal though sodden towards sundown,
Suspended in time, between pole and tropic.
When the short day is brightest, with frost and fire,
The brief sun flames the ice, on pond and ditches,
In windless cold that is the heart's heat,
Reflecting in a watery mirror
A glare that is blindness in the early afternoon.
And glow more intense than blaze of branch, or brazier,
Stirs the dumb spirit: no wind, but pentecostal fire
In the dark time of the year. Between melting and freezing
The soul's sap quivers. There is no earth smell
Or smell of living thing. This is the spring time
But not in time's covenant. Now the hedgerow
Is blanched for an hour with transitory blossom
Of snow, a bloom more sudden
Than that of summer, neither budding nor fading,
Not in the scheme of generation.
Where is the summer, the unimaginable
Zero summer?

If you came this way,
Taking the route you would be likely to take
From the place you would be likely to come from,
If you came this way in may time, you would find the hedges
White again, in May, with voluptuary sweetness.
It would be the same at the end of the journey,
If you came at night like a broken king,
If you came by day not knowing what you came for,
It would be the same, when you leave the rough road
And turn behind the pig-sty to the dull façade
And the tombstone. And what you thought you came for
Is only a shell, a husk of meaning

From which the purpose breaks only when it is fulfilled
If at all. Either you had no purpose
Or the purpose is beyond the end you figured
And is altered in fulfillment. There are other places
Which also are the world's end, some at the sea jaws,
Or over a dark lake, in a desert or a city—
But this is the nearest, in place and time,
Now and in England.

If you came this way,
Taking any route, starting from anywhere,
At any time or at any season,
It would always be the same: you would have to put off
Sense and notion. You are not here to verify,
Instruct yourself, or inform curiosity
Or carry report. You are here to kneel
Where prayer has been valid. And prayer is more
Than an order of words, the conscious occupation
Of the praying mind, or the sound of the voice praying.
And what the dead had no speech for, when living,
They can tell you, being dead: the communication
Of the dead is tongued with fire beyond the language of the
living.
Here, the intersection of the timeless moment
Is England and nowhere. Never and always.

II

Ash on an old man's sleeve
Is all the ash the burnt roses leave.
Dust in the air suspended
Marks the place where a story ended.
Dust inbreathed was a house—
The wall, the wainscot and the mouse.
The death of hope and despair,
        This is the death of air.

There are flood and drouth
Over the eyes and in the mouth,

Dead water and dead sand
Contending for the upper hand.
The parched eviscerate soil
Gapes at the vanity of toil,
Laughs without mirth.
    This is the death of earth.

Water and fire succeed
The town, the pasture and the weed.
Water and fire deride
The sacrifice that we denied.
Water and fire shall rot
The marred foundations we forgot,
Of sanctuary and choir.
    This is the death of water and fire.

In the uncertain hour before the morning
    Near the ending of interminable night
    At the recurrent end of the unending
After the dark dove with the flickering tongue
    Had passed below the horizon of his homing
    While the dead leaves still rattled on like tin
Over the asphalt where no other sound was
    Between three districts whence the smoke arose
    I met one walking, loitering and hurried
As if blown towards me like the metal leaves
    Before the urban dawn wind unresisting.
    And as I fixed upon the down-turned face
That pointed scrutiny with which we challenge
    The first-met stranger in the waning dusk
    I caught the sudden look of some dead master
Whom I had known, forgotten, half recalled
    Both one and many; in the brown baked features
    The eyes of a familiar compound ghost
Both intimate and unidentifiable.
    So I assumed a double part, and cried
    And heard another's voice cry: "What! are *you* here?"
Although we were not. I was still the same,

Knowing myself yet being someone other—
And he a face still forming; yet the words sufficed
To compel the recognition they preceded.
    And so, compliant to the common wind,
    Too strange to each other for misunderstanding,
In concord at this intersection time
    Of meeting nowhere, no before and after,
    We trod the pavement in a dead patrol.
I said: "The wonder that I feel is easy,
    Yet ease is cause of wonder. Therefore speak:
    I may not comprehend, may not remember."
And he: "I am not eager to rehearse
    My thought and theory which you have forgotten.
    These things have served their purpose: let them be.
So with your own, and pray they be forgiven
    By others, as I pray you to forgive
    Both bad and good. Last season's fruit is eaten
And the fullfed beast shall kick the empty pail.
    For last year's words belong to last year's language
    And next year's words await another voice.
But, as the passage now presents no hindrance
    To the spirit unappeased and peregrine
    Between two worlds become much like each other,
So I find words I never thought to speak
    In streets I never thought I should revisit
    When I left my body on a distant shore.
Since our concern was speech, and speech impelled us
    To purify the dialect of the tribe
    And urge the mind to aftersight and foresight,
Let me disclose the gifts reserved for age
    To set a crown upon your lifetime's effort.
    First, the cold friction of expiring sense
Without enchantment, offering no promise
    But bitter tastelessness of shadow fruit
    As body and soul begin to fall asunder.
Second, the conscious impotence of rage
    At human folly, and the laceration
    Of laughter at what ceases to amuse.

And last, the rending pain of re-enactment
  Of all that you have done, and been; the shame
  Of motives late revealed, and the awareness
Of things ill done and done to others' harm
  Which once you took for exercise of virtue.
  Then fools' approval stings, and honour stains.
From wrong to wrong the exasperated spirit
  Proceeds, unless restored by that refining fire
  Where you must move in measure, like a dancer."
The day was breaking. In the disfigured street
  He left me, with a kind of valediction,
  And faded on the blowing of the horn.

III

There are three conditions which often look alike
Yet differ completely, flourish in the same hedgerow:
Attachment to self and to things and to persons, detachment
From self and from things and from persons; and, growing
  between them, indifference
Which resembles the others as death resembles life,
Being between two lives—unflowering, between
The live and the dead nettle. This is the use of memory:
For liberation—not less of love but expanding
Of love beyond desire, and so liberation
From the future as well as the past. Thus, love of a country
Begins as attachment to our own field of action
And comes to find that action of little importance
Though never indifferent. History may be servitude,
History may be freedom. See, now they vanish,
The faces and places, with the self which, as it could, loved
  them,
To become renewed, transfigured, in another pattern.
Sin is Behovely, but
All shall be well, and
All manner of thing shall be well.
If I think, again, of this place,
And of people, not wholly commendable,
Of no immediate kin or kindness,

But some of peculiar genius,
All touched by a common genius,
United in the strife which divided them;
If I think of a king at nightfall,
Of three men, and more, on the scaffold
And a few who died forgotten
In other places, here and abroad,
And of one who died blind and quiet,
Why should we celebrate
These dead men more than the dying?
It is not to ring the bell backward
Nor is it an incantation
To summon the spectre of a Rose.
We cannot revive old factions
We cannot restore old policies
Or follow an antique drum.
These men, and those who opposed them
And those whom they opposed
Accept the constitution of silence
And are folded in a single party.
Whatever we inherit from the fortunate
We have taken from the defeated
What they had to leave us—a symbol:
A symbol perfected in death.
And all shall be well and
All manner of thing shall be well
By the purification of the motive
In the ground of our beseeching.

IV

The dove descending breaks the air
With flame of incandescent terror
Of which the tongues declare
The one discharge from sin and error.
The only hope, or else despair
    Lies in the choice of pyre or pyre—
    To be redeemed from fire by fire.

Who then devised the torment? Love.
Love is the unfamiliar Name
Behind the hands that wove
The intolerable shirt of flame
Which human power cannot remove.
  We only live, only suspire
  Consumed by either fire or fire.

V

What we call the beginning is often the end
And to make an end is to make a beginning.
The end is where we start from. And every phrase
And sentence that is right (where every word is at home,
Taking its place to support the others,
The word neither diffident nor ostentatious,
An easy commerce of the old and the new,
The common word exact without vulgarity,
The formal word precise but not pedantic,
The complete consort dancing together)
Every phrase and every sentence is an end and a beginning,
Every poem an epitaph. And any action
Is a step to the block, to the fire, down the sea's throat
Or to an illegible stone: and that is where we start.
We die with the dying:
See, they depart, and we go with them.
We are born with the dead:
See, they return, and bring us with them.
The moment of the rose and the moment of the yew-tree
Are of equal duration. A people without history
Is not redeemed from time, for history is a pattern
Of timeless moments. So, while the light fails
On a winter's afternoon, in a secluded chapel
History is now and England.

With the drawing of this Love and the voice of this Calling

We shall not cease from exploration
And the end of all our exploring

Will be to arrive where we started
And know the place for the first time.
Through the unknown, remembered gate
When the last of earth left to discover
Is that which was the beginning;
At the source of the longest river
The voice of the hidden waterfall
And the children in the apple-tree
Not known, because not looked for
But heard, half-heard, in the stillness
Between two waves of the sea.
Quick now, here, now, always—
A condition of complete simplicity
(Costing not less than everything)
And all shall be well and
All manner of thing shall be well
When the tongues of flame are in-folded
Into the crowned knot of fire
And the fire and the rose are one.

"Little Gidding" is the fourth of Four Quartets. *It summarizes not only the earlier quartets but also much else of Eliot's work as well as that of his friends ("See, they return" comes from a poem by Ezra Pound). The scope of the whole poem, from title page to last word, goes from "Four" to "one"—from multiplicity and perplexity to unity and repose.*

JOHN CROWE RANSOM 1888–1974

Ransom, a Tennessean educated at Vanderbilt and Ox-
ford, was closely associated with the Agrarians (editing
The Fugitive) and later the New Critics (editing *The
Kenyon Review*), but his tastes were catholic and his in-
terests not bound by regional or ideological prejudices.
As a poet, Ransom is honored almost exclusively for
poems issued in three small volumes between 1919 and
1927.

Bells for John Whiteside's Daughter

There was such speed in her little body,
And such lightness in her footfall,
It is no wonder her brown study
Astonishes us all.

Her wars were bruited in our high window.
We looked among orchard trees and beyond
Where she took arms against her shadow,
Or harried unto the pond

The lazy geese, like a snow cloud
Dripping their snow on the green grass,
Tricking and stopping, sleepy and proud,
Who cried in goose, Alas,

For the tireless heart within the little
Lady with rod that made them rise
From their noon apple-dreams and scuttle
Goose-fashion under the skies!

But now go the bells, and we are ready,
In one house we are sternly stopped
To say we are vexed at her brown study,
Lying so primly propped.

Ransom undermines the sentiment and the stanza (meter and rhyme) of Gray's "Elegy Written in a Country Churchyard" (p. 327) for a nicely mannered, modern ironic study of the immemorial challenge: how to write about a dead child (Ransom also wrote a poem called "Dead Boy"). See Jonson's "On My First Son" (p. 158) and Thomas's "A Refusal to Mourn the Death, by Fire, of a Child in London" (p. 1054).

Piazza Piece

❖❖❖❖

—I am a gentleman in a dustcoat trying
To make you hear. Your ears are soft and small
And listen to an old man not at all,
They want the young men's whispering and sighing.
But see the roses on your trellis dying
And hear the spectral singing of the moon;
For I must have my lovely lady soon,
I am a gentleman in a dustcoat trying.

—I am a lady young in beauty waiting
Until my truelove comes, and then we kiss.
But what grey man among the vines is this
Whose words are dry and faint as in a dream?
Back from my trellis, Sir, before I scream!
I am a lady young in beauty waiting.

Some say this poem is an exchange between Death and the Maiden. December and May seem to be likelier participants, or even a gentleman and a lady, going through the age-old rituals of courtship. The verse form is a unique adaptation of the Italian sonnet.

CLAUDE McKAY 1890–1948

McKay was born in Jamaica and came to the United
States in 1912, publishing his first volume, *Songs of Ja-
maica,* the same year; *Harlem Shadows* followed in 1922.
McKay also wrote hard-hitting novels about the Black
experience in Europe, the Caribbean, and the United
States. He also wrote the respected sociological study
Harlem: Negro Metropolis (1940).

If We Must Die

If we must die, let it not be like hogs
Hunted and penned in an inglorious spot,
While round us bark the mad and hungry dogs,
Making their mock at our accursèd lot.
If we must die, O let us nobly die,
So that our precious blood may not be shed
In vain; then even the monsters we defy
Shall be constrained to honor us though dead!
O kinsmen! we must meet the common foe!
Though far outnumbered let us show us brave,
And for their thousand blows deal one deathblow!
What though before us lies the open grave?
Like men we'll face the murderous, cowardly pack,
Pressed to the wall, dying, but fighting back!

*Although he is chiefly remembered for his prose writings, McKay could work just
as effectively in verse. In technique, this sonnet ignores all modernist innovations
and goes back to Shakespeare and Milton ("what though" comes straight from
Paradise Lost). This poem so successfully transcends its origins (in a Harlem
race riot of 1919) that it became a rallying cry for the British as well as the
Americans in the Second World War.*

ISAAC ROSENBERG 1890–1918

A poor urban Jew, Rosenberg attended the Slade
School of Art and published two volumes of strong
verse in 1912 and 1915, before going off to the war in
which he was killed.

Break of Day in the Trenches

>>>>>>>

The darkness crumbles away—
It is the same old druid Time as ever.
Only a live thing leaps my hand—
A queer sardonic rat—
As I pull the parapet's poppy
To stick behind my ear.
Droll rat, they would shoot you if they knew
Your cosmopolitan sympathies.
Now you have touched this English hand
You will do the same to a German—
Soon, no doubt, if it be your pleasure
To cross the sleeping green between.
It seems you inwardly grin as you pass
Strong eyes, fine limbs, haughty athletes
Less chanced than you for life,
Bonds to the whims of murder,
Sprawled in the bowels of the earth,
The torn fields of France.
What do you see in our eyes
At the shrieking iron and flame
Hurled through still heavens?
What quaver—what heart aghast?
Poppies whose roots are in man's veins
Drop, and are ever dropping;
But mine in my ear is safe,
Just a little white with the dust.

Through the end of the first World War, it is probable that most war literature was produced by officers. Rosenberg, however, was a common enlisted footsoldier. Much of the worst fighting of the war was in the trenches. It was there that Rosenberg spent eighteen months, and there that he died.

MacLeish spent his early career in the company of modernist expatriates and bohemians but repatriated himself during the Depression and turned his attention to problems of history and politics. His powerful *Conquistador* used the conquest of Mexico as material for an epic. He held higher appointive positions in government than any other modern American poet in this anthology, serving as Librarian of Congress for five years and briefly as Assistant Secretary of State from 1944 to 1945.

You, Andrew Marvell

And here face down beneath the sun
And here upon earth's noonward height
To feel the always coming on
The always rising of the night

To feel creep up the curving east
The earthy chill of dusk and slow
Upon those under lands the vast
And ever-climbing shadow grow

And strange at Ecbatan the trees
Take leaf by leaf the evening strange
The flooding dark about their knees
The mountains over Persia change

And now at Kermanshah the gate
Dark empty and the withered grass
And through the twilight now the late
Few travelers in the westward pass

And Baghdad darken and the bridge
Across the silent river gone
And through Arabia the edge
Of evening widen and steal on

And deepen on Palmyra's street
The wheel rut in the ruined stone
And Lebanon fade out and Crete
High through the clouds and overblown

And over Sicily the air
Still flashing with the landward gulls
And loom and slowly disappear
The sails above the shadowy hulls

And Spain go under and the shore
Of Africa the gilded sand
And evening vanish and no more
The low pale light across that land

Nor now the long light on the sea —
And here face downward in the sun
To feel how swift how secretly
The shadow of the night comes on . . .

MacLeish furnishes a commentary, much indebted to a globe or atlas, on the lines "But at my back I always hear / Time's wingèd chariot hurrying near," from Marvell's "To His Coy Mistress" (p. 229).

Ars Poetica

A poem should be palpable and mute
As a globed fruit,

Dumb
As old medallions to the thumb,

Silent as the sleeve-worn stone
Of casement ledges where the moss has grown—

A poem should be wordless
As the flight of birds.

A poem should be motionless in time
As the moon climbs,

Leaving, as the moon releases
Twig by twig the night-entangled trees,

Leaving, as the moon behind the winter leaves,
Memory by memory the mind—

A poem should be motionless in time
As the moon climbs.

A poem should be equal to:
Not true.

For all the history of grief
An empty doorway and a maple leaf.

For love
The leaning grasses and two lights above the sea—

A poem should not mean
But be.

Horace's verse epistle on the art of poetry is sometimes given the title Ars
Poetica *or* De Arte Poetica. *MacLeish appropriates the title for a critical poem
that is not very Horatian or even Roman but more in the style of what is called
the New Criticism—a study of literary works on their own terms, not so much
something you say as something you make.*

The End of the World

Quite unexpectedly as Vasserot
The armless ambidextrian was lighting
A match between his great and second toe,
And Ralph the lion was engaged in biting
The neck of Madame Sossman while the drum
Pointed, and Teeny was about to cough
In waltz-time swinging Jocko by the thumb—
Quite unexpectedly the top blew off:

And there, there overhead, there, there hung over
Those thousands of white faces, those dazed eyes,
There in the starless dark the poise, the hover,
There with vast wings across the canceled skies,
There in the sudden blackness the black pall
Of nothing, nothing, nothing—nothing at all.

Strangely, MacLeish combines light verse, apocalypse, and the familiar format of the sonnet.

WILFRED OWEN 1893–1918

Owen was killed right at the end of the First World
War. He was only twenty-five, but he had had time to
produce an impressive variety of poems, most of them
dealing with war. He was also a notable technical in-
novator, especially in rhyming. He was born in Shrop-
shire and educated at London University.

Anthem for Doomed Youth

What passing-bells for these who die as cattle?
  —Only the monstrous anger of the guns.
  Only the stuttering rifles' rapid rattle
Can patter out their hasty orisons.
No mockeries now for them; no prayers nor bells,
  Nor any voice of mourning save the choirs,—
The shrill, demented choirs of wailing shells;
  And bugles calling for them from sad shires.

What candles may be held to speed them all?
  Not in the hands of boys but in their eyes
Shall shine the holy glimmers of goodbyes.
  The pallor of girls' brows shall be their pall;
Their flowers the tenderness of patient minds,
And each slow dusk a drawing-down of blinds.

Paul Fussell's The Great War and Modern Memory *shows that the First
World War came as a distinct and horrible shock to a Europe that had been
relatively at peace for a hundred years. The new technology produced weapons of
unexampled ferocity and efficiency, and the utter horror of warfare could no
longer be ignored or camouflaged as patriotic glory.*

Dulce et Decorum Est

Bent double, like old beggars under sacks,
Knock-kneed, coughing like hags, we cursed through sludge,
Till on the haunting flares we turned our backs
And towards our distant rest began to trudge.
Men marched asleep. Many had lost their boots
But limped on, blood-shod. All went lame; all blind;
Drunk with fatigue; deaf even to the hoots
Of tired, outstripped Five-Nines that dropped behind.

Gas! Gas! Quick, boys! — An ecstasy of fumbling,
Fitting the clumsy helmets just in time;
But someone still was yelling out and stumbling
And flound'ring like a man in fire or lime . . .
Dim, through the misty panes and thick green light,
As under a green sea, I saw him drowning.
In all my dreams, before my helpless sight,
He plunges at me, guttering, choking, drowning.

If in some smothering dreams you too could pace
Behind the wagon that we flung him in,
And watch the white eyes writhing in his face,
His hanging face, like a devil's sick of sin;
If you could hear, at every jolt, the blood
Come gargling from the froth-corrupted lungs,
Obscene as cancer, bitter as the cud
Of vile, incurable sores on innocent tongues, —
My friend, you would not tell with such high zest
To children ardent for some desperate glory,
The old Lie: Dulce et decorum est
Pro patria mori.

As with his "Greater Love" (p. 1010), Owen gives the lie to a conviction from a scriptural or, as here, classical source (Horace's Ode III.2). Ezra Pound, writing at about the same time as Owen, mocked the same Horatian text in "Hugh Selwyn Mauberley."

Strange Meeting

It seemed that out of battle I escaped
Down some profound dull tunnel, long since scooped
Through granites which titanic wars had groined.
Yet also there encumbered sleepers groaned,
Too fast in thought or death to be bestirred.
Then, as I probed them, one sprang up, and stared
With piteous recognition in fixed eyes,
Lifting distressful hands as if to bless.
And by his smile, I knew that sullen hall,
By his dead smile I knew we stood in Hell.
With a thousand pains that vision's face was grained;
Yet no blood reached there from the upper ground,
And no guns thumped, or down the flues made moan.
"Strange friend," I said, "here is no cause to mourn."
"None," said that other, "save the undone years,
The hopelessness. Whatever hope is yours,
Was my life also; I went hunting wild
After the wildest beauty in the world,
Which lies not calm in eyes, or braided hair,
But mocks the steady running of the hour,
And if it grieves, grieves richlier than here.
For of my glee might many men have laughed,
And of my weeping something had been left,
Which must die now. I mean the truth untold,
The pity of war, the pity war distilled.
Now men will go content with what we spoiled,
Or, discontent, boil bloody, and be spilled.
They will be swift with swiftness of the tigress.
None will break ranks, though nations trek from progress.
Courage was mine, and I had mystery,
Wisdom was mine, and I had mastery:
To miss the march of this retreating world
Into vain citadels that are not walled.
Then, when much blood had clogged their chariot-wheels,

I would go up and wash them from sweet wells,
Even with truths that lie too deep for taint.
I would have poured my spirit without stint
But not through wounds; not on the cess of war.
Foreheads of men have bled where no wounds were.
I am the enemy you killed, my friend.
I knew you in this dark: for so you frowned
Yesterday through me as you jabbed and killed.
I parried; but my hands were loath and cold.
Let us sleep now. . . ."

The strangeness of this nightmare poem is made even stranger by a most peculiar technical device: line endings linked not by conventional rhyme but mostly by syllables that both begin and end with the same consonants but embrace different vowels (as in "hall" and "Hell"), creating a weird dissonance.

Greater Love

❖❖❖❖

Red lips are not so red
  As the stained stones kissed by the English dead.
Kindness of wooed and wooer
Seems shame to their love pure.
O Love, your eyes lose lure
  When I behold eyes blinded in my stead!

Your slender attitude
  Trembles not exquisite like limbs knife-skewed,
Rolling and rolling there
Where God seems not to care;
Till the fierce love they bear
  Cramps them in death's extreme decrepitude.

Your voice sings not so soft, —
  Though even as wind murmuring through raftered loft, —
Your dear voice is not dear,
Gentle, and evening clear,
As theirs whom none now hear,
  Now earth has stopped their piteous mouths that coughed.

Heart, you were never hot
  Nor large, nor full like hearts made great with shot;
And though your hand be pale,
Paler are all which trail
Your cross through flame and hail:
  Weep, you may weep, for you may touch them not.

Jesus said, "Greater love hath no man than this, that a man lay down his life for his friends" (John XV:13). The anatomical inventory is somewhat like the catalogue in Hopkins's "Habit of Perfection" (p. 800) but with bitter ironies.

The son of a clergyman, E. E. Cummings received two
degrees from Harvard before going off to serve as an
ambulance driver in the First World War. He wrote
plays and nonfiction prose, and he was a notable
graphic artist as well, but he will be remembered most
fondly as a versatile and original poet rather in the style
of Donne or Byron—capable, that is, of passionate love
poems and caustic satires.

anyone lived in a pretty how town

❀❀❀

anyone lived in a pretty how town
(with up so floating many bells down)
spring summer autumn winter
he sang his didn't he danced his did.

Women and men (both little and small)
cared for anyone not at all
they sowed their isn't they reaped their same
sun moon stars rain

children guessed(but only a few
and down they forgot as up they grew
autumn winter spring summer)
that noone loved him more by more

when by now and tree by leaf
she laughed his joy she cried his grief
bird by snow and stir by still
anyone's any was all to her

someones married their everyones
laughed their cryings and did their dance
(sleep wake hope and then)they
said their nevers they slept their dream

stars rain sun moon
(and only the snow can begin to explain
how children are apt to forget to remember
with up so floating many bells down)

one day anyone died i guess
(and noone stooped to kiss his face)
busy folk buried them side by side
little by little and was by was

all by all and deep by deep
and more by more they dream their sleep
noone and anyone earth by april
wish by spirit and if by yes.

Women and men(both dong and ding)
summer autumn winter spring
reaped their sowing and went their came
sun moon stars rain

---

*Cummings takes traditional themes of Everyman and Utopia ("Noplace"), tra-
ditional tetrameter couplets such as those used by Marvell and Blake, and a
modernist freedom of language, converting indefinite pronouns into three-
dimensional human characters.*

next to of course god america i

>>>>>>>

"next to of course god america i
love you land of the pilgrims' and so forth oh
say can you see by the dawn's early my
country 'tis of centuries come and go
and are no more what of it we should worry
in every language even deafanddumb
thy sons acclaim your glorious name by gorry
by jingo by gee by gosh by gum
why talk of beauty what could be more beaut-
iful than these heroic happy dead
who rushed like lions to the roaring slaughter
they did not stop to think they died instead
then shall the voice of liberty be mute?"

He spoke. And drank rapidly a glass of water

In this tour de force, Cummings welds political rhetoric and the structural music of the sonnet. Cummings was one of the great poets of satire, mockery, and caricature, and at the same time—and often in the same poem, as here—one of the great sonneteers.

HART CRANE 1899–1932

In a tragically short and sad life, Hart Crane became one of America's most ambitious and most eloquent poets, amalgamating traditions from Marlowe, Shelley, Baudelaire, Poe, Whitman, and Dickinson. Crane's father was a candy manufacturer (responsible for the original Life Savers, among other products) whose marriage to a complex and somewhat cultivated woman was turbulent and finally dissolved. Crane was tormented most of his life by difficulties with alcohol, with both parents, with friends, with lovers—male and female—and with his own craft. Through all the troubles, however, Crane sought to perfect his great gifts of vision and expression. It was on a return journey from Mexico that he jumped from a ship, probably a suicide.

To Brooklyn Bridge

How many dawns, chill from his rippling rest
The seagull's wings shall dip and pivot him,
Shedding white rings of tumult, building high
Over the chained bay waters Liberty—

Then, with inviolate curve, forsake our eyes
As apparitional as sails that cross
Some page of figures to be filed away;
—Till elevators drop us from our day . . .

I think of cinemas, panoramic sleights
With multitudes bent toward some flashing scene
Never disclosed, but hastened to again,
Foretold to other eyes on the same screen;

And Thee, across the harbor, silver-paced
As though the sun took step of thee, yet left
Some motion ever unspent in thy stride,—
Implicitly thy freedom staying thee!

Out of some subway scuttle, cell or loft
A bedlamite speeds to thy parapets,
Tilting there momently, shrill shirt ballooning,
A jest falls from the speechless caravan.

Down Wall, from girder into street noon leaks,
A rip-tooth of the sky's acetylene;
All afternoon the cloud-flown derricks turn . . .
Thy cables breathe the North Atlantic still.

And obscure as that heaven of the Jews,
Thy guerdon . . . Accolade thou dost bestow
Of anonymity time cannot raise:
Vibrant reprieve and pardon thou dost show.

O harp and altar, of the fury fused,
(How could mere toil align thy choiring strings!)
Terrific threshold of the prophet's pledge,
Prayer of pariah, and the lover's cry,—

Again the traffic lights that skim thy swift
Unfractioned idiom, immaculate sigh of stars,
Beading thy path—condense eternity:
And we have seen night lifted in thine arms.

Under thy shadow by the piers I waited;
Only in darkness is thy shadow clear.
The City's fiery parcels all undone,
Already snow submerges an iron year . . .

O Sleepless as the river under thee,
Vaulting the sea, the prairies' dreaming sod,
Unto us lowliest sometime sweep, descend
And of the curveship lend a myth to God.

from The Bridge

T. S. Eliot's "Waste Land" (p. 968), when it was published in 1922, provoked a number of responses, none stronger than Crane's prodigiously eloquent "The Bridge" (1930), which countered the myth of Waste with its own myth: the Bridge. Crane never quite achieved his impossible ambition in his own terrific voice, but it is to his everlasting credit that he conceived that ambition in the first place. (Note that: "guerdon" is "reward.")

ALLEN TATE 1899–1979

Like John Crowe Ransom, Allen Tate was a Tennessean associated with Vanderbilt University and the magazine called *The Fugitive.* He wrote studies of Confederate leaders "Stonewall" Jackson and Jefferson Davis, and he established a solid reputation as a discerning critic, intuitive but passionate. He was uncommonly sensitive to the genius of Poe and Dickinson, and he was personally close to Ransom, Hart Crane, and Robert Lowell.

Ode to the Confederate Dead

Row after row with strict impunity
The headstones yield their names to the element,
The wind whirrs without recollection;
In the riven troughs the splayed leaves
Pile up, of nature the casual sacrament
To the seasonal eternity of death;
Then driven by the fierce scrutiny
Of heaven to their election in the vast breath,
They sough the rumor of mortality.

Autumn is desolation in the plot
Of a thousand acres where these memories grow
From the inexhaustible bodies that are not
Dead, but feed the grass row after rich row.
Think of the autumns that have come and gone! —
Ambitious November with the humors of the year,
With a particular zeal for every slab,
Staining the uncomfortable angels that rot
On the slabs, a wing chipped here, an arm there:
The brute curiosity of an angel's stare
Turns you, like them, to stone,
Transforms the heaving air
Till plunged to a heavier world below

You shift your sea-space blindly
Heaving, turning like the blind crab.

   Dazed by the wind, only the wind
   The leaves flying, plunge

You know who have waited by the wall
The twilight certainty of an animal,
Those midnight restitutions of the blood
You know—the immitigable pines, the smoky frieze
Of the sky, the sudden call: you know the rage,
The cold pool left by the mounting flood,
Of muted Zeno and Parmenides.
You who have waited for the angry resolution
Of those desires that should be yours tomorrow,
You know the unimportant shrift of death
And praise the vision
And praise the arrogant circumstance
Of those who fall
Rank upon rank, hurried beyond decision—
Here by the sagging gate, stopped by the wall.

   Seeing, seeing only the leaves
   Flying, plunge and expire

Turn your eyes to the immoderate past,
Turn to the inscrutable infantry rising
Demons out of the earth—they will not last.
Stonewall, Stonewall, and the sunken fields of hemp,
Shiloh, Antietam, Malvern Hill, Bull Run.
Lost in that orient of the thick-and-fast
You will curse the setting sun.

   Cursing only the leaves crying
   Like an old man in a storm

You hear the shout, the crazy hemlocks point
With troubled fingers to the silence which
Smothers you, a mummy, in time.

        The hound bitch
Toothless and dying, in a musty cellar
Hears the wind only.

        Now that the salt of their blood
Stiffens the saltier oblivion of the sea,
Seals the malignant purity of the flood,
What shall we who count our days and bow
Our heads with a commemorial woe
In the ribboned coats of grim felicity,
What shall we say of the bones, unclean,
Whose verdurous anonymity will grow?
The ragged arms, the ragged heads and eyes
Lost in these acres of the insane green?
The gray lean spiders come, they come and go;
In a tangle of willows without light
The singular screech-owl's tight
Invisible lyric seeds the mind
With the furious murmur of their chivalry.

We shall say only the leaves
Flying, plunge and expire
We shall say only the leaves whispering
In the improbable mist of nightfall
That flies on multiple wing;
Night is the beginning and the end
And in between the ends of distraction
Waits mute speculation, the patient curse
That stones the eyes, or like the jaguar leaps
For his own image in a jungle pool, his victim.

What shall we say who have knowledge
Carried to the heart? Shall we take the act
To the grave? Shall we, more hopeful, set up the grave
In the house? The ravenous grave?

                    Leave now
The shut gate and the decomposing wall:
The gentle serpent, green in the mulberry bush,
Riots with his tongue through the hush—
Sentinel of the grave who counts us all!

---

*For people from the southern United States, at least, the Civil War remains the
great defining event. In some ways, as Mark Twain suggested, the war called
chivalry's bluff (not entirely in jest, Mark Twain blamed the war on Sir Walter
Scott). Southern writers still feel called on to address the Confederate dead, and
courthouse lawns across eleven states have monuments to those who died between
1861 and 1865.*

LANGSTON HUGHES 1902–1967

Hughes, one of the greatest and most versatile of African-American writers, was born in Missouri and wandered over much of the United States and Europe. He wrote many plays and novels but remains best known for more than a dozen volumes of poetry published in the forty years before his death in 1967. Hughes was a leader of the Harlem Renaissance in the 1920s.

The Negro Speaks of Rivers

I've known rivers:
I've known rivers ancient as the world and older than the flow
    of human blood in human veins.

My soul has grown deep like the rivers.

I bathed in the Euphrates when dawns were young.
I built my hut near the Congo and it lulled me to sleep.

I looked upon the Nile and raised the pyramids above it.
I heard the singing of the Mississippi when Abe Lincoln went
    down to New Orleans, and I've seen its muddy bosom turn
    all golden in the sunset.

I've known rivers:
Ancient, dusky rivers.

My soul has grown deep like the rivers.

Hughes's poem appeared in 1926; fifteen years later, T. S. Eliot's "Dry Salvages" (the third of Four Quartets) *was to make much the same claim about rivers.*

STEVIE SMITH 1902–1971

Glenda Jackson has given a memorable portrayal of the poet in a movie called *Stevie*. (The poet was formally named Florence Margaret Smith but preferred to use her family nickname.) She could write fiction and draw pictures, but she will be remembered as a poet of prodigious personal character, wisdom, and humor.

Not Waving But Drowning

Nobody heard him, the dead man,
But still he lay moaning:
I was much further out than you thought
And not waving but drowning.

Poor chap, he always loved larking
And now he's dead
It must have been too cold for him his heart gave way,
They said.

Oh, no no no, it was too cold always
(Still the dead one lay moaning)
I was much too far out all my life
And not waving but drowning.

Stevie Smith based her poem on the report of an actual episode. This prismatic poem has become an emblem of the ironies and absurdities of postmodern life, when appearance and reality have grown grotesquely far apart.

RICHARD EBERHART b.1904

A native Minnesotan, Eberhart was educated at Dartmouth and Cambridge. He began publishing poetry in 1930 and kept up a steady output afterwards. In 1956 he returned to Dartmouth.

The Fury of Aerial Bombardment

()◀▶()

You would think the fury of aerial bombardment
Would rouse God to relent; the infinite spaces
Are still silent. He looks on shock-pried faces.
History, even, does not know what is meant.

You would feel that after so many centuries
God would give man to repent; yet he can kill
As Cain could, but with multitudinous will,
No farther advanced than in his ancient furies.

Was man made stupid to see his own stupidity?
Is God by definition indifferent, beyond us all?
Is the eternal truth man's fighting soul
Wherein the Beast ravens in its own avidity?

Of Van Wettering I speak, and Averill,
Names on a list, whose faces I do not recall
But they are gone to early death, who late in school
Distinguished the belt feed lever from the belt holding pawl.

The airplane, a peculiarly twentieth-century development, was adapted to warfare within ten years of its invention. The combination of modern machinery and ancient myth (particularly that of Icarus) has been compelling, as is shown by Yeats's "Irish Airman Foresees His Death" (p. 863) and Jarrell's "Death of the Ball Turret Gunner" (p. 1047). The new vocabulary exploited by Eberhart also appears in Reed's "Naming of Parts" (p. 1048).

The Groundhog

In June, amid the golden fields,
I saw a groundhog lying dead.
Dead lay he; my senses shook,
And mind outshot our naked frailty.
There lowly in the vigorous summer
His form began its senseless change,
And made my senses waver dim
Seeing nature ferocious in him.
Inspecting close his maggot's might
And seething cauldron of his being,
Half with loathing, half with a strange love,
I poked him with an angry stick.
The fever arose, became a frame
And Vigor circumscribed the skies,
Immense energy in the sun,
And through my frame a sunless trembling.
My stick had done nor good nor harm.
Then stood I silent in the day
Watching the object, as before;
And kept my reverence for knowledge
Trying for control, to be still,
To quell the passion of the blood;
Until I had bent down on my knees
Praying for joy in the sight of decay.
And so I left; and I returned
In Autumn strict of eye, to see
The sap gone out of the groundhog,
But the bony sodden hulk remained.
But the year had lost its meaning,
And in intellectual chains
I lost both love and loathing,
Mured up in the wall of wisdom.
Another summer took the fields again
Massive and burning, full of life,

But when I chanced upon the spot
There was only a little hair left,
And bones bleaching in the sunlight
Beautiful as architecture;
I watched them like a geometer,
And cut a walking stick from a birch.
It has been three years, now.
There is no sign of the groundhog.
I stood there in the whirling summer,
My hand capped a withered heart,
And thought of China and of Greece,
Of Alexander in his tent;
Of Montaigne in his tower,
Of Saint Theresa in her wild lament.

Twentieth-century poets have specialized in making capacious symbols out of humble creatures (see "The Fish," by Elizabeth Bishop, p. 1043, and Robert Lowell's "Skunk Hour," p. 1058). The real mortal fate of the physical body of an unlovely actual creature permits both a close observation of nature and a well-buttressed ascent into the grandeur of conquerors, thinkers, and saints.

WYSTAN HUGH AUDEN 1907–1973

Although W. H. Auden was born in England and died there, he spent about thirty of his productive years in the United States, from 1939 onwards. A chameleon of styles and tones, he probably commanded a greater range of forms than any other twentieth-century poet.

Musée des Beaux Arts

About suffering they were never wrong,
The Old Masters: how well they understood
Its human position; how it takes place
While someone else is eating or opening a window or just
    walking dully along;
How, when the aged are reverently, passionately waiting
For the miraculous birth, there always must be
Children who did not specially want it to happen, skating
On a pond at the edge of the wood:
They never forgot
That even the dreadful martyrdom must run its course
Anyhow in a corner, some untidy spot
Where the dogs go on with their doggy life and the torturer's
    horse
Scratches its innocent behind on a tree.

In Brueghel's *Icarus*, for instance: how everything turns away
Quite leisurely from the disaster; the plowman may
Have heard the splash, the forsaken cry,
But for him it was not an important failure; the sun shone
As it had to on the white legs disappearing into the green
Water; and the expensive delicate ship that must have seen
Something amazing, a boy falling out of the sky,
Had somewhere to get to and sailed calmly on.

Someone suffering, perhaps from a painful experience, seeks consolation in a foreign art museum and discovers a highly conditional truth about suffering. Brueghel's Landscape with the Fall of Icarus *is also the subject of a poem by William Carlos Williams.*

In Memory of W. B. Yeats

I

He disappeared in the dead of winter
The brooks were frozen, the airports almost deserted,
And snow disfigured the public statues;
The mercury sank in the month of the dying day.
What instruments we have agree
The day of his death was a dark cold day.

Far from his illness
The wolves ran on through the evergreen forests,
The peasant river was untempted by the fashionable quays;
By mourning tongues
The death of the poet was kept from his poems.

But for him it was his last afternoon as himself,
An afternoon of nurses and rumours;
The provinces of his body revolted,
The squares of his mind were empty,
Silence invaded the suburbs,
The current of his feeling failed; he became his admirers.

Now he is scattered among a hundred cities
And wholly given over to unfamiliar affections,
To find his happiness in another kind of wood
And be punished under a foreign code of conscience.
The words of a dead man
Are modified in the guts of the living.

But in the importance of noise of to-morrow
When the brokers are roaring like beasts on the floor of the
    Bourse,
And the poor have the sufferings to which they are fairly
    accustomed,
And each in the cell of himself is almost convinced of his
    freedom,
A few thousand will think of this day
As one thinks of a day when one did something slightly unusual.
What instruments we have agree
The day of his death was a dark cold day.

II

You were silly like us; your gift survived it all:
The parish of rich women, physical decay,
Yourself. Mad Ireland hurt you into poetry.
Now Ireland has her madness and her weather still,
For poetry makes nothing happen: it survives
In the valley of its making where executives
Would never want to tamper, flows on south
From ranches of isolation and the busy griefs,
Raw towns that we believe and die in; it survives,
A way of happening, a mouth.

III

Earth, receive an honoured guest:
William Yeats is laid to rest.
Let the Irish vessel lie
Emptied of its poetry.

In the nightmare of the dark
All the dogs of Europe bark,
And the living nations wait,
Each sequestered in its hate;

Intellectual disgrace
Stares from every human face,
And the seas of pity lie
Locked and frozen in each eye.

Follow, poet, follow right
To the bottom of the night,
With your unconstraining voice
Still persuade us to rejoice;

With the farming of a verse
Make a vineyard of the curse,
Sing of human unsuccess
In a rapture of distress;

In the deserts of the heart
Let the healing fountain start,
In the prison of his days
Teach the free man how to praise.

Auden brings the pastoral elegy up to date. In Milton's "Lycidas" (p. 203) and Shelley's "Adonais" (p. 509), one poet mourns another by putting on the garb of a Greek shepherd, inherited from Theocritus, Bion, and Moschus. Auden puts airports in the place of sheepfolds, but he keeps one feature of some pastoral elegies: the honoring of the style of the dead. Just as "Adonais" is a Keatsian poem, using the rich Spenserian stanzas of Keats's "Eve of St. Agnes" (p. 551), Auden produces a Yeatsian poem, particularly in the third section here, which is modeled on Yeats's "Under Ben Bulben."

Lullaby

Lay your sleeping head, my love,
Human on my faithless arm;
Time and fevers burn away
Individual beauty from
Thoughtful children, and the grave
Proves the child ephemeral:
But in my arms till break of day
Let the living creature lie,
Mortal, guilty, but to me
The entirely beautiful.

Soul and body have no bounds:
To lovers as they lie upon
Her tolerant enchanted slope
In their ordinary swoon,
Grave the vision Venus sends
Of supernatural sympathy,
Universal love and hope;
While an abstract insight wakes
Among the glaciers and the rocks
The hermit's carnal ecstasy.

Certainty, fidelity
On the stroke of midnight pass
Like vibrations of a bell,
And fashionable madmen raise
Their pedantic boring cry:
Every farthing of the cost,
All the dreaded cards foretell,
Shall be paid, but from this night
Not a whisper, not a thought,
Not a kiss nor look be lost.

Beauty, midnight, vision dies:
Let the winds of dawn that blow
Softly round your dreaming head
Such a day of sweetness show
Eye and knocking heart may bless,
Find the mortal world enough;
Noons of dryness see you fed
By the involuntary powers,
Nights of insult let you pass
Watched by every human love.

Compared with the early seventeenth and early nineteenth centuries, the modern age seems deficient in the production of love poems, unless you want to count popular songs. Auden's "Lullaby" is a magnificent exception.

LOUIS MACNEICE 1907–1963

MacNeice, an Ulsterman, was educated at Merton College, Oxford. His poetry is experimental, passionate, varied, and nostalgic for a lost past. Like Archibald MacLeish, he was an accomplished writer for radio at a time (c.1935–1955) when that medium flourished.

Bagpipe Music

It's no go the merry-go-round, it's no go the rickshaw,
All we want is a limousine and a ticket for the peepshow.
Their knickers are made of crêpe-de-chine, their shoes are
    made of python.
Their halls are lined with tiger rugs and their walls with
    heads of bison.

John MacDonald found a corpse, put it under the sofa,
Waited till it came to life and hit it with a poker,
Sold its eyes for souvenirs, sold its blood for whiskey,
Kept its bones for dumb-bells to use when he was fifty.

It's no go the Yogi-Man, it's no go Blavatsky,
All we want is a bank balance and a bit of skirt in a taxi.

Annie MacDougall went to milk, caught her foot in the
    heather,
Woke to hear a dance record playing of Old Vienna.
It's no go your maidenheads, it's no go your culture,
All we want is a Dunlop tyre and the devil mend the
    puncture.
The laird o'Phelps spent Hogmannay declaring he was sober;
Counted his feet to prove the fact and found he had one foot
    over.
Mrs. Carmichael had her fifth, looked at the job with
    repulsion,

Said to the midwife "Take it away; I'm through with
    overproduction."
It's no go the gossip column, it's no go the Ceilidh,
All we want is a mother's help and a sugar-stick for the baby.

Willie Murray cut his thumb, couldn't count the damage,
Took the hide of an Ayrshire cow and used it for a bandage.
His brother caught three hundred cran when the seas were
    lavish,
Threw the bleeders back in the sea and went upon the parish.

It's no go the Herring Board, it's no go the Bible,
All we want is a packet of fags when our hands are idle.

It's no go the picture palace, it's no go the stadium,
It's no go the country cot with a pot of pink geraniums.
It's no go the Government grants, it's no go the elections,
Sit on your arse for fifty years and hang your hat on pension.

It's no go my honey love, it's no go my poppet;
Work your hands from day to day, the winds will blow the
    profit.
The glass is falling hour by hour, the glass will fall forever,
But if you break the bloody glass you won't hold up the
    weather.

---

*MacNeice seems to be foreseeing the humor of "The Goon Show" and Monty
Python. Since MacNeice was born in Belfast, it may help to keep in mind that
the bagpipe is associated with Ireland as well as with Scotland. (Note that:
"knickers" is "underpants"; "Hogmanay" is "New Year's Eve"; "Ceilidh"—
rhymes with "gaily"—is an evening celebration with singing and drinking;
"cran" is a measure of herring; "upon the parish" is "on the dole"; "cot" is
"cottage.")*

THEODORE ROETHKE 1908–1963

Roethke was born in Michigan and spent much of his mature life in the Northwest, teaching at the University of Washington. In much of his poetry, it is difficult to avoid the vegetable kingdom, from weeds to roses, from germination to fermentation; he came from a long line of foresters and nurserymen. Roethke may have taken fewer chances than his immediate forebears—fewer, even, that the more remote Hardy and Yeats—but he was a vigorous, witty, and faithful inheritor and conservator of a great tradition.

My Papa's Waltz

The whiskey on your breath
Could make a small boy dizzy;
But I hung on like death:
Such waltzing was not easy.

We romped until the pans
Slid from the kitchen shelf;
My mother's countenance
Could not unfrown itself.

The hand that held my wrist
Was battered on one knuckle;
At every step you missed
My right ear scraped a buckle.

You beat time on my head
With a palm caked hard by dirt,
Then waltzed me off to bed
Still clinging to your shirt.

Roethke, Kenneth Rexroth, and others growing up during Prohibition had a love-hate relationship with alcoholism—parental and personal. John Frederick Nims points out that the waltz (in three-quarter time) is rendered here in lines of three stresses.

I Knew a Woman

I knew a woman, lovely in her bones,
When small birds sighed, she would sigh back at them;
Ah, when she moved, she moved more ways than one:
The shapes a bright container can contain!
Of her choice virtues only gods should speak,
Or English poets who grew up on Greek
(I'd have them sing in chorus, cheek to cheek).

How well her wishes went! She stroked my chin,
She taught me Turn, and Counter-turn, and Stand;
She taught me Touch, that undulant white skin;
I nibbled meekly from her proffered hand;
She was the sickle; I, poor I, the rake,
Coming behind her for her pretty sake
(But what prodigious mowing we did make).

Love likes a gander, and adores a goose:
Her full lips pursed, the errant note to seize;
She played it quick, she played it light and loose;
My eyes, they dazzled at her flowing knees;
Her several parts could keep a pure repose,
Or one hip quiver with a mobile nose
(She moved in circles, and those circles moved).

Let seed be grass, and grass turn into hay:
I'm martyr to a motion not my own;
What's freedom for? To know eternity.
I swear she cast a shadow white as stone.
But who would count eternity in days?
These old bones live to learn her wanton ways:
(I measure time by how a body sways).

It is possible that Roethke, unconsciously or deliberately, is preserving Louise Bogan's initials in the phrase "lovely in her bones." At any rate, he and she were lovers. She, about ten years his senior, could have taught him a thing or two about poetry: "Turn, and Counter-turn, and Stand" are at once erotic and poetic (translating Strophe, and Antistrophe, and Epode).

The Waking

I wake to sleep, and take my waking slow.
I feel my fate in what I cannot fear.
I learn by going where I have to go.

We think by feeling. What is there to know?
I hear my being dance from ear to ear.
I wake to sleep, and take my waking slow.

Of those so close beside me, which are you?
God bless the Ground! I shall walk softly there,
And learn by going where I have to go.

Light takes the Tree; but who can tell us how?
The lowly worm climbs up a winding stair;
I wake to sleep, and take my waking slow.

Great Nature has another thing to do
To you and me; so take the lively air,
And, lovely, learn by going where to go.

This shaking keeps me steady. I should know.
What falls away is always. And is near.
I wake to sleep, and take my waking slow.
I learn by going where I have to go.

The complex villanelle form was used infrequently during the nineteenth century, but it was not until William Empson set a contemporary example during the 1930s that poets learned how to adapt the form to peculiarly modern needs. Here, as in Dylan Thomas's "Do Not Go Gentle into That Good Night" (p. 1050), the poet exploits the elementary energy of the patterned recurrence.

Elegy for Jane

(My student, thrown by a horse)

I remember the neckcurls, limp and damp as tendrils;
And her quick look, a sidelong pickerel smile;
And how, once startled into talk, the light syllables leaped for
    her.
And she balanced in the delight of her thought,
A wren, happy, tail into the wind,
Her song trembling the twigs and small branches.
The shade sang with her;
The leaves, their whispers turned to kissing,
And the mould sang in the bleached valleys under the rose.

Oh, when she was sad, she cast herself down into such a pure
    depth,
Even a father could not find her:
Scraping her cheek against straw,
Stirring the clearest water.
My sparrow, you are not here,
Waiting like a fern, making a spiney shadow.
The sides of wet stones cannot console me,
Nor the moss, wound with the last light.

If only I could nudge you from this sleep,
My maimed darling, my skittery pigeon.
Over this damp grave I speak the words of my love:
I, with no rights in this matter,
Neither father nor lover.

Roethke's generation of poets was the first to be routinely employed in university teaching. Roethke, Randall Jarrell, Howard Nemerov, and others developed a novel academic idiom to deal with new relationships, such as that between teacher and student. It can be a kind of love but not parental, collegial, religious, or erotic.

In a Dark Time

In a dark time, the eye begins to see,
I meet my shadow in the deepening shade;
I hear my echo in the echoing wood—
A lord of nature weeping to a tree.
I live between the heron and the wren,
Beasts of the hill and serpents of the den.

What's madness but nobility of soul
At odds with circumstance? The day's on fire!
I know the purity of pure despair,
My shadow pinned against a sweating wall.
That place among the rocks—is it a cave,
Or winding path? The edge is what I have.

A steady storm of correspondences!
A night flowing with birds, a ragged moon.
And in broad day the midnight come again!
A man goes far to find out what he is—
Death of the self in a long, tearless night,
All natural shapes blazing unnatural light.

Dark, dark my light, and darker my desire,
My soul, like some heat-maddened summer fly,
Keeps buzzing at the sill. Which I is *I*?
A fallen man, I climb out of my fear.
The mind enters itself, and God the mind,
And one is One, free in the tearing wind.

Although he was a thoroughly postmodern American, Roethke would have been at home with almost any of the lyric poets of the sixteenth and seventeenth centuries.

SIR STEPHEN SPENDER b.1909

Spender has turned out to be among the most durable
of the group of Oxford poets that emerged during the
1930s; the group included Spender's friends W. H.
Auden and Louis MacNeice. Spender's poetry, like
theirs, shows a concern for social issues and demon-
strates technical experimentation.

I Think Continually
of Those Who Were Truly Great

I think continually of those who were truly great.
Who, from the womb, remembered the soul's history
Through corridors of light where the hours are suns,
Endless and singing. Whose lovely ambition
Was that their lips, still touched with fire,
Should tell of the spirit clothed from head to foot in song.
And who hoarded from the spring branches
The desires falling across their bodies like blossoms.

What is precious is never to forget
The delight of the blood drawn from ageless springs
Breaking through rocks in worlds before our earth;
Never to deny its pleasure in the simple morning light,
Nor its grave evening demand for love;
Never to allow gradually the traffic to smother
With noise and fog the flowering of the spirit.

Near the snow, near the sun, in the highest fields
See how those names are fêted by the wavering grass,
And by the streamers of white cloud,
And whispers of wind in the listening sky;
The names of those who in their lives fought for life,
Who wore at their hearts the fire's centre.
Born of the sun they traveled a short while towards the sun,
And left the vivid air signed with their honour.

If you have a diamond-point pencil, you can have a poet inscribe a poem on an appropriate pane of glass. Edmund Wilson had Spender copy this poem on a pane for a high window, showing the air, sky, and sun (see Wilson's Upstate*).*

Bishop was a Vassar graduate who lived for many years
in Brazil. In 1946, and approximately every ten years
thereafter, she published a book of verse, many of
which were prizewinners.

The Fish

I caught a tremendous fish
and held him beside the boat
half out of water, with my hook
fast in a corner of his mouth.
He didn't fight.
He hadn't fought at all.
He hung a grunting weight,
battered and venerable
and homely. Here and there
his brown skin hung in strips
like ancient wallpaper,
and its pattern of darker brown
was like wallpaper:
shapes like full-blown roses
stained and lost through age.
He was speckled with barnacles,
fine rosettes of lime,
and infested
with tiny white sea-lice,
and underneath two or three
rags of green weed hung down.
While his gills were breathing in
the terrible oxygen
—the frightening gills,
fresh and crisp with blood,
that can cut so badly—
I thought of the coarse white flesh

packed in like feathers,
the big bones and the little bones,
the dramatic reds and blacks
of his shiny entrails,
and the pink swim-bladder
like a big peony.
I looked into his eyes
which were far larger than mine
but shallower, and yellowed,
the irises backed and packed
with tarnished tinfoil
seen through the lenses
of old scratched isinglass.
They shifted a little, but not
to return my stare.
—It was more like the tipping
of an object toward the light.
I admired his sullen face,
the mechanism of his jaw,
and then I saw
that from his lower lip
—if you could call it a lip—
grim, wet, and weaponlike,
hung five old pieces of fish-line,
or four and a wire leader
with the swivel still attached,
with all their five big hooks
grown firmly in his mouth.
A green line, frayed at the end
where he broke it, two heavier lines,
and a fine black thread
still crimped from the strain and snap
when it broke and he got away.
Like medals with their ribbons
frayed and wavering,
a five-haired beard of wisdom
trailing from his aching jaw.
I stared and stared

and victory filled up
the little rented boat,
from the pool of bilge
where oil had spread a rainbow
around the rusted engine
to the bailer rusted orange,
the sun-cracked thwarts,
the oarlocks on their strings,
the gunnels—until everything
was rainbow, rainbow, rainbow!
And I let the fish go.

We are still telling fish stories, a venerable tradition that goes from Jonah through Melville to Hemingway, James Dickey, and an episode of "The Simpsons" in which Homer catches a fabled fish called "General Sherman." Bishop, however, with characteristic profundity, goes beyond the folklore and symbolism to look closely at the far side of the actual experience.

ROBERT HAYDEN 1913–1980

Hayden received his education at Detroit City College
(now Wayne State University) and at the University of
Michigan, where W. H. Auden was one of his teachers.
Hayden himself was a university teacher, at Fisk University for about twenty years and then back at Michigan.

Those Winter Sundays

Sundays too my father got up early
and put his clothes on in the blueblack cold,
then with cracked hands that ached
from labor in the weekday weather made
banked fires blaze. No one ever thanked him.

I'd wake and hear the cold splintering, breaking.
When the rooms were warm, he'd call,
and slowly I would rise and dress,
fearing the chronic angers of that house,

Speaking indifferently to him,
who had driven out the cold
and polished my good shoes as well.
What did I know, what did I know
of love's austere and lonely offices?

As Hayden incandescently demonstrates, a good way to avoid ponderous sentimentality is to avoid outright declaration. Consider how puny this poem would be if it ended, "Love's offices are lonely and austere."

RANDALL JARRELL 1914–1965

Jarrell was born in Tennessee and died in North Caro-
lina, but significant parts of his life were spent outside
the South—childhood in California, the Second World
War in the Army Air Corps, some teaching time at
Kenyon College and elsewhere. Sometimes included as
a younger member of the Fugitive-Agrarian group and
the New Critics, Jarrell wrote some fiction and criti-
cism as well as poetry. His poetry is marked by strong
but indefinite feeling and accurate observation of the
technology of the modern world.

The Death of the Ball Turret Gunner

From my mother's sleep I fell into the State
And I hunched in its belly till my wet fur froze.
Six miles from earth, loosed from its dream of life,
I woke to black flak and the nightmare fighters.
When I died they washed me out of the turret with a hose.

---

*Bombers like the B-17 and B-24 had a plexiglass turret on their undersides for
protection against fighters attacking from below. As Jarrell noted, these fighters
were "armed with cannon firing explosive shells." He added, "The hose was a
steam hose."*

HENRY REED 1914–1986

Reed's single poem in this anthology comes from his 1946 volume, *A Map of Verona*. In addition to war poems, Reed wrote significant radio dramas and some marvelous parodies, including "Chard Whitlow," the best takeoff of Eliot's *Four Quartets*.

Naming of Parts

Today we have naming of parts. Yesterday,
We had daily cleaning. And tomorrow morning,
We shall have what to do after firing. But today,
Today we have naming of parts. Japonica
Glistens like coral in all of the neighbouring gardens,
   And today we have naming of parts.

This is the lower sling swivel. And this
Is the upper sling swivel, whose use you will see,
When you are given your slings. And this is the piling swivel,
Which in your case you have not got. The branches
Hold in the gardens their silent, eloquent gestures,
   Which in our case we have not got.

This is the safety-catch, which is always released
With an easy flick of the thumb. And please do not let me
See anyone using his finger. You can do it quite easy
If you have any strength in your thumb. The blossoms
Are fragile and motionless, never letting anyone see
   Any of them using their finger.

And this you can see is the bolt. The purpose of this
Is to open the breech, as you see. We can slide it
Rapidly backwards and forwards: we call this
Easing the spring. And rapidly backwards and forwards
The early bees are assaulting and fumbling the flowers:
    They call it easing the Spring.

They call it easing the Spring: it is perfectly easy
If you have any strength in your thumb: like the bolt,
And the breech, and the cocking-piece, and the point of balance,
Which in our case we have not got; and the almond-blossom
Silent in all of the gardens and the bees going backwards and
    forwards,
    For today we have naming of parts.

---

*Invasion is one of the unavoidable figures of war: here, as in Richard Eberhart's
"Fury of Aerial Bombardment" (p. 1023), the usual language of poetry is bar-
barically invaded by the nomenclature of mechanical contraptions. Thanks to the
many meanings of "spring" (all from a common source), the poem can glide
easily from weapon to season to elementary water. Any army is pathetic, one
without even enough equipment for training is doubly so.*

DYLAN THOMAS 1914–1953

Dylan Thomas was a fully mature poet while still an adolescent and published his first book before his twenty-first birthday. The son of a schoolteacher, he was born in Swansea, Wales. Skipping college, he worked as a writer from the age of twenty until his death, not yet forty years old, in New York. He was by far one of the greatest performers among the poets. He was in some ways alien to the austerities of the modernists before him and the postmodernists after, but one would have to be deaf and ice-cold not to respond to Thomas's magnificent voice. As his four grand poems in this anthology attest, Thomas belonged in a great tradition that includes Blake, Keats, Hardy, Hopkins, and Yeats—poets who sang ecstatically and wisely of birth, love, death, and glory.

Do Not Go Gentle into That Good Night

Do not go gentle into that good night,
Old age should burn and rave at close of day;
Rage, rage against the dying of the light.

Though wise men at their end know dark is right,
Because their words had forked no lightning they
Do not go gentle into that good night.

Good men, the last wave by, crying how bright
Their frail deeds might have danced in a green bay,
Rage, rage against the dying of the light.

Wild men who caught and sang the sun in flight,
And learn, too late, they grieved it on its way,
Do not go gentle into that good night.

Grave men, near death, who see with blinding sight
Blind eyes could blaze like meteors and be gay,
Rage, rage against the dying of the light.

And you, my father, there on the sad height,
Curse, bless, me now with your fierce tears, I pray,
Do not go gentle into that good night.
Rage, rage against the dying of the light.

This poem originated as an address to the poet's dying father. It is surely the finest villanelle ever written as well as one of the finest poems of the twentieth century in any form.

Fern Hill

Now as I was young and easy under the apple boughs
About the lilting house and happy as the grass was green,
   The night above the dingle starry,
     Time let me hail and climb
   Golden in the heydays of his eyes,
And honored among wagons I was prince of the apple towns
And once below a time I lordly had the trees and leaves
     Trail with daisies and barley
   Down the rivers of the windfall light.

And as I was green and carefree, famous among the barns
About the happy yard and singing as the farm was home,
   In the sun that is young once only,
     Time let me play and be
   Golden in the mercy of his means,
And green and golden I was huntsman and herdsman, the calves
Sang to my horn, the foxes on the hills barked clear and cold,
     And the sabbath rang slowly
   In the pebbles of the holy streams.

All the sun long it was running, it was lovely, the hay
Fields high as the house, the tunes from the chimneys, it was air
   And playing, lovely and watery
     And fire green as grass.
     And nightly under the simple stars
As I rode to sleep the owls were bearing the farm away,
All the moon long I heard, blessed among stables, the nightjars
     Flying with the ricks, and the horses
      Flashing into the dark.

And then to awake, and the farm, like a wanderer white
With the dew, come back, the cock on his shoulder: it was all
     Shining, it was Adam and maiden,
          The sky gathered again
     And the sun grew round that very day.
So it must have been after the birth of the simple light
In the first, spinning place, the spellbound horses walking warm
     Out of the whinnying green stable
          On to the fields of praise.

And honored among foxes and pheasants by the gay house
Under the new made clouds and happy as the heart was long,
     In the sun born over and over,
          I ran my heedless ways,
     My wishes raced through the house high hay
And nothing I cared, at my sky blue trades, that time allows
In all his tuneful turning so few and such morning songs
     Before the children green and golden
          Follow him out of grace,

Nothing I cared, in the lamb white days, that time would take
     me
Up to the swallow thronged loft by the shadow of my hand,
     In the moon that is always rising,
          Nor that riding to sleep
     I should hear him fly with the high fields
And wake to the farm forever fled from the childless land.
Oh as I was young and easy in the mercy of his means,
          Time held me green and dying
     Though I sang in my chains like the sea.

---

*Thomas was in some ways a primitive and in some ways a sophisticate, but in
"Fern Hill" he produced a great ode in a complex stanza that could have been
devised by Donne or Keats. The title refers to the name of Thomas's aunt's
country house, where he spent some time as a boy.*

A Refusal to Mourn the Death, by Fire, of a Child in London

Never until the mankind making
Bird beast and flower
Fathering and all humbling darkness
Tells with silence the last light breaking
And the still hour
Is come of the sea tumbling in harness

And I must enter again the round
Zion of the water bead
And the synagogue of the ear of corn
Shall I let pray the shadow of a sound
Or sow my salt seed
In the least valley of sackcloth to mourn

The majesty and burning of the child's death.
I shall not murder
The mankind of her going with a grave truth
Nor blaspheme down the stations of the breath
With any further
Elegy of innocence and youth.

Deep with the first dead lies London's daughter,
Robed in the long friends,
The grains beyond age, the dark veins of her mother,
Secret by the unmourning water
Of the riding Thames.
After the first death, there is no other.

The first thirteen lines here—more than half the poem—are a single breath-takingly apocalyptic sentence. Thomas, recalling the Welsh Henry Vaughan (see pp. 247–254) and other devotional poets of the seventeenth century, prodigiously sends the mind back to the beginning of life ("the first dead") and forward to the end of time.

The Force That through the Green Fuse Drives the Flower

The force that through the green fuse drives the flower
Drives my green age; that blasts the roots of trees
Is my destroyer.
And I am dumb to tell the crooked rose
My youth is bent by the same wintry fever.

The force that drives the water through the rocks
Drives my red blood; that dries the mouthing streams
Turns mine to wax.
And I am dumb to mouth unto my veins
How at the mountain spring the same mouth sucks.

The hand that whirls the water in the pool
Stirs the quicksand; that ropes the blowing wind
Hauls my shroud sail.
And I am dumb to tell the hanging man
How of my clay is made the hangman's lime.

The lips of time leech to the fountain head;
Love drips and gathers, but the fallen blood
Shall calm her sores.
And I am dumb to tell a weather's wind
How time has ticked a heaven round the stars.

And I am dumb to tell the lover's tomb
How at my sheet goes the same crooked worm.

Although he is one of the youngest poets in this anthology, Thomas returns to the oldest themes and techniques. It is reassuring that atavistic alliteration can be used to express the unity and economy of forces—principles accepted by modern physics and psychology alike; atoms do resemble solar systems.

GWENDOLYN BROOKS b.1917

Brooks's verse narrative *Annie Allen* won her a Pulitzer Prize. Most of Brooks's varied work in prose and verse is set in Chicago, where she grew up.

We Real Cool

◆◆◆◆

The Pool Players.
Seven at the Golden Shovel.

We real cool. We
Left school. We

Lurk late. We
Strike straight. We

Sing sin. We
Thin gin. We

Jazz June. We
Die soon.

Brooks's Chicago, even though a couple of generations newer, is at least as tough as Sandburg's (p. 912); hers, moreover, is more percussively registered in three-word sentences spoken by recognizable people.

Robert Lowell, who belonged to the same large New England family as James Russell Lowell and Amy Lowell, was a student of John Crowe Ransom and Allen Tate. Lowell's earlier poetry shows the technical finesse and the concern with large philosophical issues that were favored by the so-called New Critics. Later, moved by the example of William Carlos Williams, Lowell loosened his style somewhat and concentrated more on the details of his own life. He taught on and off at Boston University and Harvard.

Skunk Hour

Nautilus Island's hermit
heiress still lives through winter in her Spartan cottage;
her sheep still graze above the sea.
Her son's a bishop. Her farmer
is first selectman in our village;
she's in her dotage.

Thirsting for
the hierarchic privacy
of Queen Victoria's century,
she buys up all
the eyesores facing her shore,
and lets them fall.

The season's ill—
we've lost our summer millionaire,
who seemed to leap from an L. L. Bean
catalogue. His nine-knot yawl
was auctioned off to lobstermen.
A red fox stain covers Blue Hill.

And now our fairy
decorator brightens his shop for fall;
his fishnet's filled with orange cork,
orange, his cobbler's bench and awl;
there is no money in his work,
he'd rather marry.

One dark night,
my Tudor Ford climbed the hill's skull;
I watched for love-cars. Lights turned down,
they lay together, hull to hull,
where the graveyard shelves on the town. . . .
My mind's not right.

A car radio bleats,
"Love, O careless Love. . . ." I hear
my ill-spirit sob in each blood cell,
as if my hand were at its throat. . . .
I myself am hell;
nobody's here—

only skunks, that search
in the moonlight for a bite to eat.
They march on their soles up Main Street:
white stripes, moonstruck eyes' red fire
under the chalk-dry and spar spire
of the Trinitarian Church.

I stand on top
of our back steps and breathe the rich air—
a mother skunk with her column of kittens swills the garbage
    pail.
She jabs her wedge-head in a cup
of sour cream, drops her ostrich tail,
and will not scare.

The poem is dedicated to Elizabeth Bishop (see pp. 1043–1045), and Lowell said that he modelled "Skunk Hour" on Bishop's "Armadillo," which happens to be dedicated to Lowell.

For the Union Dead

>>>>>>>

"Relinquunt Omnia Servare Rem Publicam."

The old South Boston Aquarium stands
in a Sahara of snow now. Its broken windows are boarded:
The bronze weathervane cod has lost half its scales.
The airy tanks are dry.

Once my nose crawled like a snail on the glass;
my hand tingled
to burst the bubbles
drifting from the noses of the cowed, compliant fish.

My hand draws back. I often sigh still
for the dark downward and vegetating kingdom
of the fish and reptile. On a morning last March,
I pressed against the new barbed and galvanized

fence on the Boston Common. Behind their cage,
yellow dinosaur steamshovels were grunting
as they cropped up tons of mush and grass
to gouge their underworld garage.

Parking spaces luxuriate like civic
sandpiles in the heart of Boston.
A girdle of orange, Puritan-pumpkin colored girders
braces the tingling Statehouse,

shaking over the excavations, as it faces Colonel Shaw
and his bell-cheeked Negro infantry
on St. Gaudens shaking Civil War relief,
propped by a plank splint against the garage's earthquake.

Two months after marching through Boston,
half the regiment was dead;
at the dedication,
William James could almost hear the bronze Negroes breathe.

Their monument sticks like a fishbone
in the city's throat.
Its Colonel is as lean
as a compass-needle.

He has an angry wrenlike vigilance,
a greyhound's gentle tautness;
he seems to wince at pleasure,
and suffocate for privacy.

He is out of bounds now. He rejoices in man's lovely,
peculiar power to choose life and die—
when he leads his black soldiers to death,
he cannot bend his back.

On a thousand small town New England greens,
the old white churches hold their air
of sparse, sincere rebellion; frayed flags
quilt the graveyards of the Grand Army of the Republic.

The stone statues of the abstract Union Soldier
grow slimmer and younger each year—
wasp-waisted, they doze over muskets
and muse through their sideburns . . .

Shaw's father wanted no monument
except the ditch,
where his son's body was thrown
and lost with his "niggers."

The ditch is nearer.
There are no statues for the last war here;
on Boylston Street, a commercial photograph
shows Hiroshima boiling

over a Mosler Safe, the "Rock of Ages"
that survived the blast. Space is nearer.
When I crouch to my television set,
the drained faces of Negro school-children rise like balloons.

Colonel Shaw
is riding on his bubble,
he waits
for the blesséd break.

The Aquarium is gone. Everywhere,
giant finned cars nose forward like fish;
a savage servility
slides by on grease.

Since Lowell was a close friend of Allen Tate, it is certain that he meant to produce a response to "Ode to the Confederate Dead" (p. 1017). Colonel Shaw has been the subject of sculpture, music (by Charles Ives and others), and a recent movie (Glory). (Note that: "Relinquunt Omnia Servare Rem Publican" is "they give up everything to preserve the Republic"—adapted from the motto of the Society of the Cincinnati.)

Mr. Edwards and the Spider

I saw the spiders marching through the air,
Swimming from tree to tree that mildewed day
  In late August when the hay
  Came creaking to the barn. But where
    The wind is westerly,
Where gnarled November makes the spiders fly
Into the apparitions of the sky,
They purpose nothing but their ease and die
Urgently beating east to sunrise and the sea;

What are we in the hands of the great God?
It was in vain you set up thorn and briar
  In battle array against the fire
  And treason crackling in your blood;
    For the wild thorns grow tame
And will do nothing to oppose the flame;
Your lacerations tell the losing game
You play against a sickness past your cure.
How will the hands be strong? How will the heart endure?

A very little thing, a little worm,
Or hourglass-blazoned spider, it is said,
  Can kill a tiger. Will the dead
  Hold up his mirror and affirm
    To the four winds the smell
And flash of his authority? It's well
If God who holds you to the pit of hell,
Much as one holds a spider, will destroy,
Baffle and dissipate your soul. As a small boy

On Windsor Marsh, I saw the spider die
When thrown into the bowels of fierce fire:
    There's no long struggle, no desire
    To get up on its feet and fly—
        It stretches out its feet
And dies. This is the sinner's last retreat;
Yes, and no strength exerted on the heat
Then sinews the abolished will, when sick
And full of burning, it will whistle on a brick.

But who can plumb the sinking of that soul?
Josiah Hawley, picture yourself cast
    Into a brick-kiln where the blast
    Fans your quick vitals to a coal—
        If measured by a glass,
How long would it seem burning! Let there pass
A minute, ten, ten trillion; but the blaze
Is infinite, eternal: this is death,
To die and know it. This is the Black Widow, death.

Lowell combines two texts by the eighteenth-century American preacher Jonathan Edwards: "The Flying Spider" and "Sinners in the Hands of an Angry God," the latter a hellfire-and-brimstone sermon of a sort that can still be heard.

RICHARD WILBUR b.1921

Educated at Amherst and Harvard, Richard Wilbur
spent most of his long and distinguished teaching career
at Wesleyan University in Middletown, Connecticut.
He was the second holder of the annual title of Poet
Laureate of the United States. He is also a distin-
guished translator, mostly from the French.

Love Calls Us to the Things of This World

The eyes open to a cry of pulleys,
And spirited from sleep, the astounded soul
Hangs for a moment bodiless and simple
As false dawn.
  Outside the open window
The morning air is all awash with angels.

Some are in bed-sheets, some are in blouses,
Some are in smocks: but truly there they are.
Now they are rising together in calm swells
Of halcyon feeling, filling whatever they wear
With the deep joy of their impersonal breathing;

Now they are flying in place, conveying
The terrible speed of their omnipresence, moving
And staying like white water; and now of a sudden
They swoon down into so rapt a quiet
That nobody seems to be there.
  The soul shrinks

From all that it is about to remember,
From the punctual rape of every blesséd day,
And cries,
     "Oh, let there be nothing on earth but laundry,
Nothing but rosy hands in the rising steam
And clear dances done in the sight of heaven."

Yet, as the sun acknowledges
With a warm look the world's hunks and colors,
The soul descends once more in bitter love
To accept the waking body, saying now
In a changed voice as the man yawns and rises,

"Bring them down from their ruddy gallows;
Let there be clean linen for the backs of thieves;
Let lovers go fresh and sweet to be undone,
And the heaviest nuns walk in a pure floating
Of dark habits,
     keeping their difficult balance."

The pulleys seem to come, in equal parts, from George Herbert (see p. 191) and from the obsolescent, current urban practice of stringing mobile clotheslines between apartment buildings.

PHILIP LARKIN 1922–1985

Larkin chose to preserve little of his poetry, so that his reputation rests largely on three slim volumes published at approximately ten-year intervals (1955, 1964, 1974). But what a reputation he has had! It now seems probable that between the death of Dylan Thomas in 1953 and his own death in 1985, Larkin was the best practicing poet in Britain. He was a master of two rare arts: his poetry could use language that seems totally genuine and conversational, and at the same time he could craft a stanza—fully outfitted with rhyme, rhythm, and meter—quite as polished as any turned out in the seventeenth century. Larkin also wrote novels, some scattered essays and reviews, and regular jazz columns. For most of his adult life he was employed as a university librarian.

Church Going

Once I am sure there's nothing going on
I step inside, letting the door thud shut.
Another church: matting, seats, and stone,
And little books; sprawlings of flowers, cut
For Sunday, brownish now; some brass and stuff
Up at the holy end; the small neat organ;
And a tense, musty, unignorable silence,
Brewed God knows how long. Hatless, I take off
My cycle-clips in awkward reverence,

Move forward, run my hand around the font.
From where I stand, the roof looks almost new —
Cleaned, or restored? Someone would know: I don't.
Mounting the lectern, I peruse a few
Hectoring large-scale verses, and pronounce
"Here endeth" much more loudly than I'd meant.
The echoes snigger briefly. Back at the door
I sign the book, donate an Irish sixpence,
Reflect the place was not worth stopping for.

Yet stop I did: in fact I often do,
And always end much at a loss like this,
Wondering what to look for; wondering, too,
When churches fall completely out of use
What we shall turn them into, if we shall keep
A few cathedrals chronically on show,
Their parchment, plate and pyx in locked cases,
And let the rest rent-free to rain and sheep.
Shall we avoid them as unlucky places?

Or, after dark, will dubious women come
To make their children touch a particular stone;
Pick simples for a cancer; or on some
Advised night see walking a dead one?
Power of some sort or other will go on
In games, in riddles, seemingly at random;
But superstition, like belief, must die,
And what remains when disbelief has gone?
Grass, weedy pavement, brambles, buttress, sky,

A shape less recognisable each week,
A purpose more obscure. I wonder who
Will be the last, the very last, to seek
This place for what it was; one of the crew
That tap and jot and know what rood-lofts were?
Some ruin-bibber, randy for antique,
Or Christmas-addict, counting on a whiff
Of gown-and-bands and organ-pipes and myrrh?
Or will he be my representative,

Bored, uninformed, knowing the ghostly silt
Dispersed, yet tending to this cross of ground
Through suburb scrub because it held unspilt
So long and equably what since is found
Only in separation—marriage, and birth,
And death, and thoughts of these—for whom was built
This special shell? For, though I've no idea
What this accoutred frowsty barn is worth,
It pleases me to stand in silence here;

A series house on serious earth it is,
In whose blent air all our compulsions meet,
Are recognised, and robed as destinies,
And that much never can be obsolete,
Since someone will forever be surprising
A hunger in himself to be more serious,
And gravitating with it to this ground,
Which, he once heard, was proper to grow wise in,
If only that so many dead lie round.

Larkin consciously continues—with some sophistication and irony—an English tradition going back to George Herbert (see pp. 186–195), Gray's "Elegy" (p. 327), Wordsworth's "Tintern Abbey" (p. 407), and Eliot's "Little Gidding" (p. 987). The poet, situated in a sacred place, reflects on the meaning of it all. Larkin adds the modern note by giving his poem an ambiguous title, wherein "Churchgoing" dissolves into "Church Going." Larkin also wrote poems called "Going" and "Going, Going." (Note that: "pyx" is a box in which Communion wafers are kept.)

ALLEN GINSBERG b.1926

Ginsberg, the son of the poet Louis Ginsberg, was born
in New Jersey and educated at Columbia University.
He has been one of the most famous poets in the world
since the publication of his sensational first volume,
Howl and Other Poems, in 1956.

A Supermarket in California

What thoughts I have of you tonight, Walt Whitman, for I
walked down the sidestreets under the trees with a headache
self-conscious looking at the full moon.

In my hungry fatigue, and shopping for images, I went into
the neon fruit supermarket, dreaming of your enumerations!

What peaches and what penumbras! Whole families
shopping at night! Aisles full of husbands! Wives in the
avocados, babies in the tomatoes! —and you, Garcia Lorca, what
were you doing down by the watermelons?

I saw you, Walt Whitman, childless, lonely old grubber,
poking among the meats in the refrigerator and eyeing the
grocery boys.

I heard you asking questions of each: Who killed the pork
chops? What price bananas? Are you my Angel?

I wandered in and out of the brilliant stacks of cans
following you, and followed in my imagination by the store
detective.

We strode down the open corridors together in our solitary
fancy tasting artichokes, possessing every frozen delicacy, and
never passing the cashier.

Where are we going, Walt Whitman? The doors close in an hour. Which way does your beard point tonight?

(I touch your book and dream of our odyssey in the supermarket and feel absurd.)

Will we walk all night through solitary streets? The trees add shade to shade, lights out in the houses, we'll both be lonely.

Will we stroll dreaming of the lost America of love past blue automobiles in driveways, home to our silent cottage?

Ah, dear father, graybeard, lonely old courage-teacher, what America did you have when Charon quit poling his ferry and you got out on a smoking bank and stood watching the boat disappear on the black waters of Lethe?

In subject, style, and tone, Ginsberg's poem takes Whitman at his word, especially in his anti-bardic plea that the muse be "installed amid the kitchenware." That, literally, is what Ginsberg does, adding the spice of humor that Whitman usually lacks.

Despite an early life seemingly full of advantage and privilege, Plath recorded little but painful suffering in her intense and eloquent poems. She married the British poet Ted Hughes (later Poet Laureate) and was living in England at the time of her suicide.

Daddy

You do not do, you do not do
Any more, black shoe
In which I have lived like a foot
For thirty years, poor and white,
Barely daring to breathe or Achoo.

Daddy, I have had to kill you.
You died before I had time—
Marble-heavy, a bag full of God,
Ghastly statue with one gray toe
Big as a Frisco seal

And a head in the freakish Atlantic
Where it pours bean green over blue
In the waters off beautiful Nauset.
I used to pray to recover you.
Ach, du.

In the German tongue, in the Polish town
Scraped flat by the roller
Of wars, wars, wars.
But the name of the town is common.
My Polack friend

Says there are a dozen or two.
So I never could tell where you
Put your foot, your root,
I never could talk to you.
The tongue stuck in my jaw.

It stuck in a barb wire snare.
Ich, ich, ich, ich,
I could hardly speak.
I thought every German was you.
And the language obscene

An engine, an engine
Chuffing me off like a Jew.
A Jew to Dachau, Auschwitz, Belsen.
I began to talk like a Jew.
I think I may well be a Jew.

The snows of the Tyrol, the clear beer of Vienna
Are not very pure or true.
With my gipsy ancestress and my weird luck
And my Taroc pack and my Taroc pack
I may be a bit of a Jew.

I have always been scared of *you,*
With your Luftwaffe, your gobbledygoo.
And your neat mustache
And your Aryan eye, bright blue.
Panzer-man, panzer-man, O You — —

Not God but a swastika
So black no sky could squeak through.
Every woman adores a Fascist,
The boot in the face, the brute
Brute heart of a brute like you.

You stand at the blackboard, daddy,
In the picture I have of you,
A cleft in your chin instead of your foot
But no less a devil for that, no not
Any less the black man who

Bit my pretty red heart in two.
I was ten when they buried you.
At twenty I tried to die
And get back, back, back to you.
I thought even the bones would do.

But they pulled me out of the sack,
And they stuck me together with glue.
And then I knew what to do.
I made a model of you,
A man in black with a Meinkampf look

And a love of the rack and the screw.
And I said I do, I do.
So daddy, I'm finally through.
The black telephone's off at the root,
The voices just can't worm through.

If I've killed one man, I've killed two — —
The vampire who said he was you
And drank my blood for a year,
Seven years, if you want to know.
Daddy, you can lie back now.

There's a stake in your fat black heart
And the villagers never liked you.
They are dancing and stamping on you.
They always *knew* it was you.
Daddy, daddy, you bastard, I'm through.

These short lines hit the reader so hard that many think the poem has to reflect the poet's feelings for her own father. All of the available evidence suggests, however, that "Daddy" really has much more to do with the feelings of any child—female or male—for any father.

The Poems in Order of Popularity

Here is a list of the top 500 poems in English, starting with the most popular (that is, the most often anthologized), William Blake's "The Tiger."

1. *The Tiger.*   Blake
2. *Sir Patrick Spens.*   Anonymous
3. *To Autumn.*   Keats
4. *That Time of Year Thou Mayst in Me Behold.*   Shakespeare
5. *Pied Beauty.*   Hopkins
6. *Stopping by Woods on a Snowy Evening.*   Frost
7. *Kubla Khan.*   Coleridge
8. *Dover Beach.*   Arnold
9. *La Belle Dame sans Merci.*   Keats
10. *To the Virgins, to Make Much of Time.*   Herrick
11. *To His Coy Mistress.*   Marvell
12. *The Passionate Shepherd to His Love.*   Marlowe
13. *Death, Be Not Proud.*   Donne
14. *Upon Julia's Clothes.*   Herrick
15. *To Lucasta, Going to the Wars.*   Lovelace
16. *The World Is Too Much with Us.*   Wordsworth
17. *On First Looking into Chapman's Homer.*   Keats
18. *Jabberwocky.*   "Carroll"
19. *The Second Coming.*   Yeats
20. *Elegy Written in a Country Churchyard.*   Gray
21. *Ozymandias.*   Shelley
22. *Sailing to Byzantium.*   Yeats
23. *Shall I Compare Thee to a Summer's Day?*   Shakespeare

24. *Let Me Not to the Marriage of True Minds.*   Shakespeare
25. *Fear No More the Heat o' the Sun.*   Shakespeare
26. *Ode to a Nightingale.*   Keats
27. *The Love Song of J. Alfred Prufrock.*   Eliot
28. *To Helen.*   Poe
29. *"Because I could not stop for Death."*   Dickinson
30. *The Windhover.*   Hopkins
31. *Anthem for Doomed Youth.*   Owen
32. *When Icicles Hang by the Wall.*   Shakespeare
33. *Batter My Heart, Three-Person'd God.*   Donne
34. *Love Bade Me Welcome.*   Herbert
35. *Ode to the West Wind.*   Shelley
36. *God's Grandeur.*   Hopkins
37. *Do Not Go Gentle into That Good Night.*   Thomas
38. *Western Wind.*   Anonymous
39. *They Flee from Me That Sometimes Did Me Seek.*   Wyatt
40. *The Good Morrow.*   Donne
41. *Delight in Disorder.*   Herrick
42. *I Wandered Lonely as a Cloud.*   Wordsworth
43. *My Last Duchess.*   R. Browning
44. *Spring and Fall.*   Hopkins
45. *Leda and the Swan.*   Yeats
46. *The River-Merchant's Wife: A Letter.*   Pound
47. *Go, Lovely Rose.*   Waller
48. *The Retreat.*   Vaughan
49. *Ode on a Grecian Urn.*   Keats
50. *London.*   Blake
51. *And Did Those Feet in Ancient Times.*   Blake
52. *Composed upon Westminster Bridge, September 3, 1802.*   Wordsworth
53. *The Splendor Falls.*   Tennyson
54. *The Darkling Thrush.*   Hardy
55. *Lovliest of Trees.*   Housman

56. *Mending Wall.*   Frost
57. *Fern Hill.*   Thomas
58. *Adieu, Farewell, Earth's Bliss.*   Nashe
59. *Drink to Me Only with Thine Eyes.*   Jonson
60. *The Collar.*   Herbert
61. *Why So Pale and Wan, Fond Lover?*   Suckling
62. *The Garden.*   Marvell
63. *The Solitary Reaper.*   Wordsworth
64. *Break, Break, Break.*   Tennyson
65. *Crossing the Bar.*   Tennyson
66. *Mr. Flood's Party.*   Robinson
67. *Musée des Beaux Arts.*   Auden
68. *The Death of the Ball Turret Gunner.*   Jarrell
69. *Full Fathom Five Thy Father Lies.*   Shakespeare
70. *When to the Sessions of Sweet Silent Thought.*   Shakespeare
71. *Piping down the Valleys Wide.*   Blake
72. *So We'll Go No More a-Roving.*   Byron
73. *"I heard a Fly buzz—when I died."*   Dickinson
74. *Miniver Cheevy.*   Robinson
75. *To Brooklyn Bridge.*   Crane
76. *Edward, Edward.*   Anonymous
77. *Since There's No Help, Come Let Us Kiss and Part.*   Drayton
78. *O Mistress Mine.*   Shakespeare
79. *At the Round Earth's Imagined Corners.*   Donne
80. *On My First Son.*   Jonson
81. *Virtue.*   Herbert
82. *Ask Me No More Where Jove Bestows.*   Carew.
83. *Ode on the Death of a Favorite Cat, Drowned in a Tub of Gold Fishes.*   Gray
84. *The Rime of the Ancient Mariner.*   Coleridge
85. *Concord Hymn.*   Emerson
86. *The Lake Isle of Innisfree.*   Yeats
87. *Non Sum Qualis Eram Bonae sub Regno Cynarae.*   Dowson

118. *A Refusal to Mourn the Death, by Fire, of a Child in London.*   Thomas
119. *The Burning Babe.*   Southwell
120. *When in Disgrace with Fortune and Men's Eyes.*   Shakespeare
121. *To Daffodils.*   Herrick
122. *A Red, Red Rose.*   Burns
123. *To a Waterfall.*   Bryant
124. *Annabel Lee.*   Poe
125. *Felix Randal.*   Hopkins
126. *No Worst, There Is None.*   Hopkins
127. *To an Athlete Dying Young.*   Housman
128. *Among School Children.*   Yeats
129. *Fire and Ice.*   Frost
130. *I Knew a Woman.*   Roethke
131. *The Waking.*   Roethke
132. *The Force That through the Green Fuse Drives the Flower.*   Thomas
133. *When Daisies Pied.*   Shakespeare
134. *A Hymn to God the Father.*   Donne
135. *The Ecstasy.*   Donne
136. *The Canonization.*   Donne
137. *On His Deceased Wife.*   Milton
138. *The World.*   Vaughan
139. *Lines Composed a Few Miles above Tintern Abbey.*   Wordsworth
140. *To a Skylark.*   Shelley
141. *When I Have Fears.*   Keats
142. *Meeting at Night.*   R. Browning
143. *Remembrance.*   Brontë
144. *"There's a certain Slant of light."*   Dickinson
145. *Up-Hill.*   C. Rossetti
146. *London Snow.*   Bridges
147. *An Irish Airman Foresees His Death.*   Yeats
148. *Richard Cory.*   Robinson

149. *The Road Not Taken.* Frost

150. *Anecdote of the Jar.* Stevens

151. *Piano.* Lawrence

152. *Journey of the Magi.* Eliot

153. *You, Andrew Marvell.* MacLeish

154. *Strange Meeting.* Owen

155. *Thomas the Rhymer.* Anonymous

156. *The Wife of Usher's Well.* Anonymous

157. *The Flea.* Donne

158. *Still to Be Neat.* Jonson

159. *The Triumph of Charis.* Jonson

160. *The Argument of His Book.* Herrick

161. *The Definition of Love.* Marvell

162. *Ah! Sun-Flower.* Blake

163. *Lucy.* Wordsworth

164. *Rose Aylmer.* Landor

165. *The Destruction of Sennacherib.* Byron

166. *How Do I Love Thee? Let Me Count the Ways.* E. Browning

167. *Now Sleeps the Crimson Petal.* Tennyson

168. *The Battle Hymn of the Republic.* Howe

169. *A Noiseless Patient Spider.* Whitman

170. *A Bird came down the Walk.* Dickinson

171. *Recessional.* Kipling

172. *Easter, 1916.* Yeats

173. *The Emperor of Ice-Cream.* Stevens

174. *Poetry.* M. Moore

175. *Ars Poetica.* MacLeish

176. *In Memory of W. B. Yeats.* Auden

177. *The Fish.* Bishop

178. *Daddy.* Plath

179. *The Lie.* Ralegh

180. *It Was a Lover and His Lass.* Shakespeare

181. *Redemption.* Herbert

182. *On His Blindness.* Milton

183. *To My Dear and Loving Husband.* Bradstreet

184. *Bermudas.* Marvell

185. *They Are All Gone into the World of Light.* Vaughan

186. *Ode to Evening.* Collins

187. *It Is a Beauteous Evening.* Wordsworth

188. *London, 1802.* Wordsworth

189. *Ode on Melancholy.* Keats

190. *The Oxen.* Hardy

191. *Thou Art Indeed Just, Lord.* Hopkins

192. *Danny Deever.* Kipling

193. *Snake.* Lawrence

194. *Bavarian Gentians.* Lawrence.

195. *The Waste Land.* Eliot

196. *For the Union Dead.* Lowell

197. *My Mistress' Eyes Are Nothing like the Sun.* Shakespeare

198. *Poor Soul, the Center of My Sinful Earth.* Shakespeare

199. *My Sweetest Lesbia.* Campion

200. *Corinna's Going a-Maying.* Herrick

201. *On the Late Massacre in Piedmont.* Milton

202. *Peace.* Vaughan

203. *To a Mouse on Turning Her Up in Her Nest with the Plough, November, 1785.* Burns

204. *A Visit from St. Nicholas.* C. Moore

205. *The Snow-Storm.* Emerson

206. *The Owl and the Pussy-Cat.* Lear

207. *Say Not the Struggle Nought Availeth.* Clough

208. *O Captain! My Captain!* Whitman

209. *Lucifer in Starlight.* Meredeth

210. *"The Soul selects her own Society."* Dickinson

211. *In Time of "The Breaking of Nations."* Hardy

212. *Channel Firing.* Hardy

213. *The Idea of Order at Key West.* Stevens

247. *Epitath on S. P.*   Jonson
248. *Exequy on His Wife.*   King
249. *Hear the Voice of the Bard.*   Blake
250. *My Heart Leaps Up.*   Wordsworth
251. *Dirce.*   Landor
252. *I Am.*   Clare
253. *The Eve of St. Agnes.*   Keats
254. *Bright Star.*   Keats
255. *The Rhodora.*   Emerson
256. *The Year's at the Spring.*   R. Browning
257. *When Lilacs Last in the Dooryard Bloomed.*   Whitman
258. *I'll Tell Thee Everything I Can.*   "Carroll"
259. *The Convergence of the Twain.*   Hardy
260. *Spring.*   Hopkins
261. *Requiem.*   Stevenson
262. *After Apple-Picking.*   Frost
263. *Acquainted with the Night.*   Frost
264. *The Owl.*   Thomas
265. *In a Station of the Metro.*   Pound
266. *Those Winter Sundays.*   Hayden
267. *A Supermarket in California.*   Ginsberg
268. *Tom o' Bedlam's Song.*   Anonymous
269. *Adam Lay I-bounden.*   Anonymous
270. *Lord Randal.*   Anonymous
271. *The Lover Complaineth the Unkindness of His Love.*   Wyatt
272. *One Day I Wrote Her Name upon the Strand.*   Spenser
273. *O Love, Which Reachest But to Dust.*   Sidney
274. *Take, O Take Those Lips Away.*   Shakespeare
275. *On His Mistress, the Queen of Bohemia.*   Wotton
276. *The Night-Piece to Julia.*   Herrick
277. *Il Penseroso.*   Milton
278. *An Horatian Ode upon Cromwell's Return from Ireland.*   Marvell
279. *John Anderson, My Jo.*   Burns

343. *Tired with All These, for Restful Death I Cry.*   Shakespeare
344. *Like as the Waves Make toward the Pebbled Shore.*   Shakespeare
345. *There Is a Garden in Her Face.*   Campion
346. *The Funeral.*   Donne
347. *The Apparition.*   Donne
348. *The Relic.*   Donne
349. *On the Countess Dowager of Pembroke.*   Browne
350. *Prayer the Church's Banquet.*   Herbert
351. *Mac Flecknoe.*   Dryden
352. *A Song for St. Cecilia's Day, 1687.*   Dryden
353. *How Sweet I Roam'd from Field to Field.*   Blake
354. *The Little Black Boy.*   Blake
355. *A Poison Tree.*   Blake
356. *The Chimney Sweeper.*   Blake
357. *To the Evening Star.*   Blake
358. *Surprised by Joy.*   Wordsworth
359. *She Was a Phantom of Delight.*   Wordsworth
360. *Resolution and Independence.*   Wordsworth
361. *Hohenlinden.*   Campbell
362. *England in 1819.*   Shelley
363. *To — — —.*   Shelley
364. *Old Adam, the Carrion Crow.*   Beddoes
365. *Brahma.*   Emerson
366. *The Chambered Nautilus.*   Holmes
367. *Mariana.*   Tennyson
368. *The Blessed Damozel.*   D. Rossetti
369. *"After great pain, a formal feeling comes."*   Dickinson
370. *How Doth the Little Crocodile.*   "Carroll"
371. *The Man He Killed.*   Hardy
372. *Neutral Tones.*   Hardy
373. *The Ruined Maid.*   Hardy
374. *Wynken, Blynken, and Nod.*   Field

375. *The Purple Cow.*   Burgess
376. *For a Dead Lady.*   Robinson
377. *Design.*   Frost
378. *Cargoes.*   Masefield
379. *Fog.*   Sandburg
380. *Cool Tombs.*   Sandburg
381. *Grass.*   Sandburg
382. *Thirteen Ways of Looking at a Blackbird.*   Stevens
383. *Spring and All.*   Williams
384. *The End of the World.*   MacLeish
385. *Little Gidding.*   Eliot
386. *Shine, Perishing Republic.*   Jeffers
387. *Lullaby.*   Auden
388. *Bagpipe Music.*   MacNeice
389. *Elegy for Jane.*   Roethke
390. *I Think Continually of Those Who Were Truly Great.*   Spender
391. *Naming of Parts.*   Reed
392. *A Lyke-Wake Dirge.*   Anonymous
393. *My Love in Her Attire.*   Anonymous
394. *The Demon Lover.*   Anonymous
395. *Care-Charmer Sleep, Son of the Sable Night.*   Daniel
396. *When Daffodils Begin to Peer.*   Shakespeare
397. *How Like a Winter Hath My Absence Been.*   Shakespeare
398. *Since Brass, nor Stone, nor Earth, nor Boundless Sea.*   Shakespeare
399. *Spring, the Sweet Spring.*   Nashe
400. *Good Friday, 1613. Riding Westward.*   Donne
401. *Slow, Slow, Fresh Fount, Keep Time with My Salt Tears.*   Jonson
402. *The Lark Now Leaves His Watery Nest.*   Davenant
403. *The Picture of Little T. C. in a Prospect of Flowers.*   Marvell
404. *The Mower to the Glow-Worms.*   Marvell
405. *A Dialogue between the Soul and Body.*   Marvell

406. *The Night.*   Vaughan
407. *An Elegy on the Death of a Mad Dog.*   Goldsmith
408. *The Garden of Love.*   Blake
409. *The Clod and the Pebble.*   Blake
410. *For A' That and A' That.*   Burns
411. *Breathes There the Man with Soul so Dead.*   Scott
412. *Lochinvar.*   Scott
413. *Dejection: An Ode.*   Coleridge
414. *Frost at Midnight.*   Coleridge
415. *When We Two Parted.*   Byron
416. *The Ocean.*   Byron
417. *Fable.*   Emerson
418. *Days.*   Emerson
419. *Old Ironsides.*   Holmes
420. *The City in the Sea.*   Poe
421. *The Lady of Shalott.*   Tennyson
422. *The Bishop Orders His Tomb at St. Praxed's Church.*
     R. Browning
423. *Parting at Morning.*   R. Browning
424. *Two in the Campagna.*   R. Browning
425. *Cavalry Crossing a Ford.*   Whitman
426. *Thus Piteously Love Closed What He Begat.*   Meredith
427. *"I felt a Funeral, in my Brain."*   Dickinson
428. *The Voice.*   Hardy
429. *Terence, This Is Stupid Stuff.*   Housman
430. *Anne Rutledge.*   Masters
431. *The Yachts.*   Williams
432. *A Grave.*   M. Moore
433. *Still Falls the Rain.*   Sitwell
434. *If We Must Die.*   McKay
435. *Greater Love.*   Owen
436. *"next to of course god america i."*   Cummings
437. *The Groundhog.*   Eberhart

438. *In a Dark Time.*   Roethke

439. *Mr. Edwards and the Spider.*   Lowell

440. *General Prologue to* The Canterbury Tales.   Chaucer

441. *Weep You No More, Sad Fountains.*   Anonymous

442. *The Unquiet Grave.*   Anonymous

443. *Waly, Waly.*   Anonymous

444. *Whoso List to Hunt.*   Wyatt

445. *Prothalamion.*   Spenser

446. *Come Sleep! O Sleep, the Certain Knot of Peace.*   Sidney

447. *His Golden Locks Time Hath to Silver Turned.*   Peele

448. *Whenas the Rye Reach the Chin.*   Peele

449. *Come Away, Come Away, Death.*   Shakespeare

450. *Come unto These Yellow Sands.*   Shakespeare

451. *Tell Me Where Is Fancy Bred.*   Shakespeare

452. *Thrice Toss These Oaken Ashes in the Air.*   Campion

453. *The Anniversary.*   Donne

454. *Come, My Celia, Let Us Prove.*   Jonson

455. *To Penshurst.*   Jonson

456. *To My Inconstant Mistress.*   Carew

457. *The Grasshopper.*   Lovelace

458. *Alexander's Feast; or, The Power of Music.*   Dryden

459. *Huswifery.*   Taylor

460. *A Description of the Morning.*   Swift

461. *Know Then Thyself.*   Pope

462. *Epistle to Dr. Arbuthnot.*   Pope

463. *An Essay on Criticism.*   Pope

464. *A Short Song of Congratulation.*   Johnson

465. *On the Death of Mr. Robert Levet, a Practiser in Physic.*   Johnson

466. *The Vanity of Human Wishes: The Tenth Satire of Juvenal Imitated.*   Johnson

467. *The Deserted Village.*   Goldsmith

468. *The Poplar Field.*   Cowper

469. *The Indian Burying Ground.*   Freneau
470. *Holy Thursday.*   Blake
471. *Mock On, Mock On, Voltaire, Rousseau.*   Blake
472. *Holy Willie's Prayer.*   Burns
473. *The Battle of Blenheim.*   Southey
474. *There Was a Sound of Revelry by Night.*   Byron
475. *Adonais.*   Shelley
476. *Ode to Psyche.*   Keats
477. *I Remember, I Remember.*   Hood
478. *Chaucer.*   Longfellow
479. *Snow-Bound; A Winter Idyl.*   Whittier
480. *The Bells.*   Poe
481. *The Haunted Palace.*   Poe
482. *Flower in the Crannied Wall.*   Tennyson
483. *The Woodspurge.*   D. Rossetti
484. *"I never saw a Moor."*   Dickinson
485. *"Much Madness is divinest Sense."*   Dickinson
486. *Remember.*   C. Rossetti
487. *The Yarn of the* Nancy Bell.   Gilbert
488. *During Wind and Rain.*   Hardy
489. *Nightingales.*   Bridges
490. *The Habit of Perfection.*   Hopkins
491. *Carrion Comfort.*   Hopkins
492. *The Duel.*   Field
493. *The Man with the Hoe.*   Markham
494. *The Ballad of Reading Gaol.*   Wilde
495. *Into My Heart an Air That Kills.*   Housman
496. *On Wenlock Edge.*   Housman
497. *The Hound of Heaven.*   Thompson
498. *The Song of Wandering Aengus.*   Yeats
499. *No Second Troy.*   Yeats
500. *Luke Havergal.*   Robinson

ACKNOWLEDGMENTS

W. H. Auden: "In Memory of W. B. Yeats," "Lullaby," "Musée des Beaux Arts" from *W. H. Auden: Collected Poems*, edited by E. Mendelson. Copyright 1940 and renewed 1968 by W. H. Auden. Reprinted by permission of Random House, Inc. Also from *Collected Shorter Poems* by W. H. Auden. Reprinted by permission of Faber and Faber Ltd.

Elizabeth Bishop: "The Fish" from *The Complete Poems 1927–1979*, by Elizabeth Bishop. Copyright © 1979, 1983 by Alice Helen Methfessel. Reprinted by permission of Farrar, Straus & Giroux, Inc.

Gwendolyn Brooks: "We Real Cool" from *Blacks*, issued by Third World Press, Chicago. Copyright 1987 and 1991 by Gwendolyn Brooks. Reprinted by permission of the author.

Hart Crane: "To Brooklyn Bridge" from *The Complete Poems and Selected Letters and Prose of Hart Crane*, edited by Brom Weber. Copyright 1933, © 1958, 1966 by Liveright Publishing Corporation. Reprinted by permission of Liveright Publishing Corporation.

E. E. Cummings: "anyone lived in a pretty how town," "next to of course god america i," from *Complete Poems, 1913–1962*, by E. E. Cummings. Copyright © 1923, 1925, 1931, 1935, 1938, 1939, 1940, 1944, 1945, 1946, 1947, 1948, 1949, 1950, 1951, 1952, 1953, 1954, 1955, 1956, 1957, 1958, 1959, 1960, 1961, 1962 by the Trustees for the E. E. Cummings Trust. Copyright © 1961, 1963, 1968 by Marion Morehouse Cummings and © MacGibbon & Kee, an imprint of HarperCollins Publishers Ltd. Reprinted by permission of Liveright Publishing Corporation and HarperCollins Publishers Ltd.

W. H. Davies: "Leisure" from *The Complete Poems of W. H. Davies.*
Copyright 1963 by Jonathan Cape Ltd. Reprinted by
permission of Wesleyan University Press.
Walter de la Mare: "The Listeners." Reprinted by permission of The
Literary Trustees of Walter de la Mare and The Society of
Authors as their representative.
Emily Dickinson: "After great pain a formal feeling comes," from
The Complete Poems of Emily Dickinson, edited by Thomas H.
Johnson. Copyright 1929 by Martha Dickinson Bianche,
renewed 1957 by Mary L. Hampson. Reprinted by permission
of Little, Brown and Company. All other poems from *The Poems
of Emily Dickinson,* edited by Thomas H. Johnson (Cambridge,
Mass: The Belknap Press of Harvard University Press).
Copyright 1951, © 1955, 1979, 1983 by the President and
Fellows of Harvard College. Reprinted by permission of the
publishers and the Trustees of Amherst College.
Richard Eberhart: "The Fury of Aerial Bombardment" and "The
Groundhog" from *Collected Poems 1930–1986,* by Richard
Eberhart. Copyright © 1960, 1976, 1988 by Richard Eberhart.
Reprinted by permission of Oxford University Press, Inc.
T. S. Eliot: "The Love Song of J. Alfred Prufrock," "Journey of the
Magi," "The Waste Land," "Sweeney among the Nightingales,"
"Gerontion" from *Collected Poems 1909–1962,* by T. S. Eliot.
Copyright 1936 by Harcourt Brace Jovanovich, Inc., and ©
1964, 1963 by T. S. Eliot. Reprinted by permission of the
publisher and Faber and Faber Ltd. "Little Gidding" from
Collected Poems 1909–1962, by T. S. Eliot, reprinted by permission
of Faber and Faber Ltd., and from *Four Quartets,* copyright 1943
by T. S. Eliot, renewed 1971 by Esme Valerie Eliot, reprinted
by permission of Harcourt Brace Jovanovich, Inc.
Robert Frost: All poems from *The Poetry of Robert Frost,* edited by
Edward Connery Lathem. Copyright 1923, 1928, 1947, © 1969
by Holt, Rinehart and Winston. Copyright 1936, 1942, 1951, ©
1956 by Robert Frost. Copyright © 1964, 1970, 1975 by Lesley
Frost Ballantine. Reprinted by permission of Henry Holt and
Company, Inc., and Jonathan Cape Ltd.
Allen Ginsberg: "A Supermarket in California" from *Collected Poems
1947–1980,* by Allen Ginsberg. Copyright © 1955 by Allen
Ginsberg and © for Viking, 1985 edition by Allen Ginsberg,
1985. Reprinted by permission of HarperCollins Publishers Ltd.
and Penguin Books Ltd.

Thomas Hardy: All poems from *The Complete Poems of Thomas Hardy*, edited by James Gibson (New York: Macmillan, 1978).

Robert Hayden: "Those Winter Sundays" from *Angle of Ascent, New and Selected Poems*, by Robert Hayden. Copyright © 1966, 1970, 1972, 1975 by Robert Hayden. Reprinted by permission of Liveright Publishing Corporation.

A. E. Housman: All poems from "A Shropshire Lad"—Authorized Edition—from *The Collected Poems of A. E. Housman*. Copyright 1939, 1940, © 1965 by Holt, Rinehart and Winston and © 1967, 1968 by Robert E. Symons. Reprinted by permission of Henry Holt and Company, Inc.

Langston Hughes: "The Negro Speaks of Rivers" from *Selected Poems*, by Langston Hughes. Copyright © 1959 by Langston Hughes. Reprinted by permission of Alfred A. Knopf, Inc., and Harold Ober Associates, Inc.

Randall Jarrell: "Death of the Ball Turret Gunner" from *The Complete Poems*, by Randall Jarrell. Copyright © 1945, renewed 1972 by Mrs. Randall Jarrell. Reprinted by permission of Farrar, Straus & Giroux, Inc., and by Faber and Faber Ltd.

Robinson Jeffers: "Hurt Hawks" and "Shine, Perishing Republic" from *The Selected Poetry of Robinson Jeffers*, by Robinson Jeffers. Copyright 1925, 1928, renewed 1953, 1956 by Robinson Jeffers. Reprinted by permission of Random House, Inc.

Philip Larkin: "Church Going" from *The Less Deceived*. Reprinted by permission of The Marvell Press, England.

D. H. Lawrence: All poems from *The Complete Poems of D. H. Lawrence*, by D. H. Lawrence. Copyright © 1964, 1971 by Angelo Ragli and C. M. Weekley, Executors of the Estate of Frieda Lawrence Ravagli. Reprinted with the acknowledgment of Laurence Pollinger Ltd. and by permission of Viking Penguin, a division of Penguin Books USA, Inc.

Vachel Lindsay: "Abraham Lincoln Walks at Midnight" from *Collected Poems of Vachel Lindsay* (New York: Macmillan, 1925).

Robert Lowell: "For the Union Dead" from *For the Union Dead*, by Robert Lowell. Copyright © 1964 by Robert Lowell. "Skunk Hour" from *Life Studies*, by Robert Lowell. Copyright © 1956, 1959 by Robert Lowell, renewed 1987 by Harriet W. Lowell. Reprinted by permission of Farrar, Straus & Giroux, Inc. "Mr. Edwards and the Spider" from *Lord Weary's Castle*. Copyright 1946, renewed 1974 by Robert Lowell. Reprinted by permission of Harcourt Brace Jovanovich, Inc.

Archibald MacLeish: All poems reprinted from *Collected Poems 1917–1982*, by Archibald MacLeish. Copyright © 1985 by The Estate of Archibald MacLeish. Reprinted by permission of Houghton Mifflin Company. All rights reserved.

Louis MacNeice: "Bagpipe Music" from *The Collected Poems of Louis MacNeice*. Reprinted by permission of Faber and Faber Ltd.

John Masefield: "Cargoes" from reprinted by permission of The Society of Authors as the literary representative of The Estate of John Masefield.

Edgar Lee Masters: "Anne Rutledge" from *Spoon River Anthology*, by Edgar Lee Masters. Reprinted by permission of Ellen C. Masters.

Claude McKay: "If We Must Die." Reprinted from *Selected Poems of Claude McKay*.

Marianne Moore: "A Grave" and "Poetry" reprinted from *Collected Poems of Marianne Moore*. Copyright 1935 by Marianne Moore, renewed 1963 by Marianne Moore and T. S. Eliot. Reprinted by permission of Macmillan Publishing Company and Faber and Faber Ltd.

Wilfred Owen: All poems reprinted from *The Collected Poems of Wilfred Owen*. Copyright © 1963 by Chatto & Windus, Ltd. Reprinted by permission Chatto & Windus Ltd. and New Directions Publishing Corporation.

Sylvia Plath: "Daddy" from *Ariel*, by Sylvia Plath, reprinted by permission of Faber and Faber Ltd. Also from *The Collected Poems of Sylvia Plath*, edited by Ted Hughes. Copyright © by The Estate of Sylvia Plath. Reprinted by permission of HarperCollins Publishers Ltd.

Ezra Pound: All poems from *Collected Shorter Poems*, by Ezra Pound. Reprinted by permission of Faber and Faber Ltd. and from *Personae*, copyright 1926 by Ezra Pound. Reprinted by permission of New Directions Publishing Corporation.

John Crowe Ransom: All poems from *Selected Poems, Third Edition, Revised & Enlarged*, by John Crowe Ransom. Copyright 1924 by Alfred A. Knopf, Inc., renewed 1952 by John Crowe Ransom. Reprinted by permission of Alfred A. Knopf, Inc., and Laurence Pollinger Ltd.

Henry Reed: "Naming of Parts" from *Collected Poems*, edited by Jon Stallworthy. Copyright © by The Executor of Henry Reed's Estate, 1991. Reprinted by permission of Oxford University Press.

Edwin Arlington Robinson: "Miniver Cheevy" and "For a Dead Lady" from *The Town Down the River*, by Edwin Arlington Robinson. "Richard Cory" and "Luke Havergal" from *The Children of the Night*, by Edwin Arlington Robinson (Charles Scribner's Sons, publisher).

Theodore Roethke: All poems from *The Collected Poems of Theodore Roethke*, by Theodore Roethke. "I Knew a Woman" copyright 1954 by Theodore Roethke. "Waking" copyright 1948 by Theodore Roethke. "Elegy for Jane" copyright 1950 by Theodore Roethke. "My Papa's Waltz" copyright 1942 by Hearst Magazines, Inc. "In a Dark Time" copyright © 1960 by Beatrice Roethke, Administratrix of The Estate of Theodore Roethke. Reprinted by permission of Bantam Doubleday Dell Publishing Group, Inc., and Faber and Faber Ltd.

Isaac Rosenberg: "Break of Day in the Trenches" from *Collected Poems*, by Isaac Rosenberg. Chatto & Windus, Ltd., publisher.

Carl Sandburg: "Cool Tombs" and "Grass" from *Cornhuskers*, by Carl Sandburg. Copyright 1918 by Holt, Rinehart and Winston, Inc., renewed 1946 by Carl Sandburg. "Chicago" and "Fog" from *Chicago Poems*, by Carl Sandburg. Copyright 1916 by Holt, Rinehart and Winston, Inc., renewed 1944 by Carl Sandburg. All poems reprinted by permission of Harcourt Brace Jovanovich, Inc.

Edith Sitwell: "Still Falls the Rain" from *The Collected Poems of Edith Sitwell*. Reprinted by permission of David Higham Associates.

Stevie Smith: "Not Waving But Drowning" from *The Collected Poems of Stevie Smith*. Copyright © 1972 by Stevie Smith. Reprinted by permission of New Directions Publishing Corporation and James MacGibbon as Executor of The Estate of Stevie Smith.

Stephen Spender: "I Think Continually of Those Who Were Truly Great" from *Collected Poems 1928–1953*, by Stephen Spender. Copyright 1934, renewed 1962 by Stephen Spender. Reprinted by permission of Random House, Inc. Also from *Collected Poems 1928–1985*, by Stephen Spender, reprinted by permission of Faber and Faber Ltd.

Wallace Stevens: All poems from *Collected Poems*, by Wallace Stevens. Copyright 1923, renewed 1951 by Wallace Stevens. Reprinted by permission of Alfred A. Knopf, Inc., and Faber and Faber Ltd.

Allen Tate: "Ode to the Confederate Dead" from *Collected Poems 1919–1976*, by Allen Tate. Copyright © by Allen Tate. Reprinted by permission of Farrar, Straus & Giroux, Inc., and Faber and Faber, Ltd.

Dylan Thomas: All poems printed from *Poems of Dylan Thomas*. Copyright 1945 by the Trustees for the Copyrights of Dylan Thomas, and 1952 by Dylan Thomas. Reprinted by permission of New Directions Publishing Corporation and David Higham Associates.

Richard Wilbur: "Love Calls Us to the Things of This World" from *Things of This World*. Copyright © 1956, renewed 1984 by Richard Wilbur. Reprinted by permission of Harcourt Brace Jovanovich, Inc.

William Carlos Williams: All poems printed from *The Collected Poems of William Carlos Williams, 1919–1939, vol. 1*. Copyright 1938 by New Directions Publishing Corporation. Reprinted by permission of New Directions Publishing Corporation and Carcanet Press Ltd.

William Butler Yeats: All poems reprinted from *The Poems of W. B. Yeats: A New Edition*, edited by Richard J. Finneran. "The Circus Animals' Desertion" and "Lapis Lazuli" copyright 1940 by Georgie Yeats, renewed 1968 by Bertha Georgie Yeats. "Sailing to Byzantium," "Leda and the Swan," "Among School Children" copyright 1928 by Macmillan Publishing Company, renewed 1956 by Georgie Yeats. "The Second Coming," "Easter 1916," "A Prayer for My Daughter" copyright 1924 by Macmillan Publishing Company, renewed 1952 by Bertha Georgie Yeats. "The Wild Swans at Coole," "An Irish Airman Foresees His Death" copyright 1919 by Macmillan Publishing Company, renewed 1947 by Bertha Georgie Yeats. All poems reprinted by permission of Macmillan Publishing Company.

Index of Poets

INDEX OF TITLES AND FIRST LINES

Titles of poems are in italics, first lines in roman type. If title and first line are identical, or virtually so, only the title is given.